Labor in Latin America

Charles Bergquist

LABOR IN LATIN AMERICA

Comparative Essays on Chile, Argentina,
Venezuela, and Colombia

STANFORD UNIVERSITY PRESS
Stanford, California   1986

Comparative Studies in History, Institutions, and Public Policy
Edited by John D. Wirth and Thomas C. Heller

Published with the assistance of the
National Endowment for the Humanities

Stanford University Press, Stanford, California

© 1986 by the Board of Trustees of the
Leland Stanford Junior University

Printed in the United States of America

CIP data appear at the end of the book

The photographs following p. 190 appear by permission
of the following people or institutions: 2, 3, 5,
and 6, courtesy of Mariana Aylwin, Santiago, Chile;
7-12, courtesy of the Archivo General de la Nación,
Buenos Aires, Argentina; 1, 4, 13-15, courtesy
of the Library of Congress, Washington, D.C.
(13-15 are by John Vachon, from the Standard Oil
of New Jersey Collection); 16, courtesy of Foto
Rodríguez, Medellín, Antioquia, Colombia; 17, author's
collection; 18, courtesy of *El Espectador*, Colombia

To Jean and Johnny and Magola

Preface

Workers, especially those engaged in production for export, have played a determining role in the modern history of Latin American societies. Their struggle for material well-being and control over their own lives has fundamentally altered the direction of national political evolution and the pattern of economic development in the countries of the region.

This assertion, which is the thesis of the study that follows, flies in the face of much of what I learned about labor in the process of being socialized into mid-twentieth-century U.S. society. It also contradicts most of the literature on political and economic change in twentieth-century Latin America. I have been persuaded of its validity slowly as my experience widened and my research progressed, and as the social forces, political events, and intellectual trends that inform all scholarship influenced my perception and understanding of the historical evidence.

I grew up in the 1940's and 1950's in Seattle, Washington. Seattle was a new kind of company town where the marriage of clean, capital-intensive industry, the military, and the state provided an expanding number of high-paying jobs for blue- and white-collar workers in aircraft production. Like many Seattleites, my parents and relatives were recent immigrants from the farms and small towns of the Middle West. I was five years old when the Taft-Hartley labor legislation greatly curbed the economic and political power of a labor movement soon to be purged of the leftist militants who had led the struggle to organize basic industry in the 1930's and 1940's. In the Seattle of my boyhood even the memory of the powerful, radical labor movement that had set out to transform regional society in the first decades of the century had been practically extinguished from popular consciousness. Few knew about the early struggles of the Industrial Workers of the World for free speech and their explosive efforts to organize lumbermen and maritime workers, or about the general strike of 1919 that paralyzed Seattle and enabled workers to assume administrative and economic control of the city for five momentous days. By the 1950's, organized labor in Seattle was symbolized by the corrupt, bureaucratic, bread-and-butter unionism of Dave Beck and the Teamsters. As my parents and relatives moved out of blue-collar jobs or saw their real income rise during the unprecedented period of economic expansion following the Second World War, I learned an "American" history that somehow reduced the development of the U.S. labor movement to short, unintelligible descriptions of a handful of bloody confrontations in the late nineteenth century, and brief sketches of "practical, responsible" labor leaders in the twentieth. College and university training in Latin American studies in the 1960's introduced me to formal social science theory that largely ignored the role of organized labor in modern Western history and insisted on the conservative nature of the contemporary "industrial labor elite" within the working class of Latin America.

In these ways, through concrete experience and formal education, I learned to discount the role of labor in the history of the modern world. Yet at the same time I grew up with a deep respect for the working people around me. I realize now how they tried to convey to me the deepest values of a class deprived of social organization and an autonomous political consciousness: a democratic faith in the intellectual capabilities of all men; a sense of exploitation and social injustice; a suspicion of capital and government; and an elemental understanding of the power of material forces in history. I learned a trade from my uncle, a roofer, and before I got a job as a historian in 1972 I worked at a variety of industrial, agricultural, and service jobs: roofing houses, operating a printing press, driving taxis and ambulances, working on the line in a canning plant, tending bar, picking fruit, spraying pesticides, carrying mail, and loading freight. None of these jobs brought me into sustained contact with organized workers and political parties of the left, a fact that is not surprising given the containment of the bulk of organized labor within the confines of large firms in the industrial sector and the eclipse of the left in the United States following the Second World War.

Of course no one's values and world view are determined alone by an association with working people or by the necessity of depending on the sale of one's own labor in a capitalist society. An understanding of society and one's position in it develops through concrete material, political, and intellectual experience. In my case, progress toward such understanding was slow. It was retarded by the historical conditions in which I grew to adulthood. It was limited by the pervasive influence, and seemingly commonsensical logic, of a liberal vision of the world effectively propagated by the dominant culture-making institutions of an advanced, expanding capitalist society. It was delayed, later in life, by real and imagined occupational, geographical, and intellectual isolation from the daily struggle of the working class. Yet even under unpropitious circumstances like these, progress in the direction of understanding how capitalist society functions is possible. Four main sets of conditions have helped to make me personally aware of this social truth: my experience, first as a rural Peace Corps worker, then as a researcher, in Latin America, where capitalism's failures as a social system and its mechanisms of social exploitation are more nakedly revealed than in rich developed capitalist nations like the United States; my graduate work with John Johnson, the first U.S. historian to interpret modern Latin American political history in material and class terms; my exposure to Marxist analysis, which began during the struggle to stop U.S. involvement in the Vietnam War; and my understanding of the circumstances surrounding the murder of César Cauce, a former Duke University student, union organizer, and Communist Workers Party activist, who was killed along with four of his fellows by members of the Ku Klux Klan and the American Nazi Party in Greensboro, North Carolina, in November 1980.

In all these particular and personal ways the recent history of the world social system has touched my life and gradually sharpened my perception of my position in it. I have recounted them in some detail because, in a manner readers will evaluate differently, they limit and inform every aspect of the study that follows.

Quite apart from these broad ideological and perceptual considerations, the study has strengths and weaknesses related to the state of Latin American historical studies and to the use of the comparative approach. Although I am convinced that the thesis outlined and developed in the course of the study is a powerful one, the chapter essays devoted to individual countries only suggest its interpretive potential. Comparative study of the role of labor in twentieth-century Latin America is constrained not only by the underdeveloped state of the historiography on labor and Latin America in general, but by the limits imposed on primary field research by the repressive political climate in many countries of the region. The comparative approach may be the strongest feature of the study. But if it proves useful in generating important analytical questions and helpful in separating and weighing elements of historical causation, it necessarily works against an intimate knowledge of a given Latin American society and command over the literature dealing with it. The specialists who helped direct my research and who commented on the manuscript have enabled me to attenuate, not overcome, this problem.

Yet the underdeveloped state of the historiography and the limitations on historical research of the subject are also conditions that justify broad interpretive efforts at this stage. Given the magnitude of the task facing historians of modern Latin America and the political implications of all research, we cannot and should not proceed willy-nilly on all fronts simultaneously. It is in this spirit that I submit this study. I hope it will help to stimulate further research on the role of labor in modern Latin American history. And I hope that in some small way the vision of the past outlined imperfectly in these pages will help to inform intelligent and effective political activity by the working class in its continuing struggle to forge a more humane world social order.

———◆—◆—◆———

Field research on this project was funded by grants from the Social Science Research Council in 1977-78 and the Duke University Research Council in the summers of 1979 and 1980. Fellowships at the National Humanities Center in 1980 and at the Wilson Center in 1981 allowed me to read widely in the secondary literature and to write this book. Many people have commented on portions of the manuscript. I wish to thank especially John Johnson, John Wirth, David Bushnell, Tulio Halperín Donghi, John Womack, Paul Drake, John Lombardi, Richard Walter, Gonzalo Sánchez, Ariel Dorfman, Steve Ellner, Sandra McGee, Tico Braun, Cathy LeGrand, Daniel James, Ronald Newton, Emilia Viotti da Costa, Joseph Tulchin, James Barrett, Gonzalo Fallabela, David Collier, Stanley Stein, and Brooke Larson. Among my colleagues at Duke I wish to thank John TePaske, Carol Smith, Arturo Valenzuela, Gary Gereffi, Larry Goodwyn, Bill Chafe, John Cell, Bill Reddy, Jim Epstein, and Dick Fox. Although I have not been able to deal adequately with all of the criticisms and suggestions of these commentators, the study that follows, for which I remain responsible, is much the better for their efforts.

Dot Sapp typed and retyped these pages until she got her "green machine." Even with the help of a word processor she had export workers coming out her ears by the end. Yet her commitment to seeing this book to press never flagged. For that, for her humor, and for her great humanity I thank her.

C.B.

Contents

5. Colombia   274

6. On the Limits of This Study and the Promise of the Approach   376

Index   389

Ten pages of photographs follow page 190

Maps, Tables, and Figures

Maps

Tables

Figures

Labor in Latin America

1

Modern Latin American Historiography and the Labor Movement

Twentieth-century Latin American historiography suffers from two very grave deficiencies. It has failed to recognize the decisive historical role of organized labor and the labor movement in the evolution of the societies of the region. And it has failed to account for the very different ideological and political trajectories of the various Latin American labor movements—Marxist in some countries; neo-fascist in at least one; liberal, until now, in several others. Both of these deficiencies have a common root: neglect of the full social implications of the ways Latin American economies were integrated into an evolving world capitalist system in the century after 1880. After that date, the maturation of the industrial societies of the North Atlantic Basin created the enormous capital and technological resources, and internal social and political imperatives, that propelled a massive export of European capital to the rest of the world. In Latin America, elite social groups took advantage of these conditions to transform their own societies. One by one, Latin American nations came to specialize in the production of one or more primary commodities for export.

Latin American humanists and anthropologists writing in the 1930's were the first scholars to recognize and evaluate the importance of this export-oriented transformation. But it was structural economists, associated with the United Nations' Economic Commission for Latin America, who most thoroughly explored its implications for what they called the dependent (or reactive) economic development of the region. In the decades following the Second World War they constructed systematic typologies of export economies and brilliantly traced the implications of each for national economic development in the Latin American periphery of an evolving world capitalist system. Meanwhile, other Latin American social scientists and historians explored the social, political, and cultural dimensions of the region's economic transformation. All of this work, however, curiously neglected the role of organized labor and the labor movement.[1]

This failing seems especially surprising given the march of historical events in the region in the postwar period. The once seemingly common-sensical argument that industrial workers were relatively unimportant in societies whose main function in the modern world was to produce primary commodities for export lost its logical appeal after 1945. The major Latin American nations emerged from the crisis of world depression and war with rapidly industrializing economies and relatively powerful organized labor movements. In subsequent decades they became primary recipients of foreign manufacturing investment in the underdeveloped world. Yet even as the manufacturing sector in these economies came to overshadow the primary sector, most Latin American scholars insisted that industrial workers were an insignificant force for historical change in the region. Such workers, they argued, were a favored group in national labor markets. Winners among a surplus of urban workers competing for a small and very slowly expanding number of jobs in capital-intensive manufacturing industry, industrial workers were a politically conservative and socially conformist labor aristocracy. This notion was developed systematically by Latin Americanists in the 1960's[2] and persisted well into the 1970's. It was confirmed by the bulk of contributors to a major review of Latin American labor studies published in 1977.[3]

By that time the most developed societies of the region were manifestly in crisis. Rapid industrialization, under the aegis of foreign capital, entailed the progressive denationalization of domestic manufacturing industry, along with an increased dependence on imported capital-intensive

1. The most important of the works by these humanistic social scientists is the brilliant essay by the Cuban anthropologist Fernando Ortiz, *Cuban Counterpoint: Tobacco and Sugar* (New York, 1947), originally published in 1940. Mature statements by the Latin American structural economists are Celso Furtado, *The Economic Development of Latin America* (Cambridge, Eng., 1970), and Osvaldo Sunkel, with the collaboration of Pedro Paz, *El subdesarrollo y la teoría del desarrollo* (Mexico City, 1971). The most important of the other works referred to are Fernando Henrique Cardoso and Enzo Falleto, *Dependency and Development in Latin America* (Berkeley, Calif., 1979), originally published in 1969, and Tulio Halperín Donghi, *Historia contemporánea de América Latina* (Madrid, 1970).

2. Influential formulations of this position are a pair of books edited by Claudio Vélez, *Obstacles to Change in Latin America* (London, 1965), and *The Politics of Conformity in Latin America* (London, 1967), and the contributions of Henry Landsburger, especially "The Labor Elite: Is It Revolutionary?," in Seymour Martin Lipset and Aldo Solari, eds., *Elites in Latin America* (London, 1967). Exceptions to the rule are the works of Robert Alexander. Writing from a liberal, anti-Communist perspective, he consistently stresses the importance of organized labor on the modern historical development of the region.

3. Rubén Katzman and José Luis Reyna, eds., *Fuerza de trabajo y movimientos laborales en América Latina* (Mexico City, 1977). Exceptions to this generalization are the notable contributions to the volume by Elizabeth Jelin, Silvia Sigal, and Juan Carlos Torre. Their work pointed in the direction of the reassessment discussed below.

technology and machinery and on expanded imports of industrial raw materials and fuel. It quickly created serious balance-of-trade difficulties and chronic inflationary pressures. Governments relied on large-scale international borrowing to overcome these problems and to build the economic infrastructure vital to industrial expansion. Then, as they were required to meet stiffer and stiffer conditions for the renegotiation and expansion of these loans, they adopted austerity measures that were designed to be borne primarily by the working class.

That solution—the one most attractive to domestic capitalists as well—gradually drove the working class into opposition to the state, revitalized the left, and, in the open political systems typical of the major Latin American nations in the early postwar period, stymied the effectiveness of the austerity programs. Far from surmounting the problems posed by industrialization, the new strictures soon threatened the very viability of the whole process of economic expansion, and led progressively to the breakdown of open political systems, to a massive repression of organized labor and the left, and eventually to a partial abandonment of the drive toward industrialization itself. This process was discernible as early as the mid-1950's and ran its course in the relatively more advanced societies of the Southern Cone and Brazil in the 1960's and early 1970's. By the mid-1980's it was threatening to envelop the political systems of such other major countries as Mexico, Colombia, and Venezuela.[4]

The working class was thus manifestly at the very center of the crisis of postwar Latin American economic and political development. Yet so broad was the consensus over the relative unimportance and the conservative nature of organized labor among scholars of Latin America that for a long time they focused their efforts to explain what was happening everywhere but on the working class. Outstanding contributions examined the economic imperatives of "deepening" capitalist industrialization, and stressed the role models of middle-class and technocratic groups.[5] Other scholars explored the dynamics of corporativism and the state, or sought explanations of the crisis in the cultural and institutional legacy of Iberian colonialism.[6] These contributions were important, and the best of them recognized the significance of organized labor to their analysis. None of them, however, focused attention theoretically and empirically on labor itself. One book that did, a major reinterpretation of

4. A fine analysis and summary of the literature dealing with this process and its implications for organized labor is Paul W. Drake's unpublished manuscript, "Journeys Toward Failure? Political Parties and Labor Movements Under Authoritarian Regimes in the Southern Cone and Brazil, 1964-83" (1983).

5. Guillermo O'Donnell, *Modernization and Bureaucratic-Authoritarianism* (Berkeley, Calif., 1973).

6. A handy overview of this work is James Malloy, ed., *Authoritarianism and Corporativism in Latin America* (Pittsburgh, 1977).

the labor history of the region published in 1977, concluded that organized labor's role in the modern history of Latin America was a limited one indeed.[7]

The reasons for this lag between historical developments and social science theory are in themselves worthy of investigation. Did it reflect the sociology of Latin American social science, the increasingly repressive conditions for research in Latin America, the priorities of funding agencies, or the weight and prestige of theory and research agendas constructed in the developed world?

This last proposition appears to have been especially important. To a generation of scholars in the developed West writing in the decades following the Second World War, the weakness and unimportance of organized labor seemed a plausible supposition. After the war, combative Marxist-led labor movements that had been strengthened all over the West during a decade and a half of crisis in the world order were quickly contained. In country after country labor unions were transformed into relatively docile, compliant, bureaucratic organizations that were fully integrated, under the watchful regulatory eye of the state, into the legal and political life of their respective societies. The success of this general capitalist offensive against organized labor owed much to the outright repression of the political left, to the skillful manipulation of the issue of nationalism as the rivalry between the major capitalist and socialist wartime allies degenerated into the Cold War, and to the hegemony of liberal cultural values and ideology in the postwar West.[8]

Most fundamental to the success of this offensive, however, and the key to the durability of its results was a historic compromise between labor and capital. The terms of that compromise are now well known, even if the importance of its long-term implications has yet to be fully comprehended. Capital, in principle, recognized the right of workers to organize, to bargain collectively, and to strike for higher returns for their labor. Organized labor, for its part, either explicitly (as in the United

7. Hobart Spalding, *Organized Labor in Latin America* (New York, 1977). The best and most recent survey of Latin American labor history, Spalding's work differs fundamentally from the approach pursued in this volume. It emphasizes how changing external, international ties affect the common experience of the labor movements of the region, as against my stress on the meaning for labor of the internal dynamics of Latin American societies. It focuses on the relative cohesiveness of the ruling class rather than on the experience of workers in explaining the differences in the various Latin American labor movements. Most importantly, it stresses the relative lack of labor influence on national history, whereas I argue for its decisive importance.

8. The restoration of liberal cultural hegemony after the war was a direct result of the outcome of the fighting, which left the liberal capitalist powers victorious. But it was achieved only through philosophical and social concessions to domestic popular forces spawned during the world crisis that Karl Polanyi identified in *The Great Transformation* (1944). The most important of those was the compromise with organized labor discussed below. As with the labor initiatives, the contradictions within all of the social institutions of the capitalist welfare state have now become manifest, their future uncertain.

States and much of Latin America) or implicitly (as in Western Europe and parts of Latin America) renounced the goal of socialist transformation, and acquiesced to the capitalist logic of perpetual revolution in the forces of production. In particular, labor gave ground on the issue of control in the workplace in exchange for a major share of productivity gains. Capital thus eliminated the principal immediate obstacle to economic expansion in the postwar era. It tamed powerful, disruptive organized labor movements that threatened to undermine the process of capitalist accumulation. In effect, capital turned organized labor into a partner. Unions joined management in disciplining the work force and in regularizing and containing industrial conflict. In exchange, organized workers preserved their unions and watched their real wages and material benefits rise.[9]

This historic compromise has structured much of the subsequent history of the world capitalist system. How it did so is still very imperfectly understood. But that it has had enormous economic, social, political, and intellectual implications—each manifested differently over time in the various parts of the world system—is now apparent.

The viability of the postwar compromise between capital and labor in the West depended on the continual expansion of capitalism, both on a world scale and in all the separate societies where the compromise was effected. The first condition, expansion of the system as a whole, was met spectacularly over the course of the next three decades. Success in meeting the first condition, however, inevitably compromised achievement of the second. The economic implications of capital's commitment to organized labor in developed, high-wage societies forced it to shift the base of its productive operations to lower-wage economies abroad.[10] The effects of this process, which ultimately undermined both economic

9. Perspectives on the importance of this compromise are developed by Charles Maier, who stresses an "ideology of productivity" as the guiding principle of the foreign policy of the United States in the restoration of the capitalist order in postwar Europe, and David Montgomery, in his treatment of the importance of the issue of control in the workplace in workers' struggles in the labor history of the United States. Charles Maier, "Two Postwar Eras and the Conditions for Stability in Twentieth-Century Western Europe," *American Historical Review* 86:2 (Apr. 1981):327-52; David Montgomery, *Workers' Control in America* (Cambridge, Eng., 1979). The relationship of control over the organization of work to the logic of capitalist development is explored most thoroughly in Harry Braverman, *Labor and Monopoly Capital* (New York, 1974). The concept of "partnership" is advanced to explain the transformation of the European labor movements in Giovanni Arrighi's suggestive essay "The Labor Movement in Twentieth Century Western Europe," in Immanuel Wallerstein, ed., *Labor in the World Social Structure* (Beverly Hills, Calif., 1983).

10. Capitalists, of course, took other measures to circumvent their compromise with labor in the developed world. They effectively stymied the expansion of organization to other sectors of the labor force. And they promoted or acquiesced in the legal and illegal immigration into developed societies of workers from low-wage societies. In the United States this immigration was massive and to a large extent illegal, a fact that left the working class as a whole vulnerable to ethnic explanations of its class problems and impeded the legal organization of immigrant workers. These issues are explored by Alejandro Portes and John Walton, among many others. See their *Labor, Class, and the International System* (New York, 1981).

growth and the compromise with labor in the developed world, were not apparent for decades. Beneficiaries of mechanisms of capital accumulation and exchange within the world system,[11] and able to develop capital-intensive and high-technology productive and service industries in a modified international division of labor, the developed societies experienced impressive economic growth through the 1960's. Growth was particularly rapid in the developed economies of Western Europe and in parts of East Asia where wages were much lower than in the United States, and where the flow of investment from the United States into manufacturing production in the postwar decades was spectacular. By the 1970's, however, the structural effects of this massive shift in productive investment in the world system began to reveal themselves in the developed world, first in the premier capitalist economy, and then in the others. As manufacturing industry moved abroad, and domestic industry failed to modernize and became less competitive in the world market, developed Western societies began to experience declining economic growth rates, chronic balance-of-trade problems, high unemployment, and rising inflation.

The social, political, and intellectual dimensions of the historic compromise in the developed West were no less dramatic. The eclipse of a powerful political left anchored in an organized working class left capital free to pursue the implications of the compromise virtually uncontested at home, and to use the resources of the state to pursue its ends ruthlessly abroad. In its efforts to expand and protect investment overseas, the United States in particular soon found itself enmeshed in a series of costly endeavors. These ranged from publicly financed overseas investment insurance to political subversion abroad, from schools for foreign labor leaders to major international wars. Although the cost of these endeavors did not seriously undermine the political and ideological hegemony of capital in the United States, each contributed significantly to the economic problems stemming from the shift of productive industry abroad. At present it is the legacy of that economic process that is generating the most severe social and political problems in the developed West. Organized labor has seen its relative numbers decline, its economic and political power severely curtailed. In recent years the terms of the historic compromise in basic industry have broken down completely. Although

11. There is of course no consensus in liberal and Marxist economic theory over either the existence or the relative importance of such mechanisms. The position taken here draws on the propositions advanced in Paul Baran, *The Political Economy of Growth* (New York, 1957), Samir Amin, *Accumulation on a World Scale* (New York, 1975), and Arghiri Emmanuel, *Unequal Exchange* (New York, 1972). Theory aside, the operation of such mechanisms seems best to explain the developments discussed below: the rapidity with which the obstacles to capitalist expansion were revealed in Latin America in the postwar period, and the fragility of the compromise between capital and labor there; and the delay in the manifestation of both in the developed capitalist world.

organized labor as a whole has yet to reevaluate its postwar commitment to capitalism, it has joined with a coalition of social groups in the cry for industrial protection and "buy national" policies. Such policies, of course, threaten both the mechanisms of capitalist accumulation in the world system as a whole and the liberal theory of comparative advantage in world trade on which that system rests.

Still, the problems that beset developed capitalist nations today were very slow to emerge. They are more obvious now with the aid of a hindsight sharpened by the social and political pressures unleashed by the breakdown of the compromise with labor and the general economic stagnation in the developed world. For more than two blissful decades the workability of the compromise with labor—indeed its inevitability—was endorsed by public opinion and celebrated in mainstream social science theory. Scholars postulated an "end to ideology" and wrote class conflict out of their theories of development in the modern world.[12]

Such a position is no longer tenable, even in the developed world. As world economic growth began to falter and the historic compromise between capital and labor began to break down in the early 1970's, large numbers of scholars turned their attention to a reevaluation of the role of labor in the history of the modern world. It is this work that has so profoundly illuminated the terms of the postwar compromise and now enables us to begin to assess the far-reaching implications it has entailed. In Latin American studies that reevaluation has produced what one scholar has called a "boomlet" in labor studies[13] and a growing recognition of the obvious: that organized labor is central to the continuing postwar crisis in the major countries of the region. Nevertheless, the reevaluation has yet to force Latin Americanists into a major theoretical revision of traditional notions about the role of labor in twentieth-century history as a whole.[14]

Latin Americanists have ignored the historic importance of labor in large part because we have looked in the wrong place. We have applied

12. For one critique of modernization theory, and a guide to many others, see Charles Bergquist, *Alternative Approaches to the Problem of Development: A Selected and Annotated Bibliography* (Durham, N.C., 1978).

13. Thomas E. Skidmore, "Workers and Soldiers: Urban Labor Movements and Elite Responses in Twentieth-Century Latin America," in Virginia Bernhard, ed., *Elites, Masses and Modernization in Latin America, 1850-1930* (Austin, Tex., 1979).

14. Debate in the field has centered instead on the relative virtues of the "dependency" approach as outlined in the work of Hobart Spalding, cited in n. 7 above, and on the promise of the "new" labor history developed by European and North American scholars. These issues are discussed in the Conclusion. See, in addition, the exchange between Eugene F. Sofer and Kenneth Paul Erickson, Patrick V. Peppe, and Hobart Spalding, and the articles by Peter Winn, "Oral History and the Factory Study: New Approaches to Labor History," and Charles Bergquist, "What Is Being Done? Some Recent Studies of the Urban Working Class and Organized Labor in Latin America," published, respectively, in the *Latin American Research Review* 15:1 (1980), 14:2 (1979), and 16:2 (1981).

uncritically orthodox Marxist and liberal approaches to labor history that were most appropriate to the historical development of the center of the world capitalist system. We accepted a dichotomy in studies of the working class that posited a separate set of assumptions and predicted behavior for rural workers (often viewed as "traditional peasants") and industrial workers (the "modern proletariat"). Rural workers were separated conceptually and defined out of "the labor movement"; urban workers—artisans and proletarians in manufacturing industry—became the subject of "labor history." The clumsiness of such a dichotomy was apparent to many. How did one classify, for example, workers in rural Cuban sugar complexes or miners in highland Peru who moved in and out of traditional agriculture?

It is only when this conceptual dichotomy, artificial to the history of workers in the underdeveloped world, is set aside, and a new category of analysis is put in its place, that the meaning of the labor history of Latin America fully reveals itself. The primary object of early-twentieth-century Latin American labor history should be workers in export production. Sometimes more "industrial" and "urban," sometimes more "agricultural" and "rural," sometimes pure wage workers, sometimes not, it is these workers, a class formed in response to the expansion of an evolving world capitalist system in the decades after 1880, who did the most to make the Latin American labor movements. It is these workers, and those in transport and export processing linked to them in the export-production complex, whose struggles most deeply influenced the modern trajectory of the various national labor movements of the region. By the mid-twentieth century, and in countries such as Mexico and Chile much earlier, that trajectory was institutionalized within the unions and parties of the labor movement and within the pattern of labor relations sanctioned by the state. In most of the countries of the region (Cuba is a notable exception) the trajectory of national labor movements established by mid-century has held firm in our own times. The fate of workers' early struggles thus powerfully influenced the pattern through which their postwar successors have affected the political and institutional life of the various nation-states of the region.

The validity of these assertions is easily demonstrated in logical terms, although it has yet to be confirmed in detailed historical studies. The Latin American structural economists amply demonstrated the enormous importance of the export sector to the economic health and development of capitalism in the Latin American periphery after 1880. That sector provided the major opportunity for capital accumulation in the countries of the region. It determined the volume of foreign-exchange earnings, and thus the ability of a given economy to absorb imports of manufactured goods, capital, and technology. It generated, directly or indirectly, the bulk of government revenue, and consequently decisively influenced the growth and power of the state. This extraordinary economic importance continued even under the conditions of large-scale industrialization achieved in some Latin American nations by the middle of the twentieth century. In furnishing vital foreign exchange, the export sector functioned under the conditions of import-substituting industrialization as a substitute for a capital-goods industry.

No two export economies were alike, of course, in terms of their capital, labor, and technology requirements. Some proved much more vulnerable than others to fluctuations in the world market. In some, ownership of the means of production was foreign and highly concentrated; in others it was domestic and diffused. Some employed large numbers of workers; others few. Some were high-wage economies; others not. Some produced exclusively for export; others produced for both the domestic and the international market. The structural economists showed how these characteristics and many others had radically different implications for domestic capital accumulation, economic diversification, and infrastructural development in the various Latin American countries during the classic era of free trade before 1930. They demonstrated how each characteristic influenced the ability of a given society to respond to the opportunities for industrialization during the crisis of the capitalist world order and the partial breakdown of the international division of labor in the period 1930-45. Finally, they showed how these structural differences continued to influence the success of national industrialization in the modified international division of labor that took form in the postwar decades.

Clearly, this kind of structural historical analysis can easily become economistic. By divorcing the study of economic development from the human forces that economic transformation unleashed—social classes, ideas, political parties—the Latin American structural economists not only tended to oversimplify the process of economic development, but in the end were unable to explain adequately the very problem they set out to answer: why some Latin American societies were more successful than others in the pursuit of economic development as the twentieth century progressed.[15]

15. I have excluded from this discussion the influential studies of the North American neo-Marxist economists Paul Baran, *The Political Economy of Growth* (New York, 1957), and André Gunder Frank, *Capitalism and Underdevelopment in Latin America* (New York, 1967), which emerged about the same time as those of the structural economists. These authors rightly insisted on the congenital weaknesses of peripheral capitalism and made fundamental contributions to our understanding of the mechanisms through which surplus is extracted from peripheral societies and siphoned toward the industrial core of the world system. But in their preoccupation with demonstrating the failure of capitalist development in Latin America and mechanical insistence on the inevitability of socialist revolution, they proved no less economistic and deterministic than the structural economists. By denying the developmental opportunities within Latin American capitalism, the neo-Marxists found themselves unable to account for the social complexity and diversity of Latin American history, making their work of limited use in the study of those societies.

The difficulties the structural economists encountered in explaining modern Argentine economic development provide a telling case in point. According to their analysis, the livestock and grain export economy that emerged in Argentina after 1880 was uniquely favorable to national economic development. Nationally owned, modest in its capital and technology requirements, geographically diffuse, high-wage, and relatively unaffected by fluctuations in world demand over a long period of time, it should have favored domestic capital accumulation, economic diversification, and sustained economic growth. Argentina should have been the most successful example of economic development in the region, and in fact was so until about 1945. Soon after that date, however, the economy began to falter, and the nation became the first in the region to fall victim to the contradictions of industrialization in the postwar era. To this day, Argentina has failed to emerge from the long period of economic stagnation, social conflict, and political crisis that first became manifest at mid-century. Argentina's crisis of development, as we shall see, is only indirectly related to export structure. It is a crisis that must be understood primarily in terms of a powerful labor movement conditioned by that structure that since 1945 has stymied the vigorous development of Argentine capitalism and forced established groups again and again to jettison the principles of liberal democracy.

Although Latin American structuralism, by itself, proved inadequate to the task of explaining the region's economic development, it provided essential conceptual tools for such analysis. Combined with traditional Marxist premises about the role of class conflict in historical change, particularly the struggle between capital and labor in the modern era, such tools become a powerful aid in analyzing not only Latin American economic development, but the modern history of the region in general.

First of all, the economic structuralists alerted us to the overwhelming importance of workers in export production within the Latin American working class. Like owners of the means of export production in peripheral capitalist economies after 1880, export workers possessed tremendous inherent economic and political power. Contention between these two social classes forms a central theme in early-twentieth-century Latin American history, deeply influenced the pattern of economic and political change, and helped fix the basic direction of twentieth-century developments in the societies of the region.

In the second place, in pinpointing the variables that influenced economic growth, the structuralists inadvertently isolated a range of factors that encouraged or inhibited the development of working-class consciousness and organization. In the all-important export sector itself a variety of factors were involved. Geographic location and climatic conditions not only influenced the strength of social and cultural ties between export workers and the greater society, but helped determine the degree to which, as wage laborers, they depended on their jobs for their physical reproduction. Chilean nitrate workers, for example, labored in mines and processing plants in an isolated and otherwise uninhabited desert. They built informal social networks and cultural and political institutions for a class far removed from the major socializing institutions of Chilean society and utterly dependent on wages for its subsistence. The nationality of ownership in the export industry and the degree to which ownership was concentrated helped determine whether workers perceived themselves and their employers as separate, contending classes. Venezuelan oil workers, for example, quickly identified their class enemy as an international trust that manipulated the government at every turn. The capital intensiveness and technological sophistication of export production and processing influenced the organization of work and helped determine the size, concentration, skill, and wage level of the work force. The low capital requirements and simple production techniques used in Colombian coffee cultivation and processing, for example, enabled small landowners to compete successfully with large capitalist producers, and to maintain significant control over the means of production and the work process until recent times. The degree to which export production and wages reflected seasonal cycles or fluctuations in world demand and price not only gravely affected the material well-being of workers, but also shaped their sense of the fairness and rationality of the social relations that surrounded them. Such conditions, for example, laid the groundwork for the organization of the Cuban working class in sugar production. All of these variables affected the ability of capital to control or "discipline" the labor force by tapping unemployed, underemployed, or low-paid workers in the export sector and outside it during the periods of labor militancy. It was easy, for example, for management to replace striking workers in the meat-packing plants of Greater Buenos Aires, because there were waves of immigrants and underemployed workers available to take their unskilled jobs. Finally, the ethnic composition and nationality of export workers complicated their efforts to achieve internal unity as a class, and greatly affected their ability to meld nationalist and patriotic sentiments with their class perceptions in a collective struggle to improve their lives.

Nationalism also deeply influenced the broader issue of the relationship of export workers to their fellow workers and other social groups. Where export production involved a class and national dichotomy, one of national labor versus foreign capital, export workers were better able to mobilize the powerful sentiment of patriotism—a sentiment fostered by the dominant culture—in support of their class interests. In these circumstances, characteristic of Chile, Bolivia, Venezuela, and Cuba, among others, the class relationship between workers and capitalists in the foreign-owned export sector was recapitulated, in a sense, in the relationship of the whole peripheral society to the international economic system. The potential for anticapitalist alliances between labor and other social groups inherent in these analogous relationships was, in turn, greatly increased if the export sector proved unable to stimulate vigorous, sustained national economic development.

Where these structural conditions were reversed—where, that is, export production involved national capital and foreign or at least ethnically distinct labor—nationalist and patriotic sentiments could be turned more easily against labor. In these situations, illustrated in extreme form in Argentina, and to some degree in most nationally owned Latin American export economies, the class/national dichotomy in the export sector was reversed at the analogous level of the international system, and the potential for anticapitalist alliances between labor in the export sector and other social groups and classes in the larger society was greatly reduced. Such an alliance was even more unlikely if the export economy was relatively successful in directly fostering national economic development.

Of all these structural characteristics, however, the capital requirements of export production were the most important. Where those requirements were high, foreign capital was favored over national capital in the struggle for control over the means of production, capitalist relations of production tended to predominate over precapitalist ones, and concentrated rather than dispersed units of production were more likely to prevail. As a result, the structural variables that define export economies and influence their relative capacity to promote economic development over time tend to combine in patterned ways. And because these same structural variables also set the conditions for labor organization in the export sector and for class alliances between export workers and other groups, they tend to influence the development of the various national labor movements in predictable ways. Thus, for example, structural conditions such as foreign ownership and concentrated production that favor the development of cultural autonomy and class-conscious, anticapitalist labor organizations among export workers tend, at the same time, to inhibit the vigorous development of the economy as a whole. And this failure of capitalist development in turn strengthens the potential for broad, anti-imperialist alliances within the whole society. The reverse is also true. Structural variables such as national ownership, limited capital and technology demands, and diffuse geographical production systems, all of which inhibit labor organization in the export sector, tend at the same time (through their positive effects on other sectors of the economy) to promote economic development. And that economic development in turn limits the possibility for anticapitalist class alliances in the society as a whole.

If one continues to slice up historical causation in these neat and abstract ways, it is possible to locate modern Latin American societies along a continuum, defined by export structure, on which the potential for vigorous economic development functions inversely with the potential for labor organization and the strength of the Marxist left. Toward the left on such a continuum lie those export economies whose structural characteristics make them least likely to promote national economic growth and diversification; toward the right, those most likely to promote those developments. A country whose export economy falls toward the left on the continuum should also feature a historically strong, anticapitalist labor movement; a country whose export economy falls to the right, a historically weak, or ideologically co-opted labor movement. Stated differently, in countries with export economies situated on the left of the continuum the political left should be strong and the historical possibility for socialist transformation greatest. This crude set of relationships and predictions seems in fact to have considerable explanatory power. Those familiar with the history of the major nations of the region will recognize that Cuba, Chile, Bolivia, Venezuela (and perhaps Mexico[16]) fall historically to the left on the continuum, whereas Argentina, Uruguay, Brazil, and Colombia fall to the right.

Such an exercise is a useful first step in analysis. For several reasons, however, it obscures almost as much as it reveals about the individual Latin American labor movements and their influence on the development of their countries. In the first place, although the structural variables that define export economies tend to cluster, that clustering, in the real world, is never absolute. For example, foreign ownership, capital intensiveness, and technological sophistication—interrelated factors that tend to hinder domestic capital accumulation and economic diversification—may not be combined with concentrated geographical production and a small labor force, factors that also tend to have negative implications for domestic economic development. Cuba's sugar export economy approximates such a case. Conversely, domestic ownership, limited capital and technological requirements, and diffuse geographical production systems— factors that promote the development of domestic transport systems and stimulate the growth of agriculture and industry to supply the export sector—may not be combined with a high-wage labor force that helps to create a national market for domestically produced wage goods. Colombia's coffee economy fairly closely fits this pattern.

In the second place, an export economy may have a special character-

---

16. This interpretation of Mexican history is not obvious, much less widely accepted, but see the suggestive approach to the Mexican Revolution by François-Xavier Guerra, "La Révolution mexicaine: D'abord une révolution minière?," *Annales E.S.C.*, 36:5 (Sept.-Oct. 1981):785-814. I return to this issue in the Conclusion.

istic of such overwhelming importance that the predicted tendency of its impact on economic development and the labor movement, though always latent, is constantly overcome. Venezuela's petroleum economy is a good illustration. In terms of most of the variables noted above, that economy closely resembles Chile's nitrate and copper export economy. Yet unlike Chile's mineral exports, for which world demand and price have fluctuated wildly, and declined generally, in this century, the value of Venezuelan oil exports has until recently expanded geometrically. The Venezuelan labor movement initially developed under Marxist leadership and early cemented a broad anti-imperialist alliance with other social groups. But these developments were truncated after 1945, and again in the early 1960's, by liberal reformers able to win huge concessions from the oil companies, which they used to secure and maintain a compromise with organized labor and to institute significant social reforms.

Finally, and most important, is the fact that the two dependent variables derived from export structure—the potential for economic development, on the one hand, and the potential for labor organization and the growth of the left, on the other—interact historically in such complex and unexpected ways that they may in fact reverse the direction of the initial causal connection, and transform the independent variable into a dependent one. The subtle and often tragic irony of such paradoxical historical developments can be appreciated fully only in detailed historical analysis.

The chapters that follow explore the interaction between export structure, labor, and the left in the historical development of four of the larger, more economically advanced Latin American nations. The first two chapters deal comparatively with Chile and Argentina, the next two with Venezuela and Colombia. Although each chapter attempts to provide an interpretation of national history from the early nineteenth century until contemporary times, each emphasizes the period of the twentieth century when the ideological and institutional trajectory of the labor movement was fixed, and when its enduring influence on national life was clearly defined. The chapter on Chile thus concentrates on developments before 1930, whereas those on Argentina, Venezuela, and Colombia focus on the period up to mid-century.

Argentina and Colombia are treated at greater length than Chile and Venezuela, but this was not decided by their size alone (Argentina and Colombia, with populations of roughly 28,000,000 in 1983, are about twice as large as Chile, with some 12,000,000 people, and Venezuela, with 16,000,000). The depth of treatment reflects primarily the state of the existing literature on the four countries. In Argentine and Colombian labor history, the sector of the working class emphasized in this study—

workers in export production and processing—has received relatively little previous attention. Moreover, in Argentine and Colombian historiography as a whole, the importance of export workers to the evolution of the labor movement and national history has been slighted. In Chilean and, more recently, in Venezuelan historical studies, by contrast, export workers have attracted considerable attention, and their influence on the course of national life is more widely recognized.

In choosing to focus my research on these four countries and to pair them for comparative, sequential treatment I have sought to illustrate the power and range of the interpretive framework outlined in this introductory chapter. In important respects, Chile and Argentina approximate polar types among the Latin American nations. This is true in terms of both export structure and, until very recently, twentieth-century political evolution. In Chile's foreign-owned nitrate and copper export economy, organized labor evolved under Marxist leadership and ideology. The left became the strongest in Latin America. Conversely, in Argentina's domestically owned livestock and cereal export economy, organized labor ultimately became corporatist in leadership and ideology and a weak left was eclipsed by the right-wing popular nationalism of Juan Domingo Perón. The different political trajectory of the left contained within it paradoxical implications for economic development and social transformation in the two societies. In Chile the paradox was most poignant in political terms, in Argentina in economic terms. In Chile, the left's political success within a bourgeois, democratic system worked to constrain liberal capitalist economic development after 1950 and fatally undermined the left's ability to effect the transformation to socialism. In Argentina, the eclipse of the left and the rise of Peronism effectively smothered the potential for social transformation and severely eroded the country's once great potential for economic development. Thus, by the 1970's each country, by different routes and in part for different reasons, reached an economic and political impasse that was at least temporarily "resolved" through the imposition of authoritarian military regimes, the repression of organized labor, and the pursuit of neoclassical liberal economic policies. There is a strong element of convergence in these developments. As Guillermo O'Donnell[17] and others have shown, since the 1950's and 1960's all of the larger, more developed Latin American countries have faced a set of common economic and political problems generated by the exhaustion of the "easy" phase of import-substituting industrialization. Emphasis on the mechanisms of contemporary convergence, however, should not obscure the ongoing legacy of historical divergence. That divergence helps explain the great differences in the success and functioning

17. See *Modernization and Bureaucratic-Authoritarianism,* cited in n. 5 above.

of the authoritarian regimes in these two countries and has decisively influenced the nature of their current transformation.

The export economies of Venezuela and Colombia diverge in the same directions as Chile's and Argentina's do, but each has a special characteristic that moderates and complicates its influence on labor organization and economic and political evolution. Thus, on a continuum defined by export structure and twentieth-century political evolution, Chile and Argentina tend toward the poles, whereas Venezuela and Colombia lie toward, but on opposite sides of, the center. Venezuela's foreign-owned petroleum economy, unlike most other mineral export economies (especially Chile's), has experienced sustained growth and generated increasingly large government revenues since its inception in the early decades of the twentieth century. Colombia's domestically owned coffee economy, unlike most other agricultural export economies (including Argentina's), has featured very widespread ownership of the means of export production. The basic structure of the Venezuelan export economy favored the initial autonomy and organizational strength of labor and the left; its special feature helps to explain the displacement of the left by the reformist liberal governments that emerged in the 1940's and 1950's. The structure of the Colombian export economy hindered the development of working-class cultural and organizational autonomy; its special feature tended to push social and economic unrest into traditional political channels and toward the intraclass warfare of the period called *la violencia* in the 1940's and 1950's. In both countries these mid-century developments had profound implications for economic and political evolution. They resulted in organized labor movements that, in contrast to the left- and right-wing political commitments of Chilean and Argentine labor, were primarily concerned with bread-and-butter issues. In both countries, the weakness of the left (more extreme in Colombia than in Venezuela) has contributed fundamentally to the maintenance of relatively open liberal developmentalist regimes in the postwar period.

Marxists will have noted by now that in largely ignoring the standard category for analysis of Latin American labor history, the industrial proletariat, I seem to have thrown out the baby with the bathwater. Throughout the discussion of export structure I made little mention of perhaps the most important feature that distinguishes one export economy from another—the existence or not of fully developed capitalist relations of production, the existence or not of free wage workers. I did so not because I consider that issue unimportant, but because I wanted to make an important point too often slighted in orthodox Marxist Latin American labor history.

Latin American Marxists, many of them labor and political activists affiliated with the Communist parties of the region, have written many— and some of the best—studies on labor history. Unlike the majority of their academic counterparts, these militant activists never lost sight of the centrality of class conflict and the historical importance of the organized working class in the region. Moreover, and again unlike their academic counterparts, many recognized intuitively the importance of export workers to the march of labor and historical developments in their own societies. Indeed, it was from among the ranks of export workers that many of these grass-roots Marxist labor historians often sprang, it was toward export workers that they directed their organizational and political energies, and it was around export workers that they built their analyses.[18]

Many of these writers thus implicitly rejected the category of industrial workers as the primary focus for the early-twentieth-century labor history of their own societies. They did not, however, reflect deeply on the meaning of export structure for the relative success or failure of the Marxist left in organizing these workers, in developing national labor movements, and in influencing the course of national history. Part of the reason lies in the lack of comparative focus in their work, a kind of occupational hazard built into the lives of organizers and activists who depend on analytic concepts developed by others—in this case, by others outside their own societies. These activists worked with the simplistic orthodox Marxist notion that capitalism engenders a proletariat that, under the leadership of the Communist Party, gradually acquires the consciousness necessary to overthrow its capitalist oppressors and establish a socialist order. When such developments seemed to be confirmed by the course of national history, as they were in Chile, orthodox Marxists complacently and uncritically patted themselves on the back. When developments did not conform to these predictions, as in Argentina, Marxists tended to attribute the failure to tactics and leadership, or to ruling-class conspiracies, or to the ignorance of the working class. No other attitudes are possible if the main issue that determines the trajectory of Latin American labor movements is the existence of capitalist relations of production. In point of fact, however, such relations have been more, not less, developed in Argentina than in Chile throughout this century.

As we shall see, particularly in the Colombian case, the social relations of production in an export economy are fundamental to the analysis of labor history and the role of the left in Latin America. Given free wage

18. Outstanding examples of the work of these labor historians are Elías Lafertte, *Vida de un comunista* (Santiago, 1961); José Peter, *Historia y luchas de los obreros de la carne* (Buenos Aires, 1947); José Peter, *Crónicas proletarias* (Buenos Aires, 1968); and Rodolfo Quintero, *La cultura del petróleo*, 2d ed. (Caracas, 1976). These works are discussed in subsequent chapters.

labor, however, it is differences in export structure that best explain the remarkable disparity in the labor movements of Latin America, and the very unequal strength of the left in countries such as Chile and Argentina.

I discuss the strengths of this whole approach in greater depth in the concluding chapter of the volume. That chapter emphasizes ways in which the interpretive model advanced here would have to be modified to account for the historical specificity of the four countries compared. It also explores a range of other historical factors that limit the usefulness of the model in interpreting the diverse histories of the other countries in the region. The chapter ends with some reflections on the implications of the study as a whole. These, I argue, transcend the specifics of the role of export workers in twentieth-century Latin America. By placing labor at the center of historical analysis, the study raises conceptual and method-ological questions for the interpretation of the modern history of other societies as well.

Abstract model-building of the kind pursued in this chapter can help to orient research and provide historians with a way to select illuminating case studies for comparative analysis. By itself, however, such modeling is a mechanical exercise, artificially abstracted from life and incapable of touching and moving its human subject matter.

Historians are rightly impatient with such models because, more than most social scientists, they learn through training and experience to ap-preciate the complexity and untidiness of social reality and change. Social scientists learn to cut off a manageable slice of social life and to specify as precisely as possible how various factors combine to influence it in pat-terned ways. Historians, by contrast, share more fully the conviction that such fragments cannot be adequately understood apart from the whole. The difference is, of course, one of degree, but it leads to quite distinct methodological traditions.

Historians have developed methods of analysis and modes of exposi-tion that, however imperfect, should be understood as responses to the magnitude of the comprehensive task they set for themselves. Historians try to keep concrete human experience at the center of their analysis, a commitment that explains their reverence for primary sources in mono-graphic studies, and their reliance on the historiographical method in general interpretive works. This method, used extensively in this com-parative study, takes as its starting point not the absolute symmetrical de-mands of a model in search of confirmation through historical data, but rather a critical mastery of the corpus of literature written on a place and time. Historians attempt to write engagingly for the literate layman, and share a predilection for narrative and a preoccupation with prose style. These expository means reflect the assumption that general, dialectical social processes are best unraveled step by step as they unfold through time, and that interpretation should be conveyed to a general audience with a nuanced subtlety appropriate to the effort to understand such complexity.

For all these reasons, the major analytical task of this book is to illuminate the questions posed by the body of historical writing on each of the four countries compared. The measure of its success should be its ability to explain, in laymen's terms, these very different historiographical issues through a common emphasis on the human experience of workers in export production.

2

Chile

The anatomy of Chile is fine and arbitrary. . . . In image and reality, the North is the head of Chile. . . . And what a beautiful and powerful head it is! Chile's budget depended on the sweat of the nitrate shovelers and tailing scrapers of Tarapacá, Antofagasta, and Taltal. The nation was sown in the nitrate trenches. And in the trenches the Chilean was remade, acquiring the visage of a fighter.

Andrés Sabella, *Semblanza del norte chileno* (Santiago, 1955)

The Distinctiveness of Chilean History

It is customary to begin studies of Chile with an emphasis on its distinctiveness. Its geography is unique and spectacular. More than 4,000 kilometers in length, the country averages less than 180 kilometers in width. Chile's ecology ranges from the arid Atacama Desert in the north, through the Mediterranean climate of the central valley (where most Chileans live), to the rain-swept forests of the south. Bounded by sea and desert, and by the massive Andes on the east, Chile lies farthest of all Latin American countries from the North Atlantic centers of the Western civilization of which it forms an integral part. Yet of all the Latin American nations, Chile seems to have evolved politically in a way that most closely approximates patterns in the industrialized nations of the North Atlantic Basin.

Thus a second distinctive feature of Chile, one stressed tirelessly, at least until recently, by observers both Chilean and foreign: its stable, democratic political system. Unlike the new nations of the rest of Spanish America, Chile quickly stabilized politically following independence. During the nineteenth century it developed a relatively strong state and a vigorous party system. Periodic elections were held, and rules were established for the peaceful transfer of political power. This process continued in the twentieth century and, as suffrage slowly expanded, Chile developed a very wide spectrum of ideologically oriented, mass-based political parties and a reputation for democratic pluralism. Finally, it distinguished itself in 1970 by electing the first Marxist head of state in the Western Hemisphere.

The military coup of September 1973, which ended that remarkable democratic experiment and destroyed the political institutions that had made the election of such a government possible, raises serious questions about the alleged distinctiveness of Chilean political history. Looking back, the coups and attempted coups that dot Chilean history over the last 150 years now become more salient. The civil war of 1891, with its tragic parallels to the events of 1973, takes on new significance. So also does the period of military intervention and extreme political repression and instability of the years 1924 to 1932.

In fact, paradoxical as it may sound, what is unique in Chilean political history is in large part the result of an important characteristic of Chilean social development that is shared by all Latin American nations: its dependence, since the nineteenth century, on exports of primary commodities to the industrialized nations of the North Atlantic. It is this shared characteristic, as much as the legacy of Western culture and Iberian colonialism, that justifies speaking of the whole of Latin America as an analytical unit in the modern period, and that largely determined which elements of Western culture (such as a strong state and a vigorous party system) grew and developed in Chile and which elements (such as economic and social structures) remained stunted or distorted.

Thus, for all that Chilean historiography may emphasize the role of great men and the early imposition of centralized political institutions in determining the political stability and economic growth of the nineteenth century,[1] the reality is somewhat more prosaic. Although the inheritance from the colonial era, particularly the relative cultural and ethnic homogeneity of Chilean society and the absence of powerful regional interests outside the heartland of central Chile, was an important factor, the overriding determinant of early-nineteenth-century political stability was the fact that Chile, alone among Spanish-American countries, developed a viable export economy in the period 1830–60. Expanding exports of silver, copper, and wheat underwrote the community of interest within the dominant class of exporters and importers in central Chile. This class divided into contending parties over secondary issues such as the role of the Church (an institution relatively weaker in Chile than in its Andean neighbors), but it was united over the basic issues of liberal political economy and maintenance of the social status quo. Growing international trade stimulated by exports reinforced this consensus and provided reve-

---

1. In more vulgar cultural-racial interpretations, nineteenth-century Chilean political stability, economic growth, and military success are the result of a felicitous mixture of selected regional varieties of Spanish blood and culture, a sparse and proud Araucanian Indian population, and the vigorous genes and world view of Northern European immigrants. The biocultural offspring of this happy marriage became the "Prussians" or the "English" of South America.

nue to build a strong, effective state.[2] Then, as the technical limits of Chilean agriculture and mining were reached and the export economy ceased to grow (a crisis made much more serious by the worldwide depression of the 1870's), Chile was able to use the strength and resources of its early development to mount a successful war (1879–83) against its weaker neighbors, Peru and Bolivia, and annex a new and exploitable export resource base, the nitrate fields of the Atacama Desert. There followed an enormous increase in the value of Chilean exports. And although much of the ownership of the nitrate industry passed from Peruvian into British hands in the aftermath of the war, the Chilean state, from 1880 to 1930, derived huge revenues directly (through export taxes) and indirectly (through customs receipts) from the foreign trade it generated. Meanwhile, Chilean agriculturalists, merchants, and industrialists benefited handsomely as government nitrate revenues grew, and the whole economy, stimulated by the growth in the mining sector, expanded.

The nitrate export economy transformed the dynamics of Chilean politics. The issues of Chilean control of the nitrate enclave and the disposition of government nitrate revenues precipitated the breakdown of elite consensus and constitutional norms in the short, bloody civil war of 1891. But nitrate expansion also underwrote the stability and form of the political arrangements that grew out of the war. The executive would not play a direct, developmentalist role in the investment of nitrate revenues. Nitrate revenues were too central to the economic life of the nation to leave them to the discretion of one man (the president) or to the party or parties he represented. Rather, control of the state and its revenues was vested in the parliament. There, all sectors of the dominant class and their foreign allies—their weight measured by their ability to control local elections and form party alliances—could struggle over the division and destination of the spoils.

The social and political forces unleashed by the expansion of the nitrate economy in the half century following 1880 generated a third distinguishing characteristic, the most important of modern Chilean history: the rise of a strong, leftist labor movement. The implications of this de-

---

2. The point is not that there were no sectoral economic and ideological interests contending within this broader class framework. Issues such as free trade and the role of the state in economic development also divided the social elite and, like the Church issue, precipitated several attempts to bypass constitutional and political norms to impose programs and win control of the spoils of government. But these divisions were not as sharp, nor were their partisans as desperate, as in other Latin American countries, particularly the ones discussed in this volume. Political contention in Chile developed within a broader and deeper elite consensus backed by the greater legitimacy and coercive capability of the state. Each of these distinguishing political characteristics was fostered and maintained by a viable export economy. This issue is discussed separately in each of the country chapters and treated more generally in the concluding chapter.

velopment are systematically ignored in liberal historiography, yet it is the one development that most decisively sets the nation off from its Latin American neighbors. The rise of a leftist labor movement after the turn of the century destroyed the country's political stability and caused the temporary breakdown of the party system in the 1920's. In the decades following the collapse of the nitrate economy in 1930, in an environment conditioned by the exploitation of a new mineral resource, copper, the Chilean labor movement helped reconstruct the party system and pushed the entire body politic to the left. That process not only decisively influenced the course of Chilean political history, it fundamentally altered the pattern of Chilean economic development.

To summarize, then, it is the rise of a powerful, institutionalized, Marxist labor movement that most fundamentally distinguishes modern Chilean history. If the early emergence of a viable export economy in central Chile helps explain the political distinctiveness of nineteenth-century Chilean history, it is the nitrate and copper export economies that mold that legacy in the twentieth century. It is through the labor movement that the complex relationship between export structure and Chilean economic and political development becomes clear, and the meaning for modern human history of Chile's unique geography is revealed.

The Structure of the Nitrate Export Economy

The action of frigid Antarctic currents, prevailing winds, and elevated daytime temperatures makes a desert of a long strip of the central west coast of South America. In the driest part of this desert, the 700 kilometers from roughly 19° to 26° south latitude, lies a vast, elevated flatland, or *pampa*. Beneath the pampa's arid surface, in an area roughly 20 to 80 kilometers from the coast, lie shallow, discontinuous deposits of *caliche*, the raw material from which the natural fertilizer sodium nitrate can be extracted.[3] Here, far removed from populous central Chile, a huge mining and industrial complex emerged in the last decades of the nineteenth century. (See Map 2.1.)

Virtually unexploited until the nineteenth century, the nitrate fields of South America were developed in response to the changing needs and technology of European industrialization. The spread of capitalist relations of production in European agriculture, the movement of millions of people off the land into cities and factories, and the explosive growth

3. See Javier Gandarillas and Orlando Ghigliotto Salas, eds., *La industria del salitre en Chile por Semper i Michels* (Santiago, 1908), for a translation of the detailed and lavishly illustrated report of two scientists sent to Chile in 1903 under the auspices of the German government and an organization of beet-sugar producers. The origins of the nitrate industry are thoroughly examined in the classic work by Oscar Bermúdez, *Historia del salitre desde sus orígenes hasta la Guerra del Pacífico* (Santiago, 1913).

Map 2.1. Chile, ca. 1900, Showing Nitrate Fields and Major Nitrate Ports.

of population led to ever more intensive and scientific farming and a growing need for fertilizer. Guano, the fossilized bird excrement preserved on the easily accessible rainless islands off Peru's southern coast, was first tapped in the 1830's and 1840's to meet this need. But as supplies were depleted, as demand continued to grow, and as scientific understanding of plant nutrition broadened, the fertilizing qualities of sodium nitrate became widely appreciated. Nitrate was far less accessible and much more costly to produce than guano had been. But large capital investments and the application of new European technology to production and transport systems made large-scale exploitation of nitrate deposits in the deserts of southern Peru, Bolivia, and northern Chile possible after 1870. Although the bulk of nitrate production would always be used in fertilizer, nitrate served another need of the expanding capitalist nation-states of Western Europe—it furnished the raw material for gunpowder and explosives.[4]

The nitrate export economy, forcibly appropriated by Chile in 1880, profoundly influenced every aspect of Chilean society for the next half century. Part of that influence can be measured statistically. Export figures illustrate the expansion and cyclical nature of the industry, and annual employment figures tell us the number and nationality of the workers involved. Other available data allow us to estimate the industry's contribution to the national treasury and gauge the influence of those revenues on the government's fiscal policies; to sketch the evolving structure of the ownership of the production facilities; to estimate, through the figures on production costs and profits, the industry's contribution to national income and the process of capital accumulation in Chile; and to see some of the effects the nitrate sector had on other parts of the Chilean economy. The remainder of this section presents and evaluates information on these and other broad structural features of the Chilean nitrate economy.[5] Only with that structure clearly in mind can we begin to probe its implications for social and political developments in Chile.

Figure 2.1 provides information on the growth, crisis, and ultimate collapse of the Chilean nitrate export economy during the period 1880-1930. We can see that nitrate exports grew impressively, if a bit unsteadily, up to the First World War. Exports, which stood at 330,000 metric tons in 1875, topped 1,000,000 tons in 1890 and reached 2,000,000 by 1908. In 1913, on the eve of the war, they peaked at 2,750,000 tons. The

4. Mirko Lamer, *The World Fertilizer Economy* (Stanford, Calif., 1957), Chap. 3.

5. Much of this information and analysis is drawn from two excellent studies co-authored by Carmen Cariola and Osvaldo Sunkel: "Chile," in Roberto Cortés Conde and Stanley J. Stein, eds., *Latin America: A Guide to Economic History, 1830-1930* (Berkeley, Calif., 1977), pp. 273-363; and "Expansión salitrera y transformaciones socio-económicos en Chile: 1880-1930," unpublished manuscript. I wish to thank Mr. Sunkel for sending me this paper.

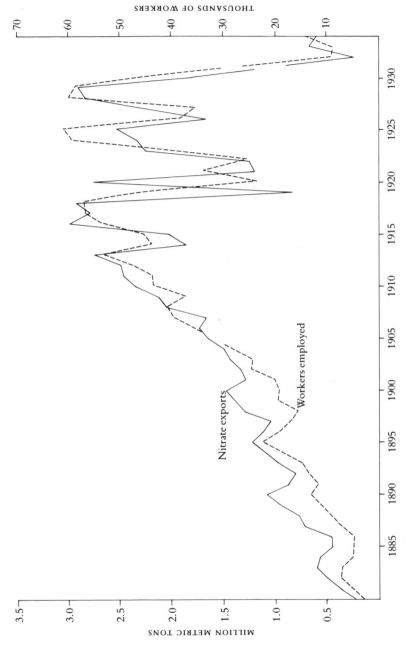

Figure 2.1. Chilean Nitrate Exports (in metric tons) and Workers Employed in the Nitrate Industry (in thousands), 1880–1934. Source: Arthur Lawrence Stickell, "Migration and Mining Labor in Northern Chile in the Nitrate Era, 1880–1930" (Ph.D. diss., Indiana University, 1979), Appendix A.

war seriously disrupted trade with Chile's major nitrate customers, and exports plummeted in 1914 and 1915. By 1916, however, wartime demand in Great Britain and the United States (which had replaced Germany as Chile's primary nitrate market) pushed exports above the prewar level, and they peaked again in 1918 at just under 3,000,000 tons. In the decade following the war the industry experienced a period of widely fluctuating demand, triggered by cyclical trends in the world economy and violent postwar changes in the level of U.S. imports. Exports fell to only 804,000 tons in 1919, shot back up to 2,750,000 tons in 1920, then fell again during the depression of 1921-22, when they averaged only 1,250,000 tons a year. The years 1923-25 saw another dramatic upswing, with exports reaching 2,500,000 tons in the latter year. After falling again in 1926 and 1927, they rose sharply over the next two years, to stand at approximately the all-time high level of 1918 at the end of the decade. But with the advent of the Great Depression, the industry virtually collapsed. At the nadir of the Depression in Chile, in 1932, nitrate exports amounted to only 244,000 tons, or less than 9 percent of their 1929 level.[6] To some extent, however, the data graphed in the figure, based as they are on yearly averages, mask the extremely volatile nature of the nitrate economy, especially after 1913. Monthly highs and lows during periods of rapid change were even more extreme.

Long-term trends in the world fertilizer economy underlay these violent fluctuations and the ultimate collapse of the Chilean nitrate economy. Chile was always the only commercial source of natural sodium nitrate. But just as the changing demands and technology of the industrial nations of the North Atlantic brought forth the Chilean nitrate economy, so they undermined and destroyed it. By 1895 European scientists had succeeded in fixing nitrogen by artificial means. Although this process was prohibitively expensive at first, new and cheaper techniques were soon developed, and the chemical fertilizer industry expanded. Finally, under the political and economic pressures of war and worldwide depression, first Germany and then the United States and other industrial powers turned to domestic suppliers to meet their needs.[7]

The wide fluctuations in world demand and prices for nitrates led the largest producers in Chile to form cartels to limit production and ensure

6. The industry slowly recovered after the Depression, and by the 1950's production again hit 2,000,000 tons, the level first reached in 1908. But nitrate never regained its central role in the economy. Struggling to maintain its 5 percent share of the world fertilizer market, the industry could contribute relatively little, proportionately, to foreign trade and government revenue. Meanwhile, mechanization cut its labor needs in half.

7. Cariola and Sunkel, "Expansión salitrera" (cited in n. 5), table 16, shows Chile's declining share of the world nitrate fertilizer market over the years 1913-24. Lamer, *World Fertilizer Economy* (cited in n. 4), p. 38, describes the changing technology of chemical fertilizers.

steady profits after 1890.[8] Although these efforts worked at cross-purposes with the interests of the Chilean state, whose nitrate revenues were tied to the volume, not the value, of exports, they met with some short-term success before the First World War. But with the rising importance of synthetics and the competition fostered by changing processing techniques within the Chilean industry itself—especially as U.S. capital and technology moved into the industry in the 1920's—the efforts of producers to moderate violent fluctuations in world demand failed. Although the Chilean government had subsidized stockpiles in an attempt to cushion the war's effect on production, it was only with the advent of the Great Depression and the collapse of the industry that it moved to take a major, direct role in the production and sale of nitrate.

Certain features of nitrate production as it developed in Chile made output in the industry especially sensitive to changes in world demand and prices. Nitrate is an extremely bulky commodity, and also one whose production was labor-intensive. Consequently, rather than invest in major storage facilities, companies found it easier and cheaper simply to dismiss their workers and reduce or close operations during cyclical downturns. Several circumstances facilitated this classic capitalist response, the first being the rapidity with which Chilean labor responded to renewed employment opportunities and higher wages in the nitrate sector during upswings. Given the relative lack of employment opportunities in agriculture and manufacturing in the nitrate enclave, laid-off men simply hung on with working relatives or friends or crowded into the port towns to await renewed employment. In more severely depressed times, nitrate workers were forced to leave the north by the tens of thousands and search for work in central Chile. But because, as we shall see, activity in all sectors of the Chilean economy was quickly affected by the fortunes of the nitrate sector, serious drops in nitrate production limited jobs all over Chile in public works, industry, coal production, and even agriculture. Widespread national unemployment and wage-cutting during these periods facilitated the recruitment of workers in central Chile once labor demand revived in the north. Recruitment was also made easier, after the turn of the century, as the development of rail lines and shipping routes increased the geographic mobility of workers eager to improve their wages and conditions of work. Real wages were higher in nitrate production than in other sectors of the Chilean economy, and workers responded avidly to the recruiting efforts of nitrate companies.

The Chilean state played an active role in ensuring the flow of labor in

8. Prices for Chilean nitrates closely paralleled changes in world demand. After exceptionally high prices at the end of the First World War, the price of a metric ton (in 1960 U.S. dollars) fluctuated between $40 and $90 in subsequent years. The all-time high was $144 in 1920. Cariola and Sunkel, "Expansión salitrera" (cited in n. 5), table 9.

and out of the nitrate enclave. It provided free transportation to workers and their families out of the north during severe depressions in the industry. As the fluctuations in production became more severe and the numbers of people involved increased, it began to provide food and shelter for the unemployed in the nitrate port towns and in the capital, Santiago. By 1913 the state was actively engaged in recruiting workers during upswings and trying to relocate and employ them during downswings.

But though the state was willing to take steps that would ensure nitrate companies their labor force and diffuse social tensions during hard times, it refused, until the labor reforms of 1924, to adopt measures that would have shifted some of the burden during depressions from labor to capital. Until that date, nitrate companies were not required to give notice to the workers they laid off, to pay them severance pay, or to contribute to the cost of their transportation out of the north.

The human cost of the cyclical unemployment in the Chilean nitrate industry can be judged from the data graphed in Figure 2.1. The work force ranged between 3,000 and 7,000 during the early 1880's, then expanded to a peak of over 13,000 in 1890. Employment reached another peak of more than 22,000 in 1895, declined in the late 1890's, then rose steeply—to reach 53,000 in 1913. After declining sharply at the start of the war, the work force increased to almost 57,000 in 1918. Employment then fell precipitously during the postwar depression of 1920-22, which saw the work force cut by more than half. Thereafter the number of workers fluctuated wildly. Employment rose to over 60,000 in 1925, fell back to only 36,000 in 1927, and then rose again in 1928-29, when it averaged about 59,000 a year. Three years later, in 1932, there were only 8,535 people still at work in the nitrate sector.

The economic insecurity of the Chilean labor force in a society tied to the boom-and-bust cycles of nitrate production was heightened by the government's inflationary policies during the nitrate era. Paper money was introduced to finance the War of the Pacific and was retained, despite an abortive attempt to return to a metal-based currency in the late nineteenth century. The government steadily expanded the paper money supply until the late 1920's. Although the economic effects of inflation and the motives of the political groups in control of Chilean monetary policy are debated in the literature,[9] there is wide agreement over the depressing effect of moderate inflation on the real wages of workers in all economic sectors. Fluctuating exchange rates and falling real wages sparked some of the most significant worker mobilizations, particularly in the nitrate sector, during the period 1890-1925.

9. The orthodoxy that the chronic inflation of the nitrate era was a result of the single-minded policy of landowners in control of the state was first challenged by Albert O. Hirschman, "Inflation in Chile," in *Journeys Toward Progress* (Garden City, N.Y., 1965), pp. 215-96.

As the nitrate economy expanded in the half century following 1880, so also did the revenues of the Chilean government. Before the outbreak of the War of the Pacific, the income of the Chilean state stood at less than 20,000,000 pesos a year. By the early 1880's that figure had doubled. Then, after an eighteenfold jump during the 30-year period 1882-1912 (to more than 750,000,000 pesos), revenues declined sharply, falling to 500,000,000 pesos during the First World War and the postwar depression. By 1922 the figure had climbed back to prewar levels, by 1924 reached the billion-peso mark, and by the end of the decade was approaching two billion pesos. Even if inflation accounted for almost half of this increase, the real expansion of government revenues during this 50-year period was spectacular.

This impressive growth was due in large part to taxes generated by the nitrate industry. By far the most important of the direct sources of revenue was the tax on exports of nitrate and iodine (a by-product of nitrate processing). This tax quadrupled during the War of the Pacific, and by the early 1880's it contributed about 20 percent of the state's ordinary income. That share rose quickly in the next several years, to hover around 50 percent for most of the period 1890-1917, then declined to 40 percent or lower as the industry entered the protracted period of crisis and sharp fluctuations in demand in the postwar period.[10] Another important direct source of revenue was the tax levied on the acquisition of nitrate lands. Nitrate capitalists claimed that they had invested £14,000,000 in such acquisitions up to 1903; this compared with an investment of only £4,000,000 in processing plants and less than £3,000,000 in railway and port facilities.[11]

In addition to these direct contributions to the treasury, the expansion of the nitrate industry stimulated the growth of foreign trade, with the result that customs revenues on imports rose dramatically. Until 1890, in fact, the government derived more income from this indirect effect of nitrate expansion than it gained from export taxes. Thereafter, throughout most of the period up to 1930, import taxes provided between a quarter and a third of the state's ordinary income.

These new and growing sources of revenue transformed the structure of state finance during the nitrate era. Internal sales, inheritance, and

10. The value of Chilean exports rose from 81,000,000 pesos in 1890 to 525,000,000 pesos in 1920; nitrate exports accounted for between 60 and 80 percent of the total value during that period. The data on government revenue in these paragraphs are taken from Cariola and Sunkel, "Expansión salitrera" (cited in n. 5), tables 6, 7, 22, 25, and 26.

11. Manuel Salas Lavaqui, *Trabajos y antecedentes presentados al supremo gobierno de Chile por la comisión consultativa del Norte* (Santiago, 1908), p. 606. Payments for the acquisitions of nitrate lands appear as extraordinary revenue in Chilean budget records; extraordinary revenue fluctuated widely from year to year, ranging from virtually nothing to more than half of ordinary income.

property taxes were reduced or eliminated in the 1890's and furnished minuscule contributions to government revenues until the 1920's. As late as 1916, during the wartime nitrate boom, only 4 percent of government revenues came from internal taxes, compared with 61.5 percent from export taxes and 27.1 percent from import duties.[12]

With these now-substantial and growing revenues at its disposal, the state was able to expand considerably its coercive apparatus and administrative control over Chilean territory. Military expenditures consistently accounted for about 20 percent of the budget during the entire period. Among all state employee groups, the one that increased the most after 1900 was the police force, the arm of government charged with preserving internal order. But substantial numbers of administrative personnel for the growing state railway system, telegraph operators, and schoolteachers were added to the public payroll as well. The growth of these groups reveals the significant efforts made by the state to invest nitrate revenues in human and material infrastructure to promote development. Large quantities of public revenues were also spent on public works, primarily government buildings.

Government tax and expenditure policies, and the influence of nitrate expansion on national markets and labor systems, combined to promote important changes in the development of Chilean agriculture and industry. During the nitrate era the rate of urbanization in Chile greatly increased. Nitrate expansion also altered the proportion of the national population living in the north. In 1805, according to census data, only a little more than one-fifth of the 1,819,223 Chileans lived in towns of more than 2,000 people. For the next 70 years, the pace of urbanization was slow; as late as 1875, only about one-fourth of the population of 2,075,971 were townsfolk. But 55 years later, in 1930, almost half of Chile's 4,287,445 people were urban dwellers. Meanwhile, the two northern nitrate provinces (virtually all of which, given the nature of economic activity in the desert, should be considered urban) more than doubled their share of national population, from 3.5 percent in 1885 to 7.7 percent in 1920.[13]

The influence of nitrate expansion on the process of urbanization was powerful and complex. Clearly, the increase in economic activity in the north, the growth of the import trade and the coastal carrying trade, and the flow of nitrate revenue through an expanded state bureaucracy into public works and human and material infrastructure all created economic opportunities for rural migrants in the cities, towns, and ports of northern and central Chile. In addition, the fuel demands of the expanding rail-

12. Brian Loveman, *Chile* (New York, 1979), p. 230. This work, the best one-volume survey of Chilean history, contains an excellent survey of the nitrate era.

13. Cariola and Sunkel, "Expansión salitrera" (cited in n. 5), table 2.

road and shipping network and of Chile's growing cities stimulated an important domestic coal industry near the southern port of Concepción.[14] But nitrate expansion also affected Chilean agriculture and industry in ways that both stimulated and responded to the urbanization process.

Carmen Cariola and Osvaldo Sunkel have persuasively challenged the idea, long accepted in the economic literature on Chile, that agriculture stagnated during the nitrate era. They have shown, on the contrary, that the whole period, at least until 1920, was one of growth, diversification, and rising labor productivity. This process was a result of a series of effects closely related to nitrate expansion. First of all, agriculture expanded geographically. The strengthening of the state and the development of transportation networks helped push the Araucanian Indians farther south and opened up new lands to wheat cultivation. Second, the growth of urban markets in central Chile and the mining areas of the north encouraged the diversification of agricultural production in the central valley. Finally, the modernization of the whole society fostered the spread of scientific techniques and the use of agricultural machinery in the countryside.

The last no doubt accounts in no small way for the increase in labor productivity in agriculture demonstrated by Cariola and Sunkel. But the increase may also be due in part to changes in tenancy and labor systems. Competition for labor generated by employment opportunities for rural workers in the nitrate zone and in manufacturing and services in the larger cities may have forced landowners to adopt more capitalist or more labor-extensive relations of production. Many landowners shifted from agriculture to ranching around the turn of the century. This response may reflect both the rising purchasing power (and meat consumption) of sectors of the Chilean proletariat and the inability of landowners to retain, without concessions they were unwilling to make, their workers on the land. After the turn of the century, the government imposed taxes on Argentine meat imports to protect Chilean livestock producers. The meat tax became an explosive political issue around which export and manufacturing workers, and urban consumers generally, mobilized dramatically during the first decades of the twentieth century.

The relationship of nitrate expansion to the growth of Chilean industry during this period is somewhat better understood, thanks in large part to the pioneering work of Henry W. Kirsch.[15] Contrary to previous inter-

14. But the demand for coal in the nitrate zone itself was not a particularly great direct stimulus in the growth of domestic production. Nitrate carriers often used coal for ballast on the return trip from Europe. In the early twentieth century only about one-fifth of the coal consumed in the north was Chilean. It was of lower quality and usually mixed with imported coal. As the century progressed, imported oil steadily replaced coal in the nitrate zone.

15. *Industrial Development in a Traditional Society* (Gainesville, Fla., 1977).

pretations, which date the country's industrialization from the 1930's or the First World War, he argues persuasively that after 1880 Chilean manufacturing moved out of the artisanal era. In the following decades, the secondary sector developed rapidly. By 1915 the number of people working in manufacturing establishments employing five people or more stood at almost 53,000. By 1924 their numbers reached 85,000.

This process stemmed from the demand for manufactured goods stimulated by the War of the Pacific, from the expansion of the nitrate sector itself and its influence on the rate of urbanization, and from the growth of a communications infrastructure that integrated and expanded the national market. Kirsch emphasizes middle-class consumption as the main market for Chilean industry, but his data show that the largest branches of manufacturing provided items like sugar, beer, glass, shoes, clothing, and matches for urban mass consumption. Kirsch demonstrates that the pace of industrial expansion was linked closely to growth and fluctuations in the nitrate export sector. He shows how the few basic industries that managed to emerge in the period (e.g. cement and locomotive production) found their markets in the mining sector or in the construction of public works made possible by nitrate revenues.

According to Kirsch, the structural characteristics that define Chilean industry in the decades following 1930 were acquired during the nitrate era. National industry primarily produced light and durable consumer goods for sale in a domestic market protected from foreign competition. The firms engaged in industrial production became highly concentrated, and many enjoyed virtual monopolies. Most depended on capital-intensive production techniques and relied on capital goods and raw materials imported from abroad. Many were foreign-owned or foreign-financed: almost half of the proprietors of manufacturing concerns during the period 1914 to 1925 were foreign-born; and about one-third of total capital invested in industry in that period was foreign.

Government policy fostered all these industrial developments. Inflationary monetary policy, by making imports more expensive, provided blanket protection for local industry. Tariff policy after 1880, although aimed primarily at producing revenue, provided some protection and set low rates on the imports needed by domestic industry. Government credit policy consistently favored large enterprises producing consumer goods. Small producers, even successful manufacturers of heavy equipment such as locomotives, were denied credit and incentives. Protected and favored by such policies, light manufacturing provided higher rates of return on invested capital than agriculture and even mining and commerce. Kirsch found no evidence of structural antagonism between foreign and domestic export-import interests, agriculturalists, and industrialists. In fact, he shows how they frequently were the same people, families, or financial groups involved in all sectors of Chilean economic and financial life, who used their control of the state to maximize short-term profits.[16]

Nitrate expansion thus exercised a powerful influence on Chilean economic development before 1930. But that influence was largely indirect, a consequence of jobs and demand opened up in the north and of government projects funded by nitrate revenues. Although the state managed to capture roughly half of the profits made in nitrate production,[17] most of the rest flowed into the hands of foreign capitalists and was remitted abroad. The scope of foreign ownership in the nitrate zone seriously undercut the direct contribution of nitrate production to capital accumulation in Chile.

Contrary to what might have been expected, the annexation of the nitrate zone in 1880 did not lead to control of nitrate production by Chilean nationals. At the start of the war, the bulk of production was located in the hinterland of Iquique in Peruvian-owned nitrate factories, or *oficinas*. Chilean policy in the newly acquired territories was designed to foster uninterrupted production and maximize revenue to a state at war. The legal dispositions developed to deal with the issue of ownership of nitrate companies and land claims in the new Chilean provinces of Tarapacá (Peru's former territory) and Antofagasta (which had belonged to Bolivia) redounded to the benefit of economic interests with access to liquid capital and to the bonds with which Peru had compensated nitrate capitalists when it nationalized the industry on the eve of the war.[18] Chilean and British capitalists had access to both. The Chileans were well established in the nitrate zone, and Chilean banks in Valparaíso financed many of the reorganized companies in the years after 1880. Chilean capitalists also had preferential access to information and personal contacts with government officials, a not unimportant advantage in the often corrupt process of entitlement and the sale of new nitrate lands. British capitalists and merchant houses, which had financed the transport and commercialization of Peruvian guano and nitrates, were also in a privileged position. In many

16. I have deleted from this discussion Kirsch's unwarranted emphasis on the cultural defects of Chilean entrepreneurs to explain this dynamic. In fact, his data and analysis show that foreign entrepreneurs acted like Chilean ones. Both responded to the opportunities for profit maximization that control of the state afforded an economic elite constrained from following patterns of investment more common in the very different economies of the North Atlantic Basin.

17. Cariola and Sunkel, "Expansión salitrera" (cited in n. 5), p. 27.

18. The Peruvian government, having almost exhausted the revenue-producing potential of its guano reserves and hard pressed by its British creditors to service its public loans, had nationalized the oficinas within its borders. It had also signed a secret defense treaty with Bolivia, wary of the reaction of Chilean and British capitalists. These interests played an important role in the events that led to Chile's occupation of Iquique, which triggered the war.

TABLE 2.1

Ownership of Companies Producing Nitrate,
by Nationality, 1878, 1895, and 1926

Nationality	1878	1895	1926
Peruvian	52%	8%	1%
Chilean	22	13	42
English	12	60	41
German	7	8	–
Other	7	11	16

SOURCE: Adapted from Arthur Lawrence Stickell, "Migration and Mining Labor in Northern Chile in the Nitrate Era, 1880–1930" (Ph.D. diss., Indiana University, 1979), p. 27.

NOTE: Stickell has based his breakdown on different kinds of data: on productive capacity for 1878; on total investment for 1895; on actual production for 1926. But despite the problems of comparability (and some internal inconsistencies in his original table), his breakdown broadly suggests the changing patterns of national ownership in the nitrate zone during the period surveyed.

cases British speculators bought the greatly depreciated Peruvian bonds and drew on their connections in Valparaíso and in London money markets to meet the Chilean government's stiff financial requirements for legalization of their status. Alfred T. North, the British "Nitrate King" who emerged to dominate production and transport in the nitrate zone in the 1880's and 1890's, was the most successful of these speculators.

But British dominance of the industry by 1895 was not so much a result of acquisitions made in the early 1880's as a consequence of access to capital needed to expand and modernize production. A potential obstacle was eliminated by the political defeat of nationalist and statist forces in the civil war of 1891. Thus, British success was the result neither of alleged cultural defects among Chilean entrepreneurs nor of ignorance or lack of patriotic sentiment on the part of the Chilean officials who reorganized the industry following the War of the Pacific. Rather, it was the logical result both of assumptions about the best way to foster capitalist exploitation of the nitrate zone, on the one hand, and of the privileged position of British entrepreneurs and commercial interests in the world capitalist system at the end of the nineteenth century, on the other.[19]

Table 2.1 shows the changing pattern of ownership in the nitrate enclave over the half century beginning in 1878. By 1895 British capitalists had largely displaced both the Peruvian and the Chilean companies, whose combined share of ownership was reduced from 74 percent to 21

19. This issue has generated much heat in Chilean historiography. A recent review of the debate, which develops the most commonsensical and persuasive explanation of the failure of Chilean capitalists to control the means of production in the nitrate enclave following the war, is Thomas O'Brien, *The Nitrate Industry and Chile's Crucial Transition: 1870-1891* (New York, 1982).

percent. British and other foreign interests owned the bulk of nitrate production facilities during the period of expansion up to the First World
War. But beginning at the turn of the century, and especially following
the war, Chilean capital recaptured an important share of ownership.
This trend was a result of a variety of factors. In the new century the industry's expansion came not in the northernmost province of Tarapacá,
where British capital was most dominant, but in Antofagasta, where
Chileans exercised more control. The war brought the elimination of
German ownership and hastened the decline of the hegemony of British
capital in the world economy. Finally, the introduction in the 1920's of a
new capital-intensive technology for processing low-grade ores enabled
U.S. capital, especially the Guggenheim interests, to capture a growing
share of nitrate production.

In some ways, however, emphasis on the issue of ownership slights the
degree to which the nitrate economy was under foreign, and especially
British, domination during the whole period. British capital built and
controlled most of the railroads and port facilities in the nitrate area. British ships dominated the carrying trade to Europe. British and German
commercial houses handled the sale of nitrate abroad and financed production in Chile. Moreover, British and other foreign managers and technicians ran not only their own nitrate oficinas, but many of the Chilean-
owned ones as well.[20]

The one sector of the nitrate industry that remained consistently Chilean was labor. Even before the War of the Pacific, a majority of the workers in the Peruvian and Bolivian nitrate zone were Chilean. The migration of rural Chileans to the nitrate zone was part of a broader historical
pattern. From colonial times on, a large segment of the rural labor force
in Chile consisted of migratory, landless workers who followed the harvest up and down the central valley. During the nineteenth century Chileans emigrated to Peru and Bolivia to work in railway construction and
the nitrate industry, to Argentina to work in the livestock industry in the
south, and to California to work in the gold fields. Nineteenth- and
twentieth-century observers alike stressed the abject condition of Chilean
rural workers, be they sharecroppers, tenants, or landless migrants. In
the face of such misery, the propensity of Chilean rural workers to mi-
grate to cities and mines or even beyond Chile's borders in search of better conditions is understandable. So, too, are the high incidence of alco-
holism among the working class and Chile's shocking infant mortality
rate. As late as the 1920's, for every 1,000 live births in Chile, 250 infants

20. Again, this predominance of foreign managers and technicians reflects the realities of
the world distribution of technical and commercial knowledge in the late nineteenth and
early twentieth centuries. By the 1920's there were many Chilean managers and technicians
in the oficinas.

died within the first year. (Comparable figures are 100 for Argentina, 153 for Venezuela, and 159 for Colombia.)[21]

Arthur Lawrence Stickell has thoroughly studied the migration of Chilean workers to the nitrate zone. His data show that despite efforts by nitrate employers to discriminate against Chileans and recruit Bolivians and Peruvians who were willing to work for less, Chileans constituted the majority of the labor force during the entire nitrate era. Foreigners were most heavily represented during the first decade of the twentieth century, when they accounted for one-quarter of the nitrate labor force.[22] The vast majority of foreign workers, some 80 to 90 percent, were Bolivians or Peruvians. Most of the others were Europeans, many of them skilled workers. The number of foreign workers slowly decreased until by the 1920's Chileans constituted more than 90 percent of the work force. The nitrate industry's low incidence of foreign workers reflected a larger national pattern. Unlike Argentina, Uruguay, and Brazil, Chile never had a large contingent of foreign immigrant workers in agriculture, manufacturing, or mining.

Life and Work on the Nitrate Pampa

The root of the distinctiveness of the Chilean labor movement lies in the special experience of workers in nitrate production.[23] Conditions of life and work on the nitrate pampa were vastly different from those in other Latin American export economies. The location of nitrate production, the structure of ownership in the industry, the demography of the labor force, the nature of the work process, and the conditions of life in nitrate oficinas and northern port towns all had important effects on workers and created among them special needs and opportunities. Their

21. Arnold J. Bauer, *Chilean Rural Society from the Spanish Conquest to 1930* (London, 1975). Nicolás Sánchez-Albornoz, *The Population of Latin America* (Berkeley, Calif., 1974), p. 200.

22. Arthur Lawrence Stickell, "Migration and Mining Labor in Northern Chile in the Nitrate Era, 1880-1930" (Ph. D. diss., Indiana University, 1979). This rich study is a social history of nitrate labor based on previously untapped company and government records. It provides much statistical information on the recruitment and demography of the nitrate labor force, on wages and prices in the north, and on health facilities and housing on the nitrate pampa. Stickell laments the radicalization of Chilean nitrate workers and tries to show that, because conditions for workers eventually improved, that development could have been avoided. On the immigration policy of the Chilean government and the recruiting programs of nitrate companies, see also Miguel Monteón, "The *Enganche* in the Chilean Nitrate Sector," *Latin American Perspectives* 7:3 (Summer 1979): 66-79. Monteón traces the response of organized workers to the companies' efforts to undermine labor unity and bargaining power by encouraging foreign and domestic immigration to the north.

23. The argument pursued here does not deny the importance of other sectors of the Chilean labor movement. Nor is it meant to slight the significance of earlier, nineteenth-century developments in working-class organization and attitudes. Rather, it calls attention to the characteristics that distinguish Chilean labor history from that of other Latin American nations.

considerable success in defining an autonomous working-class culture and in building progressive social and political institutions for their class reflects not only their determination and creativity but also the unique environment in which they worked.

One of the most striking features of this environment was the geographic mobility of nitrate workers, much of which, as noted earlier, was a consequence of conditions beyond their control. The cyclical nature of the industry, especially after 1914, forced tens of thousands of nitrate workers to leave the pampa and sometimes the north itself during periods of crisis. But workers were also extraordinarily mobile within the nitrate zone in good times as well. Stickell, who has studied company records, reports very high levels of labor turnover. Labor leader Elías Lafertte recalls in his autobiography that as a youth he was employed in more than a dozen different jobs in as many oficinas during one three-year period in the early twentieth century. In periods of expanding production and high labor demand, workers would often remain at a given job for only a few days or weeks before moving on in search of better wages or living conditions. Employers frequently lamented their inability to keep their labor force and claimed that their problems stemmed from a "labor shortage." They devised ingenious credit and payment schemes and sometimes required deposits on tools in their effort to retain workers by making it costly to move. Workers were paid only once a month, and between paydays they were advanced credit in the form of scrip, or *fichas*, which could be spent for water, food, clothing, tools, and many other items at the company store. Nitrate companies restricted commerce by outsiders and routinely expected profits from the company store to defray about 10 percent of their labor costs. At some oficinas this percentage was much higher. Especially in the early years, markups in the company stores on some items of basic consumption such as bread could be as high as 50 or 60 percent. Workers could cash in fichas only at certain times, sometimes at a discount. Still, *fugados*, the name managers gave to workers who left without settling their accounts, were frequent, and the numbers of workers who cashed in their company scrip, even at a discount, in order to move on were numerous. All these credit and payment devices—which sought to retain labor, and which served the needs of capital in other ways as well[24]—were a constant source of worker dissatisfaction and were targets of protest during the entire period.

In moving from job to job, nitrate workers took advantage of a series

24. For example, the use of scrip and the extension of credit made large shipments of cash to meet payrolls at isolated oficinas unnecessary. Deposits on tools, which usually amounted to more than a man's daily wage, could furnish, especially at large oficinas, important sums of interest-free operating capital. Finally, restrictions on commerce reduced contact by workers with peddlers and merchants in pampa towns. Oficina managers often denounced peddlers as sources of information on conditions at other oficinas and as conduits of radical ideas.

of structural conditions in the nitrate zone. In the northern desert, capital could not immediately tap a reserve of unemployed or lower-paid workers. Virtually all economic activities in the north were nitrate-related and relatively highly paid. Individually and collectively (through the Asociación de Productores del Salitre) nitrate capitalists recruited actively in southern Chile during periods of expansion in the industry. Early in the twentieth century, as we have seen, they enlisted the resources of the state in these endeavors. Despite the success of their efforts, not everyone had the stamina or could acquire the skills for many jobs in nitrate production, and capitalists never succeeded in glutting the labor market during periods of expansion. If workers could not secure satisfactory employment in the north, they could not be absorbed into agriculture or marginal urban activities there. People came north to the desert to make money. If they did not, they were wont to return as soon as they were able to families and friends, and the less costly, more benign living conditions of the south.

Because the majority of nitrate workers were single males, they were more free to protest unfair or intolerable working conditions, and more willing to move in search of better ones. Both company and, later, government recruiters sought to enlist men with families. This policy was explicitly designed to tie the worker to the oficina and reduce the value of his major bargaining chip, his ability to move and find better pay or conditions elsewhere. Despite housing incentives and the offer of free transportation for dependents (defined in some cases to include more than the nuclear family), this policy met with only limited success. The Asociación de Productores del Salitre reported that in the first five years of its recruiting operation, from 1901 to 1905, it had brought 4,567 men, 751 women, and 276 children to the north. Stickell carefully surveyed the demography of the north and concluded that on average about half of the people in nitrate oficinas were single males, only one-fifth adult females. In fact, the whole demographic structure of the nitrate provinces in the early years of the twentieth century was skewed, with roughly twice as many males as females. The preoccupation of nitrate workers with female companionship and sexual gratification found expression in a rich regional vocabulary. *Andar al palo* meant to be (or move about) without a woman. *Casarse* ("to marry") was sarcastically used in the sense of sleeping with a woman. *Hacer la cosita rica* conveyed the pleasure of copulation. *Hacer el favor* was coined to express the decision by a woman to have sex. Nitrate miners used the verb *tirar* ("to throw or shoot") to mean to copulate, and *cartucho* ("cartridge" or "stick of dynamite") to refer to a woman's virginity. Whorehouses were simply *salones*. The verb *capotear* (meaning to tease or trick a bull with a cape) meant to gang rape.[25]

25. Andrés Sabella, *Semblanza del norte chileno* (Santiago, 1955).

Sex ratios in the north and the bachelor status of most nitrate workers thus worked in two ways to encourage labor to move about: they made the consequences of quitting a job less overwhelming, and they impelled men deprived of female companionship to seek it elsewhere.

However strong the desire to move, it was the competitive and diffuse nature of nitrate production that made moving sensible. Although ownership and production became more concentrated in the industry over time, both were relatively widely dispersed throughout the entire period.[26] Even at the end of the nitrate era, in 1928, some 69 oficinas, owned by more than half as many different nitrate companies, were still in operation. The number in earlier years was much higher. Some 53 were operating in 1895, 113 in 1908, a peak of 137 in 1925. After the war the number fluctuated widely: 125 in 1919, 53 during the depression of 1922, 96 during the boom of 1925. Most nitrate oficinas after 1900 employed a few hundred workers; only near the end of the period did some employ several thousand. The existence of many competing employers in a tight labor market made shopping for the best terms of work and living conditions possible; it also limited the ability of owners to discipline workers who complained, broke rules, or joined with their fellows to secure better conditions.

The diffuse nature of nitrate mining resulted in large part from the geology of caliche deposits, which were widely scattered and of varying size and richness. Until the late 1920's, when new technology made the processing of low-grade deposits possible, oficinas often had to close or relocate once the richest ore at a site had been extracted. During periods of low world demand and prices, marginal producers closed down, only to reopen again once the profit margin allowed. In both cases nitrate workers found themselves temporarily out of work and forced to move to find it.

Scattered production facilities led to the rapid development of communications networks on the nitrate pampa. Privately owned nitrate railways measured some 860 kilometers in 1887, and twice that by 1905. Mule trails and, later, roads for truck, bus, and automobile traffic linked the scattered oficinas with each other and with the major nitrate ports. Workers used this transportation network, but until the 1920's many simply walked—searching for work in good times, relief in the ports in bad. Nitrate miners borrowed terms from the port and maritime workers

26. Firms producing nitrate worth over 1 million Spanish *quintales* accounted for 9 percent of total production in 1913, 30 percent in 1929. Producers of 500,000 to 1 million worth accounted for 21 percent of total production in 1913, 37 percent in 1929. Medium-size firms producing between 100,000 and 500,000 quintales accounted for 62 percent of total production in 1913, but only 26 percent in 1929. Small producers contributed only 8 percent of production in 1913, 7 percent in 1929. Stickell, "Migration and Mining Labor" (cited in n. 22), pp. 221 and 249.

with whom they formed close personal and organizational alliances to express their sense of constant movement on the vast pampa. Barracks in the nitrate oficinas were *buques* ("ships"). To sleep was *doblar el asta* (loosely, "to pull in the sails").

Nitrate workers developed an informal communications network of friends, relatives, and *compadres* all over the nitrate pampa and monitored conditions in the various nitrate oficinas. Although work and living conditions, as we shall see, were not good in any oficina, word spread when they were marginally better in one. Employers kept wages and expenses on labor as low as they could, but they were constrained from going below a certain minimum and were acutely aware of the competitive nature of the labor market. Wages in the nitrate zone were relatively high, and nitrate workers, especially single males, could accumulate enough savings to allow them to search for alternative work relatively quickly. Unencumbered by family obligations, single workers could pack up their clothes and tools on the slightest provocation, on getting word of better conditions elsewhere, or simply on a whim. Elías Lafertte captures all these ideas in a particularly illuminating passage:

In those days, the most characteristic phenomenon on the pampa was precisely that of emigrating from one to another oficina. Nobody put down roots and it was very difficult to find, as happens in the countryside, people who had grown old in the same place. No; the pampinos were nomadic, roving people, who didn't stay long at the same oficina. Fortunately, there was a lot of work and although the companies knew who had been fired for grave offenses, they didn't deny work to those who were simply restless. People used to take off and move at the drop of a hat. The oficinas would open then close then open again. The pampinos would change their place of work in order to earn a few pesos more, because they were interested in a woman in an oficina several kilometers away, because they found better housing, or because the food was better in another place. If anyone had taken a survey, they would have been astonished at the number of oficinas each pampino knew. I myself, by the time I was twenty, had already worked at a long chain of nitrate centers.[27]

Nitrate workers collectively expressed the harsh reality of dependence on cyclical work and the limited independence of geographical mobility in the word they chose for the activity that dominated their lives. A job, they said, was a *pega*. The noun derives from the verb *pegar*, "to stick or adhere to lightly."[28]

The willingness, even compulsion, of nitrate workers to take advantage of the opportunity to move in search of better material conditions and physical and spiritual release was a powerful statement about the nature of work and the quality of life in the nitrate oficinas. Nitrate workers contended daily with conditions that sapped their physical and mental

27. Elías Lafertte, *Vida de un comunista* (Santiago, 1961), pp. 38-39.
28. Ariel Dorfman provided me with this last shade of meaning.

health and threatened their very existence. Under these corrosive conditions workers developed attitudes and institutions first to cope with, and then to change, the nature of their lives.[29]

The typical nitrate oficina was a noisy, smoky, smelly industrial company town set incongruously in the quiet grandeur of the Atacama Desert. Seen in daylight, from a distance, the oficina must have appeared as an inconsequential dot in the vast surrounding expanse of pampa and sky. At night, however, the electric lights and the rumble of the ore crushers could be perceived from great distances through the dry desert air. At those times, even from afar, the nitrate oficina conveyed an image of power and significance.

The nucleus of the nitrate oficina was the *maquina*, or processing plant, a black metal maze of tall smokestacks, crushing machines, boilers, huge processing tanks, and drying pans. To a practiced eye the size of the slag pile behind the maquina revealed the age of the oficina. Beside the processing plant was the coal storage area, and nearby the *maestranza*, or machine shop, where skilled workers repaired the heavy railway and processing equipment and sharpened the hand tools of the miners. A bit farther on sat the *campamento*, the barrackslike housing for production workers, and still farther, segregated from workers' dwellings, the more substantial houses for managers and technical personnel. The central part of each oficina also contained the *pulpería*, the company store. Some oficinas also featured a company-run restaurant and bar where single men could take their meals and drink. Some also contained a one-room school, sometimes funded by management. Only a few had a chapel.

Stretching out into the pampa, beyond the processing plant and living quarters, lay the oficina's ore reserves and the overturned remains of mined areas. Mining operations involved the bulk of the oficina's labor force, and wages for the miners alone constituted about half of total operating costs. The mining of nitrate ore began with the work of the *barretero*, who mapped a section of the deposit by digging a grid of widely spaced holes into the surface of the pampa. Caliche usually lay between one and three meters below the surface, and it was generally necessary to blast away the desert floor to uncover it. Using a variety of iron bars with sharpened or spoonlike ends, the barretero dug a hole through the deposit wide enough for a small boy to slip down and scrape out a chamber in the

29. Although descriptions of life and work on the nitrate pampa are many and varied, I found the following four previously cited sources most useful in preparing this section: the autobiography of Elías Lafertte (cited in n. 27); the meticulous manual for prospective nitrate entrepreneurs by Semper and Michels (cited in n. 3); the report of the congressional committee on conditions in the north edited by Salas Lavaqui (cited in n. 11); and the unpublished dissertation by Stickell (cited in n. 22). I have also relied on another congressional report, published as *Comisión parlamentaria encargada de estudiar las necesidades de las provincias de Tarapacá y Antofagasta* (Santiago, 1913).

rock below the caliche to accommodate an explosive charge. "Opening" a caliche deposit involved settling on a line of advance, then exploding a series of charges to open a *rajo*, or trench. Then the nitrate miner, or *particular*, could enter the trench to separate, break up, and load the caliche into a mule-drawn cart for transport to the oficina, where the quality of the ore was judged before it was dumped into the crusher. Meanwhile the barretero, who serviced several particulares, advanced a few meters and dug a new line of holes parallel to the rajo. Once the particular had removed the caliche uncovered by the previous detonation, he set charges in the new holes and the process of excavation could begin anew. Barreteros and particulares both owned some of their tools and were among the highest-paid workers in the oficina. Their earnings were determined on a piecework basis, at rates that fluctuated according to the hardness of the ground and the ease of extraction of the caliche. Disputes between these workers and management over rates of pay and over the quality and weight of the ore delivered to the oficina were common. Success at the backbreaking, dangerous work of barreteros and particulares involved much practical knowledge and considerable skill in the use of the poor-grade and unreliable explosives manufactured at the oficina and sold to miners at the company store.

Boys of different ages, often relatives of adult workers, played important roles in the mining process. In addition to the *destrazadores*, the 8- to 10-year-olds who dug the chambers for the explosives, there were *matasapos*, 10- to 12-year-old boys who helped particulares break chunks of ore too large to carry and load. Young teenagers worked as *herramenteros*, carrying tools to workers on muleback. Older teenagers might load or drive carts, or begin doing a man's work in mining. All workers who labored in mining operations in the sun on the open pampa—the *asoleados*, as Lafertte referred to them—were paid on a piecework basis.

Processing of the caliche involved crushing the ore, dissolving the sodium nitrate in it in water, then allowing the solution to crystallize and dry in the desert air. To this basic process, known to man in pre-Columbian times, the nitrate oficina applied mechanical power, fossil fuel, and a technology that greatly increased the efficiency of the dissolving process. Water and ore were steamed in a series of dissolving vats called *cachuchos*. Operations in the processing plant were, nonetheless, very labor-intensive:[30] *paleros* shoveled the caliche into the crushers by hand, *ripia-*

30. Semper and Michels explained: "Ordinarily mechanical installations, which save on labor, are avoided because, given the high price of coal, no economies over manual labor are obtained, and because complicated machinery [can break down] in the Desert and lead to unacceptable disruption of the work process." They explained the labor intensivity of mining operations in the same way, adding that the extensive nature of the process and the often soft surface of the desert made movement of machines difficult. See *La industria del salitre* (cited in n. 3), p. 47 and pp. 80-81.

dores entered the hot dissolving vats after the water had been drained off to break loose and remove the tailings, still other workers turned the drying nitrate powder in the sun and shoveled it into burlap bags sewn by boys and women, and finally loaders carried the incredibly heavy 139-kilogram bags onto freight cars for shipment.[31] Almost all workers in the processing plant were also paid on a piecework basis, determined in part by the skill required for a given task and the difficulty of performing it, and by production in the plant as a whole. Ripiadores, whose task had to be accomplished at great speed under conditions of extreme heat, were generally the most highly paid. Most processing plants ran 24 hours a day every day of the year except September 18, Chilean Independence Day. Shifts were twelve hours long, with a total of two and a half hours set aside for lunch and rest periods. Sometimes plant workers, who generally labored in gangs charged with a specific task under the direction of a foreman, would work an additional half shift. Stickell found that these workers often labored long hours in concentrated spurts of several days, then took off a day or more to rest. Most, however, averaged more than six days a week.

Work schedules and supervision on the pampa were less rigid. Particulares were more or less free to come and go as they pleased and generally worked 7 to 9 hours a day. Supervisors were primarily concerned that they extract the caliche thoroughly. When the ore was of low quality or difficult to mine, particulares sometimes had to be contracted on a daily-wage basis. A Bedaux time-work study done in 1930 found that nitrate miners set informal production levels for a fair day's work and pay. When time cards were introduced, workers slept for a time in the trenches so as not to exceed these levels.

Work in nitrate processing, as in mining, was dangerous. It was also unhealthy, disagreeable, and strenuous. Workers had to contend with constant dust from the crushers, mud from the dissolving process (Lafertte called processing-plant workers the *embarrados*, "muddy ones"), noxious fumes, and the ever-present heat from boilers and steam lines and the sun of the desert. Machinery was often in very poor repair, and safety regulations and protective devices were almost nonexistent. A parliamentary commission sent to investigate the situation in the north in 1904 found safety and health conditions especially shocking at the older oficinas. Whereas injuries to miners resulted primarily from cave-ins and the use of unpredictable explosives, plant workers had a high incidence of lung infections and were often mutilated or burned while operating

31. Semper and Michels noted that part of the early organizational success of stevedores in Iquique resulted from the very fact that few workers could handle the weight of nitrate bags. They go on to say that in the early twentieth century the weight of bags was reduced to 100 kilograms (*La industria del salitre*, p. 90). In 1904, however, a workers' committee complained to congressional investigators that no bags weighed less than 120 kilograms, and that some were as much as 150 (Salas Lavaqui, *Trabajos*, p. 588).

the machinery. Hospital facilities and doctors on the pampa were in very short supply. Indeed, only one hospital existed in the entire nitrate region in 1912. In that year it served 1,026 patients, 326 of them classified as suffering from industrial accidents. Of these, 83 were particulares, 44 ripiadores. Most of the patients were single males between the ages of 15 and 40. Most industrial accidents were not reported and were treated in primitive facilities in the oficinas. Workers usually had to contribute one peso a month toward this service. Company compensation for accidents was infrequent. Workers early organized mutual-aid societies to sustain injured or sick members and consistently resisted the one-peso health fee deducted by management from their wages. The need for minimal safety standards, especially protective grates over the cachuchos, figured among the earliest collective demands by nitrate workers.

In his off hours, the nitrate worker had little to look forward to. Workers were assigned to miserable company housing. In the early period these structures were usually windowless hovels built of rock and tailings. Later, housing constructed of corrugated iron became common, but these buildings offered little insulation against the sweltering days and very cold nights on the desert. Single workers slept several to a room; those with families were usually housed in two-room structures. Sanitation facilities in the campamento were limited to latrines set at the end of each row of housing. Workers bought their own water, which was usually delivered in barrels by the company.

Although food and drink were more expensive in the north than in central Chile, real wages were higher there than in comparable jobs elsewhere. Single men especially, who did not have to pay rent or feed other mouths, could save significant amounts of money. Nitrate workers ate better than most other Chilean workers. They usually had meat two or three times a day, and Semper and Michels, German scientists who studied the industry in 1903, believed their diet was superior to that of workers in their homeland.

Nitrate workers were almost entirely dependent on money income for their sustenance. Even family men were denied the possibility of a garden, although some families did raise fowl and pigs, which they could carry with them if they left the oficina. Women often provided meals for single miners, but they were often prohibited from opening a small store or bar by company policy. All these factors contributed to the nomadic propensities of nitrate workers. "There are no inhabitants [of the north] rooted in the soil by [the ownership of] houses, gardens, or other reasons that constitute a love for a fixed place," wrote the manager at Oficina Humberstone in 1915. "[T]herefore, a worker has no more reasons than his convenience to fix his residence in one or another oficina. . . ."[32]

32. Quoted in Stickell, "Migration and Mining Labor" (cited in n. 22), pp. 295-96.

Despite the harsh conditions of work and life on the pampa, workers managed to build a rich social life. They traveled outside the oficinas to visit relatives and friends, participate in funerals, and attend political rallies in port towns. In the small pampa towns that sprang up along rail lines near the larger oficinas they drank, gambled, visited prostitutes, bought supplies from merchants, and discussed common needs and aspirations. It was in such towns that many gained access to labor organizers, who were often banned from the private property of the oficina.

Important social institutions developed in the oficinas as well. Lafertte acquired many of the skills he would need as a labor organizer in the sports, drama, music, and dance clubs he participated in at various oficinas. We do not know very much about these clubs, or about how fully workers participated in the activities Lafertte mentions, but though many seem to have been management-inspired and dominated by white-collar employees, some were clearly worker-inspired and -controlled.

Mutual-aid societies, often called *filarmónicas*, spread north from central Chile and existed in many oficinas. Here workers taught themselves how to play musical instruments and learned to dance. Some filarmónicas also offered night classes in elementary education. The quiet decorum of these cultural oases that workers constructed to develop their minds and social skills stood in stark contrast to the noisy, physically exhausting environment they worked in, and the loud and bawdy atmosphere of the bars and brothels where they sought release from the reality of their working lives. Alcohol was prohibited in the filarmónicas, and even the all-male dance instruction proceeded in an atmosphere of great seriousness and formality. A sympathetic middle-class journalist reacted with a mixture of condescension and awe to his dance with a well-washed, formally attired member of a filarmónica in 1904. "My partner was extremely polite, and possessed of such strong muscles, that instead of my leading 'her,' 'she' led me as if I were a feather."[33] Some of these clubs were quite large, with memberships of several hundred workers at the larger oficinas. Workers contributed two to five pesos monthly to mutual-aid funds administered by filarmónicas and by sports and drama clubs. These funds were used to sustain injured and sick members, to pay funeral expenses, and to help support workers' families for a short period following the death of a member.[34]

Organizations of this kind were essentially defensive. Through them workers sought to sustain themselves spiritually and materially under the destructive social conditions of life and work in the nitrate oficina. Soon

33. Salas Lavaqui, *Trabajos* (cited in n. 11), p. 865.
34. A worker organization in Tocopilla provided care and treatment to injured and sick members in a facility of its own that contained "several beds" and handled around 10 inpatients a month in 1904.

enough, however, nitrate workers began to form institutions that sought to change the position of workers as a class. These institutions were noisy, creative, and combative. They have left a deep imprint on the historical record.

Worker Organization in the North

All over Latin America attempts by workers in export production to organize themselves to improve their economic and social position encountered virulent private and public repression. The reasons are clear. Given the importance of the export sector to national economic health, worker organization there—with its potential to reduce capital accumulation, paralyze production in the most dynamic and important sector of the economy, and stop the main generator of government revenues—had to be prevented. In the case of the Chilean nitrate economy during the period 1880 to 1930, however, one finds that despite the brutality and intensity of the repression, attempts by workers to organize themselves, ally themselves with other sectors of the working class, and build a labor and political movement capable of exerting a major influence on national political life were remarkably successful.[35]

As in other Latin American export economies, the first workers to organize and force concessions from employers in Chile were not those engaged directly in export production, but those in the transport infrastructure that grew up to service the export economy (maritime, port, and

35. I have relied in this section primarily on the following published works: Hernán Ramírez Necochea, *Historia del movimiento obrero, siglo XIX* (Santiago, 1956), and *Origen y formación del Partido Comunista de Chile* (Santiago, 1965); Julio César Jobet, "Movimiento Social Obrero," in Universidad de Chile, *Desarrollo de Chile en la primera mitad del siglo XX* (Santiago, n.d. [1953]); Julio César Jobet et al., eds., *Obras selectas de Luis Emilio Recabarren* (Santiago, 1972); Luis Vitale, *Historia del movimiento obrero* (Santiago, 1972); Michael P. Monteón, *Chile in the Nitrate Era* (Madison, Wisc., 1982); and Peter De Shazo, *Urban Workers and Labor Unions in Chile, 1902-1927* (Madison, Wisc., 1983). The work of Ramírez Necochea, Jobet, and Vitale is built on classical Marxist assumptions about the revolutionary trajectory of Chilean workers; it demonstrates the great influence of labor, especially nitrate workers, on twentieth-century Chilean history. But because, as I argued more generally in Chapter One, such assumptions are largely borne out in Chilean history, and because these authors do not concern themselves with the very different pattern of other Latin American labor movements, they do not subject these assumptions to critical historical analysis. Monteón's work, unlike mine, emphasizes the "traditional" culture of Chilean workers and elites alike, and denigrates the accomplishments and strategies of the Chilean left. De Shazo's impressive primary research on anarchists in the urban labor movement serves as a corrective to accounts that exaggerate the role of nitrate workers and socialists, but cannot explain what so sharply distinguishes Chile's labor movement from others, such as Argentina's, where anarchism was also strong.

In clarifying my own argument, I also found very helpful the dissertation of J. Samuel Valenzuela, "Labor Movement Formation and Politics: The Chilean and French Cases in Comparative Perspective" (Columbia University, 1979). Valenzuela explains the leftist drift of Chilean labor through the narrow lens of political structure and Weberian organizational theory. His argument is analyzed in more detail in n. 43 below.

railroad workers). These workers were more skilled and better off materially than most, and they were also exposed relatively early to radical working-class ideologies. But in Chile these transport workers quickly found support among, and in turn supported, workers in the nitrate sector itself. The result was a unique Chilean working-class institution of the early twentieth century, the *mancomunal*.

Part mutual-aid society, part resistance society, part vehicle for the creation and extension of working-class culture, mancomunales responded to the needs and aspirations of workers in the nitrate economy. These organizations grew up rapidly in the major port towns of the nitrate zone in the first years of the twentieth century. Built around a nucleus of port workers, and often initially led by *lancheros*, whose task it was to ferry nitrate in small boats from the docks and load it on oceangoing ships, mancomunales quickly brought in artisans and service workers in the ports, and railway and nitrate workers on the pampa itself. Mancomunales also spread south and developed into powerful, very militant organizations in the coal-mining zone near Concepción. All mancomunales were regional organizations that brought together skilled and unskilled workers from a host of different activities to pool resources and coordinate activities.

The strike activities of these militant organizations have received considerable attention in Chilean labor historiography. Julio César Jobet, for example, has written a fine summary of the strikes they undertook after 1900, culminating in the massive general strike in the nitrate zone in 1907.[36] That strike ended in the worst massacre in Chilean labor history at Iquique on December 21, 1907. Because the nitrate strike of 1907 conveys so starkly and dramatically the nature of early Chilean labor struggles and the importance of nitrate workers in the development of the Chilean labor movement and the left in general, and because it became a symbol of the struggle of the Chilean people against foreign capital and domestic conservative forces, it has inspired a stream of newspaper articles, histories, novels, and musical scores. The massacre and the general repression of labor that followed the strike of 1907 virtually destroyed effective labor organization in the north for the next few years and ended the era of the nitrate mancomunal proper. Very soon, however, structurally similar institutions reappeared in the nitrate ports and pampa. These organizations also led strikes, but they concentrated even more on the cultural, ideological, and organizational activities that had played such an important part in the endeavors of the earliest mancomunales. These activities, as well as the dramatic mobilizations of nitrate workers around strike issues, are the main legacy of the nitrate mancomunal in Chilean

36. "Las primeras luchas obreras en Chile y la Comuna de Iquique," in Torquato di Tella, ed., *Estructuras sindicales* (Buenos Aires, 1969), pp. 57-67.

labor history. The mancomunal never succeeded in establishing enduring worker organizations at the plant level to protect and advance the interests of Chilean workers. It did something more important. It helped workers to forge an independent vision of the world around them.

The cultural and social activities of the nitrate mancomunales have seemed quaint and impractical to some later observers.[37] But through these creative and often experimental activities, nitrate workers developed—however incompletely and imperfectly—autonomous tools of organization and socialization and cracked the cultural monopoly of the Chilean ruling class. The mancomunales and their successor organizations in the north continued and extended the mutual-aid functions of earlier working-class organizations. Members contributed to different funds to sustain themselves in the event of injury or sickness, and to pay funeral costs and legal fees. Formal educational programs included night classes in elementary skills and sewing instruction for women. Some organizations went further and established consumer cooperatives. The socialist group in Iquique pursued the audacious idea of a producer and consumer cooperative, and, for a six-month period before it failed (victim of a price war and internal mismanagement), it provided the city with much of its daily bread.

A variety of activities were aimed specifically at undermining the cultural values of the larger society. Drama groups took on explicitly proletarian subjects and themes in plays written largely by Spanish anarchists. Chilean activists mounted press campaigns and organized public meetings and debates to discredit capitalists, conservative politicians, and the Church. They built both on the indifference of males in Spanish culture to formal religious activity and on anticlerical currents sanctioned within the dominant culture to encourage workers to deprecate otherworldly solutions to the problems they faced. This task was facilitated by the limited presence of the Church on the nitrate pampa, where, as one congressional commissioner lamented, priests were "very scarce indeed." Although most workers probably harbored some Catholic religious sentiment, many began to ridicule the faith openly. One woman who told a journalist touring several nitrate oficinas in the early years of the century that she was a devotee of the Virgen del Carmen, when asked why she did not display the Virgin's image in her house, explained that she had hidden it away, "because if the others see it, they'd make fun of me and my husband."[38]

Unlike anarchists and anticlericals, socialists played down the issue of

37. Such was the burden of the attacks on *recabarrenismo* made within the Chilean Communist Party in the mid-1920's. Similar attitudes also find their way into Monteón's work cited in n. 35 above.

38. Salas Lavaqui, *Trabajos* (cited in n. 11), p. 867.

the Church and concentrated instead on redefining the concept of patriotism. Workers in the nitrate economy had begun early to perceive and
to stress the structural dichotomy between foreign capital and Chilean labor. The workers' organization of Tarapacá reminded a congressional
commission in 1904 that in the north "capital in its entirety is foreign."
Foreign capital, they insisted, consistently pursued a style of action that
was "arrogant and provocative." They went on to link their interests as
a class with the larger national issue of Chilean economic well-being in
the future. "It is a fact that the nitrate pampa still owes Chile many millions of pesos, which are waiting to be transported abroad if patriotic legislation does not remedy the many flaws that prevent workers from ob-
taining the part of this wealth that migrates out of the nation rapidly and
without a single obstacle."[39] Socialists elaborated and systematized these
perceptions and carried them to their logical conclusions. At a debate
with a prominent conservative journalist in Iquique in 1913 or 1914, the
leader of the fledgling socialist party cast the British capitalists who controlled the nitrate economy and the corrupt public officials who opposed
the rights of labor as antipatriots. It was the workers who produced the
wealth of Chile and the revenue of the state; they were the real patriots,
he claimed. Aided by an audience packed by sympathetic workers, the
socialist, according to Lafertte, "won" the debate and was carried out of
the hall on the shoulders of cheering workers.

In their press, in public demonstrations, and in weekly organizational
meetings, anarchists and socialists translated their doctrinal opposition to
capitalism into terms workers could understand through their daily experience. They talked about the abuses of the ficha payment system and
linked them to the evils of private property in general. They called for
the abolition of social classes through a reorganization of production
based on cooperative worker control. Socialists advocated the nationalization of the nitrate economy and, more immediately, the redistribution
of income through progressive taxation and social-welfare programs.
Both anarchists and socialists outlined the spiritual qualities of a new society where love and freedom would prevail. Drama and revolutionary
songs reinforced these themes and became an integral part of most public
functions organized by the leftist militants.

All of these political, social, and cultural activities coalesced around the
working-class press, a key institution in the development of the Chilean
labor movement. This was especially true of the activities of the socialists
of Iquique, who held public functions in the large building that housed
their newspaper. The nucleus of the party, militants of both sexes, lived
in the building as well. They ran their newspaper as a cooperative and

39. *Ibid.*, p. 652.

relied on outside printing jobs more than advertising and subscriptions to pay the bills. The link between journalism and labor organization is most clearly shown in the career of Luis Emilio Recabarren, the man who emerged in the early 1920's as the greatest leader of the Chilean workers' movement. A typesetter by trade, Recabarren went north as a young liberal reformer to found one of the first working-class newspapers in the nitrate zone in 1903. He was radicalized through his experience in the nitrate mancomunales and spent much of the rest of his life founding and editing leftist, working-class newspapers. "Recabarren had a compulsion to found newspapers," wrote Lafertte, who edited many of them. The list of almost a dozen includes *El Trabajo* (Tocopilla, 1903-5), *El Proletario* (Tocopilla, 1904-5), *El Socialista* (later *El Comunista*; Antofagasta, 1916-27), and *Justicia* (Santiago, 1924-27). The most significant and long-lived was *El Despertar de los Trabajadores* (Iquique, 1912-27). Its name, "The Awakening of the Workers," reveals its fundamental purpose. *El Despertar*, like the other working-class newspapers of the nitrate zone, provided workers in ports and oficinas with an alternative source of information, a different view of the world. Its pages were filled with exposés of unacceptable working and living conditions, information on strikes and cultural and social activities, transcriptions of texts of European anarchist and socialist thinkers, and summaries of major speeches by Chilean militants attacking the cultural values and political monopoly of the dominant class.

Some historians have concluded that, given the high rate of illiteracy among nitrate workers, the emphasis of early labor activists on newspapers was misguided. I do not think it was. Many nitrate workers could read, and local militants probably read aloud to their friends or passed on information they had gleaned from the press in their own words. Given the respect with which illiterate and poorly educated people are taught to behold the printed word and those who can use it, a worker press must have also been a source of pride.[40]

Through the working-class press, moreover, militants built on earlier, more informal contacts between workers in nitrate ports and their nomadic friends and relatives on the pampa to establish a communications

40. The same could also be said of Recabarren's and other activists' dress, which Monteón criticizes. They did not dress as working nitrate miners, but instead (with the partial exception of Lafertte, who confesses he had a weakness for fine hats) wore modest dark suits, symbolic of education and culture. Anyone who has seen photographs of workers of the era in public demonstrations will know that those who could afford it dressed the same way. To attempt to dress as a member of the educated middle class was to affirm one's dignity. Good sources for photographs of worker mobilizations in the north can be found in the collection "Nosotros los Chilenos," especially Patricio Manns, *Las grandes masacres* (Santiago, 1972), and Mario Bahamond S., *Pampinos y salitreros* (Santiago, 1973). See also Enrique Reyes N., *El desarrollo de la conciencia proletaria en Chile (el ciclo salitrero)* (Santiago, n.d.).

network across the whole nitrate zone. Newspapers had representatives in some oficinas, and radical itinerant merchants carried newspapers, fliers, and pamphlets to others. Militants like Recabarren used these contacts to organize frequent speaking tours across the pampa. Nitrate workers often walked 25 kilometers or more to hear him speak and used the occasion to pick up radical papers and pamphlets on display. In the first years of the century, activists like Recabarren often traveled by horseback, their leftist newspapers and literature strapped behind the saddle. By the mid-1920's these tours were made in automobiles flying the huge red flags of socialism. By then rallies were often held on the open pampa at the very entrances to the major oficinas.

In all these ways (and doubtless many others hidden in the historical record), the working-class institutions of the nitrate zone gradually provided numbers of workers with the cultural tools, organizational skills, and confidence to commit themselves to collective action to change their lives. The depth of this commitment varied. Most workers, like most people everywhere, sought to avoid the sacrifices and risks of full-scale involvement. Yet what distinguishes the history of nitrate workers from that of most other sectors of the working class in Chile and in other nations is that significant and growing numbers of such committed workers emerged.

One unimpeachable indication of the growing cultural autonomy of nitrate workers is the reactions of employers in central Chile to the nitrate workers they hired during periods of crisis in the industry. Employer attitudes toward *los pampinos* were recorded in letters of complaint filed with the Office of Labor, which managed to relocate thousands of nitrate workers in jobs in public works and agriculture after 1914. Stickell surveyed these letters and found many employers uneasy with the nonconformist, assertive, and politically radical northern workers. Nitrate workers tended to refuse customary arrangements for wages, food, and conditions of work. Employers frequently expressed fear of political contamination of their local labor force. As they struggled with this problem, bureaucrats in the Office of Labor found themselves in a major dilemma. Fear of massive disorders impelled them to bring unemployed nitrate workers south; but to re-employ them risked contamination of the work force there, and to leave them in government-run hostels in Santiago was to risk politicization of the urban unemployed and the possibility of an alliance between radical nitrate workers and labor militants in the capital itself.[41]

Another indication, though a more problematic one, of the growing cultural autonomy and political nonconformism of nitrate workers is the

41. Stickell, "Migration and Mining Labor" (cited in n. 22), Chap. 4.

rising strength of reformist and leftist political parties in the north. All of these parties—Radicals, Democrats, and eventually Socialists—found proportionately greater support in the north than elsewhere. And although most nitrate workers could not vote, and most who did probably voted for left-wing Radical and Democratic candidates, the Socialist Party (Partido Obrero Socialista) founded in Iquique in 1912 managed to elect six municipal councilmen in 1915, and two national deputies by 1921. After that date, until the repression of 1926 and 1927, the electoral and congressional strength of the Communist Party (successor of the Socialist Party) expanded rapidly. Much of this success no doubt resulted from local electoral pacts with Radicals and Democrats formed to maximize the power of each in different electoral districts. Nevertheless, electoral data point to the existence in the north of hundreds of Marxist militants by the mid-1920's.[42]

It is of course difficult for historians to discover directly what most nitrate workers thought about their lives and their efforts to improve them. As late as 1927, 60 percent of workers in the industry could not read and write. In any case, unlike their class antagonists in the nitrate oficinas, workers had neither a cultural tradition of recording their problems and hopes nor much time and energy to do so. The closest thing we have to a memoir of a nitrate worker is Elías Lafertte's remarkable autobiography. Unlike the stylized autobiographies of Communist labor leaders in some other countries, Lafertte's book does not attempt to press the experiences of his early life on the nitrate pampa into an ideal, linear account of progressive radicalization and growing class consciousness. His book is honest, complex, and richly detailed. Nevertheless, Lafertte's autobiography was the product of a literate, highly politicized Marxist leader of the working class. Indeed, all the leftist writings of the nitrate era are open to the criticism that the attitudes they reflect are those of a tiny minority, far removed from the cultural values, social concerns, and political views of the mass of workers they claim to speak for.[43]

42. Arturo Valenzuela, *Political Brokers in Chile* (Durham, N.C., 1976).

43. J. Samuel Valenzuela, "Labor Movement Formation," makes this point in an extreme way. For him the trajectory of a given labor movement results from political structures and a concatenation of political events, themselves the product of the will of labor and party leaders. The implications of such assumptions for historical analysis are starkly revealed in his treatment of the settlement of an important railway strike in 1907, pp. 419-25. In his interpretation, the strike was a pivotal event in a political sequence that led to the massacre at Iquique later that year, and to the eventual eclipse of moderate social democratic leadership within the Chilean labor movement. Those events enabled more radical, leftist leaders and parties to fill the "organizational space" created by the emergence of the labor movement. Valenzuela is critical of the reformist leaders of the railway strike for not trying hard enough to "sell" a "favorable" settlement to the striking rank and file. That settlement, which was much less than the strikers demanded and was rejected by the majority, he considers favorable because *over the next several years* the exchange rate for Chilean pesos to

It is thus better to leave these sources aside for a moment, move back in time to the beginning of the century, and pursue the question from a different angle by looking at what workers actually did in their efforts to improve their lives. We have already discussed two early strategies pursued by workers on the nitrate pampa. They moved around a lot shopping for better conditions, and they organized mutual-aid societies to enrich their lives and buffer themselves and their families from natural and man-made forces beyond their control. Both of these activities implied a set of cultural values and attitudes that began to distinguish nitrate workers from other sectors of the Chilean working class, especially the rural workers whom nitrate producers mainly recruited for their labor force. Through their nomadic culture nitrate workers learned they could reject unsatisfactory conditions and, within limits, defy authority successfully. They also learned to trust in themselves, their friends, and their relatives in their search for a better life. In their mutual-aid societies workers taught themselves to pool resources and collectively confront and manage serious matters of education, health, injury, and death that no individual could handle alone.

It is ironic that the second (and more collective) approach met with approval and even encouragement on the part of owners and managers of nitrate oficinas, whereas the first (which was individualistic) encountered decided opposition from capitalists. As we have seen, nitrate managers devised schemes of payment and credit—work by the piece, payment once a month in scrip, tool deposits, and credit at the company store—to restrict the movement of their workers and the bargaining power and challenge to authority such movement entailed. But these management schemes never fully accomplished their goal. Moreover, each tended to intensify conflict between workers and management and to focus the demands of individual workers in collective ways. And though mutual-aid societies seemed to channel worker energies into innocuous cultural and social pursuits—and shouldered much of the social-welfare burden that

---

pounds sterling it would have established would have improved railway workers' real wages. Such an argument is not only ahistorical; like Valenzuela's work as a whole, it assumes that workers' past experience, current perceptions, and future expectations were relatively unimportant to the outcome; that the sacrifices and risks taken by striking workers can be measured and compensated in largely economic terms; that workers' collective understandings can be readily altered by untried leaders from a wide range of political persuasions; and that Marxist leaders of the period were not better equipped ideologically and politically than moderate reformers to take the risks involved in staying in line with militant rank and file. Valenzuela's explanation of Chilean labor formation is paralleled in his treatment of the Argentine case, pp. 366-69. He attributes the fundamentally different course of Argentine labor history to a fortuitous political event, the coup of 1930. That event is not explained within the sweep of early-twentieth-century Argentine economic and social history, nor is it related to the central problem—vital to an understanding of Argentine labor formation—of the complex causes of the anomalous course of Argentine historical development after 1930.

capital would later be forced to assume—the skills, confidence, and mutual trust workers acquired helped prepare them for the time when they would start to work collectively to overcome the man-made conditions that threatened their livelihood and embittered their lives.

Nitrate workers became involved in such collective action on a large scale as early as 1890. Many of the strikes that punctuated the next four decades began as spontaneous protests against procedures for determining pay, discounts on fichas (or the exchange rate of Chilean pesos to pounds sterling), and prices and false scales in company stores. Worker grievances have been called expressions of an "enraged liberalism" by one historian, but they were so only in a superficial sense. In the fateful strike of 1907, workers demanded the abolition of the scrip system and the immediate redemption of fichas at all oficinas without discount. Moreover, they wanted the fichas exchanged at a rate higher than the current official international exchange rate for pounds sterling to Chilean pesos. They also wanted "free commerce," adequate safety devices, free night schools, and two weeks' notice for workers fired for any reason. Finally, the logic of their protest led them to demand immunity for those engaged in collective action and legal, public recognition of the organizations they had formed to press their demands.

Each one of these demands, however, implied a challenge to the liberal principles of capitalist enterprise in general, and to the specific arrangements (often not so capitalist) through which managers sought to maximize their control and exploitation of the labor force in the nitrate zone. Universal exchange without discount of fichas for Chilean pesos at a premium rate not only threatened a major mechanism used by capital to hold its labor force on the pampa and undermined the use of inflation to cut capital's wage bill, but also violated the liberal principle of an international gold standard. Free commerce on the nitrate pampa threatened the capitalists' ability to recover through the company store part of their wage bill. It also denied capital, as the head of the Nitrate Producers' Association testified to the 1912 Parliamentary Commission, "the sacred right of property assured to us by the Constitution." That document, he explained, recognized capitalists' right to exercise "absolute dominion [over] our properties." Itinerant merchants, who sold liquor, engaged in subversive propaganda ("which they were wont to do"), or tried to lure workers away from the oficinas to other jobs, had to be dealt with sternly and expelled from the oficinas. Although it was hard for capitalists to deny the importance of safety devices publicly, workers' ability to decide where and when they were installed would challenge the supreme authority of owners to decide how best to invest capital and to dictate the way work was organized. As for schools, they might be provided at the discretion of individual employers, but they were really the business of the state, not private enterprise. Finally, insistence on striker immunity and recognition of worker organizations challenged the most fundamental principle of all—the "freedom of work," by which capitalists meant their exclusive right to purchase labor on the market and contract with individual workers as they saw fit.

The anticapitalist logic of what may appear to the mid-twentieth-century mind as liberal aspirations was inexorable. Capitalists immediately recognized what was at stake. They refused to make any concessions on principle. They sought to break worker organizations at all costs. They employed spies and established blacklists. They locked workers out. When all else failed they called on the forces of the state to protect their interests. *Carabineros*, the police force that was partially funded by capitalists on the nitrate pampa, handled smaller protests by breaking up strikes, raiding the worker press, or jailing the most militant workers. When protest grew too large for the police to handle, the state was called upon to transport hundreds of workers out of the north or to send the army and navy to "restore order." Time and time again public forces accomplished that goal by massacring striking workers, sometimes by the scores and hundreds, and at least once, the left claimed, by the thousands.

Slowly, perhaps, large numbers of workers also began to understand what their anarchist and socialist leaders already knew. Their modest efforts to better their condition involved radical principles that challenged the basis of capitalist enterprise. "Perhaps," I say, because given the immense risks involved in collective protest, workers, like their leaders, had to be cautious, practical men. Whatever they may have thought about the implications of their demands, they had to couch their inherently radical aspirations in the liberal language of the dominant culture. They had to get what they could without losing their jobs, their personal freedom, or their lives. Though workers through individual protest and collective action gradually forced concessions in the nitrate oficinas, the degree of repression to which they were exposed through the whole era must have disillusioned and disheartened many. But it radicalized many others. The single document prepared by a workers' organization published in the Parliamentary Commission's report of 1913 declared that five minutes of officially sanctioned gunfire against the peaceful striking nitrate workers in Iquique in 1907 had done more to destroy their patriotism and respect for government authority than "a half century of systematic propaganda by a thousand anarchists."[44]

Despite the entrenched strength and pull of liberal assumptions, and the great risk involved for workers who participated in leftist politics, significant numbers of nitrate workers became anarchists and socialists.

44. The commission's report is cited in n. 29; the quotations here and above are from pp. 81-82 and 137.

They did so because those anticapitalist ideologies coincided with their perceptions of the world they lived in and offered meaningful solutions to their personal needs and aspirations. Society in the north was divided into two classes, each clearly distinguishable. One bossed, the other worked. One was wealthy, the other poor. Not only was each class ethnically and culturally distinct (a condition also met in Chilean agriculture and manufacturing), but capital was foreign, whereas labor was Chilean. Capital in the north systematically exploited labor, as any worker knew who had had his caliche wrongly assessed, had exchanged fichas at discount, had seen a friend maimed by an unsafe machine, or had paid exorbitant prices for falsely weighed goods at the company store. Capital and labor were locked in a never-ending struggle in which capital, assisted by the state, gave no quarter. Nitrate workers knew that they were totally dependent on the sale of their labor; they and their families had no way to sustain themselves during depression in the industry. Improvement in the condition of their lives would have to come through collective action by the workers themselves. Workers could move about as individuals during good times, but no capitalist would sustain them in bad. Parliamentary commissions studied conditions and congressmen debated reform, but conditions in the nitrate zone changed little. Capitalism was irrational. One month there was too much work; the next, thousands were unemployed, homeless, helpless. But capitalism was not only bad for workers, it was bad for Chile. Foreigners were scooping out the irreplaceable wealth of Chile at great profit to themselves. Little that nitrate workers saw could be said to redound to the nation's benefit.

It was on this last point, and the issue of political action to enlist the support of the state to meet working-class needs, that anarchist and socialist ideology diverged. Whereas anarchists insisted on the worldwide unity of the proletariat, early Chilean socialists were more apt to stress the unity between the aspirations of workers and those of other patriotic Chileans. This position allowed socialists to countenance collaboration with progressive sectors of other classes in efforts to better the position of the working class.[45] The socialists combined in electoral coalitions with parties that had reformist, nationalist aspects to their programs. They sought to promote legislative solutions to working-class problems at the national level. However antithetical to ruling-class privilege the ideology and programs of the socialists were, their electoral tactics enabled them to turn political norms sanctioned by the ruling class to the purposes of the working class. By the 1920's socialist strategy appeared

---

45. This is true despite the prohibition of pacts with "bourgeois" parties in the platform of the Partido Obrero Socialista in 1912. Perhaps that ban was a vain attempt to stifle what was already a logical tendency, given the electoral strategy and ideological position on patriotism within the party.

to be far more effective, and much less dangerous, to the Chilean working class than the uncompromising stance of the anarchists.

Anarchists were adamantly opposed both to petitioning the state and to forming political parties to contest for state power. To do so was to legitimize the capitalist state and the electoral procedures it used to validate its monopoly of political power. Given the fact that many nitrate miners owned their own tools and maintained significant control over the work process, the anarchists' emphasis on individual freedom and spontaneous grass-roots action found a natural audience. Moreover, because most nitrate miners could not vote, and because electoral abuses such as fraud and vote-buying were in any case widespread in Chile in the early twentieth century, it is not surprising that anarchists were initially much stronger than socialists in the nitrate zone. It was anarchists, for example, who led the great nitrate strike of 1907. But systematic repression and the relative failure of direct action, coupled with the growing success of socialist union-organizing and electoral strategies in the north in the 1920's, led anarchist influence to give way slowly to that of socialist militants.[46]

Had capitalism in the north led to diversified economic development and the emergence of a complex structure of intermediate classes, had it fostered rising real incomes and widespread property ownership by the mass of workers, liberal notions might have exercised more consistent appeal. Workers came to the north to make money and improve their station in life. Individualist aspirations were encouraged by the piece-rate system and by the dominant values of Chilean society. But the export economy of the north did not lead to capital accumulation and an expanding, diversified economy there. Profits were remitted abroad or distributed through the state in the south. All the official commissions to the nitrate zone concluded that very little of this money found its way into improvements in the north. Even in the large port towns that housed the mansions of the rich and the luxurious social clubs of the foreign community, public water, sewage, health, and educational systems were grossly deficient. Savings by nitrate miners could not be invested in property. Educational opportunities were limited. Periodic crises in the industry consumed what workers could save and left them helpless, unemployed victims of economic forces beyond their control.

46. Anarchist influence was much more enduring, especially among artisans, in the manufacturing establishments of Santiago. In several industries, most notably shoe manufacturing, they were able to establish very effective organizations at the plant level. Although socialists had some success in organizing textile, tram, and construction workers, anarchists predominated in the organized urban labor movement until the end of the nitrate era, as De Shazo has effectively shown. J. Samuel Valenzuela, "Labor Movement Formation," elaborates the political implications of the contrast in effective plant-level organization in the mining and manufacturing sectors of the Chilean economy.

It is true, as Stickell argues, that by the 1920's conditions of life and work on the nitrate pampa had improved, especially in the larger, newer oficinas. But it is unlikely that improvements significantly changed the structural opportunities available for ambitious individual workers. In any case, they came too late. Some workers had already developed a vigorous, autonomous vision of the world that was successfully competing with the dominant liberal one. Anarchist and socialist leaders had proved their commitment and courage in defending working-class interests through more than three decades of systematic repression. Moreover, improvements in the condition of workers appeared as the nitrate export economy ceased to grow and began to experience the violent convulsions that further radicalized workers and culminated in the virtual collapse of nitrate production after 1930. Finally, most of the improvements came in the 1920's as a result of the direct action and militant politics of national working-class institutions and parties. The most important of these organs of the workers' movement were dominated physically and ideologically by socialist leaders whose power base lay in the north. These institutions played a large role in the insurgency of nitrate and transport workers, and of urban workers, students, and white-collar workers in the period following the First World War, an insurgency that forced the Chilean ruling class to make concessions and adopt a new strategy of labor control. In 1924, at the cost of a total breakdown of the political system, the Chilean ruling class became the first in South America to abandon the failed policy of simple physical repression of organized labor. It tried instead to curb labor's revolutionary potential through legislative means by integrating organized labor into the institutional life of the nation. It is to that remarkable story, and its unforeseen—and tragically ironic—implications for subsequent Chilean history that we now turn.

The Crystallization of a Marxist Labor Movement

The economic and ideological forces unleashed by the First World War deeply affected the strength and orientation of national labor movements all over the world. The conflict for world dominion between two blocs of the major capitalist industrial powers stimulated enormous demand for machines, ammunition, food, and raw materials. Workers took advantage of conditions of full employment and labor organizations expanded rapidly. With the armistice in 1918 pent-up civilian demand pushed prices up rapidly. Real wages lagged far behind. Labor responded by using its new organizational strength to unleash a wave of strikes unprecedented in scope and power. By 1920, however, wartime demobilization and flagging consumer demand plunged the world capitalist economy into depression. As unemployment spread, labor all over the world saw its organizational strength compromised, its ability to strike effectively impaired.

The war that generated these economic trends also undermined the liberal philosophical foundations of capitalism and, among workers, reinforced anticapitalist ideologies of the left. The war featured the spectacle of the major capitalist powers in the core of western "civilization" harnessing their liberal political systems, their new science, technology, and industrial might, to annihilate their adversaries. The outbreak of the fighting in Europe created an ideological and political crisis within the world labor movement, and proletarian unity broke in the face of national demands and loyalties, especially among the social democratic parties of the Second International. Nonetheless, the war enabled the first socialist revolution to consolidate power in Russia. As it undermined liberal assumptions, then, the world conflict provided Marxists within the labor movement (including, initially, anarchists) with ideological inspiration and renewed confidence in their ability to forge a socialist future.

This volatile mix of favorable economic conditions and positive ideological forces in the immediate postwar period exploded in a massive mobilization by the left. It created a perception, shared by radical labor leaders and the political leaders of the ruling class alike, that social revolution was imminent. As revolutionary groups within the labor movement experimented with new forms of struggle to realize this goal, ruling classes searched for new devices to avert it.

Chile, more fully than any other South American nation, participated in this worldwide drama of war and worker mobilization. Its nitrate export economy, as we have seen, was intimately affected by the changes in trade, demand, and technical innovation generated by the war. Following the severe depression of 1914 and 1915, nitrate production reached an all-time high in the period 1916-18, then plummeted into the disastrous depression of 1919-23. In terms of fluctuations in the demand for labor, postwar price inflation, and the length and severity of the postwar depression, Chile's economy was affected more seriously by the world economic forces of the period than that of any nation in South America.

Because of the structure of Chile's nitrate export economy, and because of the relative development of autonomous anticapitalist thought and organization among Chile's urban, transport, and mining workers, the ideological forces unleashed by the war affected political life and the labor movement more profoundly in Chile than in the other nations of the continent as well. Although statistics on strike activity, and on membership in radical unions and political parties, are much discussed in the literature, all are hopelessly incomplete and unreliable. All estimates agree, however, that a wave of strikes of unprecedented proportion enveloped the main Chilean cities and ports and the nitrate zone after 1918 and reached its peak in late 1919 or early 1920. Dues-paying memberships in leftist labor organizations and political parties probably expanded severalfold in the late 1910's and early 1920's. Far more important than the absolute numbers of such activists, which may have reached 20,000 or so by 1920, were the masses of workers ten times that size whom organized militants were able to mobilize in public demonstrations and general strikes in the postwar era.[47]

All anticapitalist labor organizations grew in size and broadened their influence over parts of the Chilean labor movement during the postwar period. Socialists dominated the labor organizations in the nitrate zone, anarcho-syndicalists were preeminent in Santiago, and the Chilean chapter of the Industrial Workers of the World came to predominate in the port of Valparaíso. Each group had considerable influence in the area of the labor movement dominated by the others, however. And although anarchists, syndicalists, and socialists competed with one another to expand their influence among organized and unorganized workers alike, all cooperated to excellent effect in mobilizing the working class as a whole for public demonstrations and general strikes in the immediate postwar period.[48]

But it was the socialists who moved to institutionalize their strength and influence in national labor and political organizations. For this task they were best prepared by ideology and experience. Years of struggle in the nitrate zone had convinced socialists that a solution to the problems of the working class would have to be a national one, achieved through access to the power of the state. The importance of nitrate production to national economic and fiscal life had meant repression by capital and the state so severe that maintenance of enduring organizations at the plant level in the nitrate zone had been impossible. Socialists understood how cyclical fluctuations in the nitrate economy created national problems of inflation and unemployment, how foreign ownership deprived the whole people of Chile of the wealth labor produced in the nation's most important industry. Labor leaders and organizers in the nitrate zone, like the nomadic labor force they appealed to, had built personal and political communications networks all over northern and central Chile. In the first years of the twentieth century these contacts were expanded south to the coal-producing zone and, farther, to small militant enclaves of sheepherders and meat packers in southern Chile.

47. All these statistics, which range from official counts published by the Office of Labor to later estimates based on research by scholars such as De Shazo, are collected and carefully analyzed in J. Samuel Valenzuela, "Labor Movement Formation," Chap. 7.

48. De Shazo, *Urban Workers* (cited in n. 35), provides a wealth of information on all these themes.

The vehicle used by socialists to build a national labor organization was the Gran Federación de Obreros de Chile. That timid, reformist organization, founded by railroad workers in 1909, enjoyed the toleration of government officials and possessed the rudiments of a decentralized national organization. Growing militancy among rank-and-file workers, especially in the regional section of Valparaíso, had led to a bitter strike and a change in national leadership in 1916. The next year, the FOCh held a national convention and opened its ranks to all workers. Socialist delegates enlisted the scores of worker organizations they controlled. Steadily, over the course of the next three years, the FOCh was transformed into a militant, revolutionary labor organization, the most powerful labor central in the country. This accomplishment was made possible by the numerical strength and national importance of the working-class organizations in the nitrate zone led by the socialists; by the contacts, organizational skill, and national prominence of the socialists' leadership; and by the appeal and effectiveness, within the context of Chile's political system, of the socialists' electoral tactics.

At the December 1921 FOCh convention held at Rancagua, near the huge new American-owned copper mine El Teniente, delegates voted to affiliate the FOCh with the Red International and to tie its membership politically to the Socialist Party, the Partido Obrero Socialista. The next month, representatives of that party voted to change their name to the Communist Party of Chile and to join the Third International. Affiliation with the international communist movement caused some dissent, especially from reformist elements within the FOCh. But given the ideological trajectory of the socialists, and the enormous prestige of the Soviet experiment at the time, it was probably inevitable. The most serious defector from the FOCh was the organization of railroad workers, but even these skilled and better-paid workers sought affiliation with the Red International after the split.[49]

In the changing economic and political climate of the postwar period, socialist and other labor organizations pursued a variety of tactics to expand their influence and consolidate and defend their gains. During the period of booming nitrate exports and high employment immediately following the war, union activists concentrated on job actions and organization within the working class itself. In his study of urban labor, Peter De Shazo found that the strikes of this period, in contrast to earlier ones, were more often successful. He also discovered that strike demands at this time were much more likely than in earlier years to center on measures to

49. In contrast to the argument presented here, Valenzuela ("Labor Movement Formation") places more emphasis on the personal influence of Recabarren in the takeover of the FOCh by the Partido Obrero Socialista, whereas Monteón (*Chile in the Nitrate Era*) stresses the divisiveness of the affiliation decisions.

establish and protect labor organizations and control the work environment. At the same time, however, militant elements within the labor movement began to forge contacts with other urban groups, especially those who were hurt by the economic dislocation of the postwar period and were potentially sympathetic to leftist ideological currents.

This second strategy became more important after 1919, as the nitrate economy faltered, and especially after 1920, when the postwar depression began in earnest. Spreading unemployment in the private sector and cutbacks in public spending not only eroded the bargaining position of industrial workers but threatened white-collar workers and professionals as well. Price inflation, stimulated by government advances of paper credit to nitrate producers and issues of paper pesos to make up in part for lost nitrate revenues, hurt all consumers.[50] At the end of 1919, on the initiative of the FOCh, organized workers mobilized a broad coalition of urban groups in an effort to pressure the government to reduce food prices and enact tax and educational reforms. These issues were vital to a wide spectrum of urban groups, who joined in massive street demonstrations of 60,000 to 100,000 people in Santiago in late 1919 and mid-1920. If the immediate demands of this coalition were moderate, the analyses of the situation provided by the anticapitalist orators who addressed the crowds were not. Meanwhile, white-collar workers and students were organizing and becoming more militant themselves. Teachers established a union as early as 1918, and radical students with ties to anarchists and the IWW organized in Santiago in 1919.

Into this volatile situation streamed thousands of unemployed nitrate workers in 1921. Faced with the growing threat posed by masses of unemployed workers in the north, the government rented warehouses and established hostels in the nitrate ports and Santiago and transported thousands of workers south. During 1921 and 1922, according to De Shazo, there were 20,000 unemployed nitrate workers and their families in hostels in Santiago. The FOCh organized these workers into unions, and despite the best efforts of government officials and police—and reports by government spies within the hostels—unemployed nitrate workers served as mobile shock troops for the strike actions and protest rallies of the period.

Although activities of this kind spread the radical vision of anarchists, syndicalists, and socialists to other sectors of the working class and to elements of urban middle groups, the deepening of the depression and growing public and private repression gradually sapped the strength of working-class institutions. Congress passed a residency law in 1919 that enabled government officials to deny entry to or expel foreign radicals.

50. Frank W. Fetter, *Monetary Inflation in Chile* (Princeton, N.J., 1931), Chap. 9.

Since there were few such people in Chile, the government relied primarily on police actions, state-of-siege powers, and private paramilitary groups on the right to jail labor activists, break strikes, silence the working-class press, and terrorize activist workers and students.

Meanwhile, labor organizations tried valiantly and creatively to defend workers' jobs and preserve their institutions. A huge port strike in Valparaíso to maintain an innovative work-sharing system devised by the IWW-affiliated union was finally broken by scab labor and government repression. A protracted, intermittent coal strike to avoid pay cuts and massive layoffs in an industry deeply affected by the downturn in purchases by nitrate oficinas and by other sectors of the economy was supported by FOCh revenues and a general solidarity strike, but ultimately ended in failure. Nitrate workers laid off at Oficina San Gregorio in 1921 refused management's offer of one day's pay and passage south and declared they would run the oficina themselves. When police attempted to eject them, they killed the manager and frightened off the police with dynamite. Two days later, a full-scale military operation launched from the coast forced their submission. They were robbed of their belongings by the troops, and 130 were bound and dragged across the pampa to jail in Iquique.

The repression eventually broke the postwar strike wave and temporarily shattered workers' organizations. But with the upswing in the economy in 1923, workers began to mobilize in the workplace and the streets once again. Dues-paying members of the FOCh doubled to more than 10,000 between 1923 and 1925, and the number of workers the Federación led and influenced was several times that number. Anarchist and IWW union membership and influence also expanded, especially in the case of the IWW, although their effective numbers were certainly fewer than those of the FOCh. Strike activity revived from the nadir of 1922 to reach unprecedented levels by 1925. The Office of Labor counted 19 strikes in 1922, 86 in 1924, 114 in 1925.

Judging from its strength and activities in the nitrate zone, the labor movement was stronger in 1924-25 than it was even in the immediate postwar period. Large-scale mobilization and a strike wave in the north in March 1925 resulted in the first collective contract in the nitrate industry, one that significantly improved hours and pay, established severance conditions highly favorable to workers, and recognized the FOCh as the legal representative of nitrate workers. For the first time labor unions won the right to hold meetings within the nitrate oficinas.[51]

51. The agreement, signed under the auspices of government officials, was soon broken by management; a massive government offensive against the FOCh then ensued. *El Comunista* (Antofagasta), Mar. 24, 25, 1925; *El Despertar de los Trabajadores* (Iquique), Apr. 19, 1925.

Meanwhile, the ideological influence of radical labor organizations was spreading. White-collar workers in private industry, who first organized in the north, held a national convention in 1924 and adopted statutes defining themselves as a "salaried class" and calling for the nationalization of commerce and industry.[52] One passage of that document reveals the clear influence of Marxist ideas: "Labor is the base of capital; the emancipation of employees must be the work of employees themselves; physical and mental work should not be a simple commodity; the exploitation of man by man is a crime. . . . "[53] Even organizations of medical doctors and schoolteachers, whose formal statutes were not radical, occasionally revealed "tendencies opposed to the present organization [of society]," warned the head of the Chilean Labor Office in 1926.

During the mid-1920's, the political influence of the Communist Party expanded dramatically. The party helped to organize a coalition of working-class and middle-sector groups in a National Assembly of Wage Earners to contest the presidential election of 1926. Its platform called for far-reaching social and economic reforms in the short run and contemplated as a future goal the socialization of the means of production and exchange. The coalition's candidate, a military medical doctor, captured 30 percent of the vote, almost the share won by similar leftist coalitions until the 1970's. In the congressional elections held the same year the Communist Party elected five deputies and one senator.

Faced with seemingly chronic economic disruption and threats to capitalist control in the workplace, and confronted with a growing challenge to its ideological and political hegemony and means of social control, the Chilean ruling class cast about for effective solutions to worker insurgency in the early 1920's. Capitalists organized themselves more effectively on the economic front by establishing an Asociación del Trabajo de Chile in 1921 to coordinate resistance and propaganda against radical labor. Government tolerated the activities of antilabor paramilitary groups. The repressive apparatus of the state was strengthened and its legal powers extended. But simple repression had its limits. When it had to be used repeatedly on as broad a scale as it was in Chile in the postwar period, repression undermined the legitimacy of class rule at home and tarnished the carefully constructed image of Chile as a progressive, stable society abroad.

By the 1920's some influential political leaders began to contemplate dealing with the labor problem through reform. Some members of the traditional parties advocated new laws designed to tame the economic and political threat posed by organized labor through material conces-

52. Ramírez Necochea, *Origen y formación* (cited in n. 35), pp. 102-3.
53. This quotation and the following one are taken from Moisés Poblete Troncoso, *La organización sindical en Chile y otros estudios sociales* (Santiago, 1926), pp. 50-52.

sions and institutions of control managed by the state. Others sought to accomplish the same end by working through new reformist parties that appealed to, and won support from, the growing middle class and labor. The most important of these new parties was the Liberal Alliance led by Arturo Alessandri. It managed to gain control of the lower house in congress for a time in 1918 and to win the presidency after a violent, popular campaign in 1920. Alessandri, dubbed "the Lion of Tarapacá" by his supporters, who were disproportionately drawn from the nitrate provinces, made concerted appeals to workers during the campaign of 1920. If the small number of workers who voted did not make the difference in his narrow and fiercely disputed electoral victory, street demonstrations in his favor probably assured his inauguration. Alessandri made labor reform an important part of his campaign, and in 1921 he introduced a comprehensive package of labor legislation to the congress. Alessandri's labor reforms, like most of his economic and social initiatives, were opposed and stymied in the congress by conservative elements both within his own party coalition and in the conservative parties that opposed him.[54] Conservatives themselves had become alarmed by the strike wave and the growing influence of anticapitalist ideologies within the working class, and in 1919, at the zenith of the postwar labor mobilization, they had introduced a package of labor reforms of their own.

The conservative and liberal proposals for labor reform both sought to limit the economic power, organizational autonomy, and revolutionary political potential of organized labor in Chile. Both tried to do so by granting labor certain economic and organizational concessions. For example, both outlined codes to improve working conditions, envisioned profit sharing, and granted labor the legal right to organize and to strike. Both sought to institutionalize labor conflict through schemes of conciliation and arbitration. Both would bring labor organizations under the close supervision and control of the state through systems of inspection, through legal constraints on the use of union funds, and through the specifying of conditions under which legal strikes could occur.

Yet the means each chose to achieve these common goals were philosophically distinct and procedurally different.[55] The conservative pro-

54. The appearance of these reformist parties and groups in Chile was part of a regional phenomenon, a product of greater social complexity generated by expanding international trade, foreign investment, technology transfer, and European immigration after 1880. The whole process is analyzed and given comparative Latin American treatment in the classic study by John J. Johnson, *Political Change in Latin America: The Rise of the Middle Sectors* (Stanford, Calif., 1958). Of Alessandri's coalition, Johnson says: "The objectives of the leaders varied. A few were dedicated reformers. Some sensed that the moment had arrived when it was politically expedient to institute reform measures. Others desired simply to win office by getting out more votes than the landed aristocrats and their allies could muster. They had little concern for or faith in the working group" (p. 77).

55. This discussion of the labor law projects draws on information in James O. Morris, *Elites, Intellectuals and Consensus* (New York, 1966).

posal was inspired by Catholic, corporatist philosophy and blatantly favored capital. Unions would be corporate entities formed in each separate company and could participate in profits. Once a certain proportion of workers in a given establishment voted to form a union, membership would be obligatory for all. Voting for union officers would be weighted, with employees of long standing having twice as many votes as the newly employed. Conciliation, performed by a panel of two representatives from labor and three from capital, would also be obligatory, as would arbitration in the event workers rejected the conciliatory compromise and chose to strike. Arbitration, undertaken by a government body, would be final. Workers who did not accept the outcome would be fired without indemnification. A capitalist who did not accept the outcome could be punished, but if he thought the settlement was economically prejudicial to his activities he could ignore it and lock workers out. The president of the nation could dissolve any union guilty of infringing on the right to work or of undermining the public order.

The liberal proposal was more subtle, and more favorable to labor. It combined individualist and statist principles in ways symptomatic of the philosophical transformation through which nineteenth-century liberalism responded to twentieth-century social pressures. Membership in unions was to be voluntary. A union could be formed either by workers or by employees doing similar or related tasks. Federations of unions could be formed and could engage in collective bargaining. Public employees, however, could not organize unions. Leaders would be elected by a two-thirds vote of the membership. Unions could be dissolved by the president of the nation for the same reasons as in the conservative proposal. Profit-sharing benefits would go to individuals, not to the union. Conciliation and arbitration procedures were voluntary. For a strike to be legal, the union had to go through a protracted procedure of meeting, considering, and rejecting mediation and arbitration alternatives.

Many observers have commented on the hybrid nature of the composite labor reform hammered out by a special congressional committee in late 1921 and finally passed into law under pressure from the military in September 1924. It is true that the result contained both corporatist and liberal features, but what is most striking is how it faithfully combined the most viable restrictive features of each of the original proposals. Thus, the corporate features of obligatory unionism, weighted voting by workers with seniority, compulsory arbitration, and the prohibition on industrywide federations—from the conservative proposal—were combined with the ban on public employee unionization, division of workers into separate industrial and employee unions, and meticulous state control of union elections, finances, and strike procedures—from the liberal proposal.

However onerous the economic and political controls on labor established in the compromise labor reform (some of which would backfire and redound to the organizational purposes of the left in subsequent years), the legislation entailed concessions to labor that individual capitalists and their interest groups were loath to make and risks that they were averse to taking. Congress debated the issue, turned the proposals over to committee, and failed to take action. The repression and depression of 1921-23 seemed to have broken the back of labor protest and union organizations. But the renewed militancy of labor and the need to apply severe repression again in 1924 brought the issue of labor reform back to the fore. Congress once again proved unable or unwilling to act on the labor bill and other complementary reforms, including a bill designed to blunt the growing militancy of white-collar workers by extending to them a series of social-welfare measures. Finally, in September 1924, the military intervened and pressured the congress to pass the labor legislation.

The motives of the military officers who intervened in politics in 1924 and gradually, under the leadership of Carlos Ibáñez, consolidated control of the Chilean government after 1925 were complex. The officers sought individual promotions and better pay, modern equipment, and more prestige for the military. They were appalled by the corruption and inefficiency of the Chilean political system. Most fundamentally, they were alarmed by the repressive role they were forced to play in maintaining that system and feared that militant, Marxist-led worker organizations would destroy the Chilean social system and the military's monopoly of force. By the mid-1920's, one general loyal to Ibáñez later wrote, Communist influence, especially in the nitrate zone, had succeeded in perverting "the consciousness of all workers, awakening in them feelings of greed and vengeance, stirring the lower instincts of the popular masses. . . . [T]he Chilean proletariat was on the verge of rising up, like the Russian, to destroy through blood and violence the social system of the Republic."[56] It is symptomatic of the collective concerns of the military that it was Carlos Ibáñez who consolidated political control within the military movement after 1925. Ibáñez was intimately aware of the problem of internal labor control. He had headed the School for Carabineros in 1918 and left that post to serve as Prefect of Iquique in 1919-20. There he was forced to contend with militant labor in the heart of the

---

56. Carlos Harms Espejo, *Los grandes problemas de la zona norte de Chile* (Santiago, 1930), p. 134. "Fortunately," Harms Espejo went on, "the great structural reform" of the military governments had imposed cooperation on capital and labor, thus stopping "the train of the nation on the very brink of the precipice, and preventing its fall into the abyss." On the ideology of the Chilean military generally, see Genaro Arriagada Herrera, *El pensamiento político de los militares* (Santiago, n.d.).

nitrate zone during the tumultuous labor mobilization of the postwar years.[57]

Neither labor nor capital was happy with the labor legislation imposed on them by the military in 1924, and most of the reforms remained a dead letter for several years. Anarchists denounced the whole idea of institutionalizing the labor movement within the apparatus of the capitalist state. But the Communists who controlled the FOCh counseled labor militants to take advantage of the benefits of the law and to work to change or abolish the negative features of the reform.[58] The benefits included the legal commitment to better working conditions, the legal right to organize unions and to strike, the possibility of a dues checkoff system, and a union share of profits. Reflecting on the attitudes of capital and labor toward the new legislation in 1926, the head of the Labor Office claimed that owners were beginning to recognize the necessity of labor organization. There is an appreciable element, he wrote, in favor of the new social laws, "especially the industrial union, which eliminates, within industry, free, semirevolutionary unions." Yet the attitude of workers, he noted, was "curious." They continued to belong to their semirevolutionary unions, but, at the same time, called for legal unions to win the benefits of the new legislation. By 1926, he said, 200 of the new unions had been organized.[59]

Proponents of the labor legislation had assumed that the FOCh would oppose it. Instead, the Communist Party forged alliances with groups of private employees to pressure for selective implementation of the new laws. The mobilization and electoral successes that followed help to explain the increasingly repressive stance of the military-dominated governments beginning in mid-1925. During the following two years, as control of the government passed more fully into the hands of Ibáñez, the repression of workers and their militant organizations by troops and police grew steadily more systematic and thorough.

This offensive against Marxist labor, the most severe and effective yet seen in Chile, was kicked off in the nitrate zone in June 1925.[60] There workers organized by the FOCh threatened to halt production if the

---

57. Ernesto Wurth Rojas, *Ibáñez: Caudillo enigmático* (Santiago, 1958), p. 18.

58. Since there is some debate on this point, see *El Despertar de los Trabajadores*, June 2, 1925; *Justicia*, Mar. 2, 1932.

59. Poblete Troncoso, *Organización sindical* (cited in n. 53), pp. 76-77.

60. In preparation, the government had set up an Oficina Central de Servicio de Informaciones Sociales. The new intelligence service instructed local police officials to send in lists of all organizations that participated in "working-class meetings, strikes, and demonstrations" and all members and directors of such organizations "indicating expressly which of them are foreigners and which of them devote themselves to the spread of propaganda against the established order and indicating especially those who are revolutionary syndicalists, anarchists, sovietizing Russians and Peruvians, etc." *El Despertar de los Trabajadores*, May 14 and 31, 1925.

terms of the collective contract signed three months earlier were not implemented. Owners reacted with massive layoffs of militant workers.
Faced with the likelihood of another general strike in the nitrate zone, the
government opted for repression. A full-scale military operation was
launched against militant workers at La Coruña on June 4, 1925. Estimates of the number of workers killed in this last of the great nitrate-
worker massacres and in the general repression that followed run into the
hundreds. Hundreds more, most of them anarchist and communist militants, were jailed or exiled, many of them to Chile's remote Pacific
islands.

In the years that followed, Ibáñez sought to implement the new labor
legislation through formal corporatist means. He created a progovern-
ment labor central, installed friends in the labor movement in the leadership positions of government-controlled unions, and attempted to insure the loyalty of the leadership and rank and file by extending them
palpable material benefits. Compared to the scope of similar efforts made
by Perón in Argentina twenty years later, Ibáñez's efforts seem modest
and halfhearted.[61] But in the environment of political repression and economic expansion underwritten by foreign loans (which made U.S. investment in Chile the greatest in any South American country by 1930),
Ibáñez's labor policy seemed to be effective.

By 1928 the left was broken, its once powerful union and political organizations virtually destroyed. Few could have predicted that within a
decade the left would build a more powerful successor to the FOCh, construct two mass-based Marxist parties more influential than the Communist Party in the mid-1920's, and enter into a left-center coalition
called the Popular Front that would win control of the national government in 1938.

The Trajectory of the Chilean Left

Review of the labor reform proposals of the 1920's—and of the tumultuous twelve-year period from 1919 to 1932 in which they were
drafted, fused, enacted, and enforced—reveals how the postwar insurgency of Chilean labor forced the ruling class to grant painful concessions
and redefine the channels and limits of class struggle. That process involved a total breakdown of Chile's "democratic" political system, the
writing of a new constitution that greatly strengthened executive power,
and the creation of a series of new labor institutions. Within the boundaries of this new institutional order, the four decades of Chilean history
that culminated in 1973 were played out. The struggle between capital
and labor codified in the labor legislation of the 1920's resulted in a historic compromise neither side could fully control and whose conse-

61. René Montero Moreno, *Confesiones políticas* (Santiago, 1959), pp. 53-54.

quences neither could fully predict. Although each side was able to turn parts of the settlement to its class advantage, each was compromised in ways that only became clear much later.

Two main trends define the four decades of Chilean economic history after 1930, each deeply influenced by changes in an evolving world capitalist system.[62] First, worldwide depression and war destroyed the nitrate economy that had propelled Chilean development for a half century, then helped consolidate in its stead a new, structurally similar mineral export economy around copper. Second, the breakdown in the international division of labor in the period 1930-45 stimulated the process of domestic industrialization in Chile. By the end of the period manufacturing had become the most important sector of the national economy. Both of these changes occurred within a context of agricultural stagnation, a feature of the Chilean economy that dates from the 1920's, if not earlier. During the first two decades of the period, or until about 1950, the value of export and manufacturing production slowly recovered from the nadir of the Depression. By 1950 per capita production and consumption finally surpassed the level reached in the late 1920's. During the next two decades, 1950-70, as population continued to grow, the whole economy stagnated. Copper exports leveled off, and growth in manufacturing was slight. These trends revealed the inability of the Chilean economy to respond favorably to a new phase in the evolution of the world capitalist system.[63] After the Second World War, the world economy entered an unprecedented era of expansion led by U.S. capital. A new and more complex international division of labor emerged. As multinational manufacturing corporations established branch plants in peripheral economies to supply consumer goods to the domestic market, primary exports continued to provide the foreign exchange to purchase imports of capital goods, technology, industrial raw materials, and food. Primary exports also underwrote the service on the large foreign loans peripheral economies needed to cover chronic balance-of-payments deficits and to provide material and human infrastructure for the deepening process of capitalist development. Finally, primary exports continued to generate a large share of the public revenues that allowed government to expand in order to coordinate an increasingly complex economy and provide social services to an ever more urban, and organized, civil society.

62. Structural changes in the world economic system after 1930—and the worldwide social, political, and ideological trends that accompanied them—are treated more systematically in the chapter on Argentina, and in more detail in the chapters on Venezuela and Colombia. In those countries labor in export production exerted its primary influence on the course of national life after 1930.

63. I have relied for much of the economic information in this section on Aníbal Pinto Santa Cruz, *Chile, un caso de desarrollo frustrado* (Santiago, 1959); and Markos J. Mamalakis, *The Growth and Structure of the Chilean Economy* (New Haven, Conn., 1976).

The four decades after 1930 also define a complete historical period in the evolution of the Chilean labor movement. The whole era was characterized by the resurgence of Marxist labor organizations and by the growing electoral success of the parties of the left. These political trends were molded by changing political and ideological currents within the larger world system. As in the economic sphere, they developed in two distinct phases, separated by a historical watershed at mid-century.

In the first phase, labor organization expanded under the restraints and opportunities of the complex institutional framework set up in the 1920's. By and large, that framework proved effective in curbing the economic power of Chilean labor, primarily through the laws restricting organization and collective bargaining to the level of individual companies, separating blue- and white-collar workers into distinct kinds of unions, and limiting the legal use of the strike. Weakness in the private economic sphere impelled labor to seek redress in the public political sphere, a strategy made increasingly viable by the national electoral gains of leftist parties sympathetic to the interests of organized labor. At the same time, organized groups of committed Marxists within the labor movement manipulated several of the corporatist features of the labor legislation to broaden the organizational base of labor and insure the control of unions by Marxists. Compulsory unionization (once 55 percent of the work force in a given plant voted in favor), dues checkoff, and profit sharing aided organization. Bloc and weighted voting for leadership positions favored control of unions by organized, disciplined groups of workers. These organizational and political gains of labor and the left proceeded at some cost to the militancy of leaders and rank and file. Commitment to the complex system of industrial relations socialized workers into a vast, bureaucratic system of labor law, procedures, and institutions. Successful manipulation of this system required detailed knowledge of the law, patience, and tact—requirements that sapped the energies and resources of unions, impelled them into dependence on expertise supplied by middle-class professionals of the Marxist parties, and favored the emergence of leaders who proved resistant to innovation (such as worker control) when opportunities finally arose under the Marxist government that came to power in 1970.[64]

Meanwhile, consistent with larger geopolitical and ideological trends in the world after 1930, the Marxist parties allied themselves electorally with elements of the national bourgeoisie and the middle classes. The program of this Popular Front coalition and its immediate successors re-

64. This evaluation of the effects of the legislation closely follows that of Alan Angell, *Politics and the Labour Movement in Chile* (London, 1972). On worker control under the Popular Unity government, see Juan G. Espinosa and Andrew S. Zimbalist, *Economic Democracy: Worker Participation in Chilean Industry, 1970-1973* (New York, 1978).

volved around state support for industrial growth and expansion of social services. For a decade after 1938, Marxist parties enjoyed a minority share in government. Initially, they were able to use this access to state power to expand the institutional base of organized labor and to promote both national industrial development and the material well-being of their urban working- and middle-class constituency. The number of unions expanded from about 635 to 1,880 between 1935 and 1940, and union membership went from 78,000 to 162,000 in the same period. In 1939 the Popular Front managed to establish a state development corporation, CORFO, to coordinate and promote economic development. CORFO was planned and supported by the left, but the original idea of favoring heavy industry and of funding the agency through copper taxes was diluted by U.S. opposition and financing through the Export-Import Bank. Government support for higher wages and extension of social services for urban groups helped expand the internal market for national industry during the early 1940's.

The Marxist parties accomplished these goals at great ideological, political, and economic cost, however. As they competed with one another, compromised in coalition politics, manipulated the spoils system, and succumbed to the attraction of government jobs, they undercut their revolutionary credentials and appeal. They began by sacrificing the interests of rural workers (at that time still the largest element in the Chilean working class). In 1939, under pressure from their more conservative senior partners in the electoral coalition, they halted a major organizational drive in the countryside. They ended by compromising the material interests of their own electoral base as income distribution worsened in the 1940's. This phase culminated with the postwar worldwide capitalist ideological and political offensive against organized labor and the left. That campaign split the Marxist labor and political institutions in Chile and ended with the systematic repression of the Communist Party in 1949.[65]

During the second period, the left rebuilt its institutional base and recaptured its revolutionary ideological and political momentum. It qualified its commitment to the legal strictures of the labor relations system. Illegal strikes far outnumbered legal ones. Many public employees were organized in defiance of the law. The left retained its commitment to industrialization and an electoral road to socialism, but it eschewed fundamental compromise with the dominant sectors of the capitalist system. It

65. Much of the information on politics in this section is drawn from Paul Drake's impressive study *Socialism and Populism in Chile, 1932-52* (Urbana, Ill., 1978). Brian Loveman, *Struggle in the Countryside* (Bloomington, Ind., 1976), develops the issue of rural unionization with particular force. A powerful synthesis of the postwar U.S.-led offensive against Marxist labor in Latin America is Hobart Spalding, *Organized Labor in Latin America* (New York, 1977), Chap. 6.

moved vigorously to organize the rural working class and began to stress the importance of agricultural transformation to achieve its developmentalist and redistributive goals.

The new militancy of the left precluded vigorous dependent capitalist development paced by foreign investment in Chile after 1950. The U.S.-owned copper companies, faced with militant Marxist unions that constantly escalated wage and fringe benefit demands and confronted by ever-increasing levels of direct and indirect state taxation, insisted on a "new deal" as a condition for new investment. Government policies to lighten the tax burden on copper companies became an explosive public issue in the 1950's. As pressure from the left for nationalization of the industry increased in the 1960's, the copper companies proved willing to divest under generous government offers for joint public-private control or "Chileanization." Meanwhile, the industrial sector of the economy stagnated as well. The left mobilized massive demonstrations and general strikes to protect or increase workers' real wages in a stagnant, inflationary economy and to resist policies dictated by international monetary organizations as conditions for new foreign loans. Under a withering political and ideological offensive by the left against capitalism in general, and foreign capitalists in particular, investors took their money elsewhere.[66]

As the militancy of organized labor and the Marxist parties jeopardized dependent capitalist development, it won increased support for their policies among workers and the electorate. During the 1960's, Marxists pushed the entire spectrum of Chilean politics further to the left. In 1970 they dominated the Popular Unity coalition that managed to elect Socialist Salvador Allende to the presidency. That victory allowed them to implement many aspects of the statist, nationalist, and social-welfare program first formulated in the 1930's. The Marxists encouraged unionization, presided over a significant rise in real wages, and greatly expanded some social services. They nationalized the mineral export sector, the large manufacturing firms, and the banks. These measures initially

---

66. One study done in the late 1960's concluded that Chilean economic stagnation after 1950 was not primarily a result of small market size, severe inflation, lack of capital, price controls, or bureaucratic regulations. All these were contributing factors, but the heart of the matter was that "Chilean businessmen act on the belief that *the private enterprise system (capitalism) is struggling for survival.*" Stanley M. Davis, "The Politics of Organizational Underdevelopment: Chile," in Stanley M. Davis and Louis Wolf Goodman, comps., *Workers and Managers in Latin America* (Lexington, Mass., 1972), p. 286. On copper workers, see especially Jorge Barría S., *Los sindicatos de la Gran Minería del Cobre* (Santiago, 1970); on copper policy, see Theodore Moran, *Multinational Corporations and the Politics of Dependence* (Princeton, N.J., 1974). The role of labor outlined in this paragraph is amply documented in the contemporary literature, yet has rarely been explicitly acknowledged. To do so would have been impolitic and would have involved breaking an implicit taboo in a historiography dominated by the Chilean left and its sympathizers abroad, who have preferred to place exclusive blame on labor's class antagonist for the failure of economic development in these decades.

stimulated production and greatly increased the material well-being of the bulk of the Chilean people. But increased demand outran the productive capacity of the nation as domestic and foreign capitalists divested or sabotaged production, and worker demands for wage hikes, control over the work process, and access to the land disrupted production. As problems of distribution and inflation eroded the government's popular support, it found itself besieged by the right, wracked by internal division, and stymied by constitutional, legislative, and judicial constraints on its initiatives.[67] But the majority of the Marxist leadership clung to the precepts of constitutional legality until the end. Their class antagonists did not. The government was overthrown by a military coup backed by elements of all the non-Marxist parties, foreign and domestic capitalists, the U.S. government, and a large part of the Chilean middle class in September 1973. In this tragic way, four decades of Chilean history seemed to end where they began under the government of Carlos Ibáñez: in military dictatorship, savage repression of the left, and a return to the economic and social policies of orthodox liberalism.

The Paradox of Modern Chilean History

Review of economic and political trends since 1930 thus unveils a central paradox of modern Chilean history. It was the very strength of Marxist labor and the left that spawned and nourished its great weakness: the commitment to a bourgeois legal and institutional order and the belief in an electoral road to socialism. The terms of the paradox were framed by the human forces called forth by export structure. The nitrate economy enabled workers in export production to forge an autonomous, class vision of the world they lived in. At the same time it made this vision compelling to many other groups in Chilean society. It was the appeal of this vision, embodied in a powerful insurgent labor movement, that forced major concessions from capital and a restructuring of the political institutions of the nation in 1924-25. During the next half century Marxist labor and the left engaged all their energies to turn that historic compromise to the advantage of the working class. They persisted in this formidable endeavor because, despite all the compromises and the setbacks, they were successful at it.

The success of Marxist labor and the left after 1930 hinged on their ability to turn post-1930 economic and political trends to the organiza-

---

67. The Popular Unity government has been the subject of hundreds of books and articles, but perhaps the most successful in capturing the achievements, style, and weaknesses of the regime was one of the first: *New Chile*, published by the North American Congress on Latin America (Berkeley, Calif., 1972). Fine analyses of the issues surrounding the rise and fall of the government are collected in Arturo Valenzuela and J. Samuel Valenzuela, eds., *Chile: Politics and Society* (New Brunswick, N.J., 1976).

tional and ideological advantage of the working class. When collapse of
the nitrate economy after 1930 plunged Chile into a depression more serious than that suffered by any nation in the hemisphere,[68] the left was
able to mount a telling ideological and political offensive against the hegemony of liberal thought and the legitimacy of the traditional parties.
By 1932, as Paul Drake has so persuasively and thoroughly documented,
the whole Chilean body politic began a fundamental shift to the left. Even
Conservative, Liberal, and Radical party leaders proclaimed their "socialism," a term they used vaguely and indiscriminately to express the
bankruptcy of liberal thought and policies in dealing with the crisis and
a general commitment to principles of statism, economic nationalism,
and social welfare they adapted from the philosophy and program of the
left. Meanwhile, middle-class activists and intellectuals founded new "socialist" parties of the left and right, which coalesced in 1933 into a new
political party destined to play a major role in subsequent Chilean history.
The Socialist Party adopted an explicitly Marxist ideology and a radical
program of economic nationalism and social reform, although, as Drake
has shown, strong corporatist ideological currents and "populist" styles
and strategies characterized the party's leadership through the 1940's. Beginning as a middle-class movement with significant support in the military, the Socialist Party expanded its working-class base by capturing
many of the struggling legal unions set up under Ibáñez, and by attracting anarchist and left-wing communist labor leaders into its fold. After
1950, as repression of the left in Chile intensified and the economy stagnated, the party overcame the corporatist reformist elements within it
and adopted a more consistent Marxist stance, which often placed it to
the left of the Communist Party.

The collapse of the nitrate export economy dealt a major radicalizing
blow to the Chilean labor movement. It undermined the legitimacy and
viability of the legal, corporatist unions Ibáñez had coddled. It cast thousands of radicalized miners into the volatile ranks of the working- and
middle-class unemployed in central Chile. Given the disarray with which
the FOCh and its member unions emerged from the repression of the
dictatorship—and the desperate economic straits in which workers found
themselves—organized labor took little direct part in the tumultuous political events (which included a short-lived Socialist Republic) of the early
1930's. Once economic recovery began, however, labor organizations

68. By 1932, the value of Chile's exports stood at one-eighth the level reached in 1929,
its imports at one-fifth that level. The value of nitrate exports alone fell from over a billion
Chilean pesos (at 40 to the pound sterling) in 1929 to less than 60 million pesos in 1932.
Copper exports, which had risen since the First World War to account for more than half of
the value of nitrate exports in the late 1920's, fell to about one-fourth of pre-Depression
levels in the early 1930's. A careful study of economic, fiscal, and monetary trends during
the 1930's is P. T. Ellsworth, *Chile: An Economy in Transition* (New York, 1945).

quickly revived, and workers entrusted the leadership positions of the vast majority of them to Marxist militants.

Recovery from the depression, well on the way by 1935, was paced by expansion of copper exports and the manufacturing sector. The first of these developments reinforced the radical ideological and institutional legacy of the nitrate era; the second greatly expanded the importance of urban industrial workers in national economic and political life. In many important respects, the copper industry was structurally similar to the nitrate export economy. Very capital intensive, and dependent on a highly sophisticated technology to process low-grade ores, the Chilean copper industry was even more completely dominated by foreign capital than nitrate production had been. It was also much more concentrated. In the decades following 1930, three U.S.-owned mines accounted for about 90 percent of Chilean copper exports. In the same period, copper exports furnished more than half of Chile's foreign exchange and, directly or indirectly, about one-fourth of government revenue. After bitter struggles led by the FOCh in the 1920's and by Socialist and Communist militants in the 1930's, copper workers succeeded in organizing themselves into powerful, Marxist-led unions. Since the late 1930's copper workers have played a primary role in the labor movement and in the political life of the nation.

The Marxist parties also used the radicalizing influence of the copper export economy very effectively in their appeals to other social groups. Like the nitrate economy before it, the copper economy was a classic case of a foreign-owned, extractive mineral enclave exploiting and exporting an exhaustible natural resource. It had little positive, direct influence on the process of economic development. Because of its capital-intensive nature, foreign ownership, and relatively small labor force, it fostered neither capital accumulation nor economic diversification in Chile. What capital accumulation and economic diversification did occur came by tapping the earnings of the industry through schemes of government taxation generated by leftist-influenced political coalitions. As foreign capital reacted to these impositions on its profits by curtailing investment and demanding economic concessions from Chile's governments, the nationalist, socialist solution to the crisis of Chilean development proposed since the 1920's by the Marxist left grew more logical and attractive to a broad spectrum of Chilean society.

These ideological and political trends were stimulated by the growth of the manufacturing sector after 1930 and its stagnation after 1950. The Marxist left took advantage of these developments to broaden, deepen, and radicalize the organized labor movement. Whereas the strength of the FOCh in the 1920's lay in the unity of nitrate and transport workers in the export sector, successive stages of labor unity and strength brought first manufacturing and finally white-collar workers into the organized labor movement. Thus the CTCh (Confederación de Trabajadores Chilenos) linked mining and transport workers with labor in the growing manufacturing sector in the late 1930's and 1940's. Finally, the CUTCh (Central Unica de Trabajadores de Chile), founded in 1953, brought in many white-collar unions (especially from the public sector), expanded organization in mining and manufacturing, and by the 1960's moved to incorporate agricultural workers.

The organizational success of Chilean labor after 1950, like the electoral gains of the Marxist parties, was fostered by the failure of the export economy to promote capitalist expansion and economic development even indirectly. As export production stagnated and the limits of import-substituting industrialization were reached—processes that directly reflected the strength and Marxist commitments of organized labor and the left—more and more social groups were predisposed to share the Marxist vision of national problems. These perceptions were strengthened by growing foreign control of the manufacturing sector of the Chilean economy after 1950. As a result, when the Popular Unity government proposed nationalization of the copper industry as a first step to recover national control over the economy and foster economic development, so great and wide was the consensus in support of the plan that not a single senator in a chamber still dominated by non-Marxist parties dared register a negative vote. And when that government proceeded to nationalize a substantial part of the manufacturing sector it enjoyed wide popular support.

In these ways, after 1930, the left succeeded in manipulating the institutional compromises and concessions of the 1920's to the political advantage of the working class. As it did so it undermined the hegemony of liberal economic thought and undercut the potential for dependent capitalist development in Chile. But it accomplished all this at the expense of reinforcing the legitimacy of Chile's liberal democratic political system and its own participation in it.

Much has been written about the failures of the Popular Unity government of 1970-73. Critics on the left stress its mismanagement of the economy, its rigid commitment to constitutional norms, its failure to move ahead on the issues of full democratic participation and worker control. In a historical sense, all these failures are related, the price paid by the left for its success in turning the historic compromise of 1924-25 to the advantage of the working class. In its desire to ensure its electoral future and effect socialist transformation within constitutional norms, the Popular Unity coalition adopted a short-run economic policy that rewarded the working class materially at the expense of throwing the nation's whole economy into chaos. These same concerns, and the burden of a party and union bureaucracy proud of its accomplishments and jealous of its power, made the government fatally hostile to experiments in worker participation and control, especially in the all-important copper industry. In a deeper sense, however, all these weaknesses reveal the ideological price paid by the left in the decades since 1930: uncritical acceptance of a Marxist orthodoxy that held that capitalism, by spawning a proletariat, inevitably insured the socialist transformation of society. In fact, as the history of other countries and of Chile since 1973 shows so emphatically, that is not true—at least in the short-run, decades-long terms in which political activists must work. The Marxist vision that proved so compatible with workers' experience in mineral production and so attractive to other sectors of Chilean society was neither a natural nor an inevitable result of capitalist development per se. It was the result of social perceptions of a unique set of ecological, economic, and political circumstances conditioned by Chile's peculiar export-oriented development. Rather than probing the universal cultural meaning of that exceptional historical experience and striving to make it meaningful in practice to all Chilean workers, the left simplified the reasons for its historical appeal and failed to appreciate fully the costs of its historical success. In this sense, it was a misreading of its past that led the left into the tragedy of 1973.

In failing, however, the left forced capital to jettison the liberal political and industrial relations system that, in the absence of sustained economic development, was the principal source of ruling-class legitimacy. It thus took a momentous, albeit uncertain, step toward the goal of social transformation envisioned by small groups of militant nitrate workers in the early years of the century. In September 1973, the great paradox of the development of the Chilean labor movement was starkly and tragically revealed. But it was also eliminated. If the central weakness of the Chilean left led it into a suicidal trap in that year, the structural reasons for the left's great historical strength remain largely intact. Although the copper industry is now run by a state capitalist entity, foreign control of the Chilean economy has in some ways intensified. Since 1973 the military dictatorship's orthodox liberal economic policies have fostered a massive increase in the nation's indebtedness to international banks and lending agencies.

In the 1980's, the fate of the Chilean left will depend, as it has in the past, on its ability to use the powerful cultural and institutional legacy bequeathed by workers in the nitrate era to mold domestic economic and political forces to the advantage of the great majority of the Chilean people. Success in that great project will depend in part, as it has in the past, on the health and structural tendencies of the world capitalist system. At the start of the 1980's the health of that system was in serious doubt, and structural trends have, in a sense, turned the whole of the Chilean economy into a debt-ridden enterprise analogous in many ways to the mineral enclaves of the past. It is in this sense that, although ahistorical and elitist social commentators predict a bleak future for the democratic socialist project of the Chilean working class and the parties of the left, students of the history of the Chilean labor movement in the context of the world economic system can allow themselves to be optimistic.[69]

69. These lines, like the bulk of this essay, were written in 1981 and circulated as "Exports, Labor, and the Left: An Essay on Twentieth-Century Chilean History" (Working Paper No. 97, The Latin American Program, The Wilson Center, Washington, D.C.). In 1983, as the world and Chilean economic crisis deepened, copper workers led a broad coalition of social groups into massive public defiance of the military dictatorship established in 1973. As this book goes to press, it appears that the current military regime, with its orthodox liberal economic and repressive political policies, will be repudiated like the Ibáñez dictatorship a half century before it, and that the Chilean left, after another long eclipse, will be reborn.

3

Argentina

Mr. Buckley: Since Argentina is having its problems, I thought to begin by asking: Is there anything, Mr. Borges, distinctively Argentinian about those problems?

Mr. Borges: Well, I wonder. I know very little about politics, but I think we have the right government now, a government of gentlemen, not of hoodlums. I don't think we're ripe for democracy as yet—maybe in a hundred years or so. . . .

Mr. Buckley: Why is that: Is it something distinctive to Argentinians? Distinctive to the hemisphere? Distinctive to what . . . ?

Mr. Borges: I can't tell you, since I know my own country and am very puzzled by it. I wish I understood my country. I can only love it. I can do what I can for it. But I don't pretend to understand it. I'm no historian.

"Firing Line" interview
Buenos Aires, Feb. 1, 1977

The Enigma of Argentine History

Two great puzzles preoccupy students of modern Argentine history. The first involves the paradox of Argentine economic development. How, and why, did the fastest-growing, most developed economy in Latin America in the early twentieth century practically cease to expand after mid-century? The second involves the enigma of Argentine political evolution. This puzzle is framed in different ways, but it always centers on the origins and continuing strength of Peronism. That popular, corporativist, right-wing nationalist movement has affected every aspect of Argentine society since the early 1940's. Peronism sharply distinguishes Argentine political history from that of all other Latin American countries—indeed, from that of the West as a whole—in the period since the Second World War.

Both issues are so deeply interlocked that neither can be understood in isolation. I will argue that fuller understanding of each—and of the links that bind them together—must begin with an appreciation of the evolution of a labor movement molded by the unique structure of the Argentine livestock and cereal export economy.

Argentina Before the Export Boom

The area that would become the heart of the modern Argentine export economy—the flat fertile *pampa* that radiates inland for roughly 500 kilometers from the port of Buenos Aires (see Map 3.1)—lay virtually untouched by man until late in the colonial period. For millions of years the action of wind and water slowly deposited the sediment—at Buenos Aires a thousand feet deep—that covered the broken granite base of one of the oldest land masses in the world and formed the vast treeless plain the Spaniards "discovered" in the sixteenth century.[1] Inhabited only by small groups of combative, nomadic indigenous peoples, and by the herds of wild horses and cattle descended from animals brought to the New World in Spanish boats, the pampa resisted feeble Spanish encroachments until the late eighteenth century. Effective Spanish settlement was limited during most of the colonial period to what are today Argentina's northwestern provinces. There farms and towns grew up to provide food, mules, and manufactures for the silver-mining economy of Upper Peru. It was only with the momentous transition of the world economy from mercantile to industrial capitalism beginning in the eighteenth century, and with the fundamental geopolitical readjustments that that transition brought in its wake, that the present-day heartland of Argentina became economically and strategically important to Europeans. As British trade and sea power undermined Spanish mercantilism in the New World, the port of Buenos Aires, situated at the mouth of the La Plata Basin, benefited from the reordering of trade routes. Meanwhile, the hinterland of the port responded to a growing world market for livestock products.[2] These important economic changes found political expression, first, when the Spanish Crown decided in 1776 to create the Viceroyalty of La Plata with Buenos Aires as its administrative center, and second, when exporters and importers centered in the port seized the opportunity to declare the colony's independence from Spain in 1810, during the protracted military struggle that resulted in British hegemony over the Atlantic economy after 1815.[3]

Following independence, the economic and political power of the liberal export-import interests in the port proved insufficient to exert con-

---

1. A good introduction to Argentine geography, as well as that of the other countries surveyed in this volume, is Preston James's classic study *Latin America* (3d ed.; New York, 1959).

2. Primary among these were hides and tallow, shipped to the industrializing economies of the North Atlantic, and jerked beef, which fed slaves who produced sugar in Brazil and the Caribbean for European markets.

3. For the impact of the reordering of the world economy in the eighteenth and early nineteenth centuries on the Ibero-American colonies in general and the Viceroyalty of La Plata in particular, see Tulio Halperín Donghi, *Historia contemporánea de Latinoamérica* (Madrid, 1970), and Richard Graham, *Independence in Latin America* (New York, 1972).

Map 3.1. Argentina, Showing the Pampa Region and the Location of *Frigoríficos* near Buenos Aires.

trol over the rest of the old viceroyalty. The peripheral areas broke away and became the separate nations of Paraguay, Uruguay, and Bolivia. In the area remaining—modern Argentina—the different regional economies entered into a long, painful period of adjustment to the constraints and opportunities of the industrial world economy slowly taking shape under British hegemony. The loss of traditional markets in Upper Peru and the competition of cheap imports funneled through Buenos Aires from the North Atlantic plunged northwestern and central Argentina into a long period of economic decline, social dislocation, and political instability that convulsed the nation until mid-century. The political and military struggles were not completely resolved until the nationalization of the port of Buenos Aires in 1880.[4]

The complex, protracted, and often bloody process of Argentine political readjustment to a new world order in the first half century following independence contrasts sharply with the relatively smooth transition to ruling-class consensus and stable, centralized government during the same period in Chile. Underlying this political process—which the great nineteenth-century liberal polemicist Domingo F. Sarmiento immortalized as an epic struggle between the forces of "civilization" and "barbarism" for control of the destiny of the new nation[5]—were two structural features of postindependence Argentine political economy absent in Chile. The first was the existence of a regional economy in the interior incompatible with the international division of labor emerging in the world economy; the second was the incapacity of the coastal economy tied to that new order to develop Argentine export capacity in the first half of the nineteenth century. Integration of the Argentine economy and consolidation of cultural and political hegemony over Argentine society by a united ruling class depended on the development of a dynamic export economy. But such an economy had to await the evolution of North Atlantic markets and transport systems, massive transfers of capital, technology, and labor to Argentina from Europe, and the emergence of a strong liberal state capable of preserving internal order and of meeting international financial obligations. Following independence, the merchants and livestock producers and processors of Buenos Aires and the coastal provinces to the north had neither the material resources nor the political power to accomplish this formidable task. Moreover, Great Britain was initially interested only in markets and speculative investment. It was not until the process of industrialization had matured in the

4. These developments, described at a very high level of generalization here, are carefully analyzed in major works by Myron Burgin, *Economic Aspects of Argentine Federalism, 1820-1852* (Cambridge, Mass., 1946), and Tulio Halperín Donghi, *Politics, Economics, and Society in the Revolutionary Period* (Cambridge, Eng., 1975).

5. In *Facundo* (Santiago, 1845).

leading capitalist nation that capital accumulation, technological development, and reorganization of its own internal political economy made possible the development of Argentina's export potential. In the meantime, in the words of the eminent Argentine historian Tulio Halperín Donghi, there was "a long wait."[6]

After mid-century, however, first slowly, then with gathering speed and momentum, Argentina began to realize its enormous export potential. "Civilization" triumphed, and the Argentine pampa witnessed a process of economic growth and development unprecedented in scope and duration in Latin America. That process transformed the economic, demographic, social, and political structure of the nation. It modified the language and culture of the Argentine people. And it created the structural conditions for the development, in the twentieth century, of the largest organized labor movement in Latin America.

The Promise of Argentine Economic Development

For 80 years after 1850, the Argentine economy experienced a period of export-led growth with few parallels in history. Carlos Díaz Alejandro, whose *Essays on the Economic History of the Argentine Republic* is the most important source of information and analysis on the modern Argentine economy, estimates that during the most dynamic part of this period, the half century preceding the outbreak of the First World War, gross domestic product may have grown at an average annual rate of 5 percent or more.[7] Unfortunately, reliable aggregate statistics on the period are lacking. But the Argentine economic historian Roberto Cortés Conde has assembled information that indicates the magnitude and structure of the expansion before 1914. After growing very slowly and fitfully during the 1820's and 1830's, Argentine exports of hides, tallow, wool, and meat began to expand rapidly in the late 1840's and early 1850's. Then, in the twenty-year period after 1854, total exports, virtually all of them livestock-related, grew sevenfold. After 1880, when military expeditions cleared the pampa of hostile Indians and greatly expanded the land area available for exploitation, the fast pace of export-led growth continued and its quality changed. Between 1880 and 1913 the value of Argen-

6. The phrase is the title of Chapter 3 of his *Historia contemporánea*, cited in n. 3.

7. Carlos Díaz Alejandro, *Essays on the Economic History of the Argentine Republic* (New Haven, Conn., 1970), pp. 2-3. The economic dimension of this chapter relies extensively on this rich and stimulating work. Useful overviews of Argentine economic development from colonial to modern times are Aldo Ferrer, *The Argentine Economy* (trans. Marjory M. Urguidi; Berkeley, Calif., 1967), and Ricardo M. Ortiz, *Historia económica de la Argentina* (Buenos Aires, 1974). Tulio Halperín Donghi provides a critical introduction to the literature dealing with the economic history of the period 1850-1930 in Roberto Cortés Conde and Stanley J. Stein, eds., *Latin America: A Guide to Economic History, 1830-1930* (Berkeley, Calif., 1977), pp. 44-162.

TABLE 3.1
Indicators of Argentine Economic Growth, 1880-1913

Indicator	1880	1890	1902	1913
Exports (gold pesos)	58,381,000	100,819,000	179,487,000	519,156,000
Imports (gold pesos)	45,536,000	142,241,000	103,039,000	496,227,000
Gov't revenues (gold pesos)	19,594,000	29,144,000	62,404,000	153,692,000
Foreign public debt (gold pesos)	17,388,000	161,391,000	381,083,000	308,855,000
Population	2,493,000	3,778,000	4,872,000	7,482,000
Cultivated area (ha)	1,156,000	2,996,000	9,115,000	24,091,000

SOURCE: Adapted from Roberto Cortés Conde, *The First Stages of Modernization in Spanish America* (New York, 1974), Tables 6-20 and 6-21, pp. 145-46.

tine exports expanded nine times. Meanwhile, the share of agricultural goods in these exports (wheat and corn, and to a lesser extent flax) rose to over 10 percent in 1885, over 25 percent in 1890, and over 40 percent in 1913. This astounding economic growth was accompanied by rapid expansion of the railroad network, very high levels of foreign immigration, large-scale foreign public and private investment, and the growth and consolidation of the Argentine state.[8] Table 3.1 provides a sense of the speed and scope of the changes.

In structural terms, the Argentine livestock and cereal export economy was the polar opposite of the Chilean mineral economy described in the previous chapter. The most fundamental difference involved the nationality of owners and workers in export production. Although ownership of land on the Argentine pampa by foreigners was not negligible (and probably increased somewhat around the turn of the century), Argentines owned the great majority of the huge *estancias* that produced the bulk of the nation's exports. Argentine census materials are not very helpful in elucidating the nationality of owners of rural estates, nor do they shed much light on the matter of concentration of ownership,[9] but all students and contemporary observers agree that enormous chunks of productive land were concentrated in the hands of a relatively small number of Argentine families during the nineteenth and twentieth centuries. In the province of Buenos Aires—which is about twice the size of England and makes up over half the pampa region—almost a third of the

8. Roberto Cortés Conde, *The First Stages of Modernization in Spanish America* (New York, 1974), pp. 121, 123.

9. For example, the director of the national census of 1914 claimed that the livestock census revealed a significant degree of subdivision of land and growth of smallholders in the years after 1901. Close reading of the data, however, reveals that he interchanges the terms *propiedades* (properties) and *explotactiones* (units of production). *Tercer censo nacional* (Buenos Aires, 1916-17), vol. 6, p. lv. Data from the census do reveal significant numbers of foreign owners of units of cattle production and an increase in the number of small units, but they fail to correlate nationality of ownership with the size of the land area owned. See pp. 677-91 of the same volume.

land was owned in 1928 by just over a thousand families.[10] The causes of such extreme land concentration are debated in the literature. Some economic historians attribute it to impersonal geographic and economic forces. Others argue that it was the result of the machinations of a land-owning elite that effectively controlled the legal process of distribution and sale of public lands as the frontier expanded during the nineteenth century.[11] These positions are not contradictory. Whatever their relative importance, it appears certain that the pattern of concentrated land-ownership—and the subordination of agricultural to livestock interests (a matter to be discussed shortly)—was established early, before the great expansion of export production on the pampa after 1850. This pattern has continued without fundamental change down to the present day.[12]

Although Argentine *estancieros* owned the means of production in the export sector, foreign capitalists exercised dominant (but by no means exclusive) control over the transport, processing, and commercialization of export products. British capital built and owned the bulk of the extensive railway network that linked the pampa with the coast. Foreign capital financed and owned many of the facilities and processing plants that handled Argentine staples for shipment abroad. Foreign control was especially pronounced in meat processing after 1900, when huge modern packing plants, called *frigoríficos* in Argentina, displaced the smaller, less efficient *saladeros* and *graserías* that had processed livestock products for export during the nineteenth century. Foreign capital controlled shipping

10. Jacinto Oddone, *La burguesía terrateniente argentina* (2d ed.; Buenos Aires, 1975), pp. 167-69.

11. Both of these positions move beyond the early emphasis on the traditional cultural values of the Argentine landholding elite, which allegedly made large landowners more interested in acquiring land and status than in making rational economic and political decisions to further their economic interests. The first position, developed by Cortés Conde in the book cited in n. 8 above, attributes the evolution of the large estate to the abundance of good land and the scarcity of capital and labor during most of the nineteenth century. This combination of factors, he argues, made large-scale cattle raising rational (and virtually inevitable). Jacinto Oddone is the outstanding proponent of the second position. Cortés Conde has asserted his argument in more extreme form and attempted to buttress it with detailed primary research in his recent *El progreso argentino* (Buenos Aires, 1979). That work sheds much light on the shift from livestock to agriculture in the province of Buenos Aires and on the growth of small production units exploited under rental contract. It also marshals evidence to demonstrate a vigorous market in land at the end of the nineteenth century. It does not demonstrate that any of these processes markedly diffused the concentration of landholding during the period.

12. See the careful, detailed historical studies by Tulio Halperín Donghi, Manuel Bejarano, Haydee Gorostegui de Torres, and Ezequiel Gallo in Part I of Torcuato Di Tella and Tulio Halperín Donghi, eds., *Los fragmentos del poder* (Buenos Aires, 1969). The contribution by Gallo deals with the major—and transitory—exception to the rule, the relatively diffuse pattern of landownership in the province of Santa Fe. For a dissenting view, which argues that ownership of land became less concentrated and production more diversified on the pampa in the first half of the nineteenth century, see Jonathan C. Brown, *A Socioeconomic History of Argentina, 1776-1860* (Cambridge, Eng., 1979).

and distribution abroad of most export commodities, participated in the lucrative import trade, invested in public lighting and communications systems, established banks and service industries like insurance, and—as development proceeded—invested in manufacturing industry. The large-scale penetration of foreign capital into the Argentine economy involved a heavy drain of surplus out of Argentina toward the North Atlantic. Good statistics on this sensitive issue are not available. Díaz Alejandro estimates that in the late 1920's nearly one-tenth of all nonwage income was remitted abroad.

Yet Argentine capital played an important role in most of these non-rural economic activities as well. It participated in a minor way even in the capital-intensive meat-packing industry, controlled a substantial share of grain processing and the import trade, and dominated banking. The healthy participation of Argentine capital in all these activities was made possible by Argentine control over the primary process of capital accumulation in the export economy. In contrast to the situation in Chile, Argentine appropriation of surplus generated in export production was primarily accomplished not through state taxation but through the normal mechanisms of the capitalist marketplace. Although much of this wealth was visibly and notoriously dissipated in luxury consumption by the Argentine ruling class,[13] much was reinvested in the export sector, and in commercial and financial endeavors. Meanwhile, the Argentine state limited itself to taxing the growing volume of imports generated by export-led development. It used these taxes—which fell hardest on working-class and middle-class consumers and provided more than half of the total revenue of the state—to service the huge foreign public loans it contracted to build railroads and other public works, and to finance an expanding civil (especially educational) and military bureaucracy.

If capital in export production was Argentine, however, a very high proportion of workers—again in contrast to Chile—were foreign. At the start of the export boom Argentina was very sparsely populated. The economic growth and diversification generated by export expansion cre-

13. After the turn of the century, Europeans coined the phrase "rich as an Argentine" to describe anyone with great personal wealth and lavish spending habits. At home, wealthy Argentines mimicked the European aristocracy. Copies of English country mansions and ornate Swiss chalets appeared incongruously on the pampa, and a jumble of luxurious summer homes, built in the most heterogeneous architectural styles, attested to the wealth and taste of the Argentine bourgeoisie in the resort town of Mar del Plata. The scale and solidity of the public and private buildings erected during the golden years of Argentine economic growth still set the architectural tone of the city of Buenos Aires. Photographs of the country mansions of the landholding elite adorn the glossy pages of the massive *Enciclopedia comercial*, published by the British and Latin American Chamber of Commerce (London, 1922). On Mar del Plata, see Juan José Sebrelli, *Mar del Plata, el ocio represivo* (Buenos Aires, 1970); on Buenos Aires, one can begin with James R. Scobie, *Buenos Aires, Plaza to Suburb, 1870-1910* (New York, 1974).

ated hundreds of thousands of jobs, many of which were filled by immigrants. Livestock production, especially cattle raising, involved very few workers, but after 1880, with the great expansion of cereal production on the pampa and the development of burgeoning urban economies on the coast, the immigrant stream became a flood. Between 1857 and 1930 Argentina experienced a net immigration of perhaps three and a half million people. Before the First World War more than half were Italians, about a fourth Spaniards. In 1914 on much of the pampa foreigners outnumbered Argentines two to one. In the same year three-fourths of the adult population of the city of Buenos Aires was foreign-born.[14]

Figure 3.1 graphs net annual immigration to Argentina, 1860 to 1970, and demonstrates the sensitivity of potential immigrants to changes in Argentine economic conditions and to trends and crises in the world capitalist system. Downturns came during periods of international depression (in the late 1870's and early 1930's), during domestic Argentine economic crises (1890-91 and intermittently after 1950), and during the two world wars. Upturns occurred during periods of expansion of the world and Argentine economies: the 1880's, the decade preceding the First World War, the 1920's, and the five years after the Second World War. Because the majority of immigrants to Argentina were men, males outnumbered females by a considerable margin in Argentina for a hundred years after 1860. Heavy immigration during the fifty years after 1880 also meant that the age structure of the Argentine population during those years was skewed in favor of productive adults, a circumstance that favored economic development.

It is difficult to exaggerate the influence on Argentine society of immigration during what the Argentine intellectual historian José Luis Romero aptly called the "Alluvial Era."[15] Although the absolute number of immigrants to the United States before 1930, for example, was much higher than the number to Argentina, the relative importance of immigrants (given the small initial Argentine population) was about twice as great in Argentina. Moreover, the immigration figures do not fully convey the nature of the immigration process. For every immigrant who remained in Argentina, another returned to Europe after a stay of weeks or years. The Argentine export economy attracted hundreds of thousands of seasonal workers (*golondrinas*, "swallows") from southern Europe, primarily during the summer months of the Southern Hemisphere. Many worked a few weeks or months in the grain harvest, then returned to Europe. Immigrant predominance in the labor force in export produc-

14. James R. Scobie, *Argentina* (2d ed.; New York, 1971). This book, rich in social and economic information, is the best one-volume history of the country from colonial times to the present.

15. José Luis Romero, *A History of Argentine Political Thought* (Stanford, Calif., 1963).

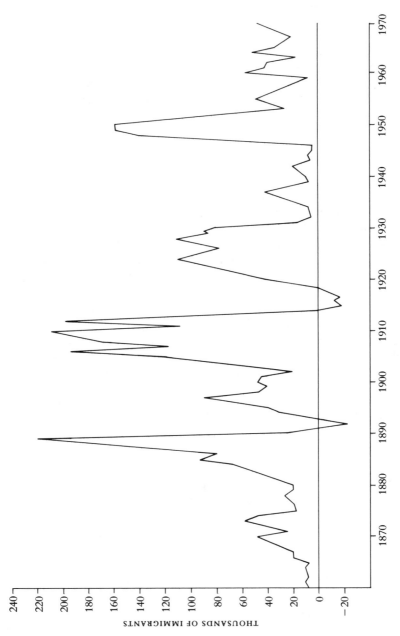

Figure 3.1. Argentine Net Immigration (in thousands), 1860–1970. Source: James R. Scobie, *Argentina* (2d ed.; New York, 1971), p. 304.

tion and in the urban economies of the coast during the first decades of the twentieth century influenced all aspects of Argentine society and decisively affected the development of the labor movement.

The structure of the Argentine export economy differed from that of Chile in other important ways as well. Whereas nitrate production was confined to an enclave far removed from the Chilean heartland, the Argentine pampa became the effective heartland of Argentina. The source of virtually all Argentine exports, the pampa also contained the great bulk of the nation's railroads and the majority of its manufacturing and service industries. By 1914 the pampa held about two-thirds—and the city and province of Buenos Aires contained 46 percent—of the nation's people.

The concentration of economic activity and people on the pampa and in its ports reflected the importance of what economists call "forward linkages" in Argentina's export economy—the transport, processing, and service activities involved in getting commodities on board ships for transport abroad. Díaz Alejandro has estimated that these activities accounted for roughly two-thirds of value added in Argentine exports.[16] The Argentine export economy was less successful in promoting "backward" and "horizontal linkages," in producing the goods needed for agricultural and livestock production and in meeting the demands of consumers for manufactured commodities. Throughout the entire period of export expansion until 1930 (with the partial exception of the years of world war and postwar depression), the Argentine economy exhibited a very high propensity to import its manufactured goods. Nevertheless, even before 1914 the development of manufacturing in Argentina was significant. Growth was most impressive in clothing and furniture manufacture and in the elaboration of construction materials (where by 1913 Argentina was meeting about three-fourths of its consumption). In 1913 about 37 percent of the processed food consumed by Argentines was produced domestically. Aside from a few very large firms in meat-packing and textiles, however, most Argentine manufacturing took place in small establishments, many of which employed fewer than ten persons and are more properly classified as artisanal than as industrial. In 1913 the census reported 48,779 manufacturing establishments, which together employed 410,201 people. More than half of these firms and their workers were located in the city and province of Buenos Aires.[17]

The poor record of Argentine import substitution before 1913, or for that matter before 1930, cannot be explained (as it can be in the case of some Latin American export economies) by shortages of domestic capital or insufficient demand. National ownership of the means of export pro-

16. Díaz Alejandro, *Essays* (cited in n. 7), Table 22, p. 423.
17. Adolfo Dorfman, *Evolución industrial argentina* (Buenos Aires, 1942), pp. 11-23.

duction provided sufficient capital for industrial investment. Capitalist relations of production on the pampa, the relatively high wage structure of the Argentine economy (the existence of which is shown indirectly by the high level of temporary and permanent international immigration), and the growing numbers of urban consumers employed in transport, processing services, and public and private construction activities combined to create a large internal market for consumer manufactures. That domestic industry did not expand further to meet these needs was a consequence of a deep and well-founded consensus among most Argentine consumers—owners and workers alike—that foreign manufactures were cheaper and of better quality than artificially protected national products in Argentina's high-wage economy. The relative lack of protection for Argentine industry during the classic era of economic liberalism in the world economy was not, as some have argued, simply the expression of the class interests of Argentine landowners, who monopolized national politics until 1916. Nor was it primarily a consequence of the limited political influence of the immigrant entrepreneurs who dominated the ranks of the industrial bourgeoisie. Even the Radical and Socialist parties, which appealed to the urban working class and won a large share of political power after 1912, steadfastly adhered to a free-trade position. And the anarcho-syndicalists, who captured the allegiance of thousands of organized urban workers early in the twentieth century, were silent on the issue of industrial protectionism. Labor unions did not endorse protection of national industry until the late 1930's. All social classes on the pampa benefited, as consumers, from Argentina's comparatively advantageous position in the international division of labor that prevailed until 1930. The costs involved in the pattern of Argentine economic development, though many, are not to be found directly in the failure to develop industry before 1930.

A final distinguishing characteristic of the Argentine export economy was its relative immunity to violent fluctuations in world demand. In contrast to Chile's mineral exports, Argentina's livestock and cereal exports remained in relatively high and stable demand even during the Great Depression. Although the demand for and price of individual export items fluctuated in response to evolving European needs and tastes, to improvements in the technology of production and transport, and to global and domestic economic cycles and political developments, Argentine producers were able to adapt to these changes.

The breakthrough to sustained growth in Argentina's livestock economy came after 1850 through wool production. Before mid-century, jerked beef was exported to the slave economies of tropical Latin America, hides and tallow to the expanding industrial economies of Europe. After mid-century, however, the growth of carpet and weaving industries in France and Belgium created an expanding market for wool, and sheep raising rapidly became the leading economic activity of the Argentine coastal provinces. At the end of the 1840's there were only about five million sheep in the coastal zone of the pampa; by 1875 the province of Buenos Aires alone contained some 46 million sheep. Exports of wool during the same period rose from an annual average of 6,000 tons in the 1840's to 120,000 tons in the 1880's. In the latter decade wool accounted for more than half the value of Argentine exports.

It was only with the revolution in transport, the development of refrigeration technology, and the expansion of European food demands after 1880, however, that economic production on the pampa acquired its modern form. Argentine livestock production adapted after that year to the growing profitability of meat exports to Europe. At first shipments of live sheep and cattle and frozen mutton dominated the meat trade, but by the turn of the century frozen beef had become an important export item, too. A few years later chilled beef (much more attractive to the British consumers who bought almost all Argentine meat exports) became the fastest-growing item in the Argentine export trade.

The shift to meat—and especially to beef—exports required a revolution in breeding and fattening techniques and drastic changes in land use and labor systems on the pampa. Blooded European stock was imported to improve herds, barbed-wire fencing crisscrossed the pampa, and better pasture grasses replaced much of the natural grassland of the open range. These changes were linked to the growth of agriculture on the pampa. As noted above, agricultural exports, primarily of wheat and corn, grew rapidly after 1880 to make up almost half the value of total exports by 1913. But agricultural development was always subordinated to the interests of large landowners and livestock (especially beef) producers. In the 1880's and 1890's these landowners began to let portions of their huge estates to immigrant tenants for grain production. The terms of these contracts severely limited agricultural diversification and security of tenure. Typically, tenant families were allowed to sow cereals (and severely restricted from cultivating other crops) on a large expanse of land for three years. At the end of their tenure they were required to leave the land planted in alfalfa and move off the land. Initially, many of these contracts were sharecropping arrangements, but by the turn of the century rental agreements became the norm.

About half of the labor demands for cereal production were met in this manner; the heavy seasonal demand for harvest labor was filled by migratory workers drawn from the coastal cities and the towns of the pampa, and from southern Europe. Through this system of temporary tenant contracts and migratory labor, Argentine landowners were able to participate in the profits of agriculture, avoid alienating land that was

rapidly increasing in value, and transform their unimproved lands gradually into pasturage suitable for production of the high-grade marbled
beef that so pleased the British consumer. The extensive nature of livestock production and the subordination of agriculture to it retarded the
growth of rural population. At the same time, onerous working and living conditions, and limited access to landownership, tended to push rural
workers toward the coastal cities where economic opportunities were
much greater and the quality of life better.[18]

The expansion of the Argentine export economy was disrupted only
temporarily by the First World War. The war initially curtailed international shipping and seriously affected the volume of Argentine exports
and imports. The sharp economic downturn reversed the direction of the
flow of capital and international migration as the British girded for war
and tens of thousands of workers returned to Europe. By 1917, however,
the economy began to benefit from wartime demand. Exports of meat
rose rapidly and Argentina began to sell manufactures such as woolen
blankets to the Allies. The war also stimulated import substitution and
promoted the growth of larger units of production in manufacturing.
But industrial expansion was constrained, as it was during the Second
World War, by the scarcity of capital goods and industrial raw materials
in a world at war.

After the war, Argentine export-led expansion continued and its structure remained basically unchanged. By the end of the 1920's the value of
exports had almost doubled from prewar levels. Large-scale immigration
revived, although it peaked at about half the level reached in the decade
before the war. Railroad construction declined, as did the influx of new
foreign investment. Both trends reflected the end to physical expansion
of the land area for export production on the pampa; to some extent they
also revealed the waning economic and financial power of the British metropolis to which the Argentine economy was closely tied. The manufacturing sector continued to grow, but little import substitution took place.
One new development in the 1920's was the emergence of a state-directed
petroleum industry. But until the 1930's, the tendency of the Argentine
economy to import complex items such as machinery, and even some relatively simple manufactures such as textiles, did not markedly change.

18. The stages of Argentine rural production during the nineteenth century, reviewed in
the preceding paragraphs, are described in Ortiz, *Historia económica* (cited in n. 7). Data on
economic cycles, 1876-1952, are summarized in Guido Di Tella and Manuel Zymelman, *Los
ciclos económicos argentinos* (Buenos Aires, 1973). A detailed analysis, based on primary materials, of the transformation of rural production in the province of Buenos Aires after 1880
is Cortés Conde, *El progreso argentino* (cited in n. 11). The classic study of the social and
cultural implications of the land tenure patterns and labor systems that evolved on the
pampa with the advent of agriculture is James R. Scobie, *Revolution on the Pampas* (Austin,
Tex., 1964).

In 1930, at the end of 80 years of export-oriented economic growth, Argentina was one of the most developed peripheral capitalist societies in the world. True, Argentine development was different from the historical pattern of capitalist development in Western Europe: most striking was the absence in Argentina of a large, integrated industrial sector. But measured against other peripheral societies, including other countries of recent settlement such as Australia and Canada, Argentina in 1930 compared quite favorably. Whether one looks at economic indicators like per capita income or wage levels, or at social indicators like literacy and infant mortality, by 1930 Argentina had far outdistanced its Latin American neighbors (except for Uruguay) and found itself not far behind Canada and Australia. Buenos Aires, which Lord Bryce described as early as 1912 as a happy mixture of the bustle and economic dynamism of Chicago and the refinement of Paris, had become one of the great cities of the world. Its wide avenues were filled with automobiles, its theaters with the latest operas and plays, its innumerable restaurants, shops, and teahouses with elegantly dressed customers. Though most Argentines did not enjoy these amenities, income distribution was probably not drastically more unequal than in industrialized capitalist societies such as the United States, and the Argentine middle class was easily the largest in Latin America. By 1930 the urban working class probably enjoyed a standard of living (especially with regard to diet) superior to that of most continental European workers, although in terms of housing and material comforts it undoubtedly ranked well below its counterparts in the United States, Canada, and Australia.[19]

The crisis of world capitalism after 1930, and the breakdown of the international division of labor it brought in its wake, stopped the growth of the Argentine export economy but did not lead to its collapse. Unlike what happened in Chile, in Argentina the volume of exports remained almost at pre-Depression levels; and though export earnings declined rapidly until 1932, they improved significantly thereafter. Table 3.2 reveals the growth of Argentine export earnings until 1929, their remarkable stability during the crisis of the Great Depression, and their decline after 1940.

Contrary to the subsequent polemics of many Marxists and Peronists, the Depression in Argentina was relatively mild, and recovery, based on the continued viability of export production and the dynamism of the manufacturing sector after 1935, was rapid and sustained. If Chile was the Latin American nation hardest hit by the Great Depression, Argentina probably escaped with the fewest economic scars. Argentine real gross domestic product declined about 14 percent between 1929 and 1932, then

19. Díaz Alejandro, *Essays* (cited in n. 7), presents some quantitative evidence on many of these comparative questions.

TABLE 3.2
*Value of Argentine Exports Averaged over
Five-Year Periods, 1900-1954*
(1950 U.S. dollars)

Period	Value of exports	Period	Value of exports
1900-1904	583,000,000	1930-34	1,481,000,000
1905-9	807,200,000	1935-39	1,479,400,000
1910-14	896,000,000	1940-44	1,192,500,000
1915-19	920,300,000	1945-49	1,180,100,000
1920-24	1,278,600,000	1950-54	937,100,000
1925-29	1,582,700,000		

SOURCE: Comisión Económica para América Latina, *El desarrollo económico de la Argentina* (Mexico City, 1959), Part I, Table 14, p. 115.

rebounded; by 1939 it was 15 percent higher than in 1929. In the words of Díaz Alejandro, the Argentine economy responded to the Depression "rather gracefully."

Recovery from the Depression was led by the manufacturing sector. Government efforts to deal with the general economic crisis, which included currency devaluation, restrictions on the use of foreign exchange, and higher tariff duties, stimulated industry. From after 1935 until the outbreak of war in 1939, the growth of industry, most of it import-substituting, was impressive. Large-scale industries, many of them foreign-owned, began to produce large quantities of durable consumer goods. The number of small-scale, nationally owned enterprises manufacturing light consumer goods mushroomed. Adolfo Dorfman has shown that whereas the number of industrial establishments grew by 1,400 between 1914 and 1935, between 1935 and 1937 alone the number increased by 8,700. The expansion of the industrial work force was somewhat less striking: 204,000 people added between 1914 and 1935; 144,000 between 1935 and 1937. Once the war broke out, the familiar wartime constraints on Argentine industry reappeared. Nevertheless, manufacturing continued to expand, although more slowly, and by 1945 it contributed almost one-fourth of gross domestic product, overshadowing agricultural and livestock production combined.[20]

In contrast, then, to the wrenching economic and social crisis experienced in Chile after 1930, the impact of the Depression on Argentina was relatively painless in economic terms. And Argentina's adaptation to the industrial opportunities presented by the world crisis was impressive. This successful response was conditioned by four sets of circumstances, each intimately related to the nature of the export economy that had propelled Argentine development before 1930. The first was the mainte-

20. Dorfman, *Evolución* (cited in n. 17), p. 148; Di Tella and Zymelman, *Los ciclos* (cited in n. 18), p. 285, n. 2.

nance of international demand for Argentina's food exports. Preservation of the whole economic complex that revolved around export production in Argentina assured continued capital accumulation, kept most people at work, and generated, albeit at slightly reduced levels, the foreign exchange vital to Argentina's capacity to import. That capacity was crucial to the effort to expand import-substituting industry. It is true that successful efforts by the Argentine landed elite, particularly livestock producers, to preserve Argentina's share of a shrinking British meat market involved concessions to British capital and manufactures that somewhat hindered the development of Argentine industry. As will become apparent, however, the major effect of these actions on the course of Argentine economic development was political and much delayed. It was revealed only with the rise to power of the Peronists after the Second World War.

The second set of circumstances revolved around the fact that, unlike Chile, Argentina consumed the same products it exported.[21] Before the world crisis Argentines ate almost half of the country's beef and wheat production, and this proportion increased in the decades following 1930. Domestic consumption of a major portion of production available for export acted as a buffer against crisis in the export sector and served to prime the pump of economic recovery in the 1930's. This advantage turned into a two-edged sword under Peronist redistributionist economic policies in the 1940's, because though expanded popular consumption greatly benefited the working class, it limited the volume of exports, particularly meat, and reduced foreign exchange earnings vital to the industrialization effort pursued by the Peronists.

Third, the cutoff in international migration eased the impact of the crisis on the Argentine working class. Outright unemployment was relatively low in the early 1930's. As recovery proceeded a modest international migration resumed, but the bulk of the employment opportunities in the new industries in the coastal cities of the pampa were filled by migrants from the depressed areas of the interior, the majority of them women. Many of these people, unorganized by political parties and established unions, eventually became important supporters of the Peronist regime.

Finally, and most generally, the Argentine export economy, unlike the Chilean, contributed directly—and very broadly—to the development of the Argentine heartland. Despite its imperfections, the impressive railway network built before the crisis served after 1930 to bind together a

---

21. Beef and wheat were the main staples of the Argentine diet. In the 1920's and 1930's Argentines consumed about 250 pounds of beef per capita per year. Comparable U.S. figures for all meat consumption, not just beef, were 150 pounds per capita per year. Other livestock and agricultural products, particularly leather and wool, were absorbed by Argentine industry.

TABLE 3.3
*Land Area Devoted to Direct Production on
the Pampa, 1930-54*
(000 ha)

Period	Agriculture	Livestock raising
1930-34	15,149	31,572
1935-39	16,013	32,373
1940-44	15,056	34,360
1945-49	13,058	36,570
1950-54	11,524	39,336

SOURCE: Comisión Económica para América Latina, *El desarrollo económico de la Argentina* (Mexico City, 1959), Part II, Table
11, p. 16.

national market for domestic industry. All of the manufacturing and service activities stimulated by a pattern of export-oriented development
that generated a high-wage urban consumer society could be adapted to
produce and distribute what was formerly imported. The skills of a large
urban work force, and the generally high level of education of the Argentine people, made adaptation to a more complex, semi-industrialized
economy easier. In all these ways, the success of Argentine export-oriented development before 1930, a success unparalleled in the rest of Latin
America, facilitated its adjustment to a new phase of inward-directed,
import-substituting industrial development in the 1930's and 1940's.

But the success of import-substituting industrialization in Argentina in
the 1930's and 1940's was not matched by an expansion of the export sector. In the decades following 1930, Argentine producers slowly shifted
toward greater emphasis on livestock production. This tendency became
pronounced after 1940 and proceeded at the expense of the area devoted
to agriculture, as Table 3.3 illustrates. This movement toward more extensive, less productive use of the land, when coupled with the failure to
make significant improvements in the productivity of agriculture and
livestock raising, explains in large part the virtual stagnation of Argentine rural production in recent decades.[22] That stagnation, in the context
of a growing population and, in some periods, of rising levels of domestic consumption, has meant a decline in the quantity of exports and lower
export earnings. Since the 1950's, foreign-exchange constraints have limited the ability of the Argentine economy to import the capital goods and
industrial raw materials needed to pursue the development of import-

22. Argentina's poor performance in this regard receives sustained attention in the report
of the United Nations' Comisión Económica para América Latina, *El desarrollo económico de
la Argentina* (Mexico City, 1959). See particularly Part I, Table 21, p. 23. Argentina's relative
failure to raise productivity in exportable grain and livestock commodities is treated in José
Alfredo Martínez de Hoz, *La agricultura y la ganadería argentina en el período 1930-1960* (Buenos Aires, 1967), Chap. 6.

substituting and basic industry. The result has been a constricting of the growth rate of the entire economy and very low increases, despite low population growth rates, in per capita gross domestic product.

There is a consensus in the literature on Argentine economic development that the failure of the rural sector to expand production lies at the heart of the dismal economic performance of the Argentine economy in recent decades. No such agreement exists concerning the causes of rural stagnation. Carlos Díaz Alejandro relies on neoclassical economic theory and careful use of historical economic information to reject the cultural, social, and economic explanations that predominate in this literature. The evolution of the large estate, he argues, was a natural function of market forces operating in the context of Argentine geography. The picture of a landowning class motivated by traditional cultural values, more interested in land rent and social status than in using economic resources in rational, entrepreneurial ways, does not fit the facts. The Argentine elite responded well to the economic opportunities presented by changing European demand for rural products. If they preferred ranching and banking to industrial pursuits it was because, given Argentina's comparative advantage in a free-trading world economy, exploitation of the land offered the highest return on investment. To allegations that land concentration and labor systems hurt the efficiency of Argentine rural production, Díaz Alejandro responds with data that demonstrate that Argentine productivity compared well with that of its international competitors (including the United States) at least until the 1920's. Why then does Argentina fall so rapidly and dramatically behind in rural productivity and expansion of output after the Depression? Díaz Alejandro's answers are basically two: the impact of Peronist policies on the prices paid for rural goods, on rural labor systems, and on rural land tenure arrangements in the postwar period; and the failure of the Argentine government to extend technical services for rural producers before, and especially after, 1930.[23]

Both of these explanations of rural economic stagnation are political. And both are persuasive, as far as they go. But the rise of Peronism and the failure of Argentine governments to foster modernization of rural production throughout this century are not the exogenous variables Díaz Alejandro makes of them. Rather, they are directly related to the structure of an export economy whose basic form was defined before the First World War. How that export structure, through its influence on the evo-

---

23. Díaz Alejandro, *Essays* (cited in n. 7), Chap. 3. This summary cannot do justice to the wealth of information and analysis that leads Díaz Alejandro to these conclusions. A similar diagnosis was reached by Martínez de Hoz in an essay first published in a volume edited by the Argentine publishing house Sur, *Argentina, 1930-1960* (Buenos Aires, 1961), pp. 189-210, and later expanded into the book cited in n. 22 above.

lution of the labor movement, helps explain the rise of Peronism is the subject of the rest of this essay. How it worked to stifle agricultural modernization (including government technical services for rural producers) is a part of that larger story that can be sketched briefly here.

The problem with Díaz Alejandro's explanation is that before the rise of Perón the rural landholding elite *was* the government. Even during the period 1916-30, when the Radical Party (which represented much more than the interests of rural landowners) controlled the executive and Socialist and Radical deputies were numerous in the congress, the landed elite possessed the political and ideological power to subvert all attempts to modify rural land and labor systems. During the whole period up to the First World War, the government pursued tax, tariff, monetary, credit, and labor policies uniquely favorable to the interests of large rural landowners. That landowning interests chose not to use even modest amounts of public moneys to foster agricultural and livestock research and extension services, when they were prepared to implement expensive public policies such as subsidizing railway construction, is explained not by their alleged cultural traditionalism (which Díaz Alejandro correctly discounts), but by the fact that they were under no effective economic, social, ideological, or political pressure to modernize production. Taxes on land and even wealth were minimal. Rural labor organization, as we shall see, was stymied. And national political forces, until Perón, never threatened their class position.

The failure of popular forces to exert significant pressure on the landholding elite before the rise of Perón largely explains the relative absence of rural modernization in Argentina and the eventual stagnation of rural production. The spectacular growth of the Argentine economy depended on expansion into previously untapped, unusually rich pampa lands until the First World War. Although technical improvements both in the breeding and care of livestock and in agricultural production accompanied this process, social relations of production that subordinated agriculture to livestock production, and denied a migratory labor force security of tenure, could not sustain and deepen the process of rural modernization. The expansion of rural production continued into the 1920's and probably would have gone on for some time longer had the world Depression not intervened. But the failure of rural modernization before Perón, as illustrated in the neglect of research and technical services for rural producers during the whole period, was congenital to the structure of Argentine export production. Those who worked the land had no opportunity or incentive to modernize, those who owned it, no need to.

It is an irony of Argentine history and a tribute to the power of the human forces called forth by export production that the same structural features that proved so conducive to the capitalist economic development of the nation in the first half of the twentieth century harbored such destructive political implications for economic development in the second. The history of the Argentine workers' movement, to which we now turn, links the separate stories of Argentine economic development and political evolution. In doing so it reveals the full dimensions of the crisis that has paralyzed not only the Argentine economy but the whole of Argentine society since mid-century.

The First Great Worker Mobilization

The history of the Argentine labor movement in the twentieth century falls into two distinct periods of mass mobilization and organizational strength. The first reached its apogee at the end of the First World War under the leadership of anarcho-syndicalists. The second developed during the Second World War and was channeled into the corporativist, right-wing nationalist movement led by Juan Domingo Perón. These two periods were separated by a twenty-year hiatus. After 1920, the labor movement quickly lost its momentum and ideological autonomy. Labor organization declined and the largest and most effective remaining workers' organizations accepted the legitimacy of the Argentine social and economic order. The early Argentine labor movement, for all its initial vitality, failed to force important ideological and institutional concessions from the ruling class. It left a shallow ideological and institutional imprint on the life of the nation. By contrast, the second era of working-class mobilization changed the course of modern Argentine history. It left a political, institutional, and ideological legacy that dominates the Argentine labor movement—and deeply influences the whole of national life—to this day.

The trajectory of the Argentine labor movement is thus fundamentally different from that of its counterpart in Chile. In Chile, labor early forged a class-specific, anticapitalist, anti-imperialist vision of its place in society. Over the course of the century it pushed more and more social groups toward its Marxist vision of the world and its socialist solution to national problems. In Argentina, by contrast, the largest anticapitalist labor movement in Latin America in the early twentieth century atrophied after 1920. When labor reappeared as a major force in national life, it did so under the banner of an anti-Marxist popular movement wedded to an ideology that assumed class harmony and accepted the basic institutions of the capitalist order.

It is around this pattern of discontinuous development and ideological metamorphosis that the central analytical questions of Argentine labor history revolve. One must account for the great appeal and initial strength of anarcho-syndicalism, yet explain the fragility, rapid decline, and permanent eclipse of this first great mobilization of the Argentine working class. One must account for two decades of ideological conformity, organizational weakness, and collective quiescence in the labor movement, yet explain the rapid mobilization of the early 1940's and the ease with which labor accepted—and has defended—an ideological and institutional order that, in Marxist terms, is theoretically at odds with the fundamental interests of workers as a class. To do so is not a simple task. Scholarly research on these questions is just beginning, and the bulk of the extant literature is descriptive and polemical.[24] In this section of the essay and the following one, I review the history of the two phases of the modern Argentine labor movement. I have tried to show how many of the puzzles in the development of the Argentine workers' movement can be clarified by placing them in the context of the economic and social trends sketched in the previous section. I argue that the precocious early development of the Argentine labor movement; its urban focus, social composition, and ideological tendencies; and its tenuous postwar strength and sudden collapse—all reflected the special structural characteristics of Argentina's rapidly growing peripheral capitalist society in the decades after 1880.

———————◆——————

Unlike their counterparts in Chile, Argentine workers in export production faced virtually insuperable obstacles in their efforts to forge working-class institutions and an autonomous vision of society. Extensive production methods—inherent in livestock raising, and imposed by large landowners on a migratory immigrant labor force in cereal cultivation—stifled the development of stable rural communities and undermined the organizational potential of rural workers. Isolated physically from one another on the vast Argentine pampa, denied ownership of the land or permanent access to it, Argentine rural workers were unable to build even the rudimentary institutions of collective life. As James Scobie showed in a classic book, the development of schools and churches, even small towns, was stunted on the livestock and cereal pampa.[25] Yet it was through institutions such as these that other rural workers, as in the United States, forged powerful working-class institutions and sustained

24. I have relied primarily on narrative histories written by activist participants representing each of the major ideological currents in the development of the Argentine labor movement. These works, which all exhibit the strengths and weaknesses discussed in Chapter One, include Diego Abad de Santillán, *La FORA* (Buenos Aires, 1933) [anarchist]; Sebastián Marotta, *El movimiento sindical argentino* (3 vols.; Buenos Aires, 1960, 1961, 1970) [syndicalist]; Jacinto Oddone, *Gremialismo proletario argentino* (Buenos Aires, 1949) [socialist]; Rubéns Iscaro, *Orígen y desarrollo del movimiento sindical argentino* (Buenos Aires, 1958) [communist]. Peronist contributions are noted below. Attempts by scholars to explain major turning points in the history of Argentine labor are discussed as the analysis proceeds.

25. Scobie, *Revolution on the Pampas* (cited in n. 18).

agrarian mass movements that were capable of influencing—and threatening—the economic and political institutions of large national states.[26]

The major exception to this pattern of social organization on the pampa was the southern region of the province of Santa Fe. The rural protest movements spawned in this region in the early twentieth century took advantage of a social and political legacy left by the immigrant smallholders who established themselves as wheat producers in the province in the 1870's and 1880's. Although the region had evolved toward the pattern of concentrated landownership and capitalist tenant agriculture typical of the pampa, in the early twentieth century it had a denser population, a more intensive agriculture (primarily corn cultivation), a more complex social structure, and greater pluralism in its political party structure than the other regions of the pampa.

Here, near the town of Alcorta in June 1912, tenant farmers launched the most successful agrarian movement in twentieth-century Argentine history.[27] Squeezed by unstable international grain prices, erratic harvests, and soaring land rents—and emboldened by the recent election of a reformist Radical political administration in the province—the tenants struck for lower rents and long-term contracts. These small capitalist farmers, the majority of them apparently Italian sharecroppers, were able to cement an alliance with the merchant intermediaries who sold their grain to the big export houses and furnished them credit. They spread their movement far beyond the province of Santa Fe. Leaders claimed the number of strikers reached 100,000 before the two-month strike was settled by government mediation and concessions from landowners. The organization founded by the Santa Fe tenants, the Federación Agraria Argentina, and its newspaper, *La Tierra*, survived the strike and continued to agitate for moderate agrarian reforms throughout the 1910's and 1920's.

It was from this same region, and southern Buenos Aires province, that landless rural laborers who had been organized into embryonic rural unions under anarcho-syndicalist leadership launched a major strike that spread across the pampa during the labor unrest of 1919. That strike,

26. Lawrence Goodwyn has developed these ideas in a major reassessment of the Populist Movement in the United States in the late nineteenth century, *The Populist Moment* (New York, 1978). Carl Solberg provides much information on the social fragmentation and abject material life of the Argentine rural working class in his "Farm Workers and the Myth of Export-Led Development in Argentina," *The Americas* 21:2 (Oct. 1974):121-38.

27. These observations on the agrarian movement begun in Santa Fe in 1912 are deduced from the rich but convoluted history by Plácido Grela, *El Grito de Alcorta* (Buenos Aires, 1956), and follow the careful survey of the structural conditions that precipitated the protest by Aníbal Arcondo, "El conflicto agrario argentino de 1912," *Desarrollo Económico* 20:79 (Oct.-Dec. 1980):351-81. Carl Solberg sketches the terms of agrarian conflict on the pampa in subsequent years in his pioneering "Rural Unrest and Agrarian Policy in Argentina, 1912-1930," *Journal of Interamerican Studies and World Affairs* 12 (Jan. 1971):18-52.

however, was opposed by both landowners and the tenants of the Federación Agraria Argentina. It was violently crushed by provincial police after five weeks of struggle. During the 1920's the petty-bourgeois FAA moved rapidly to the right. As Carl Solberg has demonstrated, *La Tierra* was sympathetic toward Mussolini's agrarian initiatives and attributed the position of landless labor on the pampa to the sloth of individual workers. Another strike by landless workers seeking union recognition and wage increases exploded in southern Santa Fe and Buenos Aires province in 1928. It was also opposed by the FAA and quickly and brutally suppressed by army troops deployed by the Radical government.

It was beyond the pampa, in the far reaches of Patagonia in 1920-21, that anarchists led the other great rural strike in modern Argentine history. Organized by urban artisans in the port of Río Gallegos, it mobilized the largely Chilean work force on the vast sheep ranches of the territory of Santa Cruz. The strike was finally crushed by army troops, who systematically eliminated hundreds of rural workers and buried them in mass graves. Osvaldo Bayer, who immortalized the strike in his three-volume history *Los vengadores de la Patagonia trágica*, reveals how different the structural conditions for labor organization in Patagonia were from those in the heartland of Argentina's rural export economy. On the vast, arid, sparsely populated plains of Patagonia, capitalists were denied easy access to scab labor and to the coercive apparatus of the state. Their workers, predominantly single males, lived in communal barracks on each ranch. During the catastrophic postwar depression in the international wool economy, these workers had literally no place to go, no alternative to their work on sheep ranches to maintain their livelihood. In Patagonia workers lived isolated from major Argentine cultural institutions in a dual-class social structure uncomplicated by intermediary groups. Their ability to identify their class antagonists and engage in successful collective action was probably also favored by the fact that the majority of them were Chileans, whereas most owners were absentee Argentine or European capitalists.[28]

These remarkable mobilizations of rural workers in Argentine export production, schematically recounted here, are the exceptions. On the vast pampa that was the core of the Argentine export economy, structural conditions proved overwhelming obstacles to effective labor organization. On the pampa the nature of rural land and labor systems tended even to limit the concentration of people and to stifle the development of rudimentary forms of community life.

Instead of fostering rural social development, social relations of pro-

28. Osvaldo Bayer, *Los vengadores de la Patagonia trágica* (3 vols.; Buenos Aires, 1972-74).

duction in the heart of the Argentine export sector tended to push workers toward the cities. There, thanks to the rapid and sustained growth of construction, manufacturing, service, bureaucratic, and professional activities fostered by the impressive development of export production, manual and clerical workers and petty entrepreneurs, many of them immigrants from Europe, found the economic and social opportunities that were lacking in the countryside. As the urban market grew in Argentina's high-wage economy, these urban activities fed on themselves.[29] A large urban economy arose to feed, clothe, house, and entertain Argentina's urban classes. In addition, the scope of the transport and processing needs of an economy based on the export of bulky livestock and cereal commodities created thousands of jobs for workers, primarily in the ports of the pampa and especially in Buenos Aires. By 1914, the working class in that city numbered almost half a million.

Argentina's economic structure during the golden age of export-oriented development thus conditioned the evolution of a class structure distinct from that which unfolded as capitalism expanded in the industrial economies of the center of the world system. The core of the Argentine urban proletariat in the early twentieth century was not made up of industrial workers divorced from ownership of the means of production and increasingly deprived of control over the conception and execution of work.[30] Except for the large and very important concentrations of workers in meat-packing and transport, most manual workers in Argentina were artisans employed in urban construction and small manufacturing establishments that utilized domestic raw materials to supply bulky, low-value commodities to the domestic market. Skilled artisans in construction and manufacturing, organized along craft lines as masons, ironworkers, typographers, carpenters, tailors, cabinetmakers, tram conductors, bakers, shoemakers, and so on, formed the core of the organized labor movement in the early twentieth century. These skilled craftsmen were able to mobilize the large numbers of unskilled workers who did the heavy and dirty work in an urban economy where hand tools and physical labor had not yet begun to be replaced by machinery and fossil

29. Arghiri Emmanuel's *Unequal Exchange* (New York, 1972) develops a powerful theoretical and historical argument to demonstrate the potential for diversified capitalist development of peripheral economies that, like Argentina's, have a relatively high wage structure.

30. Recent European and U.S. studies in labor history have persuasively demonstrated, contrary to traditional Marxist conceptions, that it is resistance to proletarianization, not the consequences of its realization, that best explains the dynamic of worker protest in Europe and the United States in the nineteenth century. Although systematic studies are lacking, such resistance probably lies at the core of the anarchist- and syndicalist-led labor protest in Southern Europe and Argentina in the first decades of the twentieth century.

fuels.[31] Only toward the end of the first period of labor mobilization in Argentina were these organizations of urban craftsmen, service workers, and laborers joined by unionized transport workers. Maritime and railroad workers achieved a significant degree of effective organization after a series of long, bitterly contested strikes between 1916 and 1918.

The nature of the middle class molded by Argentine export-oriented expansion after 1880 was also distinct from the classic pattern that emerged as industrialization proceeded in the North Atlantic. Development in Argentina strengthened the rural landowning class, not an industrial bourgeoisie. The large conglomeration of rentiers, professionals, salaried white-collar workers, and owners of manufacturing establishments consolidated in Buenos Aires in the decades following 1880 proved more interested in political democratization and access to education and the state bureaucracy than it did in pursuing a vision of social and economic organization distinct from that championed by the Argentine ruling class and the foreign capitalists allied with it. The aspirations of these middle sectors (with the exception of manufacturers, most of them native-born Argentines) presented the landed elite with a serious political—not a social—challenge. As we shall see, the solution to that challenge, which was to open the political system to all adult male Argentine citizens after 1912, had important consequences for the development of the Argentine labor movement and for the twentieth-century political evolution of the nation as a whole.[32]

Against this social and political background conditioned by Argentina's rapidly growing export economy, the early twentieth-century history of the Argentine labor movement unfolded. As happened in Europe

31. Jacinto Oddone, *Gremialismo* (cited in n. 24), pp. 275-77, provides a graphic illustration of who these workers were in his list of labor organizations from the capital represented at the fusion conference of anarchist and socialist unions held in Buenos Aires in 1906. These included saddlers, marble masons, waiters, onshore carpenters, typesetters, farriers, wood sculptors, painters, wood lathe operators (represented by Oddone), port workers, typecasters, tilers, shoe machine operators, dressmakers, carters, wagoners, owners of 1 and 2 carts, warehousemen, cooks' assistants and dishwashers, smelters and modelers, tailors, ironers, carriage makers, cutters in shoemaking, machinists, harnessmakers, silversmiths, rural metalworkers, glassblowers, railway workers, construction workers, trolleycar employees, ironworkers, electricians, shop clerks, brickmasons, photographic workers, cigarmakers, cobblers, blacksmiths, frigorífico meatworkers, sweepers, hatters, mechanics, sandalmakers, molders, domestic servants, maritime workers, day laborers in commerce, oven tenders, paperhangers, bakers, sawyers.

32. The political tendencies of the middle class, especially as evidenced by the Radical Party's relations with labor, are carefully explored in David Rock's *Politics in Argentina, 1890-1930* (Cambridge, Eng., 1975). The pioneering work of Argentine historians and social scientists presaged many of the ideas and concepts developed by Rock. See especially Ezequiel Gallo and Silvia Sigal, "La formación de los partidos políticos contemporáneos: La U.C.R. (1890-1916)," in Torcuato Di Tella et al., *Argentina, sociedad de masas* (Buenos Aires, 1965), pp. 124-76. The classic assessment of these issues in Argentine history is John J. Johnson, *Political Change in Latin America: The Emergence of the Middle Sectors* (Stanford, Calif., 1958), Chap. 6.

and other Latin American societies, Argentine workers first organized to buffer themselves from the shock of sickness and death. Mutual-aid societies, often organized along the ethnic lines of Argentina's immigrant work force, were already numerous by the end of the nineteenth century, and their numbers, members, and capital resources increased rapidly in the early twentieth century. Robert Shipley, who has produced a valuable study of the size, structure, and material condition of the working class in the city of Buenos Aires during this period, notes that at their peak around 1913, mutual-aid societies enrolled about half the working class of the capital, some 255,534 people, and reported a capital of more than 11 million pesos and paid out almost 3 million pesos in benefits a year.[33]

Parallel with the growth of these defensive institutions, workers also began to organize collectivities called resistance societies. These organizations combined the functions of mutual-aid societies with a willingness to strike to win concessions from employers. Unlike the *mancomunales* in the north of Chile, however, Argentine resistance societies were organized along craft lines primarily by skilled urban artisans. Argentine workers also sought to combine their strength and coordinate resistance activities through solidarity strikes and the formation of labor centrals. They spread working-class visions of the world in mass meetings, drama groups, and a press of their own. Working-class newspapers exposed the evils of capitalism, told the workers' side of the news, and competed with each other to promote different ideological and tactical solutions to the problems facing workers as a class.

In the development of all these activities, but especially with regard to ideology and tactics, the largely immigrant Argentine labor movement reflected the strong influence of parallel developments in Europe. Three main ideological currents predominated. One was socialism, which in Argentina initially accepted the Marxist idea of class conflict and stressed the need for organization in the workplace, but which quickly drifted toward a reformist, electoral strategy. A second was anarchism, which advocated spontaneous mass action to win concessions on the job and aspired to destroy the exploitative capitalist order and the tyranny of the state through a gigantic general strike. The third was syndicalism, which, without renouncing the vision of the anarchists, began to stress the importance of nonsectarian organization in the workplace to accomplish both the destruction of capitalism and the building of a new society of

---

33. Robert E. Shipley, "On the Outside Looking In: A Social History of the *Porteño* Worker During the Golden Age of Argentine Development, 1914-1930" (Ph.D. diss., Rutgers University, 1977), pp. 233-34. I have relied extensively on this fine dissertation for much of the quantitative information in this section. Hobart Spalding's *La clase trabajadora argentina. Documentos para su historia, 1890-1912* (Buenos Aires, 1970) provides a good introduction to the history of the labor movement during this period and reproduces scores of primary documents that convey much of the tone of the workers' movement before 1912.

free producers where liberty, abundance, and social equality would prevail.[34]

Although as early as the 1890's socialists won influence among small groups of skilled workers, in the twentieth century they failed to develop a mass working-class base. Anarchists, on the other hand, were able to mobilize large numbers of urban workers in job actions and huge general strikes; for more than a decade after 1900 they dominated the Argentine labor movement. After 1915, however, syndicalists won control of the major Argentine labor central, and it was they who conducted the pivotal strikes that brought the development of the early Argentine labor movement to a climax in the tumultuous years following the First World War.

The appeal of anarchist and syndicalist ideology to Argentine workers in this period is often attributed to the southern European origins of the large numbers of immigrants in the work force. This cultural, diffusionist explanation is correct, as far as it goes. But it neglects the concrete structural conditions that made anarcho-syndicalist ideology seem especially appropriate to workers in early-twentieth-century Argentine society. Argentine workers, like their counterparts in southern Europe, found in anarchism, and later syndicalism, a vision of the world and a program for social transformation that validated and explained their daily experience and spoke to their special needs and aspirations. Given the nature of the obstacles and opportunities they faced in their efforts to improve the quality of their lives, most Argentine workers found socialist ideology and tactics inadequate, if not irrelevant.

Socialists in Argentina advocated reform of capitalist relations of production. They struggled to pass legislation to establish safety regulations, provide accident compensation, and establish shorter hours and limits on the work of women and children. Socialists also concentrated on protecting the purchasing power of urban workers. They consistently advocated free trade and opposed the creation of "artificial" domestic industry. Socialists were able to place a deputy in congress as early as 1904, but it was not until the electoral reform of 1912 that they elected large numbers of public officials. Partly through these electoral and legislative

---

34. All of these groups had close ties to similar European movements: the socialists with the French and German social democrats; the anarchists with the anarchists in Spain and Italy; the syndicalists with like-minded workers in those countries and in France. Many Argentine militants were immigrants who had been activists in Europe. Anarchist leaders, especially, organized on both sides of the Atlantic. On the broad question of European ideological influences during the formation of the labor movement in Latin America, see Hobart Spalding, *Organized Labor in Latin America* (New York, 1977), Chap. 1. On the anarchists in Argentina and their connections with Europe, see Richard A. Yoast, "The Development of Argentine Anarchism: A Socio-Ideological Analysis" (Ph.D. diss., University of Wisconsin, 1975), and Iaacov Oved, *El anarchismo en el movimiento obrero en Argentina* (Mexico City, 1978).

efforts, but more importantly through militant job actions and general strikes led by socialists, anarchists, and syndicalists, some reformist labor legislation dealing with hours, work by women and children, and pensions was enacted into law during the first decades of the century. Shipley has shown, for instance, that by the time the eight-hour day was sanctioned by national legislation in 1925, the average Argentine worker in Buenos Aires had already won a slightly shorter work day.

From our knowledge of the unions they controlled and from analysis of electoral returns from the city of Buenos Aires after 1921, it is clear that the Socialist Party found most of its support among skilled blue-collar workers and native-born white-collar workers. It consistently outpolled the Radical Party and far outdistanced the various conservative parties in the working-class districts that were concentrated around the southern rim of the city of Buenos Aires. Yet the great bulk of the working class and almost all the immigrants did not vote. By 1914 only a tiny fraction of immigrants, a little over 2 percent, had become Argentine citizens. Most immigrants came to Argentina to make money and return home. Many of those who stayed apparently judged that the benefits of Argentine citizenship, particularly the right to vote, did not outweigh the obligations, such as liability to conscription into the army. Argentine officials did not make it easy to complete the bureaucratic process of naturalization, but even when foreigners were allowed to vote in the municipal elections of Buenos Aires in 1917, only a few more than 11,000 chose to take advantage of that opportunity.[35]

In contrast to the appeal of socialism, anarchist thought and tactics evoked a deep resonance within the Argentine urban working class. Anarchists organized and led most of the unions in the construction, manufacturing, and service trades that dominated the organized working-class movement in Argentina in the early twentieth century. Anarchist unions counted only several thousand members during this period, but these workers and their leaders were able to mobilize scores of thousands of workers in huge general strikes, notably in 1902 and 1909.

At the present state of research, we can only speculate on the reasons

35. With the opening of the political system after 1912, Socialists became a very important electoral force in the city of Buenos Aires. Socialist votes came primarily from the working class. A fine quantitative study of the class dimension of Socialist electoral strength in the capital during the period 1916-22 is Richard Walter's "Elections in the City of Buenos Aires," *Hispanic American Historical Review* 58:4 (Nov. 1978):595-624. The same author's *The Socialist Party of Argentina* (Austin, Tex., 1977) provides a scholarly analysis of the development of the party. Jacinto Oddone's *Gremialismo* (cited in n. 24) covers the same ground from the viewpoint of a Socialist activist. The evolving philosophy of the party's founder and leading light can be followed in Dardo Cúneo, ed., *Obras de Juan B. Justo* (Buenos Aires, 1947). A leftist, pro-Peronist critique of the party is Jorge Spilimbergo, *Juan B. Justo y el socialismo cipayo* (Buenos Aires, 1974).

for the widespread appeal of anarchism.[36] Anarchist activism promised community, immediate material betterment, and transcendent spiritual rewards to a working class adrift from traditional institutions of social control. Neither family, church, school, nor traditional political parties exercised great influence over an urban working class in which single adult male migrants—many of them veterans of European anarchist struggles—were unusually common. Anarchists stressed the revolutionary international solidarity of the proletariat against capital and the state to a cosmopolitan working class confronted in Argentina by a native ruling class that before 1912 exercised direct and undiluted control of government. To workers who had come to America to make money quickly, anarchism also offered effective job actions. Anarchist tactics—based on solidarity strikes and mass general strikes to win workers' demands—proved effective under conditions of rapid economic expansion and massive immigration in early-twentieth-century Argentina. Even under conditions of high employment, the expanding numbers of newly arrived immigrants desperate for work threatened the success of strikes at a single workplace. That tactic, commonly pursued by socialists, was effective only among highly skilled workers. Mass mobilization helped to intimidate and educate scab labor. The large-scale strikes organized by anarchists were not only designed to promote proletarian unity, strengthen the workers' movement through "revolutionary gymnastics," and win collective demands such as freedom for jailed activists or repeal of repressive legislation. They were also concatenations of separate workers' struggles to organize and improve wages and conditions in individual trades and manufacturing establishments. The success of these tactics was apparent to urban workers both in the expansion and growing effectiveness of unions and in the rising rate of real wages during most of the first decade of the twentieth century. Finally, anarchism held out the vision of human dignity through revolutionary struggle. It preached individual freedom, democratic social relations, and secular, scientific, rational values to a work force that still possessed its own tools, maintained its patrimony over industrial skills, and exercised significant control over the work process.[37]

After the turn of the century, the anarchist-led labor movement in Argentina confronted intermittent, often violent, government repression. If this repression initially seemed to confirm for many militants anarchist conceptions of the nature of state power under capitalism, its scope and

36. A group of young social historians associated with the Programa de Estudios de Historia Económica y Social Americana in Buenos Aires is now doing the research on popular culture that will illuminate this issue.

37. Diego Abad de Santillán, *El movimiento anarquista en la Argentina (Desde sus comienzos hasta 1910)* (Buenos Aires, 1930).

effectiveness gradually undermined the appeal of anarchist tactics to the working class in general. The government used alien and sedition acts—the Ley de Residencia of 1902 and the Ley de Defensa Social of 1910—to decapitate the Argentine labor movement periodically by deporting allegedly subversive foreigners. These measures were supplemented by frequent declarations of state-of-siege powers, which enabled the police to silence the worker press, break up workers' meetings, and jail activists by the hundreds. Right-wing paramilitary groups, often tolerated by government officials and police, complemented official repression. Civilian mobs terrorized working-class districts in 1910. That action, coupled with massive government repression in response to a general strike called by anarchists on the eve of the celebration of the centennial of Argentine independence, led to an abrupt decline in labor and strike activity after that year.

The massive political repression of the anarchist-led labor movement in 1910 was soon followed by the economic disruption and large-scale emigration precipitated by the First World War. When the workers' movement revived after 1915 and grew powerful in 1917 under conditions of rising wartime labor demand and a drastic decline in real wages, anarchist influence was overshadowed by the appeal and organizational success of the syndicalists. Syndicalism in Argentina was a meld of the ideology and tactics of militant socialists and practical anarchists. In theory it endorsed the anarchist vision of social revolution, but it sought to reach that goal through powerful, established organizations in the workplace and nonsectarian working-class unity embodied in a national labor central. Syndicalists also adopted a pragmatic approach to government in the changed political environment following the electoral reforms of 1912. The Radical government that came to power in 1916 appealed for support from both the middle and the working classes. Syndicalist leaders proved willing to negotiate with the new government and sought to enlist the power of the state—or at least to secure the state's neutrality—in the struggle between capital and labor.

Syndicalist success and strategy seem to reflect two structural changes in the composition of the organized working class itself. The first was the successful organization of transport workers. By 1917, after momentous maritime and railway strikes helped consolidate their organizational position, militant syndicalist-led railroad workers became the most numerous, and maritime workers the most effective, members of the organized labor movement in Argentina. These unions became the backbone of the syndicalist-led Federación Obrera Regional Argentina (FORA), the most powerful labor central in Argentina prior to the 1940's. The second change was demographic and cultural. By the second decade of the century, native-born Argentines, many of them the sons and daughters of the immigrants who had been flooding into Argentina since the 1880's, made up a large share of the working class. Interruption of the immigrant flow and the return of many temporary workers to Europe during the war speeded up this process. Unlike their parents, most of this second generation were citizens committed to stay in Argentina. Many had attended Argentine public schools. As a group they were more integrated into Argentine society than their parents had been, more susceptible to the influence of mainstream institutions and cultural values. The head of the syndicalist FORA at the end of the First World War, Sebastián Marotta, personified and symbolized both these changes in the Argentine labor movement. He was the son of Italian immigrants and a railway car painter by trade.[38]

Under syndicalist leadership the early Argentine labor movement came to a dramatic climax in the postwar period. David Rock has collected statistics that indicate the magnitude, and rapid collapse, of this remarkable mobilization of Argentine urban workers. The number of strikes in Buenos Aires rose to 138 in 1917, 196 in 1918, and 259 in the first half of 1919 alone. In 1917, 136,000 workers took part in strikes in the capital, in 1918, 133,000, and in 1919, 309,000. Meanwhile, the syndicalist FORA grew from a modest organization of 50 affiliated unions with something more than 21,000 dues-paying members in 1915 to a labor central that at its peak in 1920 claimed 734 affiliates with more than 68,000 dues-paying members (actual membership may have been double that figure). Yet within a year, dues-paying membership fell by more than half and at the end of 1921 the FORA itself disbanded. The number of workers involved in strikes in the capital fell from more than 300,000 in 1919 to little more than a third that number in 1920 and 1921, and then to a mere 4,737 in 1922.

A few important remnants of the once-powerful FORA survived in the 1920's, and small rival socialist, anarchist, and communist labor centrals struggled to win control over the labor movement. But whereas the FORA at its peak may have enrolled a fourth of the adult male work force of Buenos Aires, by 1922 only roughly one-twentieth of that work force belonged to unions.[39] Except for the reformist, socialist-led union of railroad workers in the 1920's, union organizations did not grow signifi-

---

38. The ideas in this paragraph are developed with great clarity in Samuel L. Baily's *Labor, Nationalism, and Politics in Argentina* (New Brunswick, N.J., 1967). Baily also notes that during the late 1910's, albeit with very uneven success, groups of white-collar workers (bank and commercial employees, telegraph and post office workers) attempted to organize themselves into unions.

39. All these estimates are drawn from Rock, *Politics in Argentina* (cited in n. 32), especially Table 6, p. 160. Rock relies on information from a variety of official and unofficial publications. As with similar data from Chile, the absolute numbers may be questionable, but the trends are clear.

TABLE 3.4
Index of Real Wages in Buenos Aires, 1914-39
(1929 = 100)

Year	Index	Year	Index	Year	Index
1914	68	1923	86	1932	104
1915	61	1924	85	1933	96
1916	57	1925	89	1934	99
1917	49	1926	90	1935	101
1918	42	1927	95	1936	95
1919	57	1928	101	1937	96
1920	59	1929	100	1938	96
1921	73	1930	91	1939	97
1922	84	1931	98		

SOURCE: República Argentina, Ministerio del Interior, Departamento Nacional del Trabajo, División de Estadística, *Investigaciones Sociales* (Buenos Aires, 1940), p. 38.

TABLE 3.5
Index of Workers Employed in the City of Buenos Aires, 1914-39
(1929 = 100)

Year	Index	Year	Index	Year	Index
1914	72	1923	80	1932	94
1915	70	1924	86	1933	98
1916	66	1925	86	1934	104
1917	61	1926	88	1935	113
1918	70	1927	96	1936	120
1919	74	1928	101	1937	126
1920	75	1929	100	1938	130
1921	76	1930	101	1939	132
1922	75	1931	98		

SOURCE: República Argentina, Ministerio del Interior, Departamento Nacional del Trabajo, División de Estadística, *Investigaciones Sociales* (Buenos Aires, 1940), p. 46.

cantly throughout the rest of the decade, and strikes became infrequent. By 1922, and for a long time afterward, the Argentine labor movement was moribund.

Part of the explanation for this extraordinary mobilization and catastrophic collapse seems to be related to trends in real wages and unemployment. Illustrative data on real wages in the city of Buenos Aires appear in Table 3.4. They show that after 1914 real wages fell drastically until 1918 and thereafter rose steadily until the Depression. Table 3.5 reveals that during the first part of the period, from 1914 to 1917, the level of employment in the city also declined sharply. After that, employment expanded rapidly until 1919, when the mild postwar depression (1919-22) caused employment in the city to level off and then decline somewhat. After 1922 the number employed in the city expanded rapidly until almost the end of the decade.

The statistics reveal the remarkable sensitivity of Argentine workers to

TABLE 3.6
Estimated Percentage of Working-Class Unemployment in the
City of Buenos Aires, 1914-30

Year	Pct. unemployed	Year	Pct. unemployed	Year	Pct. unemployed
1914	15.3%	1920	16.8%	1926	16.5%
1915	18.0	1921	18.2	1927	11.7
1916	24.8	1922	20.6	1928	9.2
1917	30.1	1923	17.5	1929	11.6
1918	20.8	1924	15.1	1930	15.6
1919	17.5	1925	17.1		

SOURCE: Robert E. Shipley, "On the Outside Looking In: A Social History of the *Porteño* Worker During the Golden Age of Argentine Development, 1914-1930" (Ph.D. diss., Rutgers University, 1977), Appendix III, pp. 346-53.

basic economic trends during the war and postwar period. During the years 1914 to 1921 workers correctly perceived their objective position in Argentina's changing economy. As soon as employment levels favored their struggle, workers threw themselves into the effort to recapture their lost purchasing power. Once employment levels turned against them and real wages continued to rise, they desisted from the costly struggle to improve their position through collective job actions.

But how does one account for the continuing quiescence of the workers' movement during the economic expansion of the rest of the decade? One way is to focus on a basic structural weakness obscured by the information on changing levels of employment: the existence of high levels of unemployment in the city of Buenos Aires during the entire war and postwar period. Robert Shipley has used Argentine Department of Labor statistics collected for other purposes to estimate the level of unemployment in the city between 1914 and 1930. His findings are reproduced in Table 3.6. These estimates are shockingly high, but even if Shipley's careful procedures (which included cross-checks with different sets of data) produced some errors, other evidence, particularly the history of major strikes, confirms that the level of unemployment in the city of Buenos Aires during the whole period was very high.

A review of the major strikes of the period reveals that the whole dynamic of the struggle between capital and labor—indeed the fate of the entire early-twentieth-century Argentine labor movement—pivoted on the existence of a large pool of unemployed workers in the densely populated coastal areas of the pampa. The most important of these strikes were waged by transport workers and meat-packers, both vital to the health of the export sector that propelled Argentine economic development. Transport workers' organizational strikes in this period were initially successful, a fact that enabled the FORA temporarily to deepen and extend organization beyond the nucleus of urban manufacturing and service workers that had formed the core of the anarchist-led labor movement in the first decade of the century. Meatworkers' struggles in the most modern and important industrial sector of the Argentine economy, however, ended in failure. Both the initial success of the transport workers and the bitter defeat of the meatworkers obeyed a dynamic defined by the major structural weakness of the early Argentine labor movement: its vulnerability to the threat of scab labor.

Mass organization of transport workers following successful strikes in 1917-19 was achieved, significantly, through a tenuous alliance between skilled and unskilled workers. Large numbers of unskilled and semi-skilled railroad and maritime workers led by revolutionary syndicalists formed alliances with small, cohesive groups of much more conservative-minded, highly skilled, and hard-to-replace workers in those same industries. Among railroad workers the latter were engineers and firemen; among maritime workers, they were ship captains, officers, and technicians. The organizational fruits of these alliances were possible in part because of the initial neutrality of the recently elected Radical government. Acting out of concern for its electoral future and a vague commitment to social justice and class harmony, this first popularly elected Argentine government initially refused to use police and troops to break up union activities and protect strikebreakers. The government was always hostile to revolutionary anarchist and syndicalist tendencies within the Argentine labor movement, however. And as organized capitalist pressure on both the government and labor increased as the workers' movement expanded in the postwar period, the government moved decisively to repress revolutionary elements and to co-opt and strengthen reformist union leadership.

The alliance of skilled and unskilled labor was strongest, and government toleration most enduring, in the case of maritime workers. After winning a tremendous organizational strike in 1916, the Federación Obrera Marítima (FOM) was able to exercise ironclad control over the labor market in its jurisdiction. Workers organized by the FOM included not only coastal merchant seamen and captains, but stevedores and longshoremen in the major Argentine ports. Under combative syndicalist leadership, the FOM dedicated itself with great discipline and sacrifice to expand union organization in Argentina during the whole postwar period. Its most effective weapon was the solidarity boycott, a powerful tool in an economy so deeply dependent on overseas trade. Although the FOM lost an important port strike in May 1921, it was not until 1924, after the back of the militant Argentine labor movement had been broken and the FORA disbanded, that the alliance between skilled and unskilled maritime workers was definitely shattered and all FOM resistance to strikebreakers crumbled.[40]

The alliance was shakier, and government neutrality more short-lived, in the case of railway workers. Cooperation between highly skilled engineers and firemen and thousands of maintenance, yard, and shop workers was strained even before their resounding strike victory over the Argentine Central Railroad in August 1917. Engineers and firemen had long been organized into a small, moderate, highly centralized union, La Fraternidad. The mass of railway workers, after a long organizational campaign led by anarcho-syndicalists, had recently formed the loosely structured, combative Federación Obrera Ferroviaria (FOF). When pressure from militant rank and file and revolutionary leaders within the FOF pushed the newly organized interunion alliance into an industrywide strike to win a long list of demands in September 1917, friction between the partners in the alliance grew intense.

The importance of these strikes against the British companies that owned the crucial transportation link in the Argentine export economy evoked intense public involvement and government concern. During the August strike, which spread south to Buenos Aires from Rosario, the second port in importance on the pampa, striking workers used every means at their disposal to bring traffic to a halt. They derailed and burned freight trains. They halted passenger trains, ridiculing passengers and forcing them out of the cars. In one case, the sole British passenger on a Buenos Aires commuter train bound for the posh El Tigre district was killed by strikers, who reportedly claimed he was a "representative of British imperialism." Troop commanders, called on by the government to control the situation without recourse to firepower, expressed a sense of helplessness in the face of mass worker mobilization. One officer notified his superiors: "There seem to be 12,000 or more men out now. Each hour the strike grows more seditious. Last night six railroad cars were burned and this morning strikers continued their work of destruction, raising railroad tracks, burning sewerage pipes, stoning stations, and destroying signals. . . . The number of troops is insufficient to cover the services needed. [S]oldiers remove strikers from the tracks only to find that others immediately take their place . . . [and] women and children sleep on the tracks all the time. . . ."[41] Revolutionary anarcho-syndicalists built on popular support for these strikes, and by the end of September 1917 they brazenly informed the minister of the interior that if the

40. Shipley emphasizes the success of the FOM in controlling the labor market; Rock stresses the electoral importance to the Radical Party of these workers concentrated in the working-class district of La Boca in Buenos Aires.

41. The information in this paragraph comes primarily from Heidi Goldberg's "Railroad Unionization in Argentina, 1912–1929: The Limitations of Working-Class Alliance" (Ph.D. diss., Yale University, 1979). The quotation is from p. 170.

companies would not negotiate, the FOF was prepared to run the trains itself. In the end, the companies were forced to submit to government mediation of the strike. But in its terms of settlement, the government skillfully rewarded the conservative elements of the union leadership and helped to discredit the revolutionary syndicalists. The engineers and fire-men won a reform of job and work codes highly attractive to them, and La Fraternidad promptly lifted the strike. The leaders of the FOF were excluded from the final negotiations, however, and, after desperately trying to prolong the strike to extract greater concessions, they were forced to capitulate and accept a moderate wage increase. Following the breakdown of the alliance, the FOF, allied with the FORA, engaged in additional strikes. Each met with violent government repression and fail-ure. After 1919 the union was powerless to prevent company firings of hundreds of its most militant members, and the largest affiliate of the FORA was gradually rendered impotent.

Among meatworkers, alliance between skilled and unskilled workers proved much more difficult to achieve than among maritime and railroad workers. Despite a heroic organizational strike that enveloped the meat-packing plants nearest Buenos Aires in 1917-18, meatworkers failed then and afterward to force even minimal, temporary concessions from em-ployers. The early organizational failures of meatworkers are a funda-mental, if neglected, aspect of Argentine labor history.[42] Meatworkers confronted in extreme form the structural obstacles to effective organi-zation faced by other sectors of the Argentine urban labor movement in the early twentieth century. Their organizational failure reveals the con-genital weakness of a labor movement that failed to develop beyond the manufacturing and transport sectors of Argentina's peripheral capitalist economy during the golden age of export-oriented development. As we shall see in the next section, meatworkers played a central role in the sec-ond great mobilization of Argentine labor that brought Perón to power at the end of the Second World War. Their failure to organize during three decades of struggle before the 1940's made them especially attentive to the opportunities and advantages presented by Perón's labor policies. Because of the meatworkers' importance to the Argentine economy, their efforts to build effective unions were a major factor in the outcome of the labor—and political—struggles of both periods of worker mobilization in twentieth-century Argentine history.

The meat-packing industry in Argentina expanded rapidly after 1890.

42. The great meatworkers' strike of 1917-18 is virtually ignored in the standard histories of Argentine labor. Part of the reason is that activist labor historians like nothing better than to chronicle labor's escalating success. The failure of the 1917-18 strike and the dismal rec-ord of subsequent efforts by meatworkers to organize themselves and win concessions from capital make meatworkers and their abortive strikes unattractive subject matter.

But it was during the first decade of the twentieth century, when Argentina's major competitors proved unable to supply the rapidly expanding British market for beef, that meat-packing assumed the capital importance it held in Argentine economic life until the 1950's. Australia and New Zealand proved too distant to take full advantage of that market; exports from the United States, which had supplied Britain's expanding market before 1900, were steadily eliminated by growing internal demand. Herein lies the major reason for the sudden expansion of the great Chicago meat-packing firms, Swift, Armour, Morris, and Wilson, to Argentina after 1905. These U.S. firms bought out existing Argentine packing houses, then greatly modernized and expanded them. By 1914 they controlled almost 60 percent of Argentine meat exports. British meat-packing firms (and one major packinghouse in which Argentine capital still held a large stake) modernized and expanded production during this same period. Yet in 1914 British firms furnished only about 30 percent of Argentine meat exports, and Argentine interests retained only 10 percent.[43]

At the beginning of the twentieth century, the meat-packing industry already featured forms of capitalist organization of production that would become typical in other industries as the century advanced. Work was organized along a continuous, mechanical disassembly line that divided the work process systematically into scores of simple, repetitive operations. Perfection of this system was already accomplished in Chicago plants by the turn of the century and was exported to the more modern and efficient plants built in Argentina by Swift and Armour in the early 1900's.

The eminent North American labor historian John R. Commons described the work process in meat-packing and pinpointed its implications for labor organization after a failed Chicago strike in 1904:

It would be difficult to find another industry where division of labor has been so ingeniously and microscopically worked out. The animal has been surveyed and laid off like a map; and the men have been classified in over thirty specialties and rates of pay, from 16 cents to 50 cents an hour. The 50-cent man is restricted to using the knife on the most delicate parts of the hide (floorman) or to using the axe in splitting the backbone (splitter); and, wherever a less skilled man can be slipped in at 18 cents, 18½ cents, 20 cents, 21 cents, 22½ cents, 24 cents, 25 cents, and so on, a place is made for him, and an occupation mapped out. In working

43. In addition to Ortiz, *Historia económica* (cited in n. 7), useful summaries of the early evolution of the Argentine meat-packing industry are Antonio M. Poz Costra, *Los frigoríficos* (Buenos Aires, 1918); Sociedad Rural Argentina, *Comercio exterior de carnes* (Buenos Aires, 1927); and James Tronbridge Critchell and Joseph Raymond, *A History of the Frozen Meat Trade* (London, 1912). The history of the most successful of the original Argentine packing plants can be followed in [Compañia Sansinena] *"La Negra" en sus cincuenta años, 1891-1941* [n.p., n.d.]. The banker Ernesto Tornquist was the first president of its board of directors.

on the hide alone there are nine positions, at eight different rates of pay. A 20-cent man pulls off the tail, a 22½-cent man pounds off another part where the hide separates readily, and the knife of the 40-cent man cuts a different texture and has a different "feel" from that of a 50-cent man. Skill has become specialized to fit the anatomy.

In this way, in a gang of 230 men, killing 105 cattle an hour, there are but 11 men paid 50 cents an hour, 3 men paid 45 cents, while the number getting 20 cents and over is 86, and the number getting under 20 cents is 144. . . .

Commons went on to explain what capital gained by this division of labor. "[C]heaper men—unskilled and immigrant labor—could be utilized in large numbers." Meanwhile, skilled workers could be granted high wages and steady employment. "If the company makes a few of these [skilled] jobs desirable to the men and attaches them to its service, it can become independent of the hundreds who work at [unskilled jobs]." Capital also squeezed much more labor faster out of a work force paid less in the aggregate. Commons cited the typical example of splitters. "In the year 1884, 5 splitters in a certain gang would get out 800 cattle in 10 hours, or 16 per hour for each man, the wages being 45 cents. In 1894 the speed had been increased so that 4 splitters got out 1,200 in 10 hours, or 30 per hour for each man—an increase of nearly 100 percent in 10 years. The wages, except for the steady-time men, were reduced to 40 cents per hour." Speedup, according to Commons, was the primary cause of the 1904 strike. The strike was defeated when skilled, steady-time workers sided with management, and when scab labor from Chicago's huge pool of unskilled immigrant workers replaced the men on strike.[44]

Such was the outcome of all attempts at meatworker organization in the United States and Argentina throughout the first three decades of the twentieth century. In the United States capital tapped waves of immigrants to break the organizational drives of meatworkers in 1886, 1894, 1904, and 1917-18. Irish were brought in to scab against German butchers, Poles and Lithuanians to break strikes mounted by German and Irish workers. After the First World War management turned to blacks and finally to Mexicans to break the organizational efforts of white immigrant workers and perfected policies of promoting racial animosity to divide

44. John R. Commons, "Labor Conditions in Meat Packing and the Recent Strike," *The Quarterly Journal of Economics* 19 (Nov. 1904):1-32. The quotations are from pp. 3, 4, 6, and 7. In addition to the "modern" organization of work they adopted, the meat-packing firms prefigured other trends in the evolution of capitalist enterprise. They monopolized worldwide production and distribution systems for meat and meat by-products and periodically divided the market among themselves. They used advertising to promote consumption of product lines (frankfurters, picnic hams, corned beef) initially unfamiliar or unacceptable to most consumers. They harnessed chemical science to preserve meat products and to exploit every bit of animal by-product, from the eyelids of hogs to the hooves of cattle. Items like these were transformed into hundreds of substances and products, many far removed from the edible meat products that formed the core of meat-packing operations and generated about three-fourths of total sales.

workers on the job and in their home communities. When these policies threatened to break down in the face of worker solidarity forged in the workplace, management resorted to extreme measures. On occasion during prolonged strikes it contracted trains to bring scab labor into the yards directly from Ellis Island or from southern states. It housed and fed scabs within the walls of the great packinghouses. It employed private armies of Pinkerton detectives and called on government police and troops to break up pickets and union meetings. It established an efficient spy system within the plants. It collected deposits from workers, which were returned only if they had not engaged in union and strike activity and had given proper notice upon separation from the company.[45]

Each of these union–busting tactics was used in Argentina as well. In the populous coastal provinces of Buenos Aires, Santa Fe, and Entre Rios, as in Chicago and Kansas City, management took advantage of the large pool of unemployed, unskilled immigrant workers to renew its work force during strikes. Faced with the solidarity between Argentine meatworkers and organized sectors of the urban labor movement, capital recruited workers in tenements and rural towns and brought in unsuspecting scabs from Uruguay to help break strikes. The companies depended on government forces to protect these workers from union pickets and relied on police and mounted cavalry to break up union meetings and rallies. In anticipation of strikes the packing companies moved cots and large stocks of food into the plants so that scabs would not have to venture outside the walls into the working-class neighborhoods near the packinghouses. Packing companies developed blacklists and spy systems. By 1921, if not earlier, Swift was using a contract in at least one of its plants (in remote Río Gallegos) that required workers to deposit with the company 30 pesos a month (about one week's pay). If the worker quit or was fired for any reason, or if he contributed "directly or indirectly to disturbances or work stoppages," he forfeited to the company all of the

45. These tactics are exhaustively described by Alma Herbst in her classic monograph *The Negro in the Slaughtering and Meat-Packing Industry in Chicago* (Boston, 1932). See also David Brody, *The Butcher Workmen* (Cambridge, Mass., 1964), and James Rogers Holcomb, "The Union Policies of Meat Packers, 1929-1943" (Ph.D. diss., University of Illinois, 1957). Meatworkers built a large organization in Chicago after 1917 under the leadership of the IWW labor organizer William Z. Foster, only to see it fall apart in the postwar depression and Red Scare that crushed the anticapitalist labor movement in the United States. Finally, after years of patient organizational work by Communists in the 1930's, United States meatworkers won company recognition and major improvements in wages and working conditions during the Second World War. These victories were part of the great labor mobilization under CIO leadership that took advantage of New Deal labor legislation to organize basic industry in the United States in the decade after 1935. Following the war, and the purge of the left wing of the CIO, the meatworkers' union adopted the bread-and-butter stance characteristic of the U.S. labor movement in the postwar period.

money he had deposited. Work at this plant was seasonal: it opened only to handle the sheep kill during the summer months.[46]

Like their counterparts in the United States, Argentine meatworkers were particularly vulnerable to these anti-union tactics because of the large percentage of unskilled workers, many of them immigrants, women, and children, in the meat-packing labor force. The 1914 census reveals that fully two-thirds of the labor force in the industry were immigrants. Symptomatic of the large number of unskilled jobs in the plants was the fact that women and children, both working for wages much lower than men, comprised almost a sixth of the labor force in 1914. With time this percentage increased so that by 1935 more than a fourth of meat-packing workers were women or children under 18 years of age.[47]

The organization of work in meat-packing created a wide gulf between skilled and unskilled workers that management could exploit through pay differentials and deliberate policies to intensify ethnic differences. Many of the unskilled foreign workers in Argentine packing plants were drawn from the least advantaged groups within the immigrant community. Newspaper accounts of early strikes stress the role of foreign activists, especially "turcos" (a generic term used to include immigrants from all the Balkan and Middle Eastern components of the Turkish Empire). These people were generally considered to be among the most undesirable and ignorant of Argentine workers. Italians, Spaniards, and "Slavs" (Eastern Europeans from Russia, Poland, and Lithuania) were also present in large numbers in the plants. Workers were often segregated by ethnicity and sex within the production process—women worked in canning and sausage making, for example, and Poles were frequently found in the cold chambers. These divisions hindered communication between groups of workers and made it difficult for activists to build plantwide organizations. Perhaps the most serious obstacle to effective organization was the fact that many skilled jobs, especially those that demanded great dexterity with the knife, were filled by native Argentines. Whereas European immigrants often possessed artisanal and industrial skills that allowed them to dominate most manufacturing trades in early-twentieth-century Argentina, native Argentine workers, inheritors of the cultural legacy of a rural work force engaged in livestock produc-

46. A copy of the contract used at Swift's Rio Gallegos plant is reproduced in Bayer, *Los vengadores de la Patagonia trágica* (cited in n. 28), vol. 2, following p. 96. The contract was probably not typical: Swift faced serious problems of labor control in remote, sparsely populated Patagonia.

47. República Argentina, *Tercer censo nacional* (Buenos Aires, 1916-17), vol. 7, p. 353; República Argentina, Ministerio de Hacienda, *Censo industrial de 1935* (Buenos Aires, 1935), p. 58.

tion for over two centuries, were able to dominate the skilled jobs in meat-packing.

It is perhaps understandable that many of these highly paid native Argentine workers deprecated the unskilled, poorly paid foreign laborers in the plants and failed to sympathize with organizational efforts and job actions. Such attitudes, logical results of the organization of work, were cultivated by management and reinforced by the cultural values propagated by mainstream Argentine institutions. Immigrants, so the line went, were responsible for social unrest and labor strife; the *criollo* (native) work force should aspire to the values of the legendary *gaucho*, the independent, self-reliant, knife-wielding cowboy whom cultural nationalists were busily making into the quintessential Argentine. The native Argentine skilled workers on the kill floors were the most strategically located of meatworkers. They handled the animal at the start of the whole production process. If they walked off the job, the entire operation ground to a halt. If they refused to stop work, it was difficult to shut down a plant without very wide solidarity among the rest of the work force.[48]

Despite these formidable obstacles to organization, Argentine meatworkers were able to mount remarkable collective actions to improve the conditions under which they labored. Different sources note strikes at individual meat-packing plants in 1894, 1915, 1917-18, 1920, 1921, 1925, 1928, and 1932. Of all these strikes, the longest, most powerful, and most promising occurred in 1917-18. It enveloped four of the five great meat-packing plants closest to Buenos Aires. These were the huge Swift and Armour plants at Berisso near the provincial capital of La Plata, situated some 60 kilometers from the city of Buenos Aires, and "La Blanca" (owned by Morris-Armour) and Sansinena's "La Negra" (owned by Ar-

48. As noted in the next section, as late as 1939, in a petition directed to the national congress, meatworker labor organizers denounced management's tactic of employing workers "who because of their limited knowledge of the language would accept the worst work conditions." As a result, "management made the foreign worker appear as the enemy of the native worker" and impeded organization in the plants. Cámara de Diputados, *Diario de sesiones de 1939*, vol. 3, pp. 118-21. The importance of ethnicity in the organization of work in meat-packing is documented for the early twentieth century in Herbst's monograph (cited in n. 45) and in Upton Sinclair's muckraking classic *The Jungle* (Cambridge, Mass., 1971; 1st ed. 1904). It is confirmed for Argentina in the 1940's by interviews I did with Argentine meatworkers in 1978. The importance of ethnic concentrations in different aspects of the production process for labor organization in general is suggested in Peter Friedlander, *The Emergence of a UAW Local, 1936-1939* (Pittsburgh, Penn., 1975). The strategic importance of skilled workers on the kill floor is well documented in the U.S. literature and confirmed for Argentina in José Peter, *Crónicas proletarias* (Buenos Aires, 1968), p. 39. U.S. meatworker and labor organizer Stella Nowicki described a situation in the Armour plant in Chicago in the early 1940's that gives the typical Argentine story a different twist. There, a tightly knit group of skilled black workers on the kill floor used their power to slow or stop production to further militant union demands. See Stella Nowicki, "Back of the Yards," in Alice Lynd and Staughton Lynd, eds., *Rank and File* (Boston, 1973), p. 87.

gentine and foreign capital) in Avellaneda, the industrial suburb just south of the city limits of the capital. At the time of the 1917-18 strike some 11,000 workers were employed in the plants in Berisso, some 4500 at those in Avellaneda. The demands of workers during the great packinghouse strike of 1917-18 help to reveal the basis of worker solidarity in meat-packing. The evolution of the strike itself demonstrates with what sacrifice and creative energy workers sought to overcome the tremendous obstacles that stood in the way of success.[49]

Whatever their pay and function in the work process, all meatworkers shared the common experience of work in an advanced capitalist enterprise. A character in one novel about meatworkers, a skilled carpenter by trade, described what it was like to exercise his craft in the box-making section (*cajonería*) of the packing plants. "Hell. To be a carpenter here you don't need to know how to plane, or ever have held a plane in your hands. Carpenters? Don't make me laugh!" The novelist explained what he meant: "In reality, in the box-making section, wood wasn't worked at all; boxes were made, nothing more. The slats arrived, cut and finished . . . in bales. The slats were put together by machine, little machines that were so exact they seemed like watches, which mathematically nailed their five nails without their operator's having to do anything more than make sure the slats were 'squared' below the hammer. It was kid's work."[50] In most meat-packing jobs it was the same. Work was devoid of creative activity. Workers repeated the same endless task throughout their shifts. To make matters worse, because of the way work was organized and the nature of the task, jobs in meat-packing were among the hardest, foulest, most monotonous, and most dangerous of industrial activities. Part of the problem was the irregular and organic nature of the raw material subject to "scientific" disassembly and processing. José Peter, who entered the packinghouses as a youth in the 1920's and who sought for two decades to build a communist labor organization in the industry, later described the disgusting nature of the work on the sheep-kill floor. There, large and small animals, some dirty and full of burrs, all passed workers on the line at the same intolerable speed.

Often it happens that animals with tumors and boils full of pus come down the line, and for all the care you take, it is hard to keep the knife from penetrating the thin layer of membrane that covers them. Then the pus spurts out on your face, it touches your mouth and eyes, and there is time only to wipe it off with the back

49. Information on the 1917-18 strike comes from a reading of the worker press (*La Vanguardia* and *La Protesta*) and the English-language newspaper *The Review of the River Plate* (all three published in Buenos Aires). The most detailed published account of the strike is Rock, *Politics in Argentina* (cited in n. 32), Appendix 3. Workers at the third big packinghouse in Avellaneda, the "Anglo" (owned by Wilson) never joined the strike. Personnel at a second Sansinena plant, located in the southern pampa port of Bahía Blanca, did.

50. Bernardo González Arrili, *Los charcos rojos* (Buenos Aires, 1927), p. 75.

of your dirty, blood-stained hand. On top of the fatigue, and the pain, comes this sickening substance—all in an environment filled with horrible odors and air contaminated with tuberculosis and brucelosis microbes which get into your lungs.[51]

Early photographs taken inside the plants confirm Peter's descriptions. They show ragged, blood-smeared workers standing barefoot on wet and bloody kill floors or working poorly dressed in the cooling and freezing chambers.[52] Among the earliest strike demands of meatworkers were calls for the provision of clean fresh drinking water, adequate facilities for workers to wash in, and company-supplied shirts, aprons, and raincoats for use on the job. In 1917 strikers also claimed a full day's pay for workers hurt on the job. If a worker were incapacitated they demanded he be compensated with a pension equal to half the average daily pay earned in the two-week period prior to the accident.[53]

All workers also suffered from the pace of the work, the abuse of foremen charged with meeting production levels, and the exactions of fines levied to ensure workplace "discipline" and prevent damage to the raw material. Strikers in 1917 demanded greater respect from foremen and, in an effort to win skilled kill-floor workers over to the cause of the strike, called for an end to the fining and dismissal of butchers who scarred or cut hides. In 1917 this tactic apparently was successful. Three weeks into the strike, 170 workers on the beef kill floor at Swift in Berisso sent the

51. Peter, *Crónicas proletarias* (cited in n. 48), pp. 55-57. Compare Peter's description with Sinclair's discussion of occupational hazards and disease in *The Jungle*, p. 98: "Of the butchers and floorsmen, the beef-boners and trimmers, and all those who used knives, you could scarcely find a person who had the use of his thumb; time and time again the base of it had been slashed, till it was a mere lump of flesh against which the man pressed the knife to hold it. The hands of these men . . . would have no nails—they had worn them off pulling hides; their knuckles were swollen so that their fingers spread out like a fan. There were men who worked in the cooking rooms, in the midst of steam and sickening odors, by artificial light; in these rooms the germs of tuberculosis might live for two years, but the supply was renewed every hour. . . . There were those who worked in the chilling rooms, and whose special disease was rheumatism. . . . There were the wool-pluckers, whose hands went to pieces . . . for the pelts of the sheep had to be painted with acid to loosen the wool, and then the pluckers had to pull out this wool with their bare hands. . . . There were those who made the tins for the canned meat; and their hands, too, were a maze of cuts and each cut represented a chance for blood poisoning. . . ." In evaluating these descriptions due allowance must be made for Sinclair's muckraking style and the nature of his and Peter's political commitments. It is perhaps revealing of the different tone of Argentine political and social life that no Argentine novel achieved the notoriety and impact of Sinclair's famous exposé. Yet whatever its literary merits, González Arrili's short novel about an early meatpacking strike in Avellaneda (cited in n. 50) portrays meatworkers with greater subtlety and their lives with greater complexity than does *The Jungle*.

52. Part 3 of the hardcover edition of Rubéns Iscaro's *Historia del movimiento sindical* (Buenos Aires, 1973) contains revealing photographs of the plants and workers during this period.

53. Strike demands were not exactly the same at the different plants struck in 1917-18. Those formulated by Swift and Armour workers at Berisso appear in *La Vanguardia*, Nov. 27, 1917, p. 3; those for workers at "La Blanca" and "La Negra" in Avellaneda in *La Protesta*, Dec. 16, 1917.

following revealing declaration to the socialist press. They affirmed their complete support of all the strike demands, and noted with pleasure "that the complete unity and solidarity which presently exists in our organization repudiates the letters that, in a moment of inexplicable confusion, several of our comrades separately sent you. Those comrades today lament having acted in that way, and as proof they sign this statement."[54]

Pay for the different categories of meatworkers was comparable to that for similar jobs in other urban industries, but work in the plants was often irregular. Although meat-packing in Argentina did not suffer from great seasonal fluctuations (as it did in the United States), demand and supply did vary considerably and workers were often recruited on a daily basis. Workers would sometimes make the journey to the plant only to find that they were not needed or could work only a fraction of the day. Strike demands during the whole period consistently called for higher pay, and in 1917 called for much higher percentage increases for the lowest-paid workers, an end to the practice of garnishing wages, and abolition of quarter days. Any worker employed for any part of a day should receive a minimum of a half day's pay. Finally, strikers proposed in their 1917 strike demands that when there was not enough work in the plants, it should be shared among all workers on a revolving basis. At least as early as 1915, when a big strike first shook the Swift works at Berisso, meatworkers demanded an 8-hour day. That issue was a primary demand in 1917 as well. It was coupled with an insistence on time and a half for overtime and Sunday work, and the establishment of May 1 as a paid holiday for workers.

In all the packinghouse strikes until the 1940's, the most sensitive strike demand was union recognition and reinstatement of organizers and militants previously fired by the companies. On this issue management proved most intransigent. At Swift, economically the most powerful of the packing companies, management delegates simply tore up the strike petition in the face of worker representatives in 1917 and refused to talk with them throughout the strike. During that strike Armour executives proved more willing to listen to worker demands. After workers had virtually shut down the company's newly opened plant at Berisso for almost three weeks, management tentatively offered workers some economic concessions if they returned to work. Company officials adamantly refused, however, to bow to the strike committee's demand that the terms of the projected settlement be committed to writing and signed by representatives of both company and union.[55]

54. *La Vanguardia*, Dec. 17, 1917, p. 2.
55. The companies refused to recognize the unions in the United States as well. The big, ephemeral union gains of 1917-18 came through the intervention of a government concerned with wartime production.

The outcome of meat-packing strikes until the 1940's hinged on the question of scab labor. Meatworkers understood better than anyone else the meaning of strikebreakers to their collective struggle. They, like all Argentine workers, called strikebreakers *borregos* (young sheep) and *carneros* (sheep for slaughter). These terms have universal significance, but they held special meaning in a livestock-export economy, especially for those who labored in the packing plants. Sheep gave up the struggle for life in the frigoríficos with a collective naiveté, a mystical docility that was incomprehensible to rational human beings. Cattle, their skulls shattered by the hammer blows of the "knocker," fell kicking and bellowing to the kill floors. Hogs literally shook the walls in ungodly protest as they were mechanically ferried, suspended by one leg, toward the man charged with slitting their throats. Sheep, on the other hand, as one novelist put it,

were the antithesis of the tumultuous pigs. They were picked up by their four feet and placed face up on arched iron platforms with their heads suspended over a little tin trough. Sixty or seventy at a time remained in this position, without one complaining. Three men went along placing them in that manner, and one man alone slitting their throats. They let themselves be slaughtered in Biblical fashion: without a mutter. Their little feet would tremble a few minutes as they bled to death while they looked with eyes full of sweet surprise at the men who were killing them. That was all. Within a few moments they were on other platforms, still on their backs, skinned and letting themselves be inspected by the veterinarians.[56]

During the 1917-18 strike workers devoted all their creative energy to defeat strikebreakers. They timed the strike, which was declared in Berisso on November 28 and in Avellaneda on December 6, to coincide with the shrinking of the pool of the unemployed in the cities as the cereal harvest on the pampa began. They used mass meetings to build and maintain solidarity with the strike. In Berisso and Avellaneda, thousands of workers met almost daily in vacant lots, in the halls of other unions, and occasionally in public theaters to deliberate over demands and strategies, share information, and applaud and criticize the revolutionary visions and strike strategies expounded by rival syndicalist, anarchist, and socialist orators. They deployed hundreds of pickets to intimidate and ridicule scabs. They canvassed working-class districts and tenements to drum up support for the strike and to educate potential strikebreakers. They derailed and uncoupled trains carrying workers and livestock into the plants. On December 1, near Berisso, a crowd of strikers boarded a passenger train and ordered off administrators, accountants, and "other high officials" en route from the plants. When the employees refused and

56. The quotation comes from González Arrili, *Los charcos* (cited in n. 50), pp. 80-81.

workers proceeded to eject them, the police intervened and ordered everyone off the train. On the platform, as police searched all passengers for weapons, workers forced the employees to take off their hats and join with them in cheers for the strike.[57]

Militants also devoted special attention to women workers. Women were among the least-skilled and lowest-paid of meatworkers. They were most vulnerable to replacement by scabs, least able to survive without work. The socialist press reported that most of the 40 percent of the labor force still working at the Armour plant in Berisso at the end of the first week of the strike were women. Working-class newspapers took care to emphasize the attendance of women at rallies, the speeches by women orators at meetings, the exemplary and heroic actions of female workers in confrontations with police and strikebreakers. In early December women decided to organize a special Women's Section in Berisso to promote female solidarity with the strike.[58]

During the 1917-18 strike, meatworkers successfully enlisted the support of the FOM and the FOF, and of other affiliates of the FORA. The maritime workers of the FOM monitored efforts to bring strikebreakers from outside Buenos Aires and on at least one occasion intercepted unsuspecting workers recruited in Montevideo, reportedly convinced them of their proletarian duty, and housed them in their union hall until they could find work or return home. The FOM boycotted companies providing fuel to the plants and refused to pilot lighters carrying stored meat to oceangoing refrigerator ships. Railway unions contributed large sums of money to the meatworkers' strike fund. The FORA, for the first time in Argentine labor history, issued strike bonds to affiliates to raise money to help supply destitute strikers and their families with food.

All these manifestations of worker solidarity were reported exhaustively in the working-class press. Contributors to the cause, like the unionized barbers who offered strikers free shaves, were honored in published lists that identified them by name. So were local merchants who donated food or extended credit to strikers. Other lists singled out scabs and "traitorous" merchants who provided supplies to the packing plants. Such merchants were boycotted by consumers and by organized workers. At one point, the bakers' union refused to supply bread to offending merchants. Even some supervisory personnel in meat-packing declared their support for the workers' struggle. On December 16, the socialist newspaper *La Vanguardia* reported on a second meeting of overseers, foremen, and employees of the Berisso plants. Those attending ratified a resolution to "not make common cause during this strike with the capi-

57. *Review of the River Plate*, Dec. 7, 1917, p. 1395.
58. *La Vanguardia*, Dec. 5, 1917, p. 1; Dec. 6, 1917, p. 1; Dec. 18, 1917, p. 2.

talists, and avoid placing any obstacle in the way of the achievement of proletarian aspirations." With this kind of support from organized labor and elements of the middle class, meatworker strike tactics began to bear fruit. By the second week of December, workers had managed virtually to halt production in Berisso and Avellaneda.

Workers achieved this goal despite the hostility of the Radical government to the strike. As soon as the workers voted to walk out, the government sent in police squads, army cavalry, and naval units to protect the plants. Army technicians helped keep cooling equipment running to preserve meat stored in the plants. Naval personnel piloted or towed the lighters that ferried processed meat to oceangoing refrigerated ships. Under the protection of public forces the packinghouses and their small resident communities of scabs were turned into armed camps. Police and soldiers joined company security forces in installing machine guns in windows and searchlights on roofs. Mounted troops dispersed pickets, shot workers who attacked drivers bringing livestock into the plants, and rode into union halls and demonstrations, wounding with their sabers scores of workers and members of their families.

The most serious violence occurred at Swift on the night of December 3. Management and the liberal press reported that workers first cut the electrical cables to the Berisso district. Then, in the ensuing darkness, hundreds of strikers stormed the plant. The charge was reportedly led by a bugler on horseback. The workers' press vigorously denied that version. It claimed management and police fabricated the story to cover up an operation aimed at terrorizing the working-class community in the tenements surrounding the plant. What seems certain is that the lights went out, a barrage of gunfire issued from the plant, and police invaded the tenements. They pulled several score workers and family members out of their homes, herded them into the fenced premises of the plant, and interrogated them for hours before turning them over to military and judicial officials for processing. Even the procapitalist *Review of the River Plate* published a workers' version of these events that claimed that of the 101 persons arrested (the majority of them "said to be Turks"), 67 had saber or dagger wounds allegedly inflicted on them by police and sailors during interrogation. A socialist congressman later filed a petition signed by 23 people protesting the police brutality during these events. All of the signers, he claimed, "except for two citizens born in Berisso, are of Russian and Turkish nationality. Several of them do not have anything to do with the packing plants. They are merchants."[59]

As the strike progressed, the Radical government came under growing pressure from management, from rural landowners and livestock pro-

59. *Review of the River Plate*, Dec. 8, 1917, p. 1463; *La Vanguardia*, Dec. 11, 1917.

ducers, and from the liberal press to guarantee the "freedom of work."[60] The packing companies threatened to close their plants and shift operations to Uruguay and Brazil. The Rural Society warned of the threat posed by the strike to the entire national economy. And the English-language *Review of the River Plate* insisted that the strike was a plot by German agents bent on disrupting the Allied war effort. To a Radical government committed to the preservation of social stability and concerned over its electoral future, another source of pressure was the potential disruption of the meat supply to the whole Greater Buenos Aires region. The manager of the frigorífico "La Negra," the most important supplier of meat to the capital, alluded to that danger in a telegram to the national interventor (temporary governor) of the province of Buenos Aires on December 15. The government, he insisted, must provide adequate protection to those willing to work. "By doing so, at the same time that the sacred rights proclaimed by the Constitution will be made effective, Your Excellency will prevent its becoming necessary to close our establishment, an extreme measure, the consequences of which, so very grave for the supply of meat to the numerous centers of population in the Province as well as to the Federal Capital, cannot escape the intelligent comprehension of Your Excellency."[61]

In an effort to counter these pressures on the Radical government, the FORA polled its affiliates for approval, then publicly demanded an end to government partiality in the strike. If harassment of peaceful pickets and the technical support supplied by public forces within the plants and on the lighters did not end, the FORA said, it would call a general nationwide strike in support of the meatworkers. Bowing temporarily to this pressure, the government met with FORA delegates and in late December ordered the removal of any army and navy personnel in the plants and on lighters and instructed police to observe a neutral, circumspect attitude toward striking workers.

Within a few days, however, the government reneged on this pledge. Whether this turnabout is best understood in terms of the growing pressure of the Rural Society and its foreign allies (as Peter Smith argues), or in terms of the government's concern for its electoral future (as Rock con-

60. Peter Smith's pathbreaking study *Politics and Beef in Argentina* (New York, 1969) provides a wealth of information on the political forces at work in the Argentine export economy during the first half of the twentieth century. I have relied on Smith's work throughout this essay for much of the information on national politics and the meat industry. On the 1917-18 strike, see pp. 72-73.

61. *Review of the River Plate*, Dec. 21, 1917, p. (a)1529. A long list of the domestic butcher shops supplied by "La Negra" appears in an advertisement in the same newspaper, Jan. 4, 1918, p. 9. The other frigoríficos also sold a significant portion of their production in Argentina. Albert Hirschman first alerted me to the possibility that production for domestic consumption, as well as for export, might have important implications for the fate of labor organization in Argentina.

tends), the threatened general strike by the FORA did not materialize. Though the FORA leadership never offered a satisfactory explanation, the failure to call the general strike probably reflected the declining effectiveness of the meatworkers' strike and the consequent escalation of divisions between syndicalist, anarchist, and socialist partisans among the strike leaders.[62] By the last week in December, scab labor had already virtually defeated the strike in Berisso, and once the large plants there resumed production, the strike in Avellaneda was severely compromised. Although the struggle continued in Avellaneda for another full month, by the end of January strikers there, desperate and disillusioned, began to return to work by the hundreds.

As the strike ended, even anarchists, who customarily attributed strike defeats to the lack of courage and commitment of individual workers, rendered tribute to the strikers. "Fifty-seven days of struggle against the greed of the bourgeoisie and its allies have forced the workers to surrender at the meat-packing plant 'la Blanca.' Further resistance was impossible. . . . To speak of this defeat makes one angry and ashamed; I'm sorry comrades, but it is true. . . . Nevertheless, I must say that it was not because they were cowards or betrayed themselves; they fell beaten by impotence, under the brutal force of the bourgeois reaction."[63]

The syndicalist FORA's evaluation of the strike, contained in a circular sent to its affiliates, was more specific about the nature of the obstacles confronted by the meatworkers and the significance of their defeat. "In the history of the class struggle in Argentina, the meat-packing strike will stand out as one of the most inspiring episodes in the life of the labor movement. Arrayed against the workers were all kinds of enemies. And this strike, because of the nature of the industry in conflict, intimately linked as it is to the interests of a class which dominates the country economically and politically, has provoked against its protagonists the most brutal of reactions."[64]

But it was the *Review of the River Plate* that inadvertently pinpointed the structural cause of the defeat as it gloated over the resumption of production at the plants in Berisso at the end of December. "The strikes of the workmen of the Swift and Armour establishments are rapidly fizzling

62. See the vague discussion in Marotta, *El movimiento sindical* (cited in n. 24), vol. 2, p. 213, and the history of the strike written by José Elías Niclison, an inspector for the National Labor Department, in *Boletín del Departamento Nacional del Trabajo* 40 (Feb. 1919) and 41 (Apr. 1919).

63. *La Protesta*, Jan. 29, 1918, p. 3. A few days later, the same writer evoked the capitulation of strikers who had worked for "La Negra": "I write under the burden of defeat. I saw how this group of lions gave up the fight. It was a moment when the soul of the multitude gathered there seemed to break apart. Not a single complaint was heard. Not a voice. Only later did I see them crying out of rage and pain. They were men." *La Protesta*, Feb. 3, 1918, p. 2.

64. *Boletín del Departamento Nacional de Trabajo* 41 (Apr. 1919):63.

out. The Swift company now has 4,000 to 4,500 men working, which is about normal strength, although on occasion they have had to employ as many as 6,000 men. . . . The majority of the hands now employed at the Armour works are new and they are delighted at having been able to find employment." "It is significant to learn," the article concluded, "that the working conditions at both the Swift and Armour establishments are the same as they were before the strike."[65]

Meatworkers in 1917-18 confronted a combination of "enemies" superior in strength to those faced by most other sectors of the urban working class. These included the international meat-packing firms, with their great economic power and their mastery of strikebreaking techniques learned through long experience in the United States; the Rural Society, the most powerful interest group in Argentina, whose influence on (and high-level participation in) Argentine governments through the 1930's Peter Smith has amply documented; and the Radical government itself, which, although it waffled briefly under the threat of a general strike, used the armed forces to protect the packing companies from economic loss and employed its police power to stymie workers' efforts to stop strikebreakers from taking their jobs. It was the pool of unemployed workers, however, that gave these "enemies" their collective strength. Meatworkers struggled valiantly to overcome this structural obstacle to which they, more than most Argentine urban workers, were tragically vulnerable.[66] Their inability to stem the tide of scab labor presaged their defeat, as it did the fate of the whole organized Argentine labor movement in the postwar period.

Within a few months of the victory over the meatworkers, capitalists organized to tap the pool of unemployed workers in a more rational, efficient manner. Their goal was to break the back of all militant labor organizations in the country. In May 1918, a leading estanciero and shipping magnate called foreign and domestic capitalists together at a meeting endorsed by the Rural Society and held at the Buenos Aires Stock Exchange. Those present included representatives of the meat-packing, railway, maritime, and grain-exporting industries. The meeting produced an organization called the National Labor Association, whose aim was to thwart the possibility of a general strike and protect the "freedom of work." With funding from member organizations (each was to contribute one percent of its total wage bill), the Association founded a Labor Exchange designed to provide workers to firms in search of compliant

65. *Review of the River Plate*, Dec. 28, 1917, p. 1569.
66. It may also be true that because many meatworkers were recently arrived foreigners, they were less able than most urban workers to find the financial resources among family and community to sustain a long strike. This consideration may help to explain the longer resistance of strikers in Avellaneda, an older, more established immigrant community than Berisso.

labor. Shipley has documented the magnitude of the Exchange's activities over the next years; tens of thousands of workers were located through its offices, many of them hired to replace militants fired for union activities. All industries were affected by the services of the Labor Exchange, but its primary impact was first to destroy the militant base of the railroad workers' FOF, and then to break the control of the FOM over the maritime labor market.[67]

At the same time that foreign and domestic capitalists organized so effectively to manipulate the labor market to their advantage, they helped orchestrate and bankroll a broad political and ideological offensive against labor and the left. As the postwar mobilization of Argentine labor reached its peak—fueled by severe domestic inflation, the news of the Bolshevik Revolution in Russia, and word of mass strikes in Western Europe—government repression and the antilabor activities of right-wing paramilitary and propaganda groups intensified. In early January 1919, police shootings of four striking metalworkers precipitated large-scale rioting in Buenos Aires. The FORA called a general strike to protest the shootings, but events soon escaped its control. For several days bands of anarchist workers and unorganized working-class youths battled with police and government troops and looted stores. These disturbances, known as the *semana trágica*, resulted in the worst repression of labor yet seen in Argentina. Hundreds of workers were killed and wounded, thousands arrested. As the repression began, government forces were joined by right-wing civilian groups that rampaged through working-class districts attacking union halls, working-class newspapers, and immigrants, especially Russian Jews. The reestablishment of public order and the settlement of the strike did not end the repression. In subsequent months, under pressure from the right, the government invoked the alien and sedition acts to arrest and deport hundreds of suspected labor activists, especially anarchists.[68]

As it had earlier in the century, the successful repression of labor in the postwar period made concessions to the organized working class through corporativist labor reform unnecessary in Argentina. As early as 1902, following the great anarchist-led general strike of that year, such legislation was in fact proposed. Drafted by the Conservative government's minister of the interior, Joaquín B. González, the proposed labor reform was similar in scope and intent to the laws promulgated in Chile in 1924-25. It would have established the legal basis for government regulation of

67. Shipley, "On the Outside Looking In" (cited in n. 33), Chap. 10.

68. A good narrative that stresses the insurrectionary anarchist component of the strike is Julio Godio, *La Semana Trágica de enero de 1919* (Buenos Aires, 1972); David Rock, "Lucha civil en la Argentina," *Desarrollo Económico* 42-44 (July 1971–Mar. 1972):165-215, emphasizes the weakness of worker organization during the whole affair.

work conditions, of labor organization, and of conflicts between capital and labor. Unions whose statutes conformed to guidelines designed to ensure nonrevolutionary, moderate activities would be legally recognized and become eligible for government subsidies to further the education and material well-being of their members. Strikes were to be managed through long and complicated mediation and arbitration procedures administered by tripartite labor courts composed of representatives of capital, government, and labor. Failure to comply with arbitrated settlements would result in fines. The legislation envisioned government inspection of work conditions and plant safety. It called for accident compensation and pension plans. Although the González labor code was endorsed by two Argentine presidents, it was opposed by most capitalists and organized workers, and was never debated in congress. In 1919 labor legislation similar in intent was introduced in congress by elements of the Radical Party. Although this initiative also received the endorsement of the president, it was also opposed by labor and was promptly forgotten as soon as the postwar strike wave receded.[69]

The Radical governments of the 1920's, however, did deal piecemeal and in corporativist fashion with the one sector of Argentine labor that achieved significant organizational success and demonstrated its strategic importance and revolutionary potential—the railway workers. Beginning with the settlement of the huge nationwide strike of 1917, the government assiduously promoted reformist leadership of railway unions and held out tangible legal and material benefits in exchange for worker discipline and political moderation. These Radical initiatives were possible because of a new spirit of compromise among railway owners and managers sobered by the extent of their losses during the strikes of 1917 and 1918 and shaken by the prospect of revolutionary leadership of a nationwide union. The initiatives eventually won support among rank-and-file workers, in part because of the effectiveness of continuing government repression of strikes after 1917 and because of the success of management, aided by the Labor Exchange, in destroying the militant base of the FOF.

The result of all these conditions was the consolidation of a new reformist railway workers' union, the Unión Ferroviaria. The new union benefited from a familiar corporativist trade-off, which has been carefully analyzed in complementary studies by Paul Goodwin and Heidi Goldberg. Through government initiatives, railroad workers gradually won higher wages, pension plans, vacations, sick pay, and legal representation

69. Iscaro, *Historia* (cited in n. 52), Part 3, pp. 123-24, 185-86; Spalding, *La clase trabajadora* (cited in n. 33), p. 554; Rock, *Politics in Argentina* (cited in n. 32), p. 198. The text of the legislation appears in Joaquín V. González, *Obras completas* (Buenos Aires, 1955), vol. 6, pp. 401-578.

before the companies and special government arbitration panels. The railroad companies, with government acquiescence, were allowed to pass new labor costs on to consumers. They also benefited from a union-disciplined labor force. Labor discipline was achieved by the union after it destroyed the decentralized decision-making and free and vigorous discussion cherished by the old anarcho-syndicalist leadership of the FOF. The Unión Ferroviaria featured full-time officials paid by mandatory union dues, strict bureaucratic procedures, control over internal communications, censorship of the union newspaper, punishment of dissent, and extreme centralization of decision-making. Basking in its legal status and able to deliver tangible material benefits to workers, the Unión Ferroviaria increased its membership to 70,000 dues-paying members by the mid-1920's. Its members accounted for almost two-thirds of the entire organized work force in Argentina during the late 1920's.[70] The railway labor legislation was an exception in Argentine labor law, however. Despite the continuing formal commitment of elements of the Radical Party to comprehensive legislation designed to curb the class potential of labor and integrate it, in corporativist fashion, into the legal and institutional fabric of the nation, it was not until the 1940's, under Perón's leadership, that such legislation became a reality.[71]

The institutional response to labor organization in Argentina in the early twentieth century was thus very different from the response in Chile. The contrast illustrates not, as some would have it, the progressive nature of the Chilean political elite or the reactionary quality of the Argentine ruling class. It reveals, rather, the congenital weakness of the early Argentine labor movement. Despite its precocious development, the Argentine labor movement never expanded into the most vital sectors of the Argentine economy. Labor organization never seriously threatened the primary process of capitalist accumulation in rural export production presided over by the Argentine ruling class. Nor did it succeed in forging important or enduring organizations in the major industry in Argentina's export economy, the foreign-owned meat-processing plants. During the first two decades of the century, with the partial and temporary exception of transport workers, labor organization was confined to

70. Paul Goodwin carefully explores the changing relationship between the railroad unions, the Radical government, and the British railroad companies in his *British-owned Railroads and the Unión Cívica Radical* (Buenos Aires, 1974). Goldberg's institutional history (cited in n. 41) follows the transformation from within the evolving railroad unions.

71. Alfredo N. Morrone, *El derecho obrero y el Presidente Yrigoyen* (Buenos Aires, 1928), lamented the continuing lack of such legislation (pp. 110-11): "Well known is the absence of a statute to regulate trade unions in our society. There is no law that deals with the particular characteristics of these associations. [There is no law] to give them legal standing and legal responsibilities."

urban activities of secondary importance to the national economy. There, the vigor and numerical strength of labor organizations were undeniable, but enduring organization of the working class as a whole was gravely undermined by structural features of Argentine society that the ruling class successfully manipulated to maintain its overwhelming advantage.

This overview of the early Argentine labor movement has emphasized the specific weaknesses of those elements of the labor force that managed to forge an autonomous vision of their place and mission in society and build effective collective organizations. In the absence of organizational possibilities in export production itself, urban labor formed the backbone of the early Argentine labor movement. But given the attractiveness of the Argentine urban economy to transatlantic and internal migrants—workers who flocked to the dynamic coastal cities of the pampa in search of relatively high-paying jobs—the organizational potential of even this sector of the working class was fatally compromised.

But the political combativeness and cultural autonomy of the entire Argentine urban working class was also undermined in more general material and cultural ways. Workers in the large coastal cities may have lived segregated by class in miserable housing, but they were surrounded by the impressive physical evidence of Argentine material progress. They may have had access to working-class newspapers and cultural institutions, but they were bombarded daily by the information, analysis, and values propagated by the liberal press, the public schools, and the Catholic Church. Argentine workers struggled for existence in an urban economy plagued by chronic unemployment. But enterprising families were able to invest savings in real estate, commerce, and services. There was a possibility for social mobility in the steadily expanding economy of the Argentine coastal cities that was almost totally absent, for example, in the Chilean north. Argentine workers were often laid off or fired for individual or collective transgressions of capital's "prerogatives," but in Argentina cyclical downturns were never severe, and work, however unpalatable, could usually be found in the vast and variegated urban economies of the coast. The collective vulnerability of workers in an irrational capitalist marketplace, so obvious in the Chilean nitrate zone—and, by extension, in the whole of Chilean society—was attenuated in Argentina. As a result, individual misfortune could more plausibly be explained as personal inadequacy in Argentina. That was precisely the explanation insisted upon by mainstream culture.

As it strove to rationalize and legitimize its position through the creation and manipulation of widely shared cultural values, the Argentine ruling class was able to appropriate the issue of patriotism and turn it against the revolutionary, largely immigrant, working class. Carl Solberg has shown how, in contrast to Chilean developments, nationalism in Argentina developed along cultural, not economic lines. Established groups and middle-class elements blamed foreigners for all the social ills that blighted the bright image of Argentine development and progress. These attitudes were focused on the early-twentieth-century labor movement. The Argentine establishment contemplated revolutionary labor with studied disbelief and patriotic outrage. Anticapitalist workers were irrational, irresponsible, un-Argentine. Workers enjoyed virtually unlimited opportunity in Argentina; their revolutionary nonconformity was a product of European social problems and ideologies inappropriate to Argentine reality. By the first decades of the twentieth century elements of the Chilean ruling and middle classes were already writing books—for example, Francisco Encina's *Nuestra inferioridad económica* (Santiago, 1912) and Ricardo Latcham's *Chuquicamata, estado yankee* (Santiago, 1926)—that questioned the pattern and future viability of Chilean economic and social development and emphasized the dangers and abuses to labor of foreign capital in mineral production. By contrast, although the Argentine establishment had begun to doubt its own ability to control the burgeoning new society its policies had helped to fashion, it applauded the theme of ex-president Carlos A. Pellegrini's 1911 classic, *The Argentine in the Twentieth Century*. Argentina possessed the capacity to become "one of the greatest nations of the earth." The only conceivable obstacle to progress, it seemed, was the nonconformist, unpatriotic, revolutionary immigrant working class. To remove that obstacle, in the name of patriotism and continued material progress, the Argentine ruling elites found a powerful, very effective tool in the alien and sedition acts.[72]

In sum, the spectacular and largely uninterrupted growth and development of the Argentine economy reinforced the cultural and ideological hegemony of the Argentine ruling class. It was hard to argue with success. By and large the middle class did not. The Radical Party never challenged the principles of liberal political economy championed by the ruling class and its foreign allies. Its impulses toward labor reform and social justice were quickly abandoned under the pressure of capitalists and the reality of electoral politics in which the ballots of the nonvoting insurgent working class did not figure. But even the revolutionary organizations of the workers found it difficult to universalize their indictment of capitalism. Railway workers had some temporary success in casting their

72. Carl Solberg, *Immigration and Nationalism, Argentina and Chile, 1890–1914* (Austin, Tex., 1970). Gladys S. Onega, *La immigración en la literatura argentina* (Buenos Aires, 1969). Shipley assembles a mass of quantitative information to illustrate the gap between the "myth" of Argentine economic and social development and the reality of the material and social conditions confronted by the working class in the decades before 1930.

demands in broader national terms, but even they were vulnerable to charges of disrupting the smoothly functioning motor of national development—of "killing the goose that lays the golden eggs," as one apologist for the status quo put it. In short, for structural reasons, the anticapitalist vision of the revolutionary Argentine working class held little appeal for other elements of Argentine society.

The cultural dependency of Argentine workers, reinforced by the structure and developmental success of the Argentine export economy, is easily discerned in the reformist ideology and consumerist activities of the Socialist Party. Significantly—and in stark contrast with the Chilean socialists—only a small fraction of Argentine socialists split from the party in 1918 and eventually joined the Third International. It was the reformist social-democratic majority that inherited control of the major surviving Argentine union in the 1920's, the Unión Ferroviaria. And it was the reformist Socialist Party, not the newly formed Communist Party, that, largely on the basis of worker votes, became a major electoral force in Buenos Aires during that decade.

Clues to the cultural dependency of the Argentine workers can also be found in the evolution of the most famous expression of popular urban culture in Argentina, the tango. The tango has preserved the rhythms, and some of the instrumentation, of the original forms working people created in the tenements and bars of the ports of the La Plata Basin after the turn of the century. Once its lyrics began to be written down and recorded after the First World War, the tango also preserved, often in highly poetic form, the working-class dialect, *lunfardo*, which Italians and immigrants from other parts of the world created out of a Spanish base to express their collective values and perceptions. The tango has never lost the aura of melancholy that led its greatest composer and lyricist, Enrique Santos Discépolo, to define it as "a sad thought that is danced." But the lyrics of tangos, unlike those of jazz, the music to which it is often compared, contain little that reveals the consciousness of workers as a class. Tango themes have preserved a preoccupation with mother and lover, with the meaning of life and death, with human perfidy and vengeance. They exude a nostalgia for place and time, and for the once incomparable nightlife of Buenos Aires. All these themes are traceable, at least in part, to the experience of the predominantly single, male, immigrant community in the large cities of Argentina and Uruguay that created the music. But the subject of work and the perception of class are totally absent from the tango. Tangos are pessimistic about the human condition, fatalistic about the outcome of human problems. At least in terms of its lyrics, the tango after 1920 expresses the emasculation of the Argentine urban working class: its proletarian forms finally appropriated and adapted by the middle and upper class *after* they had first been sanctioned in Paris; its greatest interpreter, Carlos Gardel, exhibited as a kind of musical Horatio Alger.[73]

    The history of the Argentine labor movement from 1900 to 1930 is unique and historically specific, but its outcome, evident in the 1920's, is not exceptional. In other capitalist societies, such as the United States, the "heroic" phase of labor mobilization gave way, following the repression of the immediate postwar years, to a period of relative worker quiescence and ideological conformity to mainstream cultural values.[74] In those societies like Argentina where vigorous economic growth resumed after the war, where real wages rose, and where the left was weak, liberal governments were able to contend with the challenge of organized labor through piecemeal corporativist reforms. In such societies labor forced no breakdown of political institutions and stability, and won no major institutional concessions. In South America it was Chile that was the major exception to this pattern before 1930.

    With the onset of the Great Depression, however, hints of Argentina's own historical exceptionalism first appeared, and in the course of the next half century a pattern of historical events set Argentina adrift from developments in the world capitalist system. The story of Argentine exceptionalism after 1930 is replete with irony and ends in tragedy. The labor movement plays the leading role.

The Anomalous Course of Argentine History

    After 1930 Argentina evolved politically in a manner fundamentally at odds with trends in the capitalist world economy. In the 1930's capitalist governments all over the world were forced to abandon formally the

73. The literature on the tango—next to beef, Argentina's most famous export—is vast. Argentine preoccupation with the tango, as with the gaucho, is itself a measure of a deeply fragmented national culture. Perhaps the best essay on the subject is Ernesto Sábato, *Tango. Discusión y clave* (Buenos Aires, 1963). Darío Cantón categorizes the themes of Gardel's tangos in "El mundo de los tangos de Gardel," *Revista Latinoamericana de Sociología* 69:3 (Nov. 1969):341-62. Discépolo's tangos are conveniently collected in the *Enrique Santos Discépolo cancionero* (Buenos Aires, 1977). Historians have failed to explore the relationship between the tango and working-class culture and politics. Judith Evans suggested the possibilities in a provocative oral presentation at the American Historical Association Annual Meeting, Washington, D.C., 1980.

74. Hobart Spalding has demonstrated the general similarities between the development of the labor movement in Europe, the United States, and Latin America in the twentieth century. The term "heroic" is his. Despite fundamental differences in economic structure and function in the world capitalist system, both the United States and Argentina shared two important characteristics during the period of capitalist expansion before 1930: dramatic economic and social development and large-scale foreign immigration into the work force. Both characteristics undermined the development of working-class consciousness and effective labor organization.

principles of laissez-faire liberal political economy and make concessions to the working class.[75] In Latin America, new political coalitions representing social groups and interests broader than the narrow export-import elite that had dominated politics before 1930 came to power. These new governments gradually jettisoned the principles of free trade and comparative advantage. Increasingly, they sought to solve the domestic economic and social crisis they faced through social-welfare programs and state intervention in the economy to promote industrial development. Although in practice Argentine governments in the 1930's were not immune to any of these trends (particularly in the economic sphere), their formal policies (especially toward political and social issues) moved resolutely against the tide of Western history.

The world economic crisis and the nature of Argentine government policies after 1930 nurtured the second great mobilization of Argentine workers and greatly influenced the ideological and political direction that mobilization took in the 1940's. The form and timing of labor's integration into national life under Perón in turn ensured that Argentina would participate only marginally in the great expansion of world capitalism in the decades following the Second World War. Peronist labor stymied the postwar capitalist project of the Argentine ruling class and its allies abroad. But it also thwarted the socialist potential of the Argentine working class. The result, painfully evident by the 1960's, was a tragic social stalemate viciously presided over by military force.

Understanding of the last half century of Argentine history must begin with the military-civilian coup of September 1930. The coup toppled the Radical government and in short order returned those who controlled the export economy to direct political power for the first time since 1916. In important respects these events turned back the clock on the political and social evolution of the nation. In order to maintain themselves in power in the 1930's, the conservative regimes were forced to resort to large-scale electoral fraud. For almost twenty years before 1930 members of the urban middle class had used the electoral power of the Radical Party in a democratic polity to influence some areas of public policy. More important, they had used the ballot to gain access to government jobs in a bureaucracy the party labored constantly to expand. After 1930 that access to politics was cut off. Political access was also denied the urban working class, which by 1930 included hundreds of thousands of Argentine citizens and voters. More significant for workers, however, was

75. As noted in Chapter One, Karl Polanyi was the first to recognize the scope and to develop the cultural implications of this momentous change. See *The Great Transformation* (New York, 1944).

the impact of government social policies in an era of economic crisis. Many workers, who had learned in the 1920's to content themselves with the benefits of rising real wages and the advantages of bread-and-butter unionism in an expanding capitalist economy, now saw those arrangements threatened. But as worker nonconformity grew, the conservative regimes dusted off the repressive measures perfected earlier in the century and began once more to apply them with vigor against the labor militants.

The reactionary political and social policies of Argentine governments in the 1930's were complemented by a brazen attempt by export-import interests to maintain the international economic arrangements that had fostered Argentina's spectacular development in the decades before the Depression. The cornerstone of these efforts was the Roca-Runciman Pact of 1933. In that agreement the government sought to preserve the British market for Argentine chilled beef by making extravagant concessions to British capital. British manufactures and fuels were given preferential access to the Argentine market and British investors were granted special guarantees and opportunities. In reality, this formal commitment to the old international division of labor was subverted by other types of government policies that sought to protect and promote Argentine economic interests in a world in crisis. Policies such as the abandonment of the gold standard, the devaluation of the currency, the establishment of multiple exchange rates, and the extension of credit for agricultural and industrial diversification were practical responses to the world Depression primarily designed to serve the interests of the pampean elite. But they also helped transform the structure of the Argentine economy by promoting the process of import-substituting industrialization. The remarkable growth of Argentine industry in the 1930's and early 1940's led to large-scale rural-urban migration, greatly expanded the size of the industrial working class, and increased the importance and influence of foreign and domestic manufacturing interests.[76]

76. Roca-Runciman is analyzed within the broad historical context of Argentine-British trade in Jorge G. Fodor and Arturo A. O'Connell in "La Argentina y la economía atlántica en la primera mitad del siglo XX," *Desarrollo Económico* 13:49 (Apr.-June 1973):3-66. In a provocative essay, "Crecimiento industrial y alianza de clases in la Argentina (1930-1940)," Miguel Murmis and Juan Carlos Portantiero argue that once Roca-Runciman provided protection for the basic interests of the most powerful livestock producers within the landed class, those producers used their control of the state to promote a modest policy of industrialization. Industry would take up the slack in a depressed export sector and contribute to the overall health and smooth functioning of the entire national economy during the world crisis. Most of the opposition to these initiatives came initially from provincial landowners and livestock producers whose interests were not protected by the concessions made to the British to protect the chilled beef market. The essay appears in their *Estudios sobre los orígenes del peronismo* (Buenos Aires, 1971), pp. 3-55. Here lies an important clue to the social and economic origins of the nationalist critique of cosmopolitan liberalism voiced by dissident conservatives (most important among them the Irazusta brothers) and Progressive Demo-

In Argentina, however, these important economic and social changes were not reflected in complementary political and institutional reforms. In this respect, Argentine government policies in the 1930's became an anomaly in the Western world. In other countries, political regimes felt compelled to mobilize the popular frustration behind statist solutions to the social and political crisis of the capitalist order. These solutions, nominally liberal (as in the United States), or formally corporatist (as in the fascist regimes of Europe), involved real concessions to the organized workers. They were echoed in all the major Latin American countries except Argentina. The Argentine ruling class increasingly relied on the action of the state to promote its own economic interests in the 1930's. For example, it established regulating boards to limit the production of rural commodities and raise the domestic price of meat, cereals, sugar, and wine. But it made no major ideological, political, or social concessions to popular forces at any time throughout the world crisis.

This posture was neither especially cynical nor stupid. Rather, it reflected the uncontested ideological and political hegemony of a class that had presided over the phenomenal development of Argentina's peripheral economy before 1930. That hegemony remained intact throughout the 1930's because of the ideological dependence and institutional disarray of popular forces at the start of the crisis. It was reinforced by the continuing viability and adaptiveness of the Argentine export economy throughout the Depression.

One measure of the ideological and institutional weakness of popular forces in Argentina after 1930 was the fate of the Radical Party. That party was a testament to the precocious early development of capitalism in Argentina. Its ascension to power in 1916 set Argentina apart from most other Latin American nations. Its middle-class social composition attested to the growing differentiation of Argentine urban society fostered by the expansion of the export economy. Its ideology and policies championed liberal democratic political forms, but revealed a studied reluctance to challenge the fundamental values and interests of the Argentine ruling class.

After 1916 the Radical Party functioned primarily as a vehicle providing urban professionals and white-collar workers access to an expanding state bureaucracy. Funded primarily by indirect taxes that weighed heavily on working-class consumption, the growth of the bureaucracy was easily tolerated by the ruling class during the long period of economic

crats (whose spokesman was Lisandro de la Torre). The right-wing economic nationalism of the former, which found its inspiration in Catholic corporativist thought, is cogently developed in Julio and Rodolfo Irazusta's influential *La Argentina y el imperialismo británico* (Buenos Aires, 1934). De la Torre's valiant congressional crusade against what he saw as the unholy alliance behind the organization of the meat trade is summarized in his *Las carnes argentinas y el monopolio extranjero* (Buenos Aires, 1947).

expansion before 1930. Many functions of the civilian and military bureaucracy—its role in socializing the young and repressing dissent paramount among them—directly served the interests of capital. As long as
Radical initiatives did not threaten the basic interests of the landholders
(the fitful talk of land reform did not), or curb the prerogatives of foreign
investors (only in the area of oil policy, especially at the end of the 1920's,
did that seem possible); as long as the Radical government preserved public order and kept organized labor in check (a task it learned to perform
very effectively in the years after the First World War), it was tolerated by
the Argentine ruling class. Indeed, the fact that a "reformist," "popular,"
"democratic" party governed helped legitimate the Argentine political
system and the capitalist social arrangements it presided over. And the
relative separation of the economic elite from the squabbles and corruption of day-to-day politics helped preserve its ideological and social
prestige.

With the advent of the world crisis in 1929, however, the needs of the
dominant landowning class changed and the Radical government became
the target of the general social frustration generated by the Depression.
Significantly, that frustration was focused on the political ineffectiveness
of the Radical government; it did not involve a general critical reassessment of the liberal economic principles that had promoted Argentine development so well before 1930 under conservative and Radical governments alike. The crisis demanded concerted action to deal with shrinking
government revenues and sagging Argentine export earnings. The Radical government reacted with customary ideological fuzziness, policy
confusion, and bureaucratic inertia. As public opposition to the government escalated, budgetary constraints undermined the clientelist basis of
the Radicals' traditional support.[77]

77. These considerations help to account for the controversy over the alleged personalism
and senility of Radical President Hipólito Yrigoyen. The best introduction to the coup itself
is the special issue of the *Revista de Historia* devoted to it, 3 (1958). Especially valuable are
the articles by Roberto Etchepareborda, "Aspectos políticos de la crisis de 1930," pp. 7-40,
and Ricardo M. Ortiz, "El aspecto económico-social de la crisis de 1930," pp. 41-72. Peter
Smith downplays the economic and fiscal impact of the Depression in favor of a political
explanation in *Argentina and the Failure of Democracy* (Madison, Wisc., 1974). Yet the economic and fiscal crisis was significant and the opposition of the Rural Society to the Radical
government real. The value of Argentine exports fell from 953,743,939 gold pesos in 1929
to 614,104,180 in 1930; imports fell from 861,997,355 gold pesos to 739,182,744 in the same
period (Great Britain, Department of Overseas Trade, *Economic Conditions in the Argentine
Republic, 1931* [London, 1932], Appendix V, p. 140). Whereas federal expenditures increased by 22 percent between 1928 and 1930, government revenues declined in the same
period by 10 percent; the result was a growing budgetary deficit: 214.9 million pesos in
1929, 357.0 in 1930. (República Argentina, Dirección General de Finanzas, *El ajuste de los
resultados financieros de los ejercicios de 1928 a 1936* [Buenos Aires, 1937], p. 35.) At the opening
of the annual cattle exposition of the Sociedad Rural on August 31, 1930, the Radical minister of agriculture was greeted with catcalls and whistling and was unable to finish his
speech. One reason for this hostility was the Radical government's failure to name an Ar-

Unlike what happened in most Latin American countries, then, in Argentina the world crisis weakened and discredited a supposedly reformist party of the middle class, not the traditional conservative vehicles of a ruling class in control of the export economy. The Argentine ruling class survived the initial shock of the Depression with its cultural and political hegemony intact. The middle-class Radical Party was discredited and forced to shoulder domestic blame for the international crisis. When the Radicals fell from power, the ruling class confronted no major obstacle in the way of its resumption of direct political management of Argentine society.

No element of the labor movement was able to mount effective resistance to the antidemocratic politics and liberal economic policies of the Argentine elite during the 1930's. The Socialist Party, like the Radicals, protested the political repression and the social policies of the conservative governments. Both parties, however, were ideological prisoners of the cosmopolitan liberal economic principles used effectively to justify the policies of conservative governments during the 1930's. These liberal principles—the belief in Argentina's comparative advantage and unlimited economic potential in a capitalist world division of labor, the faith in the benefits to the nation of an unrestricted flow of foreign capital, labor, and technology—coincided completely with the class interests of Argentine landowners and their foreign allies. But the growth of Argentina's livestock and cereal export economy had also promoted the rapid economic development of Argentine society and had gradually improved the material condition of most of its members. So wide and deep was the consensus over liberal economic principles that no social group proved capable of challenging the ideological foundation of the reactionary governments at the start of the 1930's. And as long as the validity of liberal economic theory remained unquestioned, its class content went unmasked, and its antinational, antidevelopmental implications in an international capitalist system in crisis remained obscured.

But the Argentine establishment could not for long expect the whole of Argentine society to view a world in crisis through the narrow lens of ruling-class interests. True, the capacity of the Argentine export economy to adapt to the world crisis initially shielded the dominant elites from fundamental criticism of their costly efforts to preserve their eco-

gentine ambassador to the United States at a time when livestock interests pinned great hope on developing a U.S. market for Argentine meat. These broader political and economic issues subsume the more concrete—but still cloudy—role that U.S. petroleum interests and their friends among the Argentine conspirators played in the coup. An intelligent recent discussion, buttressed by new research on this perennial question in modern Argentine historiography, is Carlos A. Mayo, Osvaldo Andino, and Fernando García Molina, *Diplomacia política y petróleo en la Argentina* (Buenos Aires, 1976). See also Carl Solberg, *Oil and Nationalism in Argentina* (Stanford, Calif., 1979).

nomic position. But the logic of that adaptation and the nature of those efforts ultimately called the ideological hegemony of liberal economic theory into question and laid its class content bare.

It was not the organized labor movement that performed this crucial ideological task in Argentina. Its ideological autonomy, independent political trajectory, and organizational strength had been destroyed in the early 1920's. Although competing factions led by socialists and syndicalists coalesced soon after the 1930 coup to form a new labor central, the Confederación General de Trabajadores (CGT), that organization, throughout the 1930's, played a minor and largely defensive role in the life of the nation. Dominated by the moderate socialist and syndicalist leadership of the railroad workers' unions, the CGT sought to preserve the organizational and material gains won in the 1920's through accommodation with employers and the conservative governments. But as railroad construction ceased, as competition with automobile and truck traffic increased, and as the railway companies dismissed employees during the Depression, the accommodationist leadership firmly entrenched in the Unión Ferroviaria watched its bread-and-butter strategy slowly fall apart. The union leadership was forced to accept one concession after another and ended by alienating much of its rank and file. Still, until the early 1940's the railway workers' union leadership continued to dominate the policies of the CGT. Despite escalating criticism by some of its fledgling affiliate unions, many of them led by more militant socialists and communists, the CGT leadership refused during the Depression to adopt aggressive policies to organize the growing army of industrial workers. Meanwhile, its moderate leadership helped stifle the spread of Marxist ideologies within the labor movement. Without the material and moral support of workers organized in the CGT, government repression of militant Marxist labor activists was highly effective. In addition to constant harassment of militant labor organizations—the closing of the union halls, the jailing of leaders—the conservative governments applied the alien and sedition acts to deport as many as 400 labor activists a year during the mid-1930's. Only toward the end of the decade did the determined efforts of these militant labor organizations, especially those of the communists, begin to yield organizational fruit.[78]

Unlike what happened in Chile during the world crisis, then, in Argentina the ideological and piecemeal institutional compromises that resolved the post–First World War mobilization of labor worked against the efforts of Marxist labor leaders and parties in the 1930's. Whereas the

78. Much of this analysis depends on detailed studies by Horoschi Matsushita, *Movimiento obrero Argentino 1930-1945* (Buenos Aires, 1983), and David Tamarin, "The Argentine Labor Movement in an Age of Transition, 1930-1945" (Ph.D. diss., University of Washington, 1977). The estimate of deportations appears in Tamarin, p. 156.

Chilean left capitalized on the corporativist labor laws of the 1920's and turned them to the class advantage of labor, Marxist labor militants in Argentina faced an uphill struggle against both national legislation that effectively repressed their organizational efforts and an entrenched accommodationist labor leadership that refused to support them.

The institutional barriers confronted by the left in Argentina were effective because of the broader structural economic and ideological constraints faced by Marxist labor organizers. Although the unemployment problem was not as severe as in Chile at the onset of the Depression, the crisis having temporarily cut off immigration of foreign workers into the country, the downturn in economic activity and the unemployment it caused continued to threaten effective job actions. It was not until the upturn in economic activity in the middle of the decade and, especially, the years of booming wartime demand and postwar inflation that strike activity reached large-scale proportions in Argentina once again. Difficult to measure, but probably more important to the failure of Marxist ideological and organizational efforts, was the continuing hegemony of liberal values. The hold of these values over the Argentine middle class and much of the organized labor movement doomed the efforts of labor and political activists to forge the class alliances vital to labor's struggle. Whereas important elements among white-collar workers and professionals came to adopt an anticapitalist vision of national problems in Chile, these groups in Argentina remained captive to ruling-class cultural values and liberal political economy. Before 1930 members of these groups in Argentina proved receptive to right-wing cultural nationalism, which turned their social frustrations and patriotic sentiments away from a critical assessment of capitalist society and focused them on the disruptive, anticapitalist organizations of the immigrant working class. After 1930 the growing appeal of economic nationalism to elements of the middle class reveals a more subtle difference between comparable developments in Chile.

Unlike the economic nationalism spread by the Marxist left to other sectors of Chilean society over the course of the twentieth century, the economic nationalism that slowly developed in Argentina was not an anticapitalist ideology. It did not emerge out of the struggle of the working class, nor was it propagated by the unions and political parties of the workers' movement as it was in Chile. Argentine economic nationalism focused its critique not on the social basis of ruling-class power, but rather on the legitimacy of the cosmopolitan liberal oligarchy that exercised political dominion over Argentine society. Several currents developed within the broad tradition of Argentine economic nationalism, but the most popular and influential was articulated in the 1930's by disaffected middle-class intellectuals and spread by the cultural organizations they founded to revitalize the program of the Radical Party and shape it into a vehicle capable of forging a new Argentina free of foreign influence.[79]

In content and appeal, this Argentine economic nationalism was the ideological expression of the anomalous course of Argentine political developments during the 1930's. It spoke to the special psychological and material needs of a middle class cut off from access to politics. Its growing appeal to that class—and to other social groups—mirrored the grossly unequal power of the major classes in Argentine society during the Depression. The arrogant policies of a ruling class unrestrained by alternative ideologies and popular organizations provided the new economic nationalism with its subject matter and suggested its most powerful insights. The ideological subordination and organizational weakness of the working class relieved it of popular competitors and enabled it to ignore organized labor in its plan for national reorganization.

Out of their perceptions of Argentine political reality in the 1930's, middle-class economic nationalists forged a very sophisticated understanding of the distortions of Argentine development caused by the country's historic integration into a world capitalist system as a producer of primary commodities. That process, they argued, had saddled the nation with an agricultural and livestock monoculture and had stunted its industrial development; it had led to extreme dependence on foreign capital that siphoned economic surplus abroad; it had ensconced *vendepatria* (country-selling) landowners and native sepoys subservient to foreign capital in political power and corrupted the democratic process; it had perverted *criollo* (national) culture; it had ignored legitimate social demands of the bulk of the Argentine people; it had impoverished the prov-

79. On the broad question of right-wing nationalism in Argentina, including its cultural and corporatist expressions before 1930, see the excellent synthesis by Marysa Navarro Gerassi, *Los nacionalistas* (Buenos Aires, 1968). Enrique Zuleta Alvarez's *El nacionalismo argentino* (2 vols.; Buenos Aires, 1975) emphasizes the contribution of the Irazusta brothers and their followers to right-wing nationalist thought and politics. Sandra McGee explores the social and ideological appeal of right-wing nationalist organizations before 1930 in her "The Social Origins of Counterrevolution in Argentina, 1900-1932" (Ph.D. diss., University of Florida, 1979). The nationalist current singled out for emphasis here coalesced in 1935 around the Federación de Orientación Radical de la Joven Argentina (FORJA). The account that follows of the social origins, ideology, and political impact of this group relies heavily on the sophisticated study by Mark Falcoff, "Argentine Nationalism on the Eve of Perón" (Ph.D. diss., Princeton University, 1970). The leader of the FORJA, Arturo Jauretche, provides a sample of the group's attitudes, activities, and style in his *FORJA y la década infame* (Buenos Aires, 1962), one of many publications he wrote in the 1960's and 1970's. The most distinguished intellectual associated with the group was the novelist-turned-historian Raúl Scalabrini Ortiz. The malaise he felt at the start of the 1930's is expressed in his *El hombre que está solo y espera* (Buenos Aires, 1931); his most famous historical works are *Historia de los ferrocarriles argentinos* (Buenos Aires, 1940) and *Política británica en el Río de la Plata* (Buenos Aires, 1965).

inces to the benefit of Buenos Aires; it had, in sum, subverted Argentina's great potential to become the leading nation in Latin America.

This fundamental reinterpretation of Argentine history challenged the liberal ideological hegemony of the Argentine ruling class. Because it eloquently and convincingly rationalized and universalized their plight in the 1930's, it proved especially attractive to Argentine students, intellectuals, professionals, military men, and white-collar employees. But it also eventually won adherents among other social groups: among landowners and businessmen who did not benefit directly from government policies in an economy undergoing radical change yet growing very slowly in the aggregate; among workers disillusioned with the effectiveness of both the accommodationist and the confrontational tactics of their leaders.

In the struggle for ideological dominion over Argentine society, middle-class economic nationalism enjoyed considerable advantages. It did not directly challenge the capitalist ideology of the ruling class, but only those cosmopolitan liberal aspects of it that provided such vulnerable targets during the crisis of the world system. Nor was it susceptible to the charge—manipulated tirelessly and effectively by the establishment against the Marxist left—that it was a foreign ideology, imported by unpatriotic immigrants and Soviet agents, inappropriate to Argentine reality. Middle-class economic nationalists used this charge to discredit both the Marxist left *and* the liberal and fascist elements on their right. Given the adherence of the Argentine Communist Party to the violent policy oscillations of the Comintern in the 1930's—and the fact that after the German invasion of the Soviet Union it allied itself with the liberal capitalist powers who controlled vital sectors of the Argentine economy— this charge effectively undercut much of the ideological appeal of the Communist left among Argentine workers and middle sectors. But it was also used very effectively against the liberals themselves. In detailed historical studies, middle-class economic nationalists traced the antinational, antidevelopmental implications of cosmopolitan liberal policies through the entire national period. They argued that these policies were not unfortunate results of the misguided thought of high-minded men, but the disgusting consequence of a venal process in which liberals sold out the nation for individual gain. Scrutiny of the economic policies of the regimes of the 1930's—the period the economic nationalists were to popularize as the "Infamous Decade"—confirmed this historical analysis. How else could one interpret Roca-Runciman, new concessions granted the British upon its renewal in 1936, the complementary policies that gave British capital inordinate influence in the new state banking, trade, and exchange-control institutions set up during the Depression, and the agreements signed by the conservative governments that inexplicably extended foreign monopolies over Argentine port facilities and public utilities?

Finally, middle-class nationalists criticized the Hispanic corporativism of the aristocratic cultural nationalists as a reactionary, antidemocratic, racist ideology inspired by foreign fascist models. Although, in truth, some of the leading thinkers among the economic nationalists borrowed not a little from European corporativist ideas—and in time allied themselves with forward-looking Argentine corporativists and right-wing economic nationalists—they were careful to insist on the American origins of their thought. They claimed an affinity with the philosophy of the Peruvian nationalist Haya de la Torre and admired the popular nationalism of the Mexican regime of Lázaro Cárdenas. And unlike most of their ideological rivals, they based their policy prescriptions for Argentine future greatness not on the theoretical supremacy of an abstract model of social organization, but on lessons deduced from the concrete analysis of Argentine history.

Middle-class economic nationalists were much more successful in creating the ideological tools to undermine the hegemony of liberal political economy and the legitimacy of conservative rule, however, than they were in organizing a political vehicle for implementing their program for a new Argentina. In hundreds of lectures and street meetings, in newspapers, pamphlets, and historical studies, they propagated their nationalist vision. Meanwhile, they concentrated their political activity on efforts to reform the Radical Party and capture its leadership. In this endeavor they were bitterly disappointed. True to its historical trajectory, by 1935 the party lifted the ban on electoral participation it had proclaimed after the coup of 1930 and became a junior partner in the fraudulent politics of the conservative restoration. The bulk of the party's leaders never abandoned their ideological commitment to the cosmopolitan principles of liberal political economy. By the early 1940's, as the nationalists' hopes to influence the course of the Radical Party dimmed, many began to focus their attention on the other major institution of Argentine society receptive to middle-class concerns, the military. There, especially among middle- and low-ranking officers, their propaganda found an enthusiastic audience. When the military moved in June 1943 to end the era of the conservative restoration, the most cohesive and dynamic elements of the new regime, led by Perón, shared the precepts of the economic nationalists. In fact, many of the intellectuals who had articulated and spread this new vision of Argentine society occupied important positions of power within the new government.

Middle-class economic nationalists thus both provided the cultural tool that undermined the legitimacy of the Argentine ruling class and outlined a program for the military regime that seized power in June 1943. Events were to show, however, that if that tool had not been firmly set in the powerful hand of a mobilized labor movement, the destruction of the old liberal order would have been temporary, and the nationalists' project for a new Argentina stillborn. Between 1943 and 1945 a resurgent labor movement forced middle-class nationalists to incorporate major labor and social reforms into their program for a new Argentina. In the process, however, the labor movement was harnessed in support of an ideology and a program originally designed to meet the special needs of another class. Although Argentine workers were successful in modifying both the ideology and the program to serve their immediate interests, they did so by compromising their ideological and political independence and their long-term potential to transform Argentine society.

Meatworkers and the Rise of Peronism

In the mid-1940's a resurgent labor movement consolidated the pattern of Argentine exceptionalism first evident after 1930. If the weakness of Argentine labor enabled Argentine ruling elites to pursue their liberal policies and resist popular nationalist reforms during the crisis of world capitalism in the 1930's, the growing power of labor in the early 1940's consolidated the nationalist reaction to those policies. Labor set Argentine governments on a postwar course of concessions to popular forces and nationalist economic reforms fully at odds with the liberal political economy of the postwar world order. From a world perspective the nature of the Peronist government that rode to power on the basis of labor's support in 1945-46 appears as a curious anachronism, a neofascist, developmentalist regime swimming against the tide of world history. To the majority of Argentines, however, Peronism was a progressive nationalist response to an earlier anachronism: the unreconstructed liberalism of the regimes of the 1930's. The development of the labor movement in Argentina's unique peripheral capitalist society provides the interpretive keys to understanding both of these anachronisms, and captures the dialectical relationship between them. How the labor movement placed Argentina on a course after 1945 that carried the nation against the march of world history and ended in a historical dead end is a story difficult to unravel. The most efficient and rewarding approach is to follow the fortunes of the single most important sector of the industrial labor force, the meatworkers.

Meatworkers were both typical of and, in a structural and historical sense, more important than other Argentine industrial workers in the 1940's. Like most workers in Argentina's new and expanding import-substituting industries, meatworkers were largely unorganized at the start of that decade. The history of their mobilization and organization in the early and mid-1940's thus reveals a process not unlike the one experienced by workers in Argentina's new industries during the same period. But because of their position in Argentina's export economy, meatworkers possessed inherent economic and political power far greater than that of other sectors of the industrial working class. That power, moreover, was reinforced by their symbolic importance to Argentine nationalists opposed to foreign control over Argentine society. Meatworkers' organizational struggles directly challenged the interests of the most privileged sector of the landed class and its foreign allies, the capitalists who owned the packing plants and controlled the meat trade. They combated the "unholy alliance" that had perpetrated Roca-Runciman and that bore responsibility for the whole panoply of antinational and reactionary policies instituted during the "Infamous Decade." Meatworkers, in sum, confronted the leading edge of the anti-Argentine forces that, in the eyes of economic nationalists, had perverted the course of national development for more than a century.

It is not surprising, therefore, that throughout the crucial period 1943-46 the history of meatworkers' organizational struggles is inextricably linked with national political developments and the historical fate of the nationalist Peronist regime. Meatworkers played a leading role in the process through which an insurgent labor movement first forced Argentine economic nationalists to adopt the program of social and labor reform that made the Peronist faction preeminent within the military government (June 1943–October 1945), then rescued the Peronist experiment from destruction by the liberal reaction (October 17, 1945), and finally consolidated Peronist control over the political life of the nation (February 1946). In the meantime, meatworkers' organizations, like others in the Argentine labor movement, were first stripped of their Marxist leadership (a process virtually complete by early 1945), then slowly deprived of their ideological and political independence (a painful and protracted process not fully accomplished until the end of the decade).

Meatworkers, like other Argentine workers, rendered these indispensable services to the Peronists in government in exchange for effective state support for their collective efforts to improve wages and working conditions and better the quality of their lives off the job. As they struggled to accomplish these goals, they manipulated the ideological tools available to them to conceive a nationalist and radically reformist vision for the whole of Argentine society. They attempted to use their new-found power and access to the state to implement that vision. The story of their failure to accomplish that goal reveals the congenital incapacity of the Peronists' nationalist, corporativist solution to deal with Argentina's developmental problems. And it chronicles the demeaning emasculation of the most progressive class in Argentine society.

The history of meatworker organization thus contradicts standard explanations of the process through which Argentine labor was organized, institutionalized, and "Peronized" in the 1940's. Until recently, the historiography of the period—Peronist, Marxist, and liberal alike—emphasized the active role of the Peronist leadership in the process and the essentially passive role of the mass of Argentine workers.[80] There is no doubt that Peronist leaders aspired to harness the latent power of labor in the service of a larger political project and that they successfully used the power of the state to accomplish that goal. But the history of the pivotal period 1943-46 reveals a weak and often vacillating Peronist leadership. Prisoners of a reactionary social philosophy, Peronists feared the independent power of the working class yet needed that power to surmount the powerful liberal forces arrayed against their nationalist, corporativist project. Time and time again workers forced the timid, ambivalent Peronist leaders to grant them organizational and material concessions far greater than the Peronists thought safe. That Peronists gave so much—and got away with it—owed more to the strength of the nation's economy at the end of the world war and to the bankruptcy of liberalism in Argentina in the 1940's than it did to a brave commitment to social justice or to the inherent viability of corporativist political economy.[81] For all the latitude these conjunctural economic and ideological conditions gave them, Peronist leaders often had to be pushed into the institutional and material concessions they made to labor. They had to be forced to practice the social philosophy they said they believed in, impelled into the political power they said they wanted but were almost too timid to take. Labor was the agent that pressured the Peronists into all these positions.

The rise and consolidation of Peronism is explained simplistically in much Argentine historiography as the work of a great man—a man seen as an enlightened nationalist by Peronists, as an unscrupulous political opportunist by opponents.[82] Or it is explained as the consequence of the traditional political culture of the rural-migrants-turned-industrial-

80. Murmis and Portantiero, "Crecimiento industrial" (cited in n. 76), breaks decisively with this tradition.

81. These issues are discussed systematically in the final section of the essay.

82. The Peronist interpretation, for example, is illustrated in the following early works: Partido Peronista, *El movimiento peronista* (Buenos Aires, 1954), and Enrique Pavón Pereyra, *Perón, preparación de una vida para el mando* (9th ed.; Buenos Aires, 1953). English readers were treated to a host of anti-Peronist interpretations in the early 1950's, among the most influential Robert J. Alexander's *The Peronist Era* (New York, 1951) and George I. Blankston's *Perón's Argentina* (Chicago, 1953).

workers who flocked to the Peronist banner.[83] But neither kind of explanation can fully account for the dynamic of the events of the mid-1940's.
Argentine workers, not a great man, did the most to make the history of
those momentous years. They did so as realistic and rational human
beings attempting to solve the long-standing organizational, cultural,
and material problems they faced as a class. One does not have to assume
the premodern cultural values of rural migrants to explain the "Peroni-
zation" of Argentine labor. The great cultural weakness of the Argentine
labor movement lay not in the alleged cultural defects of rural migrants,
but, paradoxically, in the modern, capitalist, liberal values instilled in Argentine workers—urban and rural alike—as the early-twentieth-century
cultural autonomy and organizational strength of the labor movement
was destroyed. The history of the rise and consolidation of Peronism is
best viewed as the struggle of workers to recapture that lost autonomy
and strength. No group illustrates this whole process better than meatworkers, nor contributes so powerfully toward its resolution.

On the eve of the military coup of June 1943, after more than a quarter
century of collective failure, meatworkers seemed on the verge of an organizational breakthrough that promised to consolidate, under Communist Party leadership, powerful unions in the industry. Before the
1930's the Communist Party had been a minor force in the Argentine labor movement and an ineffectual proponent of meatworker organization. Formed when a minority split from the Socialist Party in 1919 and
joined the Third International, the party struggled unsuccessfully against
more numerous socialist, syndicalist, and anarchist factions for control of
the fractured Argentine labor movement during the 1920's. In 1932, however, the Communists' Federación Obrera de la Industria de la Carne

---

83. This view is developed largely in the work of liberal scholars. A mature statement
by its most influential and resourceful exponent is Gino Germani, "El surgimiento del peronismo: El role de los obreros y de los migrantes internos," *Desarrollo Económico* 13:51 (Oct.-
Dec. 1973): 435-89. The impressive historical study by Samuel Baily, *Labor, Nationalism, and
Politics* (cited in n. 38), makes the same cultural assumption. Recent revisionist studies have
effectively challenged Germani's insistence on the importance of internal migrants in the
rise of Peronism but have left his cultural assumptions largely intact. These studies have
shown that organized as well as unorganized workers became strong supporters of Peronism, and that early Peronist electoral victories apparently depended more on votes from established working-class districts than recently formed ones. The most systematic review of
this literature is Matsushita, *Movimiento obrero* (cited in n. 78). Matsushita's study, like that
of Tamarin, focuses on the politics of the railway unions and the CGT and shows that by
the end of the 1930's most established union leaders had adopted a more nationalistic economic and political posture than their predecessors and had moved beyond the traditional
syndicalist emphasis on the primacy of economic versus political solutions to working-class
problems. A similar transformation in the policies of leaders of several labor organizations
is demonstrated in Joel Horowitz, "Adaptation and Change in the Argentine Labor Movement, 1930-1943: A Study of Five Unions" (Ph.D. diss., University of California, Berkeley, 1979). This transformation, part of the larger historical process analyzed in this essay,
made it easier for organized workers to accept the initiatives of the Peronists.

(FOIC) organized and led the most important strike in the packing plants to occur since the failure of 1917-18. That strike shut down the largest and most modern meat-packing plant in the world, the Anglo Frigorífico the British had built in Avellaneda in 1927. Although it spread briefly to the other plants in Avellaneda, and some workers walked out in Berisso, the strike collapsed after less than two weeks.

The strike of 1932 revealed once again the scope of the organizational problems labor organizers faced in the packing industry. The demands expressed in the strike petition were basically the same as those workers fought for in 1917-18: reinstatement of workers fired for union activity; recognition of the union; higher wages, especially for the unskilled; and a guaranteed half day's pay for all those called to report to work. The strikers were defeated by the same structural obstacles that had stymied meatworker organization fifteen years earlier. Scabs quickly filled the jobs of strikers. Police broke up picket lines, dispersed street meetings and rallies, forcibly closed down the headquarters of the FOIC, and arrested hundreds of union militants. The early support of some other sectors of the Argentine worker class quickly collapsed. Management's continuing efforts to "perfect" the organization of work within the packing plants made meatworkers especially vulnerable to these general obstacles to union organization in Argentina in the 1930's. Taylorist principles were formally introduced into the plants in the late 1920's, and the percentage of women in the work force rose substantially between the census years of 1914 and 1935. These changes resulted in two new demands in 1932 that became cornerstones of the FOIC's position during the rest of the decade: equal pay for equal work, and an end to the "standard" system that used piecework quotas and premiums to increase the work pace constantly.[84]

After 1935 Communists adopted a more moderate tactical position in their efforts to organize the packing plants. On the one hand, as the FOIC patiently spread its organizational message to meatworkers at barbecues and picnics, it sought and sometimes won minor improvements in work conditions in the plants. On the other, it orchestrated a national campaign, based on moderate legalistic demands, to convince Argentine public opinion, government officials, and the leadership of the CGT of the need for improvements in the position of workers in the packing plants.

84. The demands are reproduced in *La Vanguardia*, May 23, 1932. The continuing importance of foreign workers ("polacos y lituanos"), the central role of women in the efforts to win strike support, the failure of sympathy strikes, and the extent of police repression are conveyed in the coverage of the major Buenos Aires daily, *La Nación*, May 24, 1932, p. 5. On the "standard" and the strike itself, see Peter's account in *Crónicas proletarias* (cited in n. 48), pp. 143-71. Of 23,200 workers in the packing plants listed in the industrial census of 1935, 4,978, or more than one-fifth, were women or children under 18 years of age. *Censo industrial de 1935* (cited in n. 47), p. 58.

By 1939 the FOIC had secured a formal commitment from the moderate Socialist leadership of the CGT to make meatworker organization a major priority. The same year, the FOIC took the unprecedented step of petitioning the national government for help in the struggle to eliminate the abuses to labor in the packing plants. Backed by the Socialist Party's congressional bloc and drafted by FOIC Secretary General José Peter, the petition introduced in the Chamber of Deputies in 1939 sought to portray the meatworkers' plight as a national disgrace. Peter started from the premise that "everything related to the production and processing of meat . . . is intertwined with the most profound economic, social, and political problems facing Argentina." A case in point was the way the foreign packing companies made a mockery of Argentine law. Their union-busting tactics violated the constitution of the nation whose Article 14 granted Argentines the freedom of association. Their labor practices evaded national legislation that regulated the work of women and children (Law 11,317), stipulated hours of work and overtime pay (Law 11,544), and established compensation for industrial accidents and diseases (Law 9,688). It was ironic, Peter pointed out, that despite meatworkers' great importance to the economic health of the nation, they were among the least well paid and least healthy of Argentine workers. The foreign packing companies also refused to comply with the national legislation on severance pay, annual vacations, and sick leave (Law 11, 729). Yet meat-packing, "because of the nature of the industry, and the organization of work within it, requires perhaps more than any other industrial activity that [workers] enjoy annual vacations and sick leave benefits. . . ." Finally, Peter argued that the same hiring policies that undercut the organizational efforts of meatworkers hurt the economic interests of the nation as a whole.

The companies hire foreign workers carefully selected from among those who because of their slight knowledge of the language and the country more easily accept appalling work conditions. Through this practice they make the foreign worker appear . . . as an enemy of the native worker, since he seems to be the cause of declining rates of pay and worsening work conditions. In this way a hateful and artificial division is created between criollos and gringos. . . . But the gravest problem is that in order to accomplish such niggardly and prejudicial ends, the frigoríficos have deprived our agriculture of hundreds and thousands of trained hands, since most of the foreign workers they hire have been practiced farmers in their lands of origin.[85]

Not surprisingly, the conservative-dominated Chamber simply shelved the legislation Socialists presented to deal with the concerns expressed in the meatworkers' petition.

85. *Cámara de Diputados, Diario de sesiones de 1939*, vol. 3, pp. 118-21. The bill introduced by the Socialist deputies to deal with the conditions raised in the petition appears in the same volume, pp. 49-53.

Nevertheless, the moderate, legalistic tactics the Communists adopted in their drive to organize the packing industry in the late 1930's enabled them to take advantage of the changed climate for organization once the world war got under way. By then, Peter's formal allegations to the contrary, the historically divisive issue of foreign immigrants in the packinghouse labor force had undoubtedly become less important. Although the censuses of the period no longer break down the industrial work force by nationality, the virtual cessation of international migration into Argentina at the start of the world depression, and more than a decade of rural-urban migration, had probably diminished the importance of national and linguistic, if not ethnic and cultural, divisions among meatworkers. More important, wartime demand for exports and Argentina's booming new industries had swept away the greatest historical obstacle to labor organization in the packing industry, the existence of large numbers of unemployed workers in the populous provinces of the littoral. Finally, growing public perception of the antinational implications of conservative policies of the 1930's had created a basis for broad-based alliances in support of meatworkers' struggles against the foreign capitalists who controlled the meat-packing industry. Wartime conditions also meant that managers of the packing plants, eager to reap the high profits involved in meeting Allied contracts, grew more conciliatory toward labor. As the war progressed, an uneasy working partnership developed between Communist labor leaders and British and U.S. capitalists: both groups shared a commitment to uninterrupted production of a commodity vital to the Allied war effort. During 1941 and 1942 the FOIC was successful in remedying minor worker grievances in the plants; in those years, too, company repression of the union's organizing activities eased, and the membership of the union slowly expanded.[86]

As all these structural factors shifted in favor of the meatworkers' struggle, in late 1942 the FOIC won its first major concession from the companies and fulfilled one of its long-standing demands. After months of negotiations, the companies agreed to conform to national legislation and grant meatworkers paid vacations. Peter joined thousands of workers, company officials, and representatives of the provincial government of Buenos Aires in a lavish public celebration of this achievement held near the new "Anglo" packing plant at Dock Sur in Avellaneda on January 1, 1943. The event capped more than a decade of struggle by the

---

86. Peter later claimed much more: that the union won an effective guarantee of 60 hours of work per fortnight for each worker, pay raises, free milk for workers doing unhealthy jobs, and provision by the companies of some protective clothing. José Peter, *Historia y luchas de los obreros de la carne* (Buenos Aires, 1947), pp. 68–69. The FOIC leadership would later allege that company cooperation with the union during this period did not go far enough to enable it to maintain the loyalty of the rank and file in the competition with pro-Peronist unions.

FOIC following the disastrous strike of 1932 and signaled the start of a new era. With one stroke the union (whose dues-paying members in 1942 even FOIC leaders later estimated at only 20 percent of the meat-packing labor force) demonstrated its effectiveness to the mass of workers in the plants and won the tacit recognition of company and government officials alike.[87]

The growing prestige and strength of Communist organizations in the meat-packing industry was typical of Marxist gains in the Argentine labor movement as a whole in the late 1930's and early 1940's. After 1935, the popular-front tactics of the party and the resurgence of the Argentine economy combined to favor the success of the job actions Communists led. In December of that year Communists organized and directed a major strike in the construction industry of Buenos Aires. Aided by a general strike that paralyzed the city for two days in early January 1936, the strike succeeded. This victory brought Communists great prestige within the labor movement and began a process that, within a few short years, made them the most dynamic force within the Argentine labor movement.

During this period, Communists, like their counterparts in the CIO in the United States, adopted a policy of aggressive industrial unionism. They concentrated their efforts on food, textile, and metallurgy workers. Illustrative of the scope of their plans and organizing efforts was the federation they hoped to build among food workers. It was to be organized around a nucleus of meatworkers, and was to include unions in flour mills, breweries, and bakeries. These industrial unions would in turn be linked to organizations of rural workers in Argentina's livestock and cereal export sector and in the domestic sugar and wine industries. Although Communist organizational success fell far short of these goals, they earned a reputation for sacrifice and dedication to the workers' struggle that far overshadowed that of their ideological competitors. Communists organized and led virtually all the strikes in Argentina between 1936 and 1943. And although they lost more job actions than they won during this period, their organizational gains, especially when measured against those of their competitors, were impressive.

David Tamarin has assembled information that illustrates the gains of Communist labor organizations during this period. Whereas the members of labor organizations grew by about 18 percent between 1936 and 1941, the number of union members among industrial workers almost doubled. Communist-led organizations accounted for nearly all of this

87. The significance of the FOIC victory is stressed in the contemporary Communist press and in subsequent accounts by party members: *La Hora*, Jan. 10, 1943; Iscaro, *Historia*, Part 4, p. 69; Peter, *Crónicas proletarias* (cited in n. 48), pp. 198-99. Evidence of the growing prestige of the FOIC is revealed in the events of 1943, discussed below.

advance. The growth of the four most important Communist-led industrial unions contributed roughly 95 percent of the total expansion in union membership between 1936 and 1941. Although these organizational gains barely exceeded the growth rate of Argentina's rapidly expanding industrial labor force, they indicate trends that became explosive as the world war progressed. Despite the severity of government repression, and the economic dislocation and rising unemployment precipitated by the outbreak of the war—both of which hindered union and strike activities—between 1939 and 1942 the number of strikes and strikers recorded in official statistics doubled.[88] The war also promised to neutralize ruling-class ideological opposition to and repression of the Communist left. The logic of the Allied war effort demanded it.

As Communist organization advanced among construction, textile, metal, and food-processing workers in the early 1940's, militant Socialists expanded their influence in organizations of skilled blue- and white-collar workers. These gains emboldened a coalition of Socialists and Communists to challenge the moderate leadership of the CGT in March 1943. This effort to capture control of the labor central was unsuccessful and precipitated a major schism that split the CGT into two separate organizations. Nevertheless, the attempted takeover finally broke the grip of the moderate and passive leaders of the Unión Ferroviaria over the main Argentine labor central. It thus removed a major institutional impediment to the spread of Marxist influence within the Argentine labor movement and meant that, on the eve of the military coup of June 1943, pro-Allied coalitions of Socialist and Communist militants were in control of the most dynamic labor organizations of the country.[89]

Explanations of the military coup of June 1943 customarily focus on the depth of the ideological and political crisis of the conservative regime in a world at war. A decade of naked class rule, mercilessly exposed by economic nationalists, had fatally undermined the legitimacy of the government. The alignment of the great powers in the world war placed the Argentine ruling class in an agonizing dilemma that badly split the conservative elements in control of the state. If the traditional economic and cultural ties of members of the landed class inclined them toward the cause of the liberal capitalist Allies, their reactionary social and political stance made them sympathetic to the fascist project of the Axis powers. Meanwhile, the early course of the war, which seemed to point toward

88. Tamarin, "The Argentine Labor Movement" (cited in n. 78), p. 243. The mobilization of the Argentine labor movement in the years immediately preceding the June 1943 military coup is stressed in Murmis and Portantiero's "El movimiento obrero en los orígenes del peronismo" in their *Estudios sobre los orígenes del peronismo* (cited in n. 76), pp. 59-126.

89. Tamarin, "The Argentine Labor Movement," gives a detailed account of the origins and outcome of the split in the CGT.

Axis victory, emboldened elements within the Argentine military who shared the militarist, nationalist, corporatist, and developmentalist ideology of the fascist powers to seize political power.[90] The military conspirators enjoyed the support of diverse civilian elements outside the working class who were united by a common repudiation of both the cosmopolitan liberal economic policies and the fraudulent electoral practices of the conservative restoration.

These explanations, however, leave out an element of Argentine politics crucial to understanding the coup and the pattern of subsequent developments. Judging from the initial policies of the military junta, fear of an insurgent labor movement under Marxist leadership was a powerful motivating force in the minds of the military conspirators. Within days after taking power they closed the halls of the Communist-led unions and arrested and jailed the major Communist labor activists. But repression of leftist labor failed to stop the mobilization of Argentine workers and the ability of Marxist labor organizations to stage massive and costly strikes. The scope of the corporativist labor policies formulated in subsequent months by the faction led by Perón within the military junta must be understood in this context. The success of those labor policies, in turn, consolidated Perón in power and stamped Argentina with the institutions and political alignment that make its postwar history so exceptional. Outside the context of an insurgent labor movement under tenuous Marxist leadership the logic of this whole sequence of events—and the reluctant acceptance of its outcome by the Argentine ruling class—is difficult to comprehend.

Perón himself was always very clear about his fear of a class-conscious labor movement. And he was perfectly honest with workers themselves about the corporativist nature of his philosophy and the meaning of his program. He summarized his views succinctly in the first issue of the organ of the Secretaría de Trabajo y Previsión, the agency Perón established in October 1943 to implement his labor policy.[91] "I aspire for the Fatherland, with the most vehement desires of my heart, that the struggle between classes be replaced by harmony among all of them. . . ." This goal could be accomplished by correcting the dehumanizing influence of "tentacles of international capitalism," by developing the vast riches of Argentina, and by distributing the new wealth more equitably among the nation's people. None of these policies implied, however, an attack on

90. A thorough study of the politics of the military during this period is Robert A. Potash, *The Army and Politics in Argentina, 1928-1945* (Stanford, Calif., 1969).

91. The agency was set up under the guidance of José Figuerola, a corporativist ideologue who had helped to implement the labor policy of Primo de Rivera. Figuerola summarized his approach to labor in his *La colaboración social en Hispanoamérica* (Buenos Aires, 1943).

"accumulated effort in the form of legitimately acquired inheritance, which is the living essence of private property." On the contrary, private property needed "the most decisive protection of the State. . . ." We will not permit, he warned workers, "that the soul of Argentina fall prey to communism. . . ." "To the misguided . . . I have already appealed to their hearts. The recalcitrant, all those who aspire to spread their divisive theories and want to continue poisoning the soul of Argentines, will be made to feel the rigor with which the law punishes traitors to the Fatherland." Perón concluded this statement with a vague warning about what might happen were his corporativist policies not successfully implemented: "Woe to the country that permits hatred to grow in the heart of the working masses! Woe to the nation that tolerates governments who do not watch over the fair administration of distributive justice! Woe to the government that abandons the rudder that must guide [society] toward the necessary harmony between capital and labor!"[92]

What could happen to such a country, and what Perón claimed was in fact happening in Argentina on the eve of the military coup of June 1943, he specified in greater detail in a speech given before the Buenos Aires Chamber of Commerce on August 25, 1944. "The people themselves," began Perón, "have no leaders. And I ask you gentlemen to reflect on the issue of whose hands the mass of Argentine workers were in, and on what would be the future for that mass of workers that in large part found itself in the hands of communists. . . ." The military secret police, Perón claimed, had learned three months before the military took power that revolutionary forces in the labor movement were planning a general strike. The military government prevented the strike and could now deal with the threat to capitalism and social order, which the end of the world war would inevitably bring. There was only one good way to eliminate this "grave danger," Perón continued, because having to fight the people in the streets "is disgusting," a "thing that is done only when there is no other remedy and when the people really want civil war." That way was for the state to organize the masses and follow a real program of social justice—not giving too much, which would cause an economic cataclysm, nor too little, which would lead to social cataclysm. State authority could then control the masses "so that once they are in their place no one can escape it, because the state organism has the instrument that by force if necessary can put things in their rightful place and not permit them to get out of hand." "It has been said, gentlemen," Perón concluded, "that I am an enemy of capital, but if you look into what I have just said you will find no defender, we could say, more committed than

92. *Revista de Trabajo y Previsión* 1:1 (1944?):iii–xi.

I. . . ." A week later Perón read the same speech to a meeting of delegates from the labor unions. He added that if capitalists opposed him, as they were doing, he would not retreat an inch from his social program.[93]

Among the Marxist-led unions that most preoccupied the Peronists within the military junta that seized state power on June 4, 1943, were those of the meatworkers. Like other Communist- and Socialist-led unions affiliated with the Marxist-dominated CGT, the meatworkers' FOIC was immediately outlawed by the new military government. Within less than a week the union's headquarters in Avellaneda and Berisso were raided and closed, and its most visible leaders, Peter paramount among them, arrested. Peter was exiled to the remote interior town of Neuquén. There he remained until freed by the great general strike in the frigoríficos that began in September 1943.

The strike was carefully prepared by FOIC militants. In July they organized a series of mass meetings in Avellaneda, Berisso, and Rosario to air worker grievances and formulate strike demands. The strike petition demanded freedom for the union's leaders, respect for the union's activities, an across-the-board pay raise, equal pay for equal work, and a guarantee of thirty hours of work each week for all workers. The companies refused to negotiate. Finally, in mid-September the FOIC felt strong enough to call the workers out. And for the first time since 1917-18 meatworkers were able to shut down effectively the big plants in Avellaneda and Berisso. The military government declared the strike illegal. It used police to enforce the "freedom of work." More FOIC cadres were arrested and scores of pickets jailed. But the strike continued and production at the plants was paralyzed. Finally, at the end of September, Perón was able to convince his military colleagues in the government to allow him to fly Peter to Buenos Aires to negotiate.

In the agreement reached between the Peronists in the government and the FOIC leadership on October 3, 1943, each side sought to use the other to achieve what were in reality mutually antagonistic organizational and ideological goals. In exchange for government promises to respect the rights of the union and to support it in subsequent negotiations with the companies, the FOIC agreed to lift the strike. Peter later published

93. Juan Domingo Perón, *El pueblo quiere saber de que se trata* (Buenos Aires, 1944), pp. 157-69. It is not true, as many have contended, that Perón was simply an opportunist who said different things to different groups. Like any good politician he emphasized different parts of his program to appeal to different social groups: social justice to workers; military strength to the army; industrial development to manufacturers; the threat of Marxist labor to capitalists; anti-imperialism to economic nationalists. But the integral corporativism and anti-Marxism that provided the philosophical foundation of his thought and program was expressed in virtually all his major speeches. However different its social base from those of the classic European fascist regimes, Peronism conforms in the philosophical sense to fascism as defined in the seminal work of Ernest Nolte, *Three Faces of Fascism* (New York, 1966).

two books in which he recounted this crucial juncture in Argentine labor history, but he never elaborated the thinking behind the FOIC's decision. Perhaps the FOIC, chastened by earlier failures, had serious doubts about its ability to sustain a long strike and win concessions directly from the companies. More likely, the FOIC was constrained by the Communist Party's position and unwilling to disrupt the Argentine economy and interrupt meat shipments to the Allies. Whatever the case, the agreement proved to be a tactical disaster for the FOIC. Subsequent events revealed that by late 1943 the structural weaknesses that had impeded meatworker organization in the past were no longer sufficient to constrain rank-and-file workers from striking effectively to win their historic collective demands. If the FOIC would not lead the struggle, independent militants would—with or without the support of the Peronists.[94]

The reasoning behind the position adopted by the Peronists in the settlement of the strike is clearer. As corporativist nationalists they wanted to demonstrate to the traditional military elements within the government and to their liberal critics outside it both the magnitude of the threat from Marxist labor and their own ability to control and channel that threat. With the advantage of hindsight, Perón's negotiator with the meatworkers, Colonel Domingo A. Mercante, assessed the agreement with the FOIC as "our first triumph." Mercante attended the mass meet-

94. Peter's books are the previously cited *Crónicas proletarias* and *Historia y luchas de los obreros de la carne*. Peter's account in *Crónicas* reproduces the agreement accepted by the "Asamblea General Extraordinaria" of the meatworkers in Avellaneda. In it, in view of the assurances given by the government, the assembly resolved (p. 207): "(1) To return to work on October 4th in order to facilitate government intervention in the solution of the conflict. (2) To move to an intermediary location to consider the companies' response to the government and to the FOIC. (3) To maintain in place the Strike Committees of the various frigoríficos until the conflict is resolved. (4) To name a large Commission of workers from the different frigoríficos, presided over by comrade José Peter, and charged with representing workers in the negotiation of the strike demands." That the FOIC leadership banked on management concessions made in the interest of Allied solidarity was confirmed at the start of 1945 by U.S. diplomatic representatives in close contact with underground leaders of the union. By then pro-Perón leaders were firmly in control of powerful unions in the packing plants, and the U.S. mission was searching desperately for ways to stop Perón in his bid to consolidate his political control over the nation. Eduard Reed wrote the U.S. Secretary of State on Feb. 1, 1945: "It has seemed clear enough, from the first, that F.O.I.C. leaders were bent on availing themselves of wartime conditions to jockey the managements into negotiations for cooperation which might be tantamount to recognition and a step toward the closed shop. It has also seemed clear that, upon the appearance of Perón with his scheme of dictatorship through adding control of labor to control of the armed forces, those F.O.I.C. leaders were in high hopes to find management less stubbornly opposed to them. They thought opposition to Perón would be something they could have in common with the managements of . . . home offices in democratic countries. They thought the fight against the enemies of the democracies might be taken so seriously as to make possible a common front between them and the "frigorífico" managements in opposition to the local enemies of the democracies. They early learned that for those managements the Perón scheme of things, if an evil at all, apparently was the lesser of two evils." U.S. National Archives, Department of State, 835.5045/2-145 (hereafter, USNA/DS).

ing called by the FOIC at Dock Sur on October 3, 1943, to win rank-
and-file endorsement of the agreement to lift the strike. His description
of the meeting emphasized the size and enthusiasm of the crowd and the
great prestige enjoyed by Peter.

> When we arrived we were surprised by the multitude. Some six thousand work-
> ers were shouting *vivas* to Peter, hugging and embracing him and carrying him
> about. Peter had to circle the grounds several times in order to satisfy the workers'
> enthusiasm; then he spoke, and on the spot the strike was lifted.
>
> Although Peter did not mention the circumstance that his freedom was owed
> to Perón, that was a detail that did not escape the workers. I walked among them,
> dressed in my uniform, and no one molested me, although they eyed me with
> hatred.[95]

Cipriano Reyes, the man destined to play a major role in the organization of meatworkers and in the forging of their relationship to Perón,
later gave a very different account of the resolution of the strike. According to him, delegates from the Berisso plants opposed the lifting of the
strike in exchange for Peter's release and vague promises from the government. He claimed he grabbed the microphone from the Communist
leaders and urged workers to continue the strike. Peter's own account, on
the other hand, accords with Mercante's. He goes on to say that thousands of workers met outside the FOIC headquarters in Berisso on the
same afternoon and approved the FOIC decision to lift the strike.[96]

The exact truth of these accounts is less important than the process unleashed by the conditions under which the FOIC ended the strike. When
the union proved unable to extract concessions in subsequent negotiations with the government and the companies—and when FOIC leaders
refused to accept government offers of money and a luxurious building
for their union headquarters in exchange for their cooperation with government plans—the military regime unleashed the most severe repression
to date against the Communist-led union. On October 22, the union's
headquarters were once again raided and its leaders imprisoned. Peter
was held virtually incommunicado for six months and finally deported to
Uruguay after more than a year and a half in Argentine jails. In November 1943, FOIC funds were officially transferred to two dissident members previously expelled from the Union. In the meantime the meatworkers' struggle to win their collective demands and organize effective
unions in the plants went on unabated. But it was under Reyes' leader-

95. Mercante's oft-quoted account was published in an interview in *Primera Plana* 146
(Aug. 1965), pp. 24-30. Mercante later elevated his estimate of the size of the crowd
("20,000 or 30,000 people") and broadened his assessment of the significance of the strike
("the beginning of a general strike against the government"). Félix Luna, *El 45: Crónica de
un año decisivo* (Buenos Aires, 1969), pp. 118-19.

96. Cipriano Reyes, *Yo hice el 17 de octubre* (Buenos Aires, 1973), pp. 107-27; Peter, *Crónicas proletarias*, p. 207.

ship, not the FOIC's, that meatworkers were able to mount the massive strikes that forced major concessions from the companies—and finally won the cautious, conditional support of the Peronist leadership.

Like Peter, Reyes was born poor in the provinces. And like Peter he worked in his youth as an itinerant farm laborer on the pampa before finding work in the British frigoríficos upriver from Buenos Aires. But in contrast to Peter, who became a member of the Communist Party in the late 1920's and devoted himself to the struggle to organize the packing plants in Avellaneda throughout the Depression, Reyes spent most of the 1930's in unsuccessful efforts to climb out of the working class and establish a career in journalism. He learned his first letters from his mother in snatches of free time between his performances in a little circus his father carried to the country towns of the pampa. When the circus failed, sometime around the First World War, while Reyes was still a child, he was forced to earn his living with his hands. He moved from carpenter's apprentice to migrant farm worker, from laborer in road construction gangs to unskilled frigorífico worker. All the while he continued to read and by the late 1920's he was publishing little stories and poems in local newspapers. In time he found outlets for talents in marketing, organization, and mass publicity he must have first discovered at the side of his father during his circus days. After taking a menial job in a bakery in the town of Castelli in the late 1920's, for example, he was able to create a position for himself distributing baked goods to the surrounding countryside. In 1930 he moved to the port town of Necochea where he wrote for the local paper, supported a successful maritime workers' strike, and founded a soccer club that promptly elected him president. Somewhat later, he achieved considerable success as a writer for an independent provincial paper that devoted most of its coverage to sports events. Finally, he founded what he called "Publicidad Moderna." He outfitted a van with microphones and began to work the small pampa towns presenting a show that combined music and talk with advertising for local merchants. In 1940 he struck out for Buenos Aires with the hope of tapping the patronage of a Buenos Aires banker he had managed to meet during his travels. He hoped to land a job with a major magazine or radio station. When these plans fell through, he worked for a time as the valet of a judge in the great city. The experience, he later said, soured him on the *porteño* bourgeoisie, and he quit to join relatives who had migrated to the industrial suburb of Berisso. There, sometime in the early 1940's he took a job in the Armour frigorífico. Soon he began to apply his special talents to the problem—and the potential—of meatworker organization.[97]

97. The information on Reyes' life and organizational activities in this and subsequent paragraphs is taken from his book cited in n. 96. It must be interpreted with special care: Reyes' talents at self-promotion are everywhere evident.

Reyes entered the Armour plant at a time when conditions for labor organization were rapidly improving, and he used his organizational and communication skills to place himself at the head of the great mobilization of meatworkers between 1943 and 1946. Reyes got a job in the frigorífico's electrical power plant, where he discovered what he later called the *Huevo de Colón* of successful job actions in the packing plants. With increased mechanization of the frigoríficos after the First World War, the power plant came to overshadow the kill floors as the Achilles heel of the entire production process. Reyes worked to build the nucleus of meatworker organization around these strategic plant workers. He was also one of the first Argentine labor leaders to appreciate the power of the sitdown strike and the work slowdown to win worker demands. Industrial workers all over the world began to use these revolutionary techniques in the 1930's. Both tactics had the advantage of neutralizing the threat of scab labor to strike actions. Reyes was also quick to learn that Communist ideology was a major liability to winning support for workers' demands outside the organized working class in Argentina. He always used the rhetoric of nationalism and social justice to press strike petitions. He enlisted the support of the Catholic Church and its heretofore unsuccessful labor organizations to provide legitimacy and material support for the unions he helped build within the packing plants. Finally, Reyes understood the role of internal communication in successful strike actions. During the great strikes in Berisso in 1944 and 1945 he took his typewriter and mimeograph machine and hid on the small islands seaward from Berisso. He thus avoided arrest, maintained direction of the strikes, and distributed a constant flow of strike news that helped boost union morale and counteract damaging press reports in the mass circulation dailies.

Following the repression of the FOIC in October 1943, Reyes played a central role in the violent struggle that ensued between Communists, independent militants, and the Peronists in the government for control over the insurgent meatworker rank and file. Independent militants, led by Reyes in alliance with the Peronists, won the first phase of the struggle. Their victory was not an easy one, and it was costly for all sides. Well into 1944 Communist influence remained strong in the plants, especially in Avellaneda. Communist cadres, forced to try to outbid the militant independents, consistently threw their support behind job actions and sought to inject their political and organizational concerns into strike demands initially conceived by the independents in purely economic terms. At the same time the independent unions, forced to stay ahead of a mobilized rank and file, demonstrated a combativeness—a willingness to strike for constantly escalating demands—unprecedented in Argentine labor history. As a result of their own militance and of Communist in-

volvement in their strikes, the independents initially found it very difficult to convince the Peronist leadership that they were not really Communists. Peronists eventually realized, however, that they had no choice
but to support the independent militants. The alliance between Peronists
and independent unions in the packing plants was thus a marriage of convenience. Throughout the period 1943 to 1946 each partner constantly
jockeyed for advantage and dominance. Peronists within the government
alternately encouraged and repressed, coddled and constrained the independent unions. The unions responded with pressures of their own.

Encouragement of the independents came in the form of the sweeping
general labor legislation and social policies Peronists set in place to implement their corporativist design for labor. It also came from specific policies Peronists devised to deal with meatworkers and their special needs
and problems. Peronists set up state machinery to recognize and control
labor organizations and grant legal unions and their memberships important benefits. Workers were free to organize as long as the objective of
their unions was not "contrary to morality, the law, and the fundamental
institutions of the country."[98] In fact, legal unions also had to receive the
blessing of the Peronists in control of the labor office. Legal unions qualified for dues checkoff, subsidies for union buildings, and government
mediation of industrial conflicts. Through their legal unions members
could gain access to social security programs and win enforcement of
legislation dealing, among other things, with protection from accidents
and with pensions and severance pay. In addition to this general labor and
social legislation, officially recognized meatworkers' unions benefited
from government declarations of the legality of their strikes, police neutrality toward (and even support of) pickets, and government interces-
sion on their behalf in negotiations with the packing companies. Eventually, they also won large government subventions to pay salaries they
lost in strike actions and to provide laid-off workers with compensation
pay. On the other hand, Peronist repression of and constraints on its independent union allies were frequent and sometimes severe. They ranged
from jailings of uncooperative leaders and police raids on union halls and
picket lines to public and private exhortations for moderation in union
demands and tactics.

But the pressures within the alliance of Peronists and independent
union militants flowed in both directions. It was not until long after Peronists achieved total control of the state (following the presidential election of February 1946) that they were able through coercion and major
new concessions to establish virtually uncontested control over the meat-

98. The quotation is from the decree regulating "professional" associations signed in
early October 1945, but it guided the labor policy of the military junta throughout its
tenure.

workers' unions. After official intervention helped settle in their favor a major strike in June 1944, the independent unions signed an agreement with the government, couched in corporativist language, to refrain from new strike activity for a year. In exchange they won wage demands and the guaranteed 60 hours a fortnight that the FOIC had failed to extract from the companies eight months earlier. Yet within six months the independent unions unleashed a wave of strikes that won huge new concessions from the companies and the government. The strikes began with an industrywide walkout in January 1945 called to force company compliance with earlier agreements and win new improvements in work conditions. The companies acceded to government mediation that resulted in new concessions to workers. But they soon retaliated with a coordinated plan to cut their rising labor costs, rid themselves of union militants, and respond to uncertain postwar markets. Acting in concert, in March 1945 the companies planned to fire 17,000 meatworkers (about one-third of their total labor force). This was a prospect that neither the Peronists nor the unions could tolerate. The unions responded with a strike (eventually given legal sanction by the government) in April 1945 that paralyzed the packing industry for three weeks and resulted in major concessions to workers. The unions did not prevent most of the layoffs, but in this strike—and subsequent illegal job actions that convulsed the industry between May and September—workers won a guarantee of 86 hours of work per fortnight, large pay raises, eight hours' pay for six hours' work in the cold chambers, improved sanitary facilities, and company-provided protective clothing. At the same time the state committed itself to pay meatworkers for days lost in legal strike activity and to provide three months' salary compensation for 12,600 workers laid off between January and April 1945.

During these strikes the Peronist leadership repeatedly coaxed workers back to their jobs with promises to settle their grievances. Every time the government failed to deliver, workers struck again. Meatworkers marched on the national labor office by the thousands to pressure government officials. They defied Perón's radio exhortations to return to work. After the government declared their strike illegal in May 1945, they held out until July 2 before capitulating to new government promises to meet their demands. They then reorganized and mounted effective sectional work stoppages and plantwide work slowdowns that forced the companies into negotiations presided over by Mercante in September 1945. Finally, on September 22, these negotiations yielded the first collective contract signed between union delegates and company officials in the Argentine meat industry. With this agreement, which set up formal grievance procedures between union delegates and company officials (*co-*

mités paritarias), meatworker unions finally won legal recognition from the companies and formalized the gains they had won during the previous eighteen months of struggle.[99]

In this way, during 1944 and 1945, the alliance between non-Marxist unions and Peronist government officials liquidated Communist influence among meatworkers. Rank-and-file workers compared the terms of the struggle—and measured the scope of the benefits—under the Peronist-dominated military government with those under the conservative regimes that had preceded it. In the meat industry, as in most of the Argentine manufacturing sector, Communist-led organizations were too shallow and short-lived, and the material benefits they had won too modest, to represent serious competition in the struggle for rank-and-file loyalties with unions able to tap Peronist access to the state and the stream of benefits it offered. (Where Communist-led unions had established their effectiveness earlier, as in construction and, to a lesser extent, textiles, pro-Peronist unions had little success before 1946.)

But once independent union leaders and rank and file had committed themselves to an alliance with the Peronist state, the dynamics of that arrangement worked to undermine the independent power of the non-Marxist unions themselves. Perón could blame the companies when he failed to implement strike settlements, yet claim full credit when he succeeded in doing so. Militant independent unions were slowly but inexorably constrained by the mushrooming state apparatus and by legislation that channeled benefits only to unions sanctioned by the government. With the Marxist alternative eliminated, the independent unions allied with the Peronists in the government could press their collective aspirations in only one way. They had to become more Peronist than the Peronists themselves: more nationalist, more distributionist, more fundamentally reformist. They pursued this fateful strategy with determination and considerable success throughout 1945 and 1946.

If the alliance between independent meatworkers' unions and the Peronist leadership proved costly in the long run to the independents, it was almost fatal in the short run to the Peronists. Their corporativist labor policy—and the scope of the concessions they were forced to make to workers to insure its success—helped cement a domestic anti-Peronist coalition as strange as the international wartime alliance of liberal capi-

99. Government censorship makes the strikes of 1944 and 1945 difficult to follow in the press. I have relied primarily on Reyes' account and on the U.S. Department of State labor files, Record Group 835.504. The terms of government compensation to meatworkers are detailed in decree 9,024 (Apr. 24, 1945) and amplified and extended in decrees 20,185 (Aug. 31, 1945) and 24,097 (Oct. 5, 1945) and decree-law 6,363 (Feb. 28, 1946). See *Revista de Trabajo y Previsión* 2:5-6 (Jan.-June 1945):162-65; 2:7-8 (July-Dec. 1945):738-39; and 3:9 (Jan.-Mar. 1946):130-32.

talist nations and the Soviet Union. Communists and Socialists joined forces with the traditional conservative parties, with the bulk of the Radical Party leadership, and with the diplomatic representatives of the United States in Argentina to attempt to topple the Peronists from power and restore the liberal political and economic principles that had guided Argentine development up to 1943. The leftist parties thus united with what they themselves called their theoretical class enemies, the landowners and foreign capitalists responsible for the Infamous Decade, in opposition to the nationalist, reformist, corporativist program of the Peronists.[100] Meanwhile, the Peronists, whose program was more appropriate to the conditions of the worldwide crisis of capitalism in the 1930's and the march of the world war in the early 1940's than it was to world conditions in the mid-1940's, found themselves on the defensive as the Allies emerged victorious on the battlefronts and began to shape the institutional contours of the postwar settlement. Throughout 1945 Peronists were forced to accommodate their policies and principles as best they could to the emerging postwar liberal order. But even as they did so (for example, by finally acceding to U.S. conditions in a last-minute declaration of war on the Axis), they compromised their political prestige and ideological integrity. As liberal forces skillfully orchestrated public demonstrations and used their control of the major newspapers to discredit the regime, the military government was forced to relax its repression of the political opposition and to accommodate itself to liberal conceptions of postwar Argentine politics. The junta set February 1946 as the date for elections to replace the de facto military regime, lifted press censorship, and freed many of the political prisoners jailed during 1943 and 1944. Dragged along by the flood tide of a resurgent liberalism in the postwar world, by October 1945 the Peronist experiment seemed certain of demise. On October 9 liberal army officers forced the resignation of Perón and placed him under arrest. The advent of a postwar liberal regime seemed inevitable.[101]

100. Illustrative of this partnership was the close working relationship that developed between the Communist labor leader José Peter and the U.S. ambassador to Argentina, Spruille Braden. At the request of the president of the United Packing House Workers of America, the U.S. union, Braden urged Argentine officials to release Peter, who was deported to Uruguay on July 21, 1945. Braden to Secretary of State, Buenos Aires, June 6, 1945, USNA/DS 835.504/6-645, and July 24, 1945, 835.504/7-2445. Sometime before returning home in September 1945, Braden had an interview with Peter; once in the United States, he suggested to the president of Swift International that the company might deal with the Communist leader as a way of counteracting the appeal of the official pro-Peronist unions in the plants. Memorandum of Conversation, Department of State, Oct. 4, 1945, 835.00/10-445.

101. This and the following paragraph depend on the careful reconstruction by Félix Luna in *El 45* (cited in n. 95).

That result was thwarted by the working class in the major turning point in twentieth-century Argentine history on October 17, 1945. On that day, while an indecisive, pajama-clad Perón remained under nominal arrest in a Buenos Aires military hospital, tens of thousands of workers from the industrial suburbs of Avellaneda and Berisso walked off the job and headed for the city. When the government blocked roads or raised bridges, workers faced down the police or circumvented the barriers. By afternoon, work and normal transport in the capital had come to a standstill. Huge crowds of these workers, their numbers swollen by thousands of new recruits and sympathizers and by contingents of workers from Rosario and the interior, roamed the streets of the capital and concentrated at strategic locations: the hospital to which Perón had been transferred; the main transportation center at the Plaza Once; and the political nerve center of the nation, the Plaza de Mayo in front of the Casa Rosada (Argentina's White House). As night fell the power and resolve of the workers seemed to grow. In the flickering yellow light of thousands of makeshift newspaper torches the chanting of perhaps a quarter of a million men and women reverberated through the city, literally shaking the walls of the main government buildings.[102] Finally, just before midnight, the workers achieved their purpose. Perón was freed and addressed the multitude. A new and powerful force had made its debut in Argentine politics. Perón's next task was to try to control it.

Recent scholarly assessments of the 17th of October have emphasized the self-directed nature of the workers' collective action.[103] Certainly, the top ranks of the Peronist leadership played a marginal role. Perón himself accepted his defeat after October 9 and turned his attention during his captivity to personal problems. He planned to clear his name and marry the actress Eva Duarte, who had shared his life during his ascent to power. Mercante met with some Peronist labor leaders to assess the situation before his own arrest on the 13th, but no concrete plans were formed. Influential pro-Peronist union leaders, the meatworkers' Cipriano Reyes paramount among them, demanded that the executive committee of the CGT meet to call a general strike to win the release of all political prisoners (including Perón). At that meeting, on the 16th, pro-

102. Luna gives this conservative estimate of the numbers of workers involved.
103. For example, Luna, *El 45* (cited in n. 95), and Tamarin, "The Argentine Labor Movement" (cited in n. 78). These studies contrast with earlier, self-serving accounts like that by Reyes, *Yo hice* (cited in n. 96), and Eduardo Colom, *El 17 de octubre* (Buenos Aires, 1955). Angel Perelman, *Como hicimos el 17 de octubre* (Buenos Aires, 1961), and Alberto Belloni, *Del anarchismo al peronismo* (Buenos Aires, 1960), are accounts by participants that stress the spontaneity of the mobilization. On the making of the myth that Eva Perón played an important role in these events, see Marysa Navarro, "Evita and the Crisis of 17 October 1945: A Case Study of Peronist and Anti-Peronist Mythology," *Journal of Latin American Studies* 12:1 (1980):127-38.

Peronist trade unionists finally prevailed over the negative votes of the delegates from the Unión Ferroviaria and the strike was set for the 18th. But by the time the CGT issued its strike call, rank-and-file workers were already resolved to shut down their plants and move into the streets. A meatworker union official from Rosario assessed the situation accurately during the CGT deliberations:

> If this body does not resolve to call a general strike, let me assure you that it will be unable to contain the strike that will come from the volatile state of the workers. That is to say that if we do not lead this movement [it will happen anyway]. . . . [The workers] are only waiting for instructions from the CGT to the effect that it will take place in a coordinated manner, but I assure you that if we don't vote the strike, in Rosario they'll go out just the same.[104]

Indeed, as early as the 15th meatworkers and other industrial workers in Berisso held a huge demonstration of support for Perón where the idea of a march on the capital was enthusiastically received. By the 16th workers walked off the job at the Anglo frigorífico in Avellaneda and tested the water by marching into Buenos Aires. Meatworkers, like most other Argentine workers, had tasted the benefits of organization, improved real wages, and social legislation under Perón. They understood what was at stake in the threatened return to liberalism. Pro-Peronist union organizations and leaders helped to guide the mobilization, but they had to scramble to stay ahead of the rank and file.

Following the momentous events of October 17, pro-Peronist labor leaders moved quickly to organize a vehicle capable of translating the new-found power of the workers' movement into an effective, institutionalized political force. At the end of October they announced the formation of the Partido Laborista, and in the months that followed they developed the party into a powerful political force. Four months after its formation, the Partido Laborista provided the majority of the votes that gave Perón the presidency of the nation. The election, one of the cleanest in Argentine history, also gave the Laborites control of both houses of the Argentine congress.

The Partido Laborista was structured around the pro-Peronist unions. Its leadership was composed of union officials, and many of its candidates for electoral office were also union men and women. The party adopted a stance of critical support toward the Peronist government and articulated a program of radical reform. It called for the extension of social welfare; nationalization of major industries, transport, and utilities; and fundamental agrarian reform. Vigorous, independent, pro-Peronist unions would provide the basis for all these advances. Unions would play

---

104. Quoted in Tamarin, "The Argentine Labor Movement" (cited in n. 78), p. 93, from the minutes of the meeting published in *Pasado y Presente* 4:2-3 (July-Dec. 1973):403-23.

a central role in the running of industries, and in the governance of the nation itself.[105]

It is true that the philosophy and program of the Partido Laborista were still vague in early 1946, that its organizational structure was embryonic and weak, and that the loyalties of most of those who voted for its candidates were probably fixed more on the person of Perón than on the party. Nevertheless, the tendencies within the party's trade union leadership toward radical economic and social reform and an exalted independent role for the unions were perceived by the Peronist leadership as a major threat to their political position and corporativist plans. Once Perón had consolidated control of the government, he set out to use the resources of the state to eliminate the new-found independent organizational strength of the Argentine labor movement. What is remarkable about the struggle that ensued is not that Perón eventually succeeded in this task, but how difficult his victory was and at what cost it was consummated.

The pivotal role of meatworkers and their unions in the events of October was reflected in their influence over the Partido Laborista. Reyes, a cofounder, became vice president of the party. Of the 52 members of the party's organizing committee, five were from the meatworkers' union, the strongest representation of any union. Given their numbers and economic strength—and their powerful representation in the Partido Laborista—it is not surprising that it was around their economic struggles and political pretensions that the most important confrontation between the Peronist state and the independent unions developed in 1946. Matters came to a head during a huge industrywide strike from September to November 1946. The strike had a dual purpose. It sought to force the companies to comply with a government decree of December 1945 granting meatworkers proportional pay raises and stipulating payment of an additional month's pay following a year of service.[106] It also sought to force congressional approval of a master agreement for the meat-packing industry, the "Estatuto de la Industria de la Carne," which would regulate, to the union's satisfaction, every aspect of work and industrial relations in the packing plants: job descriptions, minimum hours, overtime pay, seniority, transfers, layoffs, vacations, safety, and grievance procedures.

The strike began with a spectacularly effective two-week slowdown that cut production in the packing plants by 90 percent. The companies responded in early October with an industrywide lockout. That action

105. Walter Bevraggi Allende, *El Partido Laborista, el fracaso de Perón y el problema argentino* (Montevideo, 1954).

106. The extraordinary year-end bonus or *aguinaldo* was extended to many Argentine workers during this period. To many, it came to symbolize Perón's largesse toward labor.

dramatized the power of the owners of Argentina's most important industry and inflamed public opinion against the packers. Labor Party congressional representatives, led by Reyes, seized the opportunity to introduce a bill in congress to nationalize the entire packing industry. A violent debate ensued both within and outside the congress. A minority in the congress, composed of elements of the Partido Laborista and the Radical Party faction that had backed the candidacy of Perón, supported the nationalization scheme and the demands of the striking meatworkers. They used the occasion to challenge the labor policies and the revolutionary nationalist credentials of the Peronist government and its partisans in the congress. Meanwhile, outside the halls of congress bloody confrontations broke out between contingents of meatworkers supporting their union officials and Peronist loyalists opposed to them. The depth of the disagreement over the definition of the movement that had swept Perón to power was symbolized, as the strike dragged on, in the separate celebrations held on the anniversary of October 17. Reyes, and much of the meatworkers' union leadership, held one demonstration, the Peronist loyalists another. In the end, on November 9, Mercante imposed a settlement that granted the wage increases and guaranteed employment security. Meanwhile, the Chamber of Deputies passed a Peronist-supported version of the master agreement, and the bill was referred to the Senate for further study. The resolution of the conflict revealed the weakness of the Reyes-led faction within the parliamentary bloc of the Partido Laborista. Almost all of the party's deputies obediently followed the compromise position dictated by Perón. But the independent power of the unions themselves was far from broken. In fact, meatworkers rejected the terms of the November 9 settlement and continued the strike for five more days until Mercante negotiated somewhat better terms.[107]

Throughout 1947 and 1948 meat-packing unions continued to disrupt production to secure compliance with past agreements, improve wages and working conditions, and pressure the government for passage of the master agreement and nationalization of the foreign-owned packing houses. Reyes used his traditional base in the meatworkers' unions of Berisso and his seat in congress to embarrass the government and agitate for the nationalization of industry as well as for sweeping agrarian reform. During the great strike of late 1946, U.S. diplomatic personnel

107. The final agreement was published in *La Prensa* (Buenos Aires), Nov. 20, 1946. U.S. diplomatic representatives interpreted the strike as an inconclusive power struggle between Reyes and Perón for control of the meatworkers' unions. One reported that the embassy had been told "in strictest confidence" by a frigorífico official that Perón himself had informed the companies "that if they would not give in to the workers' demands the Government would see that the strike was broken, and normal operations resumed." Livingston D. Watrous to Secretary of State, Buenos Aires, Oct. 11 and Dec. 13, 1946, USNA/DS 835.504/10-1146 and /12-1346. The quotations are from the first dispatch.

were convinced that Reyes was in contact with agents of the Soviet Union. Be that as it may, during 1946 and 1947 he and his partisans found themselves in alliance with remnants of the FOIC, which upon its dissolution in early 1945 had directed its militants to "bore from within" the pro-Peronist, official unions. Both groups pressed radical worker demands and kept moderate, loyalist Peronist union leaders on the defensive. Peronist government officials probably shared the assessment of Reyes' personality and politics recorded by a senior U.S. official during the 1946 strike. "What Reyes is after is really to establish a sort of labor bloc in the Chamber of Deputies. You [Spruille Braden] know enough about Reyes and his background for me not to make any special comment. However people may feel here with regard to the government, even those who are opposed to Perón are hopeful that Reyes may not be able to get control [of the] unions. He is perhaps as radical an individual as anyone in the Argentine and he could easily outdo even the communists."[108] During 1947 Reyes survived at least one attempt on his life. He was finally silenced in 1948 when government officials arrested him for allegedly plotting to kill Perón. He remained in jail until after Perón fell from power in 1955.

Reyes was only the most visible expression of meatworker nonconformity with Peronist policies, however. Throughout the late 1940's rank-and-file militants continued to exert effective pressure on the Peronist leaders of the meat-packing unions. Wildcat strikes were endemic in the industry. Workers agitated for wage hikes and new improvements in work conditions. The failure to secure the master agreement became a major embarrassment for the Peronist union officials. The absence of a provision guaranteeing the right to strike in the Peronist constitution adopted in 1948 created a major ideological crisis for the Peronist leaders of the meatworkers' unions. Finally, although meatworkers' unions and their leaders continually pressed for nationalization of the industry, the government failed to move against the foreign owners of the largest plants.

Faced with the nonconformity of much of the meatworker rank and file, the Peronist government devised ingenious methods to ensure that leaders of the meatworkers' unions were people willing to enforce the directives of the government. Some of these methods were institutional in nature. During 1947 Peronist loyalists hit on the idea of joint blue- and white-collar unions in the packing plants. The object—never publicly stated—was to introduce more conservative middle-class elements into the unions as a brake on the militancy of the meatworker rank and file. Meanwhile, recalcitrant union leaders at the separate packing plants were

108. George S. Messershmith to Spruille Braden, Buenos Aires, Oct. 28, 1946, USNA/ DS 835.5043/10-2846.

frequently superseded administratively by the national Meatworkers' Federation, and dissidents, often labeled Communists, were purged from the ranks.[109] In the end, the Meatworkers' Federation, whose traditional autonomy from the more "Peronized" and pliant CGT was maintained until 1950, was itself taken over by and affiliated with the labor central. From that point on, all evidence of an independent position vis-à-vis the government disappeared from the pages of the Federation's newspaper, *El Trabajador de la Carne.*[110]

During these same years, the flow of material benefits from the state to the meatworkers continued. Significantly, however, the great improvements in wages and working conditions achieved between 1943 and 1947 were not matched in subsequent years. Meatworker wages fell behind the rise in living costs for long periods of time, profit-sharing plans were shelved, and major new improvements in work conditions failed to materialize. Increasingly, the government sought to mollify meatworkers and insure the loyalty of their leaders through off-the-job programs and subventions funded by the state. In late 1947, Mercante, acting as governor of the province of Buenos Aires, opened a credit of two million pesos to provide health care for meatworkers and their families. By 1950 meatworkers gained access to a program of "social tourism" that Mercante set up by expropriating, in the words of the newspaper of the Meatworkers' Federation, "a great quantity of chalets in seaside vacation zones." These were turned over to the unions so that workers could vacation "in places previously reserved for the wealthy classes." Government subsidies and

109. In the first six months of 1948 the newspaper *El Trabajador de la Carne* (Buenos Aires) reported on five such interventions. In July 1948 a major schism developed within the leadership of the Federation, and the new officials installed after that date exhibited greater conformity with the policies of the government. Walter Little has surveyed the struggle within the union over the issue of critical support for the Peronist government in "La tendencia peronista en el sindicalismo argentino: El caso de los obreros de la carne," *Aportes* 19 (Jan. 1971):107-24.

110. Most of the information in this paragraph and the next is based on a reading of this newspaper, founded under the direction of Eleuterio Cardoso on Jan. 1, 1948. Cardoso himself left the paper in early 1949 to become a labor attaché in Poland. I wish to thank Mr. Cardoso for lending me his personal collection of the newspaper, for introducing me to other officials and members of his union, and for spending many hours explaining to me the nature of work in the packing plants and the appeal of Peronism in the 1940's—and afterward—to meatworkers. Cardoso began to work in the "Anglo" frigorífico as a youth in the early 1940's. He played an active role in the great mobilization of meatworkers after 1943 described in this essay. With the fall of Perón, he became a major leader in the union's resistance to the antilabor, anti-Peronist policies of subsequent liberal military and civilian governments. As secretary-general of the Meatworkers Federation, he directed the last major strike in the industry in 1962. By then the meat export industry in Argentina was in crisis and the number of jobs in the industry in decline. The 1962 strike lasted 100 days and ended with the union's capitulation. In recent decades the great integrated packinghouses of Argentina, like those of the United States, have been replaced by geographically dispersed, much smaller, and more specialized operations. Since the 1960's meatworkers have played a relatively minor role in the Argentine labor movement.

low-interest loans from government-controlled banks enabled the Meat-workers' Federation to purchase a distinguished seven-story building in the heart of the Buenos Aires business district for its headquarters. Indi-vidual meatworker unions received similar government help in establish-ing their respective headquarters near the major packing plants. Peronist union leaders were invited to gala banquets hosted by Mercante and Eva Perón to celebrate past meatworker victories. On October 21, 1949, for example, meatworker union officials reserved the glittering onetime cul-tural preserve of the *porteño* elite, the Teatro Colón opera house in Buenos Aires, to honor Perón, Eva, and Mercante. They had originally planned to invite the meatworker rank and file, the *Trabajador de la Carne* lamely explained, but decided against it when they realized that "no place existed with the capacity to hold 60,000 or 70,000 workers."

This change in the nature of benefits accorded meatworkers and their leaders after 1947 was typical of Peronist labor policies during the period and prefigured trends that became more pronounced after 1950. More and more the Peronist government resorted to symbolic and ritualistic means to perpetuate its influence and control over the Argentine labor movement. The lengths to which this strategy was carried are richly doc-umented in the pages of the *Trabajador de la Carne*. Meatworkers were asked in 1950 to look on the accomplishments they had won through struggle as a marvelous gift from Perón.

When we stop to reflect on the evolution of the conditions of life and work of the Argentine proletariat in the last half decade, and compare them with the con-ditions of the five years that preceded it, we are left simply amazed. The change wrought by the justicialist revolution has been so prodigious, the economic and social reforms so profound and rapidly effected, that at times it appears to us like a dream. . . . The revolution has come to embody the aspirations of the working class as if by an act of enchantment, since the movement from obscurity to light was effected without transition, without the least bit of sacrifice, without de-manding of workers an extraordinary effort. It seems like a miracle wrought by faith, and perhaps it is nothing else.

They were urged to place their faith in a meatworkers' trinity of sorts, composed of Perón, Mercante ("the beloved friend of the meatwork-ers"), and the "excelentísima señora doña Eva Perón, untiring defender of our union interests." In mid-1952, as Eva Perón lay near death, a draw-ing that portrayed her in a pose reminiscent of the Virgin Mary covered the front page of the meatworkers' newspaper. Its caption was meant to serve as an official epitaph for her, but it neatly summarized the thrust of Peronist labor policy as well: "Her infinite kindness, her love for the humble, and her passion for the cause of Perón makes her name be praised." By the 1950's Peronist labor policy was a caricature of its for-mer self. It had transformed the independent and vigorous pro-Peronist unions into passive instruments obedient to the dictates of Perón. It sought to substitute mystical loyalty to the person of the leader for the radical reformism of a class-conscious proletariat.[111]

———◆——◆——

By mid-century Peronist labor policy—indeed the whole of the Peronist experiment—was in serious disarray. The government found itself in a position in which it could no longer countenance continued expansion, or even maintenance, of the level of material benefits won by workers during the 1940's. Real wages, especially those of unskilled workers, which had risen dramatically between 1947 and 1948, fell steadily after that date. By 1955, when the government fell, they had returned to approximately the same levels reached in 1943, when the military government took power.[112] At the root of the problem lay the beginnings of a structural economic crisis—precipitated in good measure by the government's own economic and social policies—from which the nation, 35 years later, has yet to extricate itself. The economic crisis led the Peronist leadership to abandon the nationalist, developmentalist, redistributive political economy that had brought it to power and characterized its first years in government. After 1950 the government began to substitute rhetoric for the reality of its earlier policies, and to resort to manipulation, coercion, and venality to maintain itself in control of a government originally established with the spontaneous, democratic support of the majority of the Argentine people.

The perversion of Peronism was not, primarily, the result of intractable economic problems caused by changing world conditions after the war, as some apologists have argued. Nor was it fundamentally the consequence of personality defects of a single man, as many liberal critics imply. Its failure was congenital to the corporativist political economy put into practice by the Peronists. Based on the dual myths of class har-

111. The quotations in this paragraph and the preceding one come from *El Trabajador de la Carne*, Mar. 1950, pp. 2 and 5, Sept. 1949, p. 9, Mar. 1950, p. 5, Jan. 1951, pp. 6-7, and Jan.-June 1952, p. 1. As the union's independence from the state declined, and as its bureaucratization and the centralization of authority within it increased, the paper was published less frequently. After 1946 Eva Perón played an important role in implementing the labor policy of the regime. These activities complemented her effective efforts to organize a feminist wing of the Peronist party. The contradictions in Eva Perón's thought and activities are revealed in important recent studies by J. M. Taylor, *Eva Perón, Myths of a Woman* (Chicago, 1979), and Nicholas Fraser and Marysa Navarro, *Eva Perón* (London, 1980). The benefits accorded women by the Peronist government are highlighted in Nancy Caro Hollander, "Si Evita Viviera," *Latin American Perspectives* 1:3 (Fall 1974):42-57.

112. The figures are conveniently summarized in Spalding, *Organized Labor* (cited in n. 34), Tables 17 and 18, pp. 169 and 175. Of course, given the expansion of off-the-job social-welfare programs and improvements in working conditions, in many ways workers were still much better off at the end of the Perón regime than they were at the beginning. Workers also lost proportionately much less than other social groups after 1948; their share of national income actually increased during the 1950's.

mony and the viability of a "third way" between the extremes of capitalism and socialism, Peronist political economy foundered on its own contradictions.

Peronists came to power at a time when the Argentine economy had begun to grow at an annual rate of almost 10 percent. They governed, initially, during a period when wartime and postwar conditions in Europe and the United States created high prices for Argentine agricultural and livestock exports and shielded Argentine industry from foreign competition. Between 1945 and 1948, the volume of exports remained roughly constant but their value more than doubled. During the same period the volume of industrial production increased by one-third.[113] During his first years in power Perón was able to tap the huge (albeit restricted) sterling reserves built up in Britain during the war. He used these funds to liquidate the nation's foreign debt, to buy the British railroads and major foreign-owned public utilities, and to promote national industry. To help fund these development projects and provide government revenue to pay for extensive social-welfare measures, the Peronists established a monopoly on the sale of Argentina's main export products. The IAPI, as the state agency charged with administering this monopoly was called, enabled the government to sell these products at the high prevailing world price, pay producers a "fair" but much lower price that still provided them a modest profit, and use the large excess profit accruing to the state to meet rapidly rising government expenditures for economic development, social programs, and a mushrooming and highly paid civil and military bureaucracy.[114]

These economic and fiscal policies initially seemed to confirm the viability of Peronist political economy. They allowed the government to accomplish nationalist goals and preside over a major redistribution of wealth in favor of the working class without threatening the position of the ruling class or the principle of private property. The redistribution of wealth, in turn, stimulated internal demand for Argentina's new industries and for its rural products.

All of these policies were partly a rational response to the difficult problems of economic readjustment Argentina faced in a changed capitalist world economy. The war seriously affected the capacity of Argentina's most important traditional customer, Great Britain, to pay for its

113. These figures are taken from p. 187 of David Rock's fine synthesis, "The Survival of Peronism," in Rock, ed., *Argentina in the Twentieth Century* (Pittsburgh, 1975), pp. 179–221.

114. By 1948 Argentine officers were the highest paid in the world. Although the size of the army was reduced under Perón, the police force was expanded. Military spending more than doubled to 44 percent of government expenditures between 1941 and 1946. Marvin Goldwert, *Democracy, Militarism, and Nationalism in Argentina, 1930-1966* (Austin, Tex., 1972), pp. 102–3, 83–84.

imports. At the same time, Argentina found it increasingly difficult to balance its trade with the United States, the leading nation in the postwar capitalist system. Argentine grain exports competed with those of the United States in the world market, and domestic U.S. meat producers lobbied successfully against imports of most Argentine meat products. These considerations help to explain both particular economic strategies of the Peronist government—such as the decision to use blocked sterling to pay a high price for the run-down British-owned railroad system—as well as the general policy of favoring import-substituting industry over the rural sector in the postwar period.[115]

Many critics have argued that the root of the long-term failure of Peronist economic policies lay in the decision to tax the rural sector to promote industry at a time when the international terms of trade were uniquely favorable to Argentina's traditional exports.[116] As a result, Argentina lost a magnificent opportunity to maximize its comparative advantage in world trade, and to modernize rural production. Instead, it saddled itself with an inefficient import-substituting light industrial sector that merely replaced the traditional dependency on imports of foreign manufactures with a new dependency on imports of capital goods, industrial raw materials, and fuels. As the export of traditional commodities declined in the postwar period, the Argentine economy—including its industry—was strangled by the resulting foreign-exchange bottleneck. Stagnation of both agrarian and industrial production, evident by the early 1950's, was the outcome. This argument is theoretically sound, but, as Jorge Fodor has shown, it may overstate the actual ability of Argentina to sell its traditional exports in a postwar world in which its European customers were unable to pay in convertible currencies. In any case, the goal of Argentine economic policies was not much different from that of the other major nations of Latin America following the war. Everywhere, and with much less costly immediate results, governments sought to use the resources of the state to protect and promote import-substituting industry.

The disastrous implications of Peronist economic policies, in both the short and the long term, lay not so much in the fact that industry was promoted at the expense of the traditional export sector as in the means

115. Jorge Fodor, "Perón's Policies for Agricultural Exports, 1946-1948: Dogmatism or Commonsense?," in Rock, ed., *Argentina in the Twentieth Century*, pp. 135-61, marshals a significant body of circumstantial evidence (as opposed to hard information on the actual formulation of policy) to support the argument that Peronist initiatives simply reacted to world economic constraints.

116. Good examples are Eprime Eshag and Rosemary Thorp, "Economic and Social Consequences of Orthodox Economic Policies in Argentina in the Postwar Years," *Bulletin of the Oxford University Institute of Economics and Statistics* 17:1 (Feb. 1965):3-44; Díaz Alejandro, *Essays* (cited in n. 7); and Colin Lewis, "Anglo-Argentine Trade, 1945-1965," in Rock, ed., *Argentina in the Twentieth Century* (cited in n. 113), pp. 114-34.

the Peronists employed to reach this goal in the postwar liberal capitalist world. Peronist political economy—particularly its labor policies—seriously impaired the developmental potential of Argentina in that postwar world, yet failed to substitute for liberal political economy a viable alternative.[117]

Of greatest importance to the future economic development of the nation was the way Peronist policies affected the long-standing problem of rural productivity. By and large, Peronist initiatives worked to intensify, rather than ameliorate, that problem. The IAPI deprived rural producers of the great profits in the international grain trade in the postwar years. Peronist rural labor policies, beginning with the "Estatuto del Peón" in 1944, seriously affected the cost and discipline of rural labor by establishing a minimum wage for farm workers and encouraging their organization into government-approved unions. Peronist subsidies for light, consumer-oriented industry encouraged the migration of rural workers into the cities, yet failed to produce the farm machinery needed to help Argentina catch up with the remarkable increases in rural productivity registered in the United States, Canada, New Zealand, and Australia in the years after the war. By leaving the structure of rural ownership intact, and by taxing commerce rather than the land itself, Peronist policies destroyed the incentive of capitalist rural producers yet failed to challenge the basis of their economic power. As a result, rural producers chose not to modernize and intensify production. They continued to shift production away from agriculture into stock raising. Doing so helped them to solve their labor problems, allowed them to participate in the growing— and subsidized—internal market for meat, and enabled them to avoid the "tax" imposed by the IAPI on export products.

Peronist policies also seriously undermined the foreign-owned packing industry, traditionally a very important producer of the foreign exchange vital to the health of the Argentine economy. By 1947 the industry was in crisis, and in the 1950's it entered into a period of rapid decline. Peronist policies created three problems for the packing companies. First, those policies worked to bid up the price of cattle for slaughter. Second, they imposed exchange restrictions that interfered with profit remittance and transfers of capital. And third, they greatly increased the wage bill while weakening management's capacity to control the organization of work and the size of its labor force. The first problem resulted from increased internal demand, a product in turn of the significant redistribution of na-

117. In this sense, Fodor's dismissal of Díaz Alejandro's felicitous characterization of Peronist political economy as "a delayed response to the Depression" involves a fundamental misreading of Argentine history. That response, as argued in the course of this essay, resulted from the complex interaction of social, political, and ideological currents generated by the initial success of Argentina's export-oriented development.

tional income toward the working class after 1945. The government sought to protect urban consumers from the resulting inflation by subsidizing the operations of domestic beef suppliers. These suppliers were thus encouraged to pay rural producers high prices for cattle. Consequently, the foreign packing houses found themselves paying elevated prices for an increasingly scarce commodity. The fact that Argentines began to eat part of the meat they formerly exported contributed to the scarcity of foreign exchange. To rationalize the use of the foreign exchange available, and to prohibit the export of excess profits, the government resorted to exchange controls. These severely limited the freedom of multinational meat-packing corporations to transfer capital between subsidiaries and remit profits. Finally—and most important—Peronist tolerance of and support for the meatworkers' unions, and the government's efforts to avoid layoffs in an industry in economic trouble, struck at the very heart of capitalist enterprise: the ability to purchase labor power on the free market in the quantities deemed necessary. It also seriously curbed the power of capital to discipline the work force.

Faced with this decidedly unfavorable "investment climate" and falling profits in its unionized plants, Swift International reported it had suspended dividend payments in 1947 for the first time since the incorporation of the company in Argentina in 1918. Meanwhile, the average value of its shares traded on the New York Stock Exchange fell from $30–$35 in 1946 to less than $11 at the end of 1948. According to the company president, the decline of Swift's fortunes under Peronist economic and labor policies had not only created "great uncertainty in the minds of our shareholders, but also a general atmosphere unfavorable to United States investment in Argentina." Swift International, he pointed out, was the only Argentine corporation whose shares were listed and traded on U.S. stock exchanges. Since 1918 "United States investors, brokers, bankers, and counselors have come to regard the market for our shares as a sort of barometer reflecting Argentine business conditions and economic relations with this country."[118] By 1949, Swift International had moved its home office out of Argentina, and although Swift and the other foreign packing companies continued to operate there, they ceased to invest in and modernize their Argentine plants. Between 1948 and 1952 the total volume of meat exports from Argentina declined by more than half (from 684,000 to 294,000 tons), though the volume of cattle slaughtered (for domestic consumption and export) remained roughly the same or declined only slightly. Meanwhile, home consumption of cattle jumped

118. Joseph O. Hanson, President of Swift International, to Paul C. Daniels, Director of the Office of American Republic Affairs, Chicago, Dec. 13, 1948, USNA/DS 835.5034/12-1348.

from 68 percent of the total slaughtered in 1938 to 77 percent in 1949 and 87 percent in 1953.[119] During the 1950's the volume of meat exports handled by the foreign packinghouses declined sharply, and in the years after 1960 one by one these packinghouses closed their doors.

The crisis of the meat-packing industry, like the general economic crisis of which it was part, reveals how Peronist policies undermined the logic of the capitalist marketplace without substituting an alternative political economy capable of promoting Argentine development. The magnitude and implications of this basic contradiction were initially obscured by the dynamism of the postwar Argentine economy, by the windfall profits reaped in international trade in the late 1940's, and by the bonanza of foreign reserves inherited by the Peronists. By 1950, however, the extent of the failure of Peronist economic and social policies had become manifest. Faced with a stagnating economy and growing fiscal constraints, the government reversed virtually every aspect of its initial policies. After 1950 it moved in the direction of the cosmopolitian liberal economic orthodoxy it professed to abhor. It sought to attract foreign investors. It negotiated a loan with the United States. It signed a major agreement with Standard Oil that reversed the long-standing trend begun in the 1920's toward greater national control of the petroleum industry. It compromised its aspirations for an independent foreign policy in favor of support for U.S. hemispheric initiatives. As real wages declined after 1950, labor discipline and productivity became the watchwords of CGT directives to member unions. The government coddled landowners with subsidies, credits, and price incentives in a desperate effort to stimulate rural production.

As with its labor policy after 1950, the government attempted to substitute rhetoric and symbols for the reality of its initial nationalist and redistributive economic policies. It continued publicly to blame foreign imperialists and domestic oligarchs for the economic failures of the regime. Yet in practice it used economic incentives to encourage these same groups to invest and promote economic growth through orthodox capitalist means. This strategy ended in failure. Foreign and domestic capitalists, their economic power left largely intact by Peronist economic reforms, their labor problems magnified by Peronist social initiatives, their confidence shaken by the rhetoric of the regime and the reality of its political base, preferred to avoid risk and chose to invest elsewhere. After 1950 the deepening economic crisis slowly compromised the ideological hegemony and political legitimacy of the Peronist government. The ex-

119. Lewis, "Anglo-Argentine Trade" (cited in n. 116), pp. 121-22. Lewis also documents the stagnation of rural production in general and the decline in Argentine foreign trade in the years after 1950.

cesses of the regime—the personality cults, the pathological overtones of the enormous attention focused on the preservation of Eva Perón's body, the torture of dissidents, and the scope of corruption in the bureaucracy—all date from this period. When liberal elements in the military finally moved decisively to topple the government in 1955, few Argentines were moved to defend it. Although some union officials pleaded with Perón for weapons to arm workers to defend the regime, even that alternative foundered on the contradiction of the Peronists' corporativist social philosophy of class harmony.

The Persistence of Peronism

Had the powerful liberal forces—the pampean landowners and the domestic and foreign industrialists, bankers, and merchants—who returned to power in 1955 governed with moderation, had they been able to restore vigorous growth to the economy under liberal principles, Argentines might have been spared much of the trauma of the next quarter century.[120] That they could do neither was a result in large part of the existence of the powerful industrial unions, which survived the political eclipse of the Peronist leadership, and of their combative, cohesive rank-and-file members. This organized working class, which expanded during the Peronist regime from roughly half a million to 2.5 million workers, stood in the way of the capitalist plans of the victorious liberals.

The goals of the liberals who seized power in Argentina in 1955 were dictated by the realities of the postwar world economy. This new liberal world order was a modification of the old: it adapted itself successfully to the major economic, social, ideological, and institutional changes wrought in fifteen years of economic crisis and world war. Domestically, in all capitalist countries, these changes involved a transformation in the relationship between capital, the state, and civil society. During the crisis the state assumed a greatly expanded role in the preservation of capitalist society as a whole—in regulating the economy and attempting to promote growth, in handling the social discontent and opposition engendered by the crisis, and (in the central capitalist societies) in marshaling all social resources in a war for world hegemony. Internationally, as we

120. I have relied for much of the information in this final section on two important efforts at synthesis and analysis: Guillermo O'Donnell, "Estado y alianzas en la Argentina, 1956-1976," *Desarrollo Económico* 16:64 (Jan.-Mar. 1977):524-54; and David Rock, "The Survival and Restoration of Peronism," in Rock, ed., *Argentina in the Twentieth Century* (cited in n. 113), pp. 179-222. On the labor movement specifically, see Daniel James, "Power and Politics in Peronist Trade Unions," *Journal of Interamerican Studies and World Affairs* 20:1 (Feb. 1978):3-36; Juan Carlos Torre, "El movimiento obrero y el último gobierno peronista (1973-1976)," *Crítica & Utopia* 6 (1982):99-134; and Edward C. Epstein, "Control and Co-optation of the Argentine Labor Movement," *Economic Development and Cultural Change* 27:3 (Apr. 1979):445-65.

have seen, the crisis led to a partial breakdown in the world division of labor and an end to the unrestricted flow of capital, technology, and commodities characteristic of the pre-1930 classical liberal capitalist system.

Two aspects of these changes posed especially difficult, long-range structural problems to capital in the center of the system as the war came to an end.[121] In the advanced industrial nations, the crisis enabled workers to organize in basic industry, to force a rise in the level of returns to labor, and to expand greatly the scope of state-administered social-welfare programs. In Latin America, the crisis fostered the industrialization of the major nations and generated a consensus, backed by a broad coalition of social groups, behind state support for continued industrial development. The first of these developments challenged classical liberal domestic political economy and threatened capital accumulation in the industrial center of the world system. The second undermined the classical liberal theory of comparative advantage through trade in an international division of labor, posing a threat to the continued expansion of world capitalism based on accumulation in the center through foreign investment and trade with the periphery.

Both of these obstacles were temporarily overcome through the transfer of production by manufacturing corporations from the center to the periphery in the postwar era. This process afforded several advantages to capital in the center and rationalized the system as a whole. It gave capital an outlet for investment that could take advantage of the low wages and limited organization of workers in most peripheral societies. It enabled it to participate in the protected markets for manufactured goods in peripheral societies and qualify for government subsidies, credits, and loans there. It allowed capital to benefit, along with the bulk of the people in the center of the world system, from an expanded system of world trade based on a new, more complex international division of labor. Advanced industrial economies exchanged technology, services, sophisticated manufactures, and capital goods for raw materials and, increasingly, cheap light and durable consumer manufactures. Finally, it enabled capital in the center to maintain the process of domestic accumulation yet avoid massive social unrest and threats to its ideological hegemony. Capital was able to countenance the maintenance—even the expansion—of domestic social-welfare systems, to tolerate or preempt unions in the most advanced domestic industries (as long as increased benefits to workers were linked to gains in productivity), and, over the long haul, to weaken unions in more labor-intensive industries, which suffered both from the collapse of export markets and, later, from the competition of cheaper foreign imports.

121. These issues are discussed more generally in Chapter One.

What capital in the center, and in the world system as a whole, could not countenance was high wage levels and powerful industrial unions in the periphery. Here Argentina (like Chile) stood apart from the other major nations of Latin America in the postwar period. For specific historical reasons (discussed for Venezuela and Colombia in subsequent chapters), capital in these other nations was able to discipline industrial labor and force it into acceptable liberal arrangements after the war. All these countries were able to attract a massive flow of foreign capital and expand their economies rapidly in the years after 1945. Argentina, saddled with the labor legacy of the Peronist regime, could not.

Consequently, elimination of the Peronist unions and a reduction of the material well-being of the working class became the primary objectives of the liberal forces that overthrew Perón in 1955. For a decade capital in Argentina had been deprived of the advantages of association with the new and rapidly expanding institutions of the postwar world capitalist order. Destruction of Peronist institutions—primary among them the labor unions—would reopen the mechanisms of domestic capital accumulation and create the preconditions for an infusion of foreign capital to dynamize the whole national economy and integrate it into the expanding world system. Even Argentine industrialists could share in the enthusiasm to open the door to foreign capital. Whatever support some may have lent to early Peronist development and distribution policies, such support disappeared with the constraints on the expansion of industry evident by the mid-1950's. As did their counterparts all over Latin America, most industrialists welcomed the opportunity to associate themselves with foreign-owned manufacturing corporations. By becoming junior partners with these firms, they hoped to expand their business and profits, even as they reduced their risks. They also gained access to advanced technology, machinery, and processes, and they enjoyed the prestige— and sometimes the geographic mobility—of working for the great international firms.[122]

The caution with which the military regime that toppled Perón first approached the unions and the basic issues posed by Peronist political economy was based in large part on the fear of the unions' power and the possibility of civil war. But when the unions called an ineffectual general strike to protest early government initiatives, the government launched a full-scale offensive against the workers. Following the advice of the Argentine economist Raúl Prebisch, the government sought to stimulate the rural sector through currency devaluation and price incentives for agriculture. It eliminated government subsidies that had kept the consumer price of basic foodstuffs at low levels, abolished collective wage contracts

122. Osvaldo Sunkel, "Transnational Capitalism and National Disintegration in Latin America," *Social and Economic Studies* 22:1 (Mar. 1973):132-76; Richard Barnet and Ronald Müller, *Global Reach* (New York, 1974).

negotiated under Perón, and, as inflation skyrocketed, froze wages. The government took control of the CGT, revoked the legal status of many unions, and arrested hundreds of Peronist labor officials. Encouraged by the government, Socialists, Communists, and independent trade unionists tried to take control of the unions.

These policies failed to accomplish the liberals' economic goals, but they succeeded in achieving the one thing liberals dreaded most: they ensured the survival, and restored the prestige, of Peronism. Many workers may have been disillusioned and alienated by the course of Peronist labor policies and institutions during the early 1950's. But the scope of the attack on their material well-being and the institutions of their class after 1955 made their achievements under Perón seem like a golden age. The purges of Peronist labor bureaucrats opened the way for a shop stewards' movement that revitalized the unions and molded them into independent, militant organizations that soon proved capable of resisting the liberal attack on their wages and organizations. Perón in exile continued to direct the movement. But as the years advanced his supporters became more monolithically working-class and elements within the union movement once more defined a class-inspired program of radical reform for Argentine society.

The unions' capacity to disrupt the economy and roll back the liberals' economic and political offensives was demonstrated throughout the 1960's. Liberal regimes, military or civilian, tried every conceivable tack in their efforts to repress, split, or co-opt Peronist labor—to no avail. Labor consistently sabotaged all liberal initiatives on the economic front. After 1955 the Argentine economy suffered from spasmodic starts and stops, formidable bouts of inflation and deflation, chronic balance-of-payments crises, repeated currency devaluations, and growing structural unemployment. Through all the wild fluctuations, one thing was constant: the slow growth, if not virtual stagnation, of the Argentine economy. Despite Argentina's low population growth rate, per capita income grew fitfully and slowly. The workers' share of national wealth and the personal income of workers and middle-class elements fluctuated widely; both declined in absolute terms over long periods of time.[123]

The stalemate between capital and labor in the workplace was matched on the political front. The Peronists were proscribed from politics, yet no government, elected or imposed by military fiat, could govern effectively without them. The potential electoral strength of the Peronists—roughly one-third of the national electorate in the late 1950's—increased as the in-

---

123. Estimates of Argentine growth are vexed by conflicting sets of official statistics. The most optimistic point to a 1 to 2 percent annual growth in gross national product per capita in the years since 1955. Even these figures, however, confirm the stagnation of income in the form of wages and salaries over much of this period. See Clarence Auvekas, Jr., "Economic Growth and Income Distribution in Postwar Argentina," *Inter-American Economic Affairs* 20:3 (Winter 1966):19-38.

effectiveness of liberal economic policies continued. By the early 1970's, as significant elements of the middle class moved into their camp, Peronists approached an absolute majority.

Since the fall of Perón in 1955, Argentine society has been split into two rival camps, each with an exclusive, sectarian interpretation of the past and an uncompromising program for the future. Other Latin American societies assimilated both the historical experience with laissez-faire liberalism before 1930 and the economic nationalism and social-welfare policies of the Depression era. Argentines, prisoners of the anomalous course of their national history, could not. Coming as they did out of phase with world developments, both the liberalism of the Infamous Decade and the Peronist reaction of 1945-55 created bitter feelings in large segments of Argentine society that remained in their historical consciousness. Ideological polarization denied all post-1955 governments the measure of consensus and legitimacy vital to effective long-term policy-making.

The national frustration fostered by the economic and political stalemate after 1955 has been enormous. In part it has been nurtured by the general perception that Argentina's extensive natural resources ought to have ensured the nation a great destiny. The country's early-twentieth-century development, and the European origins of the bulk of its people, reinforced in the minds of many Argentines cultural and racial assumptions emanating from Europe and the United States about the origins of economic and political progress. Most Argentines identified with Europe and considered themselves superior to their "less cultured," "tropical," and darker Latin American neighbors. Since 1955, however, Argentina has seemed more closely to approximate First World stereotypes of Third World economic ineptitude and political instability than have the other large Latin American countries.[124] And Argentines have watched helplessly as what was perceived as an economic "miracle" propelled its major rival, racially mixed and semitropical Brazil, into a position of regional hegemony.

Faced with a collective inability to agree on rational explanations of what went wrong, Argentines of all political persuasions have turned increasingly to conspiratorial theories to account for national failure. As no political coalition proved able to marshal sufficient economic, social, or ideological power to overcome the inertia of economic stagnation and political stalemate, each political faction adopted political strategies at once more selfishly opportunistic and more prone to violence than it had in the past.

124. A typical exposition of this view is "Poor Little Rich Boy, Argentina: A Survey," *The Economist*, Jan. 26, 1980, pp. 2-26. Predictably, V. S. Naipaul focuses on the same theme in his scathing analysis of what he views as Argentine cultural pathology, *The Return of Eva Perón* (New York, 1981).

The most ominous manifestation of these general trends was the proliferation of guerrilla groups and paramilitary opposition to them in the
1960's. The guerrillas—vaguely Marxist in orientation, largely middle-
class in composition—reflected the frustration of students and professionals in a stagnating capitalist society seemingly impervious to evolu-
tionary change. The resort to guerrilla tactics revealed another serious aspect of the survival of Peronism. It was an index of the political
impotence of leftist elements denied their customary banners of economic nationalism and social justice by Peronist ideology, and isolated
from their natural constituency, the industrial working class, by Peronist
unions.

For the most part, after 1955 labor remained solidly anti-Marxist. This
attitude only partly reflected the influence of conservative Peronist leaders and the acceptance by rank-and-file workers of the corporativist assumptions traditionally elaborated in official Peronist propaganda. The
standard Peronist indictment of the Marxist left was confirmed in the
popular mind by the very course of Argentine history since the 1940's.
The Marxist parties, in alliance with the liberal ruling class, had opposed
Perón in 1945 and 1955. Peronism, not the left, was associated with the
great organizational and material victories of the Argentine working
class. The irony of Argentine history was that it seemed to confirm the
viability of Peronist political economy. Perón's initial government had
coincided with a fortuitous conjuncture of national economic trends and
exceptional world conditions. Its failure after 1950 was uncritically attributed not to its internal contradictions but to "enemies" who sabotaged
Perón's nationalist, distributive policies. Given the growing prestige of
Peronism in the years after 1955, even the Marxist left found itself forced
to contribute to this mythical vision of Peronism as a viable, revolutionary force. The historical experience and loyalties of rank-and-file workers
seemed to give Marxists no other choice. Like the independent pro-Peronist unionists before them, Marxists were forced after 1955 to become
more Peronist than the Peronists themselves. As long as Peronists and
Marxists fought a common liberal enemy this strategy was effective. But
when the Peronists returned to power in the early 1970's, it led to disaster
for the left.

Marxist labor leaders who successfully disassociated themselves from
the stigma of the international Communist movement did appear in positions of power in the Argentine labor movement during the 1960's.
This was true especially among the organizations of the "new" Argentine industrial working class—those sectors that developed under the aegis of foreign capital in the 1960's, where the legacy of Peronism was
muted and indirect. Independent Marxists also managed to capture the
leadership of some traditional Peronist unions. These Marxists were able
to use their union base to advance the political goals of the left, however,

only so long as their activities did not compromise efficient administration of union affairs or adversely affect the level of rank-and-file material benefits. Neither proved possible once the Peronists returned to national power in the early 1970's.[125] Finally, a significant left-wing movement inspired by Marxist theories of class struggle emerged as a minority position within the Peronist labor movement and the youth wing of the Peronist party itself. These nominal Peronists paid the highest price in blood when the party returned to power: many were systematically murdered and the rest purged from the party after Perón himself returned to Argentina in 1974.

The weakness and limited potential of the Peronist left and its Marxist allies were not obvious in the late 1960's, however. Guerrilla activity increased in scope and effectiveness during those years. In 1969 a volatile alliance of students and workers mounted a major insurrection in Argentina's second city, the interior town of Córdoba. The Marxist-led insurgents took control of parts of the city for several days before they were crushed in a major military operation.

With the advantage of hindsight it is clear that the bloody events in Córdoba in 1969 were not indicative of general conditions favoring mass mobilization and popular insurrection in Argentina. Córdoba was a unique place; the *cordobazo*, as the abortive insurrection came to be called, was an exceptional event.[126] Traditionally the main center of higher education in Argentina, Córdoba had a high proportion of students in its population and a long and glorious tradition of student activism. Córdoba was also the locus of the Argentine automobile industry, the most important of the "new" industries developed in Argentina after 1955 under the aegis of foreign multinational corporations. Auto workers organized in militant unions spearheaded the strikes that precipitated the cordobazo. Some of these workers were part-time students; others lived in student neighborhoods. Widely shared regional complaints completed the terms of Córdoba's exceptionalism: all classes resented discrimination by the central government against the city. Living costs were higher, housing scarcer, and public services much more inadequate than in the national capital. Elsewhere in Argentina, especially in the dominant province of Buenos Aires, where traditional Peronist leadership of the working class was solidly entrenched, the Marxist and Peronist left struggled against much greater odds in their efforts to build a revolutionary coalition in the 1960's.

Ironically, the cordobazo of 1969 precipitated not the social revolution

125. Martha Iris de Roldán has analyzed the fate of the best-known of these leaders, Agustín Tosco, in her *Sindicatos y protesta social en la Argentina (1969-1974). Un estudio de caso: el sindicato de Luz y Fuerza de Córdoba* (Amsterdam, 1968).

126. On the *cordobazo* see Elizabeth Jelin, *La protesta obrera* (Buenos Aires, 1974), and Francisco Delich, *Crisis y protesta social: Córdoba, Mayo de 1969* (Buenos Aires, 1970).

its leaders had envisioned, but the reactionary political developments that culminated five years later in the ascension to power of Perón and the virtual extermination of the left. The insurrection and its bloody repression decisively compromised the legitimacy of the military government and shook the confidence of its civilian liberal supporters. Concerted opposition to the regime's ineffective economic policies and repressive political ones, previously confined mainly to the unions and the guerrillas, now spread to much of the middle class. The Peronist party managed to capture most of the growing opposition to the military regime. Not only had the party spearheaded the opposition since 1955, it had successfully portrayed itself to a new generation of Argentines as a revolutionary popular movement capable of transforming the economy, restoring social order through policies of social justice, and returning the nation to the principles of electoral democracy.

The cordobazo thus initiated the paradoxical process through which the historical enemies of Perón came slowly to embrace him. Forced to resort to the massive use of force to contain internal dissent, frightened by evidence of the expanding power of a revolutionary alliance between students and workers, and abandoned by public opinion, which clamored for reform and free elections, the military regime and its liberal allies began the series of negotiations and mutual compromises with the Peronists that returned the party to power after the free elections of 1973. Only then did the weakness of the Marxist left and the atypical nature of the worker-student alliance at Córdoba five years earlier become clear.

Peronism returned to repeat, this time with record speed and devastating finality, the historical lesson of its first rise to power. Marxist influence in the labor movement was destroyed, the left wing of the Peronist movement eliminated. Modest social and economic initiatives, constrained this time by conditions much less favorable to nationalist economic reform and redistributionist social policies, failed to revitalize the economy but led instead to the most severe inflation yet seen in Argentina. After Perón's death in 1974, the Peronist coalition rapidly disintegrated. The economic and social policies of his successors, under the nominal leadership of his new wife, Vice President Isabel Perón, veered sharply to the right. As had happened in 1950-55, the return to liberal economic orthodoxy failed to convince capital and alienated labor. Rhetoric and an orgy of official corruption preserved the government in power for only a short time. In 1976 the familiar coalition of liberal forces and right-wing military leaders seized power once again. Given the strength of the guerrilla movement, which had been bolstered by Peronist repression of the Marxists and the left wing of their own party, the scope and nature of the repression that followed were unprecedented. Government-supported paramilitary groups complemented the activities of the military and the secret police in an internal war to "preserve Western, Christian civilization." A horrifying three-way struggle between the government, the Marxist left, and the Peronists (who maintained control of the unions) tore apart the institutional fabric of the nation. The government eventually destroyed the guerrillas. In the process it destroyed the civil rights of the bulk of Argentine people and systematically denied them the social use of their critical faculties.

Marx once said that the burden of the past weighs like a nightmare on the brain of the living. The special horror of modern Argentine history is that it began in the minds of too many as a simple bucolic success story. The terms of that success undermined the economic vigor of Argentine society and for decades destroyed its democratic promise. Argentina's social development led, through the weakness of the labor movement and the left, to the blind alley—whose end is only now completely visible—of Peronism.

The century of Argentine history set in motion by the expansion of the livestock and cereal export economy has now come to an end. That era was built on the premise, too widely shared, that liberal capitalist economic institutions would guarantee the successful development of the nation. The experiences of Peronism and of the repressive liberal governments that succeeded it have exposed the fallaciousness of that premise. Far from resolving the postwar crisis of Argentine society, corporativist and liberal capitalist solutions implemented by authoritarian regimes only intensified it. The Argentine working class played the central role in bringing the nation to the terrible impasse of recent decades. It did not make the modern history of the nation as it would have chosen. The odds are, however, that it will find its future role more suitable to its talents, and more amenable to its nature. Informed by a critical understanding of the paradox of the past, the next stage of Argentine history should have a different, more progressive ending.[127]

127. A first indication of labor's more progressive future role was the nature of the support it extended the government during the 1982 war with Great Britain. That support was conditioned by a call for the return to democratic political norms. The extremes to which the Argentine regime was willing to go in that conflict were themselves a consequence, at least in part, of the growing internal opposition, spearheaded by the unions, to the government's liberal economic and social program and its repressive political policies. The loss of the war forced the military to relinquish power through democratic elections in late 1983. The Peronists did much more poorly than most analysts predicted, and the Radical candidate emerged victorious. Several readers of this essay, completed in 1982, expressed surprise at the optimism of this last paragraph. Happily, its tone and the analysis of long-term trends it suggests are confirmed by these recent events. Given the scope of the current economic crisis, the intractability of Argentina's international debt problems, and the sensitive nature of the government's efforts to bring the military under control, however, the situation remains extremely volatile.

1. Chile. *Particulares* mining caliche.

2. Chile. *Barretero* opening a hole for an explosive charge in a bed of ore (*caliche*) on the nitrate pampa in the early twentieth century.

3. Chile. *Paleros* and other processing plant workers.

4. Chile. Bagging processed nitrate for shipment to the coast.

5. Chile. Workers in the machine shop of the Oficina Chacabuco, 1925.

6. Chile. Worker housing, Oficina Chacabuco, 1925.

7-8. Argentina. Two views of work on the beef kill floor: 7. (top) frigorífico "La Negra," 1919; 8. (bottom) frigorífico "Anglo," ca. 1950.

9. Argentina. Cutting and wrapping quarters in the cold chambers of "La Blanca," 1906.

10. Argentina. On the line butchering sheep, "La Negra," 1940's.

11-12. Argentina. Aerial views, ca. 1945: 11. (top) the frigorífico "Armour," Berisso; 12. (bottom) the frigorífico "Anglo," Avellaneda.

13. Venezuela. Tía Juana oil field, Lake Maracaibo, 1944.

14. Venezuela. Pulling drill pipe, Lake Maracaibo, 1944.

15. Venezuela. Coupling drill pipe, San Joaquin field, eastern Venezuela, 1944.

16. Colombia. Female coffee pickers (*chapoleras*) and boy during the harvest on a large estate in Antioquia, 1910.

17. Colombia. Successful smallholders in the coffee zone of western Cundinamarca, 1969.

18. Colombia. Farmers in the coffee-growing Sumapaz region of Cundinamarca study the titles of ownership to their *parcelas* just awarded them by the head of the agricultural reform agency (INCORA), 1967.

4

Venezuela

THE DANGER IS NOT BLACK BUT WHITE

. . . The danger lies in the white "misters," in the imperialists who squeeze our workers and those [like the Black Antillans] who come from abroad. Imperialism and its national allies are our principal enemies.

From the Maracaibo workers' paper
Petróleo, Aug. 29, 1936

The Historiography of a Turbulent Past

Anglo-Saxon racial and geographical determinists used to have a grand time interpreting Venezuelan history. It seemed to confirm their comfortable assumptions about the social world they lived in. Cursed with a tropical climate unsuited to white men, so their analysis went, Venezuela emerged from the colonial period an unruly, ignorant, poverty-stricken society prone to indolence and violence. Following independence, the more favored nations of South America—those of temperate clime in the southern part of the continent such as Argentina and Chile—managed to put their political houses in order, "whiten" their populations, and join in the progress emanating from the European centers of Western civilization. Not Venezuela. Like her tropical sister nations—Colombia being a good example—Venezuela wallowed in a sea of political instability, social chaos, and economic stagnation throughout the nineteenth century. Military *caudillos* (regional strongmen) led marauding ragtag armies of ex-slaves, mestizos, and mulattos in a violent and seemingly endless struggle for power. Once in power, these half-literate "generals" pompously proclaimed themselves "Saviors of the Fatherland," "Restorers of the Laws," "Regenerators of the Nation." In fact, they looted the public treasury and flouted the law. Not a few used their power to gratify colossal sexual and sensual appetites. European creditors finally grew tired of the antics of Venezuela's irresponsible political leaders, however. In the early twentieth century they induced their home governments to send naval squadrons to bombard Venezuela's coastal cities and threaten invasion of the country to secure payment of foreign loans and respect for foreign capital. Partly as a result of these threats, Venezuela finally achieved political stability and became a responsible member of the concert of nations. But this advance, and the economic progress it fostered, was achieved only through the imposition of the iron-fisted personal dictatorship of Juan Vicente Gómez. Gómez ruled Venezuela from 1908 to 1935. He imposed order, protected capital, and met Venezuela's international financial commitments religiously. Although his dictatorship was terribly corrupt and brutal, it offered the best hope for Venezuelan progress.

Interpretations of this kind reached their apogee in the early twentieth century, although they have continued to influence scholarship and inform the conventional wisdom of some Venezuelans and many North Americans. A typical exponent of these ideas in the United States in the 1920's was the distinguished economic geographer R. H. Whitbeck. Although he had never visited Venezuela himself, he confidently informed his classes at the University of Wisconsin and the readers of his influential textbook that Venezuela's turbulent political history and economic backwardness were attributable to race and climate. "Climate," he wrote, "imposes on the country all the handicaps of continuous heat and tropical disease. . . . The great preponderance of nonwhites in the population (at least 10 to 1) is, to a degree, the outgrowth of the selective action of climate. Fortunately, the cool trade winds, which blow from the sea most of the year, combined with a considerable area of high land, gives a white man's climate to a part of the northern section of the country. . . . If Venezuela is to be developed by her own people," he concluded, "the energy and enterprise must come from this highland section."[1]

Similar self-congratulatory, racist, ethnocentric interpretations of Venezuelan and Latin American history predominated in U.S. academic circles well into the 1940's. In the early 1930's, Charles E. Chapman, who helped to train a generation of Latin American historians at Berkeley, explained nineteenth-century Latin American political history as a consequence of retrograde Spanish culture and the pernicious influence of race and climate.[2] A decade later, the dean of U.S. diplomatic historians, Yale professor Samuel Flagg Bemis, devoted the first chapter of his major history of U.S.–Latin American relations to a discussion of what he called "climatic energy."[3] Graphic evidence of the pervasiveness of these views

1. R. H. Whitbeck, *Economic Geography of Latin America* (New York, 1926), pp. 59, 60.

2. See, for example, Chapman's "The Age of the Caudillos," *Hispanic American Historical Review* 12 (Aug. 1932):281-300.

3. *The Latin American Policy of the United States* (New York, 1943).

has been explored recently by John J. Johnson in a fascinating historical survey of U.S. political cartoons dealing with Latin America.[4] Revealingly, when Latin American governments imposed order and protected foreign capital, U.S. cartoonists tended to whiten their Latin American subjects, provide them with tall bodies, and give them serious Anglo-Saxon features. When, on the other hand, a Latin American country became unstable, its government adopted an anti-U.S. posture, or revolutionary groups within it grew strong, the Latin American characters in U.S. political cartoons were likely to be portrayed as small, rambunctious, Negroid children.

Throughout the nineteenth and early twentieth centuries Latin American intellectuals themselves were deeply influenced by the racist and climatic theories emanating from Europe and the United States. Because most belonged to the white social elite, a class increasingly linked to the interests of international capital, many accepted these theories uncritically. Most, however, resisted the determinism inherent in them. Because race and climate were essentially immutable, to accept their determining influence was to renounce the ability to change one's own society. It was also to deny the future prospects for Hispanic culture, the Catholic religion, and the Spanish and Portuguese languages. To accept Anglo-Saxon explanations of Latin America's political instability and economic retardation was thus to sanction the idea of future U.S. political and cultural hegemony in the region, to open the door for the potential dissolution of the fatherland itself. For these reasons, the thought of most Latin American intellectuals, though deeply influenced by European and U.S. intellectual currents, was usually more progressive. More than racial and climatic impediments to progress, Latin American thinkers emphasized cultural themes, primarily the legacy of Iberian colonialism. Most, like the Argentine writer Domingo F. Sarmiento, stressed the importance of enlightened mass education as the key to progress. Others developed the idea that material progress itself could overcome the legacy of the past. The thought of the Mexican positivist Justo Sierra reveals both the progressive nature and paradoxical implications of this position. A powerful apologist for the dictatorship of Porfirio Díaz that preceded the Mexican Revolution of 1910, Sierra argued that only through mass education and the protection of foreign investment could his country escape the Darwinian implications of Mexican and world history. Education would integrate the Indian into national culture and prepare the lower class to participate in politics and modern economic life. Foreign (including U.S.) investment in railroads, mines, and factories, if properly supervised by

4. *Latin America in Caricature* (Austin, Tex., 1981).

the Mexican elite, would bind the nation together and make it strong and vigorous enough to resist being swallowed up by its powerful northern neighbor. Finally, some exceptional Latin American thinkers, like the great Brazilian writer Euclides da Cunha, were wont to turn the racist and climatic determinism of European thought on its head. Cunha's great epic *Os sertões* (1902) is formally ambivalent on these issues. But its powerful subjective message is clear. The book is a celebration of the physical and moral superiority of Brazil's ignorant, racially mixed backlanders, a people perfectly adapted to a harsh American environment. In da Cunha even the emphasis on education takes a novel turn. It is "civilized" urban Brazil that reveals itself as truly barbaric and in need of enlightenment.[5]

The major apologist for the Gómez regime in Venezuela, Laureano Vallenilla Lanz, never achieved the international reputation of his illustrious Latin American predecessors. His life and work reveals neither the deep commitment to education of Sarmiento, the paradoxical nationalism of Sierra, nor the progressive Social Darwinism of da Cunha. He was a serious student of Venezuelan history, however, and his explanation for the political and social turbulence and lack of material progress of Venezuela's first century of existence avoided the simplistic racial, cultural, and climatic determinism of contemporary North American observers. To be sure, Vallenilla Lanz flirted with racial and cultural explanations of Venezuelan political instability. He stressed above all, however, geographical factors that could be modified by man. For Vallenilla Lanz the greatest impediment to political stability was a geographically induced regionalism. Most pernicious was the influence of the hordes of *llaneros*, the uncultured, undisciplined cowboys from the plains of the Orinoco River who swept northward into populous Venezuela again and again during the nineteenth century to overwhelm the efforts to establish national order and promote material progress. His solution to Venezuelan problems was forthright. Establishment of strong central authority would insure material progress; material progress, in turn, would promote political order and create the social conditions for real democracy.

[M]odifying the social ambiance through economic development, through the multiplication of highways and railways, through improvements in public health, through immigration of European people; that is, doing what Venezuela has been doing for twelve years with the aid of a strong government, guided by a Statesman, by a patriot who knows his duty and who, like the other great Caudillos of America, represents the very incarnation of power and maintains the peace, order, administrative regularity, [and] internal and external credit—we are preparing the country to arrive at the situation in which other nations with the same geographic structure as ours today find themselves[.] [These countries,] having passed through the same vicissitudes and having been placed under re-

---

5. The most influential works of Sarmiento, Sierra, and da Cunha are available in English translations.

gimes exactly like ours, have finally found the path that is carrying them toward the practice of the democratic principles inscribed in their constitutions since the first days of their independent lives.[6]

By this somewhat more progressive route, Vallenilla Lanz reached the same political conclusion as his academic counterparts in the United States: unconditional support for the dictatorship of Juan Vicente Gómez. Both projected onto nineteenth-century Venezuelan history an interpretation that justified the interests of the capitalist classes that benefited most from Gómez's policies. Vallenilla Lanz served as ideologue for the Venezuelan landowners and merchants favored by Gómez's orthodox economic liberalism and drastic policies of social and political repression. His academic counterparts abroad provided the philosophical rationale for the enormous expansion of U.S. capital into Latin America during the early twentieth century. Under Gómez, U.S. and European petroleum interests enjoyed cheap and virtually unhampered access to Venezuela's huge oil reserves. Thanks to the matchless investment climate created by Gómez, foreign capital made Venezuela into the premier petroleum-exporting country in the world by 1928.

The oil-based economic development fostered by the Gómez dictatorship spawned social forces that, as we shall see in detail in the remainder of this essay, progressively transformed Venezuelan society in the twentieth century. Oil production created a powerful proletariat in the oil fields and a growing middle class in the cities. These new classes burst onto the political scene following the death of the dictator in 1935. Since then, working sometimes in tandem and sometimes at cross-purposes, they have achieved a remarkable democratic restructuring of Venezuelan society.

These same social forces have also wrought a revolution in the way Venezuelans think about their past. In recent decades Venezuelan scholars have suggested a new interpretation of the nation's nineteenth-century history more complex—and decidedly more democratic—than those that held sway in the past. In one sense, then, the democratic development of Venezuelan society since 1935 seems to confirm the vision and predictions of Vallenilla Lanz, a fact that accounts for the ambivalent fascination of modern Venezuelan historians with his work.[7] In a deeper sense, how-

6. This passage, from Vallenilla's *Críticas de sinceridad y exactitud* (Caracas, 1921), is quoted in Harrison Sabin Howard, *Rómulo Gallegos y la revolución burguesa en Venezuela* (Caracas, 1976), p. 88. It is part of a polemic, addressed to Vallenilla's liberal critics in Colombia, in which he cogently defends his major work, *Cesarismo democrático*, an original interpretation of Latin American and Venezuelan history that both explains and justifies the Gómez dictatorship.

7. See, for example, the volume produced under the editorship of Germán Carrera Damas by Carlos Salaz and M. Caballero, *El concepto de la historia en Vallenilla Lanz* (Caracas, 1966).

ever, revisionist Venezuelan historians have repudiated and transcended Vallenilla's interpretation of the past, as well as the more deterministic and ethnocentric vision of his contemporaries in the developed world.

The new Venezuelan historiography, much of it explicitly Marxist, has the great merit of emphasizing the class dimensions of Venezuelan history.[8] It rejects the view that Venezuela's tumultuous first century of independent political life was the result of the racial defects and premodern cultural values of the majority of the country's people. It denies that the nineteenth century can be understood as a simple consequence of the country's climate and geography. Nineteenth-century Venezuelan history is understood instead as a painful, protracted process through which a unique colonial society underwent massive restructuring as its major classes adjusted to the changing imperatives and opportunities of an evolving world capitalist system.

Although the historiography of nineteenth-century Venezuela remains much less developed than that of the other three countries surveyed in this volume,[9] the basic outline of this revisionist approach is clear.[10] Lacking both the precious minerals and dense indigenous populations that made the highlands of New Spain (Mexico) and Peru the focus of Spain's mercantile empire in the New World, present-day Venezuela remained an unimportant peripheral Spanish colony until the eighteenth century. (Map 4.1 shows the main physical features of the part of the larger Spanish colony of New Granada that became modern Venezuela.) By 1700, however, Spanish merchants and Creole (American-born Spanish) landowners had begun to take advantage of African slave labor, expanding Atlantic markets, and the rich soils and tropical climate of the northern coastal plains and mountain valleys to reap large profits from the production and sale of tropical commodities. The most important of these was cacao, a tree indigenous to the New World, whose seeds, ground and combined with spices and sugar, found their way in the form of chocolate onto the tables of the well-to-do in Europe in the seventeenth and eighteenth centuries and into the diet of the European industrial proletariat in

8. Germán Carrera Damas has done the most to foster the development of the new historiography and turn its attention toward the study of the nineteenth century. See his *Historiografía marxista venezolana y otros temas* (Caracas, 1967).

9. As the following review makes clear, the legacy of an unusually destructive independence struggle, the late consolidation of a viable modern export economy, and the repressive dictatorial form that consolidation assumed in Venezuela seriously compromised the early development of Venezuelan historical studies. In recent decades, however, the availability of oil money for higher education and the maintenance of academic freedom have allowed professional historical studies to advance more rapidly, perhaps, than in the other three countries treated in these essays.

10. The handiest, most up-to-date guide to Venezuelan historiography is the bibliographical essay in John V. Lombardi, *Venezuela: The Search for Order, The Dream of Progress* (New York, 1982). The book itself, which covers colonial to modern times, is the best one-volume history of the country.

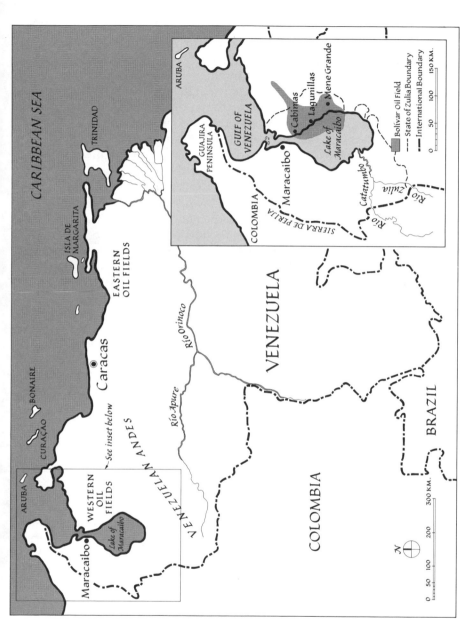

Map 4.1. Venezuela, Showing the Maracaibo Basin and Major Oil Fields.

the nineteenth century. The other commodity was coffee, whose cultivation diffused through the Caribbean Basin during the eighteenth and
nineteenth centuries. A powerful stimulant, coffee, like cacao and sugar,
was initially consumed in Europe by the rich. As industrialization proceeded, however, it became a fundamental item in the diet of European
working-class families. Coffee with cream or sugar, like chocolate, provided stimulants and calories that were easy to prepare and quickly consumed, qualities important to working-class families forced to adjust patterns of food preparation and consumption to the requirements of
factory life and female employment outside the home. Imperial policies
stimulated the production of cacao and, to a lesser extent, coffee in colonial Venezuela. The Crown enabled landowners to acquire African slaves
to cultivate these crops, and granted a trade monopoly in cacao to a
Basque merchant house. As a result, production, especially of cacao, expanded rapidly along the north coast of the colony during the eighteenth
century. A typical New World plantation society developed in this region: large estates owned by a white minority and worked by coerced—
primarily slave—labor. At the same time, on the vast plains of the Orinoco River to the south, a cattle economy grew up, spurred by the demand for leather in European industry and for meat in the slave economies of the Caribbean. Cattle ranching on the Venezuelan *llanos* was a
primitive affair, however. Huge herds belonging to a few ranchers
roamed freely over the unfenced plains, tended by a small labor force of
independent, nomadic cowboys, many of whom had fled the coercive labor systems of the northern part of the colony. (The huge expanse of
land to the south of the Apure and Orinoco rivers was never effectively
settled in the colonial period and remains very sparsely populated and
largely undeveloped to this day.)

The struggle between the major European powers for control of an Atlantic economy in transition from mercantile to industrial capitalism—a
struggle that intensified in the late eighteenth century and reached its climax and resolution in the Napoleonic wars—seriously disrupted these
colonial arrangements and culminated in the independence of Venezuela.
International warfare caused Spain's commercial network with its colonies to deteriorate and forced landowners and merchants in control of
Venezuela's cacao and coffee economy to expand their trade with contra-
bandists and slavers working out of the dynamic economies of Holland,
Britain, and the United States. Meanwhile, Venezuela's different social
classes struggled to come to terms with the unsettling ideological and political forces unleashed during this protracted period of world economic
and political change. Efforts by the major European powers to tax their
subjects more heavily in order to finance this struggle for world hegemony precipitated the great social and political revolutions of the era.

Each of these revolutions—in the British colonies that became the United States, in France, in St. Domingue (subsequently Haiti), and finally in Spanish and Portuguese America—obeyed a different social logic, and each held different meanings for the Creole elite that launched the independence movement in Venezuela. The liberal ideologies of republicanism and free trade promised to liberate Venezuelan merchants and landowners from the restrictions of Spanish political control and mercantile trade policies. Yet a war for independence might loose the social and ideological forces that had imperiled life and property in France and precipitated a slave revolt that destroyed the landed slave-owning class in nearby Haiti. Nevertheless, soon after Napoleon's invasion of the Iberian Peninsula compromised Spanish imperial authority in 1808, elements of the Creole elite in Venezuela made the first moves in South America toward independence. Simón Bolívar, one of the wealthiest of Venezuela's slave-owning cacao producers, emerged to lead this faction. Other Venezuelan Creoles judged the risks involved in war too great, or the rewards too small, to join the independence struggle. The Venezuelan independence movement thus became, from its inception, a civil as well as an international war.[11]

Members of Venezuela's other classes and castes, including slaves and mixed-bloods or *pardos*, revealed a similar ambivalence toward the independence movement. Elements of each group interpreted the ideologies of liberty and equality emanating from the great revolutions of the era differently. Most slaves had Creole not Spanish masters, and although they aimed at securing their individual freedom, most of them initially joined royalist forces when the fighting erupted. The large population of pardos, who worked as sharecroppers, artisans, petty merchants, and even professionals, had experienced increased social mobility and some access to education and the professions under the economic and legal reforms enacted by the Spanish in their efforts to revitalize their empire at the end of the eighteenth century. They continued to resent the social discrimination of the white elite, whether Creole or Spanish.

Once the fighting began, the complexity of these conflicting attitudes within and between the major classes grew. Rival royalist and independence forces wooed elements of the laboring classes through ideological and material concessions, especially the promise of freedom for slaves willing to fight in their armies. They also sequestered and expropriated property to sustain their cause. Warfare provided opportunities for personal enrichment, for social mobility, and for individual revenge that cut

11. Much of the material in this and the following two paragraphs is drawn from Carrera Damas's suggestive essay "Para un esquema sobre la participación de las clases populares en el movimiento nacional de independencia, en Venezuela, a comienzos del Siglo XIX," in his *Historiografía marxista* (cited in n.8), pp. 69-99.

across the class antagonisms and racial tensions inherited from the colonial past. Finally, the Venezuelan independence movement, and the subsequent political and social struggles that enveloped the new nation, were complicated by the influence of the *llaneros* from the cattle-producing plains to the south. This region enjoyed access to international trade, arms, and mercenaries, a ready supply of cattle to provision armies, and a relatively independent and highly mobile working class. Patriot control of the *llanos*, and of the forces that could be recruited there, eventually tipped the balance of the independence struggle in Venezuela and, indeed, in all of northern South America.

In comparative perspective, several features of the Venezuelan independence movement stand out. Landowners and merchants in the Venezuelan periphery of Spain's South American empire, like those in Argentina, had much to gain from independence. Unlike the economy of the Peruvian heartland, Venezuela's and Argentina's agricultural export economies had become closely tied to the liberal industrial capitalist order emerging under British aegis at the turn of the century. In Peru, preservation of the mining complex and Spain's trade monopoly and political control was vital to the economic health of the colony and to the social interests of merchants, miners, and the colonial administrative, military, and ecclesiastical elite. In Venezuela and Argentina, the bureaucracy of Spanish colonialism was limited and weak. It tended to restrict economic growth and constrain the interests of dominant classes. In Spanish South America it was the property-owning classes of Venezuela and Argentina that proved most receptive to liberal ideology, and it was from their ranks that the earliest and most determined proponents of independence emerged. The independence movements in Spanish South America originated in Venezuela and Argentina; after fifteen years of struggle they converged to impose independence on the Peruvian highlands.[12]

Unlike Argentina, however, Venezuela occupied a strategic position astride the Caribbean trade and communication routes that linked Spain to the heartland of its New World empire. Consequently, whereas the Argentine independence movement developed virtually unmolested by imperial forces, Venezuela was subjected to a brutal Spanish reconquest. After the reimposition of Spanish control, the struggle for independence in Venezuela became much more savage and destructive. Popular elements were often able to turn the fighting—and the partial breakdown of social control and respect for private property it brought—to their short-term advantage.

Venezuela was different from Argentina in another important respect

12. Richard Graham has clearly synthesized the main lines of this comparative approach to the dynamics of the South American independence movement in his *Independence in Latin America* (New York, 1972).

as well. It was a slave society, the only Hispanic-American slave society to win its independence through violent struggle in the early nineteenth century.[13] The class and racial tensions embedded in Venezuelan colonial society that exploded in the independence movement go far toward explaining the scope of the social, economic, and political problems Venezuela faced in the decades following independence. Social control was more severely weakened in Venezuela, economic destruction and capital flight were more widespread, and politics became, to use Halperín Donghi's phrase, more "ruralized and militarized" than in any other part of Spain's former South American empire.[14]

As in the rest of Latin America, Venezuela's break with Spain and its gradual incorporation into an industrial capitalist world order involved a painful transformation of virtually every aspect of society. It is often stressed that the highly unequal pattern of land distribution, the hierarchical and largely static class structure, and the centralized, authoritarian political culture inherited from the colonial period reemerged or were sustained during the nineteenth century. All that is basically true. Yet each of these structural features had to be accommodated to a new world order and sustained in new ways. Post-independence problems of social control, capital flight, foreign indebtedness, and the emergence of powerful new regional and military forces all had to be confronted. The influx of cheap industrial goods gradually undermined artisanal industry and forced large sectors of the population to find new livelihoods. Labor systems—most obviously the slave regime—had to be transformed. Traditional sources of credit and capital under the mercantile arrangements of the Spanish order had to be modified or replaced. Tax systems had to be revamped. The economic and social role of the Church, and its relationship to the state, had to be redefined. Land policy, especially access to corporate Indian lands and the public domain, had to be resolved. Finally, new political, judicial, and educational systems consistent with republican and liberal ideology yet compatible with ruling-class interests and Venezuelan social structures had to be created. These issues, and the struggles to decide them, generated social unrest, ideological conflict,

13. St. Domingue, a French possession, was the first Latin American slave society to win its independence. Yet the legacy of slavery, sugar monoculture, and the brutal dual struggle for independence and personal freedom prostrated the new nation of Haiti. Haiti's subsequent history gives some indication of the risks Venezuela's Creole independence leaders faced and the scope of the problems their successors had to deal with. Brazil, a Portuguese slave colony already closely tied to Britain's emerging informal economic empire, acquired independence without major bloodshed or civil commotion under the leadership of the Portuguese crown. The major Spanish slave colony, Cuba, did not achieve independence until the end of the century.

14. Tulio Halperín Donghi, *The Aftermath of Revolution in Latin America* (New York, 1973); Charles C. Griffin, "Economic and Social Aspects of the Era of Spanish-American Independence," *Hispanic American Historical Review* 29 (May 1949):170-87.

and political contention within and between the various classes of all the independent Latin American nations. They were especially pronounced in early-nineteenth-century Venezuela, where the nature of pre-independence social problems, and the long duration and destructiveness of the war, complicated all of them.

Resolution of these issues depended on the consolidation of a ruling class conscious of its needs and strong enough to capture control of the state and impose its will and vision on the rest of society. That process was most speedily completed where the economic destruction and social disruption caused by the war was slight (as in Chile and Argentina), where the landowning and merchant elite was relatively homogeneous (as in Chile), and, most importantly, where the creation of a viable and dynamic export economy within the new Atlantic economic order proved possible. A successful, expanding export economy provided local and international capitalists who controlled production and exchange in the export sector with the ideological cohesion and prestige, the economic resources, and eventually the political strength to win control of the state. The revenue generated by expanding exports then enabled this class to expand the scope and effectiveness of state power—the ability to socialize, to coerce, and to extract resources from civil society—to service its class interests and promote more export expansion. Once this self-reinforcing nineteenth-century process got fully under way, only the faltering of the export economy—a result of falling world demand or the emergence of more efficient producers elsewhere—could undermine it. In some Latin American societies, such as Chile and Argentina, this nineteenth-century process was short; in others, such as Venezuela and Colombia, it lasted beyond the turn of the century, for only then was the mutually supportive dynamic of export expansion and consolidation of effective state power under the aegis of export interests fully consummated.

In Venezuela this consolidation process foundered again and again on the rock of economic reality throughout the nineteenth century. The war for independence seriously disrupted the Venezuelan economy and complicated efforts to revive it. Cacao production on the once prosperous plantations of north-central Venezuela languished thereafter, stifled by usurious interest rates on scarce capital and by a work force increasingly unwilling to perform coerced plantation labor.[15] The cattle industry on the tropical plains of the Orinoco suffered badly from the chronic civil warfare it helped to spawn in the decades after 1810. Moreover, given the impediments of climate and geography, the Venezuelan cattle industry

---

15. The slave trade was abolished in 1820, slavery itself in 1854. The abolition process and the problems of credit and labor in Venezuela's plantation economy are treated in the pioneering work of John Lombardi, *The Decline and Abolition of Negro Slavery in Venezuela* (Westport, Conn., 1971).

could not compete with Latin American and world producers with temperate climates once demand shifted from hides and jerked beef toward high-quality meat.[16] Coffee cultivation, by contrast, expanded in the decades after 1830, and the locus of the industry shifted slowly westward onto the mountain slopes of the Venezuelan Andes. There, under the aegis of European (primarily German) commercial capital, a variety of labor and exchange systems emerged to tap the initiative and labor power of sharecroppers and small and medium producers. Exports reached half a million 60-kilogram bags in the 1870's, a million by 1914. By the end of the century coffee accounted for about three-fourths of Venezuela's expanding volume of foreign exchange and contributed (indirectly, through its influence on the level of imports taxed by tariffs) the bulk of the government's revenue.[17]

The growing importance of the coffee economy finally propelled a regional ruling class from the major Andean coffee state of Táchira into contention for national political power. Formal control of the national government was achieved with the victory of the revolutionary forces of Cipriano Castro in 1899 at a time when a drastic fall in world coffee prices threatened the industry and created widespread economic dislocation and social unrest in the coffee zone. Consolidation of that control was achieved under Castro's first lieutenant and fellow *tachirense*, Juan Vicente Gómez, in the years after 1908. Beginning in 1908, too, after a decade of depression, coffee prices began a steep upward spiral that continued for two decades. Venezuelan coffee cultivation did not expand greatly during this period, but the value of coffee exports more than doubled.[18]

From the beginning of Gómez's rule, however, the process of consolidation of control over Venezuelan society by export interests was influenced by a new product—oil—destined to mold twentieth-century Venezuelan history far more profoundly than coffee. In 1907 and 1912, Castro and Gómez awarded petroleum concessions that soon enabled European and U.S. oil companies to turn Venezuela into a major world oil producer. By 1925 the value of Venezuelan oil exports surpassed that of

16. An illuminating discussion of the wildly inconsistent estimates of the size of Venezuelan cattle herds, and of the obstacles posed by climate and geography to the development of the industry, can be found in Eduardo Arcila Farías, "Evolución de la economía en Venezuela," in Mariano Picón-Salas et al., *Venezuela independiente, 1810–1960* (Caracas, 1962), pp. 374-76.

17. Yearly data on the volume and value of coffee exports are provided in Ramón Veloz, *Economía y finanzas de venezuela desde 1830 hasta 1944* (Caracas, 1945). They must be interpreted with caution. A significant but undetermined portion of the coffee exported from Venezuela by the mid-nineteenth century was produced in Colombia.

18. This political process still awaits detailed investigation, but see Domingo Alberto Rangel, *El proceso del capitalismo contemporáneo en Venezuela* (Caracas, 1968), and *Los andinos en el poder* (Caracas, 1964). Similar and contemporaneous developments in Colombia are explored in Charles Bergquist, *Coffee and Conflict in Colombia, 1886 to 1910* (Durham, N.C., 1978), and are briefly reviewed in the next chapter.

coffee exports. Three years later they were worth three times more than all other Venezuelan exports combined. Throughout his long dictatorship, Gómez ruled in the interest of the tachirense regional elite and the international capitalists who supported him. He maintained order, protected property, and instituted orthodox liberal financial and monetary policies. As Domingo Alberto Rangel has shown, all this was second nature to a man socialized in the capitalist ethics of Táchira's coffee export economy.[19] But whereas the economic surplus generated by coffee production was suffused through the action of the market to a broad regional landowning and merchant class, the wealth returned to Venezuela from oil concessions was directly apportioned by Gómez himself, who used it to build a political base distinct from the regional capitalist class from which he sprang. He created a network of personal loyalties across the nation and built a powerful base of institutional support in a large army loyal to his person. If coffee thus helps to explain the accession to national power of a regional ruling class, oil largely accounts for the enduring personal, dictatorial form through which the power of that class—and that of its national and international capitalist allies—came to be consolidated and perpetuated.

———◆—◆———

Class struggle in a world and national economy in transition from mercantile to industrial capitalism—not the simple influence of climate, race, or culture—best explains the chaotic course of the first century of Venezuelan history and the consolidation of social and political order at the start of the second. As we shall see in the remainder of this essay, class struggle, spawned and molded by the structure of the Venezuelan oil export economy, also explains the extraordinary course of Venezuelan history in the twentieth century. The social forces generated by oil-based economic growth first undermined the legacy of the Gómez dictatorship, then set Venezuela on a path of liberal economic and democratic political development unique in Latin America.

Viewed in the context of comparative Latin American history and the historiography reviewed in this section, then, the recent development of Venezuela is richly and appropriately ironic. Contrary to the expectations and assumptions of the racial and climatic determinists of the early twentieth century, Venezuela—not the whiter, more developed societies of temperate southern South America—has registered the most impressive record of economic growth and maintenance of democratic political forms in our own time. The social element most maligned in the traditional historiography, the Venezuelan working class, contributed most to this contemporary outcome. There is poetic justice in the fact that the

19. Domingo Alberto Rangel, *Gómez, el amo del poder* (Valencia, 1975).

democratic struggle of the Venezuelan working class inspired the historiographic revolution that has challenged the racist, ethnocentric fallacies and self-serving class bias of the traditional explanations of Venezuela's past.

Oil and Development

In the twentieth century, the Venezuelan working class, spearheaded by workers in oil production, emerged as the prime mover behind and principal guarantor of the liberal economic and political order that has distinguished contemporary Venezuela's history from that of the majority of its Latin American neighbors. The central role of the labor movement in this remarkable social process has been systematically ignored in U.S. scholarship on the subject,[20] despite the fact that for some time it has been a vital issue in the work of Venezuelan political activists and academics.[21] The decisive influence of Venezuelan workers on the twentieth-century history of their nation is revealed in the separate stages of the argument that follows. In this section I describe the special nature of the petroleum export economy that has transformed Venezuelan society since the 1920's and argue that, by itself, the oil sector, a classic foreign-owned enclave, contributed to the growth but not to the development of the national economy. The turning of oil revenue to the development of Venezuelan society was a democratic political consequence of the organization of popular forces, the most important element of which was the oil proletariat itself. The following section explores the nature of life and work in the Venezuelan oil enclave. It assesses the material and human forces under which oil workers made themselves into a class capable of transforming the history of their nation. The next part of the essay recounts the organizational struggle of petroleum workers and probes the influence of that struggle on national politics during the crucial period 1936-48, when the pattern of Venezuela's subsequent development was decided. The final section highlights the role of labor in contemporary Venezuelan history.

Oil, we have learned over the course of this century, is the basic fuel and a major raw material of modern industrial civilization. It is a commodity that for two generations has intimately influenced virtually every

20. This is true despite the fact that the genesis and maintenance of Venezuela's liberal democracy has fascinated U.S. observers and stimulated a number of recent works. For a listing of the most scholarly of these, see the twentieth-century section of the bibliographical essay in Lombardi, *Venezuela* (cited in n. 10). An exception to this generalization is the work of Robert J. Alexander, especially Chapter 18 of his *The Venezuelan Democratic Revolution* (New Brunswick, N.J., 1964).

21. Note 48 below critically reviews the major contributions to this literature and assesses their relationship to the argument developed in this essay.

aspect of our daily lives. Through the internal-combustion engine it fueled a revolution in transport; through fertilizers and pesticides it fostered a revolution in agriculture. In the developed world, and increasingly outside it, the gasoline-powered automobile alone has changed the face of our physical environment, influenced our sexual mores, molded our leisure-time activities. For over half a century the automobile industry served as the primary engine for capitalist expansion within the industrialized economies of the developed world. Oil has thus helped modify the way we work, eat, dress, and play, the manner in which we make love and wage war. It has deeply influenced the scope, speed, and quality of the expansion of world capitalism in the twentieth century.

The history of demand for oil reflects its growing importance in the world economy. Oil consumption expanded geometrically as the twentieth century progressed, and for the past several decades it has been the most valuable commodity in world trade. Oil prices, meanwhile, despite massive increases in world production, remained stable or rose slowly until the early 1970's. They were then vastly increased by a cartel of producer nations. The history of oil as a commodity in international trade is thus fundamentally different from that of most other industrial minerals and agricultural products. Like the precious metal gold with which it is often compared, oil has not suffered from violent fluctuations in world demand, price, and supply. Whereas world economic cycles, international competition, and changing industrial processes have made production of other export commodities a risky business, oil, despite a geometric rise in world production, has enjoyed relatively steady markets and rising prices.

Venezuela has played a pivotal role in the history of world oil production since the discovery of its major reserves at the end of the First World War. By 1928 Venezuela had surpassed Mexico as the world's leading oil exporter, a position it maintained until the 1960's, when the bulk of world production shifted from the Western hemisphere to the Middle East. For two decades following the Second World War Venezuela was second only to the United States in oil production. Although production stabilized and then fell somewhat after 1965, just as Venezuela's share of the world oil market has declined rapidly since that date, Venezuela remains a major world supplier today.

The volume of Venezuela's petroleum production, 1918-78, is graphed in Figure 4.1; the value of these exports, 1920-73, appears in Table 4.1. Venezuelan oil production has suffered from periods of modest decline in world demand (the period 1931-33, at the start of the world depression), from wartime disruption of transport (1942-43), and from temporary gluts in world supply. But until now such periods have been brief and the economic disruption they caused in Venezuela relatively minor. The im-

Figure 4.1. Venezuelan Crude Oil Production (in thousands of barrels), 1918-78, and Workers Employed in the Oil Industry (in thousands), 1922-77. Sources: for production, 1918-73, Ministerio de Fomento, Dirección de Estadística, *Anuario Estadístico, 1973* (Caracas, 1974); 1974-78, James W. Wilkie and Peter Reich, eds., *Statistical Abstract of Latin America*, vol. 20 (Los Angeles, 1980), Table 2002, p. 231; for employment, 1922-37, Héctor Lucena, *El movimiento obrero y las relaciones laborales* (Carabobo, 1981), Table 10, pp. 118-19; 1938-73, Ministerio de Fomento, Dirección de Estadística, *Anuario Estadístico, 1973* (Caracas, 1974), Table VI-34, p. 209; 1974-77, Presidencia, Oficina Central de Estadística, *Anuario Estadístico, 1977* (Caracas, 1978).

pact of these fluctuations on the finances of the nation has been even less severe. Until the 1940's Venezuelan oil revenues derived primarily from concessionary fees (which were unaffected by the volume and value of exports) and royalties (levied on the volume, not the value, of production). Consequently, even at the nadir of the Great Depression, Venezuelan oil revenues did not decline appreciably. Since the mid-1940's, the expansion in the volume of that revenue has been extraordinary. Government revenue directly derived from the petroleum industry rose to 10 percent of government income in the late 1920's, jumped to 20 and then

TABLE 4.1
Value of Venezuelan Petroleum Exports, 1920-72
(Millions of 1938 bolívares)

Year	Value of exports	Year	Value of exports	Year	Value of exports
1920	3.3	1938	828.3	1956	3,605.3
1921	11.8	1939	843.0	1957	4,572.7
1922	15.7	1940	769.0	1958	4,054.4
1923	28.7	1941	991.6	1959	3,776.4
1924	65.5	1942	604.2	1960	3,818.6
1925	137.5	1943	694.5	1961	3,864.7
1926	246.6	1944	879.2	1962	4,136.8
1927	280.8	1945	823.0	1963	4,070.0
1928	466.9	1946	762.0	1964	5,510.8
1929	593.6	1947	2,045.4	1965	5,367.2
1930	643.1	1948	1,936.4	1966	5,057.6
1931	547.8	1949	1,891.0	1967	5,423.7
1932	531.6	1950	1,944.4	1968	5,334.0
1933	553.2	1951	2,111.3	1969	5,124.3
1934	608.5	1952	2,369.2	1970	5,335.9
1935	649.3	1953	2,557.1	1971	6,343.6
1936	684.2	1954	2,539.3	1972	6,065.6
1937	770.0	1955	3,100.7		

SOURCE: Franklin Tugwell, *The Politics of Oil in Venezuela* (Stanford, Calif., 1975), Appendix Table B, pp. 182-83.

NOTE: Between 1937 and 1963 the exchange rate of the bolívar was roughly constant at about 3.3 to the U.S. dollar; during the period 1964 to 1972 it stood at 4.3 to the dollar.

30 percent during the 1930's, and climbed to well over 50 percent for most years since 1944. (See Table 4.2.) In fact, government income has been much more dependent on the oil economy than these figures imply. Although for decades the oil companies were exempted from payment of customs duties on their imports of capital goods and supplies (a fact which led one student to estimate that before 1930 the Venezuelan government lost more revenue from potential customs receipts than it gained in oil taxes), the industry nevertheless helped stimulate a great expansion in imports. As early as 1928 oil was generating 75 percent of Venezuela's export earnings; by 1936 that figure had climbed to 90 percent, where it has remained. Customs revenue, much of it generated indirectly by oil exports, remained the major source of government income into the 1940's.[22]

In terms of its long-term ability to provide a large and expanding supply of foreign exchange and government revenue, the Venezuelan petroleum economy has had no equal among the export economies of Latin America. At mid-century, for example, when both Chile and Venezuela had populations of roughly five million people, the value of mineral ex-

22. T. E. Carrillo Batalla, *La evaluación de la inversión del ingreso fiscal petrolero en Venezuela* (Caracas, 1968), Table 7, pp. 234-35.

TABLE 4.2
Share of Petroleum Income in Total Venezuelan Government Income, 1917-63
(Millions of bolívares)

Year	(A) Total gov't income	(B) Gov't petrol. income	(B) as pct. of (A)	Year	(A) Total gov't income	(B) Gov't petrol. income	(B) as pct. of (A)
1917	72	.16	0.2%	1941	346	121.45	35.1%
1918	53	.69	1.3	1942	325	87.75	27.0
1919	57	1.31	2.3	1943	306	139.30	45.5
1920	101	1.46	1.4	1944	446	269.39	60.4
1921	82	2.21	2.7	1945	614	353.50	57.6
1922	71	7.50	10.6	1946	713	489.01	68.6
1923	88	3.78	4.3	1947	1,100	689.48	62.7
1924	102	5.91	5.8	1948	1,562	1,158.10	74.1
1925	120	20.87	17.4	1949	1,936	1,269.35	64.7
1926	172	17.88	10.4	1950	1,896	901.06	47.5
1927	182	21.43	11.8	1951	2,267	1,317.10	58.1
1928	187	46.19	24.7	1952	2,408	1,475.82	61.3
1929	230	50.34	21.9	1953	2,534	1,589.07	62.7
1930	256	47.33	18.5	1954	2,632	1,497.90	56.9
1931	210	46.98	22.4	1955	2,992	1,714.29	57.3
1932	185	45.15	24.4	1956	4,380	3,108.31	70.9
1933	172	44.18	26.0	1957	5,405	3,821.85	70.7
1934	172	52.05	30.3	1958	4,706	2,713.01	57.7
1935	203	59.30	29.2	1959	5,743	3,225.02	56.2
1936	189	63.61	33.7	1960	6,147	3,001.63	48.8
1937	274	81.78	29.8	1961	7,074	3,236.10	45.7
1938	331	118.61	35.8	1962	6,489	3,224.02	48.9
1939	341	109.47	32.1	1963	6,604	3,597.95	54.5
1940	354	97.71	27.6				

SOURCE: T. E. Carrillo Batalla, *La evaluación de la inversión del ingreso fiscal petrolero en Venezuela* (Caracas, 1968), Table 7, pp. 234-35.

NOTE: Between 1937 and 1963 the exchange rate of the bolívar was roughly constant at about 3.3 to the U.S. dollar.

ports per capita in Venezuela was already four times greater than in Chile. Government revenues derived from taxation of mineral exports were already higher in Venezuela by that date, but whereas those revenues subsequently stagnated in Chile, they doubled and then tripled in Venezuela within a decade. Moreover, huge increases were yet to come in the 1970's.[23]

There is no question that the expanding volume and value of oil exports have greatly stimulated Venezuelan economic growth, but the issue of oil's impact on the economic development of the nation is less clear. Since 1945 the Venezuelan economy has had the fastest growth rate (in

23. A provocative comparative analysis of the exceptional nature of Venezuela's oil export economy is Charles Elmer Rollins, "Raw Materials Development and Economic Growth. A Study of the Bolivian and Venezuelan Experience" (Ph.D. diss., Stanford University, 1955).

both real and per capita terms) in South America.[24] But before that date Venezuelan petroleum economy, a foreign-owned export enclave, exercised little direct, positive influence on the process of domestic capital accumulation and economic diversification. Oil production and refining is one of the most capital-intensive and technologically sophisticated of modern industries. Consequently, Venezuelan oil production depended (and still depends) on capital goods and technology imported from the advanced industrial nations. Oil production did not directly foster development of a national transportation network. Oil companies built ports and pipelines and a few roads in the oil zone, but none of these developments was very useful to other sectors of the Venezuelan economy. Before nationalization of the industry in 1975, ownership of production and transport facilities was in the hands of foreign corporations. Until mid-century virtually all of the refining of Venezuelan oil was done outside the country, much of it on the nearby Dutch islands of Curaçao and Aruba. Distribution of oil products, even within Venezuela, was largely handled by the foreign petroleum companies. As a result, given the low level of taxation of the industry before the 1940's, most of the surplus generated by oil production was remitted abroad as profits. In addition, returns to Venezuelan labor were small. Although wages in the oil fields were high by Venezuelan standards, the labor force in oil production was not large. At its peak in 1948 it numbered about 55,000 blue- and white-collar workers, about three percent of the national work force (see Figure 4.1). Especially in the early decades of oil production in Venezuela, much of the money spent on wages and salaries went to foreign managers, technicians, and skilled workers, who remitted a portion of their earnings abroad. Even as late as mid-century, much of the food and clothing consumed by workers in the oil camps was supplied through company-owned commissaries that imported these goods from abroad.

The indirect influence of oil production on Venezuelan social and economic development, however, has been extraordinary. Much of that influence is revealed in the impact of oil production on internal migration. As oil production expanded it drew workers away from agriculture into the oil zone. Petroleum production is most labor intensive during the initial phase of exploration, drilling, and construction of pipelines and port facilities. Partly for this reason, and partly also because of the relatively primitive exploration and construction techniques of the period, the labor demands of the early Venezuelan oil economy were much higher (in

24. Comparative figures, based on United Nations statistics for the period 1945 to 1968, are provided in Mostafa F. Hassan, *Economic Growth and Employment Problems in Venezuela. An Analysis of an Oil-Based Economy* (New York, 1975), Table 1, p. 10. During these years the annual rate of growth of Venezuela's real gross domestic product averaged about 7.5 percent.

comparative terms) than in later years. When production stood at about 60 million barrels in 1927, 21,000 oil workers, the least skilled among them earning wages two to three times higher than those of the average farm laborer in Venezuela, were on the company payrolls. By 1948, the peak employment year for the industry, production had expanded almost ten times, the labor force only about two and a half times. Between 1920 and 1940 the population of the oil-producing states grew faster than the other parts of Venezuela, save for the Federal District (where the nation's capital, Caracas, was located). Not all of the migrants to the oil states found jobs in the oil fields. Many ended up in the squalid boomtowns that grew up outside the major oil camps, or moved to the metropolis of the oil enclave, the city of Maracaibo. A few small oil towns saw their populations increase severalfold during the 1920's. Maracaibo, Venezuela's second city, doubled in size to 80,000 people in that decade.[25]

Although the initial effect of expanding oil production was to stimulate internal migration to the oil zone, its most enduring and important influence was to quicken the pace of Venezuelan urbanization generally. After 1940 the major economic impact of oil production was felt not in the oil enclave, but in populous north-central Venezuela, the area surrounding the capital. The expanding volume of foreign trade fostered the growth of urban import businesses, banks, and commercial services. The growth of oil revenues underwrote expansion of the federal bureaucracy (between 1938 and 1943 alone it grew from 7,000 to 47,000 employees). Oil revenues financed large-scale construction of public works and, eventually, social programs and economic development projects. All these changes had the effect of greatly improving economic opportunities and the level of public services in the cities, especially in the capital. Mass migration from the countryside to the cities was the result: in 1930 only about a fifth of Venezuela's people lived in towns of 1,000 people or more; by 1950 about half did; by 1970 roughly three-quarters did.

As oil production stimulated economic activity in the oil zone and the cities, and workers moved off the land in search of a better life, Venezuelan agriculture suffered. Some landowners tried to stem the tide of migration by raising wages; others simply held their land (which was not effectively taxed) and shifted their capital to lucrative investments in urban real estate speculation, construction, and commerce. In either case, Venezuelan agricultural products, both those for export and those for internal consumption, became more expensive—and less competitive with imports from other nations. Rising domestic food costs fueled the trend toward higher wages and prices in Venezuela; they also fostered ever

25. Much of this material is drawn from the fine history of the growth of the oil industry and its impact on Venezuela before 1950 by Edwin Lieuwen, *Petroleum in Venezuela* (Berkeley, Calif., 1954).

greater reliance on cheaper agricultural imports. The growing problems in Venezuelan agriculture were most obvious in export production. Coffee and cacao exports, which had remained at high levels in the 1910's and 1920's, never recovered from the world Depression despite government efforts to channel some oil revenue into agricultural loans and export subsidies. During the 1940's the volume of coffee and cacao exports stood at about half the level maintained in the 1920's. Meanwhile, agricultural production for domestic consumption failed to keep up with rising internal demand. By 1950 Venezuelan agriculture supplied only one-fifth of the national market for food and industrial agricultural commodities. The rest was imported. Although an agricultural reform during the 1960's and massive infusions of public moneys into agricultural development projects in the 1970's finally reversed these trends, the problems of Venezuelan agriculture, and the nation's dependence on agricultural imports, remain extreme.[26]

The expanding oil economy undermined Venezuelan agriculture in other ways as well. The growth of oil revenues during the 1930's enabled Venezuela to pursue an anomalously orthodox set of monetary and financial policies during the Depression. While countries all over the world were abandoning the gold standard, defaulting on their foreign loans, and devaluing their currencies, the government of Juan Vicente Gómez was paying off the remainder of the Venezuelan foreign debt and pursuing exchange policies that overvalued the Venezuelan monetary unit, the *bolívar*. This policy pleased import merchants and consumers of foreign goods, but it was disastrous for Venezuela's agriculturalists. One student of the Venezuelan economy under Gómez has characterized these policies as a process of "production substitution." In contrast to the process of import-substituting industrialization favored in other Latin American countries as a response to the world crisis and domestic monetary devaluations and exchange controls, Venezuelan agricultural products (already plagued by high production costs) became less rather than more competitive in the world market during the 1930's. Imports paid for by oil money replaced many items formerly cultivated at home.[27]

Venezuelan monetary and exchange policies during the 1930's also inhibited the development of manufacturing, though the country's capacity to begin to produce for itself items it imported was in any case extremely

26. Trends in export agriculture are graphed in Arcila Farías, "Evolución" (cited in n. 16), between pp. 416 and 417. The estimate of domestic agricultural production comes from Loring Allen, *Venezuelan Economic Development* (Greenwich, Conn., 1977), p. 231. Current problems of Venezuelan agriculture are surveyed in George W. Schuyler, *Hunger in a Land of Plenty* (Cambridge, Mass., 1980).

27. Eugenia Stevens Wheelwright, "The Economy of Venezuela Under Juan Vicente Gómez, 1908–1935: Policies of Underdevelopment" (M.A. thesis, University of Washington, 1979).

limited. Manufacturing establishments at the start of the crisis were few in number and essentially artisanal in nature. Most were tiny workshops geared to the processing of agricultural and livestock products. The first industrial census, taken in 1936, listed 46,855 workers in 8,025 establishments, an average of 5.8 workers per manufacturing unit. More than half of these workers were employed in food processing, most of the rest in clothing manufacturing, leatherworking, tobacco processing, glass and ceramic making, and woodworking. The only fairly large industrial establishments were a few textile mills. By 1953, the date of the next industrial census, the manufacturing sector had grown to employ 138,064 workers in 16,045 establishments (an average of 8.6 workers each), and its composition had not significantly changed.[28]

Since mid-century, however, the manufacturing sector of the Venezuelan economy has grown rapidly and its structure has been transformed. Expanding oil revenues channeled into huge public works projects during the 1950's, and into an aggressive program of import substitution (which included establishment of branch plants of foreign multinational corporations) in the 1960's and 1970's, have built a modern capital-intensive industrial sector in the economy. Manufacturing industry expanded from about 10 percent of production in the country in 1950 to 23 percent by 1974. Industrial growth has been aided by huge public investments in transportation (Venezuela, not coincidentally, now has the best highway system in Latin America), electric power, and basic industry (steel and petrochemicals). Venezuela now produces most of its own consumer goods. But it remains dependent on oil exports to pay for the huge quantities of capital goods, industrial raw materials, and technology it must import to sustain its modern industrial sector.[29]

This sketch reveals that oil production promoted the growth of the economy, not its development. The remarkable development of Venezuela's economy during the last four decades was accomplished only as the enormous wealth generated by oil production was captured by the state, distributed within the nation, and turned toward social and agricultural reform and industrial development. The transformation of the Venezuelan economy was thus primarily the result of a political, not an economic, process. That process began when popular social forces broke out of the political straitjacket imposed on them by the Gómez dictatorship. The story of their battle to forge a democratic society free of the

28. T. E. Carrillo Batalla, *El desarrollo del sector manufacturero industrial de la economía venezolana* (Caracas, 1962), pp. 11-17.

29. An informative, optimistic survey of all these developments is Allen, *Venezuelan Economic Development* (cited in n.26 above). A trenchant, pessimistic analysis of the country's developmental trajectory is Max Flores Díaz, "El capitalismo en la Venezuela actual," a paper presented at the "Seminario Imperialismo en América Latina," Universidad Autónoma de México, May 1979.

political repression, social injustice, and material poverty of the past is a dramatic one. The popular forces who fought that struggle began by supporting leaders with a socialist vision of the society they hoped to build. With time, however, they came to endorse leaders favoring a liberal capitalist society. The liberal, reformist, nationalistic policies they supported, which have so decisively promoted economic development in Venezuela during the last four decades, have not created an integrated industrial economy free from extreme dependence on oil exports for its continued expansion. Nor have they fostered significantly greater social equality. Some would argue that they have turned Venezuela into a small caricature of the advanced, consumption-oriented capitalist societies that, like Venezuela, have depended on oil to sustain continued economic expansion and political stability under liberal democratic forms. Yet these reformist policies have enabled Venezuela continually to overcome the contradictions of peripheral capitalist development that have brought countries like Chile and Argentina to economic and political impasse in the contemporary period. They have enabled Venezuela to expand and deepen the process of capitalist industrialization while legitimizing that process through mass political participation in a liberal democratic political system.

The Making of a Petroleum Proletariat

The political process that transformed Venezuela in the middle decades of the twentieth century from an autocratic dictatorship into a liberal mass democracy has its cultural and social origins in the oil enclave created under the auspices of foreign capital in the 1920's. The locus of this cradle of Venezuelan democracy was fixed by nature, the timing of its creation by historical forces beyond the control of Venezuela's workers. But the men and women who came to labor in the oil fields soon developed the cultural understanding and social institutions that enabled them to challenge the impersonal forces that determined much of their existence. And in learning to change their lives through collective action, they helped transform the history of their nation.

------------◆──◆────────

Geologists still debate alternative theories of the formation of the deposits of the liquid hydrocarbons we call petroleum, or rock oil. Most now agree, however, that the bulk of them began millennia ago as organic sediments. These deposits were buried by subsequent rock formations, transformed into liquid hydrocarbons by heat and pressure, and captured in underground reservoirs formed by the heaving and buckling of the earth. Usually these vast and discontinuous underground reservoirs are composed of porous sandstone or limestone formations surrounded by harder, nonporous rocks. Underground pools of petroleum have now been found in most parts of the world. But the largest ones exploited to date lie in areas to the north, west, and south of the Caribbean Sea in the New World and in the Middle Eastern region of the Old.

Man's knowledge of the existence of these underground deposits of petroleum is old. The prefix "Kir" in place names in Persia, the name "chapopote" in Mexico, and the term "mene" in pre-Columbian Venezuela were used by early peoples to denote places where seepage from underground reservoirs reached the surface and formed bituminous or asphalt lakes. Centuries before petroleum from shale deposits was first commercially processed for lubricants and lighting devices in mid-nineteenth-century Europe, and the first oil well was drilled in the United States in 1859, peoples in several parts of the world made use of forms of petroleum for construction, caulking, and medicinal purposes. It was only as the superior lighting qualities of kerosene became widely appreciated in industrial societies during the late nineteenth century, however, that demand for petroleum began to expand rapidly. By the early twentieth century huge capitalist enterprises emerged in the United States and Western Europe to monopolize the processing and distribution of kerosene to world markets. During the First World War, petroleum assumed the strategic and economic importance to the major industrial economies it retains to this day. After the war the proliferation of the internal combustion engine and widespread application of fuel oil to the heating and power requirements of industrial economies made demand for petroleum soar. In the scramble led by the major oil corporations for control of new sources of oil supplies in the 1920's, Venezuela assumed major importance.

Before the war, foreign investment in petroleum production in the New World focused on Mexico. In the years following the Mexican Revolution of 1910, however, the threat of nationalist economic policies and continuing social and political instability in that country led British and U.S. oil companies to cast about for safer, potentially more profitable sources of crude oil supplies to meet rising world demand. In nearby Venezuela they found promising signs of large oil reserves and a pliant dictatorship willing for a small price (sometimes paid outright in bribes) to encourage and protect foreign investment. British and Dutch capitalists affiliated with Royal Dutch Shell began to produce significant amounts of oil in Venezuela after 1918. By 1922 U.S. oil interests had bought up important concessions in Venezuela and had enlisted the support of U.S. diplomatic representatives to extract a new liberal oil law from the Gómez dictatorship that granted foreign capital cheap and virtually unrestricted access to Venezuelan oil reserves. All that remained to

ensure Venezuela's twentieth-century petroleum destiny was concrete
proof of the magnitude and accessibility of the country's oil reserves.
That proof came on December 14, 1922, when a Shell subsidiary drilling
in an abandoned hole on the eastern shore of Lake Maracaibo hit a well
which, in Edwin Lieuwen's words, "put Venezuela on every oilman's
map." The flow of the Barroso Number 2, he wrote in his classic study
of the Venezuelan petroleum economy, "began at 2,000 barrels per day
and increased rapidly until it flowed wild at 100,000, destroyed the
derrick, and blew a column of oil 200 feet into the air. It was a huge
gusher [which *The New York Times* judged] 'the most productive in the
world.' . . . " The Barroso well, the first of many great producers in
Venezuela's Bolívar oil fields, precipitated frenzied drilling by U.S. and
British oil companies in their Venezuelan concessions. By the end of the
1920's the whole eastern part of Lake Maracaibo and its shoreline was
covered by a forest of oil derricks. Venezuela had become the preeminent
oil-exporting nation in the world.[30]

Although substantial reserves of oil subsequently were found in many
parts of Venezuela north of the Orinoco, the Maracaibo Basin has remained the primary locus of the Venezuelan petroleum industry (see Map
4.1). The basin is formed by two spurs of the Andes and is dominated by
a great freshwater lake connected to the sea. The Spaniards who sailed
into the lake in 1499 and surveyed the Indian villages built on stilts over
the water originally called the region Venezuela (Little Venice). That
name was later extended to the whole of the Spanish colony, whose administrative and economic center developed some 400 kilometers to the
east of the lake in the cooler mountain valleys around Caracas. The Maracaibo Basin, whose average temperature is the highest recorded in South
America, remained very sparsely populated until the twentieth century.
The region was administered after independence as the state of Zulia.
Only its capital, the town of Maracaibo, grew significantly during the
nineteenth century. Located at the mouth of the lake, Maracaibo became
Venezuela's major coffee port, the entrepôt at which the coffee shipped
down the Zulia River from the Venezuelan and Colombian Andes was
transferred onto oceangoing ships for transport to European markets.
The torrid climate of the Maracaibo Basin, the high incidence of tropical
disease there, and the dangers of its southern and western jungles, which
were inhabited by fierce indigenous peoples, combined to make life and
work in the oil fields in the 1920's and 1930's an inferno for most oil
workers. One of their earliest collective demands asked simply for the
provision of cool, potable water to work sites far removed from oil
camps and human settlements.

30. Lieuwen, *Petroleum in Venezuela* (cited in n.25), p. 39. Lieuwen provides detailed
treatment of all of the points touched upon in this paragraph.

Early-twentieth-century oil exploration was a far cry from the extremely sophisticated scientific endeavor it has become in recent decades. Oil prospectors depended on local knowledge to locate major petroleum seeps. Once they had acquired mineral rights to surrounding lands, or, in Venezuela, a concession from the state, they simply drilled next to these seeps. Nevertheless, only large foreign companies had access to the amounts of capital needed to develop the oil potential of countries such as Venezuela in the early twentieth century. As early as 1878 Venezuelan entrepreneurs had extracted petroleum and built small works to process kerosene for the local market, but large-scale oil production required huge investments to open roads to production sites, to purchase and transport expensive drilling equipment, to contract skilled workers and technicians, to construct pipelines, pump stations, and port facilities, and to provide ocean transport to markets in the industrial world. Finally, vertical integration in an industry dominated by a few huge corporations meant that small independent oil producers could be denied access to refineries and to distribution networks that increasingly spanned the globe.[31]

Oil production, especially in the early decades in Venezuela, required a great many unskilled and semiskilled workers. Men did the heavy labor in road, pipeline, and camp construction, and the dirty unskilled labor in machine shops and around drilling rigs. Women, and some men too, provided domestic services in the camps. Most of these workers were rural Venezuelans attracted to the oil fields from Zulia and nearby states. Nevertheless, significant numbers of Venezuelan workers came from distant parts of the country, some from as far away as the island of Margarita off the country's northeast coast. Regional loyalties and identifications fostered segregated living patterns among these workers. Taciturn Andeans tended to live in one area, the more open, outgoing workers from the eastern coastal region in another. *Margariteños*, who distinguished themselves as labor activists, lived together in especially close-knit groups. One margariteño, the future Communist labor leader Manuel Taborda, later described how his group precipitated an early job action in a small British oil camp in the early 1920's. There were 122 Venezuelans working at the camp, 12 of them margariteños.

When we arrived there was no housing, so we margariteños decided to hang some sheets of zinc roofing under a wild grapevine close to the beach. In that way we protected ourselves from the rain and stored our food. We would start our fire on the sand and there we would cook our food. We would bathe on the beach and relieve ourselves in the bushes. There were no kinds of services, not even medical

31. This paragraph is based largely on the valuable account of the early development of the Mexican oil industry edited by W. J. Archer of the Pan American Petroleum and Transport Company, *Mexican Petroleum* (New York, 1922).

care. One day, while we were at work, Mister Duboy, the superintendent of the camp, saw our improvised housing and ordered it destroyed. When we got back that night, we had no place to protect ourselves from the rain, which unfortunately fell that very night. The next day, we decided not to go to work and demanded an explanation from the company. The rest of the Venezuelans supported us, and in that way we all went on strike. The explanation given by the company was that the appearance of our improvised house was undesirable. . . . The company brought in the police to force us to work, a successful ploy that got the workers back on the job, except for the twelve margariteños: we were expelled.[32]

Despite their regional identifications, no serious cultural and ethnic difference divided native Venezuelan workers in the oil fields. Rather, racial and cultural differences reinforced the nationalist sentiments most Venezuelan workers felt toward migrants to the oil fields from the British Caribbean. Several thousand of these unskilled and semiskilled workers, most of them English-speaking blacks, migrated to the Maracaibo Basin in the 1920's. Because they spoke the language of the managers, administrators, and foremen in the U.S.- and British-owned oil companies, and because they were utterly dependent on their jobs in a foreign land, workers from the Antilles tended to identify their interests with those of management, proved reluctant to participate in job actions, and often served as strikebreakers. Venezuelan workers invented a sarcastic name for conformist black workers who spoke the language of their class oppressors: combining the English words "my" and "friend," they called them *maifrenes*.[33]

Perhaps the most serious ethnic and cultural divisions among oil workers in Venezuela were those that reinforced the distinction between skilled and unskilled workers. In the early years, the vast majority of skilled workers in the Venezuelan oil fields were white foreigners. Foreign skilled workers earned twice what the few Venezuelans doing skilled work earned. Machinists, electricians, welders, and heavy-equipment operators came primarily from the United States, as did the men who dominated the most respected and highly paid of blue-collar jobs, those on the drilling rigs.[34]

Drilling crews were cohesive groups proud of their command over the wide range of skills necessary to perform their dangerous work effi-

32. The quotation is reproduced from an interview with Taborda published in Paul Nehru Tennassee, *Venezuela, los obreros petroleros y la lucha por la democracia* (Madrid and Caracas, 1979), p. 107. I comment on Tennassee's important contribution in n. 48 below.

33. A U.S. government official reported that of 2,379 immigrants to Maracaibo in 1924, 1,658 were white, 695 were black, and 26 were oriental. Wheelwright, "The Economy of Venezuela" (cited in n. 27), p. 76, presents these statistics in tabular form. Information on oil workers' housing patterns and vocabulary can be found in Rodolfo Quintero's valuable *La cultura del petróleo* (2d ed.; Caracas, 1976).

34. Lieuwen, *Petroleum in Venezuela* (cited in n.25), p. 51.

ciently. A drilling crew in the 1920's was usually made up of five men, selected by the driller himself. The driller controlled the speed of perforation and made technical decisions regarding bit types and casings to protect the hole. He also determined when the bit was spent or when technical problems made suspension of drilling necessary, forcing the crew to "come out" of the hole. At that point the crew would activate the tackle strung from the top of the derrick and begin to pull pipe from the ground. As each section of pipe emerged it was steadied by the derrickman perched high on his platform in the tower. Floormen then used massive wrenches to uncouple it. They then moved it to one side, hitched the cable to the next section of pipe, and began the operation anew. Drilling crews performed their dangerous work at high speed. Their efficiency and personal safety depended on perfect teamwork. Once all pipe was removed and a new bit screwed into place or a technical solution to a particular drilling problem decided upon, they would reverse the entire process, coupling stand upon stand of pipe together until the bit was lowered once more to the bottom of the hole. The technical problems that could interrupt drilling were many. Among the most common were deviation of the advancing hole from the vertical, caused by the hardness and inclination of the rock strata below, blowouts, caused when the bit suddenly pierced a high-pressure oil reservoir, and explosions and fires, caused when gas from the hole ignited. These were only the most spectacular and dreaded of the dangers facing the drilling crew. There was also the constant threat of being maimed or crushed in the rapid process of coupling and uncoupling long sections of steel pipe (10-inch well casing weighed 40 pounds per linear foot, and pipe sections in use in the Maracaibo fields by the 1940's reached 90 feet in length). All drilling tasks were complicated in the case of offshore wells, which became the hallmark of Lake Maracaibo oil production. Divers, who performed underwater tasks in the construction and operation of offshore rigs, earned special wage bonuses.[35]

The fact that drilling crews consisted mostly of foreigners in the Venezuelan oil fields in the early twentieth century complicated labor organization. These highly paid, skilled, and literate workers developed mutual trust and self-reliance on the job that made them a potential focus for collective action. Partly for that reason, management was usually very solicitous of their welfare. Their wages averaged two to three times those of common laborers in the industry. They were given preferential treatment in company housing, services, and benefits. This treatment, and the

35. This description of rotary drilling operations, which by the 1920's had almost totally replaced the cable tool procedures used earlier in the industry, is drawn primarily from Dorsey Hager, *Oil Field Practice* (New York, 1921), Chaps. 3 and 4.

fact that they enjoyed a significant degree of control over the way they
did their jobs, tended to separate drilling crews from the great mass of
unskilled workers in the oil fields.

In the United States, the nation that produced the bulk of the world's
oil before 1950 and remained the world's largest oil producer until the
early 1970's, the historical lack of labor militancy among drilling crews
and oil workers in general is well known. Drilling crews were the most
favored of workers in an industry whose huge profits, expanding production, and vulnerability to sabotage made granting concessions to labor both less painful and more sensible than in other industrial sectors.
As a result, labor struggles in the oil industry in the United States and in
other advanced capitalist nations have been muted.[36] A typical assessment
of the attitudes of U.S. drilling crews is this approving comment by the
authors of a Gulf Oil publication published in the 1950's.

Drilling crews are among the most dependable workmen in the world. Being for
the most part independent and self-reliant, these men show an obvious pride in
the job of keeping the bit "turning to the right." When anything goes wrong, the
roughneck is instantly at work to fix it. He is plumber, electrician, motor me-
chanic, an expert at wiring together broken equipment. . . . He is of the admirable, old-fashioned opinion that a man ought to rustle a job for himself, hold it
by hard work, and share the responsibility of making the drilling business
profitable. . . .[37]

In Venezuela such attitudes were reinforced by ethnic and cultural loyalties that tended to separate skilled U.S. drilling crews from the majority
of unskilled Venezuelan workers and link them instead to management.
In his survey of the early development of the Venezuelan oil industry,
Lieuwen noted that foreign skilled workers were usually staunch company men. Nevertheless, some of these skilled workers, who had experience in labor organizations in the United States, provided early Vene-

36. Executives of the industry leader, Standard Oil of New Jersey, liked to attribute the
relative lack of labor strife in the industry to the generous and farsighted labor relations
program founded by Jersey Standard's Clarence J. Hicks. Hicks was hired by John D. Rockefeller, Jr., to solve the company's labor problems after the Ludlow Massacre of 1914 and
bloody strikes at the company's Bayonne refinery in New Jersey in 1915. His praises are
sung in an editorial and obituary in the company's publication, *The Lamp* (Feb. 1945), pp.
1 and 23. Hicks is seen by some of his admirers as the man who complemented the scientific
management theories of Frederick W. Taylor by establishing the art of modern industrial
relations. Hicks outlined his philosophy in a book published in 1941, *My Life in Industrial
Relations* (New York). A glowing review of the history of Jersey Standard's labor relations
is Stuart Chase, "A Generation of Industrial Peace," *The Lamp* (Oct. 1946), pp. 2–14, 30–
32. Even Chase, however, recognized the structural features, noted in the text, that fostered
the relatively smooth labor relations that developed in the industry.

37. Robert R. Wheeler and Maurine Whited, *Oil—From Prospect to Pipeline. Guidebook for
Students, Mineral Owners, Investors, and Oil Company Personnel* (Houston, 1958). A similar
statement about the attitudes of U.S. drilling crews appears in Hager's 1921 publication *Oil
Field Practice*, p. 96.

zuelan union organizers in the oil fields with material support and valuable organizational knowledge.[38] And as the proportion of Venezuelans among the skilled workers in the industry increased, the barriers dividing skilled from unskilled workers diminished. The downturn in the industry in the early 1930's led to the repatriation of most foreign skilled workers, and they never again assumed the virtual monopoly over skilled jobs they held in the 1920's. The "Venezuelanization" of the work force in the industry in the late 1930's and early 1940's was in some measure a result of expanding Venezuelan production before and during the war and the demand for foreign skilled workers elsewhere. As we shall see, however, it was primarily a consequence of domestic political pressure on the companies. The declining importance of foreign workers in the Venezuelan oil industry coincided with the great mobilization and growing political impact of oil workers in the decade after 1935.[39]

The relationship between the "Venezuelanization" of the skilled labor force in oil production and the emergence of oil workers as a powerful force for the democratization of Venezuelan society is nicely framed in an allegorical novel written by Venezuela's foremost literary figure and future president, Rómulo Gallegos. *Sobre esta misma tierra*, published in 1944, reveals a profound understanding of the cultural and social forces at work in the oil enclave. It also uncannily predicts its author's—and the nation's—political future. In the novel, Gallegos paints a sympathetic portrait of an exceptional U.S. driller he names Hardman. Unlike his North American colleagues, Hardman speaks good Spanish. He soon falls in love with the novel's mestizo protagonist, Remota Montiel. Remota, the daughter of a Guajiran Indian woman, was abandoned as a

38. Rodolfo Quintero, who helped organize one of the first oilworker unions in Venezuela in the early 1930's, insisted on this point in an interview with me, Caracas, July 6 and 7, 1979. Tennassee, *Venezuela, los obreros petroleros* (cited in n. 32), provides additional evidence, pp. 134-35.

39. C. C. McDermund, *Who's Who in Venezuela* (Maracaibo, 1932), p. 180, estimated that only one-fifth of the foreign skilled workers on the company payrolls in Maracaibo in 1929 were still in Venezuela by June 1932. Corporate conceptions of the need to "Venezuelanize" the work force are discussed in *The Lamp* (Feb. 1945), pp. 16-22. Between 1939 and 1945, Creole, the affiliate of Standard Oil of New Jersey that emerged as Venezuela's largest oil producer during the war, expanded its work force in Venezuela rapidly from 6,525 to 10,072 employees. New Venezuelan workers accounted for all of the increase. Creole's "expatriate" employees (mostly U.S. citizens) declined in number from 591 in 1939 to 411 in 1943 at the height of the war, then rose to 556 in 1945. During the same period, the company's "local staff" (virtually all of it Venezuelan) burgeoned from 5,934 to 9,516 employees. These company statistics reflect the racial and cultural divisions institutionalized within the multinational oil corporations. "Expatriate" employees included white Europeans who made top pay; "local staff" was defined to include small numbers of employees from Latin America and the Caribbean along with the Venezuelan majority. Charles Sterling Popple, *Standard Oil Company (New Jersey) in World War II* (New York, 1952), p. 224. This book was commissioned and published by the company.

child by her Creole father and raised by surrogate German parents. She lived most of her young adult life in exile in New York. Upon her return to Venezuela to claim the small inheritance left her by her profligate father, however, she reveals a stubborn independence of mind and a growing sense of identification with her native land. Remota is intrigued by Hardman, but she ultimately, if somewhat wistfully, rejects his overtures. Before she breaks off her relationship with him, however, she accepts his invitation to tour the oil fields—"a country of mine enjoying a fine time in this country of yours," as Hardman puts it. Hardman explains to her the technology of oil production and introduces her to a Venezuelan driller he has trained. The driller is hard at work on an oil rig when the pair drive up. "He was a man of some forty years of age," writes Gallegos, "strong, vigorous, with brown eyes that shone with fidelity and firmness." The driller takes off his heavy glove and offers Remota his powerful, calloused hand: "Venancio Navas, at your service." Remota, it turns out, knows of the man. When she was a small child he had saved her from almost certain death when he forced her father to abandon a suicidal effort to sail down Lake Maracaibo during a violent nighttime storm. Once they were safely docked in Maracaibo her father had told Remota, "Don't ever forget that you must always be grateful for Venancio Navas." "But in reality," Venancio now tells Remota, "you need not thank me." "And let me tell you something else. Whenever you need me, for whatever reason, all you have to do is call me." As the novel proceeds, Remota forges a powerful new identity out of the disparate indigenous and European elements of her past and sets out on the waterways of the Maracaibo Basin in an ambitious and dangerous effort to build a modern, more just society for her compatriots. She enlists Venancio Navas as the pilot of her boat and her personal protector.[40]

In addition to skilled and unskilled blue-collar workers, Venezuelan oil production required a large and growing number of white-collar workers. Initially, virtually all managers, engineers, and technicians, as well as many physicians, accountants, secretaries, and clerks, came from abroad. Administration of the camps and company affairs in Maracaibo was carried out primarily in English until the 1940's. That alone gave U.S. and British citizens an advantage in the competition for white-collar jobs with the oil companies. Those Venezuelans who managed to find such jobs smarted under the social and racial discrimination inflicted on them by the Anglo-Saxons who controlled the companies. They also resented the fact that their pay scales and benefit packages were much inferior to those of their foreign counterparts. Venezuelan clerks in the industry, for example, made between 500 and 1,250 bolívares a month in 1932,

40. The quotations are from *Sobre esta misma tierra* (Buenos Aires, 1944), pp. 135-36.

roughly 65 to 151 dollars at the prevailing exchange rate of 7.75. Foreign clerks were making 175 to 275 dollars per month, or more than two times as much during the same period.[41] It is not surprising, then, that the first collective demands of organized Venezuelan white-collar petroleum workers called for an end to racial and social discrimination and equal pay for equal work.

Venezuelan oil workers revealed an acute understanding of the racial and cultural divisions that separated management and foreign skilled and white-collar workers on the one hand from the Venezuelan work force on the other. All foreigners were derisively called *musiús*. The term, said to be derived from French, had strong racial overtones and was used by the left to rally nationalist sentiment and worker solidarity across racial lines during the first great mobilization of workers in the industry in 1936. In its attempt to counteract Venezuelan animosity toward the black workers from the Antilles, who were targeted as a scapegoat, the Communist-oriented workers' paper *Petróleo* published the editorial whose headline appears at the beginning of this chapter, "The Danger Is Not Black But White."

It was the dichotomy between foreign capital and Venezuelan labor that proved to be the most important and enduring in the Venezuelan petroleum economy. Life and work in the Venezuelan oil camps, especially in the early years, reinforced workers' perceptions of this basic social division in powerful subjective ways. Removed from the rest of Venezuelan society, oil workers found their growing sense of identity and class interests reconfirmed in patterns of housing, food consumption, and recreation in the camps. Oil camps always featured segregated residential patterns. Housing for foreign managers, technicians, white-collar workers, and skilled blue-collar workers was usually clean, ample, and comfortable. Unskilled Venezuelan workers in the early years were customarily assigned rudimentary communal housing. Sometimes the companies offered no more than a large tin-roofed, open-sided shed in which hundreds of workers strung their hammocks. "The camp was divided into two sections," one Venezuelan foreman remembered,

that of the "Yankee" personnel, and that of the Venezuelan personnel, separated from each other by 500 meters; [rooms in] the "Yankee's" section were each five meters square, with two beds and places for their occupants to store equipment and other belongings. These buildings were painstakingly cared for by a special steward, who kept everything in a state of great cleanliness: he changed the mosquito netting and the bedding twice a week, and sprayed insecticide every night. These buildings contained a large dining room with two tables, bookshelves for newspapers, magazines, and books in English, a radio, a medicine kit containing all the necessary drugs, 14 very comfortable canvas chairs, . . . and two hygienic water closets, one for the North Americans, the other for their Chinese cooks.

41. McDermund, *Who's Who*, p. 180.

In contrast, the Venezuelans lived in a large communal dormitory that measured 25 by 7 meters. The dormitory was divided "by a beam held firmly in place by two pillars, so that it could sustain the weight of 506 palm fiber hammocks on each side. . . ."[42]

As for food, the North Americans had special grills to barbecue meat, and ovens to bake bread daily. Two waiters served each table. The menu was varied and included large quantities of chicken and all kinds of imported canned goods, as well as fresh vegetables and ice brought in from town. The North Americans "drank boiled and filtered water stored in special bags to keep it cool." Venezuelan workers, by contrast, always ate the same thing: meat, usually salted, boiled rice, and cassava. They usually had to eat breakfast and lunch on the run. Their water "was taken out of rusted tanks exposed to the sun and it often tasted like soap."

Recreational facilities for high-level personnel at the larger, established oil camps in the Maracaibo fields were luxurious, featuring tennis courts, swimming pools, golf courses, and fancy clubhouses for white foreign employees. A powerful scene in Ramón Díaz Sánchez's 1936 novel *Mene* depicts a worker's perception of the racial and class dimensions of these recreational facilities. A black Venezuelan oil worker returning from a day of work clearing the forest at an isolated construction site passes by the tennis courts of the main camp. He begins to watch a white woman player and to fantasize about meeting her alone on a jungle trail. As their encounter develops it is apparent to him that the woman wants him, but she resists his sexual advances. He has decided to rape her when a tennis ball flies out of the court and interrupts his daydream. He picks up the white ball, but instead of returning it to the players, he hurls it in the opposite direction. Four days later he is blacklisted by the company.[43]

The stark contrast in the living arrangements and life style of the North Americans and Venezuelans in the oil camps drew the attention of many Venezuelan novelists, journalists, and politicians in the 1930's and 1940's. Rómulo Betancourt visited many of the oil fields in the 1930's and 1940's and, with oil workers' support, built a career as Venezuela's most successful twentieth-century politician. In newspaper articles and speeches Betancourt played on the injustice of social arrangements that allowed foreign personnel to live in "California-style" bungalows while Venezuelans subsisted in what one labor inspector called "evolved matchboxes."[44] In

---

42. Quoted in Tennessee, *Venezuela, los obreros petroleros* (cited in n. 32), p. 102.

43. Ramón Díaz Sánchez, *Mene. Novela de la región petrolera del estado Zulia* (Caracas, 1936), pp. 44-46.

44. Rómulo Betancourt, *Venezuela, política y petróleo* (Mexico City, 1956), p. 87. Betancourt originally drafted this, his major work, between 1937 and 1939; it is an indispensable source for twentieth-century Venezuelan history. Typical of Betancourt's journalistic use of the contrast between housing for foreign and Venezuelan workers in the oil fields is his article in *Acción Democrática* (Caracas), Feb. 20, 1943, p. 8.

reality, domestic political pressure and organized oil workers gradually forced the companies to improve the housing available to workers. By the 1940's the communal housing of the past was no longer the norm, and in the larger camps most workers lived with their families in modest concrete-block houses. Nonetheless, many oil workers preferred to live in the oil towns outside the confines of the camps anyway. Inside company fences workers had to contend with rigid company rules that restricted their right to raise animals and food and to open small businesses. Outside the camps they were free to do more as they pleased.

Venezuelan oil workers found solace and diversion in the bars, brothels, movie theaters, and eating joints of such dirty little oil towns as Cabimas and Lagunillas, which mushroomed along the eastern shore of Lake Maracaibo in the 1920's and 1930's. In the first years of the oil boom prostitutes from Maracaibo journeyed by boat on weekends to meet with workers in makeshift whorehouses and bars, some of them run by Gómez's police. Oil workers, many of whom were single males,[45] baptized these women with names drawn from the technology of their work: "Las Cuatro Válvulas," "La Tubería," "La Cabria." Within a few years the oil towns featured established bordellos, as well as movie houses and scores of restaurants, bars, and retail stores. Immigrants from all over Venezuela and many parts of the world flooded into the oil towns. Many of those who did not land jobs in the oil fields became bootblacks and lottery salesmen, washerwomen and cooks, waiters and bar girls. In the scramble to get a cut of the oil wealth flowing through the towns in the form of wages, those who were lucky or shrewd enough could accumulate sufficient capital to open businesses and to speculate in real estate and scarce commodities. Oil wages allowed towns like Cabimas and Lagunillas to host the artistic greats of the Latin popular entertainment world in the 1930's. Carlos Gardel came, as did the Spanish singer and socialist Libertad Lamarque.[46]

As the oil towns grew, writes Rodolfo Quintero in his classic study of them, they became cities "of oil-soaked, narrow streets interrupted by wooden houses full of flies and foul odors, of naked children who bathe in puddles of dirty water and mineral oil. Streets of chaos from which one emerges surprisingly to land on a wide and level avenue with rows of great buildings. Cities where luxury contrasts with misery, hunger with the abundance of food. . . ." They became societies "created by material interests, in which to live is to race about giddily, without spir-

---

45. In 1936, for example, Lagunillas had a population of 13,922 people, 8,651 of whom were males, a ratio of 164 males to every 100 women. Antonio José Briceño Parilli, *Las migraciones internas y los municipios petroleros* (Caracas, 1947), p. 18.

46. Jesús Prieto Soto's *El chorro. ¿Gracia o maldición?* (Maracaibo, 1962) contains a wealth of information on life in the early oil towns.

itual or moral buffers. [Societies] where one has to sink or swim in a lucrative and utilitarian life."[47]

The transformation of the small villages of fishermen and farmers on
the eastern shore of Lake Maracaibo prefigured the transformation of the
whole of Venezuelan society by the oil export economy. The oil camp
and the oil town revealed in microcosm the two faces of Venezuela's oil-
based development. The oil camp served the needs of international capital and the energy-hungry capitalist economies of the developed industrial world. It was a monument to the ideal of rational economic planning. It created a clean, orderly, comfortable environment for the foreign
managers, technicians, and skilled workers charged with efficiently or-
dering capital, technology, and men to transform the natural resource of
an underdeveloped society into a commodity for export and profit. The
oil town, by contrast, grew up to meet the needs of Venezuelan labor.
There workers found relief from the fatigue and the unbending hierarchy
of their working lives. In oil towns petty local capitalists cashed in on a
small part of the great wealth being siphoned out of Venezuela by the
foreign oil corporations. The chaos of the oil towns contrasted sharply
with the manicured lawns, carefully laid-out streets, and tidy rows of
identical houses in the camps. Oil towns, with their noisy, filthy, un-
planned streets, their slapdash buildings, their miserable public services,
and their great extremes of wealth, laid bare the social reality of Venezuela's capitalist development. In oil towns workers and immigrants
struggled to survive as human beings and make their fortunes in a capitalist society. There workers drank, gambled, fought, loved—and eventually built the collective organizations that improved their lives and profoundly affected the course of Venezuelan history.

Organizing an Industry and a Nation

In the thirteen-year period between the death of Gómez in December
1935 and the fall from power of the reformist liberal party Acción Democrática in November 1948, Venezuelans forged the pattern that guides
the historical development of the nation today. During that crucial period, the Venezuelan people repudiated the political economy of the
Gómez regime. Democratic political institutions, nationalist oil policies,
and an institutionalized commitment to social reform and economic development replaced the policies of a dictatorship dedicated to the personal
enrichment of favorites, uncritical support for foreign capital, and the use
of systematic repression to maintain the social status quo. A liberal, reformist, developmentalist capitalist regime based on popular mobilization replaced an authoritarian, laissez-faire capitalist regime based on
force. This remarkable transformation involved much more than the de-

47. Rodolfo Quintero, *La cultura del petróleo* (cited in n. 33), pp. 66 and 69.

feat of those foreign and domestic interests that had supported Gómez by a popular coalition of the working and middle classes. Marxist elements within the popular coalition had to be defeated by liberal reformers, the advocates of a socialist transformation of Venezuelan society by those who sought a liberal capitalist one. The liberal-democratic pattern of Venezuelan historical development forged in the thirteen years following the death of Gómez was temporarily eclipsed by the right between 1948 and 1958, and violently challenged by the Marxist left in the early 1960's. But it has reasserted itself with renewed vigor in the quarter century since 1958. No group was more intimately involved in the process of transformation between 1935 and 1948—or more responsible for the liberal democratic outcome—than Venezuelan oil workers.[48]

Before the death of Gómez political opposition to his regime was repressed with brutal effectiveness. Conspirators in an aborted military coup in 1919 were ferreted out and reportedly hung by their testicles until

48. In conceptualizing and documenting the political and labor developments of this crucial period in Venezuelan history I have drawn especially on accounts by two rival and major participants, Rómulo Betancourt's *Venezuela, política y petróleo* (cited in n. 44), and the Communist activist Juan Bautista Fuenmayor's *Veinte años de historia* (Caracas, 1968). I have also relied on recently published secondary studies of labor and politics by Julio Godio, *El movimiento obrero venezolano, 1850-1944* (Caracas, 1980); Paul Nehru Tennassee, *Venezuela, los obreros petroleros* (cited in n. 32); Steve Ellner, *Los partidos políticos y su disputa por el control del movimiento sindical en Venezuela, 1936-1948* (Caracas, 1980); Héctor Lucena, *El movimiento obrero y las relaciones laborales* (Carabobo, 1981); and Alberto J. Pla et al., *Clase obrera, partidos y sindicatos en Venezuela, 1936-1950* (Caracas, 1982). All of these secondary works emphasize the role of the petroleum proletariat in national historical events. Godio's book, which is narrative rather than analytical, includes lengthy transcriptions of important primary documents. Tennassee's work is the first to develop explicitly the thesis, also advanced here, that oil workers played the pivotal role in the democratization of Venezuelan society. It contains the best account of the early organizational history of the oil workers, and the most detailed analysis of the events that culminated in the great oil strike of 1936. It is weaker on post-strike developments, which Tennassee confusingly conceptualizes as a transition from "informal colonialism" to "neo-colonialism." That approach does not allow him to explain very convincingly either the deradicalization of oil workers after 1937 or the fundamental role they play in the liberal evolution of post-1945 Venezuelan history. Ellner's work—although it is more concerned with politics than the labor movement and sees politicians, not workers, as the driving force in the history of the period—helps to illuminate both of these issues. It is especially rich on the period 1945-48, when oil company and government policies combined to channel the struggle led by oil workers into a liberal corporativist mold. Lucena's study argues persuasively that developments in labor relations in the oil industry set the institutional pattern for the country as a whole. Pla and his associates add little new information to the story of oil workers and national history, but their book has the virtue of presenting simultaneous developments in other sectors of the national labor movement. Though I have incorporated insights and evidence from these works published since I completed my research in Venezuela in 1979, this essay is conceptually and methodologically distinct from all of them. Through its comparative lens it focuses on the special structure of the Venezuelan oil export economy and its particular meaning for the cultural, institutional, and political development of the petroleum proletariat. And although it is based in large part on a somewhat different reading of many of the same sources employed in these other works, it also taps material from U.S. diplomatic archives.

they confessed and recanted or perished. Students who launched an important protest against the repressive policies of the regime in Caracas in 1928 were arrested and exiled or sent to work on road gangs in the interior. An invasion led by old-time regional strongmen in 1929 was defeated handily by Gómez's troops, the invaders killed or forced back into seemingly hopeless exile. Members of an embryonic communist party organized by students in Caracas in 1931 were quickly discovered by police spies, the bulk of them caught and jailed in Gómez's infamous prison, La Rotunda. According to one survivor, the inhuman conditions in which they were held—they were crowded like cattle into communal cells and denied even the means to dispose of their feces—drove several into temporary insanity. Those who survived were exiled in 1934, the poorest among them dumped at night along the Colombian border.[49]

As soon as Gómez died, however, the popular social forces repressed for so long by the dictatorship burst forth in a spasm of spontaneous rage. The popular reaction against the dictatorship was widespread, but the most serious violence erupted in the oil zone. Thirty-seven people reportedly lost their lives in Cabimas when workers led by a local barber stormed the town's government building. The next day government troops slipped out of town as angry crowds systematically destroyed all local monuments and symbols of the dictatorship. In nearby Lagunillas two government officials were killed and the rest forced to flee by crowds that surged through the streets shouting slogans against the dictatorship and destroying the brothels run by Gómez sympathizers. The next day, 150 troops sent to regain control of the town dispersed the crowds with gunfire, killing 10 and wounding 30.[50] Meanwhile, in Maracaibo crowds ransacked the houses of leading *gomecistas*. They also attacked the property of the foreign oil companies, causing many North Americans and British citizens to flee the city for the safety of ships in the harbor.[51]

Within a few days of the death of the dictator, however, Gómez's hand-picked successor, Minister of War Eleázar López Contreras, consolidated his control over the government and contained the unorganized popular protests. But the groundswell of popular reaction against the dictatorship gradually acquired more organized form. Press censorship was lifted and the exiles returning to Venezuela were allowed to enter the country virtually unmolested. A spectrum of new political parties emerged to challenge the policies of the military government and the institutional legacy

49. Details can be found in Rangel, *Gómez* (cited in n. 19), and in Fuenmayor, *Veinte años*. A sketch of the development of the Venezuelan labor movement under Gómez is Pedro Guillén Castro, "Huelgas y sindicatos bajo Gómez," *El Nacional* (Caracas), July 8, 1979. The 1928 labor legislation is treated in greater depth in Godío, *El movimiento*, pp. 72-76.

50. These details are reported in Prieto Soto, *El chorro* (cited in n. 46), pp. 209, 227-29.

51. Ellner, *Los partidos políticos*, p. 29.

of the dictatorship. Led by former students from the university protests against the dictatorship in 1928, these nascent political parties succeeded in mobilizing the support of workers and middle-class opponents of the regime in powerful street demonstrations in Caracas in February and June of 1936. The June mobilization was accompanied by a general strike that temporarily paralyzed Caracas and lingered ominously in the oil fields of Zulia before it was violently crushed by government troops and police. In Lagunillas several workers were killed or wounded in confrontations with government forces, and scores of petroleum workers were fired from their jobs.

These demonstrations of popular sentiment and strength did not achieve their full objectives. The congress, packed with former gomecistas, was not dissolved and proceeded to enact repressive legislation to limit political participation by leftist parties and enable the executive to jail or deport people suspected of communist or anarchist tendencies.

Nevertheless, by mid-1936 popular forces had won some important concessions from the government, the most important of which was a new labor law, enacted on July 16, 1936. On paper the law was among the most progressive and comprehensive in Latin America. It laid down enlightened principles governing work conditions, pay, and compensation for industrial accidents and occupational diseases. It contemplated social-security and profit-sharing plans. Written with the most important employers of Venezuelan labor in mind, the law required oil companies of a certain size to provide workers with adequate housing, medical and education facilities, and free transportation to work sites more than two kilometers from their homes. It established the principles of free commerce and free transit within the oil camps, required the oil companies to establish modest scholarship programs for workers or their children, and stipulated that 75 percent of company employees be Venezuelans. The labor law also provided for extensive state regulation of unions and industrial conflict. It set up an office of labor empowered to monitor labor organizations to ensure their apolitical intentions, internal democracy, and fiscal propriety. The office was also charged with administering complicated mechanisms for conciliation and arbitration of disputes between workers and owners.[52]

The labor law was an effort by the military to control the explosive social forces brewing in Venezuela in 1936. The final bill was a compromise worked out in congress, influenced by Mexican labor law that the oil companies flatly called "anticapitalist." Nevertheless, labor leaders expressed severe reservations about the new law. Confident of the growing organizational power of the labor movement, and correctly distrustful of

52. The law was published in a special issue of the *Gaceta Oficial*, July 16, 1936.

the intentions of the government, labor leaders claimed the law would weaken unions and lead to their control by the state. For their part, Venezuela's leading capitalists opposed virtually every aspect of the law. "The oil companies," a U.S. diplomatic official confidentially informed his superiors in Washington, "quite frankly state that they would much prefer the antiquated and 'toothless' Labor Law in effect for many years under the Gómez regime." The oil companies objected most strongly to the proposed profit-sharing scheme envisioned by the law, and to the provisions for collective bargaining and recognition of trade unions. They feared that those provisions would become "a ready medium for radical agitators," the official reported.[53]

As in the case of similar attempts by the state to institutionalize labor and regulate industrial conflict in other capitalist countries, the implications of the Venezuelan labor law of 1936 could not be immediately foreseen. Ostensibly more liberal and less restrictive than contemporary labor legislation in other countries (such as Chile), the law nevertheless granted the state extensive, and poorly defined, powers to discipline and regulate labor unions. How these restrictive powers would be interpreted and enforced, and how the benefits to labor envisioned in the law would be translated into concrete programs, remained to be seen. The influence of the labor law on the Venezuelan labor movement and, through it, on the history of the nation, was determined through struggle in the political arena and the workplace. The first great battle in that struggle was fought in the oil fields in late 1936 and early 1937.

On December 14, 1936, oil workers in the Maracaibo Basin initiated a strike that shook Venezuelan society to its foundations. Ostensibly a struggle by oil workers for recognition of their unions and improvements in pay and working conditions, the strike inevitably involved much larger political issues. For 42 days Venezuelan oil workers successfully defied the power of some of the largest corporations in the world. They threatened the finances of the government and disrupted the national economy. They built a powerful alliance in support of their efforts that transcended class lines in the oil zone and reached out to envelop workers, farmers, students, and professionals across the nation.

The oil strike of 1936 marked the high-water mark of the popular mobilization that followed the demise of the Gómez dictatorship. When the oil workers were forced to admit defeat and obey a government decree to return to work, the democratic opposition to the military government suffered a severe setback. But the strike revealed the strength and long-range political potential of the social and ideological forces galvanized by oil workers in their struggle. By demonstrating both how powerful the

53. Meredith Nicholson to Secretary of State, Caracas, June 25, 1936, and July 21, 1936, USNA/DS 831.504/66 and 831.504/67, respectively.

popular forces spearheaded by the oil workers could be and how detrimental the alliance between foreign capital and the Venezuelan state was to the Venezuelan people, the strike raised the political conscience of most Venezuelans. It put the oil companies on notice that without fundamental concessions to their workers and to the Venezuelan people they could look forward to escalating conflict in the workplace and intensifying political attacks outside it. It forced the military regime that was heir to the Gómez dictatorship to set in motion incremental political, social, and economic concessions to popular forces. The working-class institutions and popular political parties forged in the oil enclave in 1936 survived the repression following the strike and in the next years consolidated and deepened their organizational base and ideological influence in the oil zone and across the nation. Because the oil strike of 1936 sounded the death knell for the legacy of Gómez and presaged a new era in Venezuelan history, it merits our close attention.

That within a year of the death of Gómez oil workers and their allies were able to mount such a powerful organized challenge to the established power of the oil companies and the Venezuelan government attests to the optimal conditions that union organizers and political activists encountered in the oil enclave in 1936. By 1934 Venezuelan oil production had climbed back to pre-Depression levels, and by 1936 much expansion was under way. Meanwhile, the growth of the petroleum labor force, which had declined to only 8,832 workers in 1932, was well on its way to the pre-Depression levels of over 20,000 by 1936. (See Figure 4.1.) The tight labor market in oil production underlay the explosive success of petroleum worker organization during that year. However, the Marxist and social democratic exiles who streamed into the Maracaibo Basin in early 1936 also encountered what one called "excellent raw material": a militant proletariat in the oil fields, unorganized but increasingly conscious of its needs, and a body politic "uncontaminated" by traditional political affiliations, united in its hatred for the dictatorship, suspicious of foreign capital, and sympathetic to the oil workers' cause. The unions and parties that organized and flourished in Zulia in the early months of 1936 all based their appeal on three issues: democratic political rights, social justice, and economic nationalism.

With time two distinct currents emerged within this broad popular democratic movement: the Marxists, led by a core of Communist militants; and the democratic socialists, who in subsequent years evolved toward liberal reformism and coalesced in the party called Acción Democrática. By the early 1940's these two currents were sharply defined and deeply divided, and during that decade they struggled violently for control of the labor movement and the popular, nationalist political forces both had helped to create and to organize in the 1930's. But in 1936 their differences were still muted and both currents cooperated politically against a common enemy—the oil companies and their supporters within the Venezuelan ruling class, and the military government of López Contreras—to democratize the country and free it from the worst features of foreign control. Cooperation was favored as well by the fact that both the Marxists and the social democrats shared a socialist project still uncontaminated, as it were, by geopolitical realities and extranational political ties and loyalties. It was only after the failure of the 1936 strike that the emerging leader of the liberal social democrats, Rómulo Betancourt, reached the conclusion that Venezuela's geographic position, its strategic importance as supplier of oil to the advanced capitalist nations, and the small size and limited power of its industrial proletariat precluded a socialist revolution for the foreseeable future.[54] And it was only in the late 1930's and early 1940's that the Communists of Zulia became strongly affected by the party's national organization in Caracas and began to mold their labor activities and political tactics in accordance with the changing international line dictated by the Comintern.

Nurtured by this climate of unity and mutual cooperation, leftist organization and influence flourished in Zulia during 1936. Activists from both political currents joined with militant workers in the oil fields to organize vigorous blue- and white-collar unions in all the major oil camps and in Maracaibo during the first months of the year. Political organization proceeded apace. Social democrats allied with Marxists in February to found the Bloque Nacional Democrático, whose comprehensive progressive platform appealed to a broad spectrum of workers, farmers, professionals, merchants, and industrialists. The platform outlined specific measures to ensure political democratization (including respect for constitutional civil liberties, direct election of state governors, electoral reform involving proportional representation, and judicial autonomy), to promote economic development (revision of oil concessions, nationalization of foreign companies that threatened the sovereignty of the nation, "municipalization" of all public services, land reform to break up latifundia, and protection of national industry and commerce), and to advance social justice (a series of labor and education reforms, and concrete measures to promote Indian and women's rights).[55]

Social democrats also joined with Marxists in public rallies and demonstrations in Zulia to denounce the legacy of Gómez and to spread their

54. Betancourt, *Venezuela, política y petróleo*, pp. 117-19. Betancourt's conclusion was undoubtedly influenced as well by the fact that Marxists, not social democrats, already controlled the bulk of the oil workers' unions, and also by his own and his primarily middle-class party's impatience to win control of the state apparatus.

55. The platforms of the BND and of the other reformist political parties founded in Maracaibo and Caracas during 1936 are handily reproduced in Godio, *El Movimiento* (cited in n. 48), Chap. 3.

democratic, nationalist vision for change through the press and radio. They managed to alter the editorial policies of regional newspapers like *Panorama* (even its English section provided fairly sympathetic treatment of labor issues during 1936) and to transform a local radio station into "Ondas del Lago," an influential mouthpiece for labor and the left whose signal could be picked up as far away as Caracas. During the strike the station filled the airwaves with charges that the "companies enrich themselves at the cost of the sweat of Venezuelan workmen who produce all and have nothing, while the companies have all and wish to give nothing." The U.S. consul in Maracaibo quoted that phrase from one broadcast to his superiors, as well as another that proclaimed, "Fathers and mothers, children and old men and women are dying of hunger because of the uncompromising attitude of the foreign octopuses."[56]

Communists, meanwhile, founded the remarkable oil workers' newspaper *Petróleo*. With a press run of over 4,000 and correspondents in the major oil camps, *Petróleo* provided oil workers and their political allies with a stream of concrete information about working conditions and company abuses in the camps, and with news and analysis of local and regional union and political affairs. The Communists who directed *Petróleo* spread their Marxist vision in ordinary language and supported it with facts drawn from the daily experience of Venezuelan workers. The newspaper was usually flexible, sometimes self-critical, always imaginative. It focused on what it called domestic and foreign enemies of workers as a class, not on the differences that separated communists from socialists and their less radical allies.[57]

Although the editors of both *Panorama* and *Petróleo* were jailed during the strike, both papers, and another leftist newspaper, *El País*, continued to publish and promote leftist solidarity throughout the strike. They reported on company strategies to break the movement and described workers' efforts to feed their families and to curb outbreaks of violence in the oil zone. Most important, they filled their pages with manifestos and telegrams of support for the oil workers that poured into their offices in Maracaibo from workers, students, and political organizations all over the nation.

The left used these expressions of solidarity to demonstrate the scope and intensity of popular support for the oil workers' struggle. The documents they published demonstrated a widespread perception of the strike's relationship to the development of the Venezuelan labor move-

56. Reported by the U.S. consul in Maracaibo to the Department of State, Jan. 14, 1937, USNA/DS 831.5045/45.

57. *Petróleo* was edited by Espartaco González, Olga Luzardo, and Elio Montiel; underground Communists like Juan Bautista Fuenmayor contributed to the paper and participated in editorial decisions.

ment, and its significance to the march of Venezuelan history as a whole. They showed how Venezuelans in many walks of life identified their interests, and those of the nation, with the cause of the oil workers. In Caracas, *La Voz del Pueblo* summed up the views of many labor leaders in its analysis of the importance of the impending oil strike on December 5, 1936.

> The triumph or failure of the oil workers will be the triumph or failure of the Venezuelan labor movement. Their struggle is the struggle of all the workers of Venezuela. At their side, in sympathy and action, all the people must stand, because this group of men in the land of Zulia are confronting the oil companies, they are defending, in reality, the sovereignty and the dignity of our fatherland in the face of the foreign exploiter.

A group of tobacco workers in Caracas expressed their support more directly. They sent strikers a shipment of 500 packs of "Sport" and "Doble Aguila" cigarettes. An accompanying letter read, "Fate has determined that it be you, the strongest, who have headed this movement, which, because it is so popular, has become national, in order to save our honor. . . . All Caracas, all Venezuela, has its thought fixed on you."[58] In Zulia farmers and merchants donated food and merchandise to strike committees, and landlords lowered rents or suspended them for striking workers. In Maracaibo barbers and taxi drivers offered strikers free services, and the parties of the left organized a bullfight whose profits went to the unions. A Venezuelan lawyer proclaimed his solidarity with the strike by publicly renouncing his power of attorney to represent a foreign oil company. U.S. diplomatic personnel in Maracaibo reported that popular support for the strike was overwhelming, that the only "American" dentist in town had announced his intention to provide free dental care to strikers.[59]

In early January oil workers and their allies hit on a brilliant tactic to symbolize the meaning of their struggle and consolidate the multiclass national coalition emerging in support of the strike. They announced a plan to send children of strikers to live in middle-class homes in Caracas for the duration of the conflict. The idea caught on immediately. Invitations from Caracas and other cities in north-central Venezuela flooded into Maracaibo. Scores of children prepared to leave their homes in the oil zone for the capital. A steamship company offered the children free transportation; a commission of well-to-do *caraqueños* visited Zulia to arrange for the transfer. The children were given medical examinations, their parents provided with the names and addresses of their children's sponsors. A few days before the settlement of the strike, thousands of cheering oil workers and their supporters gave the first 50 "*niños petro-*

58. *Petróleo*, Jan. 16, 1937.
59. Archer Woodford to Department of State, Jan. 14, 1937, USNA/DS 831.5045/45.

leros" a rousing sendoff. The children's arrival in Caracas was greeted by another public demonstration and ample press coverage.[60]

This outpouring of public solidarity with the oil workers also found institutional expression in a congress of Venezuelan workers that convened in Caracas during the strike. The congress was organized by the Asociación Nacional de Empleados (a national white-collar union founded in early 1936 by oil company employees in Maracaibo) and by the Confederación Sindical Obrera de Venezuela (a recently organized federation of unions representing artisans and transport and industrial workers in the Caracas area). Attended by 122 delegates who claimed to represent 150,000 workers (including some farm workers), the congress convened on December 26 and devoted much of its attention to the oil strike. On December 27 the delegates passed a resolution declaring their solidarity with the strike, calling for the freedom of jailed strike leaders, commending the calm and "Venezuelanist" attitude of the armed forces, and protesting the oil companies' violations of the national labor law. The resolution also urged "progressive merchants, industrialists, agriculturalists, artisans, and all other economic forces in the country wounded by imperialist penetration" to join in a "nationalist crusade in support of the liberation and betterment of our working classes." It applauded the material support sent to oil workers by the "Pro Oil Strike Committee of Caracas." It called on all Venezuelan workers to donate half a day's pay to the strike fund on January 2, a day it proclaimed "National Day of the Oil Worker." Finally, the resolution congratulated the press and radio for echoing the "powerful anti-imperialist movement" led by the oil workers and proclaimed the oil workers' slogan, "Imperialism Will Not Advance," as a banner for all Venezuelan workers.[61]

Public and labor support for the oil workers had far-reaching consequences for Venezuelan politics, and undoubtedly stiffened the resolve of many oil workers.[62] The effectiveness of the strike itself, however, was primarily a result of the combativeness, organizational strength, and discipline of the oil workers themselves, who went into the strike with great enthusiasm and confidence. As early as January 1936, almost a year before the strike and barely a month after the death of Gómez, a Standard Oil Company official in Maracaibo reported on the excited state of the work-

60. *Panorama*, Jan. 1, 14, 15, 16, 19, 21, and 29, 1937.
61. Godio, who has inspected minutes of the congress, provides an account of the discussions in *El movimiento* (cited in n. 48), pp. 116-23. The full resolution is transcribed in Tennassee, *Venezuela, los obreros petroleros* (cited in n. 32), pp. 243-44.
62. The scope of this support and publicity not only helped the strikers materially and boosted their morale; it was used by militants to challenge the oil workers' manhood. If we cave in, wrote one militant in *Petróleo* during the last days of the strike (Jan. 20, 1937, p. 4), "What would the whole of Venezuela say, they'd call us weaklings right to our faces, and we'd suffer both from the taunts of the Yankees and from the disdain of our countrymen."

ers and concluded that despite the effective repressive measures being taken by the government against labor militants, a general strike in the industry was probably inevitable. "There is considerable unrest everywhere in Zulia," he wrote the head office of the company in New York. He said he had been "privately informed" that the government, fearing a general strike in the lake fields, had reinforced the garrison at Maracaibo with 500 additional federal troops. Officials of the state government, he went on, "have made many arrests in the fields on their own initiative, and have conscripted anywhere from 150 to 300 men, whom they shipped out of this port in Navy craft the other day. This may have the effect of forestalling any general strike; however, the agitators have already sown the seeds of discord and it is very noticeable."[63] Despite such recurring government repression, and the firing and blacklisting of labor activists by the companies, organization proceeded rapidly as the year progressed. Labor leaders learned to take advantage of the legal opportunities popular forces extracted from the state during 1936 (the rights to hold rallies, to organize under the law, and to strike) even as they perfected means to protect themselves from the continuing repression of their organizational efforts. By mid-year activists had established half a dozen vigorous local unions in the oil fields of Zulia. The largest of these, in Lagunillas, Cabimas, and Maracaibo (the last the headquarters for the marine oil transport workers' union), boasted several hundred dues-paying members. After protracted negotiations, these separate locals took a further step and federated themselves into a regional, industrywide organization. Each local preserved its autonomy but agreed to fund the umbrella organization in order to share information and coordinate activities. The federation provided effective general direction to the strike—it insured that local strike demands were basically similar and set both the date the workers walked out and the date they returned to work. Each local retained responsibility for the conduct of the strike within its jurisdiction, however. On the eve of the conflict all regular union officers resigned, and workers designated special committees (and secret backup committees) to direct the strike. As these leaders were jailed by government police, new ones appeared to take their places. Each local set up special commissions charged with channeling food to oil workers' families, defeating scab labor, and guarding against sabotage. The oil workers' unions were careful to launch their strike within the legal framework es-

63. Extracts from the letter, written by an official of Standard Oil of New Jersey's subsidiary Lago Petroleum, were sent to the Department of State from corporate headquarters on February 6. The covering letter indicated that to head off the strike the companies might be willing to grant workers a wage increase and make an eight-hour day, already in force on all but lake launches and floating equipment, universal in the oil zone. H. Walker, 30 Rockefeller Plaza, New York, to Dr. W. R. Manning, Division of Latin American Affairs, Washington, D.C., USNA/DS 831.5041/9.

tablished by the labor law; and throughout the strike, despite provocations, they were able to keep violence and destruction of property to a minimum. These tactics on the whole were very successful. Although the majority of the oil workers in Zulia in 1936 were not formally affiliated with the unions, compliance with the strike among Venezuelan blue-collar workers was virtually universal and sustained throughout.

For reasons beyond the control of the oil workers in Zulia, the strike failed to halt oil production in the Maracaibo Basin entirely and did not seriously disrupt the companies' refining operations on the Dutch islands off the Venezuelan coast. As a result, despite its long duration, the strike was much less painful to the companies and the Venezuelan government than it might have been. Standard Oil of New Jersey was able to supply its refineries, at least in part, from production sites in eastern Venezuela and Colombia. Shell's operations and those of the third large company, U.S.-owned Gulf Petroleum, were affected more severely, but like Standard Oil they had built up stocks in anticipation of the strike, used foreign skilled and Antillan labor to pump some oil, and managed to keep in operation the part of their tanker fleets manned by non-Venezuelan workers. The fact that white-collar Venezuelan workers in the oil industry chose not to strike but instead to contribute part of their wages in support of the oil workers meant that company offices and overall planning and direction of company operations were not seriously disrupted during the conflict.

Nevertheless, the strike hurt the companies severely. Exports of crude oil fell by almost half during the strike, and virtually all exploration and drilling operations came to a halt. The national government and the commerce of Maracaibo immediately felt the pinch of the falloff in tax revenues and infusions of foreign exchange. Part of the deal worked out between the companies and the government that led to the presidential decree ending the strike was a pledge by the companies to step up production to compensate for the tax shortfall experienced by the government during the strike.[64]

Historians know little, directly, about the attitudes and values of the rank-and-file petroleum workers who flooded into the unions during 1936 and supported the strike at the end of the year so effectively. Paul Nehru Tennassee has shown that rudimentary if invisible elements of organization existed among oil workers as early as a supposedly "spontaneous" strike in 1925. He found that in subsequent years some oil workers and middle-class opponents of the Gómez regime forged personal

64. *Petróleo* provides the best contemporary analysis of the weaknesses of the strike, Feb. 3, 1937; on its impact on the industry and the state I rely primarily on the report on the strike submitted by the U.S. chargé d'affaires in Caracas, Henry S. Villard, to Secretary of State, Jan. 26, 1937, USNA/DS 831.5045/46.

contacts and common political attitudes in clandestine Masonic lodges and organizations ostensibly formed to combat illiteracy. In the late 1920's a cultural organization located in Cabimas housed a library that contained works by Victor Hugo, Émile Zola, and the Colombian nationalist Vargas Vila.[65] Some labor and leftist activists, like the black editor of *Petróleo*, Espartaco González, reached their Marxist commitments after a passage through anticlericalism.[66] *Petróleo* never missed an opportunity to discredit the Church. It declared that the strike of 1936 had the important virtue of polarizing Venezuelans into a much more important dichotomy than the split between Catholics and non-Catholics. It divided them instead into "those who fight for Venezuela, for the well-being and happiness of the fatherland, for liberty and democracy, and get the name of the left; and those who are sold to foreign imperialism, who conspire against the integrity of the fatherland and democracy."[67] During the strike, Masonic Lodge No. 6 in Maracaibo announced a plan to collect funds to help feed and provide medical care for children and elderly dependents of oil workers and appealed to other Masonic lodges to join in the effort.[68] Still, pending further research the influence of these organizations and ideas on the oil workers' movement remains obscure.

Historians are on surer ground in interpreting the perceptions and class consciousness of Venezuelan petroleum workers expressed in popular language. The terms *musiú* and *maifrén* were invented or adopted by workers because they conveyed their class and racial experience in the oil camps. Evidence like this complements the valuable testimonies by oil workers of the era (such as that of Manuel Taborda, cited earlier) and helps confirm the radicalizing effect—which common sense and the insights of Venezuelan novelists also suggest—of the segregated and grossly unequal conditions of life and work in the oil camps.

The strike demands of oil workers in 1936 provide other clues to the immediate concerns and long-range aspirations of oil workers. Yet like much of the other evidence with which historians are obliged to work, they must be interpreted with care. As with the leftist press and the testimony of politically conscious labor leaders, it is difficult to separate the attitudes of militant rank-and-file workers from those of their radical, formally educated middle-class allies. The 1936 strike demands sought first and foremost to consolidate the collective organizations workers had built in the oil fields during the previous year. Leading the list were the demands for union recognition, the closed shop, and reemployment of

65. Tennassee, *Venezuela, los obreros petroleros* (cited in n. 32), pp. 135-39, 150-52.

66. Interview with Espartaco González, Maracaibo, June 21, 1979. Despite the name his father gave him, González disdained his father's politics—they were those of a petty-bourgeois merchant, he told me.

67. *Petróleo*, Jan. 6, 1937, p. 1.

68. *Panorama*, Jan. 9, 1937, pp. 1 and 6.

workers fired in previous strikes. Ending it were union demands that went further: recognition of the workers' right to bring about the dismissal of any company employee, Venezuelan or foreign, whose attitude was considered prejudicial to the interests of workers; construction, at company expense, of "ample" union halls; pay for days lost in any strike resulting from the rejection of the workers' demands. The fundamental economic demand spoke to the basic need of the unskilled majority in the camps: it called for a big increase, from 7 to 10 bolívares, in the minimum wage paid in the oil fields. Other demands were for adequate housing and medical care for all workers and their dependents. Finally, a series of demands spoke to specific worker grievances. One involved the fact that in some of the camps owned by U.S. capital no work was performed on U.S. Independence Day, July 4, though workers were required to work at regular pay on Venezuelan Independence Day, July 5. Workers demanded a series of paid holidays (those sanctioned in Venezuelan law) and double time for holiday work. Another issue was the lack of remuneration for time spent traveling to work and to isolated drilling and pumping stations. The demands here were for pay beginning from the point of departure, not from arrival at work sites, and for free transportation "with roof and seat" for all workers laboring more than one kilometer from their homes. Another demand sought to redress discrimination between foreign and Venezuelan labor in the provision of cool or iced water at all work sites. Workers rounded out their collective demands by dealing with the subject of vacations. Many Venezuelan oil workers, like their foreign colleagues in the industry, had left behind family and friends to work in the oil enclave. They borrowed a page from the benefit package enjoyed by foreign and skilled workers in the industry and demanded a full month of paid vacation. Whatever the degree of participation of rank-and-file workers in choosing and articulating these demands, workers showed their enthusiastic support for them by walking out en masse when the strike began and by staying out all through the long strike.[69]

Like similar union demands discussed in other chapters of this book, the oil workers' strike petitions were superficially liberal. Yet like all such demands they threatened the basic principles of capitalist enterprise—capital's right to hire and fire workers whenever it chose, to offer work under whatever conditions it saw fit. Recognition of that fact led the oil companies to reject the strike petitions out of hand, to refuse to negotiate with the unions throughout the strike, and to insist on a settlement that subverted the unions' organizational power. The oil strike also constituted a frontal attack on the authoritarian political institutions, antinationalist oil policies, and reactionary social program inherited by the

69. The demands are transcribed in Tennessee, *Venezuela, los obreros petroleros* (cited in n. 32), pp. 226-27.

military government from the Gómez era. Although the popular mobilization forced the government to adopt a public posture of neutrality toward the strike (even as its officials harassed and jailed strikers and their supporters on legal technicalities), the government's interest in dismantling the organized threat to its power—and in protecting the foreign and domestic class basis of that power—led it to side with the companies and seek a peaceful resolution of the strike that compromised the strength of the unions. With the blessing of the companies, the government decreed an end to the strike on January 22, 1937. The government based its intervention on powers granted the executive in the 1936 labor law to settle strikes that threatened the economic and social life of the nation. The decree ordered oil workers back on the job and granted them a single concession: the lowest-paid workers, those earning 7, 8, and 9 bolívares a day, were granted a 1 bolívar raise (2 bolívares for those without company housing).[70]

The oil workers and their allies interpreted the government decree that ended the strike as a defeat both for themselves and for the Venezuelan nation. Some militants counseled defiance of the decree and advocated continued resistance. But when the government labor inspector immediately made public his detailed report on the legality of the strikers' demands and announced his intention to enforce the 1936 labor law in all of its provisions, he diffused some opposition to the strike settlement and raised the hope that the government would implement the clauses in the labor law that set standards for oil worker housing, medical care, and transportation, assured legal protection for unions, and stipulated that 75 percent of employees in the oil industry be Venezuelan. The labor inspector's report had the effect of mollifying many of the workers' middle-class allies; but most workers decided to obey the back-to-work decree because they realized that resistance to it would be suicidal. They voted to go back to work, preserve their unions, and return to fight another day.[71]

Both the oil companies and the government were careful not to antagonize the unions and the left in the period immediately following the strike. Once operations returned to normal and the popular mobilization in support of the strike receded, however, they launched an offensive whose scope and intensity recalled the worst excesses of the Gómez era. In March 1937, the government arrested and deported 47 prominent left-

70. República de Venezuela, Ministerio de Relaciones Interiores, *Memoria, 1937* (Caracas, 1938), p. 6.

71. *Panorama*, true to its middle-class reformism, stressed the first reason; *Petróleo*, the second. A perceptive analysis of the strike settlement, and worker and public reaction to it, is the report of the U.S. consul in Maracaibo, Archer Woodford, to Secretary of State, Jan. 27, 1937, USNA/DS 831.5045/47. The report includes the complete text of the labor inspector's report.

ist and labor activists, accusing them of allegiance to Marxist principles. The list included such prominent liberals as Rómulo Betancourt and Raúl Leoni as well as Communist activists such as Rodolfo Quintero, Juan Bautista Fuenmayor, Salvador de la Plaza, and Gustavo Machado. The list was almost certainly drawn up with the aid and encouragement of the oil companies.[72] Meanwhile, the oil companies moved against grass-roots labor activists, firing hundreds and expelling them from the camps. The government of Zulia ordered the deportation of all margariteños from the state, a measure designed to remove the combative regional group that had earned a reputation throughout the oil fields for labor militancy and effective union leadership.[73] On the political front, the Bloque Nacional Democrático was denied sanction as a legal party, and the regional elections it had recently won in Zulia were nullified. The newspaper *Petróleo* was officially closed.

This drastic repression bought the oil companies and their allies only time; it was not a solution to the challenge that faced them. The oil strike had provided Venezuelans with an extraordinary education in political economy and had taught popular forces and their oppressors alike an indelible lesson in the power of labor and popular political organization. Intelligent elements within the oil companies' management and the military government appreciated this fact as thoroughly as the leftist labor and political leaders did. They realized that they would have to concede part of the enormous and expanding profits of the oil industry and a portion of their political power to popular forces if they hoped to maintain their class position and preserve the capitalist framework of Venezuelan society. That was not the heart of the lesson the Marxist leadership of labor and the left in 1936 thought it was teaching. Marxists hoped that the struggle for political democracy, social justice, and national economic development not only would win important reforms, but would consolidate a popular leftist movement capable of undermining the influence and position of foreigners and capitalists in their society in order to pave the way for socialist transformation.

The great post-1936 expansion of the petroleum industry and the resulting huge profits meant that major economic and political concessions to popular forces were relatively easy for the oil companies to make. The scope and nature of these concessions, however, had far-reaching conse-

72. The decree is published in Ministerio de Relaciones Interiores, *Memoria, 1937*, p. 33. U.S. diplomat Meredith Nicholson provided Washington with a sketch of many of the men on the list and gave several persuasive reasons for his belief in the complicity of the oil companies in drawing it up. Nicholson to Secretary of State, Caracas, Mar. 16, 1937, USNA/ DS 831.5045/50.

73. Tennassee, *Venezuela, los obreros petroleros* (cited in n. 32), p. 269, claims that by early 1938 1,500 oil workers were interned in concentration camps. His evidence, however, is thin, and it is not corroborated in any material I was able to uncover.

quences for the vitality, unity, and militancy of the left in general and for oil workers in particular. Foreign capitalists and their Venezuelan allies— who by the mid-1940's included the middle-class liberal reformers—were able to initiate programs to deradicalize the oil worker rank and file, to co-opt and bureaucratize the oil workers' unions, and finally to tailor the whole of the labor movement and the political culture of the nation to the needs of international capital. The results of all these initiatives were not simple, and they have not been (nor are they necessarily now) permanent. But they have, since the early 1940's, subverted the appeal of the Marxist left and stymied its socialist project. They have ensured until now the liberal capitalist trajectory of modern Venezuelan history.

Following the repression of 1937, the oil companies initiated policies that greatly improved the material condition of labor in the industry, attempted to ease friction between workers and management, and encouraged workers to devote their energies to personal improvement and apolitical pursuits. The oil companies also went along with government initiatives that complemented these policies. By the end of 1938 a government-administered profit-sharing program was a reality in the oil fields. New oil laws in 1938 and 1943 increased state taxation of the industry, albeit in exchange for extension of old oil concessions and grants of huge new ones. Expanded oil revenues enabled the government to extend public education and health services, and to begin a social security program for Venezuelan workers. Between 1938 and 1945 the government also gradually extended the democratic rights of unions and citizens. The labor law of 1936 was translated into administrative reality by government decree in late 1938, and in subsequent years more and more of its provisions were enforced, often to the advantage of workers and unions. Reformist political parties, most notably Betancourt's Acción Democrática, were granted legal status, censorship and other forms of repression were relaxed, and the suffrage was gradually extended.

All these reforms, conceived and put into practice by the oil companies and their allies in the government between 1937 and 1945, were a direct response to pressure from resurgent labor and leftist political forces. But even as the organizational power and ideological influence of the left grew, the leadership of popular forces split in two. On one side were the Marxists, whose influence was paramount in the labor movement and the oil fields; on the other were the social democrats, who dominated the nationalist-reformist political parties whose strength lay in the middle class. The split was intensified (and, as we shall see, in part resolved) by the position adopted by the Venezuelan Communists in support of Soviet international policy during the Second World War. At its core, however, lay the class composition of contending forces within the left.

The middle-class allies of the oil workers in 1936 had been radicalized by the alliance of a brutal dictatorship with foreign capital. The most radical political organizations of the Venezuelan middle class were formed in the oil enclave, and its most militant union organizations crystallized among the white-collar employees of the oil companies. Venezuela's foreign-owned, hugely profitable, steadily expanding mineral enclave radicalized middle-class groups mainly along nationalist, not class lines. It led them to question the developmental implications of the oil export economy and the equity of social relations primarily within, not between, the major classes that economy created. The platform of the Bloque Nacional Democrático, reviewed earlier, makes clear how the middle-class reformers sought to open up political and economic opportunities for professionals, white-collar workers, merchants, agriculturalists, and industrialists within a vigorous national capitalist order.

Inspection of the union demands of white-collar employees of the oil companies in 1936 helps to pinpoint the cultural and racial wellsprings of their collective aspirations. These demands were submitted to the major oil companies in April 1936 by the Asociación Nacional de Empleados Estado Zulia (ANDE). They reveal, frankly and explicitly, the class perceptions and identifications of the white-collar petroleum employees. The Venezuelan office workers asked for equal treatment with the foreign employees of the companies. Everyone knew, their petition stated, "the racial, moral, and social differences which the Oil Companies establish *de facto* in the treatment of their foreign personnel and their local personnel (local staff)." Equal treatment would abolish "the racial distinctions that, to the humiliation of our condition as Venezuelan citizens, are deeply ingrained in the Petroleum Companies." Specifically, the Venezuelan employees wanted to be paid by the month, like foreign office personnel, "since we consider our position as office workers incompatible with that of day laborers." They wanted a 25 to 30 percent salary increase to bring their pay up to the level of foreign employees. They wanted the same free transportation to the workplace and full month's vacation that foreign employees enjoyed, hospital benefits equal to those of foreign employees, a company savings plan, and reduction of overtime. To the companies' official reply that no such discrimination existed, the employees' organization replied that it could prove the differences in pay scales and benefits, and document the racial and social discrimination practiced against Venezuelan employees. Venezuelan employees had been denied entrance to the "residential areas and Clubs of the Companies." When they had to journey down the lake to the oil fields, "they were forced to travel on rafts . . . eating the same food as the crew." Whereas foreign employees demanded to be addressed as "Mr.," national employees were not accorded that form of address in return.[74]

Given such class perceptions, it is not surprising that the white-collar employees of the companies voted not to strike with the oil workers' unions in December 1936. Their organization, and many of its individual members, did extend the oil workers vital material and moral support during the strike, but that involvement marked the apogee of the militant collaboration between workers' and white-collar unions in the industry.

In the years following the oil strike even Marxists within the leadership of white-collar oil employee unions and the nationalist-reformist parties moderated their views and lowered their sights. As we have seen, leaders like Rómulo Betancourt came to the conclusion that they had more to gain, or at least much less to risk, by working to reform Venezuela's capitalist society through political compromise with foreign and domestic capital than they did through alliance with the Marxists. Progressive elements within the capitalist class in Venezuela, especially foreign oil interests, had good reasons for tolerating the political aspirations of these reformist liberals. The existence of a powerful Marxist-led labor movement in the vital oil sector was an immediate economic threat to capital in the workplace and a potential long-term threat to capital's—especially foreign capital's—political and ideological hegemony over Venezuelan society. The great oil strike of 1936 had made both these threats palpable. Confronted with this dual challenge to their position, progressive capitalists viewed the project of the liberal reformers as a lesser evil. With time they learned that the reforms of the liberals held for them a certain promise. Liberals might undermine the influence of Marxists in the labor movement, and reform might diffuse the popular sentiment against the oil companies shared by Venezuelans of all social classes. Given the stakes involved, and the scope of their profits in an industry they planned to expand, it was both relatively painless and eminently practical to tolerate moderate liberal reform.

It is difficult to assess the implications for worker attitudes of the reformist initiatives put into practice by the oil companies and the military government in the years following the great oil strike of 1936. Shaken by the magnitude and duration of that conflict (which management had predicted would last only a short time), the companies moved aggressively following the full-scale repression of 1937 to improve their public image and what they called their "industrial relations." Both Jersey Standard and Shell brought in high-level officials from abroad to oversee these ini-

74. *Petróleo*, Apr. 29, 1936, pp. 4 and 6.

tiatives.[75] During 1937 the companies began expensive housing projects for oil workers. Even during the oil strike the government had moved to defuse worker unrest by pledging one million bolívares to rebuild the town of Lagunillas, part of which had burned in an oil fire in 1928. The "flimsy houses, disease, and lack of sanitation or protection from the heat," a U.S. diplomat observed, "contributed to [Lagunillas's] reputation as a breeding spot for petty crimes, radicalism, and attacks on the oil companies." The companies were aided in their housing program, and encouraged to initiate public works outside the camps, by government assurances of relief from the large shipping fees they had customarily paid to port authorities for prompt dispatch of their tankers and supply ships. By 1939 Shell and Gulf were engaged in building roads in the oil zone to link the camps with Maracaibo and with nearby agricultural districts. Improved transportation, the companies believed, would moderate the rising food costs that eroded the real wages of their workers.[76]

Following the strike the companies also sponsored worker savings plans. At least at Jersey Standard's subsidiaries, these plans met with little success. They allowed workers to save up to 10 percent of their earnings and to have that amount matched by the company, but 25 percent of these funds had to be put into annuities payable only if the employee left the company after age 50. This attempt to use savings benefits to ensure worker docility and prevent job turnover was actively opposed by the unions. They lobbied instead for implementation of the government-sponsored profit-sharing plan envisioned in the 1936 labor law. So effective was this opposition that, in the words of the U.S. consul who studied the savings plan, the few "native" workers who joined it were "loath" to admit their participation. "Participation," he reported, "is a stigma in the eyes of fellow workers." Under union pressure, the government instituted the profit-sharing plan over company objections in December 1938 and made it retroactive to July 16, 1936. The plan called for very large companies (the oil corporations alone fit within the decree's definition of this category) to return 12.5 percent of their annual wage bill to workers every December 20. Half that sum went directly to the workers, the other half was deposited in a savings account with limitations on withdrawals for six years. Despite its conservative intent, the

75. These company initiatives began in 1937 as a direct reaction to the strike—not, as is sometimes assumed, as a consequence of Mexico's expropriation of the oil industry in 1938. Meredith Nicholson to Secretary of State, Caracas, Feb. 11, 1938.

76. Henry S. Villard, U.S. chargé d'affaires, to Secretary of State, Caracas, Jan. 22, 1937, USNA/DS 831.5045/44. The decree dealing with Lagunillas, which one labor militant called a "caramelo" to prepare public opinion for the bitter strike settlement, was published in República de Venezuela, Ministerio de Relaciones Exteriores, *Memoria, 1937* (Caracas [1938?]), p. 3.

profit-sharing plan was a great financial boon for oil workers. It won them a sizable increment in earnings at no sacrifice in current pay. The oil workers' unions, most of them reorganized in 1938 by Marxist leaders affiliated with the Communist Party, claimed credit for this major economic benefit. Oil workers must have agreed. By early 1939 the same U.S. official guessed that perhaps 75 percent of the oil workers in the Maracaibo Basin were unionized, with more workers joining unions every day. Each member contributed a bolívar a week in union dues.[77]

Even before the great strike, the companies had sought to promote company unions to mitigate labor problems and undercut the strength and appeal of the workers' autonomous unions. Venezuelan labor activists exposed these efforts and ridiculed them in the worker press during 1936. The company unions never experienced much success. After the strike and the wave of repression, management tried a slightly different tack. It set up committees in each of the oil fields to hear worker complaints, adjudicate differences between workers and management, and relay insolvable problems to headquarters in Caracas every week. This innovation led to occasional dismissals of particularly authoritarian foremen, but with active unions in place at the work sites, it served primarily as a conduit for worker grievances articulated by union men. The improvements that resulted probably redounded to the prestige of the unions, not the companies.[78]

After the strike the companies also expanded medical facilities for workers and made large investments in education. Technical education programs, launched by 1939, sought to enable the companies to comply with the labor law requirement that three-fourths of their employees be Venezuelans. They were most successful in training drillers. Adult education classes, designed primarily to promote literacy, apparently caught on slowly. One observer reported little interest in these classes on the part of workers in early 1938, but a Jersey Standard publication later claimed its program was "surprisingly well received by local employees" and that literacy jumped from 18 to 88 percent among its Venezuelan workers between 1939 and 1945. The companies also greatly expanded free elementary schooling for the children of oil workers. Management also invested in Spanish classes for its supervisory personnel. By 1938 Standard Oil of New Jersey had hired four Berlitz teachers to instruct its English-speaking employees in Spanish. Company personnel paid a nominal fee of one bolívar to enroll in these crash courses.[79]

77. Archer Woodford to Department of State, Maracaibo, Jan. 24, 1939, USNA/DS 831.504/92. I have drawn on this rich 20-page document throughout this section.

78. J. K. Bacon, "Memorandum on Labor Conditions," in Meredith Nicholson to Secretary of State, Caracas, Feb. 11, 1938, USNA/DS 831.504/80.

79. Popple, *Standard Oil* (cited in n. 39), p. 222.

Finally, following a twentieth-century strategy that has been extensively adopted by both capitalist and socialist regimes, the oil companies sought to undercut the disruptive political and union activity of workers by promoting sports activities. The companies built baseball diamonds, soccer fields, and basketball courts. They furnished player-employees with free sports equipment, and they encouraged "all the laborers to engage . . . in sporting activities."[80] In 1944, in Lagunillas, Shell sponsored its Fifth Olympiad for its employees. These games, commented a Caracas newspaper, were quite successful; they used sport "as a means of [promoting] spiritual unification and mutual understanding."[81]

None of these initiatives was successful in blunting the growing organizational strength of oil workers after 1938; their impact on workers' values and aspirations, however, cannot be dismissed lightly. Nowhere in the record I have reviewed is there evidence to indicate widespread worker commitment to a socialist vision of society of the kind evident, for example, in the Chilean nitrate fields by the 1920's. Venezuelan oil workers were acutely conscious of their collective interests and became militant union men. The Venezuelan oil proletariat, however, was comparatively younger in the mid-1930's than its Chilean counterpart on the nitrate pampa in the mid-1920's. Moreover, the repression under Gómez had severely constrained the cultural and political activities of Marxists in the oil fields in the decade and a half before 1935. Most important, Venezuelan oil workers' experience with capitalism was different in some respects from that of their Chilean counterparts. Except for the downturn of the early 1930's, when many Venezuelan oil workers were forced to leave their jobs, they had worked in a steadily expanding, economically healthy industry. Unlike Chilean workers, they had not experienced the radicalizing influence of severely fluctuating exchange rates and runaway inflation. Venezuelan oil workers lived in a society stabilized even during the Great Depression by the steadying influence of the oil export economy. Their earliest collective confrontations with capital (in 1925 and 1936) had met with modest success, at least in terms of wage demands. They were not the unmitigated worker disasters involving the wholesale slaughter of friends and relatives witnessed by Chilean nitrate workers in the early twentieth century. Revealingly, both before and after the 1936 strike, the Marxist leaders and radical middle-class allies of oil workers were careful to place workers' demands within an anti-imperialist and nationalist framework, not an anticapitalist one. Instructive in this regard is the following passage on the strikers' motivations and goals taken from a strike communiqué issued by the leaders of the Lagunillas union during the 1936 strike.

80. The quotation is from Bacon's memorandum cited in n. 78 above.
81. *Ahora*, Mar. 21, 1944, p. 2.

We oil workers are conscious of what we ask for, first, because we are hungry; second, because our homes are shacks that could best serve as garbage dumps; third, because our exploiters enjoy every comfort and opportunity, their children sleep in cribs, they go to secondary school or have special tutors in their homes, they have recreational centers, while our children sleep on straw mats and lack even medical care; and finally, we can't send them to school so they can become informed and free citizens.[82]

Embedded in the abstract conception of hunger as the motive force in the struggle of the working class against its exploiters in the communiqué is a detailed and concrete vision of the good life that is not antagonistic to liberal society. What, one wonders, would happen to the self-proclaimed "consciousness" of these local strike leaders should oil workers win a decent wage? What would happen should their families be able to eat well and even mimic the diet of their North American managers? What would happen if oil workers enjoyed adequate housing and medical care, if they had access to technical training and good schooling for their children, if they could take advantage of recreational facilities and long paid vacations?

Venezuelan oil workers were still a long way from achieving all of these opportunities and benefits in the early 1940's. Moreover, the fact that they continued, for the most part, to place their confidence in Communist leadership served to insulate them against the liberal cultural values percolating through Venezuela's booming capitalist society. The Marxists' social vision must have served as an antidote to the beguiling examples of individual social mobility workers observed in oil towns, a shield against the cultural influence of foreign patterns of consumption workers eyed with envy in the camps, a buffer against the conservatizing initiatives of management. But in the mid-1940's, as collective struggle in the workplace won oil workers more and more benefits of the kind the Lagunillas activists described in their strike communiqué, national and international political events conspired to destroy the influence and prestige of Marxist leadership in the oil fields.

———•——•——•———

World events caught up quickly with Venezuela's internal politics and burgeoning labor movement after 1940. The repressive Gómez dictatorship and the struggle to destroy its legacy had isolated the Venezuelan left and focused its attention on domestic affairs during the 1930's. United in a common domestic struggle, an indigenous left was able to lead the extraordinary popular mobilization described in the preceding pages. But

---

82. Sexto Comunicado, Sindicato de Obreros Petroleros de Lagunillas, Dec. 1936, in *Panorama*, Dec. 23, 1936, p. 2.

after 1940 outside influences twisted and molded the Venezuelan labor movement and the politics of the nation in ways that deeply influenced the outcome of the historical process unleashed in 1936.

The political fortunes of the liberal democratic reformers, the trajectory of the left, and the future course of Venezuelan history all pivoted in important ways on the organizational fate of oil workers during the 1940's. As long as the Marxist left controlled this powerful organized force in Venezuelan society, and the oil industry continued to expand, progressive capitalists were disposed to aid the liberal democrats in their struggle against the Marxists and to tolerate their plans for reform of Venezuelan society. But this support and tolerance was conditioned on the reformers' repudiation of socialism and on their ability to displace Marxist leadership of the labor movement.

The ability of the liberal reformers to do just that was aided by the official stance of the Communist Party during the early 1940's. By subverting local imperatives to the international line of the Party, Communists destroyed the unity of their own organization and undermined the confidence of the oil worker rank-and-file in their Marxist leaders. The Venezuelan Communist Party allied itself in 1941 with the military president (and ex-gomecista) General Isaías Medina, successor (and former minister of war) of the man who had broken the oil strike of 1936. The Communist Party preached industrial peace in the oil fields to maintain the strategic flow of petroleum to the Allies at precisely the time when expansion of the industry favored the workers' struggle. The Party won some temporary respite from company and government repression of its union-organizing activities as a result of such policies. But it also alienated many workers. In contrast to the Communists, the liberal democrats opposed the military government, persisted in their moderate nationalism, and demonstrated a willingness to resort to strikes in the oil industry to win worker demands. Their fidelity to the historic demands of oil workers won them many converts. It was not that Communist-led unions lost ground during this period. Communists deepened their influence in the Maracaibo Basin and extended their organizational strength in an important new oil zone (developed primarily by Standard Oil of New Jersey) to the east of Caracas in the states of Anzoátegui and Monagas.[83]

83. The eastern fields produced less than half as much oil as the Maracaibo Basin in the early 1940's, but labor demand in these newly opened fields was proportionally much higher than in the west. The east thus became a primary focus of the struggle to organize unions in the decade after 1936. Production in the eastern and western fields during this period is detailed in República de Venezuela, Ministerio de Minas y Hidrocarburos, *Anuario petrolero de 1956* (Caracas, n.d.), pp. 64-76. Of 22,449 blue-collar workers in the industry in 1946, 10,728 were in the State of Zulia, 9,002 in the eastern states of Monagas and Anzoátegui. Ministerio de Trabajo, *Memoria, 1946* (Caracas, 1946), Table 9.

Nevertheless, everywhere the aggressive stance of Acción Democrática attracted new militants. In addition to its preeminent position among white-collar workers in the petroleum industry—as well as among the blue-collar oil unions the social democrats had historically controlled, like the large one at Cabimas—Acción Democrática was able to organize smaller locals in both the western and eastern fields in the early 1940's.

The escalating struggle between Acción Democrática and the Communist Party for control of the petroleum proletariat undermined an auspicious attempt to forge a strong industrywide labor central in 1943. Called together by the Communist-led Unión Sindical Petrolera, the federation of oil unions founded in Zulia in 1936, delegates from oil workers' unions in both the eastern and the western fields met in Caracas in June 1943. The conference was tolerated by the government, and its delegates were courted by Communist and Acción Democrática political leaders alike. Speakers, especially Jesús Faría, the Communist leader of the Unión Sindical Petrolera, provided delegates with brilliant analyses of the importance of the oil industry to Venezuela's economy and future development. They stressed the importance of worker unity and the potential of a national industrywide organization of labor. But delegates were divided by internal disputes within the Communist Party, and by the opposition of the Acción Democrática minority. In the end they failed to construct the strong centralized national organization the Communists so urgently wanted.[84]

The weakness and disunity of oil workers' organizations evident at the 1943 conference was closely related to the coming of the world war to the Western Hemisphere. During 1942 and 1943 German sinkings of tankers in the Caribbean forced a sharp cutback in Venezuelan oil production. The layoffs that resulted temporarily weakened the petroleum unions. (See Figure 4.1.) This situation, however, proved transitory. By 1944 the Caribbean sea lanes had been freed of the threat of German U-boats and, stimulated by Allied wartime demand, Venezuelan oil production entered into a period of phenomenal expansion. During 1944 production increased by 50 percent over 1943 and reached an all-time high; by 1948 production had almost doubled the record level reached in 1944. Meanwhile, the Venezuelan petroleum labor force expanded more than threefold between 1942 and 1948. Under these buoyant economic and labor-market conditions, in early 1944 the oil unions led the call for a national convention to found a Venezuelan labor central to unify the entire organized labor movement.

The unity of the Venezuelan labor movement in 1943-44 was under-

84. Alternative accounts of the conference appear in *¡Aquí Está!* (Caracas), May 26, June 2, and June 9, 1943; and in *Acción Democrática*, June 12 and June 19, 1943.

mined, however, by a much more enduring problem posed by the war: whether the oil unions should suspend their organizational drive and economic goals in deference to the strategic needs of the Allied war effort. The collaborationist leaders of the Communist Party interpreted the Popular Front directives of the international Party to forge an alliance with the military government of General Medina. They sought to win union objectives in the workplace without resort to strikes that would interrupt the flow of Venezuelan petroleum to the Allies. Top Acción Democrática leaders proved more flexible on this issue, although they too consistently forced moderation on the party-controlled unions in the oil enclave. The issue of wartime strikes in the oil fields thus tended to divide the oil proletariat from its more moderate Communist and Acción Democrática leaders, to split the two parties internally, and, most importantly, to drive them into conflict with one another.

The drastic consequences of this disunity were set in motion at the national labor convention convened in Caracas in March 1944. The convention was attended by some 500 delegates representing 150 unions from across the country. Its call for national organizational unity, spearheaded by the Communist-controlled oil workers' unions, was enhanced by the attendance of Vicente Lombardo Toledano, the Mexican labor leader who headed the major Latin American labor federation, the Confederación de Trabajadores de América Latina. CTAL was openly sympathetic to Communist unions within the hemisphere. Jesús Faría, the Communist Secretary General of the Unión Sindical Petrolera, had served as head of the organizing committee for the convention and was promptly elected president of the convention's steering committee. Communist delegates outnumbered partisans of Acción Democrática by more than two to one. But hardly had proceedings gotten under way when Acción Democrática delegates introduced a resolution demanding parity in the leadership of the proposed labor central. In the heated debate that followed, a delegate publicly identified his group as Communist and a vote was taken that resulted in a division of the convention along strict party lines. At that point the Acción Democrática delegates walked out and immediately informed the press that the Communist delegates, by linking union affairs with a specific political party, had violated the national labor code. The next day, March 24, President Medina's minister of labor dissolved the 93 unions and three labor federations led by Communists whose delegates had participated in the voting. The government based its case, however, not on the affiliation of the offending unions with the Communist Party (a party banned by the Constitution of 1936) but on the technicality of their affiliation with a political party. President Medina proceeded to assure the Communists that his government would not impede reorganization of the unions along legal, apolitical lines. He even publicly declared his support for an end to the constitutional ban on the Communist Party.[85]

The dissolution of the 1944 labor conference marked a major turning point in the history of the Venezuelan labor movement. In the first place, it completely destroyed the unity of the Venezuelan Communist Party. Party militants believed that the dissolution decree demonstrated the bankruptcy of their collaborationist leadership. Yet the leaders of the Party clung to the carrot of future legalization of the Party and of the unions it could reorganize. As a result, just at the point when the Allies had turned the tide in the international conflict and the collaborationists' strategy seemed likely to begin to bear fruit, their control of their Party was shattered. The leadership had expected to take advantage of the prestige of the Allied victory it had steadfastly supported through the world conflict. It stood poised to exploit the amplified organizational base it had built in the climate of government toleration during the war. Instead, after March 1944 the Communist Party foundered in ideological and political disarray, its unity fatally undermined, its institutional base in the unions temporarily destroyed.

The government's action also delivered a telling blow to the strength and unity of the union movement itself. The dissolution decree temporarily destroyed the bulk of the nation's labor organizations. Especially hard hit were the oil workers' unions. Twelve of the 14 oil unions represented at the 1944 conference, as well as the powerful Unión Sindical Petrolera, were dissolved by the government decree. The government's action came at a time when the economic and political power of organized labor, especially that of oil workers, was growing rapidly. In 1944, as we have seen, the oil industry, and with it the entire Venezuelan economy, entered into a period of unprecedented expansion, and as demand for labor intensified, the bargaining position of workers grew stronger. After the setback of 1944 Venezuelan oil workers rapidly rebuilt and then extended their union organizations. But the decree of 1944 helped to ensure that the resurgent labor movement was deeply divided along political lines.

If the principal loser from the government's action in 1944 was the Communist Party, the big winner was Acción Democrática. Acción Democrática emerged from the labor convention of 1944 with the unions it controlled intact. Throughout the rest of 1944 and 1945, despite the

---

85. The best published summary of these events is Godio, *El movimiento* (cited in n. 48), pp. 173–88. Thirteen Communist-led unions whose delegates were not in the hall when the vote was taken, as well as the 41 Acción Democrática unions represented at the conference, were not dissolved.

growing political challenge the party represented to the government, officials of the labor ministry discriminated against the Communist labor leaders in the reorganization of the dissolved unions. Communist activists, like those who tried to reorganize their once-powerful union at Lagunillas, faced seemingly interminable bureaucratic delays and obstacles in their efforts to meet the requirements of the labor ministry for recertification. Meanwhile, parallel unions led by Acción Democrática partisans and dissident Communists emerged to siphon workers away from the labor organizations under orthodox Communist leadership.[86]

Some liberal scholars have been at a loss to explain the labor policy of the Medina government during this period. They point out that in dissolving the Communist-led unions in 1944 the government turned against its erstwhile allies and destroyed a major source of the government's institutional support. At the same time, government labor policy fostered the strength of the major opposition party, Acción Democrática. That party not only joined the military conspiracy that successfully toppled Medina's government in October 1945, it was able to control the government that replaced it.[87]

From the point of view of the class and political dimensions of the threat posed by labor, however, the policies of the Medina government appear quite logical. Beneath the political differences dividing the military government from Acción Democrática—differences over the speed and extent of the nationalist economic and democratic political reforms both were committed to accomplish by 1944—lay a deep and powerful consensus. That consensus, consistent with the goals of international and domestic capitalists, pivoted on the desire to eliminate Communist control over an increasingly mobilized Venezuelan labor movement. To acknowledge this underlying consensus is not to deny complementary, and positive, motives on the part of the reformers in Acción Democrática and the government. Nor is it to downplay the real differences that separated Acción Democrática from the government coalition. Medina's government inherited part of the class and institutional legacy of the Gómez dictatorship. It lost its grip on national power when its moderate, ambivalent reforms proved too much for the reactionary elements in the military and the Venezuelan ruling class who had supported the government, yet too little to stay ahead of reform-minded junior officers within its own ranks and the middle- and working-class reform forces united under the leadership of Acción Democrática. These differences help to explain the

86. *¡Aquí Está!* (Caracas), Jan. 31, 1945, p. 12, and Apr. 24, 1945, p. 12.

87. Robert J. Alexander, *Organized Labor in Latin America*, (New York, 1965), p. 144; John Martz, "The Growth and Democratization of the Venezuelan Labor Movement," *Inter-American Economic Affairs*, 17:2 (Autumn 1963), pp. 6-7.

political contention between the government and Acción Democrática, as well as the degree of commitment of each to nationalist, liberal democratic reform. But the underlying consensus explains the labor policy of the Medina government after 1944, and the essential continuity of Venezuelan government labor policy, both before and after the coup of October 1945. Acción Democrática, like the government it replaced, used the power of the state to defeat Marxist control over the Venezuelan labor movement. In contrast to Medina's government, however, Acción Democrática was constrained neither by a pro forma alliance with the Communist Party inherited from the war years, nor by the support of reactionary elements inherited from the era of Gómez. Once in power Acción Democrática could pursue its nationalist democratic reforms with vigor, its effort to displace Communist leadership in the labor movement with telling effectiveness.

Some Communists later claimed that the Acción Democrática coup of October 1945 was encouraged by the U.S. Department of State and Standard Oil of New Jersey.[88] The documented historical record, however, reveals only that both acquiesced in the coup and learned to appreciate the ways the new government served the long-range interests of U.S. foreign policy and the needs of international capital.[89]

88. Fuenmayor, *Veinte años* (cited in n. 48), p. 271.
89. The State Department records I was able to review do not confirm the contention that high U.S. officials or the corporate leaders of the U.S. oil companies operating in Venezuela actually encouraged the coup, or personally gave assurances to Acción Democrática leaders that they would not oppose it. Nevertheless, they do leave open the possibility that such encouragement or assurances were given. Three months before the coup, in July 1945, the head of Acción Democrática, Rómulo Betancourt, and the party's leading specialist on labor affairs, Raúl Leoni, journeyed to Washington, D.C. Ostensibly, the primary political object of their mission was to convince Medina's ambassador to the United States to run for the presidency with Acción Democrática support in the elections scheduled for the spring of 1946. By 1945 Betancourt was recognized in Washington as a major opposition leader, and U.S. officials debated the propriety of an official meeting between him and Nelson Rockefeller. Rockefeller, the most prominent political figure in the family that inherited the fortune of the founder of Standard Oil (the company whose direct descendant, Standard Oil of New Jersey, controlled the lion's share of Venezuelan oil production), was Assistant Secretary of State in charge of Latin American affairs in 1945. Rockefeller had met Betancourt in Venezuela in 1944, and the Venezuelan had voiced a desire to call upon him in Washington. U.S. officials were well informed of Betancourt's nationalist and reformist intentions and his anti-Communist commitments. In the end they advised Rockefeller against any "official entertainment" of an active opposition leader, but suggested he might "consider the desirability of some informal hospitality on a more or less personal basis." "The fact that Betancourt is anti–United States and anti–American big business and has had relatively little contact in this country," one official concluded, "seems to me to be a reason for endeavoring to modify his point of view." Betancourt apparently did not request a meeting with Rockefeller, and he and Leoni were officially interviewed by another State Department official. Betancourt stressed in his discussion the growing political strength of Acción Democrática and its electoral hopes in a democratized Venezuela. Memorandum, Department of State, B. C. Davis to Mr. Rockefeller, July 6, 1945, USNA/DS 831.00/7-645; Nelson A.

It is true, nevertheless, that by late 1945 both U.S. diplomatic officials and the oil company managers had good reason to fear the expanding power of the oil unions and the growing influence of the Communist Party. Both were manifested in June of that year when Royal Dutch Shell's Venezuelan subsidiary initiated an ambitious plan to reclassify skilled workers and cut their pay. The company's action unwittingly triggered a general mobilization of workers in the petroleum industry. Communist and Acción Democrática unions joined hands to combat the reclassification scheme. They seized the opportunity to demand a whole series of concessions from the companies designed to strengthen the unions and improve the wages and benefits of all oil workers. Buoyed by strong labor demand in the industry and by declining real wages under wartime cost inflation, oil workers mounted huge demonstrations in the major oil camps and flooded their union treasuries with dues. Labor unions led by both parties threatened to strike if worker demands were not met. In order to stay ahead of the mobilized rank and file and outbid their rivals for the leadership of the oil proletariat, erstwhile collaborationist Communist union leaders were forced to adopt a militant bargaining position.

The militant unity forged between the unions in the industry in June 1945 brought quick results and presaged a new era in the organized strength of the oil workers. The minister of labor arbitrated the dispute and the unions won a major victory. They forced the companies to desist from the reclassification plan and to return all workers affected by it to their original positions. They won company recognition of their shop stewards, a dues checkoff system, and company commitments to provide union halls and pay the salaries of union delegates while involved in contract negotiations. In exchange for these major concessions, the unions temporarily suspended their economic demands. Over company objections, however, they insisted that the agreement they signed on June 16, 1945, run for only five months, at which time they would reopen discussion on wages and benefits. This agreement was a virtual industrywide collective contract. It was a powerful demonstration of the organizational power and unity achieved by the oil workers by mid-1945. For the companies it boded ill for the future.[90]

Noncollaborationist elements within the Communist Party argued that the victory of the oil workers in June 1945 vindicated their position that

---

Rockefeller to Mr. Davis, July 6, 1945; B. C. Davis to Mr. Wells, July 6, 1945, USNA/DS 831.00/7-945. After the 1945 coup Rockefeller and Betancourt became "personal friends." Together they launched a major private-state capitalist initiative to modernize agrarian production and commercialize agricultural commodities in supermarket chains. The quotation is from Ellner, *Los partidos políticos* (cited in n. 48), p. 98.

90. *El País* (Caracas), June 10 and 16, 1945; *¡Aquí Está!*, June 27, 1945, p. 12.

the unity of the proletariat was forged through struggle. Collaborationists replied that the victory had come as a result of the strength of the
unions and the respectful way in which the workers' petitions were presented to government officials.[91] In fact, the more militant stance assumed
by the Communist-led petroleum unions in June was forced on them by
the combativeness of the workers themselves and by the willingness of
their Acción Democrática political rivals to carry out a strike in the industry. Their new militancy also probably reflected the pressure exerted
by the rank and file of the Party against the collaborationist leadership.
Following the disastrous outcome of the 1944 labor conference, dissi-
dence within the Communist Party grew rapidly. In February 1945 the
U.S. ambassador reported he had reliable information that, after discussion of future tactics, the regional districts of the Party had voted 92 to
27 in favor of the noncollaborationist position. "This appears to involve
a more stringent attitude toward the Medina government," he wrote,
"and a concentration on organizing Venezuelan workers along revolutionary lines."[92]

Although struggle over the leadership's dogged commitment to collaborationist policies dictated by the Comintern weakened the Party
throughout 1945, the victory against the oil companies in June greatly
enhanced the prestige of Communist labor leadership in the oil fields.
Moreover, the Party's growing strength in the labor movement was complemented in the political sphere when, following congressional action in
September, Medina's government finally legalized the Party on October
9, 1945. One week later, two days before the Acción Democrática coup,
the Venezuelan Communist Party held its first mass public meeting in
Venezuelan history.

The military–Acción Democrática coup of October 18, 1945, thus
took place at a time of surging oil-worker organizational strength and
growing Communist Party prestige. There are good reasons to believe,
however, that the primary motivations of the conspirators obeyed an internal Venezuelan logic only indirectly connected to the labor challenge
facing the international oil companies and the anti-Communist concerns
of the U.S. government as the war came to an end. Like the senior officers they revolted against, the military conspirators shared an antipathy
toward Communism, but they seem to have been animated largely by

91. Rodolfo Quintero was among the most eloquent spokesmen for the revolutionary
faction within the Party, a stance that earned him the label of Trotskyite and anarchist in the
attempts by the collaborationists to discredit him. *¡Aquí Está!*, June 13, 1945, pp. 1, 2, 13,
and July 4, 1945, p. 1.
92. On February 1, a vote on the same issue in the Political Bureau of the Party, the
ambassador continued, resulted in 14 votes in favor of the revolutionary political line and 2
against. Secret Report on the Venezuelan Internal Political Situation, Frank P. Corrigan to
Secretary of State, Caracas, Feb. 21, 1945, USNA/DS 831.00/2-2145.

personal political aspirations and corporate military concerns. Many of them also stressed, at least in their negotiations with Acción Democrática leaders, their democratic and reformist vocation.

The motives of the Acción Democrática leaders of the coup were more complex. Their commitment to nationalist and democratic reform was tempered by a keen sense of short-term political opportunities. Their overwhelming desire for political power (a desire that united their middle-class constituency) led them first to abandon their commitment to socialism (a process complete as early as 1940), then to compromise their democratic political principles (by joining the conspiracy in 1945). Party leaders correctly perceived the Communist Party as their major rival for control of the popular forces unleashed in Venezuela after 1935. During the early 1940's Acción Democrática's platform and policies embodied the nationalist-reformist aspirations of popular forces far more faithfully than those of its rival. As a result, the party's political strength expanded rapidly among middle-class elements and its influence in the labor movement grew. As the war came to an end, Acción Democrática leaders predicted a bright electoral future for their party. They realized how the conjuncture of world economic, ideological, and political forces—expanding world demand for petroleum, the influence of popular democratic forces in the West (and within the Roosevelt Administration in the United States in particular), and the rivalry between the liberal capitalist and Soviet Communist partners in the victorious wartime alliance—all worked to favor their political prospects. But when their Communist rivals resumed their militancy in the oil fields and threatened to carry the competition to lead popular forces into the political sphere, Acción Democrática's moderate leaders may have begun to worry about their ability to hold the allegiance of the left wing of their party, especially their militant partisans in the labor movement.[93] They certainly became concerned over the party's electoral future when, in September 1945, Medina's government party rejected compromise with Acción Democrática and nominated a presidential candidate (who was endorsed by a legalized Communist Party in October) unacceptable to the party's top leaders. Faced with the prospect of a meager showing in elections controlled by the government, Acción Democrática's leaders compromised their liberal democratic principles and joined the successful military conspiracy.

The circumstances of its rise to power returned to haunt Acción Democrática and gravely compromised the march of Venezuela's liberal de-

93. This is speculation informed by an appreciation of the enduring strength of socialist tendencies within the party, especially among its labor ranks in the 1940's, and by the reality of the splits suffered by the party in the competition with the Communist Party in the 1960's. Ellner discusses these issues cogently in *Los partidos políticos* (cited in n. 48), pp. 98-107.

mocracy. Three years later a reactionary military coup, led by the same officers who placed Acción Democrática in power, toppled the government of recently elected Acción Democrática President Rómulo Gallegos and returned Venezuela to ten years of military dictatorship reminiscent of the Gómez era. For three full years, however, the liberal reformers were in power. During that time they built the ideological, political, and institutional foundations for the impressive liberal edifice they returned to finish constructing in 1958.

The Foundation of a Liberal Order

The coup of October 18, 1945, was well received by Venezuelan public opinion. Acción Democrática's well-known anti-Communism won the initial toleration of many capitalists. Popular forces, with the exception of those under the influence of the Communist Party, responded enthusiastically to the prospect of democratic reform. As soon as the military situation was fully under control, Rómulo Betancourt, who was named head of a provisional governing junta, moved quickly to consolidate political power. He began with the strategic oil sector.

Betancourt immediately assured U.S. diplomats and representatives of the oil companies that the junta had no intention of nationalizing the oil industry, or of modifying existing petroleum legislation and extant concessions. He said the junta was concerned only that royalties be honestly calculated and that conflict between capital and labor in the industry be avoided. Betancourt's ability and sincerity impressed both the oil company officials and U.S. diplomats. Many of those who knew him, the U.S. ambassador reported, believed "that American interests have nothing more to fear from him or the Junta than a few relatively light concessions to labor, from which his party derived much of its political support." "Time and experience," the ambassador explained, had changed Betancourt's economic and political views. "[F]rom Marxism he has progressed to a milder concept of democratic economy. Having expressed the hope a few years ago that the oil industry might one day be nationalized, he now feels that the continent has a common destiny, and realizes that foreign capital is necessary if the country's resources are to be properly developed, and that such capital, in addition to security, must be allowed reasonable profits."[94]

Next, Acción Democrática moved to consolidate its influence over the petroleum proletariat. The coup had interrupted union plans to hold a second national petroleum workers' conference. The goal of the planned conference was to set up the industrywide labor confederation the oil

94. Confidential telegram, Corrigan to Secretary of State, Nov. 1, 1945, USNA/DS 831.00/11-145.

unions had failed to agree upon in 1943. Fearful of Communist influence in the oil unions, Acción Democrática leaders decided to put off the conference until early in the new year. In the meantime, Acción Democrática's Raúl Leoni, named minister of labor by the junta, met with petroleum union leaders and company officials on the issue of renewal of the five-month contract in the industry, which was due to expire in December. In these discussions, the union delegates agreed to delay temporarily their economic demands and accept instead a continuation of the special wartime daily pay bonus of two bolívares. They insisted, however, on immediate formal union recognition from the companies, and demanded that the companies agree to pay wages and transportation for the union delegates who would attend the upcoming petroleum conference. Their most important additional demand was a company freeze on layoffs. At Leoni's urging—he reminded the oil company officials that much of his party's support came from labor, "particularly oil workers"—the companies agreed to meet all these union demands except the freeze on layoffs. The unions compromised on this issue. But they refused to go along with the company's plan that they sign a year-long contract. Under these terms, on December 8, 1945, the companies and the unions once again signed a five-month contract for the industry.[95]

Delay of the oil workers' conference and the full-scale bargaining that would result in the first comprehensive collective contract in the Venezuelan oil industry gave Acción Democrática leaders time to consolidate their grip over the oil workers' unions. Using the power of the labor ministry to recognize unions and allow only legally sanctioned labor organizations and their members to participate in the benefits accorded by Venezuelan labor law and the petroleum contract of December, Acción Democrática quickly established new unions and managed to wrest control from Communist leaders in many others. Communist labor leaders complained that Acción Democrática partisans physically intimidated Communist labor activists, and that such violence was tolerated by local government officials. They claimed that in camps where parallel unions existed the companies openly favored Acción Democrática unions, sometimes even providing them with company telephones, radios, and trucks for use in union business.[96]

By the time the Second National Petroleum Conference convened at the end of March 1946, Acción Democrática partisans were in control of the vast majority of the petroleum unions. Two hundred delegates, rep-

95. The quotation is from Thomas Maleady to Secretary of State, Dec. 11, 1945, USNA/DS 831.504/12-1145.

96. These complaints were registered in a letter Communist oil worker leaders sent to Lombardo Toledano dated Mar. 26, 1946. The U.S. embassy got hold of a copy and transmitted it to Washington in August. Corrigan to Secretary of State, Caracas, Aug. 7, 1946, USNA/DS 831.504/8-746.

resenting 42 white- and blue-collar petroleum unions, attended the conference. Several Communist delegates attended, and some, such as Jesús Faría, even served in leadership positions during the meeting. But their influence was limited. At the inaugural session, broadcast by the national radio network and retransmitted by "Ondas del Lago" in Maracaibo, Raúl Leoni expounded Acción Democrática's philosophy that an organized labor movement and collective bargaining were the surest way to achieve cooperation between capital and labor. The conference established a powerful labor federation for the oil industry, the Federación Petrolera de Venezuela. Acción Democrática allowed Communists two of the nine positions on its executive committee. No union parallel to those recognized by the Federación would be admitted into the organization; a commission was set up to fuse parallel unions where they existed. Although some Communist delegates abstained, the conference declared its "warmest backing" for the revolutionary government. It announced that oil workers would "impede the triumph of any counterrevolutionary movement pretending to return Venezuela to a [political] situation now overcome." The delegates then turned to formulating the economic demands put off under the short-term contracts of 1945. They called for major salary hikes; extensive vacation benefits; expanded schooling, housing, and medical benefits for workers and their families; severance pay; and additional commissary privileges.[97]

After difficult negotiations with the companies in May, during which militant local Acción Democrática labor leaders and Communist activists exerted considerable pressure on their national federation leaders and kept talk of a strike alive, an agreement was reached on May 31 and formally signed on June 14, 1946. By it the wartime bonus became a part of the oil workers' regular pay. Blue-collar workers got an additional two-bolívar raise, white-collar workers a salary increase of 5 to 15 percent. Workers won 56 hours' pay for 48 hours' work, two weeks of paid vacation, bonuses for nighttime work, overtime pay, and sick pay. The agreement established the principle of equal pay for women. It also granted workers expanded hospitalization coverage. The two largest oil companies promised to implement a retirement plan within a year. The unions did not get an outright freeze on layoffs, but they won explicit rights to the substantial severance-pay benefits stipulated in the national labor law. In addition, they won housing benefits for all their dependents and free housing for a month if they were laid off, 15 days if they quit voluntarily. The companies agreed to pay workers a per diem allowance to cover time lost during job transfers, as well as the moving expenses involved in such transfers. The companies also agreed to expand the variety of low-cost items in the company commissaries and to sell workers tools at cost. Fi-

97. The quotation is from *El País*, Apr. 4, 1946, p. 1. This Acción Democrática daily gave the conference extensive coverage.

nally, the agreement regulated subcontract work in ways that made it much more difficult for the companies to avoid union labor. In exchange for these concessions, workers agreed to an 18-month contract during which no new demands could be made.[98]

The collective contract of June 1946 crowned a decade of struggle by Venezuelan oil workers. In it workers finally vindicated their strike demands of 1936. But whereas Communist militants had articulated those demands and led oil workers in the initial struggle to win them, it was under Acción Democrática leadership that the demands were finally won. The collective contract of 1946 set an enduring precedent for the relationship between capital and labor in the Venezuelan oil industry. It institutionalized Acción Democrática's liberal, corporativist philosophy of labor relations in the most important sector of the Venezuelan economy. It demonstrated the advantages of bread-and-butter unionism to the most powerful element in the Venezuelan labor movement.

In his year-end evaluation of the Acción Democrática government's labor initiatives, Labor Minister Leoni held out the collective contract in the oil industry as an example of what Acción Democrática's approach to labor relations could achieve. That contract had improved the situation of workers, and it enabled capital to plan ahead.[99] The contract confirmed Acción Democrática's philosophical approach to labor issues, an approach based on the premise that the interests of capital and labor were not inherently antagonistic. Friction between management and workers could be reduced through the centralized, hierarchical organization of each and collective bargaining mediated by a neutral state. The Acción Democrática government, Leoni had written earlier, promoted labor organization and state-supervised collective bargaining in order to "find equitable and just solutions that contribute to the maintenance of a firm and stable social peace." Improvements in the workers' economic situation, he went on, and the maintenance of industrial peace would ensure Venezuela's continuing economic prosperity.[100]

What Leoni meant by his cryptic assessment that the 1946 petroleum contract enabled "capital to plan ahead" is revealed in detail in Clause 24 of the agreement, which specified labor's contractual obligation with capital.

The Federación Sindical de Trabajadores Petroleros of Venezuela and the unions that belong to it manifest their adherence to the principle that each daily wage should correspond to a day of effective work and, in consequence, they commit themselves to assist, as they have been doing, by all means at their disposal, in the

98. Details in the contract dealing with the special conditions of marine oil workers are omitted from the summary. Tennessee, *Venezuela, los obreros petroleros* (cited in n. 32), conveniently reproduces the contract verbatim, pp. 290-301. Reports on the negotiations appear in *El País*, May 16 through 31, 1946.

99. Ministerio de Trabajo, *Memoria, 1946*, pp. v and vii.

100. *El País*, Apr. 2, 1946, p. 2.

goal of insuring that their members comply with all the obligations imposed on them by law and the regulations that govern its enforcement, the work rules the companies may establish in accordance with the law in their enterprises and establishments, and this collective contract.

The explicit language of this clause reveals the capitalist logic of the bread-and-butter unionism enshrined in labor law and practice by liberal corporativists in Venezuela and all over the Western world in the postwar era. In exchange for recognition as legal corporations before employers and the state, unions assumed management's task of disciplining the work force; in exchange for material benefits, unionized workers ceded to management control over work rules. These dual concessions enabled capitalists to increase worker productivity relentlessly through mechanization and speedup. Productivity gains underwrote both an increase in the rate of profit and expanded material benefits to organized workers.

As discussed in Chapter One, institutionalization of these principles in labor law and practice in the postwar world defined a new era in modern labor history. In the advanced capitalist societies, the great social issues of our time pivot on this compromise between organized labor and capital. The compromise led to segmentation of the labor force into an organized few and an unorganized many, fostered the bureaucratization of labor unions, and encouraged the political and social conservatism of the organized working class. Its terms implied the growing dehumanization of the work process, the deepening alienation of workers on the job, and the rise of a compensatory cult of leisure and individual consumerism. Finally, it stimulated the great expansion of the manufacturing multinational corporation into the low-wage, relatively un-unionized societies of the underdeveloped world.[101]

Venezuelan society, molded by its extraordinary petroleum export economy, adapted to the logic of corporativist liberal labor policies and bread-and-butter unionism far more readily and permanently than the other underdeveloped capitalist societies surveyed in this volume. Just as Leoni hoped, the 1946 petroleum agreement set the pattern not only for

101. As noted in Chapter One, the philosophical implications of workers' loss of control over the way work is conceived and executed are unveiled in Harry Braverman's seminal work, *Labor and Monopoly Capital* (New York, 1974). Perception of the importance of workers' struggles for control *within* the production process (as opposed to the classical Marxist conception of their struggle for control *over* the means of production) has fostered a remarkable reassessment of U.S. labor history. Case studies are developed by David Montgomery, *Workers' Control in America* (Cambridge, Eng., 1979); an attempt at synthesis is James R. Green, *The World of the Workers* (New York, 1980). Charles Maier has explored the politics of the doctrine of productivity in the reconstruction of capitalist society in postwar Europe, "Two Postwar Eras and the Conditions for Stability in Twentieth-Century Western Europe," *American Historical Review* 86:2 (Apr. 1961):327-52, and Giovanni Arrighi has assessed the disciplinary role of unions tied to the leftist parties in recent European history in his "The Labor Movement in Twentieth-Century Western Europe," in Immanuel Wallerstein, ed., *Labor in the World Social Structure* (Beverly Hills, Calif., 1983).

all subsequent collective contracts in the oil industry, but for Venezuela's entire industrial relations system in the postwar era.[102] Under the new petroleum contract the Venezuelan oil industry continued its phenomenal postwar expansion. The surplus it generated funded new benefits for oil workers, and provided a spectacular increase in government oil revenues and company profits. Government oil revenues expanded fourfold between 1945 and 1948, from 282 to 1,108 million bolívares; company profits rose from 645 to 1,060 million bolívares between 1947 and 1948 alone. The bulk of these increases resulted from a 25 percent rise in the volume of Venezuelan oil exports and a doubling of world oil prices between 1945 and 1948.[103]

The oil bonanza created a very favorable environment for Acción Democrática's liberal reforms. The flood of oil revenue enabled the party to use the power of the state to extend its liberal corporate labor policies beyond the oil proletariat to the whole of the organized labor movement. Oil revenue financed a host of material and social benefits for the unorganized working and middle class. It funded national economic development programs, which enabled the government to invest in economic infrastructure and channel cheap credit to agricultural and industrial capitalists. All these measures, discussed in more detail below, enhanced the popularity of Acción Democrática as the party moved to realize the political democratization Venezuelan popular forces had demanded since 1936. Once the new government had consolidated power, it broadened and protected civil liberties, established universal suffrage, and held free elections for a national constituent assembly, the presidency, and a new congress. Acción Democrática candidates won landslide victories in each election. A new and more democratic constitution was written and promulgated. The popularity of the government, and the economic expansion its policies helped promote, placed reactionary social forces on the defensive after 1945. Until 1948, they tolerated the progressive political, social, and economic reforms of the new regime.

On the labor front, Acción Democrática complemented its plans to deal with the oil proletariat by moving rapidly to augment its influence over the entire working class. Between October 18, 1945, and December 15, 1946, alone, the number of legally recognized unions expanded from 215 to 757, while the number of labor federations rose from none to 13. The government took a special interest in organizing rural workers. Of the 757 legal unions reported at the end of 1946, 264 were agrarian organizations. Throughout its tenure in government to 1948, Acción Democrática moved slowly on the question of agricultural reform. But it

---

102. This is the thesis developed by Lucena in *El movimiento obrero y las relaciones laborales* (cited in n. 48).
103. Hassan, *Economic Growth* (cited in n. 24), Tables 2.2 and 2.3, pp. 13 and 15.

nevertheless ceded public lands to organized rural workers, encouraged agricultural cooperatives, and established legal norms for the parcelization (with prior compensation) of inadequately exploited large estates. The weight of peasant leagues and unions helped offset the strength of industrial, and especially oil, unions in the organized labor movement and in the national labor central, the Confederación de Trabajadores Venezolanos, established with the government's blessing in 1947. Acción Democrática's influence over the agrarian labor organizations it created was (and has remained) virtually unchallenged by the Marxist left. Within industrial and oil workers' organizations, however, Communists remained a vocal and influential minority. Through control of an expanded organized labor movement, the government extended the benefits of the national labor law, offered or imposed the mediating offices of the state in disputes with capital, and promoted its philosophy of bread-and-butter unionism. Partly as a result of these initiatives, real wages rose a spectacular 31 percent in 1946, 5 percent in 1947. Meanwhile, the government used executive decrees and obligatory arbitration to reduce drastically the number and importance of strikes.[104]

Expanding oil revenue enabled the government to complement its labor initiatives by extending social services and raising the purchasing power of working- and middle-class consumers. It subsidized food prices, lowered rents and electric rates, and reduced the domestic price of gasoline and kerosene. It initiated housing projects for workers. It extended social-security coverage to public employees and some other workers. It expanded public education and health services. It started school lunch programs and nurseries for working mothers.

Finally, the government used oil revenue to stimulate national economic development. It set up agricultural and industrial development banks and joined with Colombia in promoting a regional merchant marine. Its most important initiative was the Corporación Venezolana de Fomento, organized in 1947. With a budget ceiling fixed at 10 percent of government expenditures, the Corporación advanced credit mainly to private capitalists. It invested in agriculture and irrigation programs, but its initiatives were especially successful in fostering the growth of the textile, construction, and fertilizer industries. The Corporación contributed to the more than 250 percent increase in the volume of Venezuelan industrial production between 1944 and 1948.

The integrity of Acción Democrática's whole reform program depended, of course, on expansion of the Venezuelan oil industry. Its labor

104. The information in this and the next paragraphs is drawn primarily from Betancourt, *Venezuela, política y petróleo* (cited in n. 44), which gives an exhaustive account of the initiatives of the new government, and from Ellner, *Los partidos políticos*, which provides a succinct analysis of economic and labor trends during the Acción Democrática triennium.

philosophy was built on that premise, its social and developmental programs demanded it. Once in power, Acción Democrática leaders made good on their pledge not to tamper with existing oil legislation. But they managed to pursue their long-standing nationalist position toward the industry—and increase the vital oil revenues on which their program rested—in other ways. Acción Democrática representatives had opposed the oil legislation promulgated by the Medina government in 1943 on several counts. They argued, contrary to the predictions of the Medina government, that the increase in government revenues established in the law would not achieve parity between oil company profits and returns to the government. They claimed that in effect the law condoned past malpractices. And they violently criticized the huge new oil concessions granted the companies once the law was put in place. Once in power Acción Democrática decreed a one-time extraordinary tax on the industry in 1946 to compensate the government for the failure of oil taxes to produce for the government revenue equal to oil company profits. The government also stopped granting oil concessions, contending that the huge reserves already in possession of the companies were more than adequate for major expansion of the industry. The government also acted to expand oil revenue by increasing the rate of the income tax decreed by Medina. And in 1947 it surprised the companies by demanding a portion of its royalties in kind, a move legally sanctioned in Venezuelan oil law, but never before invoked. In this way the government took advantage of postwar demand for oil to sell or barter petroleum at prices well above the official price set by the companies. Finally, the government actively pushed the companies ahead on construction of refineries in Venezuela, a policy also initiated by the Medina government.[105]

None of these policies endeared the Acción Democrática government to the oil companies. All of them threatened the long-term position and prerogatives of the companies. It was the government's labor policies, however, that by 1948 constituted the gravest immediate threat to oil company profits. As long as the postwar petroleum bonanza continued, oil company officials tolerated the government's moderate nationalism and cooperated with its initiatives to displace Marxist influence over the oil proletariat and institutionalize the philosophy of bread-and-butter unionism in the industry. In a careful study of the labor politics of this period, Steve Ellner has shown how the progressive leadership of the

---

105. Lieuwen, *Petroleum* (cited in n. 25), pp. 103-10. Acción Democrática's influential oil minister, Juan Pablo Pérez Alonzo, later claimed that this major oil legislation, enacted under the Medina regime, was written with the cooperation of the oil companies themselves. They acquiesced to increased taxation in order to regularize and greatly extend the legally suspect concessions granted under Gómez and to open up the possibility of the vast new concessions Medina in fact delivered. For a detailed discussion, see Franklin Tugwell, *The Politics of Oil in Venezuela* (Stanford, Calif., 1975), pp. 43-44.

largest Venezuelan oil company, Jersey Standard's subsidiary Creole, carried the industry toward the concessions that resulted in the historic collective contract of 1946. He documents how the companies moved rapidly after 1945 to complement Acción Democrática labor initiatives with policies of their own to blunt the appeal of Marxist labor leaders. They expanded worker benefits, tried to improve grievance procedures, placed more Venezuelans in positions of authority in management, and discriminated against Communist in favor of Acción Democrática unions. Yet even in the contract negotiations of 1945, progressive leaders within the management of the oil companies faced stiff internal opposition. Estimates of the cost to the companies of the labor concessions of that year ranged from 40 to 110 million bolívares a year, a rise of 35 to 50 percent in the companies' wage bill.[106] In the collective contract of February 1948, the scope of all these concessions—wages, medical and housing benefits, vacations, and the prerogatives of union leaders—was expanded once more. In exchange, the companies got a three-year contract, and, as the U.S. ambassador put it, no impairment of "management prerogatives." Yet the scope of the concessions to labor did not prevent the Communist minority from denouncing the unprecedented length of the contract. Their nonconformity led them to withdraw from the national oil workers' federation and in June 1948 to launch a strike among marine oil transport workers. Although that strike was disavowed by the oil workers' federation, and promptly crushed by President Gallegos (he based his action, ironically, on the same legal authority that López Contreras used to break the oil strike of 1936), conservatives within management were able to argue that the expensive concessions to oil workers and Acción Democrática unions had failed to ensure industrial peace.[107]

It was the end of the postwar oil boom, however, that did the most to undermine Acción Democrática's nationalist petroleum policies and threaten its labor policies in the oil industry in particular. By the end of 1948 world oil production caught up with demand. Venezuelan production, which had expanded steadily from 148 million barrels a year in 1942 to 490 million in 1948, dropped back to 482 million in 1949. The average price of Venezuelan heavy crude stood at $2.50 per barrel up to November 1948. By June 1949 it had fallen to less than half that price, $1.15 a barrel. During 1948 the alleged threat to Venezuela's future posed by Acción Democrática's oil policies in a glutted world market began to be discussed widely in the country's newspapers. Since 1947 the companies had

106. These estimates, published in *World Petroleum* and *The New York Times*, are quoted in Betancourt, *Venezuela, política y petróleo* (cited in n. 44), p. 338.

107. The quotation is from Donnelly to Secretary of State, Telegram No. 121, Caracas, Feb. 10, 1948, USNA/DS 831.504/2-1348.

cultivated the fear in Venezuela of Middle Eastern competition, and by the end of 1948 the prospect of world overproduction made that argument much more telling. The gains of the petroleum workers were held up not only as a threat to Venezuela's competitive position in world oil production but also as the cause for rising wage rates generally. Labor costs, it was argued, had discouraged foreign capital from developing Venezuela's recently discovered iron deposits. They also contributed to the high cost of production (and poor competitive position) of Venezuelan agriculture and industry.[108]

The wartime and postwar expansion and the drive to exploit the richest concessions granted by the Medina government after 1943 had led, as we have seen, to a rapid increase in the petroleum labor force. In 1938, 22,496 people were employed in the industry. By 1948 the number had risen to 55,170. The end of the postwar oil boom and the conclusion of the labor-intensive exploration and construction phase in the 1943 concessions left the companies at the end of 1948 with a labor force far in excess of their projected needs, yet difficult and costly to dismiss. Since 1936 the companies had resisted union and government attempts to restrict their ability to adjust their labor force in accordance with market conditions. They were successful in maintaining that absolute right, but as early as 1936 labor legislation threatened to make its exercise very expensive. The companies won a legal victory in 1938 when the Venezuelan Supreme Court interpreted the 1936 labor law in a way that limited the companies' financial obligations to the workers they laid off. In the collective contracts of 1946 and 1948, however, the companies were forced to assume costly obligations to their laid-off workers. Moreover, given the political links between the government and the oil workers' federation—and the existence of a militant minority in the oil fields that constantly questioned the good faith and effectiveness of the Acción Democrática union organizations—there is some question whether the government or the oil workers' federation could have tolerated mass layoffs politically. These speculations aside, what is certain is that after the fall of the Acción Democrática government in November 1948, the oil companies dismissed thousands of oil workers from their payrolls. Almost 10,000 oil employees, virtually all of them blue-collar workers, were deprived of their jobs in 1949, and the layoffs continued at a slower rate in 1950. (See Figure 4.1.)

As the threat to the Acción Democrática government grew stronger and rumors of an impending coup became widespread, labor leaders petitioned the leaders of the party for arms and formulated plans for a gen-

108. Lieuwen, *Petroleum* (cited in n. 25), pp. 110, 111-12, and 121; Ellner, *Los partidos políticos* (cited in n. 48), pp. 116-17.

eral strike to thwart the reactionary plans of the military. These pleas fell on deaf ears, however, and plans for a strike never received a go-ahead from top party leaders. True to their liberal commitment to class harmony, Acción Democrática leaders pinned their hopes for survival on loyal elements in the military. When the coup occurred, protest in the oil fields was fragmentary and easily suppressed by the new regime. In early February 1949, a month and a half after the coup, Acción Democrática labor leaders called a general strike to protest the march of national events. It was poorly organized, indifferently obeyed, and promptly crushed by military force. Government officials reacted to the strike by dissolving all the Acción Democrática labor organizations in the country. They later told the U.S. ambassador that they were surprised at the weakness of the Acción Democrática oil unions, and the docility with which most oil workers accepted the new political order.[109]

The Contours of Contemporary Venezuelan History

The military officers who toppled the democratically elected government of Rómulo Gallegos in November 1948, and who governed Venezuela for almost a decade, reversed virtually every aspect of Acción Democrática policy.[110] Nationalist petroleum policies gave way before an orthodox liberalism that limited government taxation of the industry and sanctioned a return to the concessionary policies (and widespread corruption) of the Gómez era. Labor organizations opposed to the government and willing to strike, in the oil industry and elsewhere, were crushed; opposition political parties were outlawed; the press was censored. In the years after 1948 thousands of labor activists and Acción Democrática and Communist political militants were imprisoned, tortured, deported, or confined in deadly tropical concentration camps. The emphasis on social programs and statist economic development initiatives characteristic of the Acción Democrática government was replaced by a commitment to more orthodox mid-twentieth-century capitalist policies of huge military expenditures and massive (and often superfluous) public works built by private contractors with personal or political ties to the government. Power within the military junta soon devolved into the hands of Lieutenant Colonel Marco Pérez Jiménez. He and a coterie of favorites, like the gomecistas before them, used control of the state to amass huge personal fortunes. The military regime that controlled the Venezuelan government after 1948 won enthusiastic support from reactionary Venezuelan land-

109. Corrigan to Secretary of State, Caracas, Mar. 11, 1949, USNA/DS 831.504/3-1144.
110. The studies of post-1948 and especially post-1958 Venezuelan developments are legion. One of the best and most pertinent to the themes discussed in this final section is Franklin Tugwell's *The Politics of Oil in Venezuela* (cited in n. 105).

owners, capitalists, and military men, and from the oil companies, other foreign investors, and the U.S. government.

The eclipse of popular forces in Venezuela after 1948 was temporary, however. The struggle against the reactionary military regime in the 1950's unified the Venezuelan left as it had in the 1930's. Within a decade liberals and Marxists drove the military from power and returned to build the democratic society they had first envisioned in 1936. Once again divergent class commitments and international loyalties divided the left. Once again liberal reformers defeated their Marxist rivals for leadership of the Venezuelan working and middle class. They were able to do so, as they had done before, by tapping the enormous wealth generated by the petroleum export economy. By taxing and eventually nationalizing the oil industry, liberal reformers in control of the state were able to finance programs to diversify and modernize Venezuela's economy, fund large social-welfare schemes, and pay the salaries of an expanding army of military and civilian employees charged with maintaining social order and administering government programs. Oil revenue enabled the liberals to pursue all these reforms without threatening the interests of property owners and investors. A major land reform in the 1960's, for example, fully compensated inefficient landowners and encouraged them to invest in more lucrative endeavors. Rural working-class beneficiaries were then organized into effective supporters of the liberal order. Similarly, nationalization of the oil industry in 1975 handsomely compensated the foreign oil companies, and they continued to profit from the sale of services and technology to the state-owned petroleum corporation. The prodigious economic growth experienced by Venezuela since 1958 and the scope of liberal social reform have validated the liberal capitalist philosophy of the reformers and contributed to their political popularity. Since 1958 Acción Democrática and other parties that share its liberal capitalist vision have relied on popular mobilization and electoral politics to legitimize their rule and discredit the reactionary forces to their right and the Marxist minority to their left.

The foundation of Venezuela's contemporary liberal capitalist order lies in the organized labor movement. After 1958 the reformers institutionalized their corporate liberal labor philosophy and deepened their control over the organizations of the Venezuelan working class. In the months following the fall of the dictatorship in January 1958, the liberal reformers moved quickly to reestablish unions all over the nation. In August they called a convention of oil workers and reconstructed the petroleum federation they had originally founded in 1946. In November they reconstituted the national labor central they had founded in 1947. The reformers' Communist allies in the struggle against the dictatorship initially cooperated in these endeavors. They accepted minority representation on the executive committees of all these union organizations. But when Marxists moved in the early 1960's to challenge the liberals' control of the organized labor movement, they were defeated just as they had been in the 1940's. Liberals used their control of the state to favor their partisans in the labor movement and relied on an expanding oil-based economy to vindicate their philosophy of bread-and-butter unionism.

Frustrated by their inability to challenge the capitalist order through control of what they viewed as their natural constituency, the organized working class, many Marxists were swayed by the Cuban example and opted for the tactics of armed struggle in the 1960's. This decision was disastrous for the Marxist left. In Venezuela Marxists confronted not a brutal, corrupt, and antinational military dictatorship like the one that fell before the Cuban revolutionaries in 1959. They confronted the successive Acción Democrática administrations of Rómulo Betancourt and Raúl Leoni, the direct descendants of the first democratically elected government in twentieth-century Venezuelan history. Those administrations acted vigorously in the 1960's to use oil revenues to expand the scope of all their earlier reforms. The Communist-led insurgency only strengthened the hand of the liberal reformers in dealing with the capitalist class.

In crushing the leftist insurgency, the Venezuelan liberals not only defeated their Marxist rivals physically, they discredited them ideologically. After the failure of the insurrection, Marxists could continue to argue, correctly, that the liberal reformers were failing to free the nation from dependency on oil, that liberal social reforms would not eliminate the structural cause of inequality and poverty, and that the liberals' commitment to political democracy was contingent on their ideological and political hegemony over Venezuelan society. Marxists could argue with Rodolfo Quintero that oil-based capitalist development was turning the entire nation into a oil boomtown, that it was creating a society with a "culture of oil" where the best in national traditions was sacrificed to a servile aping of foreign consumption patterns and to the ruthless utilitarian ethics of individual greed. Marxists could argue that though growth of Venezuela's oil dependency provided Venezuelans with the highest per capita income in Latin America, it also created the highest cost of living in the region, and destroyed the quality of people's lives. Marxists could make all these arguments, and broaden their appeal among some middle-class intellectuals and students. But none of these arguments was telling to members of the working and middle class with access to the flow of material benefits emanating from capitalist employers and a liberal state in an expanding oil-based economy. In the 1960's, by attempting to subvert the free choice of the majority of Venezuelan voters and union members, the Marxists violated a fundamental aspiration of a people that had lived under military dictatorship through most of the twentieth century.

Although the Marxist parties subsequently repudiated their violent adventure of the 1960's, they have yet to win the confidence of a large number of Venezuelan voters.

————————

After 1948 oil workers never fully recaptured the collective strength and combativeness that placed them in the vanguard of political events during the crucial thirteen-year formative period of Venezuela's modern liberal democratic order. Mechanization of the industry, already well under way in the 1940's, limited the numbers of blue-collar workers even as expansion of production resumed in the 1950's. At the same time, the proportional weight of white-collar and technical personnel in the petroleum labor force grew, and the number of foreign employees in the industry, in decline since the 1940's, fell rapidly. By the early 1970's white-collar employees made up well over half of a total labor force that had shrunk to less than 23,000, and foreign personnel within this total had fallen to less than a thousand.[111] In the decades after 1950 the relative weight of oil workers in the Venezuelan labor movement also declined. Especially after 1960, industrialization and agrarian reform programs, along with government support for the unionization of workers in industry and agriculture, increased the numbers and importance of organized workers in these other sectors of the economy. In the 1950's, after years of experience as tools in the rivalry between the Acción Democrática and Communist parties—both of which subverted the interests of oil workers as a class to party imperatives in the 1940's—oil workers were subjected to the clumsy paternalism of the Pérez Jiménez dictatorship. If the military regime refused to tolerate militant union activity in the oil fields, and did not object to the layoffs in the industry during 1949 and 1950, it was careful not to infringe on the material benefits of oil workers left on the job. The government extended these benefits in the three-year contract it unilaterally decreed in 1951. Inspired by the Peronist example, the military regime coupled the flow of material benefits to workers and pliant unions in the early 1950's with halfhearted efforts to fill workers' leisure time with "healthy" activities such as movies, concerts, and tourist excursions. It sought, in the words of one labor minister, to impart to workers a sense of "nationalism" and an appreciation for "that which is morally valid."[112] Through it all, however, most oil workers continued to harbor a political commitment to Acción Democrática, the party that had overseen their great organizational triumph in 1946.

111. Statistics on these trends through 1967 are summarized in Ministerio de Minas y Hidrocarburos, Oficina de Economía Petrolera, *Memoria, 1967* (Caracas, 1968), Apéndice Estadístico, Cuadro 1-A-213; later figures are published in the *Anuario Estadístico*.
112. Ministerio de Trabajo, *Memoria y cuenta, 1948-52* (Caracas, 1953), pp. 10-11.

After the fall of the dictatorship in 1958, oil workers played an important role in consolidating the new liberal order. In the first years they provided much of the economic and political clout behind the general strikes called by the liberals and their leftist allies to defeat reactionary conspiracies against the new regime. In the reorganization of their unions and their relations with capital and the state, oil workers once again set the pattern for the whole of the Venezuelan labor movement. Their highly centralized and bureaucratic labor federation used the corporate institutions sanctioned by the state to negotiate with the companies and win for rank-and-file workers a steady flow of material benefits without resorting to strikes.[113] In exchange, oil workers gave up collective struggle to assert control over their work and run their own union affairs. In recent decades most oil workers, like the majority of organized workers in Venezuela, have learned to content themselves with the social and political opportunities available to them in Venezuela's liberal capitalist society. They enjoy a decent standard of living and access to consumer goods. They play baseball on union teams and watch the World Series via satellite on television in their homes. They finagle to win company or state scholarships to send their children to technical school or even to college in Venezuela or the United States. They use party connections to win favors and jobs for friends and relatives. Nationalization of the industry, a process that oil workers did not initiate, has probably worked to blunt their sense of nationalism. Most Venezuelan oil workers today are good union men who vote for liberal democrats and largely ignore the Marxist left.

Looking back on the history of the left in modern Venezuelan society, one is tempted to modify the metaphor employed by the editors of *Petróleo* in 1936. The problem faced by the Venezuelan left in its efforts to overcome the nation's economic dependency on oil, preserve the best in the nation's cultural heritage, and build a more just and democratic society continues to be "white." That is, today, as in 1936, the alliance of international and domestic capital, now strengthened by major liberal reforms, stands resolutely opposed to construction of a socialist society dedicated to the goal of ensuring greater national economic and cultural independence, greater social equality, and greater control by workers over their lives. Yet perhaps the biggest problem faced by the Marxist left in Venezuela since 1936 has not been "white" but "black." It is "black" not in the racial sense referred to by the editors of *Petróleo* during the great oil strike of 1936. Racial issues greatly complicated the social prob-

113. Federación de Trabajadores Petroleros de Venezuela, *XX aniversario de la Fedepetrol* (Caracas, 1966).

lems and political stability of an independent Venezuela struggling to adjust its plantation society to an industrial capitalist world order in the nineteenth century. They served to rationalize social and political repression in the minds of Venezuelan and North American apologists for a dictatorial capitalist regime in the first decades of the twentieth century. But the modern Venezuelan labor movement has never faced the serious problems of working-class division along racial and ethnic lines that have gravely undermined the unity of the labor movement in other national settings during this century. Rather than a racial issue, the problem facing the Venezuelan left is "black" in a more abstract and structural sense. Since the 1930's, petroleum, Venezuela's black gold, has been creatively manipulated by progressive corporate managers and by liberal reformist politicians to stymie the appeal of socialism and to finance the liberal trajectory of Venezuela's capitalist development.

There is a certain irony in the ways the personal career of Espartaco González, the militant black editor of *Petróleo*, illustrates the opportunities and problems confronted by the left in Venezuela's oil export economy after 1936. In the years following the great oil strike, González gradually became disenchanted with the sectarian bickering and ineffectual policies of the national leadership of the Venezuelan Communist Party. He eventually withdrew from active politics in Zulia and became a small-scale entrepreneur. He chose an industry that developed in tandem with petroleum in the world economy, an industry that currently supplies Venezuelans with the greatest number of automobiles per capita in Latin America. Today Espartaco González owns a small factory in Maracaibo that employs some twenty workers who rebuild brake shoes.[114]

The paradox of modern Venezuelan history is that the very industry that gave birth to a powerful left stunted its child's development. Oil workers led the struggle for the political and social democratization and nationalist economic reform of Venezuelan society, not for its socialization. As long as the petroleum economy retains the historical characteristics that have made it unique among Latin American export economies, and as long as liberal democrats remain in power—issues in some doubt given the state of the world and Venezuelan economies in the mid-1980's—the Marxist left will have to content itself with making trenchant critiques of the pattern of Venezuela's oil-based development, and resign itself to a long, uphill struggle to regain its influence in Venezuela's labor movement and politics.

114. Interview with Espartaco González, Maracaibo, June 21, 1979.

5

Colombia

From radicalism to order, from infancy to middle age, from disorder to stability, from anarchic subjectivity to measured, cold objectivity, these are the historical transformations which coffee produces in Colombia. The small producers, the property owners who have, themselves, cultivated the land, have triumphed. Peace and tranquillity reign in Colombia.

> Luis Eduardo Nieto Arteta
> *El Café en la sociedad colombiana*
> (published posthumously in 1958)

Coffee and Colombian Historiography

The lines quoted above, written in March 1948 by an imaginative and perceptive Colombian historian, seemed at the time to capture the essence of modern Colombian history. In the first years of the twentieth century, after almost a century of political instability and economic uncertainty, Colombia embarked on four decades of remarkable political order and unprecedented economic growth. The rise of the coffee economy, Nieto asserted, marked this momentous transition in national life. It explained the profound social, cultural, and political transformation that created a prosperous, stable, democratic Colombia out of a poor, chaotic, violent one.[1]

The month after Nieto finished his essay, crowds of working people virtually destroyed downtown Bogotá, the nation's capital and largest city.[2] The *9 de abril*, or the *bogotazo*, as it is known outside Colombia, was the most spectacular urban expression of a vast—and primarily rural—social phenomenon that convulsed Colombian society for more than a decade after 1946. Before it ended, it claimed the lives of some 200,000 Colombians, most of them rural agricultural workers. Colombia's mid-twentieth-century civil violence mobilized Colombian workers in a fratricidal conflict comparable in its destructiveness of human life and duration to the Mexican Revolution of 1910-17. Yet unlike that other major civil war in twentieth-century Latin American history, the Colombian

---

1. Luis Eduardo Nieto Arteta, *El café en la sociedad colombiana* (Bogotá, 1958).
2. Anteo Quimbaya, *El problema de la tierra en Colombia* (Bogotá, 1967), emphasizes the ironic timing of Nieto's essay.

conflict resists comprehension as a social revolution. Colombians fought each other under the banners of two traditional political parties, the Liberal and the Conservative, formed a century earlier as expressions of contending ruling-class interests. No explicit social or economic reforms resulted from the struggle. It produced instead a simple agreement by leaders of the two parties to share national political power.

Colombians collectively express their perception of this violent social process in simple terms. They call it *La Violencia*. That generic noun describes rather than explains. But it captures the essence of what happened to Colombian society in the middle of the twentieth century far better than the self-serving rationalizations propounded by most Colombian leaders while the conflict raged, and the clumsy ex post facto theorizing of many scholars. Colombia's unique twentieth-century social evolution does not fit tidily into the usual categories of conventional social science explanation, be they conservative, corporativist, liberal, or Marxist. The Violence has confounded students of Colombian history and demolished the predictions of one of the best of them, Luis Eduardo Nieto Arteta.[3]

The problem with Nieto's analysis was not his emphasis on the importance and structure of the coffee export economy, nor his intuitive grasp of the way coffee changed the dynamics of Colombian history. In an earlier study I showed how such an approach could be developed into a systematic explanation of the transformation of Colombian economic and political life at the turn of the century, a transition marked by the greatest and last of Colombia's nineteenth-century civil wars, the War of the Thousand Days.[4] The great weakness of Nieto's vision—easier to see with the benefit of hindsight and the aid of significant new contributions to twentieth-century Colombian historiography—was his failure to appreciate the long-term, and highly disruptive, popular social forces generated by coffee expansion in the twentieth century. During the three decades after 1920 these social forces worked in complex ways to erode ruling-class consensus. They eventually found expression in uniquely tragic form in the Violence of mid-century. The dynamic of this whole social process is informed by the special feature of Colombia's coffee export economy that Nieto correctly emphasized in his essay—the existence of tens of thousands of small producers and landowners in the coffee zones. Whereas Nieto saw smallholders only as a bastion of Colombian political stability and social and economic progress, however, in

---

3. The best description of the Violence, a book that conveys its nature in vivid, sometimes sensational terms, is the best-selling study by Germán Guzmán, Orlando Fals Borda, and Eduardo Umaña Luna, *La violencia en Colombia* (Bogotá, 1962). A sophisticated, systematic recent study of the Violence (which contains an excellent critical review of the now voluminous literature on the subject) is Paul Oquist, *Violencia, conflicto, y política en Colombia* (Bogotá, 1978). Oquist's important contribution, now available in English, is discussed in more detail below.

4. Charles W. Bergquist, *Coffee and Conflict in Colombia* (Durham, N.C., 1978).

fact they also served to reinforce particularly unjust and ultimately pathological elements in Colombia's capitalist development. The social relations of production in Colombia's unique agricultural export economy generated a Hobbesian system of cultural values, preserved an archaic and destructive political system, insured the viability of a peculiarly exploitative pattern of liberal capitalist economic growth, and subverted the formation of a powerful, class-conscious labor movement capable of finding a progressive solution to the problems of Colombian development.

The influence of Colombia's coffee export economy, considered as a unique set of evolving, contradictory class relations, can thus explain the peculiar features that distinguish modern Colombian development from historical patterns in the other major nations of Latin America. Unfortunately, however, the great interpreters of the role of coffee in molding modern Colombian history have been apologists for the ruling class. Their popular, influential studies, written in the 1930's and 1940's, were imaginative and often perceptive. Yet, as their critics have progressively demonstrated, they were fundamentally uncritical and misleading. Nieto Arteta's 1948 essay falls into this category. So also does the analogous interpretation of Colombian development articulated much earlier by another intellectual socialized in the heart of the Colombian coffee zone, Luis López de Mesa.

López de Mesa's most important work, *De cómo se ha formado la nación colombiana*, first published in 1934, is a lyrical celebration of Colombian national character, an affirmation of Colombian nationalism. The book combined a lucid description of Colombian geography, a somewhat fanciful (and often racist) account of ethnic miscegenation and cultural amalgamation, and a broad survey of economic and social trends during the colonial and national periods to reach a startling—and uplifting—conclusion. The nation's historical evolution had yielded a highly commendable and uniquely Colombian adaptation to a new world environment, a "*civilización de vertiente*."

> The dominant fact of the national economy is that this republic has a "civilization of the slopes." For a long time it tried development of the hot flat lowlands . . . without being able to win out over the hostility of the tropics, which weakened and decimated the population in unsustainable proportions. In the cold flat highlands it settled as well . . . with good success for health, but with insignificant progress since these regions generally lacked fertile soils, abundant water, adequate commercial connections, and . . . exportable products with which to nourish a large civilization comfortably.
>
> All of this came to be remedied by the conquest of the mountain slopes. . . .

This ecological zone, roughly coterminous with lands appropriate for coffee cultivation, lies on the temperate intermediate slopes of the three chains of the Andes of western Colombia. According to López de Mesa, it was here—especially in the central range, the locus of the expanding coffee economy of the twentieth century—that a new racial type combining Indian, black, and predominantly white European heritage emerged to colonize the virgin forests for domestic subsistence and export agriculture. A vigorous, expansive society developed on these mountain slopes, one characterized by demographic growth, widespread land ownership, and widely shared commercial values.[5]

López de Mesa's and Nieto Arteta's essays put an appealing, progressive face on the harsh class realities of Colombia's twentieth-century coffee-based capitalist development. They argued correctly that expansion of the coffee export economy created the conditions that enabled Colombia to emerge from the economic stagnation and political chaos of the nineteenth century; that property ownership became highly diffused in the major and most dynamic coffee area as a substantial class of independent owner-operators emerged in coffee cultivation; and that in the coffee zones capitalist values were widely suffused, a vigorous, expansive society was developed, and a unique "civilization" was forged.

But López de Mesa and Nieto Arteta chose to ignore or to mystify other basic features of Colombia's coffee-based development that were well known to members of the Colombian ruling class during the 1930's and 1940's. Accumulation of capital in the most important sector of the Colombian economy depended on relations of production and exchange that grossly exploited coffee workers and small and medium producers. Colombia's ability to expand coffee production and to capture a larger share of the depressed world market during the crisis of the 1930's—as well as its capacity to mount an impressive record of import-substituting industrialization during the same period—depended on the willingness of small producers and their families to subject themselves to an ever greater degree of exploitation. Throughout this century most coffee producers have lived and labored in abject material conditions. The vigorous demographic growth of the coffee zones reflected the domestic social imperatives of family-centered, labor-intensive coffee production. Astronomical birth rates offset shocking indices of mortality and disease to produce the celebrated population growth of the coffee regions.

Relations of production in the coffee zones, and the relentless pressure of population, defined a perennial, and often violent, struggle for control

5. Luis López de Mesa, *De cómo se ha formado la nación colombiana* (Medellín, 1970). The quotation is from pp. 40-41. It is striking that in its nationalist purpose, its holistic approach, and its attention to the cultural dimensions of export agriculture, López de Mesa's essay prefigures similar, and much better known, attempts by other Latin American scholars to capture the essence of national historical evolution during the world Depression. Compare the Brazilian and Cuban classics: Gilberto Freyre, *The Masters and the Slaves* (New York, 1946); and Fernando Ortiz, *Cuban Counterpoint: Tobacco and Sugar* (New York, 1947).

of the land. Workers, sharecroppers, renters, and smallholders (these class situations often combined in a single person or family) were locked in constant combat with one another and with large landowners and merchants to improve their position and to avoid proletarianization. As the best coffee land was appropriated and viable small family farms were divided by inheritance, as the rate of exploitation increased or the opportunities to improve one's situation declined, that struggle became both more desperate and more violent.

In the main, however, the structure of the Colombian coffee export economy created enormous real and subjective barriers to effective collective organization and class action by coffee workers and small producers. Despite their creative efforts to organize to improve their condition as a class, for the vast majority these efforts were unsuccessful. Coffee producers turned instead to the traditional political parties in search of support for their individual struggles. The Liberal and Conservative parties, it is true, governed the nation in the interest of large capitalists who dominated finance, production, and exchange in the Colombian coffee export economy. Government land, labor, and credit policies consistently favored the interests of large coffee producers and exporters. But coffee workers and small producers were often able to use their party affiliations to improve their life chances significantly. And given the conditions of their labor, and the structure of their hopes for a better life, for many workers in coffee production the capitalist ideologies of the two traditional parties made sense. Both the ruling class and tens of thousands of working-class people manipulated the party system to advantage. In that complex political dynamic lies the explanation for the enduring hegemony of the traditional parties, the silent logic of the catastrophic dysfunction of the Colombian political system at mid-century.

Three years after the publication of López de Mesa's seminal essay, the Colombian socialist and social scientist Antonio García began the task of exposing this darker side of López de Mesa's coffee arcadia. In his richly detailed *Geografía económica de Caldas*, first published in 1937, García revealed the exploitative social relations beneath the deceptive surface of the "democratic" land tenure arrangements in coffee production. He showed how land, labor, exchange, and credit systems in Colombia's premier coffee-producing region left most small producers barely able to sustain themselves. He documented the shocking material conditions under which most coffee producers lived and labored, demonstrated the high incidence of endemic disease in the coffee zone, analyzed the relationship between prostitution and poverty in coffee towns and cities.[6]

Empirically, García's work was superior to López de Mesa's essay, and

6. Antonio García, *Geografía económica de Caldas* (2d ed.; Bogotá, 1978). Subsequent citations refer to this edition.

to Nieto Arteta's later extension of it. Conceptually, however, García's analysis was seriously flawed. Neither in his classic 1937 study of Colombia's major coffee region, nor in his subsequent works on the modern political and socioeconomic history of the nation, did García succeed in conceptualizing the uniquely Colombian political dynamic of the social problems he described so well. The peculiar implications of social relations in Colombian coffee production for working-class culture and social struggle, the influence of the special structure of Colombia's coffee export economy on national economic and political evolution—both escaped him. García based his interpretation of modern Colombian history on the simplistic idea that poverty and exploitation automatically breed social revolution in capitalist society. That mechanical, economistic assumption, widespread in liberal and Marxist-inspired social science in Colombia and elsewhere, is not very useful in explaining social change in any society. It is particularly misleading, however, when applied to the modern history of Colombia. Capitalist exploitation in Colombia, especially in the coffee export sector, more often reinforced conservative individualist values and institutions than it fostered radical, collective ones; more often solidified the social and political status quo than it threatened progressively to transform it. Possessed of an intimate knowledge of social exploitation in the coffee zone, yet confronted by the conservative trajectory of modern Colombian history, García resolved his intellectual and political dilemma not by reexamining his assumptions about the connection between exploitation and socialist transformation, but by making Colombian history appear more revolutionary than it actually was. He explained the failure of popular reform forces to effect meaningful social change primarily as a result of reactionary ruling-class conspiracies and betrayals of the masses by their erstwhile reformist leaders. Interpretations of this kind abound in leftist contributions to Colombian historiography. They exaggerate the historical strength of the left, distract attention from the basic causes of its weakness, and rationalize opportunistic political positions and strategies that hurt rather than enhance the long-term political potential of popular forces. García's second and most influential book, *Gaitán y el problema de la revolución colombiana*, published in 1955, illustrates each of these tendencies. Against the weight of historical evidence, García interpreted the political process that culminated in the Violence at mid-century as an aborted social revolution. He concluded his study with a passionate defense of a conservative, populist, military dictatorship.[7]

Inspired by the work of García, leftist scholars have found it easy to

7. Antonio García, *Gaitán y el problema de la revolución colombiana* (Bogotá, 1955). Vernon Lee Fluharty developed García's thesis for English readers in his *Dance of the Millions. Military Rule and the Social Revolution in Colombia, 1930-1956* (Pittsburgh, 1957).

demonstrate the class bias in López de Mesa's and Nieto's interpretation of the impact of coffee on national life. They have shown how the work of these two men simply systematized and gave literary expression and intellectual respectability to a cultural myth fabricated in the 1920's by the Colombian ruling class to buttress its ideological and political hegemony over Colombian society.[8] The idea of a progressive, democratic, dynamic society built on smallholders on the coffee slopes was supported, beginning in 1932, by a series of carefully designed coffee censuses commissioned by the National Federation of Coffee Growers, the most powerful bipartisan interest group in the country. These censuses tended to obscure the reality of social relations in coffee cultivation and demonstrated the existence of tens of thousands of small and medium coffee farms in the coffee zones. López de Mesa and Nieto Arteta applied their considerable literary skill and analytical brilliance to develop that information into an original reinterpretation of the meaning of Colombian history.

In rejecting the class content in López de Mesa's and Nieto's work, however, the left has tended to dismiss as well the powerful and original conceptual and methodological advance embedded in their thought. For despite its ideological implications, their work had the virtue of grasping the unique feature of Colombia's modern history, and of recognizing the dialectical nature of the social, cultural, political, and intellectual changes coffee produced in Colombia. In denying these strengths, the left deprived itself of the best means to orient its own analysis of modern Colombian history. It deprived itself of the opportunity to do for the Colombian working class what López de Mesa and Nieto did so effectively for the nation's ruling class: to comprehend how coffee transformed the history of the nation and enlist that understanding in the service of its class constituency.

Since mid-century the march of Colombian history itself has mercilessly revealed the deficiencies of López de Mesa's and Nieto's vision. The Violence made a mockery of Nieto's platitudes about the nation's coffee-induced political stability. The barbaric intensity that conflict assumed in the coffee zones demolished López de Mesa's lyrical description of Colombia's mountainside civilization.

Yet the traditional political form in which the Violence was triggered, channeled, and largely ended exposed glaring weaknesses in the left's own interpretation of modern Colombian history. Like Antonio García, most leftists have tried to make modern Colombian history appear to be more revolutionary than it is. They have applied pedestrian versions of universal social theory in a vain attempt to explain the twentieth-century history of a social formation whose singular structure and anomalous his-

8. This is the burden, for example, of the indictment of their work developed by Anteo Quimbaya in the study cited in n. 2 above.

torical development cry out for original analysis. Unlike García, however, who pioneered in the study of labor in coffee production, most leftists have preferred to focus their attention on the "real proletarians" in Colombian history—on oil and banana workers, on transport and industrial workers, on the minority of coffee workers whose exceptional position enabled them to organize collectively. The history of each of these segments of the Colombian working class is important. Its full meaning, however, emerges only in relationship to the primary determinant of the pattern of Colombia's modern labor and national history. It is study of the organizational fate and political trajectory of workers in coffee production that gives unity to Colombian labor history and makes the larger story of national developments in the twentieth century comprehensible.

Fortunately, recent studies by Colombian scholars have reexamined aspects of the influence of coffee on national life, making it possible to begin reassessment of the meaning of coffee export production for the Colombian labor movement and for national history in general. Fuller appreciation of that influence may enable the left in Colombia and abroad to cease trying to manufacture a revolutionary history out of conservative cloth and get on with the task of accurately understanding the past so as to help create the future. It may encourage the left to stop making invidious, spurious analogies between Colombia and countries such as Cuba, Chile, and Nicaragua, where export economies proved more conducive to revolutionary labor and political traditions. It may help the left concentrate instead on comprehending how the exceptional nature of Colombian history can guide the nation on a unique road toward a more progressive social order.

As much as the left might wish it otherwise, Colombia's main function in the world capitalist system throughout this century, particularly during the formative years of modern Colombian economic, political, and institutional development, has been to produce coffee for export. The workers who did that, more than any other social group, made the modern history of the Colombian nation.

Origins of a Partisan Political System

It is Colombia's political evolution in the twentieth century that makes its modern history so obviously different from patterns in the other major nations of Latin America. The differences can be expressed in various ways. One can point to the remarkable survival, and continuing political hegemony, of the nation's two nineteenth-century political parties, each of which shares a commitment to the maintenance of the social status quo, to republican institutions and democratic forms, and to liberal capitalist political economy. One can emphasize the failure of reformist third parties—of both the Marxist left and the corporativist right—to exercise a significant, enduring influence on the direction of modern Colombian history. Or one can stress the dynamic of the Violence at mid-century, a conflict that obeyed a traditional political logic, not a modern social one. These are different ways of saying the same thing. Each of these political characteristics is a consequence of the historical weakness of organized labor and the political left.

Analysis of modern Colombian economic and social development must come to terms with the nation's anomalous traditional politics. It is not sufficient to take the political system that emerged from the nineteenth century as a given, then show how it structured and channeled twentieth-century economic and social change.[9] An adequate interpretation of the course of modern Colombian history must explain the peculiar dynamic of Colombian politics inherited from the nineteenth century, then show how that political system was perpetuated in the twentieth. I will argue in the next section that coffee helps to account for the curious preservation of Colombia's traditional political system in this century. Explanation of the formation of that system must begin with an understanding of the special features of Colombia's social development in the colonial period and the nineteenth century.

In the mountainous western third of what is now Colombia, Spaniards confronted indigenous societies less populous and culturally advanced than those of the central and southern Andes and Mesoamerica, yet more populous and agrarian than the cultures typical of the tropical lowlands and temperate plains of North and South America. Warfare, European disease, and the imposition of Spanish labor demands and patterns of land use decimated indigenous populations all over the Americas. These forces eliminated the material base and cultural autonomy of the indigenous peoples of western Colombia during the colonial period. There, unlike the New World areas of more advanced pre-Columbian civilization, few indigenous communities survived the onslaught of Spanish colonialism. Unlike the indigenous hunting and gathering cultures of the lowlands and plains who came in contact with European settlement, however, the pre-Columbian peoples of western Colombia were not virtually exterminated. When the declining population curve of colonial Colom-

---

9. This is the strategy followed, for example, by Oquist in the study cited in n. 3 above. Joan E. Garcés, *Desarrollo político y desarrollo económico. Los casos de Chile y Colombia* (Madrid, 1972), demonstrates the failure of third parties in this century, but fails to take stock of the historiography of the nineteenth century and to account for the exceptional nature of Colombian political development in that century.

bian society was reversed in the seventeenth century, Indian peoples contributed the largest share of the genetic heritage of the new ethnic type
that became the great majority of the Colombian people. Four centuries
of Spanish colonialism in the heartland of Colombia produced a relatively densely populated, ethnically mestizo society unified by a common
Spanish culture.[10]

Colonial Colombian society developed along settlement patterns well
established before the conquest. Spaniards were drawn to the abundant
indigenous labor, fertile soil, and salubrious climate of the mountainous
highlands, particularly the easternmost chain (*cordillera*) of the three
branches of the Andes that traverse western Colombia from south to
north, and to the upper reaches of the two great river valleys, the Magdalena and the Cauca, defined by these mountain chains. (See Map 5.1.)
It was here that Spaniards founded the great privately owned cattle and
agricultural estates typical of Spanish colonialism.

Unlike other Spanish colonies, however, colonial Colombia developed
as a largely self-sufficient agrarian society. Its major population centers
were located far from ocean commerce, and its transport and communications systems were stunted by the magnitude of the obstacles posed by
the region's mountainous topography. Rugged mule trails linked the
highlands with the rivers; the rivers, navigable only by small boats propelled by human muscle power, served as the only tie between the heartland of the colony and the sea and its European metropolis. Not until the
nineteenth century—and then very precariously—did Colombians begin
to produce agricultural export commodities able to surmount the burden
of geography on the nation's economic development.

The production of precious minerals for export was a different matter.
Gold, mined in the Western and Central Cordilleras, made the colony the
major gold-producing region in Spain's New World empire. The volume
and value of gold exports, and the amount of capital invested and the
number of workers involved in gold production, however, were small in
comparison to the great Spanish silver-producing colonies of New Spain
and Peru. Colombia's gold deposits in the upper and middle Cauca Valley
were worked during the colonial and early independence periods primarily by gangs of black slaves. Gold production exercised a significant influence on the ethnic composition, social structure, and economic development of that important region of Colombia during the colonial and
independence periods. Unlike the inordinate importance of mining in the
social development of Spain's major silver-producing colonies, however,

10. These themes are treated in careful, detailed studies by Jaime Jaramillo Uribe. For a
short, synthetic statement see his "Etapas y sentido de la historia de Colombia" in Mario
Arrubla et al., *Colombia: Hoy* (2d ed.; Bogotá, 1978), pp. 15-51.

Map 5.1. Colombia, Showing the Coffee Zone and Departments in the Early Twentieth Century.

the impact of gold on Colombia's colonial and nineteenth-century society was of secondary importance.[11]

The primary axis of colonial Colombian economic, social, and political development lay in the densely populated agrarian society of the Eastern Cordillera. There, on the 2500-meter-high Savanna de Bogotá, on the foundation of the most advanced pre-Columbian civilization of northern South America, Spaniards established the administrative hub of the colony. Santa Fé de Bogotá was destined to become the capital of independent Colombia and the largest city in northern and western South America. From that base, Spanish colonialism spread north into the cold highlands and intermontane basins of the Eastern Cordillera all the way into present-day Venezuela. The largely self-sufficient agrarian society that developed in this region—more stratified and hierarchical in the south (in the modern departments of Cundinamarca and Boyacá), more fluid and democratic in the north (in present-day Santander and Norte de Santander)—became the heart of the colony. It was primarily through this densely populated, economically self-sufficient region that coffee cultivation, destined to transform modern Colombian society, diffused southward during the last half of the nineteenth century. At the end of the century, when coffee cultivation enveloped the Central Cordillera and began its explosive twentieth-century growth, the traditional regional primacy of the departments of the Eastern Cordillera was gradually undermined, and the nation, for the first time, was effectively unified.[12]

Two features thus distinguished Colombia's colonial development from the evolution of the other major colonies of Spain's New World empire: the colony's relatively homogenous ethnic composition and cultural unity; and its relative isolation from the world economic system. Neither of these characteristics was absolute. But each helps to explain the political form taken in Colombia by the social, economic, and ideological tensions generated by the painful process of Spanish decolonization and

11. Statistics on colonial Colombian gold production, based on the nineteenth-century estimates of Vicente Restrepo, are conveniently summarized in William Paul McGreevey, *An Economic History of Colombia, 1845-1930* (Cambridge, Eng., 1971), Table 7, p. 46. McGreevey provides a wealth of material and analysis in Part One of this work to demonstrate the relatively closed nature of the Colombian economy at the end of the colonial period.

12. Before 1886 the primary administrative divisions of Colombia were called states. Since that date they have been called departments. In the text I have also simplified the problems posed by the changing names and jurisdictional boundaries of the political entities to which modern Colombia pertained. Originally part of the Viceroyalty of Peru, Colombia formed the core of the Viceroyalty of Nueva Granada in the eighteenth century, and of the República de la Gran Colombia (which included present-day Venezuela and Ecuador) following independence. After the separation of Venezuela and Ecuador in the 1830's, the republic went through three more name changes until in 1886 it adopted its present official title, the Republic of Colombia. Panama separated from Colombia in 1903.

gradual incorporation into an industrial capitalist world order during the nineteenth century.

Following the independence of the colony, two contending factions, Liberals and Conservatives, emerged within the ruling class of the new nation. Liberals and Conservatives divided over the degree of their commitment to the principles of liberal political economy that undergirded the world capitalist system in the nineteenth century and conditioned successful development within it. Liberals struggled with Conservatives over the role of the Church, a major landowner and source of credit, the guarantor of ruling-class legitimacy and social control within Spain's mercantile colonial order. The two factions fought over the timing of the abolition of slavery, over the disposition of public and Indian lands, over the conditions under which foreign loans were contracted, over the character of public and private educational institutions, over the nature of monetary, banking, and tax systems, and over the degree of political and administrative centralization. These issues were defined by the Liberals' efforts to transform land and labor into market commodities that could be combined freely with capital for productive use in a world economy structured by the principles of free trade and international specialization of function.

This internal elite struggle over the principles of liberal political economy was not unique to Colombia. As we have seen in earlier chapters, it was typical of the former Iberian colonies in the New World. In some Latin American nations liberals encountered more powerful and sustained conservative resistance, or the economic results of their reforms were more immediately successful, than in others. In each Latin American society the overarching issues of liberal political economy were complicated in specific and often contradictory ways by popular class struggle, by regional interests and loyalties, and by the personal ambitions of political leaders and their clients. For all these reasons the struggle to consolidate the principles of liberal political economy produced a history of conflict and compromise within the ruling class specific to each of the distinct social formations and political entities of Latin America. In Colombia the specific details—and even some of the major turning points—of this violent process are obscured in the traditional historiography and still not fully worked out in the new.[13] But what distinguishes the Colombian version from the parallel nineteenth-century histories of the other Latin American republics is clear: on the one hand, the protracted and in-

---

13. Good recent reviews are Anthony MacFarlane, "From Colony to Nation: The Political Economy of Colombia During the First Half of the Nineteenth Century," in C. Abel and C. Lewis, eds., *Latin America, Economic Imperialism and the State*, forthcoming; and Paul Oquist, *Violencia* (cited in n. 3), Chap. 3. By new historiography I mean studies attentive to the advances of modern social science and analytical in intent.

conclusive nature of the struggle; on the other, the depth of popular politicization it entailed.

The struggle over the principles of liberal political economy remained
unresolved in Colombia until after the turn of the twentieth century. It
did so primarily because of the inability of the new nation to overcome
the pattern of isolated agrarian development established during the colonial period. Throughout the nineteenth century Colombians largely
failed in their attempts to expand exports of primary commodities to the
world economy. This was true of gold production, the only important
export of colonial Colombia, as well as of the agricultural commodities
Colombians tried to produce for the world market.

The violent civil and class conflict unleashed in the upper Cauca Valley
during the transition to a liberal order following independence gradually
destroyed the slave labor system upon which Colombia's colonial gold
production had depended. As gold mining slowly revived it acquired a
new geographical focus and relied on new modes of production. Most of
the nation's nineteenth-century gold exports were extracted from the
Central Cordillera in the huge region known as Antioquia. The bulk of
Antioquia's gold exports were produced by small- and medium-size domestic and foreign capitalist enterprises using machinery and relatively
modern techniques. These mining companies employed anywhere from
a few dozen to a few hundred free wage workers, many of whom labored
seasonally in the mines and returned to agriculture during part of the
year. The vast majority of Antioquia's mining labor force, however,
were small, independent miners. Called *mazamorreros*, after the corn-
based gruel that was the staple of their diet, these workers accounted for
some four-fifths of an estimated 15,000 gold miners in Antioquia during
peak employment years in the nineteenth century. Mazamorreros developed mining techniques and a highly mobile culture to tap the shallow
gold deposits along a thousand isolated streams and rivers on the slopes
of the Central Cordillera. Most mazamorreros were descendants of
slaves or mestizos who fled the onerous labor systems of highland agriculture; perhaps a third of them were women. They worked virtually
without capital or machinery, using hand-hewn wooden *bateas* (shallow
bowls) to pan a fourth of the gold exported from Antioquia during the
nineteenth century. Like wage laborers in the established mines, mazamorreros often engaged in agriculture, usually on subsistence plots
hacked out of the virgin forests of the rugged mountains they scoured
for gold.[14]

14. Roger Brew, *El desarrollo económico de Antioquia desde la independencia hasta 1920* (Bogotá, 1977), provides the best discussion of *antioqueño* gold mining. The figures on the labor
force are taken from pp. 52-53, those on the share of Antioquia's gold exports in total gold
and Colombian exports from pp. 131-32.

Colombia's gold-mining mazamorreros, and the merchants who supplied them and collected the product of their labor for export, played important roles in transforming the nature of *antioqueño* society during the nineteenth century. At the heart of this transformation was the celebrated movement of antioqueño farmers out of the settled highlands onto the virgin slopes of the Central Cordillera to the south. Within this advancing agricultural frontier emerged thousands of agricultural smallholders, people engaged first in subsistence agriculture, then, as the nineteenth century progressed, in coffee cultivation. The development of such an agricultural frontier, so familiar to North Americans, is rare in Latin American history. Because antioqueño colonization helped stamp the Colombian coffee export economy with its special sociological face, and because it appears to be intimately connected with the industrialization of Antioquia in the twentieth century, it is a subject of great significance not only to the history of the region, but to that of the nation as a whole.

Alvaro López Toro was the first to develop systematically the thesis that the dynamic of antioqueño colonization and of Colombia's modern coffee-based development was intimately related to the region's evolving gold export economy. In a brilliant essay, published in 1970, he argued that gold production for export in the eighteenth and nineteenth centuries generated chronic disequilibrium between the region's dynamic mining economy and its stagnant traditional agriculture. He argued that a powerful merchant class emerged to balance this disequilibrium through trade. Merchants supplied the diffuse export sector with food, tools, and clothing, and collected gold for export. Capital accumulation in the hands of merchants enabled them to displace the cultural, social, and political influence of the class of large landowners engaged in traditional agriculture in the highlands around the region's capital, Medellín. Merchants organized the colonization of the frontier beginning in the 1820's. They enlisted the support of the government in the distribution of public and privately claimed virgin land on the slopes. Much of this land went to smallholders. Merchants later fostered the transition in recently colonized areas from subsistence agriculture to coffee cultivation. They then used their control of finance and exchange to appropriate surplus in the coffee economy and turn it to industrial development.[15]

15. Alvaro López Toro, *Migración y cambio social en Antioquia* (Medellín, 1970). The classic description of the process is James J. Parsons, *Antioqueño Colonization in Western Colombia* (Berkeley, Calif., 1949). Frank Safford's "Significado de los antioqueños en el desarrollo económico colombiano," *Anuario Colombiano de Historia Social y de la Cultura* 3 (1965):44-69, emphasized the importance of gold in Antioquia's development, and questioned the bizarre thesis of cultural deprivation popularized by Everett Hagen, *On the Theory of Social Change* (Homewood, Ill., 1962). Since the publication of López Toro's essay, aspects of his thesis have been corroborated in primary research by Roger Brew, whose work is cited in n. 14, and by Ann Twinam, *Miners, Merchants, and Farmers in Colonial Colombia* (Austin, Tex., 1982).

López Toro's seminal essay analyzed this remarkable historical process primarily from the perspective of the merchant class. It is possible to read his essay, however, and the material upon which it is based, from the complementary, and more fundamental, perspective of the other major class spawned in Antioquia's gold export economy. The small farmers and dependent laborers who fled the highlands to seize the opportunities for independent gold production undermined the exploitative land and labor arrangements of highland agriculture. Mazamorreros created a market for merchants and the need for a mechanism to channel gold production abroad. Mazamorreros first opened the frontier and developed the cultural tools that proved its potential for subsistence agriculture. Merchants turned all these developments—products of the democratic struggle of antioqueño workers to improve their lives—to their own advantage. In doing so they erected a legal and political framework in which smallholder subsistence—and later export—agriculture could develop in the Central Cordillera.

If gold production can thus be shown to have exercised a pervasive indirect and long-term influence on the development of antioqueño (and ultimately Colombian) society, its short-term impact proved insufficient to transform the basically closed pattern of Colombia's agrarian development during the nineteenth century. By the last decades of that century, the volume and value of Colombia's annual gold exports had finally climbed back to the modest levels first reached during the eighteenth century, something in excess of 150,000 fine ounces valued at a little more than 3 million gold pesos.[16] Gold exports from Antioquia accounted for roughly two-thirds of all Colombian gold exports during the nineteenth century, and rose from roughly 10 to 25 percent of the nation's total exports during the last half of that century. Yet the total value of all Colombian exports, the bulk of which were agricultural, expanded only fitfully and slowly during the entire nineteenth century. Between the end of the eighteenth century and the beginning of the twentieth, the total value of Colombian foreign trade grew at a rate only slightly faster (if indeed faster at all) than the demographic growth of the nation during the same period.[17] By the end of the nineteenth century Colombia's population of

16. These figures, drawn from Restrepo's estimates summarized in McGreevey, *Economic History* (cited in n. 11), do not include contraband, which Brew thinks might have amounted to a quarter of official gold exports.

17. This is the conclusion reached by José Antonio Ocampo after a painstaking effort to reconstruct the pattern of Colombia's nineteenth-century foreign trade, "Las importaciones colombianas en el siglo XIX," in Miguel Urrutia et al., *Ensayos sobre historia económica colombiana* (Bogotá, 1980), pp. 99-142. Ocampo's work corrects some aspects of McGreevey's earlier estimates of Colombia's nineteenth-century foreign trade, but his conclusions confirm the thesis, developed in Part Two of McGreevey's work, that the Colombian economy failed to respond dynamically to the challenge of export-oriented development in a liberal capitalist world economy during the entire nineteenth century.

roughly 4 million people made it the third most populous nation in South America, yet its exports per capita were among the lowest in the hemisphere.[18]

Within this framework of secular export stagnation the turbulent and inconclusive political history of nineteenth-century Colombia took form.[19] In broad outline, the national political fortunes of the Liberal and Conservative parties—and the fate of liberal political economy—paralleled the fortunes of export agriculture. A tobacco boom during the third quarter of the century provided a tenuous material base for the merchant-led Liberal governments that managed to win precarious control of the state and transform the major institutions of the nation along the lines of liberal political economy during the 1850's and 1860's. The value of tobacco exports, produced in a small enclave in the middle Magdalena Valley, rose suddenly to average between two and three million gold pesos during most years between 1850 and 1875. But the collapse of the tobacco export economy after the latter year, coupled with declining demand and prices for Colombia's other important nongold exports (principally quinine), fatally undermined the material base, political strength, and ideological appeal of Colombian liberalism. During the 1860's and 1870's Liberals managed to defeat insurgent Conservative forces on the battlefield. In 1885, at the nadir of the depression in export agriculture, a divided and discredited Liberal party offered only token resistance to a Conservative restoration.

The accession to power in Colombia in 1886 of a Conservative regime bent on restoring Church privileges and pursuing economic and monetary policies bitterly opposed by import-export interests and dramatically at odds with liberal economic orthodoxy in the Western world reversed the direction of nineteenth-century Colombian history. Thereafter, until the start of the twentieth century, Colombia followed a political course anomalous in the pattern of late-nineteenth-century developments in the other nations of the region. In all the other major countries of Latin America (Chile and Argentina are good examples) governments devoted to the principles of cosmopolitan liberal political economy consolidated themselves in power after 1880. Whatever the precise political form these regimes assumed, they all presided over the expansion of viable national export economies, constructed the bases for effective national government, and expanded the institutions of ruling-class consensus and ideological hegemony. Even in nations such as Venezuela where export-

18. In 1971 McGreevey estimated average annual per capita exports for the late 1890's at only about four current U.S. dollars: *Economic History* (cited in n. 11), Table 13, p. 104.

19. The analysis of nineteenth-century politics sketched in the remainder of this section is developed and documented in my *Coffee and Conflict*, cited in n. 4. I do not attempt here to recapitulate fully the argument developed in that book.

oriented economies and polities were not yet fully consolidated, the proponents of liberal political economy were not forced onto the defensive by reactionary conservative forces as they were in Colombia. The strength in Colombia of conservative forces opposed to liberal political economy at the end of the nineteenth century revealed the entrenched character of a traditional agrarian society only temporarily and superficially affected by export-oriented economic development during the entire nineteenth century.

In this way, the boom and bust and long-term failure of export agriculture structured the political history of the nation during its long nineteenth century. Agricultural export cycles defined the period of liberal hegemony during the third quarter of the century, and the extraordinary resurgence of conservative forces in the fourth. The ephemeral successes and enduring failure of export agriculture thus perpetuated and intensified the struggle between Liberal and Conservative elites. In the process, however, politics in Colombia acquired a life and logic of its own, a form and dynamic unique within the nations of the region.

The outstanding feature of the political system formed in Colombia during the nineteenth century was the high degree of popular participation in the struggle between ruling-class factions for control of the state. That participation was the result of the willingness of political leaders to mobilize popular forces in the battle for political hegemony. Their readiness to do so reflected the enduring inability of each faction to impose its will and vision on the whole of Colombian society. In the absence of viable export-based development, the resources of the state, meager as they were, proved decisive in tipping the balance of power between the contending political factions. The conquest and preservation of state power nonetheless depended on the ability to defeat rivals through electoral means or outright warfare. And that ability, in turn, depended on broad popular support. Political elites mobilized the artisans and rural agricultural laborers who made up the great majority of Colombian society because they were not afraid of the social consequences. During the course of its incessant nineteenth-century internecine struggles, the Colombian ruling class was occasionally confronted with embryonic horizontal class alignments, or with evidence that the duration and intensity of civil violence threatened a breakdown of social control. On those occasions elite factions quickly forgot their differences and united to eliminate the threat to their class dominion. Such occasions were rare, however, and with time virtually all social tensions were diverted into the clientelistic channels of the two great political parties. This outcome reflected, at least in part, the relative ethnic and cultural homogeneity of Colombia's precapitalist agrarian society. Popular forces were denied a collective base on which to build a separate identity and an independent vision of the world.

To mobilize the popular classes who gave their blood in the interminable struggle between the factions of the elite, political leaders resorted to a variety of means. These ranged from outright economic coercion of dependent rural workers to ideological appeals to Christian values and democratic ideals shared by the popular classes. They included the promise of paternalistic aid, the possibility of clientelistic spoils, the likelihood of justice in the courts. During hard times and civil commotion the simple opportunity to trade the certainty of poverty and personal insecurity at home for the fortunes of war might induce rural workers to enlist in one or another army or local guerrilla force.

Political and social elites were not the only potential beneficiaries of sectarian political struggle, however, nor the popular classes its exclusive victims. Individual members of the elite could lose their lives or part with material fortune in civil warfare. Members of lower strata could improve their life chances through participating in political struggle. But only elements of the ruling class could hope to improve both their individual fortunes and the position of their class faction in the struggle over liberal principles and political hegemony.

The mobilization of popular social strata in chronic civil warfare gradually polarized Colombian society into two opposing multiclass blocs of political antagonists. For members of the working class, political affiliation began over issues as concrete and rational as access to land or physical protection. But once a man had killed in the name of one party, or seen his friends or relatives despoiled at the hands of the other, loyalty to the political collectivity became something more complex, abstract, and emotional. With time, identification with one or the other party became hereditary. Political loyalties passed from father to son as a complex of rational material calculations and memories of transcendental deeds and injustices. Party affiliation began to crystallize a peculiar Colombian political geography. At the level of the departments, as a result of regional ruling-class social and economic interests, one or the other political collectivity became predominant. At the municipal level, local strongmen, Liberal or Conservative, manipulated economic power and ties to the national party to distribute favors and the benefits of control over police and the courts. Even at the level of *veredas*, the subdivisions of Colombian *municipios* (counties), smallholders or sharecroppers of one political affiliation might enlist the support of local urban politicians and lawyers in their resistance to large landowners—or to other rural smallholders—of opposite political loyalties.

These then were the essential features of a unique political system forged in a century of inconclusive conflict over liberal political economy in a culturally homogeneous agrarian society still largely isolated from the world market. Colombia emerged from the nineteenth century with a polity deeply divided into two opposing parties, each cemented together by clientelist ties and hereditary partisan loyalties sealed in blood on a hundred battlefields during three generations of civil struggle.

But if the Colombian political system provided rival elite factions with powerful party vehicles in their still-inconclusive struggle for political hegemony, if it channeled popular social tensions in traditional political ways, it was by no means entirely functional for ruling-class needs. It periodically disrupted civil life and impeded economic development and private accumulation. It created a dynamic of its own that limited the maneuverability of politicians and moderate factions in the pursuit of consensus and compromise over issues vital to the class as a whole. The depth of popular politicization, the dynamic of clientelism, and the legacy of civil warfare rewarded the most partisan and opportunistic leaders within the two traditional parties. The Colombian political system thus retarded, and always complicated, the historical evolution toward consensus within the ruling class around the principles of liberal political economy.

The catastrophe that befell the nation at the end of the nineteenth century plainly revealed the dangerous threat to elite interests of the political system they themselves had molded. During the 1890's the long-sought consensus over the issues of liberal political economy that had divided the elite throughout the century seemed finally within grasp. Coffee exports expanded five times between 1886 and 1896, and by the last year they stood at over half a million 60-kilogram bags valued at more than 10 million gold pesos.[20] During this period, bipartisan liberal reformers, united by their interests in the coffee export economy, joined forces in opposition to the sectarian Conservative regime that had consolidated control over the state during the crisis of export agriculture in the 1880's. But their concerted efforts to institutionalize economic and political reforms and avert a new civil conflict ended in disaster. A sharp decline in world coffee prices plunged the Colombian economy into crisis at the end of the 1890's. Moderate liberal reformers lost control of their respective parties to extremist sectarian leaders, and the nation was plunged once more into civil war. The great war that enveloped Colombian society between 1899 and 1902 was the largest civil conflict fought in Colombia or any other Latin American nation during the nineteenth century. But it ended, after

20. These are official government statistics. República de Colombia, Ministerio de Industrias, *Memoria, 1927* (Bogotá, 1927), p. 228. The actual volume and value of coffee exports may have been higher. Estimates greater by more than 20 percent were reported by British consular officials. See Table 8 in William Paul McGreevey, "The Transition to Economic Growth in Colombia," in Roberto Cortés Conde and Shane Hunt, eds., *The Export Sector and Economic Development in Latin America*, forthcoming.

the death of some 100,000 Colombians, with the military defeat of the Liberal forces. Colombia entered the new century with its still modest coffee export economy in crisis, and the struggle over the principles of political economy still unresolved.

Only after the war did the bipartisan liberal reformers finally emerge victorious. The war discredited the extremist leaders of both parties. It left in its wake unprecedented human and economic destruction, monetary chaos, the incipient collapse of elite social control, and, with the separation of Panama in 1903, the dismemberment of the nation. Following the war, in the context first of gradual recovery, then of remarkable expansion of the coffee export economy, moderates from both parties were able to overcome the partisan dynamics of the Colombian political system and institutionalize the liberal political and economic principles that have guided the development of Colombian society ever since.

Finally, then, after almost a century of civil war and unsuccessful export-oriented development, Colombian society stabilized politically and began the dynamic phase of export-oriented development that had eluded liberal leaders for so long. The bitter, protracted nineteenth-century transition to elite consensus and export-oriented economic development left a powerful political legacy, however. It saddled Colombians with a unique political system that has endured to influence every aspect of Colombian society to the present day.

Coffee soon ushered in a new era of ruling-class consensus, political stability, and export-oriented development. But coffee did not transform the political system Colombians inherited from the nineteenth century. Rather, it reinforced its socially most destructive features. In the special structure of Colombia's coffee export economy—and the social forces it called forth—lie the reasons for Colombia's anomalous political development in this century, the primary cause of the stubborn survival of a destructive political system forged in the struggles of the last.

The Development of a Coffee Economy

Paced by a dynamic coffee export sector, the Colombian economy has turned in a record of growth and diversification during this century virtually unmatched among the other countries of Latin America. The primary basis for this dramatic economic growth before mid-century was an export sector whose special structure favored domestic capital accumulation and fostered expansion even during the crisis of the world economy in the 1930's. Full explanation of the impressive economic development of the nation during the last three decades, however, lies a step further removed from export structure. Unlike its counterparts in other major Latin American nations, the Colombian ruling class has not been forced to compromise its principles of political economy in response to organized working-class pressure in recent decades. Throughout this century, it has been able to take full advantage of the changing opportunities for liberal capitalist development within an evolving world system. Coffee both promoted economic growth and at the same time inhibited the organization and cultural autonomy of the popular forces that elsewhere challenged liberal principles and undermined the political legitimacy and cultural monopoly of the ruling class. This section of the essay looks briefly at the first issue—how the structure of the coffee export economy directly promoted Colombian economic development. Once the structure of the coffee export economy is clear, and the direct influence of coffee exports on the nation's economic development established, we can turn to the larger, more complex question of the relationship between the coffee export economy and the political history of the nation. That history pivots on the development of the Colombian labor movement, which is in turn defined by the organizational fate of workers in coffee production.

Colombian coffee exports expanded dramatically for a half century after 1900. By 1905 they had recovered from the end-of-the-century depression and the dislocation of war to reach levels first attained in the mid-1890's, some half a million 60-kilogram bags per year. Thereafter, a gradual improvement in world prices (they reached 10 cents a pound in 1910, 15 cents in 1920, and an extraordinary 28 cents at their peak in 1926) stimulated explosive growth in the Colombian coffee economy. Within eight years, in 1913, exports reached a million bags; in another eight years, in 1921, they topped 2 million. By 1930, as world coffee prices plummeted, exports reached 3 million bags. Eight years of world depression, during which coffee prices averaged about 10 cents per pound (and fell as low as 8 cents per pound in some years), translated not into a decline but rather into an increase of 1 million bags to the level of 4 million by 1937. Coffee exports reached 5 million bags in 1943, after which the rate of expansion slowed. Despite record high prices between 1945 and 1956, it was not until 1953 that exports topped 6 million bags. They stayed at roughly that level until the 1970's. (Figure 5.1 summarizes trends in the volume and value of Colombian coffee exports, 1870-1970). Colombia's coffee exports expanded at a rate of more than 7 percent per year in the 1910's and 1920's, and 5 percent during the Depression of the 1930's.[21]

The rapidly growing value of Colombian coffee exports stimulated an

21. José Antonio Ocampo and Santiago Montenegro, "La crisis mundial de los años treinta en Colombia," paper given at the conference "The Effects of the 1929 Depression on Latin America," St. Anthony's College, Oxford, Sept. 20-23, 1981, p. 14.

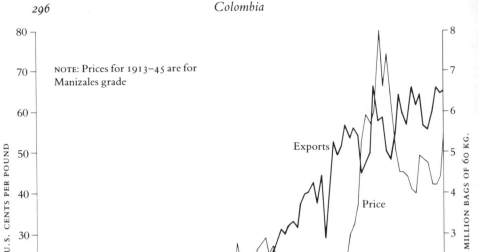

Figure 5.1. Colombian Coffee Exports and Prices of Colombian Coffee on the New York Market, 1870-1970. Sources: 1870-1945, Robert Carlyle Beyer, "The Colombian Coffee Industry: Origins and Major Trends, 1740-1940" (Ph.D. diss., University of Minnesota, 1947), Appendix Tables I and IV; 1946-70, Federación Nacional de Cafeteros de Colombia, División Commercial.

enormous increase in Colombian foreign trade between 1905 and 1929. In the period 1905-9 the annual value of Colombian exports and imports averaged about 26 million dollars; by 1925-29 that value averaged 200 million, an eightfold increase. During the first three decades of the century, despite considerable expansion of gold, banana, and (after 1925) petroleum exports, coffee exports rose from 40 to more than 70 percent of the value of Colombia's total exports. That percentage declined somewhat owing to the sharp drop in coffee prices during the Depression, but by the 1940's it rose again to about 70 percent, and in the 1950's approached 80 percent. Customs duties levied on the imports made possible by the expansion of coffee exports provided a major proportion of the government's revenues during the first half of the twentieth century. Between 1912 and 1928 alone, annual ordinary government income (that is, excluding loans) expanded from 14 to 61 million pesos. Customs duties provided two-thirds of government revenues at the start of this period, between one-third and one-half of those revenues during the 1920's and 1930's. Only in the 1940's did the weight of customs revenues in the national budget begin to be offset by direct taxes.[22]

The remarkable expansion of the coffee export economy enabled the Colombian government to become a major recipient of the flood of finance capital emanating from New York banks in the years preceding the Great Depression. U.S. loans to Colombian government entities, more than half of them to departments and municipios (especially those of the coffee-producing regions) totaled some 260 million dollars during the 1920's. No Latin American nation witnessed such a rapid rate of increase in the value of foreign investments during that decade. U.S. indemnification for the loss of Panama, 25 million dollars, paid to Colombia in installments in the mid-1920's, and spent on railway construction, added to the influx of foreign capital.[23]

Foreign loans fostered a revolution in Colombian transport. Railroad trackage, much of it serving the coffee trade, doubled between 1913 and 1929; the number of passengers and the volume of freight these rail lines carried expanded eight times during the same period. Highways suitable for automobile and truck traffic were virtually nonexistent in 1913; they had expanded to some 1,500 kilometers by 1929. Large-scale aerial cable systems were built to carry coffee out of the Central Cordillera down to the Magdalena and Cauca rivers. After 1919 airline service expanded to link Colombia's larger cities. Large-scale construction of transportation systems and other projects financed by foreign loans to provide electrical, telephone, and sewage systems as well as public buildings for Colombia's major cities stimulated the whole economy and created tens of thousands of jobs outside agriculture. Among these new free-wage workers, those employed in railway and river transport were among the first, and, as it developed, the most successful, in organizing unions to improve wages and work conditions.

Meanwhile, foreign capitalists also invested directly in the Colombian

22. These included a modest income tax instituted in 1936. A convenient source for statistical information on trade in the 1920's is José Alberto Pérez Toro, "La gran depresión de 1930 en Colombia," *Comercio Exterior* 12:11 (Nov. 1980), pp. 3-75. Statistics on the national budget and the sources of government revenue are summarized in Jésus Antonio Bejarano, "Fin de la economía exportadora," *Cuadernos Colombianos* Nos. 6, 7, and 8 (1975), Tables 24 and 25, pp. 292-93.

23. An overview of U.S. investments in Colombia during this period is J. Fred Rippy, *The Capitalists and Colombia* (Durham, N.C., 1931). A detailed recent analysis of these trends, based on the primary documents of the Kemmerer mission which helped reorganize Colombia finance in the early 1920's, is Paul Drake, "The Origins of United States Economic Supremacy in South America: Colombia's Dance of the Millions, 1923-33," Working Paper No. 40, Latin American Program, The Wilson Center, Washington, D.C., 1980, pp. 1-77.

economy. These investments, almost exclusively from the United States, focused on export activities that, unlike coffee, required large infusions of capital and depended on sophisticated technology. This was true of the banana enclave located along the Caribbean coast near Santa Marta, where the U.S.-based United Fruit Company expanded production rapidly during the first decades of the century. It was also true of petroleum production, focused primarily in the middle Magdalena River near the port of Barrancabermeja. There, Tropical Oil, an affiliate of Standard Oil of New Jersey, began commercial production for export after 1925. Between 1913 and 1929 U.S. private investment in Colombia, most of it in petroleum, a smaller amount in bananas and gold production, expanded from an estimated 2 or 4 million dollars to 20 million. The foreign-owned banana and oil export enclaves employed several thousand workers by the end of the 1920's, but they contributed only a small percentage of Colombia's export earnings, which remained dominated by coffee. (Bananas accounted for 6 percent of the value of total exports at their peak in the late 1920's; oil, some 17 percent during the same period; precious metals, 5 percent.) In the foreign banana and oil export enclaves Colombian workers found conditions favorable to collective organization. It was there that they mounted a series of spectacular strikes that temporarily shook the foundations of the Colombian political order in the late 1920's.[24]

While the quantitative growth of the coffee export economy and the impact of its rapid expansion on foreign trade, government revenue, and foreign investment can be statistically measured, the structural characteristics that economy assumed in the course of this century are not so easily established. There is no debate over the nationality of ownership of the means of coffee production. Although no statistics exist to measure the proportion of foreign owners of Colombian coffee farms, all observers agree that though foreign ownership was not negligible (and may have increased in certain periods such as the 1920's), it was never extensive. The overwhelming proportion of Colombian coffee farms, large and small alike, remained in the hands of nationals.

The issue of the relative concentration of ownership in the industry is quite another matter. Because this issue lies at the heart of the myth of Colombia's smallholder civilization, and of the debate over the economic and political influence of smallholders on the course of national developments, its illumination is vital to an understanding of modern Colombian history. Yet because the issue has been purposely obscured by the Colombian ruling class, and systematically misinterpreted by many left-

24. The figures in these paragraphs are from Rippy, *The Capitalists*, pp. 177-78, 152.

TABLE 5.1
Coffee Properties Classified by Number of Trees in the Major Colombian Coffee-Producing Departments, 1932

Department	Number of farms with the following numbers of trees:					Total no. of properties
	Fewer than 5,000 trees	From 5,001 to 20,000	From 20,001 to 60,000	From 60,001 to 100,000	Over 100,000	
Antioquia	24,434	3,531	518	65	41	28,589
Caldas	36,475	3,411	260	23	5	40,174
Cauca	12,194	283	—	—	—	12,477
Cundinamarca	12,474	922	257	68	91	13,812
N. de Santander	5,128	2,416	352	38	38	7,972
Santander	1,500	1,128	303	51	63	3,045
Tolima	9,610	2,670	369	62	60	12,771
Valle	18,477	1,514	71	3	4	20,069
Other dep'ts	9,264	1,046	96	14	19	10,439
TOTALS	129,556	16,921	2,226	324	321	149,348
Pct. of farms	86.75%	11.33%	1.49%	0.22%	0.21%	
Pct. of trees	48.79%	24.67%	12.57%	5.51%	8.46%	

SOURCE: Censo Cafetero, *Boletín de Estadística* 1:5 (Feb. 1933):122.

ist scholars, that task is not an easy one. It must start with critical analysis of the major source available to historians, the vexed coffee censuses of the middle decades of the twentieth century.

The first of these systematic coffee censuses, published in 1932, apparently demonstrated that the structure of ownership of the means of coffee production in Colombia was highly diffused (see Table 5.1). That census showed that of the 149,348 coffee farms tabulated, 87 percent, containing about half of all coffee trees, were small, with fewer than 5,000 trees. Somewhat larger coffee farms, containing 5,000 to 20,000 trees, accounted for another 11 percent of all coffee farms and a fourth of all trees. Finally, large coffee farms, those with more than 20,000 trees (a few hundred of them with more than 100,000 trees) made up only 2 percent of the coffee farms but contained the other fourth of the trees.

The census takers preferred to tabulate the number of farms; they chose not to explore the structure or tenancy of ownership. In their evaluation of their census the officials of the National Federation of Coffee Growers expressed surprise and great satisfaction over the degree of property division in the coffee economy they claimed to observe in the statistics.

All of these interesting and truly surprising data demonstrate that the coffee industry is not only the fundamental and decisive factor in our national economy, but that it constitutes at the same time an admirable element of social equilibrium, since because of the very nature of its organization, and circumstances exceptionally favorable to providing adequate and almost permanent work to women and

TABLE 5.2

*Coffee Properties Classified by Number of Trees in Cundinamarca
and Tolima, 1932 and 1939*

	Number of farms with the following numbers of trees:					
	Fewer than 5,000 trees	From 5,001 to 20,000	From 20,001 to 60,000	From 60,001 to 100,000	Over 100,000	Total no. of properties
Cundinamarca						
1932	12,474	922	257	68	91	13,812
1939	25,826	3,874	406	76	88	30,270
Tolima						
1932	9,610	2,670	369	62	60	12,771
1939	22,555	5,021	511	68	62	28,217

SOURCE: Table 5.1 and "Censo Cafetero en los Departamentos de Cundinamarca y Tolima," *Boletín de Estadística*, no. 24 (Apr. 1943):62.

children, it is accomplishing on its own, automatically, without need for laws or for expropriations, the phenomenon of property division.[25]

In fact, any of the farms listed in the census might have been owned and operated by the same person, administered by an absentee owner, rented, or sharecropped. Moreover, the same person, extended family, or firm might own several of the farms counted separately.

This failure to address the issue of tenancy, repeated in the partial coffee census of 1939, has been interpreted cynically by several scholars in recent years. These observers have argued that property in the coffee zone was much more concentrated than the 1932 and subsequent census data implied, that the thousands of coffee workers cultivating one or two hectares and less than 5,000 trees were poverty-stricken farmers forced to labor much of the time on neighboring large coffee estates, that precapitalist forms of tenancy and labor service were the norm in Colombian coffee production during the first decades of the century. All of these points, as we shall see, are correct, yet at the same time fundamentally misleading.

As coffee cultivation expanded in Colombia during the 1930's, the number of small coffee farms mushroomed. At least that is the conclusion to be drawn from a comparison of the 1932 census and the coffee census of 1939, which was completed for only two major coffee departments, Cundinamarca and Tolima (see Table 5.2). Judging from the increase in the number of trees cultivated in these departments during this seven-year interval, coffee production probably increased about 75 percent. During the same period, however, the number of coffee farms in these two departments doubled. Table 5.2 reveals that there were increases in the number of coffee farms of all sizes *except* the largest, those of 60,000 and those of over 100,000 trees. In Cundinamarca the fastest

25. Editorial, "El censo cafetero," in *Boletín de Estadística* 1:5 (Feb. 1933), p. 117.

rate of increase was in the 5,000- to 20,000-tree category; in Tolima it was in the small farms (fewer than 5,000 trees). The 1939 census, like the previous one done by the National Federation of Coffee Growers, tells us nothing directly about the ownership of these thousands of small, medium, and large coffee farms. Like the census of 1932, it obscures the question of tenancy.

The next census, taken in 1955 under the auspices of the Economic Commission for Latin America and the Food and Agriculture Organization of the United Nations, was based on a large, representative sample of coffee farms in Colombia. Like the previous censuses, the ECLA/FAO census of 1955 demonstrated the continuing diffuseness of coffee production in Colombia. It estimated that there were 214,270 producing coffee farms in the country, plus an additional 20,204 new farms with trees (under three years old) not yet in production. That was an increase in producing farms of 65,122 over the figure in the national coffee census of 1932. The number of producing coffee farms increased in all Colombian departments between 1932 and 1955. The big gains, however, came not in the Central Cordillera, in the major coffee-producing departments of Caldas, Antioquia, and Valle, where all observers agree small farms were historically more common. They came instead in the two other important coffee-growing departments, Cundinamarca and Tolima, departments that had the largest concentration of big coffee farms in 1932.[26] Cundinamarca and Tolima alone, with increases of 13,808 and 13,749 farms respectively, accounted for 42 percent of the national expansion in the number of producing coffee farms between 1932 and 1955; Antioquia, with a rise of 1,732 producing farms, Caldas, with 4,021, and Valle, with 1,420, together accounted for only 11 percent of that increase. (All of the rest of the increase came in the minor coffee-growing departments, which combined produced only 15 percent of Colombia's coffee in 1955.)[27]

Far more important than this information, however, was the fact that for the first time, the ECLA/FAO census clarified the issue of tenancy arrangements in the Colombian coffee economy. These data are summarized in Tables 5.3 and 5.4. Because the census used a different measure of farm size from the previous coffee censuses (hectares instead of num-

26. Absalón Machado, *El café. De la aparcería al capitalismo* (Bogotá, 1977), Table I, pp. 90-93, shows that comparison with the less formal figures on coffee farm size collected by Diego Monsalve in 1925 reveals that the rapid growth of smaller coffee farms in these departments dates at least from the 1920's. During that period, however, the numbers of large coffee farms also increased, albeit at a slower rate.

27. Adapted from Table 12, p. 26, of Comisión Económica para América Latina y la Organización de las Naciones Unidas para la Agricultura y la Alimentación, *El café en América Latina. Problemas de la productividad y perspectivas. I. Colombia y El Salvador* (Mexico City, 1958) (hereafter cited as CEPAL, *El café*).

TABLE 5.3
Number and Production of Colombian Coffee Farms According to Size, 1955

Size of farm	Number of farms	Pct. of all farms	No. of metric tons produced	Pct. of all production
Up to 1 hectare (fewer than 2,500 trees)	77,245	36.3%	19,129	5.3%
1.1 to 10 hectares (2,500 to 25,000 trees)	123,719	58.1	207,639	57.9
10.1 to 50 hectares (25,000 to 125,000 trees)	11,429	5.4	108,637	30.3
50.1 to 100 hectares (125,000 to 250,000 trees)	447	0.2	13,734	3.9
100.1 to 200 hectares (250,000 to 500,000 trees)	79	—	4,426	1.2
More than 200 hectares (more than 500,000 trees)	51	—	4,996	1.4
TOTALS	212,970	100.0%	338,561	100.0%

SOURCE: Comisión Económica para Américan Latina y la Organización de las Naciones Unidas para la Agricultura y la Alimentación, *El café en América Latina. Problemas de la productividad y perspectivas. I. Colombia y El Salvador* (Mexico City, 1958), Table 18, p. 30.

TABLE 5.4
Percentage of Producing Colombian Coffee Farms According to Type of Administration and Size, 1955

	Up to 1 hectare (fewer than 2,500 trees)	1.1 to 10 ha (2,500 to 25,000)	10.1 to 50 ha (25,000 to 125,000)	More than 50 ha (more than 125,000)
Owner administrator	87.7%	77.9%	57.1%	14.3%
Administrator	2.0	4.6	17.2	71.4
Sharecropper	6.3	16.8	24.3	14.3
Administration by contract	3.9	0.7	1.4	—

SOURCE: Same as Table 5.3, Table 23, p. 33.

ber of trees), I have entered in parentheses in the tables an equivalent measure in trees. The census computed an average in Colombia of about 2,500 coffee trees per hectare.[28]

This crucial information on tenancy, buried in a small table in the census of 1955, reveals the pervasiveness of land ownership by small- and medium-scale producers in the Colombian coffee economy at mid-century. It also establishes, with the help of some additional information, the importance of family-owned-and-operated farms in Colombian coffee production. Estimates of the size of viable family-owned coffee farms in

28. CEPAL, *El café*, Table 17, p. 29. The density of coffee trees, typically much higher in the Eastern Cordillera, varied widely. This procedure is used only to enhance comparability of the figures in the censuses and to illustrate broad trends.

Colombia range from 5,000 to 20,000 trees, 2 to 8 hectares.[29] Farm size is, of course, only one criterion. Viability depended on the size of the family and its age structure, the fertility of the land, the age of the coffee trees, the degree of the family's indebtedness, the extent of land in noncoffee production, the price of coffee and other commodities, and so on. On farms smaller than two hectares, however, few coffee-growing families could sustain themselves even under optimal conditions, and some of their members would have to work off the farm for others. This information means that the bulk of the farm units referred to in Table 5.4 in the 1.1 to 10 hectare size, 78 percent of which were owned by their operators, were probably owner-operated family farms. Table 5.3 suggests that the number of such farms in 1955 was in the tens of thousands.

It is of course risky to project this vital information on the importance of smallholders back onto the 1932 and 1939 censuses. It is quite likely that ownership was much less widespread in 1932, and that sharecropping, still important in 1955, was much more prevalent in the earlier period. But the 1955 coffee census demonstrated what the earlier censuses done by the National Federation of Coffee Growers had implied. It showed that land ownership was very widespread in Colombian coffee production and that small family farms made up the most numerous and important unit of Colombian coffee production. It seems likely that over the whole period, 1932 to 1955, property ownership in the Colombian coffee economy was also widespread and that large numbers of owner-operated family farms existed. At any rate, the historical trajectory of coffee production in Colombia during these decades led to that result by 1955. To deny this central feature of Colombian coffee production is to miss the most important historical facts implied in the censuses of the 1930's and confirmed in the census of 1955. Ownership of the means of production in the Colombian coffee economy was national, and, if highly unequal, very widespread. Each of these characteristics, as we shall see, deeply influenced the modern political and labor history of the nation. Each of them also had important implications for Colombian economic history in the twentieth century.

Because of its special structure, the Colombian coffee export economy proved highly conducive to national economic development. The fact that ownership of coffee production units was national and spread among tens of thousands of individual Colombians meant that much of the economic surplus and foreign exchange generated by coffee exports stayed

29. The best discussions of this issue I have seen are Richard Loxley Smith, "Los Cafeteros: Social and Economic Development in a Colombian Coffee Municipio" (Ph.D. diss., University of Oregon, 1974), pp. 88-92; and in Chapter 3 of Nicolás Buenaventura, "Proletariado agrícola," in *Estudios Marxistas* 1 (Apr.-June 1969):1-85.

within the country. From the beginning, it is true, foreign merchant capital financed much of the expansion of Colombian coffee production. Foreign import, roasting, and distribution firms, based in France, Germany, England, and increasingly the United States, captured a large share of the value added to Colombian coffee as it moved off the farm for processing in Colombian towns and cities and was then shipped and sold in the consumer markets of the North Atlantic. None of these activities, however, was monopolized by foreign capital.

Colombians owned the bulk of the coffee-husking plants, called *trilladoras*, where coffee beans, already semiprocessed, dried, and selected on farms, were stripped of their parchmentlike husks, sorted, graded by women workers called *escogedoras*, and bagged for export. The Colombian government came to own most of the railroads (some built with Colombian capital, others financed with foreign loans) that carried coffee down the slopes to the Magdalena River, and up the Cauca Valley and hence to the sea at Buenaventura, the Pacific port that eventually came to handle the bulk of Colombian coffee exports after the opening of the Panama Canal in 1914. Colombians shared in the ownership of the steam-navigation companies that transported coffee down the Magdalena to the country's major Caribbean port at Barranquilla. As early as the 1890's, Colombian merchants established export-import houses, engaged primarily in the coffee trade, in New York and some European cities. In the 1920's, as U.S. import firms threatened to monopolize Colombia's domestic and international coffee trade, large Colombian coffee producers and coffee exporters organized effectively to capture greater control over the Colombian coffee economy. The National Federation of Coffee Growers, established in 1927, moved decisively in the 1930's and 1940's to control the internal price of coffee and to extend credit to producers. The Federation built facilities to store and process coffee and developed aggressive programs to ensure the high and uniform quality of Colombian coffee exports, to broaden Colombia's international coffee market, and, finally, to create a Colombian merchant marine (the Flota Gran Colombiana, established with Venezuela in the 1940's) to ensure Colombian participation in the international coffee-carrying trade. In all these ways Colombian capitalists managed to capture profits generated in the production, processing, and transport of coffee. The involvement of foreign capital in all these operations was significant. But Colombian capitalists were able to tap an important and increasing share of the opportunities for capital accumulation within the industry.[30]

30. For detail on these themes see Robert Carlyle Beyer, "The Colombian Coffee Industry: Origins and Major Trends, 1774-1940" (Ph.D. diss., University of Minnesota, 1947); Marco Palacios, *Coffee in Colombia, 1850-1970* (Cambridge, Eng., 1980); and Bennett Eugene Koffman, "The National Federation of Coffee-Growers of Colombia" (Ph.D. diss., University of Virginia, 1969).

Students of Colombian economic history have long stressed the contribution of small-scale coffee production to the country's economic development in the twentieth century. Contrary to what occurred in many other Latin American export economies, they note, where initially most earnings were remitted abroad, or were concentrated in the hands of a few and squandered in luxury consumption of foreign imports, earnings from coffee production in Colombia were widely, if thinly, spread. Smallholders, especially those who owned family farms, broadened the market for basic goods and services. They created, for example, a demand for improved educational systems for their children, for the hand-operated coffee depulping machines every small coffee farm required, and for the nationally made cotton clothing and fiber sandals most coffee workers wore by the 1940's. These ideas seem to be confirmed in the relatively higher literacy rates in major coffee departments such as Caldas, or in the industrialization of Antioquia, a process in which foreign capital played little role until after mid-century.[31]

Other scholars, however, have discounted the importance of coffee smallholders, whom they consider too impoverished and self-sufficient to stimulate new industrial demand. They argue that Colombia's impressive record of industrial development since the 1920's resulted from the other side of the structure of the Colombian coffee economy, from the opportunity for domestic capitalist accumulation in a coffee economy characterized by extreme inequality in access to the means of production and by commercial monopoly over the means of exchange.[32] These two arguments, whose relative importance in stimulating Colombian economic developments awaits empirical study, are complementary, not mutually exclusive. It is likely that the structure of production, processing, and commerce in the Colombian coffee economy both fostered accumulation in the hands of Colombian capitalists and broadened the national market for agricultural and industrial production. Capitalists—the Ospina family of Antioquia being a good example—were involved simultaneously in the production and commercialization of coffee and in the development of manufacturing industry. At the same time, the geographical spread of coffee production, its relatively simple technology, and its diffuse pattern of production fostered the development of a national market and the creation of the "backward, forward, and horizontal linkages" U.S. economist Albert Hirschman first observed in Colombia

31. William Paul McGreevey systematically developed these ideas (first applied to Cuban history by Fernando Ortiz in the work cited in n. 5) in Chapter 9 of his *Economic History,* cited in n. 11. The importance of smallholders in the economic evolution of the nation is persuasively advanced in the work of Hugo López. See his "La inflación en Colombia en la década de los veintes," *Cuadernos Colombianos* No. 5 (1975), pp. 43-139.

32. The most systematic exposition of this view is Mariano Arango, *Café e industria, 1850-1930* (Bogotá, 1977).

and later developed into a celebrated explanation of the unequal development potentials of different export economies.[33]

Historically, however, the structure and dynamics of Colombia's coffee export economy had a richer, more complex impact on economic development than either of these ideal positions suggests. For example, it was an increase in working-class consumption in the coffee-producing regions that helped make it possible for Colombia to become a major recipient of foreign finance capital in the 1920's. Payment of the flood of foreign loans contracted by Colombia's national, departmental, and municipal governments during the 1920's was guaranteed by revenues from indirect taxes on items of mass consumption. The departmental governments, which were the major recipients of these loans, guaranteed payment with moneys from taxes on tobacco, liquor, and the slaughter of livestock; the national government, for its part, paid for foreign loans with customs receipts, the bulk of them generated by imports of textiles consumed by the working class. These foreign loans, as we have seen, were invested in the construction of transport systems and public works. The loans thus stimulated economic development in two ways. They helped to unify a national market for domestic agricultural products, construction materials, and manufactures. And they deepened the national market by creating tens of thousands of relatively high-paying jobs for workers who previously had worked in agriculture, subsisting largely outside the money economy. Thanks to the rapid growth of the coffee export sector, and the foreign loans it made possible, Colombia's per capita gross domestic product was expanding by the last half of the 1920's at a rate in excess of 5 percent a year. During this same period, 1925-29, industrial production grew almost 20 percent, while capital investment in industry increased almost 50 percent, a difference which created an excess of installed capacity that was turned to import substitution with the advent of the international Depression.

But the economic change fostered by the coffee export economy was not simply quantitative. As Jesús Antonio Bejarano showed in a seminal essay published in 1975,[34] it precipitated a qualitative transformation in

33. Albert Hirschman, "A Generalized Linkage Approach to Development, with Special Reference to Staples," *Economic Development and Cultural Change*, 25, supplement (1977):67-98. McGreevey points out the connection between Hirschman's experience as a consulting economist in Colombia and his thinking about the linkage effects of export economies in "The Transition" (cited in n. 20).

34. Bejarano, "Fin de la economía exportadora" (cited in n. 22). As a rich and powerful interpretation of the impact of coffee-paced growth on labor demand and precapitalist social relations of production, Bejarano's essay stands as one of the outstanding contributions to twentieth-century Colombian historiography. To the extent, however, that Bejarano implies that the contradictions in Colombia's capitalist development, revealed in the 1920's and pinpointed in the writings of progressive intellectuals such as Alejandro López, led to the

the nature of Colombia's peripheral capitalist society. During the 1920's demand for labor in export and domestic agriculture, in public works and railway and highway construction, and in a small but burgeoning industrial sector undermined the precapitalist productive relations that predominated in Colombian agriculture, especially in the all-important coffee sector. This process, analyzed in more detail below, had tremendous implications beyond its meaning for the capitalist economic development of the nation. It triggered the first great mobilization of Colombian rural workers, compromised the unity of the Colombian ruling class, and unleashed the social and political struggle that convulsed Colombian society in the 1930's and ended in the Violence of the 1940's.

Even as it worked to drive forward this disruptive social and political process in the decades after 1930, however, the coffee export economy continued to foster the economic growth and diversification of the nation's economy. As we have seen, despite the drastic fall in world coffee prices during the Depression, the volume of Colombian coffee exports continued to expand rapidly. Carlos Díaz Alejandro, who has compared the performance of Latin American economies during the world crisis, provides the following indicators of the export quantum for major nations of the region during the period 1932-33 to 1952-53 (1928-29 = 100).[35]

	1932-33	1938-39	1948-49	1952-53
Argentina	85	70	57	41
Brazil	93	162	175	133
Colombia	100	132	160	177
Chile	36	87	97	89
Mexico	60	49	44	58
Venezuela	91	145	368	491

Actually, these figures, which include all exports, understate the role of coffee in increasing the export quantum in Colombia during the 1930's, a decade during which Colombian banana and petroleum exports (especially the former) fell far below pre-Depression levels.[36]

---

transformation of political economy under the Liberal regimes of the 1930's, the essay is misleading. Those intellectuals may have wanted to end the political economy of the Conservative "seignorial republic," but the political change in 1930, and the social and economic policies of the 1930's, reflected not so much the rise to power of a national industrial bourgeoisie as they did the defense of the interests of a ruling class formed in the export-oriented development of the first decades of the century and faced by 1930 with a challenge on two fronts: first, the need to adjust to the economic imperatives of the world crisis; second, the need to diffuse the social and political threat posed by an insurgent rural working class. These issues are discussed in more depth in the next section of the essay. The figures in the previous paragraph, cited by Bejarano, p. 356, are from Comisión Económica para América Latina, *El desarrollo económico de Colombia* (Mexico City, 1957).

35. Carlos F. Díaz Alejandro, "Algunas notas sobre la historia económica de América Latina, 1929-1950," Table I, p. 202, in Miguel Urrutia et al., *Ensayos sobre historia económica colombiana* (Bogotá, 1980).

The impressive performance of the Colombian coffee economy during the Depression is partly explained by the nature of coffee production. The coffee tree is a perennial that begins to produce about three years after planting. The species commonly grown in Colombia until recent decades, the *arábigo*, reaches maximum production after about 12 years. Then, although its production slowly declines, proper care can make it produce well for another 10 or even 20 years. To some extent, then, the post-1930 increase in Colombian coffee production can be explained by the coming to maturity and continuing productiveness of trees planted during the period of high prices that preceded the world crisis.

Still, coffee plantings expanded rapidly in Colombia during the Depression as well. The 1939 coffee census revealed an 89 percent increase over 1932 in the number of coffee trees under cultivation in Cundinamarca. For Tolima the increase was 57 percent.[37] This expansion was favored in part by monetary devaluation, a policy championed by the large growers of the National Federation of Coffee Growers.

The primary reason for the expansion of coffee production during the 1930's, however, lies in the social relations of production in the Colombian coffee sector. Expansion pivoted on the ability of small producers to withstand the decline in returns to their labor, on their willingness to exploit themselves and their families in order to produce more coffee despite its low market value. Writing in 1934, the president of the National Federation of Coffee Growers, future national president Mariano Ospina Pérez, pinpointed the locus of Colombia's competitive superiority in a world market suffering from excess production and low prices. "Colombia, because of the enormous parcelization of its coffee properties and the multiplicity of crops grown within each coffee farm, is in a very favorable position to endure a price war. [E]ven supposing that a great part of the coffee harvest were lost or that the price of coffee were to fall considerably, the people of the coffee zone could count on a considerable part of the products they need for their subsistence."[38] Ospina thus defended the policy of no restrictions on coffee exports and opposed efforts to bring Colombia into a pact with Brazil, the world's largest coffee producer, to limit exports. Whereas Brazil was forced to destroy hundreds of thousands of bags of coffee after 1930 in a futile attempt to raise the world price, Colombia, by then the world's largest producer of mild coffee, was able to sell virtually all of its production on the world market at

36. See José Antonio Ocampo, "Comentarios," Table 3, p. 216, in Miguel Urrutia et al., *Ensayos sobre historia económica colombiana.*

37. *Boletín de Estadística* 24 (Apr. 1943):60.

38. From his report to the Sixth National Congress of Coffee Growers, quoted in Ocampo and Montenegro, "La crisis" (cited in n. 21), pp. 22-23.

a price somewhat higher than Brazilian coffee. As a result, Colombia's share of the U.S. market, by far the most important in the world, rose from 23.1 percent in the period 1925-29 to 30.4 percent in the period 1933-37. Meanwhile, Brazil's share of that market fell from 61.8 to 51.9 percent.[39] Colombia's success owed something to climate and soil, but it was related as well to the careful, extremely labor-intensive process of coffee harvesting and processing by small producers, and to the policies of the National Federation of Coffee Growers, which developed effective measures to ensure the high uniform quality of Colombian coffee exports.[40]

The expanding volume of Colombian coffee exports during the 1930's stimulated economic demand within the nation and provided the foreign exchange vital for imports of capital goods and industrial raw materials. The growth in coffee exports thus played a major role in enabling Colombian industrial production to expand at a rate faster during the 1930's than that of other large nations in Latin America. Díaz Alejandro provides the following average annual percentage growth in the value of manufacturing production for the major nations of Latin America during the period 1929-39: Argentina, 3.1; Brazil, 5.0; Chile, 3.3 (a figure for 1927-39); Colombia, 8.8; Mexico, 4.3. During the next ten years, 1939-49, Colombia's industrial performance was only slightly less impressive. The figures are Argentina, 3.5; Brazil, 7.2; Chile, 4.8; Colombia, 6.7; Mexico, 7.5.[41]

The reasons behind the extraordinary growth of Colombian industry during the world crisis are complex. José Antonio Ocampo has shown that excess industrial capacity, devaluation, tariff protection, increased demand, and the ability to import capital goods and raw materials all played a role. If the pre-1929 coffee boom largely explains Colombia's excess industrial capacity at the start of the world crisis, pressure by the Federation of Coffee Growers helps to account for the politics of devaluation. Growing national demand (including, as Ocampo notes, the willingness of Colombia's mass of consumers to buy inferior nationally made manufactures) and relatively high capacity to import are both directly related to expansion of coffee production during the world crisis. That expansion, in turn, owed much to the widespread nature of production and land ownership in Colombia's coffee export economy.

39. Ocampo, "Comentarios," Table 5, p. 218, in Urrutia et al., *Ensayos* (cited in n. 35).

40. Colombian harvesting and processing techniques are discussed in the next section. The Federation required that coffee exporters deposit a percentage of the exports in inferior beans, called *pasilla*, in its warehouses. This coffee was destined for national consumption. On the genesis and development of the Federation and its policies, see Koffman, "The National Federation" (cited in n. 30).

41. Díaz Alejandro, "Algunas notas" (cited in n. 35), Table IV, p. 203.

By the time wartime conditions induced Colombia to join in an international agreement with the United States and Brazil to control volume and price in the coffee trade, Colombia had significantly increased its share of the U.S. market. That agreement, signed in 1940, assured Colombia its market in the United States, but it kept prices artificially low as the war stimulated demand. The agreement thus deprived the Colombian economy and its industry of a great deal of foreign exchange while the war was in progress. With the end of the war, however, and the termination of the international coffee agreement, coffee prices shot up to unprecedented heights after 1946 and remained at that level for a decade. (See Figure 5.1.) The internal demand and foreign exchange generated by the postwar coffee boom stimulated the rapid growth of Colombian industry as it had in the 1920's. In the midst of major civil conflict in the coffee regions, coffee exports—and consequently Colombian foreign exchange earnings—continued to expand in the postwar era.

Since the war, however, the fate of Colombia's economic development has depended as much on an indirect legacy of coffee-based twentieth-century social evolution as it has on the direct contribution of coffee production to national economic development. In recent decades, Colombia, like the other Latin American nations, has had to adjust to a new division of labor in the world capitalist system. The decentralization of manufacturing industry in the world economy has promoted both the expansion and the denationalization of Colombian industry. Within this pattern of industrial development, coffee has served as the Colombian surrogate for heavy industry. It has continued to provide foreign exchange to purchase the growing volume of capital goods and industrial raw materials needed by Colombian industry and to service a foreign debt that has ballooned in the process of the nation's postwar expansion. But Colombia's relative success in pursuing this model of development has depended as well on the organizational weakness of the Colombian labor movement and the impotence of the political left. Coffee ensured that both remained minor impediments to the postwar liberal developmentalist plans of the Colombian ruling class. To appreciate how it did so we must retrace our steps to the era of the 1920's. During that decade Colombian workers first forged powerful organizations and began their struggle to change the order of things in Colombia's booming coffee export economy.

Coffee Workers and the Fate of the Labor Movement

Contrary to the assertions of many scholars, the weakness of the Colombian labor movement is attributable neither to the paucity of European immigration nor to standard conceptions of the failure of leftist leadership.[42] The history of the Colombian labor movement—its late gestation, its explosive and ephemeral strength in the late 1920's and early 1930's, its institutionalization and deradicalization by the Liberal governments between 1930 and 1945, and its repression and co-optation in the years of the Violence after 1945—obeys a dynamic buried deep in the structure of Colombia's coffee export economy.

Between 1920 and 1950 many coffee workers and small producers gradually emerged victorious in the battle to free themselves from oppressive precapitalist labor systems and win control of the means of coffee production. They persisted in this struggle through three decades of alternating economic bonanza, depression, and boom, during which Conservatives and Liberals alternated in control of the national state, and small progressive parties on the left gathered momentum only to collapse. Economic and political change forced workers in coffee production to adapt their tactics to maximize their advantage during the course of the

42. The argument that the absence of European immigration accounts for the lack of class consciousness and political autonomy of the Colombian labor movement is stated forcefully by Marco Palacios, *El populismo en Colombia* (Medellín, 1971), p. 29. "The fact is that the working class could never develop organizational and ideological independence. . . . Contributing in good measure to this [failure] was the absence of migratory flows similar to those experienced by the nations of the Southern Cone, which would have lent a progressive influence and might even have made possible the ideological definition of the working class and the [constitution] of modern forms of political culture." That European immigration did not so simply influence the development of Latin American labor movements is clear in comparative perspective. The strongest left in South America emerged in Chile, where the role of European immigrants was marginal; one of the weakest lefts on the continent developed in Argentina, where the influence of European immigrants was overwhelming. In Colombia, as elsewhere in Latin America, the influence of European working-class ideologies and European anarchist, socialist, and communist activists was important in the development of the workers' movement. That influence, however, was mediated by export structure in the decisive ways each of these essays seeks to illustrate. Palacios correctly stresses the importance of worker identification with the two traditional political parties in frustrating the development of the parties of the left. I have tried to explain such identification in material and class terms, not accept it as a traditional cultural artifact that is a given.

Comparative perspective can also act as a corrective to the excessive, divisive, and destructive voluntarism of much Marxist analysis. Contrary to assertions in many of the Marxist contributions cited in this section, the historical failure of the Colombian left was not a simple consequence of inadequate leadership. As we shall see, it would be hard to show that Colombian Marxists—or, specifically, the members of the Colombian Communist Party—were more guilty of the failure to lead than their counterparts in other countries. Yet that is the argument advanced in the official history of the Communist Party, *Treinta años de lucha del Partido Comunista de Colombia* (Bogotá, 1960), and developed in the popular and otherwise insightful history of the Colombian labor movement by the Communist author Edgar Caicedo, *Historia de las luchas sindicales en Colombia* (3d ed.; Bogotá, 1977), pp. 57-61. Leftists like Caicedo frequently allude to the importance of small property ownership in Colombia. They also recognize the power of liberal ideology over the Colombian working class. But they do not explain why these obstacles to leftist influence have been so inordinately large in Colombia. Nor do they explore the meaning of each for the history of the Colombian left and its strategy for the future.

struggle. Inexorably, however, as they progressed toward their goals, they abandoned the collective strategies that won their early victories. At great cost to themselves and to their society, the collective struggle of workers in coffee production degenerated into private, individual affairs sanctioned by traditional politics. The transformation of their struggle inevitably turned coffee workers against one another. After mid-century it left their class oppressors free to forge a new ideological and political consensus and successfully consolidate an industrializing peripheral capitalist order.

In winning the battle for the land, these workers in coffee production thus lost the struggle to transform the exploitative capitalist society in which they labored. They helped instead to modernize that society, and to reinforce the liberal values and institutions on which it rested. As they achieved their individual victories they helped destroy the power of an organized labor movement in which they were potentially the most important part. As their own collective organizations languished, the unions of their early allies in the foreign-owned export enclaves and in transport and manufacturing industry were left exposed to the corporativist and repressive designs of the state. As they gravitated toward the traditional clientelist politics of the Liberal and Conservative parties, their allies on the political left who had championed and organized their early collective struggles abandoned the fight and cast their fate with the corporativist reformers of the Liberal party.

Finally, in winning their battle for the land, coffee workers and small producers left the structure of commerce and credit in the coffee economy untouched. Domestic capitalists gradually shifted their control over the means of coffee production to a monopoly over the means of coffee exchange. Coffee workers won greater control over the work process and the means of production, only to be exploited more efficiently and easily through capitalist control over coffee commerce. The profound yet Pyrrhic victory of coffee workers, well advanced by mid-century, left a conservative ideological, political, and institutional legacy that the working class and the parties of the left have yet to overcome. Only now, after three decades of impressive industrial development and the capitalist reorganization of agricultural production (including coffee cultivation), is the left beginning to learn how to transcend it.

The weakness of organized labor and the political left in our own time thus has its locus in the democratic struggles of coffee workers in the three decades after 1920. The outcome of that struggle was not determined by the ethnic and cultural origins of a working class untouched by European immigration. It was not a consequence, primarily, of the oft-cited timidity and political errors of the Colombian left. Nor, as we shall see, was it the simple product of especially intelligent, manipulative, or repressive strategies pursued by elements of the Colombian ruling class.[43] It pivoted on the special features of the social relations of production in the motor of the Colombian economy before 1950. It was the product of the hopes and the resolve of the men and women who produced coffee for export.

———————◆——◆———————

Coffee production, as it developed in Colombia in the late nineteenth and early twentieth centuries, depended on a bewildering variety of labor and land tenure systems, all of which shared a central characteristic. They tended to confuse the neat capitalist dichotomy of ownership and free

43. This is the argument advanced in the other major surveys of Colombian labor history, all of which focus on the relationship of labor to the state to explain the liberal trajectory of the Colombian labor movement. Unlike the official Communist version described in note 42, these works, to a greater or lesser degree, attribute the co-optation of the left and the successful liberal institutionalization of labor not to the failure of leftist leadership but to the successful leadership of the Colombian ruling class. Miguel Urrutia's *Development of the Colombian Labor Movement* (New Haven, Conn., 1969), for example, is an intelligent defense of the corporativist liberal institutions that govern Colombian labor relations today. It celebrates the steps through which labor gave up its radical political tendencies and won the support of the state through the efforts of the Liberal party, which held power in the 1930's and early 1940's. These efforts were a consequence of the political weakness of those Liberal governments vis-à-vis the right. Progressive Liberals granted concessions to labor and the left in order to preserve themselves in power and accomplish their reformist mission. Quite apart from the special problem posed by the clientelist dynamic of Colombian politics addressed in this essay, it can be more plausibly argued that the weakness of the reformist Liberals within their own party and vis-à-vis the Conservative opposition came about precisely *because* of their alliance with the labor movement and the left, a step some Liberals were willing to take as progressive members of a ruling class threatened by the rural insurgency described below. The French political scientist Daniel Pecaut argues in his *Política y sindicalismo en Colombia* (Bogotá, 1973) that the "liberal logic" of the Colombian labor movement developed out of the gradual and limited incorporation of organized labor under the Liberal governments of the 1930's and 1940's. One of the few students of the Colombian labor movement to view its history in comparative perspective, Pecaut recognizes that this liberal dynamic developed because of the country's "continuing export potential," its "limited industrialization," and the "weakness of [its] popular classes." But he explains that weakness not as a function of the structure of the coffee economy, which is where his attention to Colombia's position in a world capitalist economy and to ECLA theory might be expected to lead him; rather, he concentrates completely on the changing politics of ruling-class fractions and the passive role of a working class he defines to exclude its most important component, the coffee labor force. Finally, Manuel Moncayo and Fernando Rojas, who write from a Marxist perspective in their *Luchas obreras y política laboral en Colombia* (Bogotá, 1978), see the Colombian labor movement as a victim of the ever more comprehensive effects of corporativist legislation enacted under Conservative and Liberal governments alike. Their exhaustive analysis of the intent of this legislation is a major contribution to Colombian labor studies. But since they do not address the question of why liberal corporativism was comparatively successful in Colombia, one is left with the impression that the Colombian ruling class was simply smarter than, say, the Chilean. Each of these studies enhances understanding of the developing relationship between organized labor and national political and institutional change, but none sees the struggle of Colombian workers as the primary motor behind these changes. None views the liberal corporativist incorporation of the Colombian labor movement from the comparative perspective of the making of a working class in a peripheral economy distinct from the others in the hemisphere.

wage labor. The cultural and ideological result of the peculiar land and labor arrangements in Colombian coffee production was the making of a rural working class in the coffee zones torn between the individualist aspirations of petty capitalists and collective democratic values forged in the struggle for progressive social change. Most of the time, in most places, individualist capitalist aspirations prevailed.[44]

The least modern of the social relations in coffee production were those in the oldest coffee zones, the zones developed in the Eastern Cordillera in the nineteenth century. We know most about these relations in the area to the southeast of Bogotá where the huge coffee haciendas founded at the end of the nineteenth century became the focus of large-scale worker protests during the 1920's and early 1930's. Typically, permanent workers on these estates, called *arrendatarios* or *estancieros*, were granted the use of a small portion of land, a *parcela*. On the parcela, the arrendatario and his family could grow crops such as corn, plantains, yucca (a starchy tuber), and sugarcane for their sustenance, raise fowl and livestock, and construct a house, usually a modest affair made of split bamboo and thatch. In exchange for the use of this land, the arrendatario was obligated to work a certain number of days on the lands of the hacienda, usually in the coffee groves. Depending on the size of the parcela, its location, the quality of its soil, and current practice on the hacienda, the labor obligation of the arrendatario could range from a few days a month to most of them. By the 1920's the arrendatarios' obligatory work on the hacienda was remunerated, usually at a rate below the standard wage for free labor in the region. Arrendatarios also enjoyed access to the woodlands of the hacienda and many had the right to pasture an animal or two on hacienda lands.

In addition to these permanent workers, who numbered in the hundreds of families on the largest estates, the large coffee hacienda relied on day laborers called *jornaleros* or (more graphically) *voluntarios*, who sold their labor freely to the large coffee capitalists. These workers were hired temporarily during periods of peak labor demand. Many were impoverished small farmers from the densely populated highlands of Cundinamarca and nearby Boyacá. *Enganchados* (literally, "hooked") by labor contractors for the large estates, they came down to the subtropical coffee zone for a few weeks during the coffee harvest in April and May. Housed in rude barracks, and fed as part of their wage, voluntarios were usually paid by the piece, the number of *cuartillas* (wooden boxes that held some 50 pounds of ripe coffee) they harvested. Women and children, often

44. The best and most systematic discussion of the social relations of production in the Colombian coffee economy in the early decades of the twentieth century is Absalón Machado's *El café* (cited in n. 26). See also the rich material uncovered by Palacios, *Coffee in Colombia* (cited in n. 30).

from the families of permanent hacienda workers, joined these temporary workers in the coffee harvest. Jornaleros were also hired for the *des-
yerbe* or weeding of coffee groves, a task usually performed twice a year,
and for the pruning of coffee trees to increase their productivity and facilitate the harvest by limiting their height.

Finally, the owners of large coffee estates in Cundinamarca entered
into relationships with another kind of worker, especially during periods
of expansion of coffee cultivation. These were *colonos*, workers who
agreed to open new lands for coffee cultivation under contract with the
large estate owners. Typically, a colono agreed to clear the forest and
plant and cultivate coffee trees during a specified number of years, usually three or four, until the trees became productive. During that time he
and his family could grow food crops between the coffee plants. At the
end of this period he sold the trees, usually at a specified rate per tree, plus
all other *mejoras* (improvements)—such as plantain or banana trees, often
used to shade coffee, patches of sugarcane and yucca, his house—and expressly renounced all claim to the land. This renunciation, specified in
contracts of sale of new coffee trees, was of fundamental importance to
the coffee hacendado.[45]

Large coffee estates in Cundinamarca and elsewhere were often
founded on vague and faulty title to the land. Typically, they reached
enormous size by expanding into public lands or *baldíos*. Public lands
were allocated to private individuals throughout the nineteenth and early
twentieth centuries primarily on the basis of land certificates issued by
financially pressed national governments to discharge obligations to soldiers, public works contractors, and creditors. These certificates were
often bought up at great discount by merchants and large landowners,
who used them to secure title to a specific lot of public land. Colombian
land law also contemplated allocation of public lands to another kind of
colono, homesteaders. These laws, passed primarily under the Liberal
governments of the 1870's, envisioned alienation of public lands to small
farmers who occupied and cultivated lands in the national domain. Those
who could prove they had occupied and used the land for a certain number of years became eligible for a grant of land several times larger than
the size of the plot they effectively occupied. In reality, as Catherine
LeGrand has shown in a comprehensive study of the alienation of Colombian public lands, most of the land distributed in this manner, much
of it in the previously unclaimed slopes of the coffee zone, was granted
in huge chunks to large landowners. Moreover, recipients of these poorly
defined land grants often proceeded, illegally but successfully, to extend

45. Samples of these contracts from the 1890's are discussed in Bergquist, *Coffee and Conflict* (cited in n. 4), pp. 29-32. Antonio García noted similar arrangements in Caldas in the
1930's: *Geografía* (cited in n. 6), p. 311.

their holdings far beyond the limits of the original grants. This process often brought them into conflict with squatters, who claimed rights to public lands as colonos. But the legal costs, survey requirements, and bureaucratic delays involved in adjudication procedures—and the control by large landowners over local political and police authorities and their willingness to use violence—usually resulted in the defeat of small colonos and their eventual incorporation into the dependent work force of the coffee estates.[46]

De facto control over uncultivated land in the coffee zones was made de jure in part through the contracts with colonos described above. By renouncing any pretense of claim to the land as baldíos, colonos were forced to hand large coffee hacendados a double boon. They gave up new coffee groves just at the point when the heavy labor demands of clearing and planting began to bear fruit in the first coffee harvest. And they provided large landowners the legal basis—cultivated land—for acquiring title to huge new tracts of public lands. The magnitude of this dual injustice, which denied the letter of the public land laws and deprived coffee workers of the chance to become independent producers, was not lost on colonos of either kind. Those who squatted on public land acquiesced only after struggle. Many refused to move and often engaged in protracted legal disputes, which were almost invariably decided against them. Those who contracted with the big landowners to open up new lands for coffee cultivation, and were forced to renounce any claim to the land, had already concluded it was futile to try to circumvent the pretensions of coffee hacendados and contest their control over local political, judicial, and police authorities. As we shall see, the issue of faulty title to the land and the dream of acquiring a freehold through possession and effective use of public-domain lands became part of the collective memory of dependent workers on the great coffee estates of Cundinamarca and neighboring Tolima. When the balance of power between the classes in coffee production shifted in the 1920's and 1930's it was around these issues that coffee workers mounted the largest sustained mobilization by rural workers in Colombian history.

In the newer coffee zones of the Central Cordillera, labor and tenancy arrangements were typically more modern, and often more favorable to coffee workers. Not only were independent small and medium-sized family farms (discussed below) more common, but medium-sized and large coffee haciendas were usually worked by sharecroppers and renters. For these workers access to a plot of land to grow subsistence crops and coffee often involved taking responsibility for the cultivation and harvest of a specific number of coffee trees (apportioned according to the number

46. Catherine LeGrand, "From Public Lands Into Private Properties: Landholding and Rural Conflict in Colombia, 1870-1936" (Ph.D. diss., Stanford University, 1980).

of productive workers each family could muster, at a rate often calculated at 1,000 trees per adult worker). Sharecroppers on these estates received a part of the coffee harvest, usually half, in exchange for cultivating and harvesting the trees under their care and processing the coffee they produced. (If they did not depulp and dry their coffee they received less, sometimes a third of the coffee harvest.) In some places they were obliged in addition to work a certain number of days on estate lands, at rates of pay standard for the region. In still other localities they were required to share a portion (often a fourth) of the food crops they produced on their subsistence plots with the estate owner. As Absalón Machado and others have shown, by the 1920's the varieties of sharecropping and rental agreements in both the Central and the Eastern Cordilleras were many, and some were more onerous to sharecroppers and renters than others. These agreements, usually made verbally before the 1940's, resist systematic investigation by historians. They included specific arrangements for coffee processing, and access to hacienda pasture and food crops, stipulations about credit advances, and so on. All were based on the principle that in exchange for access to the land, the sharecropper or renter had to relinquish a portion of the product of his labor to the landowner. In few instances did sharecroppers contribute a portion of the capital involved in coffee production.[47]

In the Central Cordillera, and increasingly in the Eastern Cordillera as time progressed, small and medium-sized family farms made up the bulk of coffee production units. These ranged from tiny plots, unable to provide for the subsistence needs of family members, to fairly large enterprises that depended on hired labor during the harvest and on sharecropping or rental arrangements to farm a portion of family-owned land during the year. Typically, however, the smallholder and his family furnished the bulk of the labor in production of food crops and coffee on these farms. During the first half of the twentieth century, as we have seen, these small, family-owned-and-operated farms became the most important producers of coffee in Colombia.

The pattern of life and labor on these small family farms is consistently ignored in the literature on the social relations of production in the Colombian coffee economy. Inspired by Marxist theory, most of that literature presupposes the steady differentiation of "peasant" producers into a few large capitalists and a proletarianized many.[48] That process is especially visible in the Colombian coffee economy in the decades since mid-

47. In addition to the sources in n. 44, see the succinct discussion for Caldas in García, *Geografía* (cited in n. 6), pp. 310-11.

48. Absalón Machado's otherwise admirable and instructive study (cited in n. 26) is a good example of these widespread tendencies. So preoccupied is he with showing the concentration of land in the coffee sector, and with demonstrating the evolution of precapitalist labor systems toward capitalist ones in the decades before 1950, that he fails to stress the

century. But before 1950, the outstanding feature of coffee production in Colombia was the development and persistence of the small family coffee farm. The nature of life and work on these farms merits our close attention. In the collective experience of these most numerous and important Colombian coffee producers lies the source of the cultural values and a certain political consciousness that deeply influenced the development of the Colombian labor movement and the modern history of the nation as a whole.

The secret to the growing preeminence of small family coffee farms in Colombia lay in the nature of the production process. Successful production of high-quality coffee in Colombia required neither large capital investments nor the application of sophisticated technology. But it did require very heavy inputs of labor in all phases of coffee cultivation and processing. As early as the 1890's large coffee producers increased the efficiency of their operations by investing in large-scale depulping and drying machinery run by steam and fueled by imported petroleum products. These investments, however, only marginally reduced labor costs, which typically accounted for more than three-fourths of the cost of coffee production in Colombia until the mid-twentieth century.[49] Small coffee farmers depended on rudimentary tools and machinery, on the ingenious use of natural resources and energy supplies, and on the full employment of the labor power of all family members in order to compete successfully against large-scale coffee producers.

For a century now, small coffee farmers in Colombia have relied on a handful of simple iron and steel tools to accomplish the multitude of tasks vital to their survival.[50] From the beginning, the clearing of the land

---

most important fact that emerges from the coffee censuses he analyzes—the growth and persistent viability of the small family farm. A lucid review of the debate over the differentiation of petty commodity producers and a powerful challenge to the orthodox Marxist position is Carol Smith, "Does a Commodity Economy Enrich the Few While Ruining the Masses?" (unpublished paper, Center for Advanced Study in the Behavioral Sciences, Stanford, Calif., 1981).

49. Even as late as 1955 the CEPAL coffee census estimated that labor represented more than 75 percent of the cost of coffee production in Colombia: CEPAL, *El café*, Table 74, p. 81. That was an average for all farms. Most of these labor costs were involved in cultivation, not processing. Large farms (over 50 hectares) spent less than small (1 to 10 hectares) in processing, 3 percent versus 9.4, but more in cultivation, 76 percent versus 68.4.

50. Except as noted, most of the material in the following pages is based on personal experience. My contact with the culture and history of Colombian small coffee producers began in 1963 when I was assigned for two years as a Peace Corps volunteer to a small coffee county in northwestern Cundinamarca. Charged with promoting modern agricultural techniques, I participated in the diffusion of pesticides such as Aldrin (now banned in the United States for its carcinogenic properties) and hybrid seeds such as those for corn developed for Colombian agriculture on experimental farms financed by the Rockefeller Foundation. The conventional wisdom in the developed world regarding the use of chemicals in agriculture and the promise of the so-called "Green Revolution" has now been subjected to telling critique. Small coffee farmers have always been able to provide, for those willing to listen, a fairly complete education in the sound and efficient use of agricultural resources.

on the heavily forested slopes of the coffee zones depended on primitive techniques, on the use of hand axes and fire. Even after the 1940's, when bulldozers and tractors became common in roadbuilding and in commercial agriculture in Colombia, the steep and broken terrain of the coffee zone prohibited the use of machinery in the clearing and cultivation of most coffee land. The weeding of coffee trees and other food crops in the coffee zone is still done with hoes and sharpened flat metal shovels called *palas*. Colombian agronomists schooled in the agricultural techniques of the developed world often ridicule the way small coffee farmers plant their crops in vertical rows straight up the side of their mountainside fields. Unlike contour plowing, that procedure does nothing to prevent erosion and the landslides that are the scourge of steep-slope farming. But since plowing these slopes, even by animal traction, is impossible, small Colombian farmers know that by planting vertically, the back-breaking task of cultivating between the rows by scraping off weeds at the surface with the *pala* can be performed standing almost erect and moving up the slope. Planting on small coffee farms is still done with a variation on a pre-Columbian tool, the iron-tipped *barretón*, whose sharp, heavy wedge-shaped tip is mounted on a long straight hardwood handle. The barretón is plunged into the soil to form a hole for kernels of corn, coffee seedlings, or sugarcane cuttings. The other indispensable tools of the small coffee farmer are the *peinilla* and the larger, heavier *machete*. Both are used to fell secondary growth in fields being readied for planting, to clear pastures of weeds, to open and clear trails. The peinilla is employed to cut down and fashion *guadua*, the large bamboo that is the basis of most construction on the small coffee farm, to gather *palmicha*, the wild fronds for roof thatching, to carve handles for tools and the wooden supports for animal packs, and to accomplish a hundred other tasks, from harvesting plantains to cutting firewood. Although most coffee farmers who could afford it owned a shotgun or rifle, or more recently a handgun, the peinilla remains the most common weapon in the coffee zones. It hangs, protected in its decorated leather sheath, or *vaina*, at the waist of nearly every adult male in the rural areas of the coffee regions, within hand's reach for use in the many different tasks he undertakes in a typical day.

The techniques of small-scale coffee cultivation in Colombia have evolved in ways admirably suited to the terrain of the coffee zone, appropriate to the capital resources of small farmers, and protective of the fragile ecology of the coffee slopes. Until recently, few small coffee farmers used chemical fertilizers and pesticides. The practice of planting food crops between coffee seedlings made maximum use of cleared land and helped stabilize recently denuded soil. The custom of planting shade trees to protect mature coffee trees had several advantages. The large root systems of shade trees helped prevent erosion; their leaves furnished organic matter to the coffee plants below. Shade not only assured the slow ripening of coffee beans (a consideration in their flavor), it retarded the growth of the coffee tree, ensuring an adequate supply of nutrients and prolonging its productivity. The practice of allowing pigs and barnyard fowl to forage in the coffee groves helped eliminate insects and fertilized the grove.

The cultivation of coffee trees and their harvesting involved huge labor demands and tapped the resources of all family members. Men and older male children did the heavy labor involved in clearing, planting, and weeding the groves. Women and children of both sexes played an important role in the harvest. Coffee was picked as it ripened—a protracted, time-consuming task—although the bulk of the crop was brought in over the course of a few weeks of intensive labor. The beans were depulped in small hand-operated machines of Colombian manufacture, then washed into a hollowed-out log where they fermented until the mucous film around the bean dissolved. Once washed, the beans were ready for drying, a process that often took several days during the rainy season that usually accompanied the coffee harvest. The beans were spread in large flat wooden trays that could be easily covered from the rain or brought indoors. The dry beans, greenish behind their thin parchmentlike shells, were then given an initial selection by women and children who picked out broken and imperfectly depulped beans. This defective coffee, called *cacota*, was used for domestic consumption on the farm or sold at reduced price in the coffee towns. The rest was sacked in burlap bags and loaded on mules or horses for transport along rugged trails (often made virtually impassable by the rain) to coffee towns sometimes several hours distant. There, the smallholders' coffee might be sold to storekeepers, to representatives of export firms, or, as time went on, to the local officials of the National Federation of Coffee Growers. Until the 1940's the most important coffee towns had one or two trilladoras, the small dehusking plants where the parchment skin of the coffee beans produced by smallholders and most large growers alike was removed by large machines, and where the beans were completely dried and subjected to a final, and very labor-intensive, selection process.[51]

On all family coffee farms coffee was only one of many crops. On the smallest it was a crop of secondary importance.[52] The first priority of the

51. In the early twentieth century some of the largest producers had husking mills on their estates. By the 1940's, the increased efficiency of selection done by machine sharply reduced the number of escogedoras employed in trilladoras. Greater investment in machinery also fostered the centralization of processing in large cities and reduced the number of mills in operation.

52. Chapter IV of CEPAL, *El café* (cited in n. 27), provides a full discussion of the diversified nature of agricultural and livestock production on Colombian coffee farms by size. See especially Tables 24 to 29.

small coffee farmer was to feed his family. Plantains and a variety of bananas, yucca and *arracacha* (another root crop of the manioc family), corn, and beans were the staples of most coffee workers. Corn, grown whenever possible, often with slash and burn techniques on marginal land off the coffee farm and rented for that purpose, was consumed in soups and a variety of breads (especially the bleached, unsalted *arepa*), and was eaten with great relish, just before maturity, as corn on the cob (*mazorca*). Corn enabled the family to raise the chickens, ducks, turkeys, and pigs that were the main sources of animal protein on coffee farms. These fowl and animals were usually slaughtered only on special secular occasions and some religious holidays. The rest of the time soups and starches were garnished with small portions of salted beef or pork purchased weekly in the small towns of the coffee zone. Only the largest and most prosperous families in coffee production could afford the luxury of raising dairy or beef cattle. Nor did most coffee farmers cultivate vegetables. They might plant hot peppers, but the few vegetables they consumed—tomatoes, onions, garlic, Chinese parsley (*cilantro*), and potatoes, as well as condiments such as salt and cumin—they usually bought in town. Many coffee growers planted citrus and mango trees and supplemented their diet, especially in newly developed coffee zones, with a variety of wild fruits and vegetables, animals, birds, and fish. Wild vegetable products were also widely used in the rich tradition of home remedies upon which coffee families depended to cure or alleviate injuries and disease.

Finally, many family coffee farmers, especially those with farms of some size in the lower, warmer parts of the coffee zone, also cultivated sugarcane. Typically, sugarcane was harvested at different times throughout the year during lulls in the cycle of labor in coffee, corn, and other food crops. Sugarcane was often collected in a way similar to coffee. Only the mature stalks of the plant were cut and processed at any one time. Processing was done with small wooden (later, iron and steel) presses called *trapiches*, driven traditionally by animal power and increasingly in recent times by small diesel engines. The juice was boiled in a series of vats over a large adobe fire chamber fueled by dried pressed cane stalks and firewood. Sugarcane thus processed yielded *panela*, the brown sugar cakes universally consumed by the Colombian working class until refined sugar slowly worked its way into mass consumption in recent decades. It also produced *miel*, the molasses that formed the base of the fermented and distilled alcoholic beverages widely consumed in the coffee zones. Miel mixed daily with water and starter in large earthen jugs made *guarapo*, a tart, fermented drink consumed throughout the day by those doing heavy work in the sun. Allowed to become sufficiently alcoholic, guarapo could be transformed in homemade stills into anise-flavored *aguardiente* or rum. Despite sustained efforts by public officials to fine and punish makers of distilled liquor not produced and taxed under government monopoly, and despite the propaganda of private businessmen interested in expanding the market for bottled beer and soft drinks, home production of guarapo and aguardiente continued to satisfy the bulk of the rural market for beverages until recent times. Chopped sugarcane also supplemented the diet of mules and horses where pasturage was limited. These animals, as well as pigs and turkeys, were also fed the *cachaza* skimmed off cane juice as it was boiled to make miel and panela. Sugar products in excess of domestic needs, like all the other agricultural and livestock commodities produced on small family coffee farms, were sold or traded to neighbors and relations, or marketed in the coffee towns.

Small coffee farmers never engaged in home textile production as rural families in other sectors of the Colombian economy traditionally did. Unlike the small tobacco farmers in Santander during the eighteenth and nineteenth centuries who produced textiles in their homes for distribution in other regions, and the wool spinners and weavers of highland Boyacá and Cundinamarca, coffee farmers depended from the beginning on industrially manufactured (and initially imported) cotton cloth for most of their clothing needs. Women and female children did, however, fashion much of their own clothing by hand until the use of imported treadle sewing machines became widespread in recent decades. Males customarily had their cotton pants made by tailors in the towns, a practice that continues to this day, despite the fact that the shirts, fiber sandals (*alpargatas*), leather shoes, and rubber boots coffee workers wear are manufactured in the factories of the nation. Small children, especially among the most impoverished coffee families, often still wear little or no clothing.

Families in possession of small coffee farms traditionally manufactured many other items they consumed and used in their work from local materials. Some cultivated maguey or *fique* to produce fiber to weave ropes. Most gathered tropical vines to lash together the bamboo beams of farm buildings and the hanging bridges they constructed over streams and rivers. Coffee workers fashioned the large round gourds of the *totumo* tree into tough thick-skinned bowls for drinking and for a score of different uses as dippers, skimmers, and containers. Women wove natural fibers from a variety of plants into baskets to collect the coffee harvest, into the famous *jipijapa* (Panama) hats once exported from Colombia to the developed world in quantity, and into the mattresses most coffee workers slept on. Women made candles and soap from tallow purchased from butchers in the towns. They packaged stacks of panela and cold lunches in wrapping stripped from banana plants. With time coffee families depended more and more on the purchase of commodities in the marketplace. They bought corrugated iron roofing, cement to lay floors and build coffee-processing tanks, petroleum products to run trapiche motors and light their lanterns, plastic containers to collect coffee beans. They also began to purchase a variety of imported consumer goods including watches and transistor radios. Yet even today the self-sufficiency and frugality of most families in coffee production, and their creative use of the natural resources around them, are impressive.

To a traveler coming down from the cold highlands, coffee workers live in what first appears as a subtropical paradise. Range after range of mountains stretch into the distance as far as the eye can see. Falling away for a thousand meters below one's feet, the nearest of the coffee slopes appears as a riot of vegetation—the many-hued and -textured greens of its shade and coffee trees, stands of bamboo, and patches of cane and young corn accented by the red, orange, and purple pastels of *cámbulos*, *acacias*, and other large flowering trees. As one descends into the warm air, the fragrance and color of orange and coffee blossoms, of bougainvillea and wild orchids intoxicate the senses. But within this land of eternal spring a human and social reality emerges that is often not pretty. The same benign climate that nourishes the lush vegetation of the coffee slopes hosts a variety of insects and tropical diseases that mine the health of man. The human inhabitants of the coffee zone live in primitive material conditions. And the social and political reality of their lives can be mean and frightening.

Sanitary and health conditions on most family coffee farms are deplorable and have changed little in a hundred years. Housing itself, however rudimentary, does not pose major health problems. The split bamboo walls of most dwellings allow air to circulate. Dirt floors are easily swept with homemade twig brooms. Cooking is usually done on a raised hearth over an open fire. Some farms have adobe ovens for baking. The washing of clothes, the other major domestic task performed by women, is done by hand, often on the banks of nearby streams and rivers. On almost all small coffee farms, however, the open-air privacy of the *cafetal* serves as a vast latrine. That custom helps replenish the fertility of the soil, but it contributes to the general contamination of water supplies in the densely populated coffee zones, and leaves coffee workers, many of whom still go barefoot some of the time, vulnerable to soil-transmitted intestinal parasites such as hookworm, as well as to waterborne internal parasites, especially the insidious amoeba. Nearly everyone in the coffee zone today suffers from intestinal parasites. A doctor who sampled the population of the coffee-growing municipio of La Mesa, Cundinamarca, in 1920 found that an astounding 95 percent of its inhabitants suffered from *anemia tropical*, or ancylostomiasis. Antonio García, whose economic geography of Caldas is a rich source of statistics on health in the heart of the coffee zone, found a similar incidence of the disease there in 1937. In some coffee zones malaria and yellow fever were endemic until recent decades, when major government programs coordinated by the United Nations eradicated the mosquito populations on which their propagation depended. Traditionally, both the birth and the death rates in the coffee departments have been higher than in other parts of the country, where the rural population, if poorer, was healthier.[53]

Until recent decades, most coffee workers never saw a doctor. Midwives oversaw the birth of children, *sobanderas* massaged severe sprains and set broken bones, *rezanderas* were commissioned to brew potions and recite chants and prayers to free young children of the evil spirits said to cause chronic diarrhea. As time went on, rural coffee workers complemented home remedies with modern medicines sold by small-time druggists in the coffee towns. But even today medical doctors, health facilities, and medical supplies are scarce in the coffee zones, and most poor workers still depend on their own resources and folk medicine to treat their ailments.

Coffee workers have traditionally sought alleviation from disease and pain through recourse to religion. Most women still attend mass on market days, and the Catholic rituals of baptism, confirmation, and funeral services mark the lives of most individuals. Although many men are cynical about the destination of the financial exactions of the Church (which customarily charges for its services, and frequently solicits special contributions as well) and about the sexual morality of many priests, most, Liberal and Conservative alike, share a faith in the supernatural (not only a Christian God, but the special powers of the dead) and a vague commitment to the dogma of the Church. Most fear the consequences of the death of unbaptized children, for example, and seek to confess when they are mortally ill.

Although the nuclear family sanctified by Catholic marriage bonds was more common in the coffee zones than in some other areas of rural Colombia, many cohabitants, especially among the poorer farm families, were not formally married. Most who maintain informal liaisons today claim they are too poor to finance a decent marriage ceremony, an event traditionally accompanied by much food and drink and a party of more than a day's duration. One investigator writing in the 1920's found a strong correlation between rising coffee prices and increased frequency of marriages in the department of Antioquia. In booming and newly developing coffee zones, where migrants and seasonal laborers converged

53. Machado, *El café* (cited in n. 26), p. 51. On ancylostomiasis, see García, *Geografía* (cited in n. 6), pp. 217-18; on birth and death rates, pp. 202-3. As late as 1955 the CEPAL coffee census estimated that less than 8 percent of all coffee farms between 1 and 10 hectares had a bathroom, only 8.5 percent a latrine. CEPAL, *El café*, Table 61, p. 75.

from other regions of Colombia, adult males far outnumbered adult females in the population, a fact that contributed to the notorious incidence
of prostitution and venereal disease in coffee towns and cities.[54] Marriage
ties did not prevent some coffee farmers, especially the more prosperous
among them, from fathering illegitimate children and maintaining more
or less open liaisons with other women. A few males divided their time
and resources between more than one family. The complexity of sexual
relations and formal and informal ties between couples often generated
conflict between partners and their relatives, especially over the issues of
illegitimate children and inheritance. The seduction of women or their
abuse by males who failed to provide for their families or mistreated them
often precipitated serious interpersonal violence between the male relatives of aggrieved women and their alleged offenders. These disputes are
but aspects of the pervasive undercurrent of interpersonal tensions and
conflict that have traditionally characterized social life in the coffee zones,
especially where small farms are numerous.[55]

At the heart of these tensions was the constant struggle for control of
the land. Possession of a freehold, the bigger the better, was the goal of
every coffee worker. That aspiration is often dismissed in Marxist and
liberal scholarship as an anachronistic, irrational impulse inherited (along
with other traditional cultural values) by "peasants" from precapitalist social formations.[56] It is true that as petty commodity producers, Colombian coffee smallholders were swimming against the tide of history. But
to neglect the dynamics of their successful struggle for control of the land
in the decades before 1950 is to ignore the most significant determinant
of national historical trends during the twentieth century. It is also to fail
to recognize that their struggle was but a specific expression of goals
shared by all workers in all societies: the desire to control one's own life,
to decide how and when work is done, and to appropriate the full value
of one's labor. Although the implications of land ownership were compromised by relations of credit and exchange in the Colombian export

54. García, *Geografía* (cited in n. 6), Chapter IV, provides an excellent discussion of the
strength of the family in smallholder coffee production. On the frequency of marriage, and
the age at which it was customarily contracted by men (late) and women (early) in Caldas
in the 1930's, see pp. 194-96; on the high percentage of single males in the coffee work force
and the incidence of prostitution and disease in Caldas, see pp. 209 and 223-25. The relationship between coffee prices and marriages is advanced in Diego Monsalve, *Colombia cafetera* (Barcelona, 1927).

55. The best published work on the sources of interpersonal conflict and political violence in a Colombian coffee town is Jaime Arocha's provocative study *La violencia en el
Quindío* (Bogotá, 1979). It is discussed in more detail below.

56. This position, central to the thought of both liberal modernization theorists and orthodox Marxists, informs the otherwise penetrating research and analysis of migrant rural
workers' attitudes in contemporary Colombia developed under the leadership of Nicolás
Buenaventura. See his "Los temporeros," *Estudios Marxistas* 9 (1975):3-32. This work is discussed in detail in the final portion of this essay.

economy, to own a viable family farm was a goal within the grasp of many workers in coffee production before mid-century. Colombian coffee workers pursued that goal relentlessly, primarily by individual means, but also through collective organization. Their abortive collective efforts, favored by exceptional structural conditions in the late 1920's and early 1930's, have attracted the attention of many students of Colombian history. Their individual strategies, ignored in the work of most scholars, were more prosaic. But it was these individual strategies that produced the major changes in the social relations of coffee production before mid-century and influenced most deeply the pattern of national labor and political history.

Landless and dependent coffee workers could acquire, augment, and sustain a freehold in different ways. They could colonize new land and win title to it through official procedures. They could organize to force large landowners to divide their estates and sell out. Or they could purchase land on the market. This last strategy was the most common. The politics of official distribution of public lands in the coffee zone, even in the Central Cordillera, favored large landowners, and over the years the struggle one observer appropriately called "the battle of the axe versus officially stamped legal paper" was usually won by educated large landowners, merchants, and professionals. The parcelization of large coffee estates as a result of collective struggle by dependent coffee workers, discussed below, affected several score coffee haciendas and a few thousand coffee workers and their families in important regions of Cundinamarca and Tolima. Neither process, however, can account for the general fragmentation of landholding in all coffee zones revealed in the census data and the statistics on tenancy by the 1950's.

Successful pursuit of ownership of a smallhold involved families of coffee workers in a lifetime struggle in which ingenuity, hard work, and a good measure of luck all played a role. The ingenuity included successful cultivation of a wide range of interpersonal relationships (from the choice of a spouse and of godparents for children to the ability to gain sympathetic terms from relatives, friends, merchants, landowners, local political bosses, and government officials). Members of socially mobile families had to balance the expenses of material gifts and a certain liberality in the entertainment of strategic individuals with the desperate need to save in order to accumulate. That dilemma involved them in a complex and ever-changing social calculus that preoccupied coffee families, especially heads of households, throughout their lives. All family members had to cooperate and work hard to execute the multitude of agricultural, domestic construction, and artisanal tasks required for successful small farm operation. A healthy family blessed with children, who happened to rent or agree to sharecrop land suitable for coffee production at a time when international coffee prices were low, and then saw prices rise as the new coffee trees it planted came into full production, enjoyed optimal conditions for success in the struggle to accumulate capital and purchase land. Those families that suffered the loss or partial incapacity of one or both parents, were barren of children, or invested in coffee production at an inopportune point in the unpredictable cycle of world coffee prices were almost certain to fail in the pursuit of a freehold. A family affiliated to one of the factions of the two major political parties in a municipio where the other party or rival faction was in the majority might be harassed by neighbors, merchants, and local officials in one historical era, only to see the tables turned as its own party or faction won control of national politics and local affairs.

In their struggle to survive and control enough land to ensure their independence, coffee families found themselves in constant and often violent competition with their neighbors, large landowners and small. Part of the reason lay in the structure of production in the coffee zone. Many smallholders depended not only on the use of cultivable land in the possession of others but also on access to water, trapiches, pasturage, and woodlands outside the boundaries of their own plots. Larger landowners depended on the labor of those without a viable family freehold. Failure to meet an obligation, or disagreement over the value of mejoras made on rented or sharecropped land, could lead to lasting grievances and protracted litigation between neighbors. Small coffee farmers, precisely because the margin between success and failure in their struggle was so narrow, were constantly denouncing their neighbors for alleged breach of verbal contracts, or for damages allegedly incurred when pigs, mules, or cattle trespassed property and ate or damaged crops. Coffee farmers were encouraged by the structure of their situation to be tempted to use their wits to take advantage of their rivals at every conceivable opportunity. Some stole from others, if they thought their action would go undetected. Most tried to cheat landowners of part of their portion in sharecropping agreements. Others sought to change boundaries of property, since property was typically unsurveyed and vaguely delimited in deeds by references to landmarks like trees and stones and the course of creeks. In the constant struggle with his neighbors, a small coffee farmer depended for success to a sizable degree on his manliness and tact. In areas far removed from effective control by civil and ecclesiastical authorities, those capable of intimidating their fellows or of winning their respect, those able to bully their neighbors or impress them through equanimity and courage, had the best chance of surviving to reach old age, the best chance of acquiring, expanding, and maintaining a freehold.

Those who labored in coffee production thus saw the central myths of capitalist and Christian ideology played out on an intimate scale before their eyes during the course of their lives. If they were successful, they attributed their fortune to hard work, intelligence, frugality, and the moral virtue of their family and its members. If they failed they blamed themselves or their rivals or attributed their misfortune to fate. As small property owners they identified with the capitalist, Christian values championed and disseminated by the Liberal and Conservative parties. Their loyalty to the two traditional parties, however, was not simply a consequence of the coincidence between ruling-class ideology and the vision of society fostered in their daily experience. The clientelist structure of party politics and the competitive struggle between the parties for control over local affairs was enlisted by individual smallholders in their efforts to create a social field of hierarchical interpersonal relationships favorable to their interests. Through allegiance to one or the other of the major parties or its factions, coffee workers secured a host of strategically placed allies in the struggle to accumulate capital and control a portion of the land. That such an affiliation also placed them in conflict with a host of rivals and competitors of different political affiliation did not weaken their partisanship. In a local structure of power completely at the mercy of partisan politics, one was potentially better (and no worse) off as a partisan of one of the possible victors in political struggle than he was as a neutral, exposed in a Hobbesian world without political allies. Victory of one's party or party faction could mean everything from relief from military conscription for a teenage son, to effective police protection from belligerent neighbors, to the favorable resolution of legal disputes. For a wealthier small farmer it could mean access to government jobs or advanced education for his children, a favorable decision on the location of a rural road, or any of a hundred other political or legal favors.[57]

To be successful, then, a coffee smallholder had to become something of a rural Colombian Renaissance man possessed of a Machiavellian understanding of politics and human nature. He had to be accomplished in the arts of agriculture, animal husbandry, construction, and simple mechanics; he had to be an astute judge of men and a master of human psychology. But unlike those ideal urban types of early modern Mediterranean capitalist society, he was primarily a worker, who depended not on command over the means of exchange, but on control over the means of production and the work process in his struggle to survive and accumulate capital. To the extent he was able to mobilize and coordinate the intelligence and muscle of a large family (while keeping his rivals at bay), to the degree he was favored by natural, economic, and political forces

57. A rich source on the mechanics of traditional political clientelism in a Colombian coffee municipio is Steffen Walter Schmidt, "Political Clientelism in Colombia" (Ph.D. diss., Columbia University, 1972).

beyond his control, he succeeded in his goal of acquiring and maintaining a freehold. In Colombian coffee production before mid-century neither heavy capital investment nor command over advanced technology was sufficient to compensate for the inefficient use of and control over human labor on large coffee haciendas. Consequently, many landless families involved in rental and sharecropping arrangements were able to transcend their position at the expense of large landowners. But the coffee smallholder (like the large before mid-century) was incapable of revolutionizing the means of coffee production. His success was dependent on his superior ability to mobilize the labor power of his family. Ironically, then, the success of a socially mobile family in coffee production during one life cycle undermined its ability to perpetuate that success in the next. Like Sisyphus, the family able to accumulate a modest portion of land during the lifetime of one head of household saw that resource fractured by inheritance with his demise, and watched the struggle begin anew, as each child sought to expand his or her meager inheritance into a viable independent family production unit.

Some observers have seen only the corruption of mythic antioqueño values in this pattern of life and labor in smallholder Colombian coffee production. In his novel *La cosecha*, set in Líbano, Tolima, in the midst of the Depression, the reactionary anti-Communist intellectual J. A. Osorio Lizarazo painted a sordid description of the material poverty, physical deterioration, stupidity, and moral decay of coffee smallholders and their families. The novel had the virtue of correcting the rosy romanticism of the ruling-class vision of life in the heart of the coffee zone. But Osorio degraded and dehumanized coffee workers and their struggle for control of the land. In a cynical passage typical of his tone of moral condescension, Osorio alluded to several of the features of interpersonal relations and cultural values fostered by the structure of smallholder coffee production. If he exaggerated and saw only one side of these relationships and values, he nevertheless captured something of their unity and their links to the material forces at work in small-farm coffee society.

Work and tilling the soil were the factors that established the sentiment of property and it was that sentiment that subverted the errant masculinity of the first settlers and the ancestral nomadic tendencies, which propelled them into the conquest [of the land]. The new generation had become brutalized by the absolute predominance of elemental instincts, it fell to reproducing itself at an astounding rate, like the very trees of the forest, it let initiative languish. The men vegetated, completely tied to the land, they engaged in transactions in which they tried to swindle each other, they practiced hospitality on a grand scale, they got drunk on Sundays and pompously cultivated the savage supremacy of sex. The uniformity of the struggle established a spontaneous solidarity, broken, nevertheless, by the egotism that propitiated the intensity of effort. Children were a pretext to create artificial kinship ties tending toward personal gain. . . . And in that way they tried to deceive each other with small transactions involving machetes or oxen and they began to traffic in properties.[58]

Contrary to Osorio Lizarazo, most smallholders were neither physically destroyed in the production of coffee nor dehumanized in their struggle for control of the land. They survived as a class and emerged partially victorious in that struggle precisely because, despite enormous obstacles, they developed their human faculties and potential so fully. If the terms of struggle reinforced their individualism, their receptivity to the ideological message of the ruling class, and their conformity to the clientelist politics of the traditional parties; if it left them resistant to collective organization and leftist ideology and carried them inexorably toward fratricidal conflict—it was not because smallholders were rendered less human by their experience and their struggle. It was because their intelligence and enormous energy were channeled by the structural imperatives of their existence into a destructive individualist dynamic beyond their control. It was the very success of coffee smallholders that sealed their fate as a class and ensured the decline of popular social and political forces in Colombia during the 1930's and 1940's. That process castrated an insurgent labor movement, led to the co-optation of the political left, and ended in the Violence at mid-century.

The story of the mobilization of Colombian workers, particularly coffee workers, in the late 1920's and 1930's has been told and retold with increasing detail and sophistication by Colombian historians in recent years.[59] Before the First World War, in contrast to developments in Chile

58. J. A. Osorio Lizarazo, *La cosecha* (Manizales, 1935), p. 66.

59. Among the general surveys that attempt to place these labor developments into the context of the broader history of the Colombian labor movement, those by Urrutia (*Development* [cited in n. 43]) and Pecaut (*Política y sindicalismo* [cited in n. 43]) are the most important. A good narrative history of popular protest in Colombia, written by a Communist activist who played a major role in the labor struggles of the 1920's and 1930's, is Ignacio Torres Giraldo, *Los inconformes*, 5 vols. (Bogotá, 1978). Recent contributions to the literature on the great banana strike of 1928 include Fernando Botero and Alvaro Guzmán Barney, "El enclave agrícola en la zona bananera de Santa Marta," *Cuadernos Colombianos* 11 (1977):309–89; Judith White, *Historia de una ignominia: La United Fruit Co. en Colombia* (Bogotá, 1978); and Catherine LeGrand, "Colombian Transformations: Peasants and Wage Laborers in the Santa Marta Banana Zone, 1900-1935," paper presented at the Latin American Studies Association Meeting, Washington, D.C., 1982. On the mobilization of coffee workers, see especially the pioneering work of Hermes Tovar, *El movimiento campesino en Colombia* (Bogotá, 1975); Machado's *El café* (cited in n. 26) and Palacios's *Coffee in Colombia* (cited in n. 30); books by Pierre Gilhodes, *Las luchas agrarias en Colombia* (Bogotá, 1974), Gloria Gaitán, *Colombia: La lucha por la tierra en la década del treinta* (Bogotá, 1976), Darío Fajardo, *Violencia y desarrollo* (Bogotá, 1979), and Gonzalo Sánchez G., *Las Ligas campesinas en Colombia* (Bogotá, 1977); the chapter "Land Use and Land Reform in Colombia" in Al-

and Argentina, labor organization in Colombia was confined to a few mutual-aid societies, primarily among the artisans of the larger cities. Although at different times in the nineteenth and early twentieth centuries Colombian artisans mounted powerful political protests and violent street demonstrations in defense of their livelihoods and honor,[60] it was not until after the First World War that they developed permanent collective organizations aimed at improving their working conditions and wages. The delayed development of the Colombian labor movement, like that of neighboring Venezuela, reflected the limited nature of Colombia's historical links to the world economy.

Under the impetus of expanding coffee production, however, the Colombian labor movement began to blossom. With the end of the world war, in the context of the worldwide efflorescence of the labor movement, worker protests exploded in the major Caribbean ports of Colombia. Organized by anarcho-syndicalists and supported by river and railway transport workers and urban artisans, a general strike shook Barranquilla in early January 1918 and spread to the port cities of Cartagena and Santa Marta. The strikes jolted public opinion throughout Colombia, led to the imposition of a state of siege in the entire Caribbean coastal region, resulted in a government decree regulating strike activity that set the precedent for much subsequent labor legislation, and encouraged workers at the huge United Fruit complex near Santa Marta to submit

bert Hirschman's *Journeys Toward Progress* (New York, 1965), pp. 131-213; the testimony of Communist organizer Victor J. Merchán, "Datos para la historia social, económica y del movimiento agrario de Viotá," *Estudios Marxistas* 9 (1975):105-16; the analysis of the struggle for the land in Tolima by Alejandro Caballero, "Violencia y estructura agraria," *Estudios Marxistas* 12 (1976):5-31; and the recent paper by Marco Palacios, "La propiedad agraria en Cundinamarca, 1880-1970," given at the Conference on El Mundo Rural Colombiano, Fundación Antioqueña para los Estudios Sociales, Medellín, 1981. We will know more about the nature of worker mobilization on the great coffee estates once the dissertation in preparation at Harvard University by Michael Jiménez is complete.

60. The history of these protests deserves much closer study. Historically, artisans were inordinately important in Colombia's relatively populous society and closed economy. Their protests, moreover, follow a pattern, coming as they did when liberal initiatives reduced barriers to foreign trade, or when rapid export expansion suddenly undermined artisans' position. The role of artisans in the late-eighteenth-century revolt of the Comuneros and the political events of the early 1850's is well known if still inadequately researched in Colombian historiography. Artisans mounted a large-scale revolt in Bogotá in 1893 at a time when the full initial effect of Colombia's first coffee boom must have seriously cut into their livelihood. They demonstrated violently again in Bogotá in 1919, this time in protest of the decision by the government to purchase army uniforms abroad. Finally, it is not unlikely that artisan unrest during the post-1945 coffee boom contributed to the great urban riot called the *bogotazo* in April 1948. The best discussion of this issue is Gonzalo Sánchez, *Los "Bolcheviques" de El Líbano* (Bogotá, 1976). Some detail on the 1893 events in Bogotá can be found in Bergquist, "Coffee and Conflict in Colombia, 1886-1904" (Ph.D. diss., Stanford University, 1973), pp. 74-75. On the 1919 affair see Urrutia, *Development* (cited in n. 43), pp. 62-64.

their first petition for improvements in working conditions and wages. During 1919 continuing labor unrest in the coastal zone, small strikes by artisans in the major cities of the nation, and large-scale, coordinated strikes by railway workers in the nation's nerve center and economic heartland, the department at Cundinamarca, combined to encourage passage of legislation to regulate labor conflict. These laws, passed in 1919 and 1920, sought to restrict strike activity to the simple peaceful refusal to work, provided for the deportation of foreigners who advocated or participated in strike disorders, established mechanisms for conciliation and arbitration of industrial conflict, and prohibited strikes (and made arbitration compulsory) in labor disputes in public services, including transport. Through this legislation, and the establishment of an Office of Labor in 1923, the Colombian ruling class attempted to defuse and regulate the novel wave of strikes that shook Colombian society in the immediate postwar period.[61] The laws seemed to accomplish that end effectively during the short postwar depression. But in the context of the spectacular coffee-based expansion in the middle and late 1920's they proved ineffective. After 1923 an insurgent labor movement seized upon the favorable conditions for worker organization and protest. Massive strikes first erupted in the foreign-owned export enclaves, then spread ominously to the heart of the coffee export sector itself.

The most important of these conditions was an unprecedented demand for labor. The expansion of employment in coffee production itself was clearly the most significant element in this process. As early as 1906, when coffee exports stood at only half a million bags a year, the *Revista Nacional de Agricultura* estimated that there were 12,000 permanent workers and 100,000 harvest workers in coffee production. In 1914, when coffee production had slightly more than doubled and much expansion was under way, the same source gave an estimate of 80,000 permanent workers, 240,000 harvest workers.[62] There are no such estimates of the coffee labor force available for the 1920's. It is probable that the trend (already evident in the 1914 estimate) was toward a greater reliance on permanent workers (sharecroppers, estancieros, and smallholders), who spent a part of their time in coffee production throughout the year and furnished the bulk of the labor at harvesttime. Were the (perhaps exaggerated) estimate of 1914 projected to the end of the 1920's, when coffee exports had almost tripled, it would yield a number approaching a million workers—almost an eighth of the total population of Colombia—engaged in full- or part-time labor in coffee production. A more conservative estimate of the cof-

61. These events are traced in some detail in Urrutia, *Development* (cited in n. 43), Chap. 5. The legislation, like all Colombian labor law, is effectively mined for its class content in Moncayo and Rojas, *Luchas obreras* (cited in n. 43), Chap. 1.
62. Cited in Bejarano, "Fin" (cited in n. 22), p. 258.

fee labor force results from calculating the number of adult workers (or the adult equivalent of younger workers) needed to harvest the some 500 million trees in production in Colombia at the end of the 1920's. As noted previously, standard contracts at that time in Caldas assigned about 1,000 trees to the care of each adult worker in families expected to devote some time to subsistence food production and furnish all labor needed to harvest the trees. This procedure yields an estimate of about 500,000 workers involved most of the time in coffee production at the end of the 1920's, an estimate that may still be too high given the lower productivity of trees outside Caldas, particularly on farms in the Eastern Cordillera. Still, whatever the absolute number, it is clear that the work force in coffee production was very large, and that it increased rapidly throughout the 1920's.

There was also a very rapid rise in the number of workers in certain other sectors of the Colombian economy, especially after 1925 when the full effects of the influx of foreign capital began to be felt. Workers in labor-intensive public and private construction, in transport, in the foreign-owned oil and banana enclaves, and in artisanal and industrial manufacturing increased by the thousands during the 1920's. Hugo López estimated that between 1925 and 1928 alone the labor force expanded by 140,000 workers. He calculated that of these new jobs more than 42 percent were in agriculture, 11 percent in manufacturing, 12 percent in construction, 8 percent in mining, and some 26 percent in government, commerce, and transport.[63] Most of these workers were attracted out of traditional agriculture by better working conditions and by wages for unskilled labor sometimes more than twice those paid to day laborers in agriculture. Large coffee producers seem to have held their own in this growing competition for labor until about 1927. But as world prices and their profits began to slump after that year, they filled the air with complaints of "labor scarcity," and unveiled desperate and sometimes bizarre schemes to increase their supply of cheap, dependent labor. These included plans for forced work on coffee plantations by urban juvenile delinquents, projects for Asian immigration, and calls for the use of heavy machinery in public construction projects. It was traditional agriculture, however, that was hit the hardest by what large landowners insisted on calling the "shortage of hands"—by which they meant their inability to attract and hold workers under the conditions of work and pay they had offered in the past. Large estates engaged in domestic food production lost workers to coffee production, construction, and transport. Small-scale food producers left the land for higher wages in the national labor market. Consequently, as demand for food by a wealthier working class

63. López, "La inflación" (cited in n. 31), p. 95.

grew, food production for domestic consumption stagnated or declined. The squeeze on domestic food production was also intensified as many coffee producers, large and small alike, responded to the extraordinary level of coffee prices and directed more of their land and labor away from domestic food production toward coffee cultivation. Price inflation was the result of all these trends. Despite a sixfold increase in food imports between 1922 and 1928, as well as the passage of an emergency law to remove tariff barriers on many food imports, food prices and the cost of living rose precipitously.[64]

These dual conditions—the extraordinary demand for labor and the rising cost of food and other commodities—gave Colombian workers the leverage and the resolve to mount a major effort, individually and collectively, to change the condition of their lives. As a result primarily of their individual efforts—the pressure they exerted on employers through thousands of individual decisions to demand better terms for their labor or quit their jobs and move on in search of better pay and conditions— real wages rose throughout the decade and work conditions improved in many areas. Workers' collective efforts were less successful in the short run. But the massive strikes they engaged in, and the collective organizations they built, decisively influenced the course of Colombian history in the decades after 1930. These strikes occurred first and most spectacularly in the oil and banana enclaves. There living and working conditions combined with the explosive cultural, ethnic, and nationalist dimensions of foreign-owned capitalist enterprise to favor collective organization under Marxist leadership. First oil and then banana workers mounted the great, sustained strikes that culminated in the infamous slaughter of perhaps a thousand striking banana workers and their families near Santa Marta in December 1928. It was the worst labor massacre in Colombian labor history.[65] Coffee workers faced much greater obstacles to organization. Yet gradually after 1925, especially on the large estates of southern Cundinamarca and northern and eastern Tolima, they mounted the great-

---

64. Quantitative information on prices and wages appears in Bejarano, "Fin" (cited in n. 22), pp. 406-9, and López, "La inflación" (cited in n. 31), p. 100. See also Miguel Urrutia and Mario Arrubla, *Compendio de estadísticas históricas de Colombia* (Bogotá, 1970).

65. The great strikes, particularly the banana strike of 1928, loom large in the labor historiography of Colombia and in the iconography of the Colombian left, and I have purposely downplayed their importance in this account. The banana strike was immortalized in a work of the great Colombian novelist Gabriel García Márquez, *One Hundred Years of Solitude*. There is no more suggestive source on the cultural impact of life in the banana zone on the Colombians who experienced it. The labor movement in Colombian banana production evolved under structural conditions similar to those explored in the chapters on Chile and Venezuela. But the banana enclave was as exceptional in the experience of the Colombian working class as the work of the great Marxist novelist socialized in the heart of the Colombian banana zone is in the literary tradition of his homeland. See Charles Bergquist, "Gabriel García Márquez: A Colombian Anomaly," forthcoming in *The South Atlantic Quarterly*.

est sustained collective challenge to the domestic ruling class ever witnessed in Colombia.

In the long run, the great strikes in the foreign-owned enclaves, and the continuing militancy of Colombian workers in oil and banana production, probably influenced Standard Oil of New Jersey and United Fruit to curtail their Colombian operations and expand elsewhere.[66] Whatever the precise role of militant labor in the process, Colombian petroleum production increased very slowly and fitfully after 1930 and banana exports fell from 10 million bunches in the late 1920's to half that level in the 1930's. Had Colombia become a major oil exporter or continued to expand banana production, the history of its labor movement might have been different. Communist activists from both enclaves—and their allies among river and port workers—were the most militant components of the organized labor movement throughout the 1930's and early 1940's.[67] It was coffee, however, rather than either of these other export commodities that continued to propel the Colombian economy after the 1920's. And it was the struggle of coffee workers that decided the fate of the Colombian labor movement.

66. U.S. oil companies operating in Colombia continually complained that the complexity of Colombian oil legislation, the indecisiveness of government oil policies, and the pretensions of Colombian workers were obstacles to their expansion. The importance of the last consideration is revealed in stark form in the comments made before State Department officials by an executive of Texas Petroleum in 1948. He expressed the company's continuing frustration with Colombian labor, especially "its determination to share in the management [of the company]." He said the company would "not stand for this" and would "pull out of Colombia rather than submit to it." He urged a cutoff in all U.S. loans to Colombia if its government did not act decisively to curb labor's excesses. Restricted Memo, U.S. Department of State, Sept. 13, 1948, USNA/DS 821.504/9-1348. For its part, United Fruit alleged that disease on its Colombian plantations forced it to expand production in Central America. But continuing labor unrest in the Colombian banana zone also played a role. In 1934 Colombian banana workers launched another major strike against the company. The Liberal government agreed to mediate. The settlement denied workers their primary demand, abolition of the piece-rate system, but it extended them substantial wage and other benefits. The terms enabled the Liberal government to undermine Communist control over the banana workers' unions, but it also alienated the management of the company. The strike petition appears in *El Espectador* (Bogotá), Dec. 11, 1934, pp. 1 and 3; the settlement, in *ibid.*, Dec. 24, 1934, pp. 1, 3, and 6. Petroleum exports represented 17 percent of the value of all Colombian exports in 1925-29; 20 percent in 1935-39; 15 percent in 1945-49; and 14 percent in 1955-59. Banana exports were 6, 5, 2, and 4 percent respectively in these same periods. McGreevey, *Economic History* (cited in n. 11), Table 26, p. 207.

67. U.S. officials reporting on Colombian labor often emphasized this fact, and sometimes linked it with a racial explanation of the relative militancy of Colombian workers. Reporting on the Sixth Congress of Colombian Workers held in the city of Bucaramanga near the oil enclave in December 1943, the U.S. consul noted that despite the ostensible Liberal majority among the delegates, a Communist from the banana zone, Carlos Arias, was elected president of the Congress. "The relatively large number of delegates and participants of the colored race mostly from the coastal regions conspicuous . . . in all the proceedings of the congress reflected the social consciousness of this racial group and their strength in the Colombian labor movement." J. Brook Havron to Department of State, Dec. 10, 1943, USNA/DS 821.50/142.

Coffee workers on the great estates of southeastern Cundinamarca began to agitate for better conditions as early as 1918. It was toward the end of the 1920's, however, as labor demand turned in their favor, that they embarked on the escalating and gradually successful struggle to liberate themselves from the precapitalist arrangements under which they labored and to win control of the land. This collective struggle, which stretched into the mid-1930's and beyond, obeyed a dynamic different from that which governed the mobilization of free wage workers in the foreign enclaves and the transport and manufacturing sectors of the Colombian economy. If, like those struggles, it began with collective efforts to improve working conditions and increase the economic returns to labor, it was at once more complex, and potentially more threatening to the interests of the Colombian ruling class, than those simpler struggles within the familiar structure of industrial capitalist relations. Whereas the collective efforts of the free wage workers in Colombian society were rapidly undermined by the downturn in international coffee prices after 1928 and the coming of the Great Depression—circumstances that brought in their wake a cessation of foreign lending, severe cutbacks in government spending and public-works construction, and a precipitous decline in economic activity in general—these same conditions only made the struggle of coffee workers on the great coffee estates more intense, more radical in content, and more violent.

This was true for several reasons. The coffee bonanza of the mid-1920's and the national labor demand it generated enabled coffee workers to force the owners of large coffee estates to liberalize the terms under which dependent workers labored. Large coffee producers were both willing to make these concessions in order to expand production, and able to make them because of the extraordinary level of coffee prices and their own profits. At the same time, their arrendatarios were encouraged by the high price of coffee and domestic food commodities to devote ever more time to cultivation of the parcels of land in their possession, and to sell their coffee and surplus food production on the market. Coffee hacendados were forced to tolerate these activities—and the de facto reduction of the labor time their workers put in on hacienda lands—because short of resorting to violence they had no choice.

This dynamic awaits detailed investigation. It was eloquently analyzed in the reports of Labor Office investigators,[68] however, and can be de-

68. See, for example, the remarkably clear analysis in the circular from J. R. Hoyos Becerros, Head of the Labor Office, to the principal coffee growers of Cundinamarca, dated January 4, 1929, in *Boletín de la Oficina del Trabajo* 1:1 (Aug. 1929):1-11. Urban migration and labor demand in public works, he noted, had created a critical labor shortage on the large coffee estates. "Given the shortage of hands, the estancias—relatively quite large—of the arrendatarios have become real competitors of the haciendas. That competition reaches such extremes that in some cases the estancia is charged with such small rent, sometimes practically nothing, that the arrendatario resists working on the hacienda at the going rate in the region" (p. 5).

duced from the nature of the collective demands, articulated by workers on a few large estates, that made their way into the public record. For example, thanks to the work of Hermes Tovar, Absalón Machado, and others, we know that workers on coffee estates in Quipile, Cundinamarca, presented petitions as early as 1925 that included demands for better food and housing and for shorter hours for freely contracted workers; for reduction of the labor tasks involved in payment of arrendatario land rents; for termination of uncompensated labor performed by arrendatarios in tasks beyond those specified in their contracts for agricultural labor; and for an end to the ejection of arrendatarios from their parcelas without fair compensation for improvements.[69] In 1927, the demands of arrendatarios on the huge coffee estate "El Chocho" in Fusagasugá, Cundinamarca, went further. They demanded freedom to sell their coffee and other food produced on their parcelas outside the hacienda, payment of land rent in money only, the fixing of land rent only every three years under the supervision of government labor inspectors, stipulation of the legal terms under which arrendatarios could be legally dispossessed of the land they occupied, establishment of legal guidelines for the compensation of improvements, and an end to fines for alleged infractions of contract obligations. They demanded as well an understanding that they would work voluntarily, at the prevailing free labor wage, on hacienda lands, that the hours of such work be the same as those established by the government in public works projects, that those engaged in such work be covered by the national laws regarding work-related accidents, that such workers be provided with rain gear when needed, that those without timber on their parcelas be granted access to hacienda woodlands for their construction needs, and finally that the hacendado issue each arrendatario a written copy of rental agreements and contracts. In addition, these arrendatarios put the hacienda owners on notice that in making these demands they did not renounce any rights or prerogatives that future laws might add to their "rights as workers." They ended their petition with the most revealing demand of all. They advised the owners that if they could not accede to these demands, a plan should be worked out so arrendatarios could "acquire ownership, by means of a bank, mortgages, and amortizations customary in these cases, of the lots of land they rent today."[70] Neither of these petitions was immediately successful, and workers on estates like these were forced to press their demands far into the future before they succeeded in winning the last of them. But the demands reveal a dynamic in the struggle between the classes on the great coffee estates that at the peak of the coffee boom decisively favored labor.

After 1928, as world coffee prices turned downward and labor demand in the Colombian economy slackened, coffee hacendados took the offen-

69. Machado, *El café* (cited in n. 26), pp. 247-48.
70. Tovar, *El movimiento* (cited in n. 59), pp. 76-80.

sive against their workers. Yet because of the special nature of coffee production on the large estates, economic depression tended not to help them turn the struggle with their workers to their temporary class advantage. Instead, their desperate efforts to preserve their position only stiffened the resolve of their workers, forced workers to broaden their collective organization, and radicalized worker demands.

The decline in coffee prices threatened the economic viability of the large coffee estates and jeopardized the very existence of the coffee hacendados as a class. They were burdened by mortgages and debts incurred in coffee expansion,[71] faced with the growing competition of more efficient small family coffee producers within their own estates, and stymied by the higher wages free laborers had come to expect. They attempted to solve their dilemma through the only means available to them: they attacked the recently won autonomy of their dependent labor force. By prohibiting the cultivation of coffee on parcelas, by banning the sale of agricultural commodities outside their haciendas, and by ejecting recalcitrant arrendatarios from their land, coffee hacendados hoped at one stroke to eliminate their competitors and recreate a cheap, abundant supply of dependent labor on their estates.

In executing this strategy, however, coffee hacendados faced obstacles not confronted by industrial capitalists. The latter customarily react to economic downturns by simply firing workers unwilling to accept reduced wages or more exploitative working conditions. Usually these workers drift away into a depressed free labor market and join others similarly dismissed in a desperate search for a way to sell their labor and preserve their existence. Industrialists then tap this pool of unemployed workers to reconstitute their labor force at regressive wage levels and under more exploitative conditions of work. But coffee hacendados confronted a class of workers at once less dependent on the sale of their labor and deeply entrenched in their position on the land. Worse, by the late 1920's dependent coffee workers were themselves also petty capitalists, primary-commodity producers in effective control of the land, cultivating products for the national and international markets. These workers, who before 1927 sought primarily the liberalization of work conditions to strengthen their position as independent producers, now refused to return to their former position as dependent laborers. The result was a running battle between the classes on many of the large estates that became more intense, not less, as the Depression deepened.

At first glance it would appear that the solution available to employers of free wage labor in other sectors of the Colombian economy would have aided coffee hacendados in their efforts to resolve their labor prob-

71. This is a theme that runs through the literature. See especially Palacios, *Coffee in Colombia* (cited in n. 30).

lem. In pursuit of subsistence, many unemployed workers, prominent among them those dismissed from public works construction, returned to the land. Coffee hacendados sought to take advantage of this influx of laborers desperate for work and access to the land to grow food. They intensified their efforts to eject intractable arrendatarios from the land and tried to replace them with a cheaper, more compliant work force.

Several factors inhibited the success of this grand project, however, and tended instead to produce militant class alliances between the jornaleros and arrendatarios on large coffee estates. The most important was the stubborn opposition of arrendatarios, who proved extremely difficult to dislodge effectively from the land. Some of these workers, who had learned to pursue their demands for liberalized work conditions collectively in the late 1920's, now joined together to develop ingenious tactics to resist dispossession. Depending on which strategy seemed likely to serve their interests most effectively, they mobilized alternatively as workers, renters, or colonos and appealed to the state for protection and satisfaction of their rights under three different bodies of law. They organized work stoppages and rent strikes, or claimed that the land they occupied and cultivated on the great estates was really part of the public domain. The last strategy caught coffee hacendados, whose title to the land was often faulty, in a legal quandary, threatening them with loss of their holdings through judicial procedures under public land law. The second strategy presented hacendados not only with legal problems, but with insoluble financial difficulties as well. They could perhaps evict a few arrendatarios and pay them, as prescribed by law, for their mejoras. But strapped as they were financially, they could not buy out their renters en masse, a situation arrendatarios fully appreciated and moved to exploit by acting in concert. Finally, work stoppages were not effectively countered by hiring new free wage workers. Even under the falling wage rates of the early 1930's most coffee hacendados could not afford production under a free wage system. Inefficient producers, they had been able to get by paying as little as a hundredth part of their potential wage bill thanks to the dependent labor system in force on the large coffee estates in the 1920's. (That at least was the estimate proffered by the Head of the Office of Labor after inspection of the books of some large coffee estates in the 1930's.)[72] Moreover, arrendatarios devised effective ways to counter the threat posed to their position by newly hired workers. On the one hand, they effectively intimidated workers willing to accept onerous labor contracts; on the other, they enticed many of these workers to join them in struggle. The first tactic was successful because owners could offer loyal and newly hired workers little protection on the vast domain of their iso-

72. J. V. Combariza to Ministro de Industrias, Bogotá, June 20, 1930, in *Boletín de la Oficina del Trabajo* 1:7 (June 1930):414.

lated estates. The success of the second reflected the common objective of all coffee workers. All wanted access to the land to grow food under favorable conditions, and the most favorable condition imaginable was that of a freeholder. Jornaleros joined arrendatarios as prospective colonos by laying claim to a freehold in the huge expanse of uncultivated land contained within most large coffee estates.[73] The fact that some of the workers who returned to the coffee estates had been exposed to labor organization and working-class ideologies fertilized these budding alliances between jornaleros and arrendatarios and injected into them advanced organizational tactics and systematic ideas about the injustice of capitalist society. It did not, however, imbue them with Marxist ideas regarding the socialization of the means of production. Despite the efforts of the Socialist and Communist activists who helped coffee workers organize and tried to orient their struggle by advocating the virtues of collectivization, the goal of an independent freehold remained paramount in the minds of most coffee workers.[74]

All this is not to imply that coffee workers in the late 1920's were very successful in turning back the capitalist offensive launched against them, or that coffee hacendados were helpless in the struggle against their increasingly organized and militant workers. The contrary is true. Coffee hacendados used their control over local politics to pursue their interests in increasingly violent and effective ways. Local police arrested striking arrendatarios and physically evicted them from the land. Local mayors and judges refused to enforce laws regulating indemnification for mejoras. Claims by workers to land that they alleged was part of the public domain ran afoul of local functionaries and were hopelessly bogged down in the national bureaucracy. Bands of thugs in the service of big landowners terrorized arrendatarios and colonos. They threatened workers and their families at gunpoint, burned their houses, destroyed their coffee trees, and turned hacienda cattle loose on their food crops. By the first years of the 1930's, armed confrontations between organized coffee workers and hacienda administrators and local police were common in the coffee zones of southeastern Cundinamarca and several parts of Tolima. Poorly armed coffee workers were usually the losers in this unequal confrontation. By 1933 several score workers had died in the struggle for the land, hundreds more had been wounded, and thousands had seen

73. By mid-1930 the Head of the Office of Labor declared that over the past two or three years the problem posed by workers claiming colono status on the large coffee estates had grown to huge proportions. "The working masses involved in this situation are huge in number, and the extent of the lands they occupy measures in the thousands of hectares." *Ibid.*, p. 416.

74. I have relied on evidence in the studies cited in n. 59 for the interpretation advanced in this section.

themselves despoiled of the fruits of years of painstaking labor on the land.

But they persisted. Thrown off their parcelas in one part of a hacienda, they moved at night and joined with others to fell the big trees in another part of the hacienda and begin cultivation anew, asserting their status as colonos. Plots of land belonging to those who were jailed were tended by their families or by sympathetic neighbors and friends. Workers driven off one hacienda joined with better organized workers on the next and renewed their struggle.

Faced with the growing insurgence of workers who refused to fulfill their labor obligations and disrupted the production of those willing to work, coffee hacendados turned increasingly to the state for solution of their problems. They blamed the labor unrest on subversive agitators, called for troops to restore order on their properties, and organized powerful interest groups to coordinate the offensive against labor, influence public opinion, and press government officials for effective solutions to their labor problems. Throughout the whole period of large-scale collective labor unrest on the big coffee estates (roughly 1925 to 1935), the balance of political forces at the national level decisively favored the interests of coffee hacendados as a class. High-level government officials might remonstrate against coffee hacendados, try to prod them into concessions to their militant workers, and attempt to mediate agrarian conflict. These officials continually pointed out the conservatizing virtue of parcelization and urged the big coffee growers of Cundinamarca to imitate their class brothers in the heart of the coffee zone in the Central Cordillera—that is, to leave coffee production to smallholders and concentrate their energies on controlling coffee commerce and finance. But the resolution of the labor problems on the large estates, slowly accomplished through basic changes in national land law and credit institutions, jealously guarded the class interests of the large estate owners. And although for a time organized coffee workers found allies in the national labor movement, where unions supported them and where small reformist and leftist political parties championed their interests in the press and sometimes in the congress, the partial victories they won in the mid-1930's were decided primarily on the ground, as a result of their own efforts.

Nevertheless, the insurgent labor movement on the great coffee estates in the late 1920's and 1930's always had a profoundly conservative meaning whose true dimensions were slowly revealed as coffee workers succeeded in their struggle for control of the land. Through government and private initiative, one by one the huge coffee estates that were the locus of collective worker protest after 1925 were bought up by the government and public banks. Their owners were fully compensated, and the land was broken into small parcels and sold to the coffee growers who cultivated them. On some estates coffee hacendados were forced to finance parcelization themselves, but the results were the same. Coffee workers became coffee smallholders, property owners who, like the majority of the coffee labor force in the rest of the country, found their deepest aspirations best expressed in the liberal values of the dominant culture, their needs serviced through the clientelist dynamics of traditional politics. Effectively channeled from the beginning into a legal struggle bounded by Colombian law, coffee-worker protest was now sublimated into a desperate struggle by smallholders to pay off their loans to banks and landowners and make their parcelas into going concerns. As the huge coffee haciendas that depended on precapitalist labor systems were slowly eliminated, coffee production in southeastern Cundinamarca and various parts of Tolima evolved toward the pattern of diffuse production units, owned and operated by smallholders and their families, that was becoming increasingly typical of the Colombian coffee economy as a whole. And with this change, the Colombian labor movement was stripped of its most explosive component in the early 1930's and forced to accommodate itself, as best it could, to the overwhelming weight of conservative political forces in Colombian society.

Neither the conservative implications of worker protest on the great coffee estates, however, nor the congenital weakness of the Colombian labor movement embodied in the social relations of production in the rest of the coffee export economy was obvious in the 1920's and early 1930's. The rapid development of the Colombian labor movement after the First World War, the explosive mobilization of Colombian workers during the coffee bonanza of the mid-1920's, the spectacular strikes led by Marxist labor leaders in the foreign-owned export enclaves, and the spreading organization of coffee workers on the great estates in Cundinamarca at the doorstep of the national capital in the late 1920's—all convinced political leaders on both the left and the right of the power of the workers' movement and the revolutionary threat it posed to capitalist society in Colombia. After the world war, first utopian-socialist and then Marxist parties emerged to channel the workers' movement politically.

Meanwhile, the Colombian ruling class, confronted for the first time by an organized and politicized class antagonist, cast about for effective ways to crush the workers' movement. In the process it became hopelessly divided over the alternative solutions of massive repression versus modest reform and co-optation. Little work has yet been done on the cleavage within the elite during this crucial period in Colombian history. We know, however, that as early as 1920 the bipartisan forces that had consolidated the liberal political and economic institutions which guided Colombia's coffee-based export development after 1910 began to contemplate ways to confront the challenge of a radical labor movement through social reform. What those moderate reformers within the Liberal and Conservative parties feared most was the polarization of Colombian politics into a reactionary repressive bloc, led by the right wing of the Conservative party, and a revolutionary socialist movement, formed out of an alliance between a Marxist labor movement and the left wing of the Liberal party. Such polarization, they feared, could trigger once again the partisan political exclusivism and civil conflict that had threatened and delayed the capitalist program of the Colombian elite at the end of the nineteenth century.[75]

Although the emergence of such a revolutionary coalition was successfully thwarted, the fears of the moderates within the elite proved a prescient analysis of the course of Colombian history during the next three decades. Despite the determined efforts of these bipartisan reformists, who managed to win control of the Colombian government at the start of the world crisis in 1930 and initiate legislation to defuse and institutionalize the labor movement, the Colombian ruling class split irrevocably over the issue of how to cope with insurgent labor. As the progressive leadership within the Liberal party moved to capture the labor movement and institutionalize it through modest reform and corporativist labor legislation, reactionary leaders within the Conservative party opposed concessions to popular forces at every turn. In the late 1920's Liberals effectively used the issue of repression of the left and labor to discredit the Conservative governments, split the Conservative party, and win the election that brought the party to national power in 1930. Conservatives in their turn wielded the issue of the Liberal governments' concessions to labor and the Communist left in the 1930's and early 1940's to discredit and split the Liberal party and regain national power in 1946.

There is an uncanny logic to this pattern of alternating rule by the factions of the Colombian ruling class during the three decades after 1920. It is a logic not fully captured in interpretations that emphasize the personalities of preeminent political leaders, the dynamics of Colombia's partisan political system, and the fortuitous events that always mark and seem to fundamentally change the course of political history. Nor is it a logic very closely linked to the macroeconomic and social changes (such as rates of industrialization and urbanization and changes in literacy and newspaper circulation) so central to the explanatory modes of liberal modernization theorists. Finally, it is a logic whose fundamental terms are not defined in Marxist treatments that purport to see in the ascension

75. See, for example, the revealing letters by Eduardo Santos, Luis Cano, and L. E. Nieto Caballero to Carlos E. Restrepo, Bogotá, June 20, 1920, and by Carlos E. Restrepo to Eduardo Santos, Luis Cano, and L. E. Nieto Caballero, Medellín, June 30, 1920, published in José Fernando Ocampo, *Colombia Siglo XX*, vol. 1 (Bogotá, 1980), pp. 314-21.

to power of the Liberal party in 1930 the emergence of an industrial bourgeoisie.[76] Understanding of Colombian history in the period 1920-60 emerges with clarity only when viewed from the perspective of the labor movement and the changing imperatives faced by a peripheral ruling class deeply enmeshed in the changing realities of an evolving world capitalist system.

By the end of the 1920's the Colombian ruling class perceived the insurgent labor movement as a threat to its ideological and political hegemony. It is easy to see with hindsight that the scope and strength of that movement was in reality quite limited. But contemporaries daily witnessed the novelty of a labor movement exulting in new-found strength, radical promise, and unbounded enthusiasm. By 1926 the Colombian labor movement had acquired some national unity and direction under the leadership of the Partido Socialista Revolucionario (PSR). A Marxist party affiliated with the Comintern, the PSR was formed out of early socialist cadres and dissident left-wing Liberals. Its top leadership, composed primarily of typesetters and journalists, organized and led the great strikes in the export enclaves in the middle and late 1920's. By 1927 leaders of the PSR were crisscrossing the nation promoting labor organization and radicalizing workers in multitudinous rallies in river ports and coffee towns as well as major cities. The popular appeal of the PSR's most celebrated public speaker, young María Cano, reveals something of the tenor of the insurgent labor movement of the time. A poetess born into a distinguished Liberal newspaper family of Medellín, she early developed a concern for the plight of the working poor. By the late 1920's she had become a symbol of insurgent labor, a speaker capable of electrifying the crowds of workers who flocked to hear her passionate rhetoric and the simple truths of her newly discovered Marxism. Workers at these rallies responded to her enthusiasm in kind. They cheered the Socialist Party and the advent of a new era of social justice. They christened her the "Flower of Work," the "Revolutionary Red Flower of Colombia."[77]

The class fears kindled in the minds of Conservative government officials by the growing insurgency of labor and the revolutionary rhetoric and leadership of the PSR in the late 1920's seemed to be confirmed in developments like those in the town of Líbano, Tolima, in 1929. Gonzálo

---

76. Illustrative of the first two approaches is Robert Dix's informative survey of twentieth-century Colombian politics, *Colombia: The Political Dimensions of Change* (New Haven, Conn., 1967); a provocative and particularly intelligent example of the last is Bejarano's "Fin" (cited in n. 22).

77. Ignacio Torres Giraldo, the companion of María Cano during these memorable national tours, who subsequently became a leader of the Colombian Communist Party and a major interpreter of Colombian labor history, effectively conveys the nature of the time and sympathetically interprets the character and intellectual development of his subject in his fascinating biography *María Cano: Apostolado revolucionario* (Bogotá, 1972).

Sánchez has shown that in that exceptional coffee municipio artisans created a remarkable revolutionary culture in the 1920's. They published radical newspapers, baptized their children in the "Santo Nombre de la Humanidad Oprimida," and set out in 1929 to organize rural coffee workers for the violent seizure of state power.[78] The abortive insurrection in which the workers of Líbano took part in mid-1929 was echoed in only two or three other towns along the Magdalena River and was promptly defeated by government forces. It was part of a wildly impractical plan developed by Marxist and radical Liberal leaders of the PSR to seize national power in conjunction with a simultaneous revolt in Venezuela.[79] The events in Líbano hardly represented an effective immediate challenge to capitalist rule or to the stability of the Conservative government. But they confirmed to many political leaders of both the left and the right the radical potential of the Colombian labor movement. Those who doubted had only to contemplate the insurgent coffee workers of Cundinamarca and parts of Tolima who were occupying the largest coffee haciendas in the country, questioning the basis of Colombian land law, and successfully, and almost daily, confronting the repressive forces of the state in coffee municipios just a few kilometers from Bogotá.

Throughout the late 1920's the Conservative governments responded to the challenge of labor primarily through repression. They insisted that labor insurgency was the simple product of a vast Bolshevik conspiracy. They pushed draconian laws through congress to ferret out and punish Marxist revolutionaries. They violently repressed striking workers. But the repression, effective against individual strikes and their leaders, was not very successful against the movement as a whole. And such repression exposed the Conservative governments to sustained attacks on their morality and nationalist credentials.

78. Sánchez's brilliant little book, *Los "Bolcheviques"* (cited in n. 60), recovers some of the ritual and world view of the revolutionary artisans of Líbano, a municipio that ranked third in national coffee production in the late 1920's. The cultural syncretism at work in the efforts of these artisans to cement their collective solidarity and forge an alternative vision of the world in a Catholic culture is revealed in the following words, recited at the baptismal ritual of a female child (pp. 78-79): "Your mission places special demands on you and those like you, since you are to open the way to a new social order and march toward the future in which the advent of a new life will rest on Justice flowing from the Socialist spirit. You will walk on the path of the ideal of Justice and you will stay apart from the columns of those who surrender to the fatalism of slavery with the cowardly thought that 'this is the way we have found the world and this is the way we shall leave it.' You will have faith in Justice and love for humanity. Instead of being a slave, may you illuminate with your flaming body the feast of tyranny. You are the priest called forth from the innermost recesses of your good Mother and part of the new generation liberated by the courageous efforts of the proletariat. Listen to the supplication of the modern worker: from tyranny, as from disease and hunger, set us free, even though it may be necessary to sacrifice our own existence." Líbano's apparently exceptional political culture needs further explanation. The municipio was much more isolated from the national market than comparable coffee counties; it was traditionally a Liberal island surrounded by Conservative municipios.

79. See Chapter 4 of this volume.

The most passionate of those attacks came from Jorge Eliécer Gaitán, the Liberal politician whose assassination in 1948 triggered the *bogotazo*. In 1929 he walked before congress carrying a small skull. It was a child's, he asserted, murdered by Colombian soldiers in the massacre of striking banana workers at the United Fruit installations in 1928.

More traditional leaders of the Liberal Party reacted to an insurgent labor movement at the end of the coffee boom in colder, more calculating terms. Future Liberal president Alfonso López publicly and candidly pleaded with the head of his party in 1928 to seize the opportunity to make the Liberal party into an intelligent, progressive instrument for the defense of established interests by denouncing the repression of the working class and recognizing the just aspirations of labor. Doing so, he argued, would enable the party to avoid eclipse by the left, and possibly catapult its democratic leadership into the full exercise of national power for the first time in half a century.[80]

The insurgency of Colombian workers in the late 1920's thus disconcerted and discredited the Conservative regime, emboldened the revolutionary left, and forced the Liberal party to modernize its social philosophy and rediscover its vocation for governance. Moreover, with the advent of the Great Depression, the social threat posed by the labor movement did not disappear in Colombia. If, as in other nations, the organized strength of urban and transport workers and free wage labor in the foreign enclaves was undermined by the economic downturn after 1928, the insurgency of rural coffee workers only gathered momentum and carried the threat to the heartland of the traditional Colombian coffee bourgeoisie.

It was a more immediate threat to ruling-class interests, however, one superimposed on the long-term problem posed by labor insurgency, that triggered the political crisis of 1930 and led to its resolution in the momentous transfer of power that put a Liberal-dominated government in control of the state for the first time in almost half a century. After 1928, the Conservative government proved incapable of sustaining the flow of foreign investment capital into the Colombian economy. Foreign investment to promote Colombia's development was the central pillar of the liberal economic and political institutions cemented into place by the bipartisan coalition after 1910. The abrupt cessation of foreign lending after 1928 threatened not only Colombia's immediate economic prosperity; it undermined the foundation of the entire social, institutional, and ideo-

---

80. This remarkable open letter of April 25, 1928, and a subsequent one dated May 20, 1928, in which López emphasized the financial mismanagement of the Conservative regime and its implications for social revolution in Colombia, illustrate the interpretation advanced in this section. They are reproduced in Ocampo, *Colombia* (cited in n. 75), vol. 1, pp. 332–45.

logical framework of Colombia's post-1910 export-oriented development. Subsequent events were to reveal that cessation of foreign lending obeyed causes far beyond the power of the Colombian ruling class or either of the political parties to remedy. But in the minds of contemporaries it was the Conservative regime, ironically the most successful in Colombian history in attracting foreign investment in the mid-1920's, that bore the brunt of the blame for the crisis of foreign lending as the world Depression deepened. In addition to the criticism of its ineffectual repressive labor policies, then, the Conservative regime was saddled with the political burden of an economic crisis beyond its control. The party foundered and divided over this dual challenge to its political hegemony, and the election of 1930 was won by a Liberal-dominated bipartisan coalition led by the principal architects of the institutional order established in 1910. The platform of the victorious Liberal party proclaimed an "open door for foreign capital" and affirmed that "agriculture is the axis and foundation of our national life." The choice of the Liberal presidential candidate was predicated on his intimate contact with U.S. bankers and the hope that he could induce them to reopen the floodgates of U.S. investment in Colombia.[81]

The Liberal-dominated government that came to power in 1930 embarked on a broad front to meet the dual labor and economic challenge confronting the Colombian elite at the start of the Great Depression. On the economic front, however, it was gradually forced by the reality of the world situation to reconsider its commitment to orthodox liberal principles and its hopes for a revival of large-scale foreign investment. Like other liberal regimes in Latin America during the world crisis, it reluctantly abandoned the gold standard, defaulted on the foreign debt, devalued the currency, raised the tariff, and pursued a panoply of other policies that tended to foster the industrialization of the nation in the 1930's. These policies are best understood, however, not so much as the handiwork of a mythical "national industrial bourgeoisie," but as the practical response of large coffee growers and exporters, bankers, and industrialists with largely compatible class interests to the exigencies and opportunities posed by the crisis in the world economy.[82]

81. On the platform see the brief discussion in Bergquist, *Coffee and Conflict* (cited in n. 4), pp. 256-57. Presidential candidate Enrique Olaya Herrera's special credentials are revealed in the explicit speech on the economic problems facing the country that he delivered before the cream of the Colombian elite at the Jockey Club in Bogotá ten days before the election. It is reproduced in Ocampo, *Colombia* (cited in n. 75), vol. 1, pp. 345-60.

82. Again, that the political economy pursued by the Liberal regimes of the 1930's promoted industrial growth reveals not so much the ascendancy of an industrial bourgeoisie as an attempt by export interests, bankers, and industrialists (who in Colombia were often the same people) to promote their class interests in the face of continuing world depression and the insurgency of rural workers. Colombian liberals like Alfonso López, son of one of the

The labor- and land-law initiatives of the Liberal governments of the 1930's and early 1940's should be viewed from this same perspective. They were not primarily designed to broaden the national market and promote more efficient capitalist agricultural production. They were conceived primarily to eliminate the social threat embodied in an insurgent labor movement. The labor legislation of 1931 opened the way for the rapid organization and institutionalization of labor in transport, manufacturing, and enclave export production. The body of labor law perfected between 1930 and 1945 sought to eliminate the revolutionary potential of these workers and reduce conflict in industrial relations. These laws established norms for the legal recognition of unions, recognized and restricted the right to strike, and regulated conflict between capital and labor through complex procedures for state-supervised conciliation, mediation, and arbitration.[83]

Similarly, the land-law reform drafted in the early 1930's and passed in 1936 sought to eliminate rural conflict between landowners and workers. Essentially, it legalized the status quo in the countryside. It validated the suspect titles of many large landowners, and regularized procedures for defining public lands and distributing them to colonos.[84]

These legal initiatives, given philosophical expression in the constitutional reform of 1936, were complemented by a range of other policies designed to curb the revolutionary potential and autonomy of the labor movement. These included significant and highly successful efforts to eliminate labor insurgency on large coffee plantations through government-sponsored or -supported parcelization programs,[85] initiatives to counter leftist labor organization in the countryside and cities by organiz-

largest coffee exporters in the country, differed in their approach to labor from their counterparts in nations like Argentina not because they more completely represented emerging industrial interests, but because they faced a mobilized labor movement, one which threatened the functioning of the export sector itself. In the end, as we shall see, the agricultural reform law enacted during López's presidency worked primarily not to transform Colombia's inefficient agrarian structure, but to eliminate the social threat to the interests of Colombia's large landowners.

83. On the intent of these laws see the alternative interpretations of Urrutia, *Development* (cited in n. 43), Part III; Moncayo and Rojas, *Luchas obreras* (cited in n. 43), Chap. 2; and Pecaut, *Política y sindicalismo* (cited in n. 43), Part II. None of these interpretations recognizes the importance of the rural workers' movement to this whole process, nor the essential unity of labor and land-reform law.

84. The land law drafted in 1933 at the height of labor insurgency on the coffee estates was more favorable to colono rights and more drastic in its definition of public domain lands than the law passed in 1936, after the wave of rural conflict had crested. See LeGrand, "From Public Lands" (cited in n. 46), for a discussion.

85. Detail on the parcelizations can be found in Palacios, "La propiedad agraria" (cited in n. 59), pp. 64 and 85. Of the 71 haciendas affected by labor conflict registered by the Labor Office between 1925 and 1930, 41 eventually experienced parcelization. By 1936 the Banco Agrícola Hipotecário, the government of Cundinamarca, and the national government had financed the parcelization of 28 coffee haciendas. After that, private parcelization, often financed by the Banco Agrícola Hipotecário, increased.

ing workers into Liberal-dominated unions,[86] and policies to promote the loyalty of organized labor as a whole to the Liberal governments through official sanction and government subvention of a national labor central (the Confederación de Trabajadores Colombianos).[87] Central to all these Liberal initiatives was the policy, formalized in 1936, of alliance with the single most important political force in the Colombian labor movement in the 1930's and early 1940's, the direct descendant of the Partido Socialista Revolucionario, the Communist Party of Colombia.

The decision of the Communist Party to link its fate with the corporativist reformers of the Liberal party in 1936 had serious repercussions for the development of the Colombian labor movement. That decision, which remained official Communist Party policy until the late 1940's, is often interpreted by the modern Colombian left as a grievous error. According to this view, the Communists' change in tactics doomed the development of a strong, autonomous labor movement, made labor dependent on official favor, and after 1945 rendered workers' organizations more vulnerable to attack from the right.[88] As we shall see, Communist acquiescence on the labor front and the Party's informal alliance with the progressive wing of the Liberal party—policies that brought the Colombian Party into line with the international directives of the Comintern— contributed to each of these outcomes. Proponents of this view, however, often push their indictment too far. The historical failure of the Colombian left was not simply a problem of leadership. Those who argue such a case tend to overestimate the potential strength of a labor movement constrained by the structure of Colombia's coffee export economy, ignore both the progressive and conservative dynamics of protest by the coffee workers on the great estates (who were the most combative sector of the labor movement in the early 1930's), and fail to appreciate both the magnitude and the failure of the left's efforts before 1936 to organize workers in the most important sector of Colombia's economy, coffee production, transport, and processing.

86. A rich account of these anti-Communist unionizing activities by the organizer of many of them is Julio Cuadras Caldas, *Comunismo criollo y liberalismo autóctono* (3d ed.; Bogotá, 1938).

87. For detail on this issue, as well as the broader problem of the Liberal alliance with the Communist Party, and Conservative and Church reaction to it, see Alvaro Tirado Mejía, *Aspectos políticos del primer gobierno de Alfonso López Pumarejo, 1934-38* (Bogotá, 1981).

88. According to the official Communist Party interpretation, formulated during the Cold War as a denunciation of "Browderism" (so called because of the alleged influence of the social democratic reformism of the head of the U.S. Communist Party), the Colombian Party leadership incorrectly interpreted the international Party line and became a virtual appendage of the Liberal Party. In fact, similar policies were adopted by all the Communist parties of Latin America in the decade following 1936, and their results were uniformly disastrous for the development of Latin American labor and for the growth of the Communist Party. Rather than critically assess the full meaning of its historic support of Soviet foreign policy, the Party prefers to fix the blame on Browder and the leaders of the other national parties during the period.

These efforts, undertaken both by Communists and by dissident Liberals in the short-lived Unión Nacional Izquierdista Revolucionaria (UNIR) led by Jorge Eliécer Gaitán, succeeded in organizing worker protest on the large coffee estates in the 1930's. The Communist Party, in particular, fostered the organization of scores of rural workers' leagues in which jornaleros, arrendatarios, and colonos joined forces in the struggle for control of the land. In the mid-1930's Communist activists tried valiantly to broaden their organizational base among workers in coffee production by linking rural leagues with organizations of coffee transport and processing workers in a grand alliance at the core of the Colombian export economy. Between 1934 and 1936 Communist cadres devoted the bulk of their considerable energy to the organization of a National Coffee Strike, which, after a series of false starts, finally got off the ground in the Central Cordillera during the peak of the harvest and processing season in Caldas in January and February 1935. Unlike many of its modern critics, then, the Colombian left in the mid-1930's had the virtue of recognizing where the locus of its weakness lay and the courage and resolve to try to overcome it.

The results of all these efforts, however, were not very impressive. True, collective struggle by rural coffee workers resulted in permanent organizational gains in some localities. Yet collective protest involved only a small minority of coffee municipios. In the rest the battle for control of the land was decided by individual initiative and partisan struggle within the boundaries of traditional politics. Moreover, even where Communist and dissident Liberal activists had the greatest organizational success, as they did in the southeastern Cundinamarcan coffee municipios of Viotá and Fusagasugá, respectively, the terms of success gradually undermined the position of the left. As organized rural coffee workers won control of the land they worked, they ceased to be a force for radical social and political change. Communist organizers, more consistently committed to social transformation than the dissident Liberals of UNIR, struggled with the ideological and political dilemma posed by the objectives of rank-and-file coffee workers and their own uncritical commitment to the virtues of collectivization throughout the 1930's. By mid-decade they had been forced to abandon their early efforts to organize landless coffee voluntarios in opposition to the arrendatarios who employed them, and to recognize instead the hunger for a freehold that united both groups in opposition to coffee hacendados. Yet they were acutely aware of the conservatizing influence implicit in the achievement of parcelization. And they struggled mightily to reconcile somehow the results of victory in the struggle for the land with their own vision of a collectivist future for the nation. "We need to feel that we are owners of the land," an organizer from Viotá informed readers of the Party's national newspaper *El Bolchevique* in 1935, "but to feel we are owners not because we have possession of it, but rather because we know how to defend it."[89] By 1938 the Party had resigned itself to full support for the principle of parcelization and devoted itself to criticizing the usurious terms offered workers by the Liberal government and the public and private banks.[90] The Party's position on parcelization was not simply a consequence of its alliance with Liberalism after 1936; it was a direct response to the reality of rank-and-file coffee workers' objectives.

The limits of the organizational drive by the left were starkly revealed in the National Coffee Strikes of the mid-1930's. Planned well in advance, the strikes sought to include "pickers, escogedoras, muleteers, and coffee production and processing workers in general."[91] Strike demands in 1934 included a 40 percent wage increase, an 8-hour day, Sunday rest with pay. They declared that workers in possession of land should have the right to cultivate any crop they wished, that all political prisoners should be freed, and that the right of all coffee workers to organize independently should be recognized.[92] In a few scattered localities workers in coffee production joined with urban coffee-processing workers to support these demands. But such alliances were rare. In most places the Communists' strike call went unheeded, a fact publicly admitted by the Party leadership in late 1934.[93] Nevertheless, the Party resolved to redouble its efforts in 1935. It would concentrate primarily on organizing the female work force in the coffee trilladoras.

In the mid-1930's some forty trilladoras existed in the coffee zone. Most of the larger coffee towns had more than one. These were usually small establishments employing anywhere from a dozen to several score workers. Cities in the coffee departments, such as Medellín, Manizales, and Pereira, had several large trilladoras, each of which employed more than a hundred workers. One source estimated that there were about 3,500 workers in the trilladora labor force in 1936. About 85 percent of these workers were escogedoras.[94]

Among the most exploited of Colombian coffee workers, escogedoras worked by the piece in some trilladoras, by the hour in others. In the oldest mills, where piecework predominated, they sat at small wooden ta-

89. *El Bolchevique* (Bogotá), Mar. 24, 1935, p. 4. This failure by orthodox Communists to grapple theoretically with the universal and progressive dimensions of coffee worker control over the production process continues into the contemporary era. I discuss its implications in detail in the final portion of the essay.

90. *Tierra*, Jan. 14, 1938, pp. 3 and 8.

91. *El Bolchevique*, Aug. 4, 1934, p. 1.

92. *El Bolchevique*, Sept. 22, 1934, p. 1.

93. Exceptions noted were the municipios of Florida, Restrepo, and Viotá.

94. The figures on the numbers of trilladoras and the size of the work force are from the *Anuario general de estadística* (Bogotá, 1936) as given in Machado, *El café* (cited in n. 26), pp. 136-37.

bles and regulated the flow of unselected beans down an incline before them. Paid about 40 centavos per *bulto* of 70 kilos of selected coffee beans, only the most accomplished escogedora might cull as much as one and a half bultos of high-grade coffee a day. The maximum wage of the fastest coffee escogedora was still well below the average wage of males in urban industry, and most escogedoras earned between one-half and two-thirds of that wage. Pieceworkers, many of whom were teenagers, were at the mercy of foremen who monitored their output. Foremen could claim that an escogedora had failed to pick out enough poor quality beans and require her to rework the lot before payment. At the newer trilladoras, escogedoras were paid by the hour, but work in these more mechanized plants created new kinds of problems. Many escogedoras could not accustom themselves to the dizzying speed of work at the conveyor belts that moved the unselected coffee past them. Some, one later claimed, habitually took over-the-counter drugs to settle their stomachs. Others found themselves docked for the time they were unable to work during the frequent power outages at the plants. Speedup and improved hulling machinery increased the output of escogedoras at mechanized trilladoras severalfold. Wages in these plants, however, were only slightly higher than the average wage in trilladoras where the selection process was not mechanized.[95]

Both Communist and UNIR activists were involved in organizational strikes at trilladoras in the major coffee towns and cities of Pereira, Chinchiná, Montenegro, Finlandia, Manizales, Santa Rosa, and Palestina in early 1935. The workers' petitions in these strikes usually sought wage increases, an eight-hour day, and coverage under national legislation governing compensation for industrial accidents. But they also demanded improvements in the organization of work and work conditions. At Pereira, for example, women pieceworkers demanded the right to elect the hulling machine operators who determined the volume and quality of the beans they selected. They also sought the right to begin work earlier, at six o'clock in the morning, demanded that wage workers be docked less for time lost during electrical power outages in the plants, insisted that women employees not be required to move heavy coffee bags to and from their work sites, and declared they needed better, cleaner sanitary facilities.[96]

95. The information in this paragraph draws on Antonio García's admirable description of the evolution of processing machinery, selection techniques, and wages in *Geografía* (cited in n. 6), pp. 457-68 and 326-31; on a remarkable interview with a 17-year-old escogedora union leader, Lilia González, published in *El Bolchevique*, Feb. 16, 1935; and on a personal interview with Bárbara González, a veteran escogedora and *salonera* (floor supervisor) who began work in a trilladora in Manizales at age 12 in 1922 and spent more than 40 years working in non-unionized trilladoras in that city, in Chinchiná, and in Santa Rosa (Chinchiná, Aug. 15, 1980).

96. *UNIRISMO* (Bogotá), Jan. 31, 1935, p. 2; *El Bolchevique*, Feb. 2, 1935, p. 2.

The women involved in these work stoppages confronted massive opposition from trilladora owners and local government officials. Employers fired suspected union members, locked workers out, threatened to have their coffee hulled outside Colombia, and appealed to railway officials for tariff reductions to move unprocessed coffee to trilladoras in areas unaffected by labor unrest. Government officials, especially mayors, banned meetings of striking escogedoras. They unleashed police to disperse and arrest pickets, break up union meetings, and dismantle collective kitchens set up to feed workers on strike. Several workers were killed in clashes between strikers and local police during January and February 1935. Scores of women were beaten and/or arrested. Communist labor activists were ferreted out and transported in cages to trial in the cities of the coffee zone. Sensational press reports in the major dailies of Colombia, far from emphasizing these injustices, played instead on the fears of male readers and the anti-Communism of the Colombian middle and ruling classes. Striking women workers were described in one headline as trying to "strangle" a truck driver bringing coffee into a strikebound trilladora. Communist conspirators were accused of setting fire to a large trilladora that burned to the ground during the strike.[97]

Throughout these strikes, escogedoras received strategic and material support from organized transport workers and artisans in coffee towns. Some of these unions struck in solidarity, others donated funds, others offered their union halls for meetings and shielded women strikers from government repression. (According to the accounts in both the Communist and the UNIR press, male workers were the victims of police gunfire during these confrontations; women suffered from wounds inflicted by sabers and billy clubs.) This support, and the determination of the escogedoras themselves, enabled some of the strikers to win small wage increases at several trilladoras in the Central Cordillera during the first months of 1935. Nevertheless, once the strikes were over employers dismissed union activists, and the newly organized unions proved incapable of protecting their hard-won gains. By November 1935, Antonio García concluded his survey of unions in the heart of the coffee zone by noting that only two organizations of escogedoras existed in the whole of Caldas. Together they represented only 8 percent of the escogedora labor force in the department. A year before, he reflected, officially unrecognized organizations of coffee escogedoras had constituted the bulk of the labor unions in Caldas.

The reasons for this organizational failure lie partly in certain structural features of Colombian coffee production and processing. Once coffee had

97. Fairly detailed coverage of these strikes appears in the pages of *Pluma Libre*, a *gaitanista* weekly published in Pereira, in *La Voz de Caldas* (Manizales), in the Communist and UNIR papers cited earlier, and in the major Liberal daily, *El Espectador*.

been dried it could be stored almost indefinitely before husking. It could also be exported unhusked. The fact that hulling mills were highly dispersed in Colombia meant that growers and exporters could move coffee through towns unaffected by strike activity. Finally, escogedoras seem to have been especially vulnerable to union-busting tactics and strikebreakers. Charged in Colombian culture with primary responsibility for care of the family, women who lost their jobs were denied the geographic mobility available to most men in their search for new employment. Moreover, the better machinery of the modern trilladoras being built in Colombia in the 1930's cut the need for labor in the selection process roughly in half. In fact, Antonio García implied that the motive for the strikes of 1934 and 1935 may have been the rationalization of production and the decline in the number of jobs available to escogedoras.[98] Be that as it may, although escogedoras did not give up the struggle to organize themselves, they remain un-unionized even today.[99]

In this way the organizational efforts of the left in Colombia's coffee export economy met with failure. Like the vast majority of rural coffee workers, escogedoras proved resistant to union-organizing efforts. These workers also remained electorally indifferent to both the Communist Party and the UNIR throughout the early 1930's. The congressional elections in early 1935 following the coffee strike revealed the depth of rural Colombians' loyalty to the traditional parties. Except for pockets of support, such as the municipios of Aracataca (in the heart of the banana zone) and Viotá (an exceptional part of the coffee region), Communist electoral support remained minuscule in rural areas.[100] Gaitán's UNIR had fared no better in most of rural Colombia, and in 1935 he first declared his party's abstention from the elections, then decided to dissolve the UNIR and return to the Liberal fold. In the mid-1930's, then, not only the Communist Party (whose action can be explained by international directives) but the UNIR (whose decision cannot) elected to join forces with the Liberal party. At least in part the decisions of both parties were motivated by their organizational and political failure in the coffee zone. Neither had been able to mobilize a powerful working-class constituency able to subvert the political hegemony of the traditional parties in the heart of the Colombian economy.

By the end of the 1930's the threat posed to the Colombian ruling class by an insurgent labor movement had been eliminated. That result

98. García's observations are from *Geografía* (cited in n. 6), pp. 336 and 314. The material I was able to uncover does not support his intriguing idea on the motivations of the strikers, however. That question, like analysis of these strikes as a whole, is worthy of much more investigation.

99. A major organizational strike enveloped the trilladoras of Honda, Tolima, in mid-1944, for example. Though it led to short-term wage hikes, it failed to secure protection for union personnel, and the unions there consequently did not endure.

100. *El Bolchevique* provides electoral returns and comment on May 25, 1935, p. 4.

owed more to the intrinsic weakness of Colombian labor and to the dynamic of social and political life in the coffee economy than it did to the reforms and initiatives pursued by the Liberal regimes after 1930. But with the apparent success of Liberal labor and land reforms, important segments within the Colombian elite began to abandon their support of corporativist labor legislation and land law reform. And as the Second World War came to an end, and the imperatives and opportunities posed for capital by the restoration of the liberal world order took form, a consensus emerged within the Colombian ruling class that the labor and agrarian reforms of the 1930's had become costly, even dangerous, anachronisms.[101]

Between 1944 and 1946 the labor and agricultural policies pursued by the Liberal regimes of the 1930's were largely reversed. In the context of rising coffee prices and a demobilized rural labor movement, coffee growers won legislative means to facilitate the re-creation and extension of dependent labor systems on large holdings. Law 100 of 1944 protected landowners from the pretensions of sharecroppers who declared themselves colonos, authorized them to prohibit cultivation of all but subsistence food crops in sharecropping contracts, provided for the rapid assessment and payment of mejoras, and required workers to abandon the land immediately once their contracts expired.[102] The labor legislation of 1945 (Law 6 of that year) granted organized labor increased material benefits and for the first time protected union leaders from dismissal from their jobs. It also protected striking workers from scab labor, declaring that while a legal strike was in progress employers could not make new work contracts. But the law also severely limited the potential power of unions by making the plant-level union, not the industrywide federation, the fundamental unit in Colombian labor law. It greatly expanded the definition of public services in which strikes were prohibited. And it extended the range of mandatory conciliation and arbitration procedures. Under the public-service regulations of this law, the single most powerful and militant labor union in Colombia, the bastion of Communist strength in the labor movement, the River Transport Workers Union, was crushed by the government when it struck in defense of a work-sharing plan at the end of 1945.[103]

---

101. From the perspective of a demobilized labor movement, neither the Liberal party's decision to choose Eduardo Santos over Darío Echandía as presidential candidate for the term 1938-42, nor the more conservative course of López's second government and its growing illegitimacy, nor the tenacious resistance of the party hierarchy to the candidacy of Gaitán in 1946 appears in the enigmatic light often cast on it in the liberal historiography that deals with this period.

102. Machado, *El café* (cited in n. 26), pp. 331-48.

103. Throughout the late 1930's and early 1940's this industrial union, with 39 affiliates, engaged in a valiant struggle against the river transport companies and three Liberal presidents to preserve its power and protect its members' jobs in the face of declining river cargo. That decline reflected growing navigational problems caused by silt from the eroding coffee

The deep division within the Liberal party by the mid-1940's, which split the party in the electoral campaign of 1946 and enabled the Conservative party to regain national political control, reflected in large part the lack of elite consensus over the benefits and advisability of continuing the labor- and social-reform policies of the 1930's. That division was sealed and complicated by the politics of Jorge Eliécer Gaitán. Following his failure to launch an effective rural movement for reform and his return to the Liberal party in the mid-1930's, Gaitán slowly built a mass political constituency in the major cities of the nation, especially Bogotá. These cities were growing as urban service and manufacturing industries expanded and rural political and social tension intensified after 1930. Gaitán offered the urban poor and the struggling middle class an appealing vision of what was wrong with Colombian society and a vague program of reform. He divided Colombian society into the *pueblo* and the *oligarquía*, the *país nacional* and the *país político*. The great undifferentiated mass of people in the país nacional (which Gaitán defined to include everyone except the economic and political elite) worked, sacrificed, and struggled, yet went unrewarded in a grossly unjust social system. Gaitán embodied in his program and in his person, in his demagogic political style, and in his passionate and often violent oratory the social and ideological schizophrenia of the middle class. He championed the principles of private property, hard work, social justice, and public morality. His message also appealed to a largely unorganized urban working class deprived of an autonomous vision of its place in society. That class was socialized into the liberal values and Catholic morality of a mainstream culture reinforced by the dynamics of small-farm coffee society. Yet it was freer of the clientelist arrangements that kept most rural workers in the fold of the traditional party leadership. Gaitán won a huge following in the cities, learned to manipulate urban crowds creatively and effectively, and decided, against the odds, to launch an independent presidential campaign in opposition to the Liberal party's official candidate in 1946. His strategy was first abetted and then taken advantage of by the most sectarian elements in the Conservative party. At the last minute they launched a Conservative candidate of their own whose class background and ties to the coffee economy and to industry made him acceptable to political elites of both parties. The Conservative candidate won the election over a majoritarian

slopes, and intensified competition from alternative land transport systems. For the union's account of that struggle see "Manifiesto de Fedenal," *El Diario Popular* (Bogotá), June 20, 1945, pp. 3-4. U.S. officials watched developments in this Communist-led union with care. Nelson R. Park to Secretary of State, Barranquilla, Oct. 19, 1940, USNA/DS 821.504/117; Lane to Secretary of State, Bogotá, Oct. 27, 1942, USNA/DS 821.504/129; James D. Bell, "Special Report on Colombian Confederation of Workers," Aug. 14, 1945, USNA/DS 821.504/8-1445.

but divided Liberal party; Gaitán captured the most urban votes, but came in third.[104]

Like the Liberal party itself, by the mid-1940's organized labor and the Communist Party were also deeply divided by the changing labor policies of the Liberal political elite. As the leaders of the Liberal party abandoned the pro-labor, corporativist reformism of the 1930's, unions and Communists split over the issue of continued support for the official leadership of their erstwhile Liberal party ally. The increasingly reactionary stance and the union-busting policies of the Liberal government that paved the way for the Conservative restoration of 1946 thus signaled a return to the repression of organized labor and the left, and, by dividing the labor movement, also facilitated that process.

The repression of labor greatly intensified under the steadily more reactionary Conservative regimes of the late 1940's and early 1950's. The labor policies of these governments, undertaken in the context of a postwar strike wave with the clear objective of placing Colombia in an advantageous position for the resumption of foreign investment in the postwar period, were supported by the moderate leadership of both of the traditional parties. The labor initiatives of the late 1940's proceeded on two levels. On the first they attacked the power of the existing organized labor movement. During 1948 government decrees required unions to seek government approval for union meetings and meeting agendas, undermined the immunity of labor leaders fired by their employers for union activities (employers who did so were simply subject to fines), and took from the courts and placed in the hands of the executive the power to declare public-service strikes illegal. In mid-1948 the government set up a special commission to write a new Labor Code, which was completed and promulgated in 1950. The code systematized most of the restrictive labor initiatives of the previous five years and added some new ones. It established the single-company union as the basis of Colombian labor organization. It regularized and expanded the restrictions on public-service strikes, gave the executive power the faculty to declare such strikes illegal, and extended the provisions for their compulsory arbitration. A major new departure in the Code was a ban on sit-in strikes. In addition, new provisions governing collective contracts required that workers give up the benefits of existing contracts when they chose to negotiate new ones. Finally, government labor policy eliminated the re-

104. Most of the ideas in this paragraph are creatively developed in a major revisionist study of Gaitán and the bogotazo by Herbert Braun, "The *Pueblo* and the Politicians of Colombia: The Assassination of Jorge Eliécer Gaitán and the *Bogotazo*" (Ph.D. diss., University of Wisconsin, 1983). I have emphasized the contextual and class dimension of a political analysis that in Braun's hands is psychological and cultural.

strictions on parallel unions. That innovation was vital to the other dimension of the postwar labor initiatives, the stimulation of a new kind of unionism.

Under this new philosophy, typical of trends in the labor movement all over the Western world, labor would give up its political concerns and any pretense to control over the production process in exchange for a share of productivity gains. Promoted by the Catholic Church, by government policy, and by many of Colombia's industrialists, the new unionism developed under the legal protection accorded the single-company union in Colombia's new labor laws. In the late 1940's and early 1950's unions devoted to these principles, grouped under the tutelage of a new labor central, the Unión de Trabajadores Colombianos (UTC), emerged to dominate the burgeoning industrial sector of Colombia's rapidly expanding postwar economy. This labor central, since the 1950's the largest in Colombia, early won the approval and support of U.S. government officials and the conservative leadership of the major U.S. labor federations.[105]

By the late 1940's the whole period of Colombian history defined by the rise of an insurgent labor movement in the 1920's and the crisis of the world capitalist system (1930-45) was complete. In ways no single political leader or faction could have fully foreseen, the disunity of Colombian political elites over the labor question, and the alternation in power of the traditional parties, served ruling-class interests admirably. Under the corporativist Liberal initiatives of the 1930's the labor movement was effectively deradicalized and institutionalized under Colombian law. Under the repressive Conservative initiatives of the late 1940's, a weakened and domesticated labor movement was reduced to political and ideological impotence. Virtually all the leaders of both parties were united in their attitude toward labor by the late 1940's. All envisioned a weak non-Com-

105. The consensus of opinion in Mariano Ospina's bipartisan cabinet on the need to "confront" Colombian labor and correct the "demagogic, uneconomic, unscientific social and labor legislation" is reported in a confidential dispatch from Willard L. Beaulac to Secretary of State, Bogotá, Sept. 16, 1948, USNA/DS 821.504/9-1648. Beaulac solicited this report on the labor policy of the government by reminding the foreign minister of a point he made to Colombian officials earlier: that unsatisfactory treatment of the labor problems facing U.S. companies "raised the question of whether Colombia was entitled to receive loans from the United States." This document was drafted three days after the memorandum on Tropical Oil's suggestions for dealing with its labor problems cited in n. 66. On the labor laws, see Moncayo and Rojas, *Luchas obreras* (cited in n. 43), Chap. 3. On the genesis and expansion of the UTC, see Urrutia, who emphasizes its distance from the Conservative party and celebrates its apolitical economistic orientation (*Development* [cited in n. 43], Chap. 12), and James Backer, who traces its links to the Church, "La historia de la influencia de la iglesia sobre el sindicalismo colombiano," *Razón y Fábula* 22 (Nov.-Dec. 1970):6-27. Early contacts between U.S. officials and the Catholic advisers of the UTC are revealed in John C. Wiley to Secretary of State, Feb. 28, 1945, and Jan. 21, 1946, USNA/DS 821.504/ 2-2846 and 821.504/1-2146 respectively. A critical examination of UTC membership claims is Alvaro Delgado, "En torno de la crisis de la UTC," *Estudios Marxistas* 9 (1975):33-65.

munist labor movement, confined to the pursuit of bread-and-butter unionism, led by responsible bureaucratic leaders, and efficiently regulated by the state. Such a labor movement would guarantee Colombia's successful integration into the postwar world capitalist order.

But political institutionalization of that consensus and coordinated pursuit of this postwar vision were delayed for almost a decade. For if the division of the elite and the alternation in power of the traditional parties in 1930 and 1946 worked to demobilize labor and channel class conflict into traditional political paths, that very process gradually assumed a dynamic not entirely functional even to ruling-class interests. Alternation in power of the traditional parties unleashed the sectarian potential of the Colombian political system. As class conflict was directed into traditional political channels it gradually carried political events and control of public policy out of the hands of moderate leaders in both political parties. By the end of the 1940's the Conservative and Liberal parties, and the majority of the Colombian people, were locked in violent political conflict. For the Colombian ruling class the violence at mid-century proved only a temporary impediment to the institutionalization of a postwar liberal capitalist order. But for the Colombian working class the frightening civil convulsion known as the Violence proved an unmitigated and enduring disaster.

The Violence and Small Farm Coffee Civilization

The Violence, defined as the period of civil commotion that disrupted Colombian society between 1946 and 1966, was not a single, uniform social phenomenon. It took on different dimensions and shades of meaning as it enveloped parts of Colombian society with greater or lesser intensity over two decades of national history. The first, most important, and most intense phase of the Violence was the period 1946 to 1953, when more than three-fourths of its almost 200,000 victims lost their lives. This period was the most "political" and "traditional" of its phases. That is, whatever their other motives, partisans in the struggle rationalized their actions within the terms of the traditional struggle between the Liberal and Conservative parties for control of political power. A Conservative regime, increasingly partisan and violent in its pursuit of political hegemony and public order, governed the nation during this period. Liberals contested that power in a major urban riot (the bogotazo) and on the battlefield (especially on the cattle-producing plains of Meta and Boyacá east of the capital). But the most important and enduring form of Liberal resistance, characteristic of the political contention in the rural coffee-growing heartland of the country, was through ad hoc armed groups and guerrilla bands that attacked Conservatives and the repressive forces of the state in sporadic confrontations using hit-and-run tactics. This whole period was characterized by very rapid economic growth paced by extraordinarily high coffee prices, by price inflation, and by declining real wages for rural and urban workers.

In mid-1953 the Conservative government was overthrown in a military coup backed by moderate leaders of both of the traditional parties. The military government succeeded in pacifying much of the country through conciliatory political policies, a proclamation of general amnesty for Liberals willing to lay down their arms, and a vague program of social reform. By 1956, however, the military regime had evolved toward full-blown dictatorship. Its program for political and social reform had taken on a formally corporativist rationale and design that threatened the liberal political and economic institutions of the nation. It found itself enmeshed in an economic and fiscal crisis brought on by a dramatic fall in coffee prices. And it was confronted by a recrudescence of partisan conflict in the countryside that it proved powerless to control. During 1957 the leaders of the Liberal and Conservative parties joined forces to topple the dictatorship and institutionalize a political solution to the Violence. They agreed to share political power and all political posts equally. In 1958 the nation returned to civilian rule under this formula. For 16 years thereafter Liberals and Conservatives alternated in control of the presidency and all other political and administrative government offices were divided equally between them. The events of 1957 and 1958 closed the period of the Violence proper. During this second and less intense phase, roughly the years 1954 through 1957, some 16,000 people lost their lives. The political agreement between the parties removed the partisan excuse for the violence and restored ideological and political consensus within the ruling class and effective authority to national political institutions.

Traditional politics played little direct role in the third and least intense period of the Violence, when it became more "economic" and "criminal," and in exceptional areas, more "revolutionary." Between 1958 and 1966, a period of depressed coffee prices and relatively sluggish economic growth, some 17,000 to 18,000 people lost their lives in the Violence. During this phase the struggle was waged primarily between the Colombian army and organizations of fierce bandits in the central coffee zones, and between Colombian army units aided by U.S. counterinsurgency teams against Marxist-led rural communities in isolated regions in the mountains of central and southern Colombia.[106]

106. For clear, detailed treatment of the politics of this whole period see Dix, *Colombia* (cited in n. 76). Oquist, *Violencia* (cited in n. 3), provides a good discussion of the diversity of the Violence and furnishes the figures on the number of victims which I have adapted to the periodization used here. See his Table VI-1, p. 322. The material on the Violence is extensive, but see, in addition to Oquist, the review by Russell W. Ramsey, "Critical Bibliography on La Violencia in Colombia," *Latin American Research Review* 8:1 (Spring 1973):3-44. The best work on the Violence after 1958 is Gonzálo Sánchez and Donny Meertens, *Bandoleros, gamonales y campesinos* (Bogotá, 1983).

The Violence was thus a many-faceted process whose social and political features and geographical focus changed as it evolved over two decades of time. The complexity of the Violence, however, should not obscure its essential unity. It was primarily, although not exclusively, a social phenomenon that obeyed the exclusivist, partisan, clientelist dynamic of Colombia's traditional political system. And it was a social phenomenon focused primarily, although not exclusively, in the coffee zones. These two unifying characteristics were interrelated.[107]

The potential for violent civil confrontation inherent in the partisan dynamics of the Colombian political system was unleashed by the alternation in power, in 1930 and 1946, of the two traditional parties. These crucial political turning points, engineered by moderate bipartisan leaders in the face of vital class imperatives, triggered a life-and-death struggle by party rank-and-file for exclusive control at the local level. Politics in rural Colombia was not about the philosophical ideals and sectoral and class interests of the contending national parties. It concerned the political and personal resources one could marshal in the struggle to improve one's social position and avoid proletarianization. From the beginning, political contention at the local level was deeply enmeshed with the struggle for the land and other forms of property, for access to jobs and credit, and for protection from police and the law. The stakes in this struggle in the rural areas (where most Colombians still lived in the 1940's and 1950's) forced local rank and file to support the most sectarian and opportunistic leaders of the parties at the national level, those willing to use their power and talents for exclusively partisan ends. As these leaders consolidated control over the parties, or (in the case of the party in power) over the national government, and used their influence for partisan ends, the vicious circle of partisan struggle at the local level intensified. It led inexorably toward violent intimidation and resistance between opposing blocs of partisans, some aided by the weight of the institutions of the state, others forced to resist them. The abuse of and resistance to government authority slowly led to the breakdown of effective government at both the local and the national levels. Crimes against individuals and property perpetrated by local officials, police, and the army in the name of party went unpunished. Retaliation was common, and its authors often managed to escape unapprehended. With the breakdown in public authority and social control on the local level, the struggle for individual gain became a nightmare of land grabbing, robbery, and extortion. The means used to accomplish these material ends degenerated from polite and subtle persuasion to armed threats, house burnings, and brutal slayings. Once the Violence began in a region it fed on itself. Relatives,

107. There is a consensus in the literature on the first proposition, much qualitative evidence but no systematic analysis to support the second, and very limited and partial recognition of the third.

friends, and co-partisans avenged the crimes against victims by retaliating against their alleged authors, against those authors' families and friends, or simply against those identified with the opposite political party. In doing so they often simultaneously accomplished cherished material goals and settled old social debts and long-smoldering personal grudges.[108]

Most people in regions affected by the Violence engaged in none of these acts. But many tried to take advantage of them in one way or another. They encroached on lands abandoned by victims or tried to purchase them at a low price. Landowners paid armed groups for protection and bought out frightened arrendatarios and sharecroppers and neighboring smallholders at ridiculous prices. The reverse was also true, if largely unrecognized in the literature on the Violence. Larger landowners were less desperate and had more alternatives open to them than smallholders and landless workers. Administrators of large estates had little to gain and much at risk by remaining on lands threatened by land-hungry workers on every side. Both were less likely to subject themselves to the terror and insecurity of life in areas where violence was endemic. Many sold out for what they could get to local merchants or to their sharecroppers, renters, and nearby smallholders.[109] Only a few people in violence-ridden regions—the criminal and depraved, or those maimed psychologically by the violence itself—seized upon the breakdown of social control, legal authority, and political order to terrorize and torture their victims and perpetrate the mass murders, decapitations, mutilations, and sex crimes that received such full attention in the contemporary press. But opportunistic national political leaders manipulated the partisan passions enflamed by such accounts to consolidate their power within the parties.

108. Many of these themes, painfully familiar to all those who have lived in the coffee zones, are given lucid treatment by Jaime Arocha in *La violencia en el Quindío* (cited in n. 55). That book is an anthropologically oriented study of homicide in a major coffee municipio located in the Quindío, the part of the old department of Caldas that today is the newest and most productive part of the Colombian coffee zone. On what he calls "la impunidad institucionalizada," see p. 16; on the conflict between neighbors in defense of property, pp. 100-101; on the struggle for the land as motive in violent confrontations, pp. 140-41; on the politicization of the local police and the militarization of local government during the era of the Violence, pp. 146-47; on electoral intimidation, pp. 148-49; on the confusion between political partisanship, the struggle for personal gain, and the desire to defend one's honor and dignity, p. 141.

109. The direction of land tenure changes in the coffee zones during the Violence awaits systematic study. Although the evidence points to land concentration in the later phases of the Violence, it may be that significant diffusion also occurred, especially during its early stages. Personal knowledge confirms that was the case in Vergara, Cundinamarca, a municipio with a smallholder Conservative majority. There local partisan conflict and Conservative political hegemony at the national level after 1948 resulted in the loss through sale of the bulk of a huge hacienda owned by a Liberal family, the Silvas, in the northeastern part of the municipio. The land was sold in small parcels on favorable terms to former renters and sharecroppers and to Conservative smallholders from other parts of the municipio. For other illustrative examples, see Sánchez and Meertens, *Bandoleros* (cited in n. 106).

And at the local level these sensational accounts helped rationalize more civilized forms of violence—economic coercion and the application of legal tools for personal and partisan ends—practiced by the "decent" and the well-to-do.

The political aspects of the Violence and the sensational coverage of its most bestial expressions distracted contemporaries—and many subsequent scholars as well—from the material and class dimensions that lay at its core. Yet the Violence, more than anything else, was the ultimate political expression of the ongoing struggle for land and social mobility in the coffee zone. By the late 1940's that struggle had become both more desperate and less collective than it had been in the early 1930's. More desperate because lands suitable for coffee cultivation had largely been appropriated and put to use by that time. (Herein may lie the primary reason for the drastic decline in the rate of growth of coffee exports after mid-century.) More desperate as well perhaps because subdivision of family-owned farms through inheritance rendered many farms unviable, at a time when growing competition for land appropriate to coffee cultivation intensified and made reconsolidation of viable family farms more difficult. (That at least is one way to account for the end to the remarkable growth in the number of small coffee farms sometime between the late 1930's and the early 1950's that is revealed in the coffee census data.) More desperate, finally, because at the end of the 1940's small coffee producers and workers were no longer as self-sufficient as they had been two decades earlier. They depended more on purchases in the market for their subsistence needs and devoted more land to coffee instead of domestic food production. Postwar price inflation thus left them particularly hard pressed to feed themselves. Yet high coffee prices lured them, as it did large growers and domestic food producers, to devote even more of their land to coffee production.[110] Landless and migrant wage workers were the most vulnerable to price inflation. Totally dependent for their subsistence on the market, they lacked both organizational means to pressure employers for higher wages and access to the land to provide for subsistence needs.[111]

The struggle became more individualistic because, by the 1940's, coffee workers were deprived of the support of the collective organizations at the local level and the leftist parties at the national level who sought in the

110. This last is the central thesis advanced by Arocha to explain the Violence of the late 1940's. His argument is suggestive, but lacks a solid statistical base. See *La violencia* (cited in n. 55), pp. 31-34.

111. Arocha found in his sample that landless workers were more likely than smallholders to be both the instigators and the victims of violent confrontations, but that the margin of difference was greater among instigators. He also found that a high percentage of victims of violent acts were immigrants into the municipio (*La violencia*, pp. 90-91). On the basis of their evidence, Sánchez and Meertens conclude that the leaders of bandit gangs were usually smallholders, whereas their followers were usually landless laborers.

1930's to organize and orient their struggle. These organizations were
never very widespread at the local level, and their activities in the 1930's
were most influential in areas peripheral to the core of the coffee zone in
the Central Cordillera, the area that became the primary focus of the Violence after 1948. Nevertheless, the existence of the national leftist parties
in the early 1930's had made a difference. They sent organizers into isolated areas and coordinated activities nationally. Their newspapers collected and propagated alternative information and projected a different
vision of reality. They used the courts and the congress to defend the
rights of organized workers and their leaders. Vociferous champions of
insurgent labor, they helped to force the Liberal leadership to proceed
slowly and cautiously to consolidate the party's political hegemony after
1930. And it was not until the class threat posed by labor and the left in
the early 1930's receded that the Conservative leadership, initially divided
and disconcerted by the loss of national power, adopted the intransigent
partisan political stance that characterized its dominant faction throughout the late 1930's and 1940's. After 1935, however, the partisan struggle
between the traditional parties intensified at the national level and a revitalized Conservative leadership turned its heavy fire against labor and the
left. As both the Communist Party and Gaitán's UNIR gave up the difficult struggle to organize workers in the export sector and scurried into
the Liberal fold for protection, they left the unorganized coffee labor
force with little alternative to traditional partisan channels to defend its
interests and pursue its goals.

There is as yet no quantitative study that demonstrates with precision
that the Violence was primarily a phenomenon of the coffee zones. That
proposition is amply supported in the descriptive and qualitative literature on the subject. But since the Violence was more than a civil conflict
in the coffee zones—one that included such disparate phenomena as the
bogotazo and the struggle in the cattle-producing llanos to the east of the
national capital—the qualitative evidence tends to obscure the extent to
which, from the beginning, the Violence was mainly a product of the
coffee zones. The most systematic quantitative study of the Violence unfortunately does not address the question of its relationship to coffee production. In that study Paul Oquist demonstrates that municipios under
the established electoral hegemony of one or the other of the traditional
parties were less likely to experience the Violence than those where the
electoral control of one party or the other was weaker or where there was
real competition between the parties.[112] That quantitative evidence supports the contention, assumed throughout this essay, that the Violence
was directly related to the struggle for political control at the local level.
So does the fact, also demonstrated quantitatively by Oquist, that muni-

112. Oquist, *Violencia* (cited in n. 3), Table II-24, p. 88. I do not review here Oquist's
careful evaluation of the quality of his statistics or his definition of terms.

TABLE 5.5

*Deaths Attributed to the Violence in Colombia, 1946-57, and
Coffee Production, 1955, Ranked by Department*

Deaths attributed to the Violence		Coffee production	
Department	Deaths, 1946-57	Department	Tons
Antiguo Caldas	44,255	Caldas	117,202
Tolima	30,912	Antioquia	59,600
Antioquia	26,115	Tolima	56,075
Santander (Norte)	20,885	Valle	50,042
Santander (Sur)	19,424	Cundinamarca	28,547
Valle	13,106	Huila	15,498
Meta	5,842	Santander (Norte)	10,484
Boyacá	5,359	Santander (Sur)	9,582
Huila	4,111	Cauca	9,464
Cundinamarca	4,037	All other	12,719
(Bogotá)	2,585		
Cauca	2,236		
All other dep'ts and lesser administrative units	2,386		

SOURCES: Paul Oquist, *Violencia, conflicto y política en Colombia* (Bogotá, 1978), Table VI-2, p. 322; Comisión Económica para America Latina y la Organización de las Naciones Unidas para la Agricultura y la Alimentación, *El café en America Latina. Problemas de la productividad y perspectivas. I. Colombia y El Salvador* (Mexico City, 1958), Table II, p. 25.

cipios in which liberals were electorally strong were most likely to experience violence after 1946 when political control shifted in favor of the Conservative party. Nevertheless, as Oquist acknowledges, the correlation between the relative degree of electoral competition and experience of the Violence is weak: large numbers of municipios with low political competition experienced high levels of violence; and large numbers that did not were politically competitive. Oquist, however, did not attempt to correlate his statistics on the geographical distribution of Violence-caused deaths by municipios with coffee production by municipios. Had he, it seems likely that he might have found very high correlations between the two. This supposition emerges from the aggregate statistics on the geographic distribution of Violence-caused deaths by departments presented by Oquist, and the volume of coffee production by departments derived from the coffee census of 1955. Table 5.5 presents these data on deaths during the period 1946-57, when the Violence was most intense and most closely obeyed traditional partisan political dynamics.

A very close correlation between the major coffee-producing regions and the numbers of deaths from the Violence emerges from this table. Absent as important loci of the Violence are the departments of the Atlantic Coast (Magdalena, Bolívar, and Atlántico) and the southern highlands (Nariño), where coffee production has always been unimportant. The three most important coffee departments in 1955, all in the Central Cordillera—Antiguo Caldas, Antioquia, and Tolima—rank first, third,

TABLE 5.6
Deaths Attributed to the Violence in Colombia,
1958-66, Ranked by Department

Department	Deaths
Tolima	5,251
Valle	5,016
Antiguo Caldas	3,606
Antioquia	2,127
Huila	733
Santander (Norte) } Santander (Sur)	649
Cauca	457
Cundinamarca	334
Meta	166
Boyacá	142

SOURCE: Oquist, *Violencia*, Table VI-3, p. 323.

and second in number of deaths attributed to the Violence. Two older, and in 1955 less important, coffee departments—the two Santanders—rank next in the number of such deaths. And all the other important coffee departments figure as important foci for the Violence, although its relative intensity does not correlate very closely with their importance in coffee production (Valle, Huila, Cundinamarca, and Cauca).

The major anomalies in this correlation are instructive. The relatively high incidence of Violence-related deaths in the unimportant coffee-producing departments of Meta and Boyacá reflects the exceptional nature of the Violence on the eastern plains, where liberals from the Eastern Cordillera joined with local co-partisans in confronting the Colombian army in large-scale operations. Cundinamarca, a coffee-producing department that had slipped to mid-rank in production by 1955, suffered a relatively low number of deaths caused by the Violence. That fact may reflect the legacy of collective organization among coffee workers in the southeast. (The deaths reported for Bogotá are primarily those of the bogotazo.) Finally, although Valle experienced relatively fewer Violence-caused deaths than the other major coffee-producing departments before 1958, its rank order in the number of deaths attributed to the Violence after 1958 is much higher. (See Table 5.6.) During this period the Violence was almost exclusively confined to coffee-producing departments. Most violent were the four major coffee-producing departments in 1955, all located in the Central Cordillera. Within this region, however, the relative intensity of the Violence shifted to the south away from Caldas and Antioquia to the departments of Tolima and Valle.

These same two departments, Valle and Tolima, also lead the list of those ranked by the number of parcelas or plots of land abandoned as a result of the Violence (Table 5.7). These statistics, published by Oquist,

TABLE 5.7
Parcelas Abandoned Because of the Violence in
Colombia, 1946-66, Ranked by Department

Department	*Parcelas* abandoned
Valle	98,400
Tolima	54,900
Cundinamarca	50,400
Santander (Norte)	38,400
Antiguo Caldas	36,800
Huila	27,100
Santander	26,600
Boyacá	26,400
Antioquia	16,200
Cauca	3,000
All other	14,648

SOURCE: Oquist, *Violencia*, Table VI-4, p. 323.

are, as he notes, less reliable than his data on deaths. The parcelas in question apparently included farms owned and operated by the victims, as well as lands they rented or occupied under sharecropping and dependent-labor arrangements. The data imply that abandonment of land as a result of the Violence was most common in areas affected most severely by violence in the phase after 1957. For many departments there is little relationship between the relative intensity of the Violence (as measured by deaths) and abandonment of land because of the Violence. Nevertheless, the figures tend to confirm the widespread supposition that the Violence was accompanied by large-scale changes in land tenure, changes confined primarily to the important coffee-producing departments.

The magnitude of the tragedy that befell the Colombian rural working class during the Violence cannot be measured in these numbers alone. For every fatality produced by the Violence, there were scores of people scarred emotionally and psychologically by a process that had no transcendent class or redeeming philosophical meaning. For all these victims of the Violence, for those who were despoiled of their possessions, and even for those who gained materially from the turmoil, the experience confirmed a vision of human behavior and society as mean, cruel, and unforgiving. Few Colombian workers learned the power of collective, cooperative behavior during two decades of violence. They found confirmed instead their worst suspicions about the motives of their fellow man.

The Violence is often interpreted by the left, albeit not very clearly or convincingly, as a ruling-class conspiracy against the working class.[113]

113. The clearest and most extreme expression of this view is perhaps Antonio García, *La dialéctica de la democracia* (Bogotá, 1971). Variations on this theme in works by Camilo Torres, Orlando Fals Borda, and others are lucidly criticized by Oquist, *Violencia* (cited in n. 3), pp. 25-30.

That interpretation seems plausible because of the effect the Violence had on the labor movement. The Violence did for the rural working class after 1946 what the simultaneous ruling-class legal and political offensive against organized labor did for the urban working class. It rendered it ideologically, organizationally, and politically impotent. The civil warfare that raged in the Colombian countryside for at least two decades after 1946 pitted Liberal and Conservative workers in cruel and costly struggle against each other. The Violence reinforced the emotional ties felt by rural workers to one or the other of the traditional parties, taught them to depend on partisan clientelist channels of traditional politics for protection and the satisfaction of their material aspirations, and strengthened the feelings of mutual hostility and suspicion between members of the rural working class. The flight of rural workers from the Violence in the countryside to the security of the cities facilitated the concentration of land, and, by eliminating many smallholders, smoothed the way for more extensive capitalist relations of production in agriculture. It also furnished the growing industrial sector of the Colombian economy with a flood of cheap, and culturally conservative, new workers. These workers, embued with Catholic precepts and individualist values, proved especially receptive to the blandishments of the new unionism. They furnished the economistic cadres for the UTC.

But simple interpretations that attribute the genesis of the Violence to insidious ruling-class conspiracy distort the causal complexity of that process. They attribute not only a design, but an intelligence, to ruling-class intentions that do not hold up against the historical record. And they demean the Colombian rural working class. Colombian workers were not duped into the fratricidal conflict that proved so costly to their class and to their nation. They, like their ruling-class oppressors, were locked in a historical drama beyond their full control. Unlike their class exploiters, however, Colombian rural workers succumbed to the dynamic of the Violence for progressive reasons. They fell to the Violence as they struggled for elemental human freedoms: the freedom to control their own lives and the product of their labor. It can be more plausibly argued that the Colombian rural working class, not the ruling class, most directly "caused" the Violence. Therein lies the devastating irony of the process that lacerated a vibrant, energetic, resourceful, and progressive class, and rendered it impotent before the march of Colombian history.

The Meaning of Contemporary Colombian History

In the wake of the tragedy that befell the working class at mid-century, the pattern of Colombia's historical development has finally turned against the interests of the ruling class. The very success of its liberal capitalist policies, pursued unhampered by a strong labor movement since mid-century, has slowly undermined the historical foundation of its ideological and political hegemony over Colombian society.

The validity of these assertions is not readily apparent. The growth and diversification of the Colombian economy, fostered historically by national ownership of a rapidly growing coffee economy, and sustained, thanks in part to smallholder coffee production, during the world crisis, has continued throughout the postwar era. Despite the great poverty and social inequality that have prevailed during this whole period, and the growing contradictions of Colombia's economic development in recent decades (revealed, for example, in the denationalization of Colombian industry and finance and the steady growth of the foreign debt), sustained economic growth has provided enough real social mobility to nourish the liberal cultural values propagated by the basic institutions of Colombian society. The hundreds of thousands of rural working- and middle-class people who fled the countryside in the decades after 1946 have operated in the cities much like the coffee smallholders many once were. They have manipulated family resources and personal and political contacts in a desperate individual struggle to get ahead in the world. If they have tended increasingly since 1958 not to vote in the largely uncompetitive elections between the parties under the Frente Nacional, they have retained nevertheless an identification with the traditional parties and have continued to rely as best they can on clientelist political channels in their struggle for social mobility.

The influence of liberal cultural values propagated by the ruling class through church and school and political party—tempered by the historical experience of tens of thousands of coffee smallholder families, and reinforced and twisted in the nightmare of the Violence—is manifest in the contemporary behavior of working-, middle-, and ruling-class Colombians in striking ways. It is revealed in the notorious incidence of petty and violent crime in Colombian cities and the high level of homicide in many rural areas. It is evident in the intensity of small-scale commerce, the ubiquity of "con" artists, and the alacrity with which working- and middle-class Colombians responded to the risky opportunities of the international drug trade. (Many observers speculate that the value of illegal marijuana and cocaine exports from Colombia now exceeds that of coffee.) At the highest levels of society these same values find expression in the frenetic activities of real estate speculators, industrial monopolists, and corrupt public officials and politicians. Behavior like this, of course, is widespread in all contemporary capitalist societies. But the intensity of its expression in contemporary Colombia, especially at the level of working-class behavior, is extreme. And not entirely negative. Working- and middle-class Colombians contemplate the reality of ruling-class economic behavior and the corruption of the political and judicial institutions of the state with complete and informed cynicism. Working-class Colombians are not resigned to their fate in a grossly unequal society. Nor are they very submissive to authority in an unjust social system.

But though there is little evidence yet of the emergence of alternative cultural values within the working class, and though it is true that the electoral hold of the traditional parties seems secure, the historical conditions that have sustained existing values and traditional politics are crumbling. The expansion of Colombia's capital-intensive, consumer-goods-oriented industrial sector under the aegis of international capital has not freed the Colombian economy from dependence on coffee exports and infusions of foreign loans. Nor has it created nearly enough jobs for the nation's rapidly expanding working class, or significantly improved the pattern of income distribution in the country.[114] But it has created for the first time in Colombian history a large and increasingly combative urban working class. That class demonstrated its potential political power, growing organizational unity, and ideological capacity to transcend simple bread-and-butter issues in a massive general strike that shook Colombian society in 1977.[115]

Meanwhile, the development of capitalist agriculture has slowly transformed relations of production in the rural areas. In the decades since mid-century there has been steady concentration of landholding patterns in Colombian agriculture, an increase in mechanization and capitalist investment in agriculture, and a corresponding growth in the number of landless wage workers in the countryside. Even coffee production, which historically proved so resistant to pure capitalist forms and favored the growth and maintenance of small producers and the family-owned and -operated farm, has witnessed in recent decades a revolution in production techniques, tenancy, and labor systems. The application of capital

114. On the contradictions see Konrad Matter, *Inversiones extranjeras en la economía colombiana* (Medellín, 1977). On the success of the Colombian ruling class in partially overcoming them through a return to more orthodox liberal political economy in the 1960's, see Carlos Díaz Alejandro, *Foreign Trade Regimes and Economic Development: Colombia* (New York, 1976). The weakness of the labor movement goes a long way toward explaining the success of the Colombian ruling class in implementing policies designed to curb inflation by squeezing real wages and to resolve balance-of-payments problems through export promotion and diversification. That success, however, owed much as well to the coffee bonanza of the 1970's, when coffee prices trebled and exports expanded by one-third to 9 million bags. It also reflected the emergence of the illegal drug trade. All these factors have combined to enable the Colombian regime to pursue, successfully to date, liberal political economy in the contemporary period without resort to full-blown authoritarian political institutions.

115. On the significance of this event see Oscar Delgado, comp., *El paro popular del 14 de septiembre de 1977* (Bogotá, n.d.), and Arturo Alape, *Un día de septiembre. Testimonios del paro cívico de 1977* (Bogotá, 1980).

and advanced techniques to coffee production has, since mid-century, slowly undermined the competitive position of coffee smallholders.[116]

These trends have been greatly facilitated by the introduction and spread since the 1960's of a new species of coffee tree in Colombia, *café caturra*. Caturra coffee trees grow rapidly without shade and require heavy infusions of chemical fertilizer. Drastic pruning of the tree encourages heavy yields during the short lifespan of the plant. Pruning also makes the harvest, concentrated over a short period, easier and less time-consuming. *Caturra* coffee production in Colombia is increasingly undertaken on level and rolling land previously used for pasture or the production of food crops. But whether it is grown on land suitable for machine cultivation or on steep slopes, the groves are not usually weeded. Increasingly, large capitalist coffee farmers rely on chemical herbicides to eliminate the plants that compete with *caturra* coffee trees for nutrients in the soil. Although little investigation has been done on the subject, these changes in coffee-production techniques may have grave implications for the ecology of the coffee zones and the health of coffee workers. What is certain is that they have accelerated the proletarianization of the coffee labor force.[117]

The free wage-labor force in coffee production, mainly migrant workers employed during the short periods of intense labor demand, has grown dramatically in recent years. These workers travel from farm to farm, municipio to municipio, to work in the coffee harvest, which varies in season from region to region. Most also work as migrant laborers in other kinds of agriculture, such as sugar and cotton. Unlike their historical counterparts, these workers, who now number in the hundreds of thousands, are landless and dependent primarily on their wages for subsistence. Like all migrant workers they confront serious problems to effective collective organization. But the fundamental historical barrier to their ideological formation as a class in direct opposition to the interests of capital has now been virtually eliminated.

116. One discussion of these issues, which contains a brief treatment of the coffee census of 1970, is Hernán Pérez Zapata, *Enjuiciamiento de la política agraria y cafetera* (Bogotá, 1978). For a fascinating discussion of smallholders' imaginative cultural efforts to understand and resist proletarianization, as well as some evidence of the ongoing efficiency and ecological soundness of petty commodity agricultural production in Colombia, see Michael T. Taussig, *The Devil and Commodity Fetishism in South America* (Chapel Hill, N.C., 1980).

117. By 1980 approximately one-sixth of the area planted in coffee in Colombia was of this new type, denominated "café tecnificado al sol" in the literature of the Coffee Federation. The proportion was much higher in the heart of the coffee zone, reaching more than one-fourth in Caldas, almost a third in Antioquia. *Economía Cafetera* 11:12 (Dec. 1981). For a critical, polemical discussion of recent Colombian coffee policies, see Héctor Melo and Iván López Botero, *El imperio clandestino del café* (Bogotá, 1976). The information on production techniques is from interviews with coffee workers in Chinchiná, August 1980.

Thanks to the pathbreaking work of a research team headed by Nicolás Buenaventura, we have a clear idea of the changing class position and perceptions of this large and important sector of the Colombian working class.[118] The experience of these workers reveals in microcosm the changes that have affected, to one degree or another, the entire Colombian rural working class since mid-century. The migrant workers, like the rural working class as a whole, have been progressively denied access to the means of production and subsistence as capitalist relations of production have expanded in Colombia since mid-century.

The team devised a revealing questionnaire and probed the condition and attitudes of 338 migrant agricultural workers in several municipios in the middle Cauca Valley in the mid-1970's. The sample of workers was not selected by any rigorous formula. About a fourth of these workers said they labored exclusively in the coffee or sugar harvest, the rest responded that they worked as migrants in any kind of agriculture. About a fourth said they traveled all over the country in pursuit of agricultural work. The rest said they usually did not journey beyond the one or two municipios closest to their own. The interviews were conducted by educated middle-class leftists sympathetic toward the workers' struggle. Some of the interviews were conducted with the support of leaders of working-class organizations actively engaged in promoting collective protest of working conditions in the region. The primary investigator was a distinguished Marxist scholar affiliated with the Communist Party of Colombia. For all these reasons, if the sample of workers surveyed is skewed, it would appear the bias lies in a "progressive" direction. The workers interviewed were more likely than most migrant workers to be involved in union activities, have contact with leftist parties, and be sympathetic to the politics of their interviewers. It is this built-in bias in the survey that ensured the rich and candid participation of the interviewees, and gives special authority to the "conservative" implications of many of the survey's findings.

The survey graphically reveals the extent of the proletarianization of the agricultural working class in Colombia in recent decades. Its most startling findings, however, probe the depth of the cultural values of a rural working class formed historically in a coffee economy defined by relations of production that blurred the distinction between capital and labor, featured very widespread ownership of the means of production, and allowed worker control over the production process. Asked if they had once been "owners of a small farm in the countryside" (*dueños de finca en el campo*), 39 percent responded that they had been. But only 12 percent

118. Nicolás Buenaventura, "Proletariado agrícola, 'temporeros,'" *Estudios Marxistas* 9 (1975):3-32.

could say that they now possessed such a farm.[119] The 39 percent were then asked if the farm they once held enabled them to earn a living, or if they had to do outside work. More than two-thirds said it had been sufficient, that they had not had to work for others.[120] The entire sample was asked whether their fathers had been small landowners. Sixty-one percent said they had been.[121] Asked if they presently owned their own homes (had clear title to them), almost a third said they did.[122]

Most of these migrant workers faced long periods of unemployment during the year. Over half had been out of work for a month at a time in the previous year; more than a fourth had been unemployed during six consecutive months during that time. Asked about the various ways they supplemented their income as migratory wage workers, a fourth responded that they had plantings of their own or raised animals. Another fifth said they rented out a part of the house they lived in. Another fifth said they worked as peddlers on the streets. And 40 percent said they supplemented their wages by collecting what was left in the fields after the harvest. Some of these said that they, in turn, sold part of these leftovers to others.[123]

Asked about their aspirations and plans for the future, these workers revealed to Buenaventura and his team that they were in his words "too tied by the semislave, semiworker economy of their work," that they did not "really want to regain possession of the land as a solution, just a minimal portion of it." "[T]heir whole horizon," he concluded, "is a parcel of land, hopefully 'titled.'" The migrant workers were asked whether they hoped to *"independizarse"* (a term Buenaventura revealingly and incompletely interpreted as meaning to "cease being poor") by acquiring a small farm or a business, or whether they hoped instead to find a steady job in the city. More than three-fourths chose a small farm or business. Of these, the overwhelming majority (84 percent) chose a small farm over a business.[124]

The investigators then probed the attitudes of the migrant workers interviewed toward the crucial issue of land reform. They asked them

119. *Ibid.*, Table 1, p. 11. Of these, 12 percent apparently had title to the land, 9 percent were in possession of land as colonos, 10 percent were sharecroppers, and 8 percent were renters. I have rounded these and other percentages cited from the survey to the nearest whole number.

120. *Ibid.*, Table 2, p. 11. Many of the questions asked in the survey were paired in this manner.

121. *Ibid.*, Table 4, p. 13.

122. *Ibid.* Another 15 percent owned their house on agricultural land extended them under some kind of sharecropping contract, 41 percent said they rented, and the rest, 13 percent, said they lived in barracks for workers or in boardinghouses.

123. *Ibid.*, Table 6, p. 16.

124. *Ibid.*, Table 10, p. 22. The quotations are from pp. 21 and 12.

whether they thought the land produced best or better as it was presently distributed or if it would produce more or better if it were distributed in a different way. Ninety-two percent chose the latter proposition. Asked what way they thought best, 70 percent responded "It would be better divided up into family-owned farms"; only 30 percent thought it best "organized into cooperatives or community enterprises."[125]

That response, which Buenaventura labeled the "peasant" position versus the "worker" position, disappointed him. Nevertheless, throughout the survey the interviewed workers gave fairly positive responses to questions concerning the importance of worker organization and union activity. Although 56 percent thought that the best way for workers to get ahead was for each to defend himself as best he could, 44 percent thought the best way was through cooperative efforts and worker solidarity. Asked how workers hurt their own position, 83 percent affirmed that it was because they worked too cheaply, and only 17 percent thought it was because they complained too much and made demands on employers.[126] Finally, more than three-fourths of the workers thought unions helped rather than hurt workers, although most were critical of "political" unions. Yet more than 70 percent denied the proposition that all politics was the same and affirmed that there were politics which favored the rich, others which favored the poor.[127]

These worker responses eloquently summarize the rich formative experience of a class of smallholders in coffee production that has most profoundly influenced the development of Colombian society in this century. That experience was a fact, although it is systematically ignored in Colombian historiography and denied in much Marxist scholarship.[128] Marxist scholarship, the parties of the left, and most of all the Colombian working class are poorly served by a labor and national history that ignores its most important subject and places the blame for the weakness of the left and the reason for the failure of social transformation everywhere but at its source.

125. *Ibid.*, Table 11, p. 23.
126. *Ibid.*, Table 13, p. 23.
127. *Ibid.*, Tables 15 and 16, pp. 26-27.
128. Even leftists forced to come to terms with this experience too often fail to probe its full implications. Nicolás Buenaventura, for example, expresses surprise in finding in his survey that the attitudes of the workers he interviewed cannot be easily dismissed as products of dominant ruling-class ideology (*ibid.*, pp. 22-23). He notes in his conclusion the importance of the fact that the workers' desire to become smallholders "does not appear to be determined by the simple influence of bourgeois reformism" (p. 30). Since, as Buenaventura notes, worker attitudes are not determined "naturally, and from their [objective] class position" (p. 22), where else but to the historical experience of the class are we to look for the origins of these attitudes?

But it is not simply that Colombian historiography has denied workers in coffee production their rightful place at the center of twentieth-century Colombian history. In doing so it has failed to undertake the vital task of evaluating the historical experience of the class that has contributed the most to the current state of affairs in Colombian society. In the negative aspects of that experience lies the primary source of the working-class cultural values that continue to guarantee the ideological dominion of the liberal ruling class, the ongoing political hegemony of the traditional parties, and the enduring obstacles to combative collective organization of the working class.

Yet in the struggle of coffee workers for the control of the land lies also an affirmation of progressive values universally shared by all workers and imperfectly realized in any society—capitalist or socialist—today. Coffee workers struggled for control over the means of production and the full product of their labor. But they struggled as well for the freedom to work in the ways they saw fit. Coffee workers, small property owners, arrendatarios, and sharecroppers realized that last goal most perfectly. And in doing so they demonstrated, against formidable historical odds, the power of unalienated human labor. Working with limited productive means, insufficient capital, and a rudimentary technology, they historically measured their humanity and efficiency against their large and richly endowed capitalist rivals and won. In their victory lies a lesson for all leftists convinced of the virtues of collectivization without full worker control. In it lies a powerful testament for all those striving to eliminate material want in underdeveloped societies. In it, finally, lies part of the answer to the excesses of industrial civilization, capitalist and so-called socialist alike, bent on destroying the natural systems on which we all depend in an unnecessary and self-defeating effort to transform them. In the bittersweet legacy of the coffee workers' struggles lie the keys to Colombia's recent past and the promise for its future.

6

On the Limits of This Study and the Promise of the Approach

Readers of these essays on Chile, Argentina, Venezuela, and Colombia have seen just how complex—and historically specific—the relationship between export structure, labor movement formation, and national economic and political development, outlined so simply and abstractly in Chapter One, is in point of fact. I hope they will have also come to appreciate, as I have, the heuristic value of such an approach. Once attention is directed to workers in export production, the great influence of labor on twentieth-century developments in these countries begins to reveal itself. Once attention is focused on the structure of export production, the pattern of that influence gradually becomes clear.

These chapters were written to stand alone as individual examples of the potential of the interpretive framework outlined in Chapter One. When the volume is considered as a whole, however, its interpretive sum should be greater than that of its separate country parts, and the thesis of each chapter should appear in more plausible light. The chapters use the lever of comparison to build a cumulative argument for the proposition that the postulated relationship between material forces (export structure) and human consciousness (labor movement formation) is not a coincidence of fortuitous correlation; that it is, rather, a product of the logical connections sketched out in Chapter One and the causal links I try to document through concrete historical evidence in the individual chapters.

Nevertheless, the country essays reveal aspects of that relationship not identified in the paradigm outlined in the introductory chapter. The most important of these is the influence of political systems, forged in the post-independence period, on the social developments unleashed by the consolidation of export economies after 1880. Clearly, the socialist and electoral trajectory of the twentieth-century Chilean labor movement cannot fully be comprehended outside the strong state and multiparty political system in place in the country before the nitrate boom began. By contrast, in Argentina, the absence of a strong, traditional party system inherited from the nineteenth century, especially the lack of a powerful, centrally organized conservative party, affected twentieth-century historical developments in a very different way. It left the Radical party without a national conservative counterweight in the early decades of the century. It led the Argentine elite to bypass the party system and throw its weight behind a military solution to the crisis of 1930, and to continue to resort to that strategy intermittently in the decades since. The decidedly modern cast of Venezuelan politics after 1936 was made possible in part by a weak nineteenth-century party system whose remnants were virtually swept away by the brutal personalistic dictatorship of the first decades of this century. Finally, the strong bipartisan political system forged in nineteenth-century Colombia cut channels into the body politic so deep that twentieth-century social developments have yet to find enduring expression outside the political monopoly of the two traditional parties.

The consolidation of the state and the emergence of distinct political systems in the various Latin American republics in the nineteenth century are problems that Latin American historians and social scientists have yet to conceptualize and study very thoroughly. I have tried to advance in the direction of such explanation by emphasizing the political dynamics of the success or failure of the several new nations in developing agricultural or mineral exports for the world market in the decades following independence. It is apparent from my treatment of these issues, however, that the consolidation of the state and party systems, the evolution of modes of political mobilization, and the forging of political cultures in nineteenth-century Latin America was a very complex process, influenced as well by ecological, demographic, economic, social, and intellectual patterns inherited from the colonial and pre-Columbian periods. Detailed comparative treatment of the nineteenth-century political histories of these new nations would reveal the influence of other factors as well—the role of geopolitics, of the vision of individual leaders, of the fortuitous outcome of battles, and so on. In both theoretical and empirical terms, treatment of these nineteenth-century political issues remains the least developed part of the argument advanced in the essays. Only in the case of Colombia, no doubt because my previous work focused on the nineteenth-century political economy of that country, does the interpretation begin to suggest the full complexity of the relationship between early export developments and the evolution of nineteenth-century political systems. The essay on Colombia also reveals most clearly the extent to which the party systems forged in the nineteenth century worked to channel the social forces unleashed by the export-oriented transformation of Latin American societies that are the focus of this book. It thus serves to highlight an important theoretical issue not addressed in the interpretive paradigm outlined in the introductory chapter, one that I have dealt with primarily on an ad hoc basis in the country-specific chapters of the study.[1]

———————◆－◆———————

How useful, then, is the approach developed in this volume in interpreting the modern histories of the other nations of Latin America? Until the value of the paradigm is tested in detailed historical analysis of these other countries, the answer must be qualified and tentative. It is clear, however, that the framework should reveal much more about the historical evolution of some countries than of others. The approach should prove most useful in understanding the modern history of countries where a single export economy, or a series of structurally similar export economies, molded economic and social development over a long period of time. It should thus prove to be a much more powerful tool of analysis

1. A stimulating alternative approach to the formation of nineteenth-century Latin American political systems is advanced in the work of J. Samuel Valenzuela. He argues that political variables explain the consolidation of nineteenth-century party systems and the formation and ideological trajectory of the various labor movements of the Western world. For Chile (which along with France is the primary focus of his study) he contends that nineteenth-century elite political cleavage over the role of the Church resulted in a well-developed, multiparty system before the emergence of the labor movement at the end of the century. Exactly how conflict over the role of the Church explains this political outcome in Chile, yet contributes to chronic civil war and the development of an entrenched two-party system in Colombia, or to chronic civil war and the consolidation of a personalistic dictatorship in Mexico is not made clear in the analysis. More persuasive is Valenzuela's contention (shared by many students of Chilean history) that this well-developed party system served to channel the labor movement toward electoral politics. Valenzuela shows how even conservatives were willing to play this electoral "game" because of their political control over their dependent agricultural work force. The implications of Valenzuela's explanation of labor movement formation in Chile and Argentina are discussed in Chapter Two, notes 35 and 43.

Less extreme, and more compatible with the general argument of this volume, is the position on the role of political variables in the formation of the Latin American labor movements developed in the important work in progress of David and Ruth Berins Collier. The Colliers are not concerned with the process of state and party formation in nineteenth-century Latin American societies; they take those systems as a given. Rather, they focus on the process of labor movement incorporation in eight countries of the region, and trace its implications for political developments in recent decades. This work emphasizes the contrasting mobilizational and control-oriented modes of labor incorporation adopted by contending political factions in their struggle for control of the state. Such an approach results in fascinating comparisons of the political results of labor incorporation in countries with very different economic and social characteristics. It tells us little, however, about the causal dynamics of incorporation, especially the role played in that process by labor movements of such divergent strength and ideological autonomy over time as those compared in this volume. David Collier and Ruth Berins Collier, "Unions, Parties, and Regimes in Latin America: An Introduction," paper presented at the Rutgers University Political Science/ Political Economy Workshop, March 1984; and Ruth Berins Collier, "Popular Sector Incorporation and Political Supremacy: Regime Evolution in Brazil and Mexico," in Sylvia Ann Hewlett and Richard S. Weinert, eds., *Brazil and Mexico: Patterns in Late Development* (Philadelphia, 1982).

for a Bolivia or a Cuba,[2] for example, than for an Ecuador or a Paraguay. The approach should also prove more meaningful in areas of Latin America where the legacy of pre-Columbian societies and Iberian colonialism is relatively weak—in an Argentina or a Venezuela, more than in a Peru or a Guatemala. The four countries dealt with in this volume were all peripheral parts of pre-Columbian and colonial Latin America; they were among the regions most completely transformed during the integration of Latin America into an industrial capitalist world order after 1780, and especially after 1880. The approach should work better for Latin American nations less large and regionally diverse, and less fully developed economically in the modern period, than Mexico and Brazil. It may also prove less useful in interpreting the modern histories of the smallest, least autonomous, and most underdeveloped countries of the region, those of Central America and the Caribbean, than it is for the four countries compared in this study.

It is likely, however, that the approach can reveal a great deal about the modern histories of all the countries of Latin America. By focusing on the experience of export workers, it can discover the wellsprings of the ideological and political forces that make each of the national labor movements of the region distinct. By emphasizing the influence of export structure on the whole of peripheral Latin American societies over time, it can reveal the constraints and opportunities under which the class alliances, so central to the question of labor's wider influence on the course of national economic and political development, took form and evolved. Comparative focus on export structure, and on the workers who performed the major task of Latin American societies in the world economy for a long time after 1880, will not by any means answer every question about the Latin American labor movements. Nor can it fully explain the different courses of the national histories in which these movements play such a decisive part. But I believe that it is a powerful and subtle tool of analysis that can illuminate most aspects of both of these subjects.

The utility of the approach, however, will depend in large part on the spirit in which it is applied. As the four case histories presented in this volume demonstrate, the paradigm should be used heuristically to gain interpretive leverage over a concrete and specific national history, a discrete and complex national historiography. The usefulness of the approach cannot be decided casually; it will be determined only by investigators willing to immerse themselves fully in the historiography of these separate nations and willing to undertake primary research. For each

2. June Nash's remarkable book on Bolivian tin miners, *We Eat the Mines and the Mines Eat Us* (New York, 1979), demonstrates the potential of the approach for that country. Cuba, as Fernando Ortiz (see Chapter One, n. 2) originally suggested, may be the prototypical case for such analysis.

country the framework of analysis will have to be modified substantially to take into account political variables and all the special characteristics noted above.

For Mexico, to take a particularly complex and fecund example, it may prove fruitful to begin detailed historical analysis of the prerevolutionary period with only two important notions borrowed from the paradigm in mind: first, that the labor movement should be conceptualized to include miners and transport workers in the mineral export economy of the north, the artisanal and industrial workers of the cities (including the textile workers in the foreign-owned mills of the central region), the plantation workers of the tropical agricultural enclaves, *and* (here is the major modification of the paradigm outlined in Chapter One) subsistence agriculturalists living in communities that predate the Conquest whose livelihood and cultural and institutional autonomy were threatened by the rapid advance of capitalist and export agriculture; second, that however diverse Mexico's export-oriented development after 1880, most of the country's export economies resembled the foreign-owned, capital-intensive, extractive type represented in this volume by the mineral export economy of Chile. Consequently, however complex and specific its historical expression in Mexico, one should expect to find a relatively developed sense of class and cultural autonomy within the early labor movement, and a relatively great propensity for multiclass alliances of the reformist, nationalist, and anti-imperialist kind. That both of these developments happened earlier in Mexico than in Chile, and found expression in a violent social revolution rather than in an incremental electoral history, points to the need to consider conditions unique to Mexican history. These would include the existence and vitality of long-standing agrarian communities, the social legacy of the struggle against Spanish colonialism, the history of nineteenth-century civil war and territorial despoliation at the hands of the United States, and the special dictatorial political form under which rapid export-oriented development took place in Mexico in the decades prior to the revolution of 1910.

Once the revolution began, as an increasingly sophisticated and detailed Mexican labor and national history reveals, the role of workers and the process of their incorporation into national life become central themes in the history of the nation. What has not yet been demonstrated systematically is the extent to which the workers' struggle can illuminate much broader issues in modern Mexican historiography: most generally, the ideological trajectory and institutionalization of the revolution itself over the next several decades; more specifically, the fate of the various revolutionary coalitions in the 1910's and 1920's, the advent of sweeping social, economic, and political reforms in the 1930's, the dynamics of economic "miracle" in the decades after 1940, and the origins of the grave crisis of contemporary Mexican political economy.

———————◆ ➤ ➤———————

Whatever the specific utility of the approach pursued in this volume to Mexican history, however, and whatever the verdict on its generalizability, in modified form, to the other nations of the region or beyond,[3] the essays in this book raise issues that transcend the question of the particular strengths of the interpretive paradigm I have relied upon. These revolve, in the first instance, around the problem of applying concepts and methods derived from developments in world historiography to Latin American studies. More broadly, however, they include methodological and political issues raised in the whole enterprise of trying to place labor at the center of modern Latin American history.

The developments in world historiography to which I refer are customarily called in shorthand terms the "new social" (or labor) history, on the one hand, and "world-system analysis" or, more narrowly, "Latin American dependency thought," on the other. It can be argued that each of these developments constitutes a major, albeit partial, breakthrough in the way we understand the historical evolution of the modern world; that each is an intellectual analogue of social struggle by dispossessed classes and nations within a world social system; that each, unfortunately yet understandably, has developed largely in isolation from the other; and finally, that creative fusion of these two historiographical developments could so broaden and deepen our vision of the historical process that we could begin to rewrite the history of the modern world in a way both more accurate and more attuned to the interests of the majority who worked the hardest to build the modern world social system yet benefit least in it.[4]

Those familiar with these two schools of modern historical studies will have seen how gingerly and disproportionately I have borrowed from each in this study. Social history, especially its most modern applications, remains very poorly developed in the field of modern Latin American

3. The approach may prove a useful springboard for study of other Third World societies, which, like Latin American countries, but under formal colonial control, were integrated into an industrial world order as producers of primary commodities for export. It is also possible that the concept of a manufacturing export sector as the most important part of some industrial capitalist economies, and of workers in such industries as the most important element in the making of national labor movements there, will prove useful to the comparative study of labor in the developed capitalist world.

4. The argument in this section is presented in more detail in Charles Bergquist, "Latin American Historical Studies in the 1980's: One View," in "Trends and Priorities for Research on Latin America in the 1980's," Working Paper No. 111, The Latin American Program, The Wilson Center, Washington, D.C., 1982.

history. And though I seized every opportunity to use those few relevant studies I could find, and attempted through primary research and through interpretation to advance a bit on my own, the results of these efforts are modest indeed. Nor does the study depend primarily on concepts drawn directly from world-system analysis; it relies instead on insights from the work of its Latin American precursors, the structural economists whose work is evaluated in the introductory chapter. What little social history informs the study is focused on a group—export workers—whose significance in the historical process, although ignored in the work of the Latin American structural economists, is nevertheless implicitly predicted by it. I have kept both these important historiographical advances at arm's length, and drawn on them very selectively, because I believe that despite their strengths, both have serious limitations when applied uncritically to an underdeveloped field of history.

The great contribution of the new social and labor history developed by European and North American scholars in recent decades has been to expand the range of historical source materials to include the workaday documents of civil society, and to uncover demographic, social, and cultural processes that lie deep beneath the surface of the economic, institutional, intellectual, and political issues which have traditionally preoccupied historians. The best of the new labor history has enriched and modified the concepts and optimistic assumptions of early Marxism in light of the failure of social revolution in advanced capitalist societies. It stresses the defensive institutions that working people collectively created to resist the dehumanizing tendencies of capitalist relations of production. It explores the ways workers adapted the powerful instruments of hegemonic ruling-class culture to serve working-class needs. It broadens our understanding of the complex problems raised by concepts like proletarianization and class consciousness. All of these issues address the special problems of labor historians confronted with the growing conservatism and quiescence of the industrial working class in advanced capitalist societies following the historic post-1945 compromise discussed in the Introduction.

It is important that Latin Americanists recognize the geographic and historical specificity of the issues the new labor history set out to illuminate. For, although these problems are in some sense universal, and although they are vitally important to the study of the Latin American working class, it is nevertheless true that the political quiescence, social conservatism, and cultural dependency of the working class is more pronounced, and that the cultural and corporativist mechanisms for ensuring that state of affairs are more developed and secure, in advanced capitalist societies than in Latin America.

The new social and labor history is also more suited to the state of historical studies in advanced capitalist societies, and to the level of their economic, technical, institutional, and human resources, than it is to those of underdeveloped historical fields and societies. The new social history is the end product of a long and sequential development process in a discipline that began writing biography and political and institutional history, moved through economic and intellectual history, and today prides itself in advancing into the fields of social and cultural history. Without the benchmarks that traditional historiography provides, social historians can founder in a sea of primary information and address issues unrelated to important aspects of historical change. Social history is also expensive. It involves huge investments of time by highly trained professional historians who take advantage of the magnificently organized and stocked repositories, libraries, and computer centers of the developed world.

For all these reasons, I believe Latin Americanists not only must look hard at the costs involved in applying the new social history to our field, but at the appropriateness of the issues it sets out to answer. It seems to me that we must devise ways to target the social and labor history we do, and at the same time contribute to the economic and political and institutional history of an underdeveloped field. The approach developed in this volume is one way to do that; it may or may not be judged a viable one; it certainly is not the only one. But it has as its goal a historiographical principle that goes far beyond its specifics, that of using concepts and methods from the new labor history in ways appropriate to the nature of its Latin American subject matter and to the historiography and material constraints of an underdeveloped field.

The new social history is vital to fuller understanding of a major issue this study has had to address: the process of human cognition and the creation of collective cultural understandings that traditional Marxist analysis both identified and enormously simplified under the heading of class consciousness. Throughout the study I wrestled more or less unsuccessfully with this issue, whose full elucidation would require a massive amount of primary investigation by highly trained and unusually perceptive social historians. Perhaps the most important contribution of the volume in this respect is to advance a set of useful criteria for selecting topics for some of that research.

The contributions of world-system analysis to our understanding of the historical process have been of a very different order from those of social history. This work has effectively undermined the cultural (and racial) assumptions that historically informed mainstream Western thought. It has shown how development and underdevelopment in a world capitalist system are dialectically related historical phenomena, the one part cause and part consequence of the other. It has argued that the continuing underdevelopment of the Third World is not so much a function of traditional cultural values that preceded contact with European imperialism as the cultural, political, and material consequence of unequal exchange and specialization of function in a world division of labor that disproportionately benefits core capitalist nations.

Although this study shares these assumptions, it contributes very little directly to the global historical concerns that have come to preoccupy world-system analysts. It sheds little light on the dynamics of the famous long waves in the world economy, on the issue of ascent or decline within the hierarchy of nation-states within the world social system, or on the relationship between those two phenomena, on the one hand, and the degree of mobilization and the relative strength through time of the world and national labor movements on the other.[5] I have tried to keep all these issues in mind and bring them into the story of the individual countries as necessary. Yet although the study relies heavily on the changing international context of an evolving world capitalist system, it makes no real theoretical or empirical contribution to understanding the global causal dynamics of any of these phenomena.

The study does address, however, what I believe is a major contradiction within world-system analysis. The bulk of the neo-Marxist economists and sociologists who work within this approach hope to contribute through their scholarship to the creation of a world socialist order. Yet they focus so singlemindedly on the global structural "logic" of the world system that they neglect the concrete dynamics of class struggle within national societies, and they fail to come to terms with the issues of human consciousness and agency whose importance social historians have so convincingly demonstrated. This contradiction is revealed starkly in the prose of most world-system analysts. Like most social-science writing it is artless, abstract, technical, and utterly devoid of life. It fails to appeal to the very class whose struggle, world-system analysis contends, drives global capitalism forward and which alone has the power to transcend it.[6]

I have tried to surmount the problems evident in much world-system analysis by building on the concepts and methods of an intellectual tradition that developed out of the specific historical experience of Latin America. Leaving aside the conservative ideology of the Latin American structural economists, and also the issue of the class interests their studies

5. I attempt to show the importance of labor history for all these issues in "Placing Labor at the Center," the introduction to Charles Bergquist, ed., *Labor in the Capitalist World Economy* (Beverly Hills, Calif., 1984).

6. Illustrative of all these issues is Samir Amin et al., *Dynamics of Global Crisis* (New York, 1982).

ostensibly served, their work had the conceptual virtue of recognizing and explaining a fundamental historical reality in the region: the reactive nature of Latin American economic development, and the very different potential for development of Latin American nation-states over time. These economists addressed a set of problems whose importance was perceived by all social classes in the region in the postwar period, the issue of industrial transformation and the promise it seemed to hold (even in capitalist form) for eliminating material want and more equally distributing income. However insufficient and narrow their conceptual framework, these economists developed a method of analysis appropriate to the resources of the societies they studied. Understanding that the root of development problems was historical, but lacking good economic histories of the region, they set out to write an economic history of their own. Since they recognized that that was a mammoth task far beyond their immediate resources, they developed a sophisticated comparative approach that enabled them to weigh elements of historical causation and to pinpoint issues for systematic research.

This study has attempted to turn this conceptual scheme and comparative method more fully to the interests of the working class. It broadens the emphasis on export structure to address the central political issue of its meaning for working-class consciousness and labor movement formation. It expands the question of economic development by linking it to the related issues of social and political transformation. It approaches these issues through the comparative study of the impact of changing world economic, ideological, political, and cultural forces on the social struggle between capital and labor in the various national societies of the region. Whatever its limitations, the intent of this volume is to specify ways to focus the deeper vision of the new social history within the broader view of a world capitalist system in ways appropriate to Latin American social reality and the state of its historiography.

To the extent these essays succeed in elevating labor to a central place in the national histories of Chile, Argentina, Venezuela, and Colombia, they raise important conceptual and political questions not only for modern Latin American history but for modern historical studies as a whole. Admittedly the essays are too one-sided and focus too little on the role of the ruling and middle classes in the historical process. But perhaps these excesses can be excused in the context of a historiography that has for too long left working people out of its central concerns. If workers occupy a pivotal place in the modern history of the underdeveloped capitalist countries surveyed in this volume, one begins to wonder about the re-

ceived wisdom regarding the modest role of labor in the modern history
of other Latin American and Third World societies, and in the history of
the industrial world itself.

Placing labor at the center of modern history works to empower not
capitalists and their world system, but the working people who have
struggled most consistently to democratize that system. It dignifies the
people unacknowledged in the bourgeois history of great men, ignored
in the neo-Marxist history of abstractions, disdained in the neocorpora-
tivist history of the structuralists, and demeaned in the social history that
ignores politics and regales the working poor with paternalistic sops
("they have a history too"). If the essays in this volume succeed in showing that workers' struggles fundamentally influenced the course of the
national histories of Chile, Argentina, Venezuela, and Colombia, if they
demonstrate how those struggles illuminate the central issues in the historiography of these nations, if they unveil the democratic goals of
working people and the complexity of the reasons for their failure to realize fully their aspirations in the past, they reveal to us concretely how
working people make their own history. They remind us all that, with
the courage of democratic convictions, and a clearer understanding of the
past, we can collectively create a better future.

Left unresolved in this study is the question of how a history that
places workers at the center of its concerns should be written and diffused. To realize its potential such work must learn how to use the social
sciences and the humanities, analysis and narrative, in ways capable of
linking intellect and emotion in the human agency of the working class.
Most studies in the social sciences and history, even those that focus on
the working class, are read only by a narrow minority of professionals.
There is irony in the fact that the professionals in this tiny sector of the
working class are the only members of the class whose conditions of employment, of the way they sell their labor, require them to read such
work. Until we learn to broaden the appeal of historical scholarship,
studies like this one will not be widely read among the very class it takes
as its subject. Until we learn to write a history that is read by the majority, the broadest implications of the example set by the militant nitrate
miners, meatworkers, and oil and coffee workers whose struggles fill
these pages will be left unrealized.

Index

Index

Library of Congress Cataloging-in-Publication Data

Bergquist, Charles.
  Labor in Latin America.

  Bibliography: p.
  Includes index.
    1. Labor and laboring classes—South America—
History.   2. Trade-unions—South America—History.
I. Title.
HD8256.B47 1986   331'.0968   84-51648
ISBN 0-8047-1253-0 (alk. paper)
ISBN 0-8047-1311-1 (pbk. : alk. paper)